Old Testament Life and Literature

GERALD A. LARUE

University of Southern California, Los Angeles

Old Testament Life and Literature

Allyn and Bacon, Inc.　Boston

Preface

THIS book is concerned with the literature, history and religious thought of the Old Testament and the Apocrypha. The approach to these themes is chronological and utilizes literary and historical analytic methodology, as well as the results of archaeological, anthropological, geographical and Near Eastern studies.

The contents of this book have been tested during the past seven years in elective classes which ranged in size from fifteen to ninety-five, and which were composed of freshmen, sophomores, juniors and seniors (and occasionally graduates), of varying religious traditions. Included were Protestants from all the large, and many small, denominations, Roman Catholics, Jews, representatives of the Eastern Churches, Christian Scientists, Latter Day Saints, Seventh Day Adventists, fundamentalists, conservatives, liberals, Moslems, Buddhists, those without religious background, humanists, agnostics and atheists. Some students were religion majors; most were not. Their influence is reflected on almost every page of the book not only in format, but in ideas that have been modified through discussion with, and research by, these students.

The sketch of the development of human life in the ancient Near East in Part Two has been included in response to a persistent query from students: "Where do the Hebrews" (or "Where does the Old Testament") "fit into the pattern of human development?"

The book has been designed to be read with the Bible—students have called it "a working textbook." The underlying assumption is that the student will have an open Bible at hand to consult passages listed in the margins, for there are few biblical quotations and biblical narratives are sketched only when necessary.

Maps, pictures, diagrams and charts are placed in relationship to the discussion, because students believe that this is where they belong—not gathered at the center or the end of the book. Extended outlines at the beginning of certain sections and chapters are provided because students requested them. These outlines provide summary introductions and are useful for review.

The bibliography includes some resource materials drawn to my attention by students who were eager that I should be familiar with the work of scholars from their particular religious traditions. I have not thought it necessary to segregate authors according to their theological persuasions; if the work is listed, it is because it has something to say that merits attention.

Foreign words and technical terms are introduced and defined because these are words students will encounter in books listed in the bibliography. Biblical study, like other disciplines, has developed its own vocabulary with which the informed person should be familiar.

Nor have I spared detail. Each year entering students are better informed in the fields of history, literature, art, anthropology and languages. Those from parochial schools and those with extensive religious training assure me that they do not wish to repeat in college classes what they have studied with scholar priests, rabbis and ministers. Detailed analyses of certain parts of the Bible may be used for depth study.

There is some repetition. The brief treatment of the text and canon in Part One is expanded in Part Ten, where the issue of canon belongs chronologically. The basis for the separation of I and II Isaiah is introduced in Chapter 18 in the discussion of the work of Isaiah of Jerusalem, and again in Chapter 23 where the work of the anonymous prophet of Babylon is presented. Such repetitions serve as "re-enforcements" in the learning process (to quote the psychology majors), and keep before the student the principles of literary and historical analysis which underly the organization of the book.

Some readings are repeated for study in different contexts. For example, Isaiah 9:2–7 and 11:1–9 are said to be the work of Isaiah of Jerusalem by some scholars and therefore should be read in the context of the eighth century; other scholars argue for an Exilic provenance, and when read in an Exilic setting the passages take on a different coloration. We read them in both periods, for the question of the time of writing is not settled. Parts of Deuteronomy are listed for double reading, first as general background to the understanding of the book, and again, in relation to specific themes.

Insofar as possible I have avoided any theological interpretation that might suggest the book is inclined toward one or another denominational or dogmatic point of view. It is the prerogative of the instructor and the class to introduce specific interpretative themes and principles. The book is, therefore, devoid of any desire to convert anyone to a specific theology or religious outlook. My fundamentalist and ultra-conservative students challenge this thesis on the ground that the analytical method is in itself a product of "liberal" or "modernist" scholarship, and the use of this approach throughout the book is tantamount to an attempt to "convert" the reader. In response, I can only admit that I am committed to the analytical method as the best tool for understanding the literature and hence the religious thought of the Bible. To their credit, these students have gone along with me on the basis that it is well to be informed about differing approaches to the Bible, and with the understanding that as long as they knew and understood the methodology set forth here they were as free as any other student to present their views. I have found that the deepest understanding of biblical religious concepts consequently develops in the classroom rather than out of summary statements in textbooks. I have not sought to develop any formal introduction to biblical theology. The average student has no problem in recognizing pertinent issues such as the relationship of religion to society, or trust in God and the problem of international relations, or themes such as concepts of sin and salvation, *if he reads his Bible.* Read in context, in a good translation of the original writer's or speaker's words, religious concepts have relevance and can be grasped in their full strength; presented in textbooks or summarized form, most students have complained that these dynamic beliefs "sound like pedestrian preaching," or appear "blatantly dogmatic." I have followed their advice and simply introduced religious themes in historical and literary contexts, leaving the larger discussion for the classroom.

Two former students have been directly associated with the preparation of the manuscript, and I am most grateful to them: Leanne Lachman carefully read the entire manuscript and offered many valuable suggestions, and Margaret Ann Bennett worked diligently at the production of maps, charts and sketches.

I am deeply indebted to professional colleagues who read the manuscript and offered constructive, helpful criticism: Professor J. Kenneth Kuntz of Wellesley College, Professor Douglas Eadie of the University of Redlands, the Rev. Professor H. McKemie, s.j., of St. Louis University, Professor H. E. Yeide of George Washington University, Professor Henry Thompson of Syracuse University, Professor Robert Anderson of Michigan State University and Professor Alan Pickering of the University of Nebraska. Where I followed their counsel I am sure the book has been improved, and where I did not, perhaps I was unwise. Professor Toivo Harjunpaa, Pacific Lutheran Theological Seminary, Berkeley, California, and Professor Dimitri Zaharapoulos, Holy Cross Greek Orthodox Theological School, Brookline, Massachusetts, were particularly helpful in matters pertaining to the canon.

Gary Folven, Associate Editor of Allyn and Bacon, has been a source of continued support, encouragement, and help. To our wonderfully patient secretaries, Judy (Mrs. Kenneth K.) Kidd, Sheila (Mrs. Alvin A.) Koski, and Karen (Mrs. Brian Dennis) Drought, I can only continue to say "thank you" for typing and re-typing page after page of manuscript, and Susan Prindle has provided valuable assistance and guidance in the final stages of the book.

GERALD A. LARUE

Contents

PART FOUR: THE MONARCHY

PART FIVE: THE DIVIDED KINGDOM

PART SIX: THE LAST 100 YEARS OF JUDAH

PART SEVEN: THE EXILE

Illustrations

A Word to the Reader

TO get the most from this book, you will need a Bible, preferably in modern translation. Keep the Bible at hand, for few passages are quoted and the writer has assumed that you will read the biblical references.

The first two parts of the book form a prolegomenon, a summary of important background material, and an introduction to significant problems and methods of approach essential to proper understanding of the biblical text. These parts are designed to set the biblical period within the context of cultural development in the ancient Near East. These pages should be read quickly and then consulted from time to time as the methods of study and analysis described in these chapters are utilized to analyze some specific writing.

Marginal notations refer to passages that must be read for proper understanding of the text. Passages noted within the text are important for tracing themes or concepts.

Footnotes are suggestive, not exhaustive, and direct you to references that will aid in deepening and expanding your knowledge of the biblical period and of scholarly probing. Some sources will contain extensive lists of resource material for further study.

Sketch maps, designed to assist in understanding topography, relationship of countries, national boundaries, and the like, include only essential details. If you require further information, you may wish to consult one of the many excellent Bible atlases listed in the Bibliography at the back of this book.

Charts placed at the beginning of some sections (and occasionally at the head of some chapters) summarize major historical developments within the period under discussion. An abridged historical chart appears at the end of the book.

A consistent effort has been made to introduce you to the "scholar's workroom" by providing, where feasible, differing expert opinions or some of the reasons why a writing is given a specific date or is treated as a composite work. More exhaustive information can be found in the analytical commentaries on specific books listed in the Bibliography.

Detailed analyses of portions of the biblical text are provided for those who may wish to explore in some depth the literary structure and development of a particular book, or who may wish to examine the principle of "continuing or progressive interpretation" introduced in Part One, Chapter 3, and employed extensively throughout this book.

The Bible and How We Study It

What Is the Old Testament?

THE Old Testament is a collection of selected writings composed and edited by members of the Hebrew-Jewish community between the twelfth century B.C. and the beginning of the Christian era. It includes such diverse materials as prophetic oracles, teachings of wise men, instructions of priests and ancient records of the royal courts. Some material is historical, some is legendary; some is legalistic, some is didactic. For the most part the literature was written in Hebrew, but a few passages were written in Aramaic, a kindred language which came into common usage among the Jews during the post-Exilic era (after the sixth century B.C.). The Aramaic portions include Dan. 2:4b–7:28; Ezra 4:8–6:18, 7:12–26; Jer. 10:11; and one phrase in Gen. 31:47 "Jegar-sahadutha," translated "Heap of Witness."

The term "Old Testament,"[1] or more properly "Old Covenant," is a Christian designation, reflecting the belief of the early Christian Church that the "new covenant" mentioned in Jer. 31:31–34 was fulfilled in Jesus and that the Christian scriptures set forth the "new covenant," just as the Jewish scriptures set forth the "old covenant" (II Cor. 3:6–18; Heb. 9:1–4). Jewish scholars prefer the term "Tanak," a word formed by combining the initial letters of the three divisions of the Hebrew Bible: Torah (Law), Nebhiim (Prophets), and Kethubhim (Writings).

The Bible, as we know it today, is the end product of a long process of writing, editing and selecting of literature primarily concerned with Jewish religious concepts, and, as such, it has a long literary history. It cannot be assumed that a group of men composed writings echoing what they thought God was dictating. The Bible reflects historical situations, human events, men's reactions to these happenings, and the belief that God was also involved in events.

The literary history of the Bible can be said to have begun in the time of Solomon when two men, or groups of men, produced what was to become the nucleus of the Old Testament. One concentrated on the story of David, drawing, no doubt, from court records and other sources, to produce a rather matter-of-fact and intimate account of

---

[1] The earliest use of the term "Old Testament" is attributed to Melito, Bishop of Sardis about A.D. 180. Tertullian, a Roman centurion who became a Christian, is believed to have been the first to designate the Christian writings as the "New Testament" (about A.D. 200).

David's rise to power, the weaknesses and strengths of the man and his family, and the successful coup by which his son, Solomon, gained the throne. The other writer or writers delved into the oral and written traditions of the past to enrich the understanding of the present. Stories of patriarchal ancestors, songs and folk-tales of the tribes, explanations concerning the origin of the world, and accounts of the action of God in the affairs of men, were gathered and woven into a saga explaining how the nation Israel came to be, and how God, who had acted in the past on behalf of his chosen people, was acting in the present and could be counted upon to act in the future. The theologized tradition or "sacred history," as it has been called, was probably utilized in the festivals and cultic rites of the temple.

But the writing did not stop in the tenth century. New events and new monarchs required the extension of national history, and a developing theology saw new facets of the relationship believed to exist between God and the nation. Some materials were undoubtedly discarded over the years, for the Bible reflects selectivity of materials, as we shall see. Study of the sacred literature and new historical events developed new insights and resulted in the addition of new materials: an extension of the creation narrative, detailed genealogies to account for various nations, and new traditions about the patriarchs to explain how history had developed. Even David's story was reinterpreted as David became, more and more, the prototype of the ideal king and, ultimately, of the Messiah. Other literary forms were added: sermonic utterances of the prophets, teachings from the schools of the wise men, devotional hymns of the temple, parables, and material related to the nation's understanding of itself and its divine purpose.

Differing theological insights are often apparent, so that as one writing reflects a universalistic spirit, another stresses particularism. Over and over again, however, it is made clear that the writers believed that traditions of what God had done for his people in the past symbolized what he could be counted upon to do in the future. Thus, a people in captivity to the Babylonians could see that as God once delivered others from the Egyptians, he would do the same for those presently enslaved. The literature had, therefore, a dynamic rather than a static quality; being more than a record of the past, it constituted a narrative of the activity of God on behalf of his people.

In its present form, the Old Testament opens with religious traditions concerning the origin of the world and of mankind. In broad literary strokes, the transition is made to the beginnings of the Hebrew people with the adventures of the patriarchs—Abraham, Isaac, and Jacob—as they dwelt in the land of Canaan. Because of famine, the Hebrews migrated to Egypt where Joseph attained high office and his descendants were treated well. Change in Egyptian leaders altered their attitude to the newcomers, and the Hebrews were pressed into virtual slavery. Led by Moses, they escaped to the wilderness. After Moses' death, under the leadership of Joshua, a successful invasion of Canaan gave them control of the land, a mastery maintained with great difficulty and many wars. Ultimately, internal and external pressure became so great that a single leader, a king, became a necessity. Under Saul, David, and Solomon, Canaan was united into a single empire.

When Solomon died, the Hebrew kingdom split into northern (Israel or Ephraim) and southern (Judah) sections, and during the next few centuries the great prophetic figures (Amos, Hosea, Isaiah, etc.) proclaimed their messages. Israel fell to the Assyrians in 721 B.C. and was absorbed by the Assyrian empire, never again to become a nation. In 586 B.C. Jerusalem was conquered by the Babylonians and Judaeans (Jews) were taken into exile in Babylon, where they managed to maintain their identity.

Release came with the conquest of Babylon by the Persians under Cyrus the Great in 539 B.C. The exiled Judaeans were permitted to return to their homeland, reestablish themselves, and rebuild Jerusalem. Two leaders in the restoration movement, which reached its peak about the middle of the fifth century, were Ezra and Nehemiah. For two centuries, or until the coming of the Greeks under Alexander the Great in 333 B.C., Judah was ruled as a Persian province and the Jews enjoyed comparative freedom in matters of religion and social conduct. The introduction of Greek culture brought drastic changes.

When Alexander died in 323 B.C., his kingdom was divided among his generals and Judah was eventually controlled by the Seleucids of Syria. From this time onward, Greek social and cultural patterns made inroads into Jewish life, causing anguish and suffering to those who opposed change. Unable to endure the situation any longer the Jews rebelled and won freedom. For a short time, under Maccabaean leadership, Judah enjoyed the status of an independent nation, only to come under the control of the Roman empire. Here we leave the Old Testament period and enter the Christian era. However, as we shall see, there is far more than history or the interpretation of historical events within the literature of the Old Testament.

DEVELOPMENT OF THE CANON

Writings accepted as authoritative for faith and teaching are said to be *canonical,* and when gathered together constitute a *canon.* The term "canon," the Anglicized form of the Greek word *kanon* designating a rod used for measuring, is related to a Semitic root appearing in Hebrew as *kaneh,* meaning a "reed." Used metaphorically in reference to religious matters, it signifies the measure or guide or standard for principles of belief and practice.

The number of books constituting the canon of Old Testament Scripture varies among different religious groups. The Jewish Bible contains twenty-four books;[2] the Protestant Bible, thirty-nine books; the Eastern Orthodox Bible, forty-three books; and the Roman Catholic Bible, forty-six books. The difference between the Jewish and Protestant versions is easily explained: one book in the Jewish Bible

[2] Josephus, the Jewish historian of the first century A.D. in his first book against Apion (*Contra Apion*), section 8, mentions twenty-two books. He unites Ruth and Judges, and Jeremiah and Lamentations.

entitled "The Twelve" (Dodecapropheton), actually contains twelve prophetic writings which, in Christian versions, are counted individually, and four other writings which are treated as individual units in Jewish Bibles are each sub-divided into two books by Christians (I-II Samuel, I-II Kings, I-II Chronicles, Ezra-Nehemiah). The additional books in the Orthodox and Roman Catholic Bibles include writings not accepted as canonical by Jews and Protestants, who place them in a collection known as "The Apocrypha." (See Chart I.) The term "Apocrypha" as applied to writings is first known to us through the work of Clement of Alexandria (*Stromata* iii, 5), a Christian theologian-philosopher living in Egypt at the close of the second and beginning of the third centuries A.D. In the preface to his translation of Samuel and Kings (*Prologus Galeatus*) in the fourth century, Jerome, the great Christian scholar who made the Latin translation of the Bible known as the "Vulgate" (see Part Ten), applied the term to books found in the Greek translation of Hebrew scriptures but excluded from the Jewish canon.

Etymologically, "apocrypha" is derived from a Greek word meaning "hidden" or "concealed." The explanation as to why certain books were hidden may give to the word "apocrypha" either a complimentary or derogatory significance. In one sense, the books were hidden because they contained esoteric knowledge to be revealed only to members of a particular group. In another sense, they were concealed because they were heretical writings not acceptable in the canon of scriptures. How parts of the Apocrypha came to be accepted by some and rejected by others is part of the story of the development of the canon. (See Part Ten.)

It is estimated that close to 1,000,000 Jews lived in Alexandria, Egypt, during the third century B.C. Having been separated from Palestinian Judaism for many generations, the Alexandrian Jews spoke only Greek and could not understand the Hebrew scriptures. According to a legend preserved in "The Letter of Aristeas,"[3] in response to a request that the Jewish scriptures be translated into Greek, seventy Jewish scholars (another tradition says seventy-two) went to Egypt and translated the first five books of the Bible (the *Law* or *Torah*). These books, believed to be the work of Moses, had achieved a relatively fixed form and canonical status during the fifth century B.C.

Subsequently other Jewish writings were translated: first the prophetic writings (the *Prophets* or *Nebhiim*), which had almost achieved canonical standing, and finally the *Writings* or *Kethubhim*, which incorporated all other authoritative religious documents. The tradition of the translation by the seventy was extended to include the entire Greek version which came to be known as "The Seventy" or in the Latin form as *Septuaginta*, now Anglicized to "Septuagint" and given a numerical abbreviation LXX.

[3] A Greek document, probably written in Alexandria, Egypt, during the second century B.C. Cf. Moses Hadas, *Aristeas to Philocrates* (New York: Harper and Brothers, 1961).

CHART I. THE BOOKS OF THE OLD TESTAMENT

Jewish	Protestant	Roman Catholic
The Law (Torah)	Genesis	Genesis
	Exodus	Exodus
Genesis	Leviticus	Leviticus
Exodus	Numbers	Numbers
Leviticus	Deuteronomy	Deuteronomy
Numbers	Joshua	Josue (Joshua)
Deuteronomy	Judges	Judges
	Ruth	Ruth
The Prophets (Nebhiim)	I Samuel	I Kings (= I Samuel)
	II Samuel	II Kings (= II Samuel)
The Former (Earlier)	I Kings	III Kings (= I Kings)
Prophets:	II Kings	IV Kings (= II Kings)
Joshua	I Chronicles	I Paralipomenon
Judges	II Chronicles	(= I Chronicles)
I Samuel	Ezra	II Paralipomenon
II Samuel	Nehemiah	(= II Chronicles)
I Kings	Esther	I Esdras (Ezra)
II Kings	Job	II Esdras (Nehemiah)
The Latter Prophets:	Psalms	†Tobias (Tobit)
Isaiah	Proverbs	†Judith
Jeremiah	Ecclesiastes	Esther (with additions)
Ezekiel	Song of Solomon	Job
The Twelve:	Isaiah	Psalms
Hosea	Jeremiah	Proverbs
Joel	Lamentations	Ecclesiastes
Amos	Ezekiel	Song of Songs
Obadiah	Daniel	†Book of Wisdom
Jonah	Hosea	†Ecclesiasticus
Micah	Joel	Isaias
Nahum	Amos	Jeremias
Habakkuk	Obadiah	Lamentations
Zephaniah	Jonah	†Baruch (including the
Haggai	Micah	Letter of Jeremiah)
Zechariah	Nahum	Ezechiel
Malachi	Habakkuk	Daniel
	Zephaniah	Osee (Hosea)
The Writings	Haggai	Joel
(Kethubhim)	Zechariah	Amos
	Malachi	Abdias (Obadiah)
Psalms		Jonas (Jonah)
Proverbs	**The Apocrypha**	Micheas (Micah)
Job		Nahum
Song of Songs	*I Esdras (or III Esdras)	Habacuc
Ruth	II Esdras (or IV Esdras)	Sophonias (Zephaniah)
Lamentations	*Tobit	Aggeus (Haggai)
Ecclesiastes	*Judith	Zacharias (Zechariah)
Esther	*Additions to Esther	Malachias (Malachi)
Daniel	*Wisdom of Solomon	†I Machabees
Ezra	*Ecclesiasticus	†II Machabees
Nehemiah	*Baruch	
I Chronicles	Letter of Jeremiah	
II Chronicles	*Prayer of Azariah and	
	*The Song of the Three Young Men	
	Susanna	
	*Bel and the Dragon	* Books accepted by The Eastern Orthodox
	Prayer of Manasseh	Church but not included in the Jewish Canon.
	*I Maccabees	† Books accepted by **Roman Catholics** but not
	*II Maccabees	included in the Jewish Canon.

The contents of the Law and the Prophets had been determined by usage in the Jewish community prior to the LXX translation, but the limits of the Kethubhim had not been defined and books were included that were not to achieve canonical status among all Jews.[4] When the Christian Church began to move into the Greek-speaking world during the first century A.D., the scripture used by the missionaries was the LXX. The authors of the New Testament Gospels drew upon the LXX to prove that Jesus was the Messiah and the fulfillment of Jewish prophecy, using some passages which the Jews argued had been inadequately translated from the Hebrew to the Greek (particularly Isaiah 7:14; compare with Matt. 1:23). The destruction of the Temple by the Romans in 70 A.D. gave Judaism a new direction, centering in scripture rather than sacrificial rites, so that it became imperative to define the limits of the authoritative writings. Consequently, in 90 A.D. at Jamnia (Jabneh), situated west of Jerusalem near the Mediterranean, a council met under the leadership of Rabbi Johanan ben Zakkai to determine the Jewish canon. Long debates ensued over the Song of Songs, Esther, Ecclesiastes, and Ezekiel. The books agreed upon by the Council constitute the Jewish canon of today. Concerning other writings, both Jewish and Christian, the Council stated:

> The Gospel and the books of the heretics are not Sacred Scripture. The books of Ben Sira and whatever books have been written since his time, are not Sacred Scripture. (Tosef Yadaim 2:13)

Meanwhile the Christians continued to use the LXX including books of the Apocrypha rejected by the Jamnia Council. There was, however, some uneasiness among Christian scholars concerning certain of the books and just prior to the Protestant Reformation questions were being raised about the authority of the Apocrypha. Seeking to go back to ancient sources, Protestant reformers accepted the Jewish canon and relegated the Apocrypha to the status of writings without authority for doctrine, partially, no doubt, because certain unacceptable doctrines were based upon these writings.[5] For Protestants, the writings of the Apocrypha are separated from canonical scriptures and held to be non-authoritative for doctrine.

The Roman Catholic Church took the opposite stand at the Council of Trent held in Tridentum, Italy from 1545 to 1563 and, partially on the basis of traditional usage among Christians, declared the books of the Apocrypha, with the exception of I and II Esdras and the prayer of Manasseh, to be canonical and pronounced anathema upon all who denied their status. The accepted books are labeled "Deuterocanoni-

---

[4] The Qumran Jewish community located near the Dead Sea, which produced the so-called "Dead Sea Scrolls," included among their writings all of the books of the Old Testament (with the possible exception of Esther), the book of Enoch and Jubilees, plus numerous writings of their sect including "The War of the Children of Light versus the Children of Darkness," many hymns, and a community rule book. It should be noted that at least some members of the early Christian community used the book of Enoch (cf. Jude, vss. 14–16).

[5] For example, the doctrine of Purgatory (cf. II Macc. 12:43–46).

cal"[6] by Roman Catholic scholars who restrict the use of the term "Apocrypha" to designate writings purporting to be inspired but not accepted into the Roman Catholic canon. The latter writings are labeled "Pseudepigrapha" (False Writings) by Protestant scholars. Later, in 1672, at the Council of Jerusalem, the Eastern Orthodox Church accepted I Esdras, Tobit, Judith, the Wisdom of Solomon, Ecclesiasticus, Baruch, the Prayer of Azariah and The Song of the Three Young Men, Bel and the Dragon, and I and II Maccabees into the canon, for reasons that are not completely clear.[7]

Thus, the term "Old Testament" has a wider and a narrower meaning, depending upon who uses it. This book will discuss the literature common to Jewish, Protestant, Roman Catholic, and Eastern Orthodox Bibles, and the writings called the "Apocrypha" by Protestants and Jews or "Deuterocanonical" by Roman Catholics.

WHY DO WE READ?

For those with religious training received in Church or Synagogue, the answer to the question "Why do we read?" may seem obvious. One reads for religious, theological, devotional, or inspirational reasons, for spiritual edification, to nourish and nurture faith. The Jew recognizes Tanak as God's word revealed to Israel, requiring neither supplement nor fulfillment. It is used in public and private worship linking the individual Jew to the household of faith throughout history, providing strength in time of need, offering hope in moments of darkness, and giving assurance that the Covenant made with God in the past has relevance today.[8]

For the Christian, the Old Testament is that part of Holy Scripture known and quoted by Jesus and the New Testament writers. Often, it is viewed as the prologue to the New Testament, as a document which, pointing forward to Jesus, is to be interpreted in the light of the New Testament, where Old Testament promises find fulfillment.[9] Through the Bible God speaks to man, and one may read of God's outreach or search for man, or, to reverse the idea, man's search for God.[10]

The very reverence and respect paid to the Bible in services of

[6] Indicating that they were written later. The other books in the canon are called "Protocanonical."

[7] See The Old Testament Canon, Part Ten, chap. 31 for greater detail.

[8] Cf. Leo Trepp, *Eternal Faith, Eternal People* (New Jersey: Prentice-Hall, 1962), pp. 78 ff.; H. J. Schoeps, *The Jewish-Christian Argument* (New York: Holt, Rinehart, and Winston, 1963), p. 4. For a different evaluation, cf. J. L. Liebman, "New Trends in Jewish Reform Thought," *Reform Judaism* (Cincinnati: Hebrew Union College Press, 1949), pp. 58–65.

[9] Cf. Aldo J. Tos, *Approaches to The Bible: The Old Testament* (New Jersey: Prentice-Hall, 1963), pp. vii f.; H. C. Kee, *The Renewal of Hope* (New York: Association Press, 1959), pp. 49 ff.; A. Richardson, *A Preface to Bible Study* (Philadelphia: The Westminster Press, 1944) pp. 65 ff.

[10] R. M. Brown, *The Bible Speaks to You* (Philadelphia: Westminster Press, 1955), pp. 15 ff.; E. P. Blair, *The Bible and You* (New York: Abingdon-Cokesbury, 1953), pp. 27 ff.; S. Mowinckel, *The Old Testament as the Word of God*, trans. by R. B. Bjornard (New York: Abingdon, 1959); John T. Wilkinson, *Principles of Biblical Interpretation* (London: Epworth Press, 1960).

worship by Jew and Christian symbolizes its importance. The approach of the Synagogue or Church directs attention to the essentially religious nature of the Bible, to the fact that the Old Testament is the product of a community of faith reflecting theological convictions, and to the subsequent fact that this ancient document is still a powerful factor in shaping and sustaining beliefs. However, the purposes of Bible study as defined or understood by religious organizations do not determine the goals of the classroom.

Often hailed as a "literary classic," the Bible has been approached as great literature, and there have been those who have read with deep appreciation, particularly in the King James Version, the magnificent prose and poetry appearing in many passages. Biblical themes have been compared with those of other literary masterpieces.[11] The impact of the Bible upon the literature of the Western world has been traced and recognition given to the permeation of our culture by this great document.[12] Such an approach may ignore the intention of the authors of the Bible and the relevance of what they said to their own time, or, in stressing literary characteristics, may slight the religious convictions of the writers.

The remarkable historical record preserved in the Old Testament[13] has led archaeologists and historians to study it for contributions to the understanding of Near Eastern history. The great American archaeologist, W. F. Albright, has commented upon the significant role the Bible has played in the identification of Palestinian sites,[14] and in some instances the Bible has led to the discovery of ancient places by describing locations.[15] But, as archaeologists would be quick to assert, the Bible is more than an historical record or a guide to buried cities.

Beyond the study of the Old Testament for the contribution it may make to personal and corporate piety or to literary, historical, and archaeological studies, is the recognition of the role this body of writings has played and continues to play in shaping human concepts and values through the adherents of three great religions that acknowledge its authority: Judaism, Christianity, and Islam. To study these ancient writings is, therefore, to study works that for centuries have influenced social, literary, musical, artistic, ethical, moral, and many other aspects of society.[16] Understandably, no single introduc-

[11] Mary Ellen Chase, *The Bible and the Common Reader* (New York: Macmillan, 1944); C. A. Dinsmore, *The English Bible as Literature* (New York: Houghton Mifflin, 1931); Joseph Frank, *Literature from the Bible* (Boston: Little, Brown & Co., 1963).

[12] L. A. Nelson, *Our Roving Bible* (New York: Abingdon-Cokesbury, 1945).

[13] Records preserved in II Sam. 9–20 and I Kings 1–2 have been recognized as unique documents, conveying to the reader a sense of factuality that indicates intimate familiarity with the events described. Cf. John Bright, *A History of Israel* (Philadelphia: Westminster Press, 1959), p. 163.

[14] Wm. F. Albright, *The Archaeology of Palestine* (Baltimore: Penguin, 1960), pp. 227 ff.

[15] Nelson Glueck, *Rivers in the Desert* (New York: Farrar, Straus, and Cudahy, 1959), pp. 30 ff.

[16] Areas of academic inquiry affected by the Old Testament include: art, archaeology, comparative literature, ethics, history, music, philosophy, psychology, sociology, and, in a controversial way, biological and geological sciences, to name but a few.

tory volume has been able to deal with the relationship of the Bible to all of these themes.[17]

It is the purpose of this volume to introduce the literature of the Old Testament, the vehicle by which the concepts of the ancient Hebrew-Jewish community are conveyed to us, in terms of the situations out of which these writings developed (so far as they can be known), giving attention to the beliefs and commitments of the authors. Whether or not one believes that the religious, social and ethical concepts of the Old Testament are acceptable as authoritative guides for present day belief and conduct must remain a personal matter. If, from such study, one committed to the religious teaching of Church or Synagogue can gain enriched awareness of the foundations of his convictions, or, if one without such commitments can develop sensitive understanding of the basis of another's beliefs, and, if both are able to broaden their appreciation of concepts that are fundamental to western religious thought, perhaps this will be enough to answer the question, "Why read?" But, to read with understanding the words of another is, to some degree, to apprehend the person. If, through empathy and imagination, the barriers of time and space can be transcended and some identity with the writer—his mood, his situation, his thinking, his values, and the generating sentiment of his writing—can be attained, then it is possible to discover, not only another sentient human being, but, to an extent, oneself. The question then becomes, "Why not read?"

[17] Cf. H. H. Watts, *The Modern Reader's Guide to the Bible* (New York: Harper and Brothers, 1959); W. Irwin, *The Old Testament: Keystone of Human Culture* (New York: H. Schuman, Inc., 1952) for volumes cognizant of the cultural aspects.

2
How Do We Read?

THERE was a time when it was believed that the best way to read the Bible was to begin at Genesis and read straight through. Today we know that the Bible was not written in the sequence in which we find it, but developed slowly over hundreds of years. Consequently, passages written centuries apart may now appear side by side. To appreciate the development of Hebrew religious thought, and to understand concepts in terms of the time in which they were recorded, it is essential to read biblical passages in chronological order insofar as we are able to determine that order. During the past one hundred years or so, a methodology, which may be termed "historical-literary," has been developed. This approach seeks to do two things: to determine the specific time in history in which each part of the Bible was written, and to classify various literary genres (such as funeral laments or oracles of doom).

Basically, the historical-literary method recognizes that, because literature develops within definite historical contexts, specific problems, life situations and cultural patterns are often reflected. For example, a Psalmist wrote:

> By the waters of Babylon,
>> there we sat down and wept,
>> when we remembered Zion.
> On the willows there
>> we hung up our lyres.
> For there our captors
>> required of us songs,
> And our tormentors, mirth, saying,
>> "Sing us one of the songs of Zion!"
>>> Psalm 137:1–3

Whoever wrote these words was captive in Babylon and in poetic form expressed unhappiness and nostalgia for Jerusalem (Zion). Reading the complete poem makes it apparent that the writer was one of the Hebrew people living in Babylon after the armies of King Nebuchadrezzar of Babylon had overrun the Near East and enslaved many peoples, and before Cyrus the Great, having defeated the Babylonians, permitted the people to return home (cf. II Chron. 36). The Psalm comes from the sixth century B.C.

Unfortunately, all biblical literature cannot be dated as easily as Ps. 137. Biblical scholars must employ, wherever possible, the techniques developed by historians to ascertain the period out of which a writing came, the specific life situation which prompted the writing, and the accuracy or reliability of any report of a past event.

THE PROBLEM OF HISTORY

Like other historians, the biblical scholar seeks to fix with certainty the factual nature of a reported event. He reaches conclusions by examining all relevant data from written sources, archaeological discoveries, sociological and anthropological research and, in some instances, geography. His conclusions must be true to all available facts and must be credible. For instance, II Kings 18:13 ff. reports the attack of the Assyrian King Sennacherib upon Jerusalem during the reign of King Hezekiah. How can we know that this event occurred? Fortunately, confirmation has come through the archaeologist's discovery of the Taylor Prism, a hexagonal clay cylinder on which Sennacherib had inscribed an account of his military victories. At one point the siege of Jerusalem, including the name of King Hezekiah of Judah, is mentioned. Such coincidence of data provides what one scholar has labeled "controlled history."[1] Having achieved a fixed "fact" in history, the historian next seeks to arrange other data around the event to establish a chronology on the basis of deductive reasoning.

Because the deductive process involves movement from the known to the unknown, from the factual to the probable, from fixed data to the schematic arrangement of related data, results are always tentative. Therefore, it is necessary to preface each section of this book with the acknowledgment, "Here is where we stand in the light of the evidence available at this particular moment. Tomorrow may bring new information that will necessitate a change in this conclusion."

In dealing with written records of the past, the biblical historian must evaluate the testimony he utilizes. Although it is clear that the Bible reports events with a high degree of accuracy, it cannot be assumed that all biblical history is accurate. For example, archaeological research has demonstrated that the city of Ai, reported in Josh. 8 to have been conquered by Joshua, was a heap of ruins centuries before Joshua's time.[2] Each event must be assessed individually. The scholar asks, "How did the writer of this account know of the events he reports? Was he an eye-witness? Did he talk to eye-witnesses, and if so,

[1] Cyrus H. Gordon, *Introduction to Old Testament Times* (New Jersey: Ventnor Publishers, 1953), pp. 11 f.

[2] None of the several hypotheses set forth to explain this apparent error is completely satisfactory, for either the motives of the biblical writer are questioned or he is accused of a high degree of confusion. One theory labels the account a fabrication designed to explain the heap of ruins at Ai; another suggests that the men of Bethel (a city about a mile and a half away) made a stand at Ai before falling back to Bethel; and a third suggests that the account of the fall of Bethel was transferred to Ai. Cf. John Gray, *Archaeology and the Old Testament World* (New York: Harper and Row, 1962), p. 93; G. E. Wright, *Biblical Archaeology* (Philadelphia: Westminster Press, 1962), p. 81.

how long after the event? Is he recording an old, written tradition or an oral source?" The further a report is from the event it describes, the greater the possibility of error or interpretation affecting its accuracy. Phrases such as "in those days" or "even to this day" reveal that the writer is conscious of reporting an event long after the time when it was supposed to have occurred.

How did the historian build his records in ancient times? Testimony was gathered from written and oral sources and, by exercising judgment as to the worthiness or appropriateness of the materials, the compiler blended them into a more or less homogeneous, connected narrative. In time, other writers might add to or reinterpret the account, regardless of the fact that the new material might contradict some details of the earlier accounts. The anointing of Saul is reported three times: once as a private ceremony (I Sam. 9:27–10:1) and twice as a public ritual (I Sam. 10:17–24, and 11:15). There are two accounts of the death of the Philistine giant, Goliath. In one, David is the conqueror, killing Goliath with a sling stone (I Sam. 17); in the other, Goliath dies at the hand of one of David's warriors, Elhanan (II Sam. 21:19). Still later, the writers of the books of Chronicles, who compiled their histories in the fifth century B.C., were troubled by the conflicting records and solved the dilemma by reporting that Elhanan killed Goliath's brother, Lahmi (I Chron. 20:5).

Beyond the establishment of historical fact (the "happenedness" of an event) is the recognition of the point of view of the reporter. Like recorders of other national or religious documents, biblical writers not only selected events and details which best served their purposes, but also reported with national and religious bias. Battles and national events are reported to be under the control of the God of Israel, just as writers in other nations reported victories and conquests as ordained by their gods. For the Hebrew writer, Israel was the chosen people, peculiarly blessed, and written history echoed and reinforced this belief.

The biblical record, therefore, contains more than a listing of happenings and, like other historical writing, interprets data in the light of national and religious convictions. Events did not just happen. Battles were not won through superiority of armaments or numbers, but because the deity was personally involved. History had meaning— the fulfillment of promises made to the patriarchs, the development of the holy nation, the blessings that were to come to the chosen nation as the people served and worshiped their God. The nation *per se* and the people as part of the nation were involved in a divine-human relationship, and it was essential for national welfare that this relationship be recognized and appreciated. To what extent cultic observances made use of this interpretation of history is not fully known, but there can be little doubt that a passage like Deut. 26:5–9 contains a recitation utilized at sanctuaries, reflecting awareness of the relationship of the nation's history to the deity. "History" in the biblical sense reflects a national setting and relationship to a religious community, a "community of faith" as it has sometimes been called, and thus presents a particularistic interpretation. The events are there, together with the delineation of the meaning of the events for the nation.

HISTORY AND LEGEND

Around great figures in history, the heroes of a nation, legends invariably seem to rise. Shortly after Abraham Lincoln's death, descriptions were published of private conversations between certain individuals and the president. Upon study by literary experts and historians, it was demonstrated that these accounts were legends, not history. Even during the lifetime of heroes legends may develop. In 1959 it was reported that, out of his great love and respect for British justice and law, Sir Winston Churchill provided £1,000 for the defense of a Nazi general on trial in Britain for war crimes. A letter from Sir Winston's secretary quickly discredited this story. Churchill had not contributed any money to the defense of any war criminal, and, further, war criminals had not been tried in Britain. Investigating stories of Bible heroes is somewhat more difficult.

Semi-nomadic peoples, such as the Hebrews were prior to their invasion of Canaan, could not very well maintain written records. As David D. Luckenbill has observed, "History begins with the vanity of kings."[3] Formal history begins when a monarch starts to record agreements reached with other nations, victories in battles (sometimes greatly exaggerated), laws introduced or reforms instituted, on parchment, papyrus, clay or stone. Even with such documents the historian seeks confirming evidence of the recorded event. At this moment there is no external evidence of the events reported in the Bible prior to the Hebrew invasion of Palestine. The excavation of cities in Canaan has indicated that an invasion did take place. For example, at Tell Beit Mirsim (believed to be Debir) an abrupt cultural change was ascertained. Below the destruction layer Canaanite buildings and artifacts were found, and above, the pottery, buildings and defenses of the Hebrew conquerors. From that point onward, archaeological documentation of Hebrew habitation was available.[4] Concerning the pre-invasion or Mosaic period and the activities of the Patriarchs, evidence that at best can be labeled tangential has been recovered. The actual existence of the Patriarchs—Abraham, Isaac, Jacob, and others—cannot be proven or disproven. The stories of their adventures must be treated largely as legend, containing here and there accurate memories of a tradition but preserving these memories in writings produced many years after the events they purport to describe—writings designed to dramatize the convictions held by the Hebrew people concerning God's activity in human affairs.

The birth story of Moses (Exod. 2:1–10), probably recorded during

[3] David D. Luckenbill, *The Annals of Sennacherib* (Chicago: University of Chicago Press, 1924), p. 1.

[4] Cf. C. C. McCown, *The Ladder of Progress in Palestine* (New York: Harper & Brothers, 1943), pp. 91 f.; Wm. F. Albright, *From Stone Age to Christianity* (New York: Doubleday-Anchor, 1957), pp. 284 f.

the tenth century B.C., reflects the pattern found in the birth account of King Sargon of Agade who lived near the end of the third millennium B.C. The Sargon account reads:

> Sargon, the mighty king of Agade, am I.
> My mother was a changeling,[5] my father I knew not.
> The brothers of my father loved the hills.
> My city is Azupiranu, which is situated on
>   the banks of the Euphrates.
> My changeling mother conceived me, in secret
>   she bore me,
> She set me in a basket of rushes, with bitumen
>   she sealed my lid.
> She cast me into the river which rose not over me.
> The river bore me up and carried me to Akki,
>   the drawer of water.
> Akki, the drawer of water, lifted me out
>   as he dipped his ewer.
> Akki, the drawer of water, took me as his
>   son and reared me.
> Akki, the drawer of water, appointed me as
>   his gardener.
> While I was a gardener, Ishtar[6] granted me
>   her love,
> And for four and . . . years I exercised
>   kingship.[7]

The similarity of the Moses and Sargon accounts is obvious. Actually both stories reflect literary patterns often associated with heroes. The life of the hero is threatened when he is still a child; he escapes; he is unrecognized until he achieves his full status as a messiah or savior of the people. Very often his life pattern reflects the way in which a people consider their early history, for they look back upon their humble and troublous beginnings and marvel at what they have become. The life of the hero embodies the struggle of a nation or a group to achieve greatness.[8] Having detected the hero motif in the Moses literature, one must consider the question of how much of the Moses cycle may be labeled "legend," and how much "history."[9]

Similar problems confront the scholar in the patriarchal narratives. Were Abraham, Isaac and Jacob real persons? Are their stories factual or legendary, embodying a fictionized history of the Hebrews, symbolizing the way the Hebrews looked back at their nomadic origins from

[5] The term "changeling" conveys no meaning. It is possible the term meant "vestal" or one associated in some way with temple personnel.

[6] Ishtar was the goddess of vegetation, fertility, and love.

[7] Trans. by E. A. Speiser, in James B. Pritchard (ed.), *Ancient Near Eastern Texts* (Princeton, New Jersey: Princeton University Press, 1950), p. 119. Used by permission.

[8] Cf. Lord Raglan, *The Hero* (New York: Vintage Books, 1956); Otto Rank, *The Myth of the Birth of the Hero* (New York: Vintage Books, 1959); Joseph Campbell, *The Hero with a Thousand Faces* (New York: Meridian Books, 1956).

[9] The Moses story reflects accurate details concerning adoption procedures as known from Mesopotamian documents, cf. B. S. Childs, "The Birth of Moses," *Journal of Biblical Literature*, LXXIV (1965), 109–122.

the vantage point of their settled life in Canaan? Archaeological contributions provide no definite clues for determining whether or not these men ever existed. A Babylonian business contract from the beginning of the second millennium B.C. refers to a certain Abarama (Abraham), son of "Awel-Ishtar," but there is no possible way to link him with the Abraham of the Bible.[10] Two Abrams, one associated with Egypt and the other with Cyprus, are mentioned in Ugaritic administrative texts. The references demonstrate that the name was known in the periods often associated with the patriarchs. The name of Jacob appears as the name of a Hyksos king (Y'qb-Hr) about 1700 B.C. and, in an Egyptian list from the time of Pharaoh Thutmose III (ca. 1480 B.C.), a Palestinian town called Jacob-el (Ya'qob-el) is found, but these inscriptions do not help us very much.[11]

Moreover, the biblical texts confuse the problem. Genesis 10 lists Noah's descendants and some of the "sons" can be identified as geographical areas. "Cush," mentioned in Genesis 10:6, is the area in North Africa south of the first cataract of the Nile known as Nubia. "Egypt" is called a son of Ham, and another son is called "Canaan," the area known today as Palestine. Among Canaan's children is one called "Sidon" (Gen. 10:15), the name of a Phoenician seaport in northern Canaan. Abram (Abraham) is listed as one of the descendants of Shem, but among Shem's children we find areas listed as individuals —Elam, which is near Susa in Persia, and Asshur, which is Assyria. Among the immediate ancestors of Abram named in Gen. 11 is Nahor, his grandfather, and Terah, his father. Nahor appears to be the city called Til-nakhiri, and Terah, Til-turakhi in Assyrian texts.[12] The name "Haran" refers to a person in Gen. 11:27–30 but to a place in subsequent verses (Gen. 11:31–32; 12:4–5). When do people really become people and stop being symbolic representations of places? The pattern goes on and Esau becomes Edom and Jacob becomes Israel.

On the other hand, within the patriarchal narratives are accurate details relating to the age which they describe. Aspects of nomadic life could easily have been discovered by writers observing peoples who continued to dwell in the steppes and retained ancient desert customs. However, the Nuzi texts from the second millennium B.C. record practices similar to some reported in the patriarchal accounts. So far as we know at this moment, these specific practices were not observed by Canaanites or settled Hebrews and belong only to the early part of the second millennium. In the marriage agreements discussed in the Nuzi texts, a childless wife is obligated to provide a maiden for her husband so children should be born to him. Such a ruling explains why Sarah gave Hagar, her Egyptian maid, to Abraham (Gen. 16). The apprehension which Abraham expressed when he expelled Hagar and her child (Gen. 21:11) is, perhaps, explained by the Nuzi legal ruling that the handmaiden who bore a child for her master could not

[10] George A. Barton, *Archaeology and the Bible* (Philadelphia: American Sunday School Union, 1916), pp. 352 ff.

[11] Cf. John Bright, *op. cit.,* p. 70.

[12] *Ibid.*

be driven out.[13] Those who would place Abraham in the fourteenth or fifteenth century muster other evidence.[14] Thus, although the Abraham stories may be labeled legendary to separate them from the historical, it should be remembered that a legend may be centered in real people and embody historical data. On the other hand, the record of a few accurate details does not guarantee the reliability of all reports. If biblical traditions actually go back to patriarchal times, then it must be assumed that a long period of oral transmission ensued before the accounts were recorded.[15] Legends are important, not merely because they may contain accurate data, but because they provide us with an appreciation of the way in which people thought, and an understanding of what they believed at the time the legend was recorded. Legend belongs in the history of human thought.

One characteristic that helps to distinguish legend from history is the tendency of those who record legend to use terms to indicate the great age of the account without being specific as to when, precisely, the event occurred. Gen. 19:36–38, which describes in most uncomplimentary terms the origin of the Moabite and Ammonite peoples, twice uses the phrase "to this day," indicating that the story is being recorded long after the event it appears to report. Gen. 22:14 concludes the story of Abraham's near-encounter with child sacrifice with the phrase, "as it is said to this day," to indicate that the place name known in the writer's time actually originated in "olden times."

Another distinguishing feature lies in the tendency of historical writings to deal with matters of public importance, events that affect the political and public welfare of the group. In legend, the account centers in and around a person who may embody or dramatize the spirit of the group for whom the tale is recounted.

In the discussion of the hero or central character the miraculous or the incredible is often incorporated to heighten the story. The principle of credibility must be applied to evaluate the possibility or the probability of the miraculous having occurred. At this point an understanding of the *Weltanschauung,* or world view, of the people of Old Testament time is important, for it was an accepted belief in the Near East that divine powers intruded in human affairs to alter and upset the ordinary pattern of existence. It seems only natural that literature of this period, whether it be Hebrew or Egyptian, Babylonian or Assyrian, should reflect such a belief. Thus, when we read of an iron axehead floating to the surface of a pond (II Kings 6:3–6), or of a magic jar of oil which continued to produce oil until all available containers were full (II Kings 4:1–6), the principle of credibility

13 Cf. James B. Pritchard (ed.), *Ancient Near Eastern Texts* (henceforth *ANET*) (Princeton, New Jersey: Princeton University Press, 1950), p. 220.

14 Cyrus H. Gordon, "Hebrew Origins in the Light of Recent Discoveries," A. Altmann (ed.), *Biblical and Other Studies* (Cambridge: Harvard University Press, 1963). See also Cyrus Gordon, "The Patriarchal Age," *Journal of Bible and Religion,* XXI (1953), 238–243; and *Introduction to Old Testament Times,* pp. 1–119.

15 Raglan, *op. cit.,* pp. 13 ff., limits folk-memory to a period of 150 years. On the other hand, Eduard Nielsen, *Oral Tradition* (London: S.C.M. Press, 1954), believes that the written records of the Old Testament prior to the sixth century B.C. (the Exile) were negligible and that the writing, which must be dated in the post-Exilic era, is dependent upon oral tradition.

compels us to label these accounts legendary, not forgetting that to the non-scientific mind of earlier times such events were explicable on the grounds of belief in supernaturalism. To question the supernatural as it appears in the Bible is disturbing to some, but what would be labeled legend in Greek or Roman or other non-biblical writings deserves the same label when found in the Bible.

Different types of legends can be recognized in the Bible.[16] The *aetiological* legend explains why something is the way it is. For example, Gen. 11, the story of the tower of Babel, explains why men who are related through a common father, Noah, speak different languages. The explanations must be approached in the light of the time when they were recorded. In one sense, because aetiological legends attempt to answer the qustion "why" about the environment, they might be said to mark the beginnings of science, without a scientific methodology. The *ethnological* legend is concerned with relationships existing between certain groups at a certain point in history and attempts to explain that relationship in terms of past events. For instance, Canaan, one of the sons of Noah, is condemned by a curse to slavery in Gen. 9:25 because his father, Ham, looked upon Noah's nakedness. Actually, the account was written after the Hebrews had established their kingdom and exerted their authority over Canaan. The legend explains, in terms of a curse, why the slave-master relationship developed. *Etymological* legends explain why certain places bear the names they do (see Gen. 19:22; 21:31). *Ceremonial* legends explain why certain rituals are performed in the Hebrew cultus (cf., Exod. 12:26 ff.; Exod. 13:14 ff.). *Geological* legends are concerned with the explanation of certain natural phenomena. The pillar of salt, a landmark probably well known in Old Testament times[17] is explained by the legend of Lot's wife (Gen. 19:24–26). The literary categories devised by modern scholars enable the reader to appreciate the creative genius of the Hebrew writers, even though such classifications may seem to pour this genius into fixed molds. But the Hebrews were not bound by patterns and, on occasion, differing types of legends are combined (cf., Gen. 32:30, a combination of etymological and ceremonial legends).

The necessary separation of legend and history does not imply that legend is to be thought of as deceit or falsehood. It is not the function of legend to deceive, but to portray dramatically real beliefs and convictions held by people concerning origins and to answer the question "why" concerning certain characteristics of the time. How legends were used by the Hebrew people is not known for certain, but it is possible that some were recited at sanctuaries associated with the individual hero at cultic festivals.[18]

[16] Hermann Gunkel, *The Legends of Genesis* (Chicago: The Open Court Publishing Co., 1901), pp. 24 ff. (republished in 1964 by Schocken Books, New York).

[17] Some modern scholars identify the pillar with the stone outcropping on the mountain ridge to the southwest of the Dead Sea known as the Jebel Usdum. Cf. Curt Kuhl, *The Old Testament, Its Origins and Composition*, trans. by C. T. M. Herriot (Richmond: John Knox Press, 1961), p. 43.

[18] "Legend" in *The Interpreter's Dictionary of the Bible* (New York: Abingdon Press, 1962).

Myth, which is classically but somewhat narrowly defined as "stories of the gods," is distinguished from legend by the divinity of the central figure or figures. As there is no true polytheism in the Old Testament (only echoes, cf., Deut. 32:8–9; Ps. 82:1), only the creation accounts (Gen. 1–3), the story of the sons of God (Gen. 6), and perhaps Job 1–3, are placed in this category. The flood accounts and the story of the tower of Babel are combinations of myth and legend.

More broadly defined, myth is the description of any action of the deity in human affairs. Such a definition tends to embrace almost every Old Testament statement about the activity of God and, thus merging with what is generally classified as "theology,"[19] would nullify any attempt to analyze Old Testament literature.

A third definition seeks to interpret myth in terms of ancient Near Eastern thought patterns and lay stress upon aetiological factors. Like other peoples of the Near East, the Hebrews conceived of the world as a flat disc beneath the solid vault of heaven which met the earth or sea at the horizon. Such a concept, we know, was based upon optical illusion, but peoples of early times had developed neither instruments nor techniques for scientific investigation of their environment. To explain the beginnings of life or why things are as they are, the Hebrews, like others, developed explanations which modern scientific and historical knowledge render unacceptable, but which reveal to us how people thought and what they believed. Only as we are cognizant of the ancient belief in a three-story world (heaven above, earth, and Sheol, the place of the dead, below) and are sensitive to the tendency to interpret experience and "reality" in mytho-poeic terms can we begin to understand how the Hebrew writers responded to their world.

It would seem preferable to recognize in myth a literary vehicle developing out of the creative and sensitive spirit of man, as man, in awareness of the totality of his experiences, including change, decay, death, birth, the cycles of nature, and strange, unexpected happenings, sought to make sense of, or give order to, or give significance to his experience. This deep awareness of his environment and of his experience led to the presupposing of creative powers which, in primeval time, "in the beginning," brought order into being by overcoming chaos.[20] What happened "then" had relevance for "now." As chaos was defeated "then," so it must be overcome "now." Once the normal time span, whether it be the cycle of the year or some other period, had run its course, it had to be renewed; life had to be re-energized

---

19 G. von Rad, *Old Testament Theology*, trans. by D. M. G. Stalker (New York: Harper and Brothers, 1962), I, 105 f.; E. Jacob, *Theology of the Old Testament*, trans. by A. W. Heathcote and P. J. Allcock (New York: Harper and Brothers, 1958), pp. 11 f.

20 The struggle between benevolent and malevolent forces could be witnessed in the battle between sterility and fertility in the land, light and darkness in the heavens, life and death in nature.

EGYPTIAN COSMOLOGY. *Egyptian cosmology pictured Nut, the sky goddess, arched to form the heavens; Geb, the earth god, reclining so that the curvature of his body symbolized valleys and hills; and Shu, the air god, separating heaven and earth and supporting the heavens. The arch of the sky is also represented by the figure of Nut as the heavenly cow with Shu in the same posture beneath the animal figure. (Based on the fifteenth century B.C. papyrus of Ani, the so-called "Book of the Dead.")*

and recharged; re-creation had to ensue, symbolically, through the defeat of chaos.[21]

The myth, which conveys beliefs about what happened at the beginning, had environmental significance. Events of the first creation were re-enacted through ritual and ceremonial cult drama, and in this re-enactment the worshiper was a participant. He was, so to speak, *there,* involved in the renewal of life. Myth is a literary expression relating the ideal to the real, binding that which took place in the ancient past to the ritual act of the present. As such, it becomes for the believer the foundation of reality, for he is linked physically, emotionally, intellectually, spiritually and socially with fundamental beginnings, with his own primeval origins. Such a definition emphasizes that, for people in Old Testament times, myth was a living reality. It was more than a story told about ancient times; it was a reality experienced as words, articulated, took form and meaning in cultic dramatization.[22]

All biblical mythology does not fit into the seasonal or cultic drama pattern.[23] Where remnants are found of ancient myths reflecting the battle between chaos and order, or between God and the primeval monster of the deep (cf. Isa. 27:1, 30:7, 51:9–10; Ezek. 29:3–5, 32:2–6),

[21] The cyclic pattern was apparent in lunar changes, seasonal periods, rhythms of birth and death, etc.

[22] Cf. T. H. Gaster, *Thespis, Ritual, Myth and Drama in the Ancient Near East* (New York: Henry Schuman, 1950), pp. 3–72; H. and H. A. Frankfort, "Myth and Reality," *Before Philosophy* (Baltimore: Penguin Books, 1959); B. S. Childs, *Myth and Reality in the Old Testament* (London: S.C.M. Press), pp. 13–27; C. Kerenyi, "Prologomena," in C. G. Jung and C. Kerenyi, *Essays on a Science of Mythology,* trans. by R. F. C. Hull (New York: Harper and Row, 1963).

[23] G. H. Davies, "An Approach to the Problem of Old Testament Mythology," *Palestine Exploration Quarterly* (London: Office of the Fund, 1956), pp. 89 f.

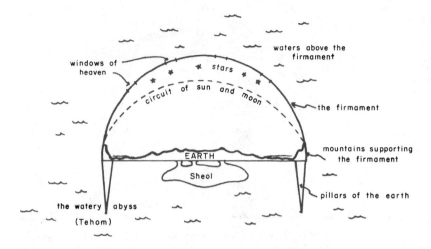

HEBREW COSMOLOGY. *Because no depictions of the Hebrew concept of the universe have been found, any reconstruction is conjectural and is dependent upon the interpretation of information found scattered through the Bible. The flat earth is a disc, the heavens, like an inverted bowl, are solid, holding back the waters above the firmament, and only as the windows of heaven were opened could these external waters fall upon the earth. Above the firmament and the external waters was the court of heaven. Outside the heaven-earth complex was the water abyss (Heb.:* Tehom) .

the myth has been "historicised" and God's enemy, whether it be Egypt or Babylon, is described as the monster of chaos, or the myth is related to a past event, such as the Exodus from Egypt (Ps. 74:13 ff.) .[24]

Other categories of biblical literature are: fable, in which animals and plants are the *dramatis personae* and a moral is drawn or a lesson taught (cf. Judg. 9:7–15); fiction, which may also teach a lesson (Jonah, Ruth); and apocalyptic literature, which deals with the end of the age (Daniel). Each category of literature has its own purpose and conveys in its own way the writer's intent. It must be assumed that different forms of literary expression were not employed accidentally. To understand what each writer is attempting to say, it is important to recognize the literary form utilized, for problems develop when myth is treated as history or when fiction is accepted as fact.

POETRY

Writers of the Old Testament were not limited to expression in prose; poetry was extensively employed. In modern translations, large portions of what used to be printed as prose are now in poetic form. It is estimated that, whereas only 15 per cent of the Old Testament appeared as poetry in the King James version of 1611, in the Revised Standard Version of the Bible about 40 per cent of the text is printed

24 Cf. Artur Weiser, *The Old Testament: Its Formation and Development,* trans. by D. M. Barton (New York: Association Press, 1961), pp. 57 f.

as poetry.[25] Translators of the 1611 edition were limited in their understanding of Hebrew word rhythm and, unless a writing was specifically identified as a "song" or "psalm," it was printed as prose.

The discovery of the major key to the understanding of Hebrew poetry is attributed to a British scholar, Bishop Robert Lowth, who in 1753 published a work titled *De sacra poesi Hebraeorum praelectiones academicae*.[26] In this book Lowth called attention to what he labeled *parallelismus membrorum,* or parallelism, wherein the thought patterns of one part of the verse are expressed in another part of the verse in different terms.[27] For example:

> The heavens are telling the glory of God;
>> and the firmament proclaims his handiwork.

> Ps. 19:1

The thought of the first line is repeated in the second: the word "heavens" is paralleled by the word "firmament," the verb "are telling" means the same as "proclaim," and the Psalmist believed that "the glory of God" was manifested in "his handiwork." This precise echoing of the concept of one line in the following line is called "synonymous parallelism." Where the second line expresses the antithesis of the first line, thus emphasizing the thought, the form is called "antithetical parallelism,"[28] as in:

> A soft answer turns away wrath,
>> but a harsh word stirs up anger.

> Prov. 15:1

The principle which lies behind the Hebrew verse has been succinctly stated by T. H. Robinson: "Every verse much consist of at least two 'members,' the second of which must, more or less completely, satisfy the expectation raised by the first."[29] Rhyme as we know it in English poetry is not a dominant characteristic of Hebrew poetry (see Gen. 4:23, the "Song of Lamech" in which each line ends in an "i" sound). Sense rhythm or parallelism was not the creation of Hebrew poets, for the same characteristics are found in Egyptian, Babylonian and Canaanite poetry predating Hebrew poems.[30]

Like the poetry of other peoples, Hebrew poems made use of hyperbole to express emotions in superlative terms ("my bones burn

[25] James Muilenburg, "The Poetry of the Old Testament," *An Introduction to the Revised Standard Version of the Old Testament* (New York: Thomas Nelson and Sons, 1952), pp. 62 f.

[26] An English translation was made by G. Gregory in 1847, *Lectures on the Sacred Poetry of the Hebrews.*

[27] The importance of the repetition of thought patterns for interpretation of the text had been recognized by Jewish scholars at a much earlier date. See G. B. Gray, *The Forms of Hebrew Poetry* (London: Hodder and Stoughton, 1915).

[28] Other types include "stairlike parallelism," "emblematic parallelism," "introverted parallelism." Cf. C. A. and E. G. Briggs, *A Critical and Exegetical Commentary on the Psalms* (New York: Charles Scribner's Sons, 1912), I, Introduction.

[29] Theodore H. Robinson, *The Poetry of the Old Testament* (London: Gerald Duckworth & Co., Ltd., 1947), p. 21.

[30] Cf. *ANET,* pp. 406 ff. (Egyptian), pp. 434 ff. (Babylonian), pp. 129 ff. (Canaanite).

like a furnace"—Ps. 102:3) and employed highly figurative language and similes to convey impressions (The righteous man is "like a tree"—Ps. 1). Poetry is used for love songs (Song of Songs), taunt songs to mock the enemy (Judg. 5:28–30), praise songs (Ps. 145), wisdom sayings (Proverbs), prophetic oracles, and many other types of expression.

PROBLEMS OF TEXT AND AUTHORSHIP

In attempting to understand a particular writing, whether it be prose or poetry, the biblical scholar seeks to discover, wherever possible, who wrote the material, when, where, why, to whom or for whom, and under what circumstances. This methodology received the title of "higher criticism" to distinguish it from "lower criticism" which is concerned with manuscript or textual study.

In lower criticism, the history of a particular writing is depicted as a stream, the source of which is the "autograph" or the original copy as it left the author's hand. (See Chart II.) As autographs are no longer available we must depend upon the accuracy of those who through the centuries have copied and recopied the words. Until the discovery of scrolls in caves near the Dead Sea in 1947, the earliest Hebrew manuscripts of the Bible known to translators were from the ninth century A.D. Textual experts, comparing manuscripts, find variances. Copyists, being human, made many simple errors in the process of transmission. An early copyist's error might affect hundreds of subsequent manuscripts. For example, if a weary scribe let his eyes drop from one line to another ending in the same word thereby omitting several intervening lines (*haplography*), and his uncorrected manuscript was copied and

_____ CHART II. MANUSCRIPT TRANSMISSION _____

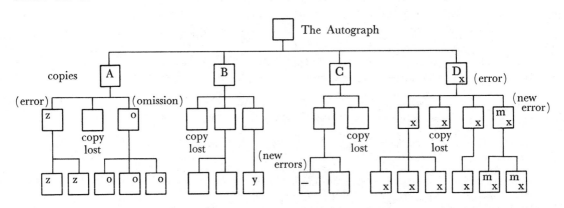

The greater the distance between an individual manuscript and the autograph the greater the possibility of the manuscript containing copyists' errors. Once an error had been made, those who copied tended to reproduce it. A scholar with an impressive number of manuscripts representing the "D" family in the above chart and with few manuscripts from A, B and C must evaluate the material to determine whether the D evidence should be allowed to outweigh the other evidence. Meanwhile he may be confronted with dozens of individual textual problems in the A, B and C families.

recopied, a textual critic would have to decide whether the intervening lines appearing in some manuscripts were added by a later writer, or had been inadvertently omitted by an early copyist. Sometimes a line or word is copied twice (*dittography*), and on occasion a scribe will do what many modern typists often do, invert a word (*metathesis*). The lower critic compares manuscripts, recognizes "families" by the relationship of spelling patterns and errors, learns to distinguish between careful and careless copyists, and uses every skill and tool he possesses to provide the most accurate manuscript.

The higher critic focuses attention upon the author. He seeks to discover all that he can concerning the time of the writing, the cultural setting, the situation which prompted the writing and the nature of the group for whom the writing was intended. Sometimes the author's identity is easily ascertained, for an editor may have prefaced the work with a statement of identification. However, a name placed at the beginning of a book may not signify the author. The name Joshua stands over one book of the Bible which is certainly not by Joshua, for Joshua's obituary appears in the last chapter. The book is about Joshua. The same thing may be said about the first five books of the Bible which are called the "Books of Moses." Moses' death is recorded in the last chapter of Deuteronomy, so he cannot be the author of these verses, and, as we shall see presently, other matters make it quite clear that while Moses is the central character, he is not the author of these books.

Even when a book does appear to be the work of the individual named in the title, additional material may have been added. The book of Isaiah refers to King Uzziah (ch. 6) and King Ahaz (ch. 7), both of whom lived in the eighth century B.C. when Isaiah prophesied. Chapter 45 contains a reference to King Cyrus of Persia, who, in the sixth century B.C., released the Hebrew people from their captivity in Babylon. Because of differences in style, in details reflecting a different historical setting, and in messages directed to people in a different life situation, Chapters 40 onward are believed to be the product of someone living in Babylon two centuries after the time of Isaiah of Jerusalem. The book of Isaiah is, therefore, a composite work. It is the task of the higher critic to attempt to discover, wherever possible, the work of the original writer and to study that writing in terms of the historical period out of which it came. He must apply the same methods and questions to the later additions.

3

The Analysis of the Pentateuch

PERHAPS the portion of the Bible which best demonstrates the results of the historical-literary approach is the Pentateuch.[1] The five books were named by the Jews of Palestine according to the opening Hebrew words:

   I.   Bereshith: "In the Beginning"
  II.   We'elleh Shemoth: "And these are the names"
 III.   Wayyiqra': "And he called"
 IV.   Wayyedabber: "And he spoke"
  V.   Elleh Haddebarim: "These are the words"

The names now used in the English translations are from the Septuagint:

   I.   Genesis: the beginnings of the world and of the Hebrew people
  II.   Exodus: departure from Egypt under Moses
 III.   Leviticus: legal rulings concerning sacrifice, purification, and so forth of concern to the priests, who came from the tribe of Levi
 IV.   Numbers (Arithmoi): the numbering or taking census of Israelites in the desert
  V.   Deuteronomy: meaning "second law," because many laws found in the previous books are repeated here

These writings, which begin with the creation of the world and trace the development of the Hebrew people through the patriarchal period up to the invasion of Canaan, were believed from very early times to be the work of one person—Moses.[2] There were those who questioned the Mosaic authorship. About A.D. 500 a Jewish scholar wrote in the Talmud[3] that the last eight verses of Deuteronomy which tell of Moses' death must have been written by Joshua.[4] By the time of the Protestant Reformation, Roman Catholic and Protestant scholars were

[1] The term "Pentateuch" was used as early as the third century A.D. by Origen in reference to the first five books of the Bible—the Torah. The word is formed from the Greek terms *pente*—five, and *teuchos*—scroll. Scholars also use the words "Tetrateuch" to refer to the first four books, "Hexateuch" for the first six, "Septateuch" for the first seven books, and "Octateuch" for the first eight books.

[2] See II Chron. 25:4; Luke 2:22; 24:44.

[3] The Talmud is a vast collection of expositions on, or interpretations of, the Torah, representing the discussions of rabbis and schools from about the first five centuries A.D.

[4] Baba Bathra 14b-15a: "Joshua wrote . . . eight verses of the Law."

discussing the difficulty of maintaining the Mosaic authorship of the Torah.

Part of the problem lies in the fact that at no point in the Pentateuch is it stipulated that Moses is the author; certain portions are said to be by Moses, but not the total writing. On the other hand, there is good evidence that Moses could not have been the author. In Gen. 14:14, Abram is said to have led a group of men to the city of Dan, but elsewhere it is stated that this city did not come into existence until the time of the Judges (Judg. 18:29), long after Moses' time. The conquest by the Gileadites of the area called Havvothjair took place in the time of the Judges (Judg. 10:3–4), yet it is reported in the Pentateuch (Num. 32:41; Deut. 3:14). The time of the Hebrew monarchy is reflected in Gen. 36:31, yet this passage is set in a discussion of the patriarchal period. How could Moses write of conditions that did not come into being until long after his death?

There is some indication that whoever wrote certain parts of the Pentateuch was in Palestine, within the territory which in Moses' time had not yet been entered. Gen. 50:10, Num. 35:14, and Deut. 1:1, 5, 3:8, 4:46 speak of places which are located "beyond the Jordan," which is to say on the east side of the Jordan and outside of Palestine proper. Such a statement could only be uttered by someone on the western side of the Jordan river, and Moses, we are told in Deut. 34, never entered that land.

Other evidence also suggests that Moses did not write the Pentateuch, and that many different writers made contributions to it. There are contradictory statements, one of the most obvious of which concerns the number of animals Noah took into the ark. In Gen. 6:19 Noah is told to take two of every kind of living creature—one male and one female—but in Gen. 7:2 seven pair of clean animals and birds are required. Would a single writer be so inconsistent?

Num. 35:6–7 specifies that Levites were to receive certain territorial inheritances, but Deut. 18:1 makes it quite clear that they are to have no inheritance. According to Exod. 3:13–15 and Exod. 6:2–3, the personal name of God, "Yahweh,"[5] was revealed for the first time to Moses on the holy mountain. Prior to this revelation, Yahweh was known only as "Elohim,"[6] or as "El Shaddai."[7] On the other hand,

[5] The personal name of God is represented in Hebrew by the consonants YHWH, often called the "tetragrammaton" (four letters). On the basis of Greek transcriptions most scholars believe that the proper pronunciation of the word is "Yahweh" (often spelled in the German form "Jahveh"). This name became so sacred that it was not to be uttered, and the term "adonai" meaning "Lord" was read in its place. Most English translations use the form "LORD" for the Hebrew YHWH. The form "Jehovah" is an English hybridization composed of the consonants J-H-V-H and the vowels from "adonai" producing JaHoVaH. Cf. Theophile J. Meek, *Hebrew Origins* (New York: Harper & Brothers, 1950), pp. 82 ff.; R. Abba, "The Divine Name Yahweh," *Journal of Biblical Literature*, LXXX (1961), 320–328.

[6] "Elohim" is usually translated "God" in English versions. The general term for any deity is *"el"*. The form "Elohim" is a plural, and the fact that it is used as a singular noun to refer to the God of Israel may reflect an awareness that the various manifestations of deity (*el*) are but extensions of a supreme "El," or "Elohim" embodying them all.

[7] This term, often translated "God Almighty," means "God of the Mountains." Cf. Wm. F. Albright, "The Names Shaddai and Abram," *Journal of Biblical Literature*, LIV (1935), 180 ff.

however, Gen. 4:26 indicates that from very early times men called upon God by his personal name of Yahweh, and in numerous places the patriarchs use the name Yahweh (see Gen. 22:14, 26:25, 27:20, 28:13). Would a single author make statements so contradictory? In fact, the very manner in which divine names are used prior to the revelation of Yahweh's name in Exodus raises problems. In certain sections of Genesis "Elohim" appears exclusively (Gen. 1:1–31, 9:1–11); in other places "Yahweh" appears alone (Gen. 4:1–16, 11:1–9). It would appear that different traditions have been brought together.

Some stories appear more than once, in what scholars have called "doublets." For example, in Gen. 15:5 Abraham is promised many descendants, and in Gen. 17:2 the promise is needlessly repeated. In Gen. 12:11–20 Sarah pretends to be the sister of Abraham. This same story appears in a slightly different setting in Gen. 20:1–18, and is told again with Isaac and Rebekah as central actors in Gen. 26:6–11. In the last two examples, Philistine kings are mentioned and the Philistines did not settle in Palestine until the twelfth century. How are such repetitions, contradictions and anachronisms best explained?

By the seventeenth century a number of scholars had wrestled with the problems of the Mosaic authorship of the Pentateuch. Carlstadt, a leader of the Reformation movement in Germany, wrote a pamphlet in 1520 arguing that Moses did not write the Pentateuch, for the style of writing in the verses reporting Moses' death (Deut. 32:5–12) was that of the preceding verses. In 1574, A. Du Maes, a Roman Catholic scholar, suggested that the Pentateuch was composed by Ezra, who used old manuscripts as a basis. Thomas Hobbes, the English philosopher, concluded in 1651 that Moses wrote only parts of Deuteronomy (*Leviathan* III:33). In *Tractatus theologico-politicus* (1677), Baruch Spinoza, the Jewish philosopher, recognized as one of the founders of modern biblical criticism, reached a conclusion much like that of Du Maes, that Ezra compiled Genesis to II Kings from documents of varying dates. Shortly afterward, Richard Simon, a Roman Catholic priest, often called "the father of biblical criticism," gathered together the substance of critical analyses up to his time and raised the problem of literary history, thus opening the door to the application of techniques used in the study of non-sacred literature to the Bible.

In the eighteenth century Jean Astruc, a celebrated physician, published a treatise on Genesis in which he postulated that Moses used two major sources in writing the book of Genesis.[8] The source in which the name "Elohim" is used for God, Astruc called "A," and that which used "Yahweh" was labelled "B." Ten fragmentary sources were also recognized and given alphabetical designations. Additional criteria for defining sources were worked out by J. G. Eichorn, sometimes

---

[8] Astruc, son of a Protestant minister who was converted to Catholicism, served as physician to King Augustus III of Poland and then to Louis XV of France, ultimately becoming regius professor of medicine at Paris. His work, *Conjectures sur les mémoires originaux dont il paroit que Moise s'est servi pour composer le livre de la Genèse,* was published in Brussels and Paris in 1753 and later appeared in German. He published several other theological essays, as well as a number of important medical treatises.

called "the father of Old Testament criticism"[9] or, on the basis of his five volume "Introduction" to the Old Testament, "the father of the modern science of introductory studies."[10]

Others built upon these foundations. In 1806–7 W. M. L. DeWette, a German scholar, published a two volume introductory study of the Old Testament in which he suggested that the book found in the temple in 621 B.C., during the reign of King Josiah of Judah (II Kings 22–23), was the book of Deuteronomy. In the work of Julius Wellhausen, who built upon the research of K. H. Graf and Wilhelm Vatke, the most significant analysis of the Pentateuch was made. The thesis known as the Graf-Wellhausen theory, or as the Documentary Hypothesis, still provides the basis upon which more recent hypotheses are founded.

The Graf-Wellhausen analysis identified four major literary sources in the Pentateuch, each with its own characteristic style and vocabulary. These were labeled: J, E, D and P. The J source used the name "Yahweh" ("Jahveh" in German) for God, called the mountain of God "Sinai," and the pre-Israelite inhabitants of Palestine "Canaanites," and was written in a vivid, concrete, colorful style. God is portrayed anthropomorphically, creating after the fashion of a potter, walking in the garden, wrestling with Jacob. J related how promises made to the patriarchs were fulfilled, how God miraculously intervened to save the righteous, or to deliver Israel, and acted in history to bring into being the nation.[11] E used "Elohim" to designate God until the name "Yahweh" was revealed in Exod. 3:15, used "Horeb" as the name of the holy mountain, "Amorite" for the pre-Hebrew inhabitants of the land, and was written in language generally considered to be less colorful and vivid than J's. E's material begins in Gen. 15 with Abraham, and displays a marked tendency to avoid the strong anthropomorphic descriptions of deity found in J. Wellhausen considered J to be earlier than E because it appeared to contain the more primitive elements.

The Deuteronomic source, D, is confined largely to the book of Deuteronomy in the Pentateuch, contains very little narrative, and is made up, for the most part, of Moses' farewell speeches to his people. A hortatory and emphatic effect is produced by the repetition of certain phrases: "be careful to do" (5:1, 6:3, 6:25, 8:1), "a mighty hand and an outstretched arm" (5:15, 7:19, 11:2), "that your days may be prolonged" (5:16, 6:2, 25:15). Graf had demonstrated that knowledge of both J and E were presupposed in D, and having accepted DeWette's date of 621 B.C. for D, argued that J and E must be earlier. J was dated about 850 B.C. and E about 750 B.C.

The Priestly tradition, P, reveals interest and concern in whatever pertains to worship. Not only does P employ a distinctive Hebrew

[9] H. F. Hahn, *Old Testament in Modern Research* (Philadelphia: Muhlenberg Press, 1954, Fortress Press, 1966), p. 3.

[10] A. Weiser, *The Old Testament: Its Formation and Development*, trans. by D. M. Barton (New York: Association Press, 1961), p. 2.

[11] The characteristics of the individual sources will be discussed in greater detail later.

vocabulary but, influenced by a desire to categorize and systematize material, develops a precise, and at times a somewhat labored or pedantic, style. Love of detail, use of repetition, listing of tribes and genealogical tables, does not prevent the P material from presenting a vivid and dramatic account of Aaron's action when an Israelite attempted to marry a Midianite woman (Num. 25:6–9) or from developing a rather euphonious and rhythmical statement of creation (Gen. 1). The Graf-Wellhausen hypothesis noted that P contained laws and attitudes not discernible in J, E, or D and reflected late development. P was dated around the time of Ezra, or about 450 B.C.

The combining of the various sources was believed to be the work of redactors. R^{je}, the editor who united J and E around 650 B.C. provided connecting links to harmonize the materials where essential. R^d added the Deuteronomic writings to the combined JE materials about 550 B.C., forming what might be termed a J-E-D document. P was added about 450–400 B.C. by R^p, completing the Torah. This hypothesis,[12] by which the contradictions, doublets, style variations, and vocabulary differences in the Pentateuch were explained, can best be represented by a straight line.

900	850	800	750	700	650	621	600	550	500	450	400
/---	--/---	--/---	--/---	--/---	--/-	--/-	--/---	--/---	--/---	--/---	--/
	J		E		R^{je}	D		R^d		P	R^p
								(JED)			(JEDP)

Variations in the Graf-Wellhausen theory have been proposed since it was first expounded in the nineteenth century. Research into the composition of the individual documents produced subdivisions such as J^1, J^2, J^3, etc. for J, and E^1, E^2, and so on, for E until the documents were almost disintegrated by analysis.[13] New major sources were recognized by other scholars. Professor Otto Eissfeldt discovered a fifth source beginning with Gen. 2 and continuing into Judges and Samuel which he labeled "L" for "Lay" source.[14] R. H. Pfeiffer of Harvard University identified an "S" source in Genesis, so labeled because Pfeiffer believed it came from Seir (in Edom) or from the south.[15] The great Jewish scholar, Julian Morgenstern, singled out what he believed to be the oldest document, "K," which, while in fragmentary form, preserved a tradition of Moses' relationships with the Kenites.[16] Martin Noth of Germany argued for a common basic

[12] For an excellent summary of the Graf-Wellhausen thesis, see J. Wellhausen, "Pentateuch and Joshua," *Encyclopaedia Britannica*, 9th ed. For greater detail see J. Wellhausen, *Prolegomena to the History of Israel* (New York: Meridian Books, 1957).

[13] See, for example, C. A. Simpson, *The Early Traditions of Israel* (Oxford: Basil Blackwell, 1948).

[14] Otto Eissfeldt, *The Old Testament, an Introduction*, trans. by P. R. Ackroyd (New York: Harper and Row, 1965).

[15] R. H. Pfeiffer, *Introduction to the Old Testament* (New York: Harper & Brothers, 1941).

[16] J. Morgenstern, "The Oldest Document in the Hexateuch," *Hebrew Union College Annual*, IV (1927), 1–138.

source "G" (*Grundlage* for "ground-layer" or "foundation") upon which both J and E are developed.[17]

Along with developments stemming from the basic hypothesis, there have been challenges to certain aspects of the theory, including the dating of Deuteronomy[18] and the pattern of development of the sources.[19] Other scholars, particularly those representing conservative theological positions, have taken issue with the documentary hypothesis, arguing for the integrity of the Pentateuch and supporting Mosaic authorship.[20] Most present-day scholarship accepts the basic premises of the documentary hypothesis—namely, that different source materials are to be found, that the labels J, E, D, P, are acceptable for major sources, and that the order of development is that proposed in the Graf-Wellhausen thesis.

But much development away from the hypothesis has taken place too. Back of each of the four sources lie traditions that may have been both oral and written. Some may have been preserved in the songs, ballads, and folktales of different tribals groups, some in written form in sanctuaries. The so-called "documents" should not be considered as mutually exclusive writings, completely independent of one another, but rather as a continual stream of literature representing a pattern of progressive interpretation of traditions and history.[21] Perhaps this idea can best be illustrated by reference to the account of the plagues in Egypt in Exod. 7 ff. The J account tells of the hardening of Pharaoh's heart, of Yahweh's threat to befoul the waters of the Nile and kill the fish, and of the execution of this threat (Exod. 7:14–15a,

[17] For an extended discussion of these developments, see Hahn, *op. cit.*, pp. 1–43, or C. R. North, "Pentateuchal Criticism," *The Old Testament and Modern Study*, H. H. Rowley (ed.) (Oxford: Clarendon Press, 1952).

[18] A. C. Welch, *The Code of Deuteronomy* (London: James Clarke & Co., 1924).

[19] Cf. Yehezkel Kaufmann, *The Religion of Israel*, trans. and abridged by Moshe Greenberg (Chicago: University of Chicago Press, 1960) where an order J-E-P-D is proposed.

[20] For a good survey of opposition from Jewish scholars, cf. Felix A. Levy, "Contemporary Trends in Jewish Bible Study," *The Study of the Bible Today and Tomorrow*, ed. H. R. Willoughby (Chicago: Univ. of Chicago Press, 1947), pp. 98–115. Protestant scholars defending the Mosaic authorship include W. H. Green, *The Higher Criticism of the Pentateuch* (New York: Charles Scribner's Sons, 1895); James Orr, *The Problem of the Old Testament* (New York: Charles Scribner's Sons, 1906); Gleason L. Archer, *A Survey of Old Testament Introduction* (Chicago: Moody Press, 1964). Roman Catholic scholarship has moved from opposition to an acceptance of the basic tenets of the analytic method. Cf. *Rome and the Study of Scripture* (St. Meinrad, Indiana: Grail Publications, 1962) for official statements from the encyclical *Providentissimus Deus* of Leo XIII to reports from the Biblical Commission, 1961; R. A. Dyson and R. A. F. MacKenzie, "Higher Criticism," *A Catholic Commentary on Holy Scripture* (New York: Thomas Nelson and Sons, 1953), pp. 61–66; Jean Steinmann, *Biblical Criticism*, The Twentieth Century Encyclopedia of Catholicism (New York: Hawthorn Books, 1958), pp. 81 ff. A good summary with bibliography by C. U. Wolf, "Recent Roman Catholic Bible Study and Tradition," appears in *The Journal of Bible and Religion*, XXIX (1961), 280–289.

[21] The phrases "progressive interpretation" and "continuing interpretation" will be used interchangeably to underscore the dynamic nature of the biblical material. Concepts and traditions did not remain static but were subject to reinterpretation and could be given new dimensions and new significance at a later date in the light of new experiences and insights. In the example involving Moses and Aaron given above, the roles of the two heroes undergo changes and Aaron assumes a more meaningful role commensurate with the growing importance of the high priesthood in the Jewish community.

CHART III. THE COMPOSITION OF THE TORAH

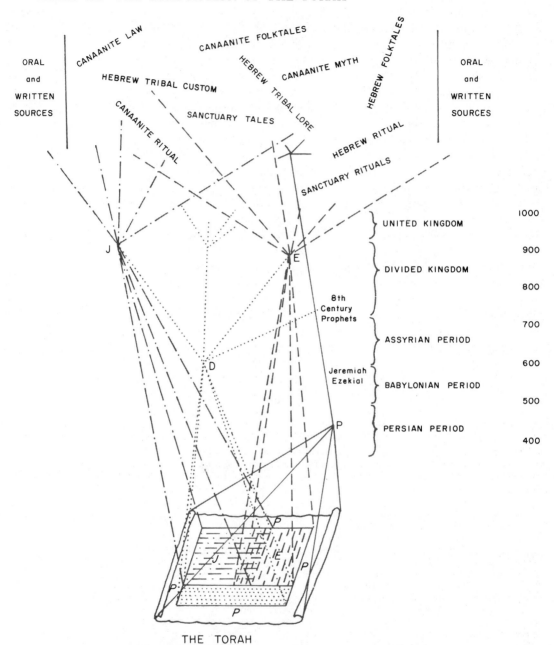

THE TORAH

16–17a, 18, 21a, 23–25). The E writer reinterpreted the story, adding to the account the rod of the wonder-worker and Moses' threat to strike the water and turn the Nile to blood—a threat which he fulfills (Exod. 7:15, 17b, 20b). The Priestly author made other changes: Aaron, not Moses, is the wonder-worker, and it is Aaron who waves the rod not only over the Nile but other rivers, canals, ponds and pools, and all waters are turned to blood, including water stored in containers. The P writer explains that this terrible plague did not change Pharaoh's mind, for Pharaoh's priests can perform the same miracle. The important change made by the P editors is that Aaron, the symbol of the high priesthood in Israel, acts as the priest-magician-agent of God, performing the divine will. The interpretive pattern can be traced quite easily through the subsequent plagues by reference to the lists which delineate the contents of the various sources (see pp. 139 ff., 173 ff., 357 ff.) .

The process of progressive interpretation did not exclude the incorporation of new materials, and some of the new material may have had a long history—oral or written—in circles outside of those which produced the earlier writings. For instance, in 1929 a Canaanite temple library, which can be dated from the fourteenth century B.C., was discovered at Ras es-Shamra, a site on the Syrian coast. The religious documents were found to contain words most familiar to us through Priestly writings of the Pentateuch, suggesting that part of the P material may be based upon sources as ancient as those used in J. Thus, we are confronted with a literary problem that is more difficult than the simple straight line analysis would suggest. Not only do we have materials coming from different periods of time and from different groups within society, and not only are these materials brought together and blended at different periods of history, but those who added the extra materials employed an interpretive principle in accordance with their theological convictions expanding, and, in a sense, expounding the writings with which they worked. Further, at some points the fusion of materials is so complete that it is impossible to distinguish sources—particularly where J and E are combined.

Because the documentary hypothesis is the most widely accepted of all theories of Pentateuchal analysis, this book will utilize, in principle, the conclusions reached by this method of research. One important change in the thesis accepted by many scholars will be observed: J and E, dated in Wellhausen's time in the ninth and eighth centuries respectively, will both be placed in the tenth century, for reasons to be discussed later. Such a change does not deny that additions were made to each in the years before they were combined, but implies that the time of Solomon's reign best fits the period for the accumulation of the core of J, and the early years of the divided kingdom are most appropriate for the writing of E.

It should be remembered that the documentary hypothesis, no matter what form it takes, is nothing more than an hypothesis—a proposition—assumed to explain certain facts (in this case doublets, contradictions, etc.) , which provides the basis for further investigation. There is no way of proving that a J collection ever existed. Such a body of writings is assumed on the basis of evidence previously discussed.

4

Other Methods of Approach

OTHER patterns of approach to biblical literature have been developed and most of these supplement the historical-literary method. Each new methodology causes the scholar to reconsider familiar material in the light of new evidence or from a different angle of vision. The results of the multiple approach have been new insights into and a clearer understanding of biblical life and literature and a diminishing dogmatism about what any individual or group of scholars might consider to be "firmly established conclusions."

THE DEUTERONOMIC HISTORY

A somewhat different study arrangement of part of the Pentateuch has been proposed by Martin Noth.[1] Deuteronomy is combined with Joshua, Judges, I and II Samuel, and I and II Kings as part of an immense Deuteronomic history extending from Moses to the destruction of Judah by the Babylonians in the sixth century. The work, Noth believes, was composed by an individual who skillfully blended a variety of source materials into a single work. The point of view is Judaean, and the interpretive key to the whole is found in Deut. 4:44–30:20. The book of Deuteronomy is, according to this analysis, to be studied as part of an historical collection rather than simply as part of the Pentateuch. Noth's thesis will be acknowledged in this book.

CULTIC INTERPRETATION

A different approach, stressing the use of the Old Testament in worship, provides important clues for understanding the literature.[2] Just as myth can be interpreted as the spoken or recited portion of a

---

[1] Martin Noth, *The History of Israel*, trans. by S. Godman, rev. by P. R. Ackroyd (London: A. and C. Black, 1960), p. 42.

[2] A. Bentzen, *Introduction to the Old Testament* (Copenhagen: G. E. C. Gad, 1958), II, 76 ff.; J. Pedersen, *Israel, Its Life and Culture* (Copenhagen: Povl Branner, 1940), pp. 725–745; G. E. Wright, "Cult and History," *Interpretation*, XVI (1962), 3–20; Martin J. Buss, "The Meaning of 'Cult' and the Interpretation of the Old Testament," *The Journal of Bible and Religion,* XXXII (1964), 317–325.

ritual, and drama or sacrifice or other physical performance as the enactment of the myth, the cult may be recognized as the structure of the organization making possible the ritual performance. Within organized religious structure, within the cult, the traditions of the past were transformed into ritual acts; therefore, to understand the significance of the tradition one must understand its relationship to the cult. Large portions of the Old Testament lend themselves to this mode of analysis.[3]

Three great annual festivals were observed in ancient Israel: the Feast of Unleavened Bread (Passover)[4] in the spring, the Feast of Weeks (or Harvest or Pentecost)[5] in the early summer, and the Feast of Ingathering (Booths)[6] in the fall (Exod. 23:14–17, 34:18–23). The Unleavened Bread celebration appears to have combined a nomadic pastoral festival when a lamb was sacrificed (celebrated on the first day of the festival) and an agricultural feast of unleavened bread occupying seven days, perhaps borrowed from the pre-Hebrew Canaanite inhabitants of Palestine. The Feast of Weeks, an agricultural harvest celebration, included the offering of "firstfruits" through which the total harvest, represented in the first reaping, was symbolically presented to the deity. During the festival of Booths, celebrated at harvest, the people lived in huts made of boughs, much as some families in the Near East do today at harvest time. Unleavened Bread was associated with the escape of the Hebrews from Egypt, Booths with the wilderness wanderings, and Weeks, ultimately, with the giving of the Torah, or with Noah's covenant.[7] In addition to these major observances, numerous other cultic rites may have taken place at local shrines.[8]

Participation in the cult ceremonies had individual and national significance. For the individual, when the ritual was successfully completed, it marked the achievement of harmonious relationships with life-giving powers and with all life within the locale, the attainment of personal communion with the deity, and the participation in rites of community re-invigoration.[9] For the nation the rite marked the renewal of life-power and of divine human relationships, and symbolized divine blessing for those belonging to the cult. What had happened in the past had meaning for the present; deliverance in the past, successfully re-enacted, was related to blessing, forgiveness, favor and deliverance in the present.

3 For example, the Psalms.

4 Also called "Yahweh's passover" (Exod. 12:11, 27; Num. 28:16).

5 For titles cf. Exod. 34:22; Num. 28:26; Deut. 16:10; II Chron. 8:13, "weeks"; Exod. 23:16, "harvest"; Num. 28:26, "firstfruits"; and among Greek-speaking Jews "Pentecost," cf. Tobit 2:1; II Macc. 12:32.

6 Also called "the feast" in I Kings 8:2, 65; Isa. 30:29; Ezek. 45:23, 25; "Feast of Yahweh" in Lev. 23:39; Judg. 21:19.

7 Both associations are reported in late literature. Cf. the Talmud: *Pesahim* 68b and in the Pseudepigrapha: *Jubilees* 6:17.

8 Sites associated with the patriarchs such as Beer-sheba, Hebron, Bethel and Shiloh.

9 Cf. Gaster, *op. cit.* pp. 3–33; M. Eliade, *The Sacred and the Profane* (New York: Harcourt, Brace and Co., 1959).

Such an approach to Old Testament literature tends to give scant attention to the analysis of sources. Emphasis is placed on blocks of literature and the usage of these literary units in cult rites. For example, it is argued that the annual festival of Weeks, celebrated at Gilgal, dramatized the deliverance of Israel from Egypt and the crossing of the Sea.[10] Chapters 1–5 of Joshua are based upon this ritual and clearly demonstrate that the miraculous passage through the waters was enacted by a procession through the Jordan River. This kind of approach renders the attempt to distinguish the sources of Josh. 1–5 relatively unimportant.[11]

ORAL TRADITION

A number of Scandinavian scholars have moved away from the patterns of literary analysis previously discussed and have laid stress upon the importance of oral tradition in the transmission of Old Testament materials.[12] One scholar, Eduard Nielsen, has argued that written Old Testament records prior to the Exile (sixth century) were negligible. This thesis rests upon a number of presuppositions. It is assumed that prior to the Exile writing skills were confined to a group of specialists whose services were employed primarily in formulating business contracts, legal texts, and inscriptions on monuments. Cult legends, traditions and laws were transmitted orally. For example, Isa. 8:16 records the prophet's intent to "bind up" his words with his disciples, and it is assumed that the "binding" is in their memory. When Jeremiah's words were written down because he could not deliver them in person and the scroll was destroyed by the king, Jeremiah seemed to have no trouble in reiterating his message, apparently in the same words (Jer. 36). Because there was no real dependency upon the written record, memory was cultivated and could be relied upon.

Where traditions were recited before a group, certain controls were placed upon the reciter, tending to "freeze" the form of the narrative and guarantee accuracy: controls from the professional body of which he was a part, and controls from listeners familiar with the tradition. Stereotyped forms tend to aid in memorization, and oral tradition may thus become as fixed as written records.

Certain criteria help to distinguish oral forms. For example, where only a single written prose record exists, the following clues point to an oral tradition back of the written form: a monotonous and rhythmic style, the repetition of expressions, changes of style in a single sentence which would ordinarily be caught and remedied in a written work, and use of catch words and other mnemonic devices. When there are doublets with discrepancies, one must undertake the difficult task

[10] The Hebrew designation, *"yam suph"* meaning "Sea of Reeds," has traditionally been translated "Red Sea." Cf. Num. 33:10 ff. However, cf. Exod. 14:10–15:21 where only the term "Sea" appears.

[11] For example, see below, the section on "Torah and Cult" in chap. 26.

[12] E. Nielsen, *op. cit.*; A. Bentzen, *op. cit.*, I, pp. 102 ff.

of determining the relationship of the accounts to each other and to the earlier oral or written traditions.[13]

It is further presupposed that any written traditions that may have existed probably were not carried to Babylon by the Exiles; thus the whole pre-Exilic tradition, fortunately committed to memory, was perpetuated through oral tradition. Only after the destruction of Jerusalem was it finally reduced to writing.[14] Such a thesis does not deny that traditions from different sources were ultimately blended, but it does reduce to unimportance the results of source analysis.

Up to the present time there has been no widespread acceptance by scholars of this particular hypothesis of the oral traditionalists. No one will question that oral forms lie back of the written materials, but few will accept the sixth century B.C. date for the beginning of written records. We will give limited attention to literary forms but we will not attempt to investigate the complicated and demanding subject of the oral traditions that lie back of the written records, except insofar as this study relates to "form criticism." (See below.)

FORM CRITICISM

Form criticism, or "form history,"[15] is a method of literary analysis seeking to go behind the written documents to the underlying oral traditions. Certain presuppositions, drawn from the study of folk literature, are basic to the method.[16] It is assumed that folk memory tends to operate with small units, often no more than a line or two. These units grow out of folk events, and each unit has a characteristic pattern associated with the event, whether it be a wedding, a birth celebration, a funeral, a celebration of a victory over an enemy, or a liturgy accompanying an act of worship. Each unit, coming out of its own particular life setting,[17] tends to have its structure or form fairly well fixed insofar as structural pattern, length and tendency[18] are concerned. That is to say, the form associated with a wedding would differ from that utilized for funeral situations. Custom determined what details were "proper" or "right" for each. So long as the community interest in the event commemorated is kept alive, the oral unit will survive.

Within the Old Testament, certain features suggest the validity of such an approach: the priests gave instruction, the prophets uttered oracles, the wise men spoke their aphorisms, the judges pronounced verdicts, the choristers sang their psalms. For each situation there was a proper pattern of utterance. As we shall see, analysis of the cultic use of the Psalms depends heavily upon the recognition of poetic forms

---

13 Cf. E. Nielson, *op. cit.,* pp. 36 f. for details.

14 Between 586 B.C. and the Maccabaean period, *Ibid.,* p. 39.

15 A translation of the German *"Formgeschichte."*

16 First applied to the Bible by Gunkel.

17 A translation of the German *"Sitz im Leben."*

18 A translation of the German *"Tendenz"* meaning "aim" or "purpose." Tendency may include entertainment, excitation to action, etc.

associated with specific situations. It is the purpose of form criticism to recognize stylistic features, to analyze them in terms of life settings and tendencies, and to trace the history of the form or the way in which its use developed within biblical literature.

The significance of this study for understanding oral tradition is obvious, for its aids in understanding how the literature could be preserved through the patriarchal period and even through the time of the Babylonian Exile. It is also significant for literary criticism, for not only does it draw attention to the important pre-literary stage of biblical materials, but it provides the basis for better understanding of the significance of Hebrew-Jewish literary patterns.

ARCHAEOLOGICAL AND LINGUISTIC STUDIES

Archaeological and language studies, special areas of research, have made significant contributions to the understanding of the Bible.

Archaeological research, concerned with the scientific study of the ancient past, may conveniently be divided into three areas: field work, analysis (some of which will also be done in the field) and application (some of which will also be done in the field). Field work consists of the discovery, excavation and identification of sites. Ancient cities were generally located near adequate water and agricultural resources and on trade routes. For purposes of defense, and perhaps to avoid flood waters, the cities were often built on hilltops. During the hundreds of years that these sites were occupied, they suffered destruction by enemies, earthquake, and fire, only to be rebuilt and reoccupied. As layers or strata of cultural deposit accumulated, the height of the mound or tell[19] rose higher and higher. Many tells have been mapped and some have been identified. Often local Arabic names echo ancient biblical designations.[20] Sometimes careful descriptions of the location in ancient records, including the Bible, make identification possible. Excavation of ancient sites involves careful removal of cultural layers, accurate cataloging of soil characteristics, artifacts, buildings, walls, etc. Analysis, which begins on the site and is continued after excavation, comprises dating of pottery vessels and sherds or pieces, identification of buildings, and interpretation of all like data significant for understanding the history of the site. Application, which may also begin on the site, is the use of information resulting from the excavation for better understanding of some aspects of the Bible or Near Eastern history and ecology. From archaeological research has come knowledge of nations heretofore unknown (such as the Hittites),[21] a staggering amount of linguistic knowledge of Semitic languages including Ugaritic or Canaanite and

19 "Tell" is the Arabic word for mound, cf. Albright, *The Archaeology of Palestine*, p. 16.

20 E.g., Tell Dotha which is ancient Dothan, Tell el-Jazar which is Gezer.

21 The Hittites are mentioned in the Bible (Gen. 23:3 ff.; 26:34; II Sam. 11; Ezek. 16:3, 45), but up until archaeologists provided evidence of the great Hittite nation they were assumed to be a tribal group. Cf. O. R. Gurney, *The Hittites* (Baltimore: Penguin, 1952).

Akkadian, and also of non-Semitic languages such as Egyptian, Hittite and Sumerian, some of which have helped in providing better translations of the Bible and all of which have made available vast quantities of textual data. In addition, many historical details omitted from the Bible are recovered and, what is perhaps equally important, many historical details provided in the Bible are confirmed.[22] In a broader context, the recovery of household items, tools, jewelry, toys, weapons and cultic items, and the uncovering of homes, temples, industrial plants and other facets of daily life have put flesh and bone on biblical personnages, revealing them as individuals with responsibilities, interests and concerns parallel to those of our own time. The fruits of archaeology will be utilized throughout this book.[23]

From specialists in language have come translated texts of myths, prayers, hymns, historical documents, wisdom writings and other literature of the great neighboring nations of Palestine. Cuneiform tablets relating beliefs about creation, the flood, gods and goddesses have provided important information for understanding the Bible. Such knowledge makes it possible to comprehend the flow of ideas and the impact of one culture upon another, without ignoring the distinctiveness of each. Biblical literature is best understood in the context of the literature of the ancient Near East, for not only are relationships of concepts recognized, but the distinctiveness of Hebrew-Jewish writings is made clear.

A further contribution of linguists is in the provision of better texts and translations of the Bible. Some portions of the Bible have suffered in transmission.[24] On occasion a word appears only once in the Bible and its meaning is not clear.[25] Through comparative linguistics and manuscripts studies, better and clearer Bible texts and translations are available. We will employ the results of such research.

[22] For an excellent summary of archaeology and biblical history, see Walter G. Williams, *Archaeology in Biblical Research* (New York: Abingdon Press, 1965), pp. 115–127.

[23] For an analysis of the importance of archaeology for Old Testament chronology, see G. E. Wright, "Archaeology and Old Testament Studies," *Journal of Biblical Literature*, LXXVII (1958), 33–38.

[24] Cf. passages in Job 23–24.

[25] E.g., the Hebrew term *"pim,"* a measure of weight, occurs only in I Sam. 13:21. For a brief discussion of problems of translation, see Harry M. Orlinsky, "The Hebrew Text and the Ancient Versions" and Wm. F. Albright, "The Language of the Old Testament" in *An Introduction to the Revised Standard Version of the Old Testament* (New York: Thomas Nelson and Sons, 1952), pp. 24–40.

PART
TWO

Before There Was an Israel

PROLOGUE

All human events occur within dimensions of space and time. Prerequisites for adequate evaluation of happenings are knowledge of the physical environment or stage-setting and comprehension of historical antecedents or factors preceding the event. Because biblical history is centered in the Near East in general,[1] and in Palestine[2] in particular, it is important to know the geographic features of the total area. Less than 2,000 years are encompassed in the biblical period, so to understand the history of the area prior to the arrival of the Hebrews, archaeological and historical knowledge of the pre-Hebrew eras is necessary.

[1] The area encompassed by the Near East has been defined by H. W. Hazzard, *Atlas of Islamic History* (Princeton Oriental Series, Princeton: University Press, 1951) as extending from 25 degrees East (the western border of Egypt) to 63 degrees East (the eastern border of Iran), and from 42 degrees North (north of European Turkey) to 13 degrees North (the south coast of Arabia).

[2] Palestine includes land on both sides of the Jordan River extending from the Mediterranean Sea to the Syrian and Arabian Deserts, and from the Leontes River in the North to the Wadi el Arish and Ezion Geber in the South.

5

The Land

AS the land-bridge between Africa and Asia, Palestine early became a thoroughfare for wandering peoples, tradesmen, and armies. Over its highways came products and ideas from Egyptians, Hittites, Assyrians, Babylonians, Persians, Aegeans and desert nomads. In itself, the land gave no promise of great wealth, for its mineral resources were modest and its limited agricultural potential ranged from poor to excellent, depending upon the area. Its value lay in its strategic location. From earliest times, it served as an inter-continental cultural link, and when great nations developed and expanded, it became a buffer state, a cushion, between the people of the Nile and those of Asia Minor or Mesopotamia.

In climate and terrain, Palestine is not unlike parts of Southern California. Both have long coastal plains flanked by inland mountains beyond which lie the desert. Both have inland bodies of water below sea level and both have temperatures ranging from temperate along the beaches, to cool in the highlands, to torrid on the deserts in summer. Nor is there dissimilarity in agricultural products, providing adequate water is available.

Geographers[1] divide Palestine into four strips running length-wise through the land: maritime plains, central highlands, Jordan valley and Transjordan plateau, but within these major partitions there are several subdivisions. The long, almost unbroken coastline provides few locations suitable for harbors; consequently, the peoples of Palestine were not, for the most part, oriented toward the sea. In the north the island of Tyre and the coastal city of Sidon, which became Phoenician possessions, had adequate port facilities, but mountains press close to the shore, providing scant acreage for agriculture and making direct communication with the hinterland difficult, and it is natural that the interests and industries of these cities were primarily maritime.[2] Further south at Acco, a natural bay bordered by a broad fertile plain

[1] For geographic and geophysical details, see Denis Baly, *The Geography of the Bible* (New York: Harper and Brothers, 1957). For a more general treatment, see Denis Baly, *Palestine and the Bible*, World Christian Books (London: Lutterworth Press, 1960); "Palestine, Geography of," *Interpreter's Dictionary of the Bible*.

[2] Perhaps the failure of the Sidonese to come to the rescue of Laish, a possession, when the Danites attacked reflects the westward orientation of this seaport (cf. Judg. 18:28 f.).

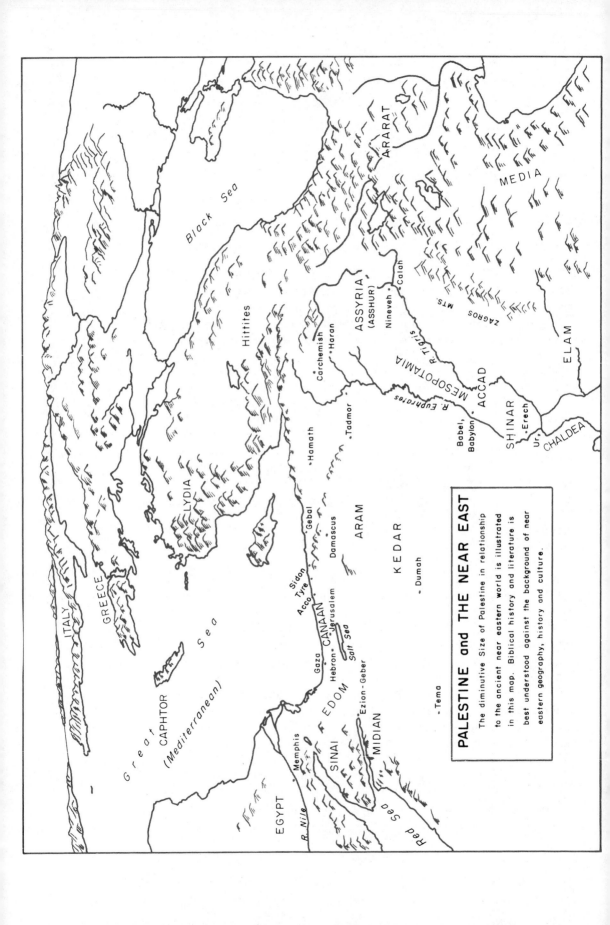

PALESTINE and THE NEAR EAST

The diminutive Size of Palestine in relationship to the ancient near eastern world is illustrated in this map. Biblical history and literature is best understood against the background of near eastern geography, history and culture.

THE SHEPHELAH WEST OF HEBRON. *Olive trees dot the slopes of the hills which have been terraced to prevent erosion. In the rich bottom land between the hills the cultivated fields bear various kinds of grains and vegetables. The houses on the hill to the right are constructed of native limestone.*

formed an adequate but poorly sheltered harbor with access to major inland highways. Below Mount Carmel, which breaks into the coastline, was the heavily forested Plain of Sharon which, in turn, merged into the more southerly Philistine Plain.[3] Small harbors were located at Dor, Joppa (used by Solomon, II Chron. 2:16), and Ashkelon. The Philistine Plain broadened to the south, and inland the sandy seacoast became a gently undulating hinterland, well watered, and ideal for growing grains, olives and grapes. This hilly country, called Shephelah or "lowland" in the Bible (cf. I Kings 10:27; Jer. 17:26, 32:44, 33:13), reaches a height of 1,500 feet in the south, and can only be seen as "low" when viewed from the central highlands.

Running as a backbone throughout the length of Palestine are the central highlands, grouped into three clusters. The upper Galilean hills in the north are rugged and high (nearly 4,000 feet). In lower Galilee, to the south, the hills are not so high and fertile valleys between permit cultivation of vineyards, orchards and olive groves. At the foot of the hills, the Plain of Jezreel spreads southward to the Carmel range, linked to the Plain of Acco by the Kishon River. The strategic importance of the highway that ran through Jezreel is

[3] For the Philistines, see below, chap. 7.

45

demonstrated by the powerful fortified cities that protected it: Jokneam, Megiddo, Taanach, Ibleam and Beth Shan.

The hills of Samaria, or the Ephraim highlands, form the next cluster. One arm of these mountains, the Carmel range, extends westward to the Mediterranean, separating the Plain of Acco from the Plain of Sharon. At the center are the mountains Ebal and Gerizim, with the road linking Samaria and Shechem running between. Further south the Ephraim highlands become the Judaean hills, rising gently from Jerusalem (2,600 feet) to the hills above Hebron (3,000 feet) and descending abruptly further south to Beer-sheba (1,200 feet). Beyond Beer-sheba the hills become part of the desert, the Negeb or "dry land" (Gen. 12:9, 13:1; Deut. 1:7).

Survival in the Negeb depended upon careful hoarding of water, despite the fact that on occasion late spring rains may leave surface pools standing in May. Westward, the Judaean hills became the Shephelah, descending to the Philistine Plain. Strategically located fortresses in the Shephelah formed a first line of defense for the important hill cities of Hebron and Jerusalem.

The Jordan River, formed by a union of streams from the watersheds of Mount Hermon, flows southward in a huge geological rift or fault called in Arabic the Ghôr ("the valley"). The rift begins in Lebanon and extends into the Red Sea at the Gulf of Aqabah and into Africa. From Mount Hermon the Jordan flows into Lake Huleh, a warm, swampy area of reeds and papyrus, 229 feet above sea level.[4] From Huleh the waters descend rapidly for ten miles to the Sea of Chinnereth (Num. 34:11; Josh. 13:27) or Chinneroth (Josh. 11:2, 12:3; I Kings 15:20),[5] a sparkling, fresh water lake 695 feet below sea level. From the lake the river meanders and twists through a jungle of tamarisk, oleander, and other shrubs (cf. Jer. 12:5) to enter the Salt Sea[6] sixty-five miles to the south at 1,285 feet below sea level, the lowest exposed spot on the face of the earth. Here the waters are trapped, escaping only by evaporation and leaving a sterile, heavily saline body of water, useful in ancient times as a source of salt (Ezek. 47:11) and for the tars that floated to its surface.[7] South of the sea, the land begins a gradual rise to a height of 656 feet above sea level midway to the Gulf of Aqabah. This area, known as Wadi el Arabah (the valley of the desert), contained valuable mineral resources.

The high plateau of the Transjordan area is cut horizontally by four streams. The northern river, the Yarmuk (not mentioned in the Bible), forms the southern boundary of the fertile tableland of Bashan, an area famous for cattle (Ps. 22:12, Amos 4:1) and timber

---

4 The modern State of Israel has drained Lake Huleh and utilized the area for agriculture.

5 Later called "Sea of Galilee," "Sea of Tiberias," and "Lake Gennesaret" (I Macc. 11:67).

6 Best known today as the "Dead Sea," a designation not used in the Bible. In addition to "Salt Sea" (Gen. 14:3; Num. 34:12; Deut. 3:17), the waters are called "Arabah Sea" (Deut. 3:17; 4:49), and "Eastern Sea" (Ezek. 47:18; Joel 2:20; Zech. 14:8).

7 P. C. Hammond, "The Nabataean Bitumin Industry at the Dead Sea," *The Biblical Archaeologist*, XXII (1959), 40–48.

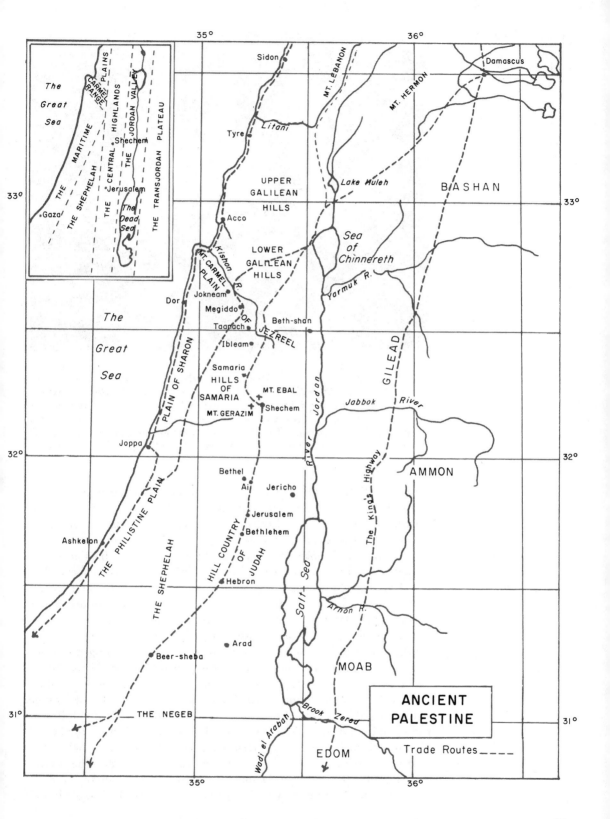

ANCIENT
PALESTINE

Trade Routes _ _ _ _ _

SALT CRYSTALS AT THE SALT (DEAD) SEA. *Driftwood that floats down the Jordan River and into the Dead Sea soon becomes coated with salt crystals. The sea waters are the densest in the world (25 per cent solids) and contain chlorides of sodium, potassium, magnesium and calcium, as well as other minerals. The high salinity imparts to the waters an oiliness that can be felt and seen. The waters in the photograph reveal something of their oily nature.*

(Isa. 2:13, Ezek. 27:6) . The hill country of Gilead, stretching from the Yarmuk to a line just south of the Jabbok (Nahr ez-Zerga) [8] was ideally suited to grape and olive culture. South and east was Ammon, which extended to the Arnon River (Wadi Mojib) , and between the Arnon and the brook Zered (Wadi el-Hesa) was Moab. The broad tableland in these two areas was most suited to raising sheep, but could produce food crops (cf. Ruth 1:1) . Further south was Edom, a semi-desert region through which ran important trade routes. Below Edom was the land of Midian and the Arabian Desert.

Four major trade routes crossed through Palestine from north to south, linked by a cross hatch of minor roads. One, coming down out of Syria and following the coastline, was joined by a second road from the north, which, having followed the Litani River for a distance, skirted the base of Mount Carmel and cut through the Carmel range below Megiddo to join the coast road below Joppa. A third followed the same inland route from the north but went south from the Sea of Chinnereth to link Shechem, Jerusalem, Hebron and Beer-sheba with southern roads leading to Egypt or the Gulf of Aqabah. The Transjordan highway came from Damascus and passed through key cities of Bashan, Gilead, Ammon, Moab and Edom, to the Gulf of Aqabah and

[8] River names in parentheses are modern Arabic labels.

then followed the eastern side of the gulf, along the coast of Arabia to the Arabian Peninsula. The portion of this road linking Damascus and Aqabah was called "The King's Highway" in the Bible (Num. 20:17, 21:22) and was protected by a line of forts.

Water is and was the key to life and survival in Palestine. During the rainless summers, the land dries up and the hills become sere and brown. The winter rains, which come in isolated storms, bring life to the land, flooding the wadis, or stream beds which are ordinarily dry, with torrents of rushing water. The midpoint of the rainy season is January, and the early and late rains mentioned in the Bible refer to showers coming in October and November and in April. Abundance of rain meant good crops, good pasture and good life. In normally arid areas and during periods of little rainfall, the hoarding of water in catch basins and cisterns made existence possible. Moisture absorbed into the subsoil of the hills penetrated until reaching a hard pan of rock, and the collected waters flowed out on the lower hillsides as springs. Subsurface pools and streams were tapped by wells. Because herbage dried up in summer, pasturage for flocks was sought in the highlands, making part of the population mobile. Cities, built near springs and wells, were in dire straits when these failed.

Palestine's geographical divisions extended northward into Syria. Here, the coastal region became a narrow strip broken by rocky spurs projecting from the Lebanon mountains, which rise abruptly from the seaboard to heights of 10,000 feet. On these mountains grew the famous cedars, prized for building throughout the Near East.[9] To the east is the broad valley of Beqa'a through which the Orontes and Leontes Rivers flow before turning westward to the Mediterranean, and on the eastern edge of Beqa'a is the Anti-Lebanon range, of which Mount Hermon[10] (9,000 feet) forms the southern spur. As part of the land bridge linking Africa and Asia, Syria, like Palestine, felt the impact of foreign powers.[11] The coastal road, linking important ports, was supplemented by an inland route that followed the rivers through Beqa'a.

Far to the north, the huge peninsula Anatolia or Asia Minor jutted out from the mainland toward Greece, separated by the Black Sea from the cultures inhabiting the European steppes and river basins. The southwest coastal region facing upon the Aegean, with arable lands and forested hill country, became the home of the Lydians. The center of the peninsula is a vast, rocky, mountainous wasteland with few arable areas along river valleys. In this forbidding region the powerful Hittite nation was located. The mountains of Anatolia extend eastward toward the Caspian Sea to form the arc-shaped Taurus and Anti-Taurus ranges.

In the inland highlands of Armenia, the Euphrates begins, flowing westward as if to enter Hittite domain, then south to Aram, and

9 Cf. II Sam. 5:11, 7:2, 7; I Kings 5–7.

10 For other designations, see Deut. 3:9; 4:48; Judg. 3:3.

11 Inscriptions on the Dog River, north of Beirut, by Egyptians, Hittites, Babylonians, Assyrians, Persians, Greeks, Romans, etc., provide an impressive summary of the country's international relationships.

A CEDAR OF LEBANON. *Cedars were prized
as building material, particularly important for massive pillars and for interior
finishings, and were exported from Syria
to all parts of the ancient Near East. They
still grow near the area where David and
Solomon obtained cedars for the royal
buildings, and are the most magnificent
trees grown in Syria.*

finally southeast to form a boundary of the Arabian desert and enter
the Persian Gulf. In the half-circle of the middle Euphrates, where
numerous streams pour down from the hills to increase the river's flow,
the Hurrians settled,[12] the Mitanni kingdom was established,[13] and
the city of Haran where Abraham lived and where his father died
(Gen. 11:31, 32), was located. The waters move more slowly as they
approach lower Mesopotamia, and where they pour into the Persian
Gulf huge deposits of alluvial soil have accumulated.

The Tigris River, to the east, begins in the mountains of Armenia
and, fed by numerous tributaries, moves toward the southeast to join
the Euphrates and empty into the Persian Gulf. The area between the
Tigris and Euphrates was called by the Greeks "Mesopotamia" ("between the rivers"). In ancient times, lower river regions appear to
have consisted largely of marsh and lagoons with islands of solid earth
upon which the earliest human settlements were founded. In the area
between the rivers, the mighty kingdoms of Sumer, Babylon and
Assyria were located. East of the Tigris, a wide grassy undulating

12 For the relationship of the Hurrians to Horites and Hittites, cf. John Bright,
op. cit., pp. 53 ff.

13 For the Mitanni, cf. John Bright, *op. cit.*, pp. 99 ff.

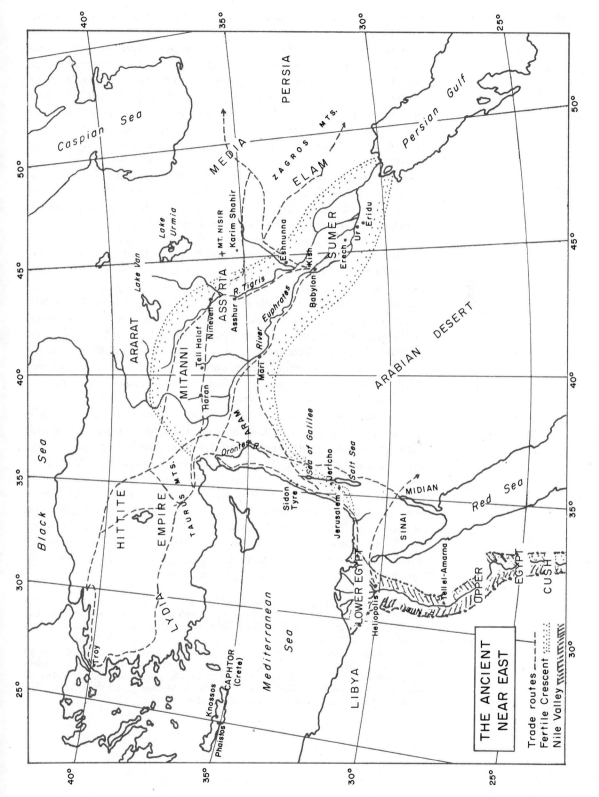

THE ANCIENT
NEAR EAST

Trade routes ------
Fertile Crescent ·······
Nile Valley ⊔⊔⊔⊔⊔

51

plateau rises steadily toward the Zagros Mountains and here Persians and Elamites settled.

By drawing curved lines from the Persian Gulf through Mesopotamia and following the Euphrates to Aram, then down through Palestine, James Henry Breasted over fifty years ago sketched what he labeled "The Fertile Crescent," the relatively narrow belt of arable land skirting the desert. Merchants and armies traversed this route that linked Mesopotamia to the north, the west, and the south (Egypt), and as they passed through Palestine, they brought this little country into direct relationships with her neighbors.

Egypt was the only great power to threaten the southern border of Palestine. Although the nation was centered in the Nile valley and delta, called the "blackland" to contrast it with the "red land" of the desert, territorial control included the rugged hinterland of the Sinai peninsula where valuable turquoise and mineral deposits were located and through which ran roads linking Egypt by land to Mesopotamia and Asia Minor. Egypt's northern borders were at the Wadi el Arish, the Brook of Egypt (Num. 34:5; I Kings 8:65; II Kings 24:7).[14] Egypt proper, the long strip of black soil along the two banks of the Nile stretching from the first cataract to the Mediterranean, was the result of the political union of Lower Egypt (the delta) and Upper Egypt (the area from the delta to the first cataract).[15] Steep cliffs and barren land separated the fertile region and the people of the second and third cataracts from Egypt, and forbidding deserts limited communication from east and west to caravan trade.

Consequently, Egyptian commerce flowed northward with the Nile toward the delta where, by land and sea, the nation was in touch with the outer world. Egyptian agricultural economy depended upon the annual rise and fall of the Nile. This mighty river, originating 2,000 miles southward near the equator in the Mountains of the Moon, was channeled to irrigate fields along its banks. When its flow, swollen by equatorial rains, swept down to inundate the land, there was promise of good crops and a bountiful year. Overabundance of water destroyed canals and dams; too little water meant famine. The river, together with the other dominant natural feature related to agriculture, the sun, held an important place in Egyptian religion.

14 Other references to this border label it "The River Egypt" (Gen. 15:12; Judith 1:9), and "Shihor" (Josh. 13:3; I Chron. 13:5) which may refer to the same stream. The "Brook of the Arabah" of Amos 6:14, may be another designation or may indicate a separate valley.

15 Cf. John A. Wilson, *The Burden of Egypt* (Chicago: University of Chicago Press, 1951), chap. 1; also in a paper-bound edition titled: *The Culture of Ancient Egypt*, Phoenix Books (Chicago: University of Chicago Press, 1956); Walter A. Fairservis, *The Ancient Kingdoms of the Nile*, A Mentor Book (New York: New American Library of World Literature, 1962), chap. 1.

The People, from the Paleolithic to the Chalcolithic Periods

OUR study will concentrate on the biblical period which embraces less than two millennia of human history, but long before the Hebrews entered the historical scene there were people living in the Fertile Crescent and Egypt. To grasp the magnificent human heritage that fell to the Hebrews and those who lived during the biblical period, the next two chapters will provide an overview of ancient Near Eastern history as reconstructed out of the researches of historians and archaeologists, first, from the Paleolithic to the Chalcolithic periods; and next, from the Early Bronze to the Late Bronze periods.

As elsewhere in the Near East, evidence of human habitation can be found in Palestine dating to the Paleolithic period, or Old Stone Age, which lasted hundreds of thousands of years.[1] Paleolithic man was a nomad, depending upon natural resources for sustenance, following migrations of wild animals and harvesting wild grain wherever it chanced to grow. Possibly his itineraries followed some generally established pattern, terminating in a periodic return to a family cave. On the basis of stone artifacts (implements made from wood, fibre or leather are seldom preserved), the earliest Paleolithic period, which extends from more than 300,000 years ago to approximately 70,000 years ago, can be divided into three parts.

During the so-called "Pebble" or "Chopper" period, water-smoothed pebbles or chunks of rock were roughly shaped by chipping one end into a cutting edge. Such tools have been found in the Jordan River valley just south of the Sea of Galilee and at a hillside site midway between Tiberias and Nazareth. In the later Bifacial period, hand-axes were formed by working both sides of a flint block to make a point or cutting edge, and such tools have been found in Galilee, near Jerusalem, and in the desert regions in southern Palestine. Hearths and burned bones reveal that man had mastered the use of fire (approximately 200,000 years ago), and circles of stones, which may have served as seats, spaced around the fire suggest that the glowing

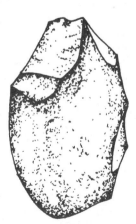

PEBBLE TOOL

[1] For details cf. Kathleen Kenyon, *Archaeology in the Holy Land* (New York: Frederick A. Praeger, 1960); E. Anati, *Palestine Before the Hebrews* (New York: Alfred A. Knopf, 1963).

_____ CHART IV _____

Years B.C.	Archaeological Period	Cultural Features			Specific Locations
300,000 to 70,000	Lower Paleolithic	Pebble tools Man discovers fire (200,000) Bifacial tools	N O M		Tabunian Cave on Mount Carmel Yarbrud in Syria
70,000 to 35,000	Middle Paleolithic	Mousterian flaked flints Neanderthal Man	A D I C		Galilee, Palestine Mount Carmel, Palestine
35,000 to 12,000	Upper Paleolithic	Blade industries "tepee" type dwellings figurines, bone and ivory jewelry	L I F E		Wadi en-Natuf, Palestine Shanidar, Iraq Zawi Chemi, Iraq Karim Shahir, Iraq
12,000 to 10,000	Mesolithic	Natufian micro-flints New weapons and tools Primitive agriculture Rock drawings and wall paintings Beginnings of sea travel	H A M L E T	L I F E	Wadi en-Natuf, Palestine Deir Tasi, Egypt Jarmo, Iraq Tell Hassuna, Iraq
10,000 to 4,500	Neolithic	Extensive agriculture Domestication of animals Extensive trade Early shrines	V I L L A G E	L I F E	Jericho, Palestine Deir Tasi, Egypt Jarmo, Iraq Tell Hassuna, Iraq

4,500 to 3,300	Chalcolithic	Copper and stone tools
		Pottery of varied styles
		Beginning of ziggurats
		Development of writing,
		   and mathematics
		Cylinder seals used
		Time of the "Flood"
		Egyptian nomes unite to
		   form upper and lower Egypt
			C
			I
			T
			Y
			/
			S
			T
			A
			T
			E
			S
				K
				I
				N
				G a
				D n
				O d
				M
				S
					al Badari, Egypt
					el Amrah, Egypt
					Tepe Gawra, Iraq
					Tell Halaf, Iraq
					Eridu, Iraq
					Beer-sheba, Palestine
					Dead Sea Region

embers provided a center for family gatherings.[2]

The third period, named Tabunian after the Tabun cave on Mount Carmel, and Yabrudian after a site in Syria, is characterized by superior skill in shaping tools and by new and more varied imple-

[2] For evidence of much earlier use of fire in other parts of the world, cf. Grahame Clark, "The Hunters and Gatherers of the Stone Age," *The Dawn of Civilization,* Stuart Piggott (ed.) (New York: McGraw-Hill Book Company, Inc., 1961), p. 36.

ments. Variances in tool patterns at different sites (as at Carmel and Yabrud) indicate that each group created and maintained local traditions and techniques. Comparable materials are found in Europe.

In the Middle Paleolithic period, extending from about 70,000 to 35,000 years ago, man's tools improved. Having learned to take thinner flakes from flints, he could make more precise shapes and a greater variety of implements were developed. The people of this culture, first discovered at Le Moustier in France and named Mousterian, are related to Neanderthal man and are similar to (but still different from) modern man. In 1923, Mr. F. Turville-Petre, an Oxford student, excavating a cave near the Sea of Galilee on behalf of the British School of Archaeology, discovered four pieces of the skull of a young man amid mineralized animal bones and flint tools of the Mousterian type. This find, labeled "Galilee man," was the first of such discoveries in Palestine. "Carmel man," whose remains were found shortly afterward in caves in the Carmel mountains, proved to be another offshoot of Neanderthal man. Taller than Neanderthal, walking upright, probably possessing speech, Carmel man left flint tools, bone ware, an amazingly preserved four-sided spear point of wood, and numerous burials which, by their very nature, reflected deep concern for the dead and perhaps the expression of some form of religious feeling. The dead were entombed in the floor of the cave, sharing in death the same habitation as the living. Bodies were placed on the side in the "sleep" position and there is some evidence that food was interred with the body, suggesting belief in afterlife.

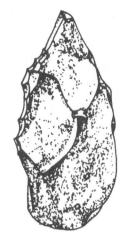

BIFACIAL HAND AXE

The final stage of the Paleolithic period, the Late or Upper Paleolithic which extended from about 35,000 to between 10,000 and 15,000 years ago, has provided the earliest evidence of man-built structures. Small mounds of earth and rock or excavations into the earth provided the outline of the dwelling above which walls and a roof were constructed, possibly out of branches or perhaps out of animal skins, after the fashion of the American Indian tepee. It is possible that these structures were occupied for part of the year, and in inclement weather Upper Paleolithic man returned to his cave. Well-made flint tools, carved ivory, pendants, necklaces and bracelets of shells, bone, ivory and stone testify to the creative skill of these people. Carved figurines of pregnant females may represent amulets used to facilitate childbirth, or, in view of the later development of the worship of the mother goddess, they may be early evidence of the beginnings of this cult.

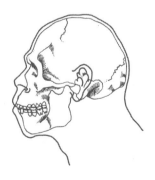

CARMEL MAN *differed from the typical Neanderthal type found in Europe and had physical characteristics closer to Homo sapiens. The thick ridge of the brows or occipital protuberances, the heavy nasal structure and the lack of any true chin development are typical Neanderthal features. Carmel man shows the slightest hint of a developing chin and above the protruding brows is a higher forehead, more akin to Homo sapiens. This sketch is after E. Anati in* Palestine Before the Hebrews *(New York: Alfred A. Knopf, 1963) p. 103.*

55

Comparable Paleolithic evidence has been found in Egypt where Bifacial and Mousterian artifacts were recovered on terraces overlooking the Nile, at oases, and on the shores of ancient lakes.

Sometime between 14,000 and 12,000 years ago, the Mesolithic period or Middle Stone Age began in the Near East, and with it came a veritable social and technological revolution probably due, in part, to changes in climate at the close of the last Ice Age. The most dramatic evidence in Palestine has come from a site ten miles northwest of Jerusalem in the Wadi en-Natuf, which has given the name "Natufian" to the culture. In 1928, in a huge cave some 70 feet above the *wadi*, Miss Dorothy Garrod found evidence of a center of flint industry characterized by tiny crescents and triangles of flint known as micro-flints. Natufian sites, since found in other locations, suggest long periods of uninterrupted occupation and reveal a uniformity in art, industry, burial customs and artifacts that indicates close communication among groups, although it must be admitted that each site has its own distinctive features. Massive implements, such as huge basalt mortars weighing hundreds of pounds for grinding grain, were produced, as well as such delicate objects of bone as fish hooks, barbed harpoons and pins. A wide variety of tools, including adzes, sickles and picks, suggest the beginning of agriculture. Rock carvings portray men using lassoes and nets, and the imprint of matting on clay floors indicates the weaving of fibers.

During this period the bow and arrow were used and, with better tools and weapons and having learned how to store food, it is possible that life became somewhat easier, providing time for artistic expression. Rock drawings and wall paintings depict men and animals with the precise pictorial representation so often characteristic of primitive art, but Natufian man moved beyond this phase into schematic and symbolic representation and geometric patterns. Skeletons were often decorated with necklaces, pendants, breast ornaments and headdresses of shell and bone. The curious custom of separating the skull from the rest of the skeleton has been variously interpreted as a cannibalistic rite, evidence of ancestor worship, a skull cult, or simply as an interesting hobby of collecting tokens of victory over enemies. Sea travel had begun, probably on rafts of bamboo or papyrus at first and later on more sophisticated ships, and the Near Eastern world was drawn more closely together.

The Neolithic or New Stone Age began between 12,000 and 10,000 years ago (10,000–8,000 B.C.) and is characterized by settled communities in which man, having developed agricultural skills, was no longer dependent upon natural resources for food. Excavations at Jericho, directed by Miss Kathleen Kenyon, produced impressive evidence of the development of village culture prior to the invention of pottery. Floors surrounded by stone and earth humps were found in the earliest levels, but solid structures soon began to appear. Circular houses, with pounded earth floors cut below the level of the surrounding terrain, had upper walls of upright poles and elongated, cigar-shaped bricks sloping inward to form domed roofs. Woven reed mats covered the floors. Around this community, a wall of free-standing

THE NEOLITHIC TOWER AT JERICHO. *The steel grating at the top covers the opening to a narrow inner staircase that winds to the entrance at the bottom.*

stone had been built, over six feet wide in some places and still standing to a height of twelve feet. A huge tower more than thirty feet high with an interior staircase was built against the inner wall. Such structures indicate the existence of fully developed, cooperative community life as early as the sixth and seventh millennium B.C.

Subsequent layers of occupation reveal new living patterns. Houses become rectilinear with plastered floors and walls. Bones of goats, pigs, sheep and cattle point to domestication of these animals. Obsidian, turquoise and cowrie shells were imported from Syria, the Sinai peninsula and the Mediterranean for manufacture of tools and ornaments. In a shrine, a piece of volcanic stone from the Dead Sea area was placed in a niche, perhaps foreshadowing the sacred standing pillars mentioned in the Bible.[3] Clay figurines and human skulls with features skillfully modeled in fine clay reveal artistic tendencies and,

[3] Called in Hebrew *massebah* (plural: *masseboth*). Such pillars are usually associated with Canaanite worship (Exod. 23:24; 34:13; Deut. 7:5; 12:3; II Kings 10:26 f.), or with apostasy in the Hebrew cult (I Kings 14:23; II Kings 17:10; Hos. 10:1-2) and are expressly forbidden in the Torah (Lev. 26:1; Deut. 16:22).

FIFTH MILLENNIUM MODEL OF A MAN'S HEAD.   *This plaster figure was found at Jericho. The eyes are of shell and the hair and beard have been painted in with simple brush strokes.*

perhaps, if these items are cult objects, association with worship. Later, in the Neolithic period (fifth millennium), pottery-making begins. From this period have come three almost life-sized plaster statues built on reed frames, representing a man, woman, and child. The male head, which alone was recovered intact, is a flat disc of clay about one inch thick, with shells for eyes and brown paint for hair. It is possible that a divine triad is represented.

In Egypt during the Tasian period (named for Deir Tasi in Middle Egypt) which began between 10,000 and 7,000 B.C., man began to cultivate grains, including wheat, barley and flax. In a large Neolithic village near the southwest edge of the delta at Meremdeh Beni-Salamah, oval huts of unbaked mud bricks and a large central granary were found, indicating the development of co-operative enterprise. Woven plant fibers and ornaments of shell, bone and ivory reflect manufacturing and artistic skill. Similar settlements have been found in the Fayum, an ancient oasis west of the Nile.

Near the Caspian Sea and in the upper reaches of the Tigris River, Paleolithic, Mesolithic and pre-pottery Neolithic materials have been recovered, largely from caves. At Mesolithic sites below Lake Urmia (Karim Shahir, Zawi Chemi, Shanidar), circular dwelling foundations of stone with hearths, storage bins, grinding stones and other implements, together with bones of sheep, cattle and dogs, indicate the beginnings of settled culture. These sites may have been occupied only seasonally. At Jarmo in eastern Iraq, a Neolithic site marked the transition to year-round living at one location. No pottery vessels were found. Crude representations of animals and female figures in unbaked clay point to artistic interests perhaps associated with the worship of the mother goddess or the use of fetishes to aid in childbirth and, possibly, to domestication of animals.

Similar patterns of developing society have been observed elsewhere. At Tell Hassuna, south of Mosul, adobe dwellings built around open central courts with fine painted pottery replace earlier levels with crude pottery. Hand axes, sickles, grinding stones, bins, baking ovens and numerous bones of domesticated animals reflect settled agricultural life. Female figurines have been related to worship, and jar burials within which food was placed, to belief in afterlife. The relationship of Hassuna pottery to that of Jericho suggests that village culture was becoming widespread.

The Chalcolithic Age (*chalcos,* copper; *lithos,* stone) extended from the middle of the fifth to near the end of the fourth millennium B.C. During this period the art of smelting and molding copper was developed, and stone and bone tools were now augmented by a limited supply of implements made of this new substance. The skill developed by smiths in the handling of copper is amply illustrated in the several hundred beautifully fashioned cultic items from the end of the Chalcolithic period that were discovered in a cave near the Dead Sea in the spring of 1961.[4] Villages and towns of varying size were now spread throughout Palestine and permanent houses were built of stone, mud-brick and wood, although cave living was still common, and near Beer-sheba there was a whole village with underground living and storage quarters. A rich variety of stone, pottery and copper artifacts, fine flint work, paintings and carvings mark cultural growth in this period. New burial patterns were developed. Often the dead were interred in large storage jars, and at other times bodies were cremated and the remains placed in specially made pottery urns and interred in caves.

In Mesopotamia, at Tell Halaf on the Khabour River, a tributary of the Euphrates, hard, thin pottery with a beautiful finish produced by high firing at controlled heats was found. This pottery from the middle of the fifth millennium is decorated with geometric designs in red and black on a buff slip, but animal and human figures also appear. One figure appears to represent a chariot, thus indicating the use of the wheel. Houses were constructed out of mud brick, but reed structures plastered with mud were also built. Cones of clay, painted red or black or left plain, were often inserted in the mud walls to form mosaics and to protect the wall from weathering.

A small shrine of mud brick from Eridu belongs to the same period. Only foundations and a plastered floor remain, but it is surmised that the upper structure was plastered and painted. Later in the period the shrine was covered over with earth, and a second temple was built above it, placing the new building considerably above the surrounding plateau.

A more pretentious structure from the beginning of the fourth millennium was found at Tepe Gawra, near modern Mosul. Three large buildings of sun-baked brick were located on an acropolis and designed to frame three sides of an open court. Inner rooms were painted in red-purple, and exterior walls were red on one building, white on another and brown on the third. A fourth millennium temple was built at Uruk upon a staged, elevated mound, 140 by 150 feet at the base and 30 feet high. This man-made, mountain-top home for the gods was of pounded clay and layers of sun-dried brick and asphalt. Surmounted by a white-washed temple (65 x 150 x 14 feet) and approached by a steep stairway and a ramp, this structure is known as a ziggurat (from the Assyrian-Babylonian *ziqquratu,* meaning "to be raised up," hence "a high place") and is the prototype of loftier and more magnificent ziggurats of later periods.

For the first time the cylinder seal is found. Each of these small stone cylinders had distinctive patterns inscribed on its surface, and when rolled over soft, moist clay left a raised design, which could be used as a sign of ownership. About the middle of the fourth millennium, pictographic writing was developed and incised upon clay tablets. As the use of writing increased pictographs became more and more stylized, finally being reduced to wedge-shaped symbols or what is

---

[4] Cf. P. Bar-Adon, "Expedition C—The Cave of Treasures," *The Expedition to the Judean Desert, 1961* (Jerusalem: Israel Exploration Society, 1962), pp. 215 ff.

A HEARTH OR INCENSE BURNER *found in one of the caves near Beer-sheba. The burner was set in the center of the mud floor and consisted of an arrangement of large pebbles in the form of what has been called "a magic square." Each stone bears a mark in indelible red color, and it is possible that the hearth was used in divination by a priest-magician in the Chalcolithic age. The excavators lifted out the entire section of the floor that contained the hearth and mounted it in a special frame for study and display.*

called cuneiform writing. Cuneiform characters were impressed upon a tablet of moist clay with a stylus, and if the document required a signature, a cylinder seal was used. The tablet was baked or allowed to dry, forming a permanent record.

The precise identity of these Mesopotamian people is not known for sure, but on the basis of the sexegesimal arithmetical system utilized on some of the clay tablets, a system also used by the Sumerians, and from references to gods worshiped by the Sumerians, it is presumed that they were Sumerians. Where they came from and when is unknown,[5] but they are neither Semites nor Indo-Europeans, and they refer to themselves as "the black-headed people."

In Egypt the Chalcolithic period is represented by Badarian culture, first found at al Badari. Unusual, ripple patterned pottery was produced in a variety of finishes. Green malachite ore, so important for the beautification of the eyes, was ground on slate palettes that were

[5] S. N. Kramer, "Sumer," *The Interpreter's Dictionary of the Bible* believes that the Sumerians probably came from the Caucasus mountains in the last quarter of the fourth millennium. E. A. Speiser, "The Sumerian Problem Reviewed," *Hebrew Union College Annual*, XXIII (1950–1), 339 ff.

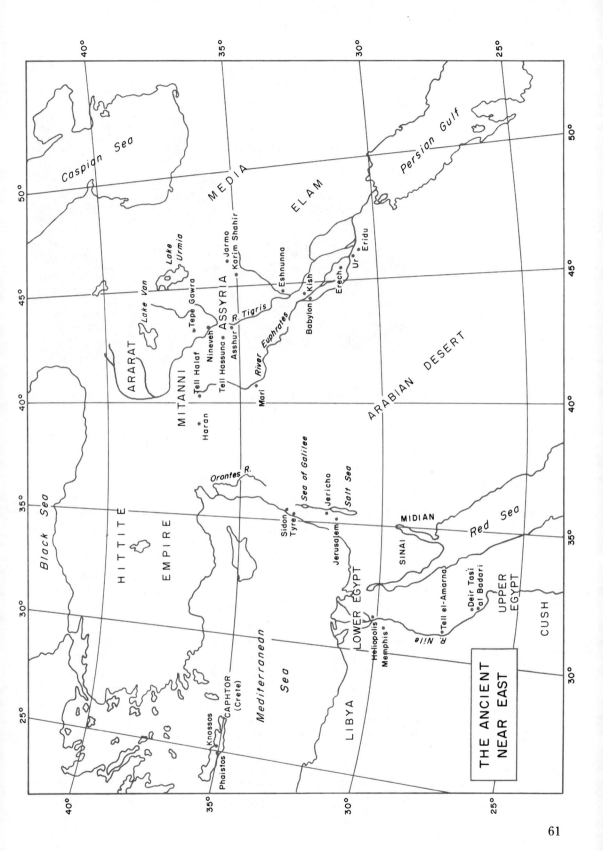

THE ANCIENT
NEAR EAST

Caspian Sea

MEDIA

ELAM

Persian Gulf

Lake Urmia

Lake Van

Jarmo

Karim Shahir

Eshnunna

ARARAT

Tepe Gawra

ASSYRIA

R. Tigris

Kish

Erech

Ur

Eridu

Tell Halaf

Nineveh

Asshur

Babylon

River Euphrates

MITANNI

Tell Hassuna

Mari

ARABIAN DESERT

Haran

Orontes R.

Sea of Galilee

Jericho

Salt Sea

Black Sea

HITTITE

EMPIRE

Sidon

Tyre

Jerusalem

MIDIAN

Red Sea

SINAI

Mediterranean

Sea

LOWER EGYPT

Deir Tasi

al Badari

Tell el-Amarna

UPPER EGYPT

R. Nile

Heliopolis

Memphis

CUSH

CAPHTOR (Crete)

Knossos

LIBYA

Phaistos

BURIAL URNS FROM THE PLAIN OF SHARON. *The deceased person was cremated and the ashes and bones were placed in these clay house-shaped ossuaries. Each urn is individualistic in design and structure, which may indicate stylistic variations in the architecture of the dwellings of the period. The significance of the "nose-like" projection is not known.*

often ornamented. Skeletal remains indicate that the Badarians were a stocky people and that they believed in some form of afterlife, for the dead were buried in a flexed or sleeping posture with food and equipment.

The succeeding culture, beginning with the fourth millennium, was called Amratian, after el-Amreh near Abydos, and was centered in Upper Egypt. A new people, tall and slender, appear. Some features of their artifacts demonstrate borrowing from the Badarians, but the extensive use of copper, magnificent flint work, and artistic expressions in slate, ivory and clay mark unique developments. Amratian dead were buried in oval pits in tightly flexed positions. In addition to the usual grave furnishings, ivory and clay figurines of women and slaves were included, leading to the hypothesis that these were miniature substitutions for an older practice of sacrificing living individuals to serve an important individual in the afterlife.

The Gerzean period began in the middle of the fourth millennium, and for the first time written documents appear in Egypt. Local towns or districts (later called "nomes" by the Greeks) were formed, each with a local symbol that was often mounted on ships to designate district of origin. By conquest, units were joined into larger districts. Gerzian tombs were elaborate: the poor were buried in oblong graves with a ledge at one side to hold funerary offerings, the rich in tombs

A CLAY VESSEL ABOUT 11¾ INCHES HIGH FROM
THE LATE GERZIAN PERIOD. *The figures are in
deep red against a cream colored background.
The wavy handles on each side are known as
"ledge handles" and are characteristic of vessels
of the same period found in Palestine.*

lined with mud brick. Gold is found for the first time along with silver
and meteoritic iron.

Within the next half millennium significant administrative changes
occurred. Gerzean districts of Upper Egypt united under a single ruler
who wore a tall white helmet as a crown. Delta nomes united under a
king who wore a crown of red wicker-work. By 2900 B.C. the two areas
had become one, and the single ruler wore both red and white crowns
and was known as "King of Upper and Lower Egypt."

7

The People, from the Early Bronze
to the Early Iron Ages

MANETHO, the Egyptian priest-historian of the third century B.C., writes of Egyptian history in terms of dynasties. Modern historians, without abandoning Manetho's pattern, prefer broader designations of Protodynastic, Old, Middle and New Kingdoms to mark periods of outstanding prosperity and development, with "Intermediate Periods" to designate eras of weakness.

During the Protodynastic period (c. 2900–2700 B.C.) widespread commercial interests brought Egypt into touch with Syria and Mesopotamia, resulting in interchange of products and skills. Now a new concept of monarchy developed in united Egypt. The pharaoh was recognized as a god; consequently, Egyptian government became a pharaoh or god-centered bureaucracy with a powerful priesthood. Memphis, near the junction of Upper and Lower Egypt, was the capital and nearby Heliopolis the headquarters of the priesthood. Godship and immortality are closely linked concepts; hence increasing importance was placed on the burial of the Pharaoh. Royal tombs of the first dynasty were underground pits lined with brick and roofed with timber and matting. About the central chamber, small offering rooms were clustered, and adjacent to the royal tomb were graves of servants. In time a superstructure, a rectangular shell with sloping sides called a mastaba (platform), was added.

During the Old Kingdom (c. 2700–2200 B.C.), which encompasses the third to sixth dynasties, the great pyramids were built. For Djoser, the first monarch, a royal mausoleum was erected by the gifted priest-magician-engineer-architect, Imhotep. Five mastabas of diminishing size were imposed one upon the other to form the famous step-pyramid. Succeeding monarchs built larger and smaller pyramids. Egyptian territorial control was extended to Nubia in the south and Palestine and Syria in the north and east, and the resultant trade and inflow of products and wealth brought higher standards of living and better education to the common people. Schools of wise men produced aphorisms similar to those preserved in the book of Proverbs. However, huge building projects, expensive military forays, and perhaps royal indolence brought Egypt to a point of weakness and foreigners, possibly Amorites,[1] gained control of the land. This dark page in

[1] The name "Amorite" is related to the Akkadian *Amurru* which designated inhabitants of Amurru, a land west of Mesopotamia, the precise whereabouts of

— CHART V —

POLITICAL AND CULTURAL FACTORS

Years B.C.	Archaeological Period	Egypt	Mesopotamia	Palestine
3300–2000	Early Bronze or Early Urban	PROTODYNASTIC PERIOD (2900–2700) : Unification of Egypt OLD KINGDOM (2700–2200) : Mastabas and pyramids, Extensive literature FIRST INTERMEDIATE PERIOD (2200–1990) : Amorite Invasion	EARLY DYNASTIC PERIOD (2800–2360) : Founding of great cities, Development of writing, Primitive democracy yields to monarchy, Flood legends, great epics OLD AKKADIAN PERIOD (2360–2180) : Semitic control—Sargon of Agade, Gutian invasion, Sumerian Renaissance	EARLY URBAN PERIOD: Walled cities, Under Egyptian control, Amorite invasion about 2200
2000–1500	Middle Bronze	MIDDLE KINGDOM (1990–1786) : Theban rulers, Extensive trade, Building, writing, art, literature flourish SECOND INTERMEDIATE PERIOD (1786–1570) : Hyksos control	Elamites and Amorites in control, Rise of Assyrian Power, Time of Hammurabi, References to "Habiru", Cassites control Babylon, Hittite attacks	Canaanite invasion, Eighteenth century invasion by Hyksos, Horse and chariot introduced, Time of Abraham and patriarchs
1500–1200	Late Bronze	NEW KINGDOM (1570–1290) : Expulsion of Hyksos, Time of Akhenaten, Reference to 'Apiru, Time of Hebrew Exodus, Invasion by Sea People	Hittites master smelting of iron	Under Egyptian and Hittite (?) control Invasion by Philistines, Invasion by Hebrews
1200–586	Iron Age			The time of the Hebrew Kingdoms

A GRANITE BOWL FROM THE EARLY PROTODYNASTIC PERIOD. *Long before men learned to form vessels out of clay and bake their products for lasting hardness, they worked the hard stone to form vessels of simple form and beautiful shape. Similar stone vessels have been found in Palestine.*

Egypt's history is classified as the First Intermediate Period (c. 2200–1900 B.C.). Despite the "darkness" of the era, or perhaps as a result of it, a remarkable literary document "A Dispute Over Suicide" was written.[2] A man, weary of life, argues with his soul the merits of self-destruction after a fashion that calls to mind the unhappy lot of Job and the philosophy of Ecclesiastes.

In Mesopotamia, the Early Bronze Age embraces both the Early Dynastic (c. 2800–2360 B.C.) and the Old Akkadian (c. 2360–2180 B.C.) periods. Such great cities as Shuruppak, Eshnunna and Erech were founded in the Early Dynastic era. Writing developed away from pictographic forms and a tremendous literature was produced. Shortly after 2500 B.C., a chronology of rulers known as the Sumerian King List cataloged kings who reigned before and after the great flood. Reigns of tremendous length (43,000 to 18,000 years) were ascribed to the eight antediluvian monarchs, a familiar literary device by which "history" is extended into the distant past and vast periods of time encompassed by simply listing names (cf. Gen. 5). The flood is reported next, after which kingship was again established at Kish. At first, post-diluvian dynasties embrace vast periods of time (24,510 years), but as the period in which the writing was composed is approached, more reasonable figures begin to appear (100, 99, 491, 25 years).

A Sumerian flood story relating the adventures of Ziusudra, a priest-

---

which is unknown. (As a result of Amorite movements, Amorite cities and states sprang up in the area of Aram. M. Noth, *The History of Israel*, p. 24, contests the hypothesis that these invaders were Amorites.) In the Bible the term sometimes refers to a Canaanite tribe (Gen. 10:16; Exod. 3:8) and at other times designates the pre-Hebrew inhabitants (Gen. 15:16).

[2] Cf. *ANET*, p. 405; D. W. Thomas (ed.), *Documents from Old Testament Times* (henceforth *DOTT*) (New York: Thomas Nelson and Sons, 1958), p. 162.

king who escaped in a boat, was later incorporated in the Gilgamesh Epic as part of a literary struggle with the issues of life and death. Gilgamesh (another Sumerian hero-king) hears the story from Utnapishtim, who has replaced Ziusudra as the hero of the flood.[3] Other myths relate stories of gods and goddesses and, with hymns and prayers, provide valuable insights to religious beliefs and practices.

Additional documents record business affairs, the building of temples, legal issues, and taxation problems. Earliest Sumerian cities appear to have had a form of "primitive democracy," according to Thorkild Jacobsen.[4] Everyday business affecting the community was handled by a committee of elders, but major issues were voted upon by the adult free men. In an emergency, one person could be appointed leader *pro tem.* The unwieldy nature of this arrangement yielded to the centralization of authority in one individual, a leader or governor, who was recognized as the representative of the particular god of the city. In this capacity his duties included concern for religious matters such as sacrifice and temple building and for community welfare, which involved maintenance of irrigation channels and a protecting army. The will of the gods was sought in all matters.

Graves of common people were pits into which the body, wrapped in matting or placed in a wooden or clay coffin, was placed, usually on one side in the sleep position with a cup placed before the face. So-called "royal" burials at Ur were most lavish. Huge underground pits in which a stone burial chamber for the "king" or "queen" was erected contained the bodies of guards, servants and animals. Within the tomb chamber, the royal bodies were lavishly attired, and large quantities of gold and silver household items, weapons and personal jewelry were placed nearby. Because the names of these monarchs are not found in any list of royal personages known to date, it has been suggested that they may have been individuals appointed king or queen for sacrificial ceremonies of fertility rites. Artistic talent is demonstrated in exquisite work in stone, copper, silver, gold, electrum and lapis lazuli. Harps and lyres indicate enjoyment of music. Sculpting was highly developed. The Early Dynastic was a period of great art and literature.

The Old Akkadian period began when Semitic peoples, who had been moving into the area for many years and whose names began to appear with greater frequency in Sumerian documents, assumed kingship. Only minor cultural changes took place and Sumerian customs were continued, but the Semitic tongue was the language of the land, although a Sumerian cuneiform script was used. Sargon, the Semitic king of Agade, brought Mesopotamia under his domain in a series of conquests and extended his kingdom through Syria to the Mediterranean. His dynasty ended with the invasion of the Gutians, a people from the eastern Caucasus about whom little is known. Their control lasted for only 100 years, then Sumerians resumed power and introduced a short-lived cultural renaissance lasting until about 1960 B.C.

---

[3] Cf. *ANET*, pp. 44 f., 60 f. *DOTT*, p. 17 f.

[4] T. Jacobsen, "Primitive Democracy in Ancient Mesopotamia," *Journal of Near Eastern Studies,* II (1943), 172.

The corresponding period in Palestine is the Early Bronze or Early
Urban period (c. 3300–2000 B.C.), a time when villages became walled
towns encircled by cultivated fields and grazing grounds, each with its
dependent hamlets. Beth Yerah, Megiddo, Beth Shan, Shechem, Gezer,
Lachish, Jericho and Ai were among the powerful centers. Well built
homes, large public buildings and granaries were protected by heavy
walls of stone or mud brick. No single power united the land,
although much of the time, Egyptian garrisons with petty princes
controlled key cities. Canaanite, a Semitic language, was written in a
syllabic script influenced by Egyptian writing. Egyptian influence can
also be seen in pottery patterns. A unique pottery with a red and black
burnish of unusual beauty, known as Khirbet Kerak ware after the
site where it was first found, reflects the intrusion of a people from the
north whose identity is not yet known. Of religious beliefs, little is
known. At Megiddo a large circular stone altar was uncovered (see
photograph) upon which pottery fragments and animal bones were
found, suggesting a place of offering. A large rectangular temple was
found at Ai. Burial caves, often containing between twenty-five and
fifty entombments, suggest family tombs utilized over long periods of
time. Jugs, juglets and bowls found in the graves may have contained
food, liquids and unguents.

The final years of this period in Palestine are marked by the same
decline noted in Egypt. Waves of desert people swept into the land,
and battles decreased the number of city dwellers. Established patterns

AN OPEN-AIR CANAANITE ALTAR FOR BURNT OFFERING FOUND AT MEGIDDO. *The
huge circular altar comes from the last years of the Early Bronze Age and is
twenty-nine feet in diameter and six and a half feet high. At the base of
the six steps that lead up to the altar, animal bones were found. An adjoin-
ing sanctuary can be seen in the lower right hand portion of the photograph with a square altar with four steps.*

were abandoned and new pottery, weapons, architecture and burial customs were introduced. The newcomers are usually identified as Amorites. Having destroyed the towns, these pastoral nomads were content to dwell in unwalled communities. Family-tomb burials ceased and individuals were interred in local cemeteries. Variations in funerary practices indicate that the newcomers represented different tribal groups with individualistic customs.

The resumption of the city-state marks the end of Amorite control. The newcomers who dominate the Middle Bronze Age (c. 2000–1500 B.C.) are broadly identified as Canaanites, a Semitic people whose origins are not known. The Amorites appear to have been content to dwell with the Canaanites, but once again new weapons, pottery and interment patterns are introduced. Heavy walls reinforced with towers protected the towns. Large dwellings, some with upper stories, were constructed. The dead were placed with pottery and bronze weapons in oblong stone lined trenches and covered with stone slabs. Pottery was fashioned in new shapes on a fast wheel, covered with a deep red slip and highly burnished. For the first time, bronze appears in abundance.

During the Middle Kingdom, which coincides with the twelfth dynasty (c. 1990–1786 B.C.), Egypt was ruled by Thebans. If Abraham's visit to Egypt is dated between the twentieth and nineteenth centuries, it occurs when Egyptian splendor was at a peak. Nubia was held by Egypt, and Sinai was exploited for metals and stone for statuary. Egyptian engineers constructed a canal linking the Nile and the Red Sea so that trade from Arabia and Mesopotamia flowed by seaway into Egypt to meet merchants and ships from the Mediterranean. Egyptian art found expression in buildings, ornaments and tomb paintings. Literary talent abounded. Coffin texts, religious documents, were written in the lids of coffins. The "Tale of Sinuhe," with its important description of Palestine and Syria, is from this era.[5]

The Second Intermediate period, during which art, architecture, literature and economy entered a period of decline, lasted from the thirteenth to seventeenth dynasties (c. 1786–1570 B.C.). The nation, weakened by internal political strife, was easy prey for a people of mixed stock, known as the Hyksos,[6] who seized and held rule for 150 years (c. 1700–1570 B.C.). Excavations in Palestine indicate that the Hyksos built city walls of beaten earth with a sloping face, encircled their cities with dry moats, utilized the horse and chariot for rapid troop movement, and employed the composite bow and arrow. In the literature of the period, other migrations are mentioned—the Hurrians[7] and Habiru (who will be discussed below)—and it is pos-

---

[5] *ANET*, p. 22 f.

[6] Manetho identifies these people as "Hyksos" which he interprets to mean "shepherd kings." Modern scholars believe the name means "rulers of foreign countries."

[7] A people called Horites, Hivites and Jebusites in the Bible and who were the dominant element in the Mitanni kingdom, located in the Middle Euphrates region. For a fine summary see E. A. Speiser, "Hurrians," *The Interpreter's Dictionary of the Bible*.

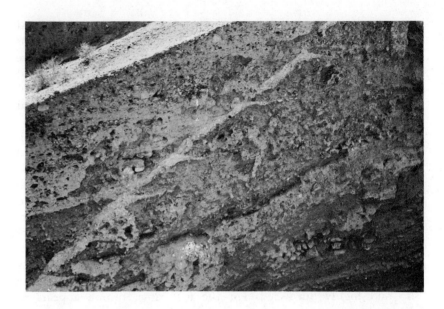

HYKSOS GLACIS (SLOPING RAMP) AT JERICHO. *The sloping face of the Hyksos glacis begins in the lower left-hand corner of the photograph and can be traced upward to the top of the picture. When the Hyksos came to Palestine they constructed cities on the tops of ancient tells, and introduced a new structural concept in defence works. The slope of the tell was hardened by pounding and packing the earth (terre pisée) and the packed surface was coated with a thin coating of plaster (visible in the picture). The city wall was built at the top of this glacis making attacks very difficult.*

sible that some of these may have joined the Hyksos movement.[8] Josephus identified the Hyksos with the ancestors of the Jews and their expulsion by Pharaoh Ahmose with the Exodus.[9]

The New Kingdom (eighteenth to twentieth dynasties) began with Ahmose, lasted from approximately 1570 to 1290 B.C., and constitutes ancient Egypt's most glorious period. Ahmose, using the new weapons introduced by the Hyksos, unified the nation and extended its borders from the fourth cataract of the Nile to the Euphrates. Once again art, architecture and religion flourished. A vigorous commercial policy brought new products from foreign nations. Royal marriages were made with foreign princesses.

A few of Ahmose's immediate successors are worthy of comment. Queen Hatshepsut, mother of Thutmose III (1490–1436 B.C.), who by law could not officially reign, donned royal robes, wore the double crown, and for eighteen years (c. 1486 to 1468) conducted affairs of state and engaged in extensive building. At her death, Thutmose III disfigured his mother's monuments and then turned his attention to the expansion of the empire, conducting campaigns into Palestine and Syria. His successor, Amenhotep II (c. 1436–1410), an athlete and

8 Kenyon, *op. cit.*, pp. 182 ff.
9 *Contra Apion* I:14, 16.

warrior, held the territories and, when Amenhotep III (c. 1400–1364) became king, Egypt was at a peak of power.

Amenhotep IV (c. 1370–1353), son of Amenhotep III, served as co-ruler during his father's declining years, but altered his name to Akhenaten when he came to power and made dramatic changes in religion and government. Sun worship, central in Egyptian history, was continued, but the center of worship was moved to a new city, Akhetaten (El Amarna), thus depriving ancient worship centers of power, prestige and wealth. The various animal manifestations of the sun were abandoned, and only the sun disc (Aten) was recognized. A hymn to the sun, bearing striking parallels to Ps. 104, may have been composed by the monarch. The well-being of the nation faltered under Akhenaten, and control of Palestinian provinces, as indicated in the El Amarna letters,[10] was slipping away through political intrigue and invasion by a people called the 'apiru.

Only four other pharaohs will be mentioned. Seti I (c. 1302–1290 B.C.) conducted campaigns in Palestine and Syria. Rameses II (c. 1290–1224 B.C.) fought the Hittites in an attempt to regain Syria and Palestine, but had to be satisfied with Palestine. Both Seti and Rameses were involved in building programs at Per-Rameses (the House of Rameses) and Pi-Tum, called Raamses and Pithom in Exodus 1:11. Mernephtah (c. 1224–1214 B.C.) campaigned in Palestine, and in his fifth year published his conquests in Canaan on a victory stele, mentioning the cities of Ashkelon, Gezer and Yenoam, and going on to announce "Israel is laid waste; his seed is not." The grammatical structure of the claim indicates that a people rather than a country is meant by "Israel." Rameses III (1195–1164 B.C.) came to the throne following a number of contenders who held brief rule after Mernephtah's death. New invaders, the "Sea People," threatened the land. Among these were the "Peleste" who settled the Philistine plain after a sea and land battle. A pictorial and verbal record of the encounter has been preserved in Rameses' mortuary temple at Medinet Habu.

The next 700 years of Egyptian history are marked by strife within the nation and decline in international power. Only for brief periods does Egypt exert real influence beyond her own borders, and because these periods affect biblical history, they will be considered in their proper sequence.

Political changes were also taking place in Mesopotamia. After the Neo-Sumerian period, Elamites and Amorites controlled Southern Mesopotamia. Of the Amorite rulers, the most distinguished was Hammurabi, a military, administrative and economic genius who united the country. His famous law code, reflecting, in part, earlier codes, contains many regulations not unlike those found in the Bible, indicating a broad common pattern of dealing with legal issues in the Near East. Administrative, trade and commercial, building and agricultural matters appear in documents of this period. A religious text contains a myth in which man is formed of clay in the image of the

---

[10] Cf. *ANET*, pp. 483 f.; *DOTT*, pp. 38 f.

A LIMESTONE RELIEF OF AMENHOTEP IV (AKHENATEN) AND QUEEN NEFERTITE. *The rays of the sun stream from above and terminate in hands, two of which present the symbol of life, the* ankh, *to the Pharaoh and his wife.*

gods.[11] Another myth relates the story of creation by the chief god of Babylon, Marduk. Representing the forces of order, he defeats the powers of chaos and forms the world and man, utilizing in part the bodies of defeated gods. The leader of the opposition forces, Tiamat, is split in half: one part of her divided body is arched to form the heavens and the other part stretched out to form the earth and sea. The sun, moon and stars are made to mark the divisions of the year. The blood of the rebel god Kingu, the consort of Tiamat, is mingled with clay and man is formed with the express purpose of serving the gods.[12] During this same period, reference to a people called "Habiru" is found in diplomatic correspondence.

Toward the middle of the seventeenth century, Cassites from the eastern mountains overcame Babylon and succeeded in establishing a kingdom that lasted into the twelfth century. The Cassite period is most obscure, but it is clear that they were under pressure from two other peoples, Hittites and Assyrians.

The Hittite nation, centered in Anatolia, arose during the second millennium (the period of the Old Empire),[13] when Indo-Europeans took control of the existing native population and established a feudal nobility under a monarch with limited powers. Some attempts at

11 Jack Finegan, *Light from the Ancient Past,* 2nd ed. (New Jersey: Princeton University Press, 1959), p. 62.

12 *Enuma elish,* cf. *ANET,* pp. 60 ff.; *DOTT,* pp. 3 ff.

13 S. Moscati, *The Face of the Ancient Orient* (Chicago: Quadrangle Books, 1960), p. 158.

THE HITTITE WEATHER GOD TESHUB *holding a hatchet (thunderbolt) in his upraised right hand and a trident (forked lightning?) in his left. He wears a short fringed tunic with a wide belt. His horned helmet is reminiscent of the bull figures often associated with him. The statue was found at Til Barsip.*

expansion were made around 1800 B.C., but it was not until the sixteenth century that the Hittites pushed into Syria and then eastward to Babylon. In the New Empire (c. 1460–1200 B.C.), Hittite power again affected Syria and Upper Mesopotamia, incorporating the kingdoms of the Mitanni[14] and engaging in clashes with Egyptians. Hittite documents indicate that wars generally ended with settlement treaties which clearly reveal the use of diplomatic strategy. One contribution of these people to Near Eastern culture is the use of iron. Between the fourteenth and twelfth centuries, Hittites used iron for weapons, holding a virtual monopoly on this product. Weakened by internal problems and by the invasion of Syria by Sea Peoples, the Hittite empire finally fell under attacks from less civilized peoples from the North. Hittite power was never again a threatening force in the Near East. After the collapse of the Hittite empire in the twelfth century, iron came into common use in Palestine, first among the Philistines, then among the Hebrews.[15]

The Philistines, the Peleste branch of the Sea People, settled in Palestine in the twelfth century BC. While it cannot be proven beyond all shadow of doubt, it is believed on the basis of pottery similarities that they are related to the Mycenaeans whose beginnings go back to the nineteenth century when waves of Indo-Europeans invaded Greece. During the fourteenth and thirteenth centuries, the Mycenaeans developed a tremendous export industry and their pottery was shipped to important Mediterranean centers. In the twelfth century some upset seems to have occurred in Mycenaean life, perhaps an earthquake, disrupting normal settled life. Bands of people usually associated with Mycenaeans began to roam the seas, apparently seeking a new place to settle. These "Sea People," as they are called in Egyptian literature, first threatened the delta during the reign of Rameses II and were defeated by his successor Mernephtah. The participants are called Danaans and Achaeans, names used by Homer to designate Greeks.[16] It appears that Cyprus, Ras es-Shamra, and the Hittite country, were also attacked at this time.[17]

A second wave of Sea People, which broke into two parts, followed the first. One group, the Tjikal or Tjeker, struck north Syria. The other, the Peleste or Pulusatu, attacked Egypt. After a bitter land and sea battle they were prevented from entering Egypt proper and were

[14] Both Hurrians and Mitanni were mountain peoples from Armenia. Cf. John Bright, *op. cit.*, pp. 55 f.

[15] Wm. F. Albright, *The Archaeology of Palestine*, p. 110.

[16] Among the Egyptian mercenaries were a group of Sea People known as "Sherdans." Cf. Y. Yadin, *The Art of Warfare in Biblical Lands* (London: Weidenfeld and Nicolson, 1963), pp. 248 ff.

[17] Michael C. Astour, "New Evidence on the Last Days of Ugarit," *American Journal of Archaeology*, LXIX (1965), 253–258.

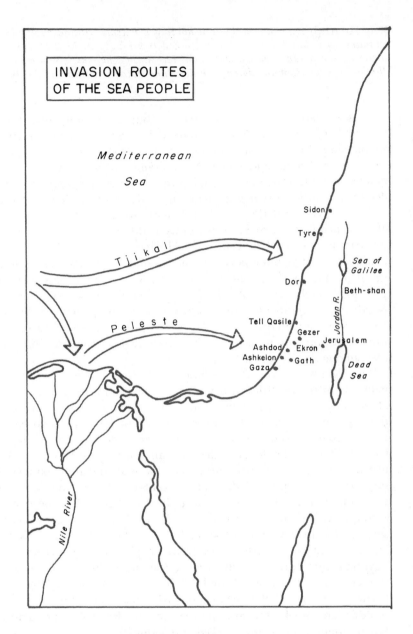

INVASION ROUTES
OF THE SEA PEOPLE

Mediterranean

Sea

Sidon

Tyre

Sea of
Galilee

Tjikal

Dor

Beth-shan

Jordan R.

Peleste

Tell Qasile

Gezer

Jerusalem

Ashdod

Ekron

Ashkelon

Gath

Gaza

Dead
Sea

Nile River

held to the area known as the Philistine Plain in southern Palestine. Here they settled in five major cities: Ashkelon, Ashdod, Ekron, Gath and Gaza, but their activities and holdings were much more extensive as revealed by excavations at Tell Qasile, Gezer, Beth Shan and elsewhere. The northern group settled the seacoast around Tyre and Sidon, an area ultimately called "Phoenicia" by the Greeks.[18]

We know something of Philistine dress. Rameses III depicted the sea battle in his mortuary temple at Medinet Habu and the Philistines are

[18] The term "Phoenicia" is the plural form of the Greek word "Phoenix" and seems to mean a dark red or purple color. Cf. Michael C. Astour, "The Origins of the terms 'Canaan,' 'Phoenician,' and 'Purple,'" *Journal of Near Eastern Studies*, XXIV (1965), 346–350.

A POTTERY SARCOPHAGUS FOUND AT TELL FAR'A, *a site about ten miles inland on the Philistine plain. The lid, in the form of a human face and arms, may reveal Egyptian influence, but the high headdress suggests that the coffin was for a Philistine burial.*

shown wearing kilts and armored vestments. On their heads were high feathered headdresses with chin straps and they carried huge round shields, bronze swords and spears. Those who attacked by land were similarly attired and came in horse drawn chariots and carts drawn by oxen. The same feathered headdress is depicted on a sarcophagus from Tell Far'a.

It would appear that the Philistines were organized along the city-state pattern with local rulers for each unit. Little is known of their industry, apart from the characteristic pottery and the reference to the control of the iron industry (I Sam. 13:19 ff). Whatever their language may have been, it would appear that they soon adopted the Canaanite tongue, for they appear to have had little difficulty in communicating with the Hebrews.[19] Like other peoples in Palestine, they suffered the pressures of the great powers around them, utterly disappearing from history after the neo-Babylonian period (sixth century) and leaving only their name to designate the territory they partially occupied (Palestine).[20]

One other people, the Assyrians, were destined to play an important role in Near Eastern and Hebrew history. The nation was located in the foothill region of the Kurdistan mountains at the middle course of the Tigris, and both country and capital city were named after the god Asshur. Excavations at Asshur show the site to have been occupied in the early third millennium but Assyria did not begin its rise until the second millennium with the decline of power of the first Babylonian Dynasty. Language and religious beliefs were like those of Babylon. In the second half of the eighteenth century B.C. under King Shamsi-Adad, the city-state of Asshur began to develop in power and independence, ultimately to become the basis for the formation of the Assyrian Empire, which lasted until the end of the seventh century B.C. Under Tiglath Pileser I (c. 1100 B.C.), Assyrians took possession of land as far as Lake Van on the north and Syria and the Mediterranean Sea on the west. The events of the next centuries are obscure, but in the ninth century under Ashurnasirpal II, when a military machine renowned for its efficient ruthlessness was developed, Assyria again became a threat in the Near Eastern political affairs. Because Assyrian growth directly affects the Hebrew people, subsequent Assyrian history will be discussed in context.

[19] However, cf. G. E. Wright, "Fresh Evidence for the Philistine Story," *The Biblical Archaeologist* (henceforth *BA*), XXIX (1966), 70–86.

[20] The territory possessed by the Philistines is called "Pelesheth" in the Bible (cf. Exod. 15:14; Isa. 14:31; Joel 3:4), "Palaistine" by the Greeks, and subsequently "Palaestina" by the Romans, which became "Palestine" in English.

The Hebrews

Who Were the Hebrews?

ACCORDING to biblical tradition, the Hebrews are peoples descended from Shem, one of Noah's sons, through Eber, the eponymous ancestor, and Abraham. Gen. 7:22 f., reports that the flood destroyed all life except that in Noah's ark; consequently, the whole human family descended from Noah and his sons: Japheth, Ham and Shem. As yet, not all of the names of eponymous ancestors in the family lines can be identified,[1] but some probabilities are listed in Chart 6.

From Shem, through Arpachshad and Shelah came Eber, the eponymous ancestor of the Hebrews, and from his descendants through Peleg, Reu, Sereg and Nahor came Terah, the father of Abram and his brothers Nahor and Haran. It becomes clear that if "Hebrews" are descendants of Eber, then others besides those of Abraham's line would be included (see Gen. 10:25–27).

Read Gen. 12–25

With Abraham the story of the Hebrews begins, and it is clearly stated that Hebrew origins lay outside Canaan. The summons to leave his ancestral home and journey to Canaan is accompanied by a promise (Gen. 12:2) that becomes a submotif in patriarchal accounts, re-appearing again and again (cf. Gen. 13:14 f., 15:5 f., 18:10, 22:17, 26:24, 28:13 f., 32:12 f., 35:9 ff., 48:16), finally taking covenantal form (Gen. 17:14 ff.). The promise has two parts: nationhood and divine blessing or protection. The precise location of the nation-to-be is not specified but was, of course, known to those hearing or reading the account. The promise of blessing signified the unique and particularistic bond between Yahweh and his followers, so that the enemies of Abraham or the nation were enemies of Yahweh, and those befriending Abraham and/or the nation would be blessed. With this assurance, Abraham journeyed to Canaan, Egypt, the Negeb, Hebron, Gezer, Beer-sheba and back to Hebron where he and his wife Sarah died.

The descriptions of Abraham are not uniform: at times he appears as a lonely migrant, at others as a chieftain, head of a large family, or as a warrior. Factual details about the patriarch are difficult to establish, for his real significance lies in what is often called "inner history," through which those who looked to Abraham as a forefather gained

---

[1] G. von Rad, *Genesis*, trans. by John H. Marks (Philadelphia: Westminster Press, 1961), pp. 142 f.

—— CHART VI. THE TABLE OF THE NATIONS IN GENESIS 10–11 ——

Noah
- *Shem*
  - Elam (Elamites)
  - Asshur (Assyrians)
  - *Arpachshad* (A Chaldean location?) — *Shelah* (unknown) — *Eber*
    - *Peleg* (unknown) — *Reu* (A Mesopotamian group or city) — *Serug* (A Mesopotamian group or city) — *Nahor* (the city, Til-nakhiri) — *Terah* (the city, Til-turakhi)
      - *Abram*
      - Nahor
      - Haran
    - Joktan (unknown) — The descendants of Joktan appear to be South Arabian peoples or locales.
  - Lud (Lydians)
  - Aram (Arameans)
    - Uz (A city in the Syrian desert)
    - Hul (An Aramean tribe or village?)
    - Gether (An Aramean tribe or village?)
    - Mash (An Aramean location or tribe or village?)
- Ham
  - Cush (North Africa)
    - Seba (In northern Africa, bordering the Red Sea)
    - Havilah (A city in Arabia?)
    - Sabtah (A city in Arabia?)
    - Raamah (A city in Arabia?)
      - Sheba (in South Arabia?)
      - Dedan (in North Arabia?)
    - Sabteca (in Arabia?)
  - Egypt (North Africa)
  - Put (North Africa)
  - Canaan (reflecting Egyptian domination)
- Japheth
  - Gomer (Cimmerians of the sixth century B.C.?)
  - Magog (Scythians?)
  - Madai (Medes)
  - Javan (Ionian Greeks?)
    - Elishah (A colony on Cyprus? South Italy? North Africa?)
    - Tarshish (A colony of Eastern Mediterranean people in Spain?)
    - Kittim (Cypriots?)
    - Dodanim (A Mediterranean people? Rhodians?)
  - Tubal (A people in Asia Minor?)
  - Meshech (A people of the upper Euphrates called Mushki in Assyrian texts?)
  - Tiras (An Aegean people?)

Bracketed statements reflect scholars' attempts to identify the peoples. The Hebrew heritage (in italics) is traced through Shem to Abram (Abraham).

understanding of themselves as "people of the promise" and attained a sense of destiny and an appreciation of their particular relationship to their deity. We have noted earlier that some Abrahamic traditions coincide with information coming from Nuzi, which would place Abraham in the Middle Bronze era.

We read that Abraham, in response to a divine summons, left Mesopotamia and journeyed to Canaan with his wife, Sarah, and nephew, Lot. It is clear that the people were meant to recognize themselves as a community originating in a commission from God and in the unwavering, unquestioning obedience of Abraham. The journey itself was more than a pilgrimage, for it constituted the starting point of a continuing adventure in nationhood. Nor are the travelers without vicissitudes, but throughout famine, earthquake, fire and war, they are protected by Yahweh.

Gen. 14, in which Abraham is called a "Hebrew" for the first time, records a battle between the patriarch and kings of countries or areas as yet unidentified for certain and associates him with the Canaanite king of Jerusalem. It is possible that reliable historical data are preserved here.[2] The account of the destruction of Sodom and Gomorrah may also rest in some memory of a shift in the earth's crust that destroyed the cities of the plain. Tradition associates Abraham with Hebron, and if Jebel er-Rumeide is the site of this ancient city, it is evident that a powerful city was located here in the Middle Bronze period.[3]

Abraham's adventures in the Negeb, the problems of grazing and watering rights, and the digging of a well at Beer-sheba[4] echo genuine problems of the shepherd. The episode involving Sarah and King Abimelech (a doublet of Gen. 12:10 ff.) introduces Sarah's relationship to Abraham as both wife and sister, a relationship which in Hurrian society provided the wife with privileged social standing. It may also be interpreted as an historic link with the cultures of the upper Euphrates.[5]

The close relationship between the Hebrews and the people of the desert and steppes is recognized in the story of Ishmael, the nomadic first son of Abraham; but it is through Isaac, the second son about whom so very little is recorded, that the Hebrews trace their own family line. Both Isaac and his son Jacob maintain a separateness from the people among whom they dwell, taking wives from among their own kin in Haran (Gen. 24; 28). The story of Jacob, who becomes Israel, and his twin brother Esau, who becomes Edom, is colored with rivalry, trickery and bitter misunderstanding but also contains echoes of Hurrian custom. In Hurrian law, birthright could be purchased, and some of the terminology associated with Isaac's blessing of his sons reflects Hurrian patterns.[6]

2 E. A. Speiser, *Genesis*, The Anchor Bible (Garden City, New York: Doubleday & Co., Inc., 1964), pp. 105 ff.

3 Gerald A. Larue, "The American Expedition to Hebron, 1965," *The Journal of Bible and Religion*, XXXIII (1965), 337 ff.

4 Possibly located at Tell Sheba, an unexcavated mound just east of the modern town.

5 Speiser, *Genesis*, pp. 91 ff.

6 *Ibid.*, pp. 212 f.

The stories about Jacob also accord with Nuzi (Hurrian) law for it is recorded that a man may labor for his wife.[7] In dealing with his uncle Laban, Jacob's trickery was matched by his uncle's deceptive acts. There is no condemnation of chicanery but, rather, the attitude that to best a man in a business contract revealed cleverness. When Jacob's hopes to inherit his uncle's estate were dashed by the birth of male heirs, he broke contract and fled, and it was only when a new contract was made that relationships were healed. The account of Jacob's night wrestling with an angelic visitor has probably come down to us through various recensions, for it now contains two aetiological explanations: one concerning the name "Jacob–Israel" and the other giving the reason why the ischiatic sinew is not eaten by Hebrews. Other traditions associate Jacob with Bethel and Shechem.

Joseph, the son of Jacob, was sold into slavery by jealous brothers and rose to high office in Egypt. When his father and brothers migrated to Egypt to escape famine, they were regally received and encouraged to settle. Documents attesting to the custom of admitting nomadic groups into the country in time of famine are known from Egypt, and the Joseph stories reflect many accurate details about Egyptian life and may be derived in part from Egyptian tales, as we shall see. The pharaoh under whom Joseph rose to power is not identified.

It is quite possible, as A. Alt has argued, that the patriarchs were founders of separate cults or clans in which distinctive names for the deity were compounded with patriarchal names.[8] Hence, the deity was known as "the Shield of Abraham" (Gen. 15:1), "the Fear of Isaac" (Gen. 31:42, 53), and "the Mighty One of Jacob" (Gen. 49:24). Individual representations were later fused and equated with Yahweh, and individual clan heroes were placed in an historical sequence and made part of a single family line from Abraham to Jacob (Israel).

Read Exod. 1–6

After what appears to be an extended period of time, the Hebrews increased in numbers and became a mighty multitude, and a pharaoh who was indifferent to the Joseph traditions inherited the throne and persecuted the Hebrews, pressing them into virtual enslavement. Moses, a desert refugee from Egyptian justice, became associated with the Kenite people. On the slopes of Mount Sinai in a dramatic encounter with Yahweh, he was commissioned to act as deliverer of the Hebrews. In the clash with Pharaoh, the god-king's power was overshadowed by Yahweh through a series of horrendous events in which

Read Chs. 7–11

the Nile was turned to blood and plagues involving frogs, gnats, flies, cattle, boils, hail, locusts and darkness are ultimately climaxed by the death of all the first-born children of Egypt. This final act, associated in tradition with the Passover festival, persuaded Pharaoh to release the Hebrews. Shortly after the Hebrews departed, Pharaoh changed his mind and pursued them. At the Sea of Reeds, Yahweh permitted the Hebrews to pass through the waters unscathed but overwhelmed

---

[7] Cf. G. Cornfeld (ed.), *Adam to Daniel* (New York: The Macmillan Company, 1961), p. 85.

[8] A. Alt, *Kleine Schriften zur Geschichte des Volkes Israel* (Munich: C. H. Beck'sche Verlagsbuchhandlung, 1953), I. See also J. Bright, *op. cit.*, pp. 88 ff.

the Egyptians. The Hebrews pressed into the wilderness to Mount Sinai where the law was given and there they entered a covenant with Yahweh. After an abortive attempt to seize Canaan by penetrating from the south, they moved eastward and, after many setbacks, took up a position on the eastern side of the Jordan, just north of the Salt Sea. Here Moses died, and under his successor, Joshua, the attacks on Canaan were launched.

Read
Num.
14:39 f.

PROBLEMS WITH DATES AND PLACES

Efforts to date the patriarchal period have not been particularly rewarding, for biblical chronology is complex. In the P source, 215 years pass between the time of Abraham's journey to Canaan and Jacob's migration to Egypt (see Gen. 12:4b, 21:5, 25:26, 47:9), and the period spent in Egypt is given as 430 years (Exod. 12:40 f.), making a total of 645 years before the Exodus. As we shall see, most scholars date the Exodus near the middle of the thirteenth century, so that Abraham would leave Mesopotamia at the beginning of the nineteenth century, and Jacob's journey to Egypt would occur about 1700 B.C. Unfortunately, date variations occur in some manuscripts. In the LXX, Exod. 12:40 includes time spent in both Egypt and Canaan in the 430-year period (some manuscripts read 435 years). According to this reckoning, Abraham's journey would fall in the seventeenth century and Jacob's in the fifteenth century.

The early nineteenth century date for Abraham places his departure from Mesopotamia at the time of the Elamite and Amorite invasion. It harmonizes with the conclusions of Nelson Glueck, who found that between the twenty-first and nineteenth centuries B.C. the Negeb was dotted with hamlets where inhabitants, having learned how to hoard water, engaged in agriculture and tended small flocks. Such settlements would provide stopping places for Abraham and his retinue.[9] The seventeenth century date for Jacob's settlement in Egypt coincides with the Hyksos invasion of Egypt, lending support to Josephus' hypothesis, for Hebrews may have been part of this movement.

The second pattern of dating would place Abraham in the time of Hammurabi of Babylon and would give strength to the argument that the mention of King Amraphel of Shinar in Gen. 14:1 is a Hebraized reference to Hammurabi. Abraham would, therefore, be in Canaan during the Hyksos period, and Joseph would have risen to power in the Amarna age. The close of the Amarna period brought to power leaders hostile to Akhenaton and possibly also to those he had favored.

Whatever the correct date for Abraham may be, he represents the beginning of the nation to the Hebrews. Yahweh's promise to the patriarch and his successors is considered to be the guarantee of national existence (Num. 32:11). There are no references to Abraham in the writings of the eighth century prophets, for then stress was laid on the Exodus as the starting point of the nation. In the seventh and

[9] Nelson Glueck, *Rivers in the Desert*, pp. 68 ff.

MIDDLE BRONZE AGE POTTERY FROM THE EXCAVATION OF HEBRON. *If Abraham went to Hebron during the time of the Hyksos, he would have found a city surrounded by a massive stone wall with huge reenforcing towers. Graceful clay jugs, bowls, and juglets, like those pictured above, would be in common use.*

sixth centuries, and in the post-Exilic period, the Abrahamic tradition came to the fore once again.

Efforts to determine the date and route of the Exodus have been disappointing. Josephus placed the Exodus at the time of the over-throw of the Hyksos by Ahmose in the sixteenth century, a date that is far too early. Biblical evidence is limited. I Kings 6:1 reports that Solomon began building the temple in the fourth year of his reign, 480 years after the Exodus. Solomon's rule is believed to have begun near the middle of the tenth century, possibly about 960 B.C. Thus, the date of the Exodus would be: 960 minus 4 (4th year of reign) plus 480, or 1436. In that case, Thutmose III would be the pharaoh of the oppression, and his mother, Hatshepsut, might be identified as the rescuer of the infant Moses. The Hebrew invasion of Canaan, taking place forty years later or about 1400 B.C., might be identified with the coming of the 'apiru.[10]

Another theory is based on the reference to the building of Pithom and Raamses in Exod. 1:11. It was noted earlier that both Seti I and Rameses II worked at the rebuilding of these cities, and that Rameses is the best candidate for the Pharaoh of the Exodus (1290–1224 B.C.). If the Exodus took place between 1265 and 1255, the invasion of

[10] Jack Finegan, *Light From the Ancient Past,* pp. 118 ff.

Canaan would occur in Mernephtah's reign, and some encounter between Egyptians and Hebrews would be the basis for his boast of annihilating Israel.

Attempts to chart the course followed by the fleeing Hebrews is equally frustrating. No one knows for sure the location of Mount Sinai, and the site chosen for the holy mountain determines, in part, the route suggested. Attempts have been made to identify stopping places mentioned in Num. 33:1–37,[11] but the identifications can be no more than conjectures, for biblical descriptions are vague without distinctive landmarks.[12]

The traditional site of Sinai, Jebel Musa, near the southern tip of the Sinai peninsula, has been widely accepted since the fourth and fifth centuries A.D., although there was some confusion over which mountain in the cluster of peaks was Sinai. The traditional route to Jebel Musa begins in Egypt, crosses the Sea of Reeds (identified either at the tip of the Red Sea in the Gulf of Heroonpolis [Gulf of Suez] or as one of the papyrus swamps above the gulf), and goes southward along the western edge of the Sinai peninsula before turning inland to Jebel Musa. From Sinai, the Hebrews would move to the north along the Gulf of Aqabah toward Ezion Geber and Kadesh Barnea.

Sinai has also been identified as Jebel Helal, located in the northern part of the peninsula. The route to this mountain goes from Egypt across the marshy swamp area and follows the Way of Shur, one of the major trade routes of the ancient world, to Jebel Helal and Kadesh Barnea. Another route to this same mountain goes over the land strip of Lake Sirbonis (which becomes the Sea of Reeds), northward along the Way of the Philistines, the coastal route, then southward to Kadesh Barnea and Jebel Helal.

Some have insisted that the descriptions in Exod. 19:16 suggest volcanic disturbances and that Sinai must be sought among volcanic mountains, probably those in the Midianite areas on the eastern side of the Gulf of Aqabah. One choice among these mountains is El Khrob which preserves the name Horeb. The Exodus route would then follow the Way of Shur to Kadesh Barnea and Ezion Geber and down the coast to El Khrob. Sinai has also been located in Edomite territory, for Judg. 5:4 and Deut. 33:2 locate the mountain in Seir. Jebel Faran on the west side of the Wadi Arabah has been suggested as a possible choice, and mountains in the Petra area have also been suggested. In this case the Hebrews would have traveled along the Way of Shur, by way of Ezion Geber, into Edomite territory.[13]

Although, for the scholar, there are innumerable problems associated with the Exodus tradition, this memorable event became a central factor in the interpretation of the Hebrew faith. Here Yahweh had demonstrated his loyal, redeeming love to the people whom he had chosen as his own. In the darkest days of the Exilic period, the

---

[11] G. E. Wright, *Biblical Archaeology,* p. 64; C. Kraeling, *Bible Atlas,* pp. 107 ff.

[12] Y. Aharoni, "Kadesh Barnea and Mount Sinai," *God's Wilderness* (New York: Thomas Nelson and Sons, 1962), p. 118.

[13] For a detailed statement of conjectures on Sinai and the Exodus route, cf. Kraeling, *op. cit.,* chap. 6.

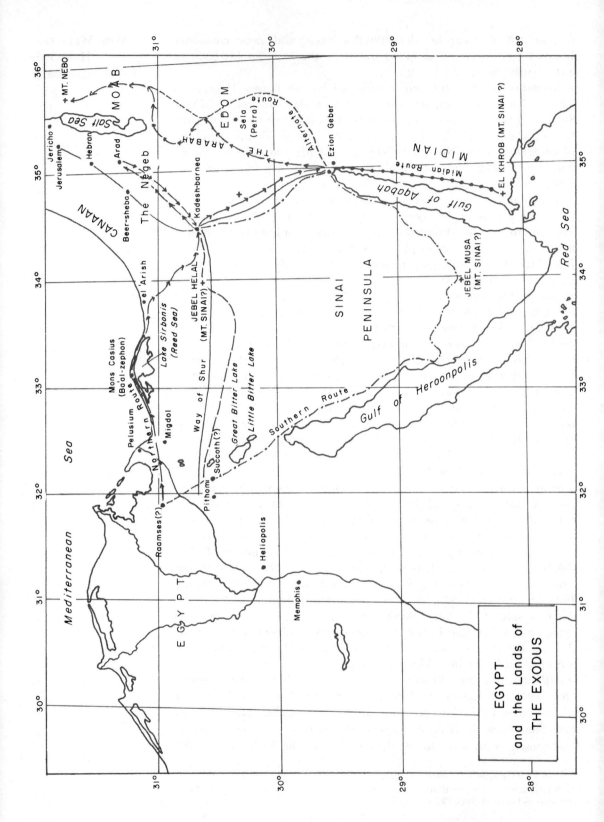

EGYPT
and the Lands of
THE EXODUS

memory of the Exodus event became a source of hope, for it was believed that Yahweh would deliver his people from bondage in Babylon even as he had rescued them from Egypt.

A somewhat different tradition of Hebrew beginnings is reflected in Ezek. (16:3 ff.), where mixed ancestry—Amorite, Hittite and Canaanite—is attributed to the Jerusalemites. But here we have a unique situation, for Jerusalem was a Jebusite stronghold which did not become a Hebrew city until the time of David (II Sam. 5). The firstfruits liturgy (Deut. 26:5) traces Hebrew ancestry to the Aramaeans, but the designation appears to be used in a broad rather than a specific sense.

Etymological analyses of the term "Hebrew" ('ibrī) have given little help to the study of origins. The term has been related to a root, meaning "to go over" or "to go across"; hence, a "Hebrew" would be one who crossed over or one who went from place to place, a nomad, a wanderer, a designation that would fit some aspects of patriarchal behavior. A similar term, habiru, is found in cuneiform documents from the twentieth to the eleventh centuries, often used interchangeably with another word, SA.GAZ. At times the Habiru appear to be settled in specific locations; at times they serve in the army as mercenaries, or are bound to masters as servants. The El Amarna tablets refer to invaders of Palestine as 'apiru, a word bearing close relationship to the terms habiru and "Hebrew."[14] Extensive research has led many scholars to the conclusion that the term "Hebrew" was first used as an appellative to describe foreigners who crossed into settled areas and referred not to a specific group but to a social caste. If the word "Hebrew" parallels habiru or 'apiru, we know that these people on occasion were employed, at times created settlements of their own, and at other times attacked established communities. The suggestion that the terms 'apiru, habiru and "Hebrew" relate to those who have renounced a relationship to an existing society, who have by a deliberate action withdrawn from some organization or rejected some authority, and who have become through this action freebooters, slaves, employees or mercenaries presents real possibilities.[15] In the Bible the word Hebrew becomes an ethnic term used interchangeably with "Israelite."[16]

Perhaps the best that can be said is that the Hebrews of the Bible appear to be one branch of the Northwest Semitic group, related linguistically to Canaanites, Edomites and Moabites, who moved from a semi-nomadic existence to settled life in the Bronze Age.

[14] Cf. T. J. Meek, *Hebrew Origins*, chap. 1. For the suggestion that the term 'apiru means "donkey driver, caravaneer" cf. Wm. F. Albright, "Abram the Hebrew: A New Archaeological Interpretation," *Bulletin of the American Schools of Oriental Research* (henceforth *BASOR*), No. 163 (1961), 36–54.

[15] E. F. Campbell, "The Amarna Letters and the Amarna Period," *BA* XXIII (1960), 15; G. E. Mendenhall, "The Hebrew Conquest of Palestine," *BA* XXV (1962), 71 f.

[16] For an extended discussion of the 'Apiru-Habiru-Hebrew problem, cf. Mary F. Gray, "The Habiru-Hebrew Problem in the Light of Source Material Available at Present," *Hebrew Union College Annual*, XXIX (1958), pp. 135–202; Moshe Greenberg, *The Hab/piru*, American Oriental Series, XXXIX (New Haven: American Oriental Society, 1955).

A SACRED PILLAR OF WHITE LIMESTONE *from what is believed to have been the temple of El (Ba'al) Berith at Shechem. There is no way of determining the original height of the stone. It has been restored to what the excavators believe was its original position.*

It is clear from biblical tradition that, at the beginning of their history, the semi-nomadic Hebrews with flocks of sheep and goats were at the point of moving into a settled way of life. The patriarchs are chiefs of large families or clans living, for the most part, in peace among their neighbors with whom they enter covenants. From family and clan beginnings came tribes linked to one another by ancestral blood ties. Bonds between clans or tribes were so strong that the group might be described as having an existence of its own, a personality embodying the corporate membership. This phenomenon of psychic unity, labeled "corporate personality" by H. Wheeler Robinson,[17] placed particular responsibilities upon each member of the group. Because group life was a unity, injury to a single member was injury to all demanding repayment by the next of kin, the go'el.[18] Blood shed was tribal blood requiring redemption by the next of kin. Should

[17] H. Wheeler Robinson, "The Hebrew Conception of Corporate Personality," *Werden und Wesen des Alten Testaments*, J. Hempel (ed.), B.Z.A.W. LXVI, 1936, pp. 49 ff. See also J. Pedersen, *Israel: Its Life and Culture* (Copenhagen: Povl Branner, 1926), Vols. I–II; Aubrey R. Johnson, *The One and the Many in the Israelite Conception of God*, 2nd ed. (Cardiff: University of Wales Press, 1961); and Aubrey R. Johnson, *The Vitality of the Individual in the Thought of Ancient Israel*, 2nd ed. (Cardiff: University of Wales Press, 1964).

[18] *Go'el* comes from a root meaning "to recover" or "buy back" or "redeem," and thus means "redeemer," "restorer" and, in a sense, "protector." For a brief discussion, cf. Roland de Vaux, *Ancient Israel, Its Life and Institutions*, John McHugh, trans. (New York: McGraw-Hill Book Co., 1961), pp. 21 f.

a man die without offspring, his next of kin had to bring the widow to fruition, and the child born to her became the child of the dead man, the one carrying his name (Ruth 4:4–10). As the father was at the head of the family, so the tribal chief and elders led the larger group, seeking the well-being, peace and psychic health of the members. The corporate nature of the group afforded great protection, for wherever a member went, he was backed by the strength of the tribe to which he belonged. Fear of reprisal tended to be—but was not always—a restraining factor in violation of social mores (Judg. 19–20). When the head of the household died, the widow and orphan were cared for by the next of kin and ultimately by the total group.

Tribal and family religion centered in holy places where a local priesthood tended shrines, kept altar fires burning, and shared in offerings (I Sam. 2:12–17). The father seems to have acted as ministrant on behalf of the family (I Sam. 1). Offerings were made and a meal shared through which the participants were bound more firmly together. There is no evidence that the deity was believed to participate in the meal. Agreements made at holy places were witnessed by the deity who guaranteed fulfillment of terms (Gen. 31:51 ff.). The shrine of Ba'al-berith (Judg. 9:4) or El-berith (Judg. 9:46), the "covenant god" at Shechem, may have been a holy place where covenants were made in the presence of the god.

An important custom in Hebrew society was the practice of hospitality. A guest was honored and entertained, even at considerable expense to the host (Gen. 18:1–8, 24:28–32). Once under the host's roof, or having shared food, the guest was guaranteed protection (Gen. 19, Judg. 19). Should a stranger settle in the community, he enjoyed most of the rights and responsibilities.

From time to time new groups were grafted into the family tree of Hebrew tribes, and the heritage of the larger group became that of the adopted ones, as when the Calebites united with the tribe of Judah (Josh. 14:6–15, 15:13). When confronted by common problems or enemies, tribal federations were formed (see Judg. 4–5). On the other hand, when a famine or food shortage occurred, one group might leave to seek new territory (Gen. 13). Tribal activity in Canaan is portrayed as a twelve-tribe federation,[19] often called an amphictyony, after Greek tribal federations.[20] However, clear distinctions between Greek and Hebrew patterns must be recognized. Greek cities united in an amphictyony centered about a shrine where peoples from the surrounding cities worshiped and where decisions affecting the participating members were made. The Hebrew amphictyony was centered in the Ark of Yahweh, a moveable shrine. Some scholars have argued

[19] The scheme develops out of the twelve sons of Jacob—six from Leah: Reuben, Simeon, Levi, Judah, Issachar, Zebulun; two from Zilpah: Gad and Asher; two from Rachel: Joseph and Benjamin; and two from Bilhah: Dan and Naphtali (cf. Gen. 29:16–30:24; 35:16–20). The final grouping for division of the land includes: Asher, Benjamin, Dan, Ephraim, Gad, Issachar, Judah, Manasseh, Naphtali, Reuben, Simeon and Zebulun. More than twenty variant lists occur within the Bible.

[20] Martin Noth, *The History of Israel*, pp. 87 ff.; John Bright, *A History of Israel*, pp. 142 f.; Murray Newman, *The People of the Covenant* (New York: Abingdon Press, 1962), pp. 102 ff.

—— CHART VII. A CHART OF TRIBAL LINEAGE ——

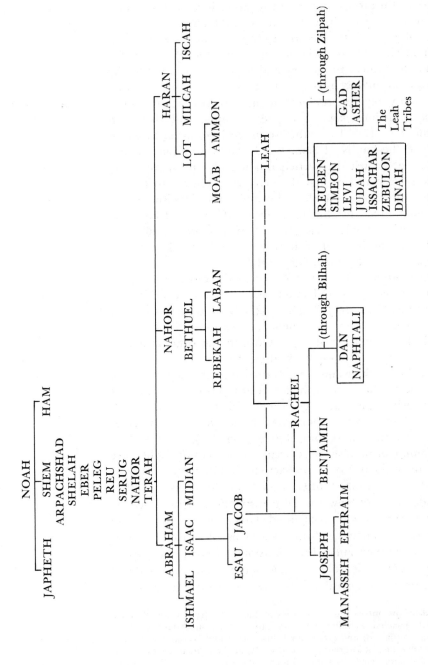

Sometimes the tribes are listed genealogically (Gen. 35:23; I Chron. 2:1–2); sometimes in cultic formation (Num. 2–3; Deut. 27:12); and sometimes geographically (Num. 34:14–28; I Chron. 6:54 ff.; Ezek. 48:1 ff.). Usually twelve tribes are mentioned, but the identification of the tribes varies: in one Dinah is listed in place of Benjamin (Gen. 29–30), and in Chronicles both halves of the tribe of Manasseh are counted (I Chron. 2–3; 6:54–80). Some lists mention only ten tribes (Deut. 33:6 ff.; II Sam. 19:43); one gives eleven tribes (I King 11:31); and in Gen. 46:48 ff. there are thirteen.

that a primitive amphictyonic ritual was observed at the shrine at Shechem,[21] but the hypothesis rests only upon probabilities. A six-tribe federation, which preceded the twelve-tribe grouping, has also been postulated involving the Leah tribes: Reuben, Simeon, Levi, Judah, Zebulun and Issachar.[22]

21 Cf. Noth, *op. cit.*, pp. 92 f.; Newman, *op. cit.*, pp. 108 ff.
22 Cf. Noth, *op. cit.*, pp. 88 f.; Newman, *op. cit.*, p. 102.

9
The Settlement of Canaan

THE Hebrews entered a land with its own highly developed culture. During the Late Bronze and Early Iron Ages, Canaan was dotted with strong, walled, industrial and trade centers surrounded by orchards, vineyards, grain fields and pasture land. Wool and flax were woven and dyed with the rich purple obtained from the Murex shellfish. Wine, dried fruits, grain and milk products were also produced. Minerals from the Wadi Arabah were smelted and fashioned into ornaments, tools and weapons for sale and exchange. The rich lived in magnificent villas built around central courts; the poor dwelt in hovels massed together. Slaves captured in battle, and the poor who sold their families and themselves to meet debts, contributed to the power and wealth of the few.

Canaanite religion, a fertility or nature religion, reflected the major concerns of the populace—increase and productivity. Until recently, information about Canaanite belief was drawn largely from the negative statements in the Bible, but since 1928 new data has been forthcoming. While plowing a field, a farmer discovered a Canaanite necropolis at Ras es–Shamra in northern Syria at a point along the seacoast to which the "finger" of Cyprus appears to be pointing. Excavations began in 1929 under the direction of Claude F. A. Schaeffer of France and have continued since with only a brief interruption during World War II. The necropolis belonged to the ancient city of Ugarit, known to scholars from references in the El Amarna texts. The city was destroyed in the fourteenth century by an earthquake and then rebuilt, only to fall in the twelfth century to the hoards of Sea People. It was never rebuilt and was ultimately forgotten. One of the excavator's most exciting discoveries was a temple dedicated to the god Ba'al with a nearby scribal school containing numerous tablets relating the myths of Ba'al written in a Semitic dialect but in a cuneiform script never before encountered. The language was deciphered and the myths translated, providing many parallels to Canaanite practices condemned in the Bible and making it possible to suggest that the religion of Ba'al as practiced in Ugarit was very much like that of the Canaanites of Palestine.

The texts[1] portray a divine hierarchy headed by the benign father-

[1] A translation of the texts by H. L. Ginsberg appears in *ANET*. See also G. R. Driver, *Canaanite Myths and Legends,* Old Testament Studies, III (Edinburgh: T.

— CHART VIII —

Years B.C.	Archaeological Period	Conditions and Events in Palestine	Condition and Events Outside of Palestine
1500–1200	Late Bronze Age	Canaan: a province of Egypt dotted with powerful walled cities city-state plan of government extensive trade and industry flourishing nature religion Hebrews invade from the east (thirteenth–twelfth centuries) Philistines invade from the west and occupy coastal region (twelfth century)	EGYPT: weakened by war against Sea People unable to control Palestine HITTITE nations collapses
1200–922	Early Iron Age	Philistines establish city-states Hebrews struggle to hold territory: period of the Judges war with Canaanites: battle of Taanach battles with Moabites, Midianites, Amalekites, Philistines an abortive attempt at Hebrew kingship the tribe of Dan is forced to migrate the war against Benjamin	ASSYRIA: Under Tiglath Pileser I holds Syria until 1100 EGYPT: still weak

THE CANAANITE GOD BA'AL. *A limestone stele found at Ras es-Shamra portrays Ba'al wearing a conical headdress with horns, a short kilt, and a sword strapped to his side. His upraised right arm is poised to hurl a thunderbolt, and his left hand holds a spear of lightning, stylized to represent a tree. He stands above the undulating hills, or perhaps the waves of the ocean. The small figure below the tip of the sword is, perhaps, the donor of the stele.*

god El, a rather subordinate figure in some of the myths, and the mother goddess, Astarte, who appears in the Bible as Ba'al's consort. The numerous children include: Ba'al, the god of rain or weather and fecundity; Yam, the sea god; Mot, god of death; Koshar or Kothar, the artisan god; Shemesh, the sun god; Anat, the sister-consort of Ba'al; and numerous other minor figures. One myth reflects the seasonal cycle which must have been basic for cultic observances. It tells of a battle for sovereignty of the land between Ba'al and Yam, in which Yam, defeated by magic weapons supplied by Kothar, is confined to the ocean bed. (Compare Prov. 8:29; Ps. 89:9 f.) The triumphant Ba'al builds a castle and, in a victory feast, extols his prowess in battle and his role of lord of the land. During the banquet, messengers from the uninvited Mot bring a challenge to Ba'al, and when Ba'al and Mot meet, the god of life is overcome by the god of death. Without rain Mot's deathly powers begin to encroach upon the fertile land. El descends from his throne and sits on the ground pouring ashes on his head and, in a ritual act, gashes his face, arms, chest and back (cf. I Kings 18:28). Anat too, conducts mourning rites, weeping over hill and mountain as she searches for the dead god. Finally, having discovered Ba'al's fate through the sun god, Anat encounters and defeats Mot, grinding him and scattering his remains. In some manner not explained, Ba'al was revived and life returned to earth. For the seasonal pattern of the ritual, Ba'al's death symbolized the aridity of summer; the defeat of Mot symbolized the time of harvesting crops and fall sowing; and the rebirth of Ba'al symbolized the coming of the autumnal rains. Numerous "stage directions" point to some form of dramatic enactment.[2] Within this and other myths, gods perform sexual and cultic acts prohibited in the Hebrew religion, suggesting that some biblical prohibitions may have been directed against participation in Canaanite religion as much as against some violation of accepted mores.

As a god of productivity, Ba'al was well suited for the social and economic climate of Canaanite business society. There can be little doubt that the prophetic idealization of the wilderness period and the outcries for justice for the widow and orphan reflect Canaanite social mores which made it possible to seize every opportunity to profit from the death of a neighbor's father or husband. On the other hand, in another Canaanite tale in which a certain Dan'el (or Daniel) is a

---

& T. Clark, 1956); T. H. Gaster, *Thespis;* Cyrus H. Gordon, *Ugaritic Literature* (Roma: Pontificium Institutum Biblicum, 1949).

[2] Cf. Gaster, *Thespis,* pp. 3 ff.

symbol of those who maintain social order, Dan'el judges the cases of widows and orphans, and this text sets forth the responsibility of a son for his father, so that it should not be assumed that Canaan was without any moral code.

THE INVASION OF CANAAN

The only written reports of the Hebrew invasion of Palestine are found in Joshua and in the first chapter of Judges, both of which are part of the Deuteronomic history, and in Num. 13; 21:1–3, a combination of materials from J, E and P sources.[3] It is clear that Joshua did not write the book bearing his name, for some passages reflect a post-conquest point of view (cf. "to this day" in Josh. 4:9; 5:9; 7:26; 9:27; 15:63) and Joshua's death and burial are reported in Josh. 24:29 f. A number of inconsistencies and repetitions (cf. Josh. 3:17 and 4:10 f.; 4:8, 20 and 4:9; 6:5 and 6:10; 8:3 f. and 8:12; 10:26 and 10:37; 10:36 and 15:14) have led some scholars to extend Pentateuchal sources into Joshua, but so thoroughly has the Deuteronomist integrated and overwritten the work that the analyses are not very satisfactory.[4] As a result, serious difficulties are encountered in any attempt to reconstruct the invasion history.

The general picture presented in the book of Joshua is that of a swift, complete conquest by invaders who were enabled, through Yahweh's miraculous intervention, to overcome the most powerful Canaanite fortress without difficulty, and who engaged in a program of massive annihilation of the Canaanite populace. Despite this picture numerous passages reveal that the conquest was not complete (cf. 13:2–6, 13; 15:63; 16:10; 17:12), and the impact of Canaanite life and thought through the period of the monarchy reveals the continuation of strong Canaanite elements within the culture.

The Deuteronomic interpretation of the invasion in terms of a holy war adds further problems to our efforts to understand what actually happened. Holy war was waged under the aegis of the deity. Battles were won not by might of human arms, but by divine action. The hosts of heaven assisted human soldiers who represented the family of worshipers, and battles were waged according to divine directions.

A GODDESS FIGURINE. *A contemporary bronze cast made from a mold found in a Canaanite shrine from about 1500 B.C. uncovered at Nahariyah, which is located along the Palestinian coast, north of Acco. It is quite probable that priests or smiths at the shrine manufactured figurines for sale to worshipers. The goddess, who may be Astarte, wears a horned headdress, like the goddess Hathor of Egypt, a tall peaked cap, and, perhaps, a string of beads.*

[3] For a possible reference to a pre-Mosaic conquest of Shechem, cf. Gen. 48:22, and see G. E. Wright, *Shechem, The Biography of a Biblical City* (New York: McGraw-Hill Book Company, 1965), p. 20.

[4] In chapters 1–12, only 5:13–14, 9:6–7, and 10:12–13 are attributed to J, and most of the rest is taken to be a combination of D and E.

Read
Josh.
1–12,
23–24

Ritual purification was essential. Conquered peoples and properties came under the ban or *herem* and were "devoted" to the deity.[5]

The Joshua story opens with the Hebrews poised for attack on the eastern bank of the Jordan. Joshua, appointed by divine commission as the successor of Moses, sent spies into Jericho and, upon their return, made ritual preparations for the holy war. Sanctification rites were performed, for the people had to be a holy people (3:5). Miraculously, the Jordan River was crossed (ch. 3) and the purified people entered the land promised by Yahweh. The rite of circumcision was performed, signifying the uniting of all to Yahweh[6] and Passover was observed. Assurance of success came with the appearance of the commander of Yahweh's armies. Through ritual acts, Jericho's walls collapsed and the city was taken and devoted to Yahweh. Violation of the *herem* by Achan interrupted the smooth annexation of the land at Ai, and it was not possible for the invasion to proceed harmoniously until he and all encompassed in the corporate body of his family were exterminated. Subsequently Ai fell. Gibeon, through a ruse, was spared destruction. A coalition of frightened monarchs from Jerusalem, Hebron, Jarmuth, Lachish and Eglon attempted in vain to halt Joshua's progress. Next, the Hebrews moved through the Shephelah, then northward into Galilee, completing the conquest north and south. The conquered territory was divided among the Hebrew tribes. Joshua died after making a farewell speech and performing a covenant rite (which interrupts the sequence) at Shechem.

Archaeological research has provided only limited assistance for the reconstruction of the invasion history. Excavation at Jericho produced no evidence for the period of the Hebrew attack because erosion had washed away all remains,[7] but there is no reason to doubt the tradition that Jericho fell to the Hebrews. The problem of Ai mentioned earlier must remain unsolved. Of the cities of the southern coalition both Lachish (Tell ed-Duweir) and Eglon (possibly Tell el-Hesi) have produced evidence of destruction in the thirteenth century; Hebron (Jebel er-Rumeide) is being excavated; Jarmuth (Khirbet Yarmuk) has not been explored; and Jerusalem, if it fell in the thirteenth century (cf. Josh. 15:63), was rebuilt and reoccupied so that it had to be reconquered when David came to the throne (II Sam. 5:6–9). Other sites, Bethel (Beitan), Tell Beit Mirsim (possibly Debir) and far to the north, Hazor (Tell el-Qedah) reveal thirteenth century destruction, supporting the thesis of a Hebrew invasion.

[5] The term *herem* comes from a root conveying the sense of separation and designates that which is set apart for holy purposes, devoted to the deity, or placed under a ban. Consequently, all living things were killed, all objects burnt, and metal items consecrated to the deity. Exceptions do occur, and at times the property becomes booty (cf. Josh. 6:18–21; 8:26 f.; 10:28, 35, 37, 39 f.). For the *herem* among Moabites, see the Moabite Stone, p. 167.

[6] Circumcision was widely practiced in the Near East and was an Egyptian as well as a Hebrew custom. In the earliest period, it may have been a puberty ritual by which the male youth was admitted to manhood. Among the Hebrews, it signified membership in the covenant community (cf. Gen. 17:11). Cf. "Circumcision in Egypt," *ANET*, p. 326.

[7] K. Kenyon, *Digging Up Jericho* (New York: Frederick A. Praeger, 1957), pp. 256 ff.

Judg. 1:1–2:5 gives a different portrait of the invasion, which parallels certain parts of the account in the book of Joshua,[8] but which omits any reference to the role of Joshua and simply announces his death in the opening verse. Battles for both southern and northern territories are reported, but individual tribes struggle for the territory allocated to them in Joshua, and the impression of united action by an amalgamation of all tribes is missing. It is possible that this account, which may have taken written form as early as the tenth century, preserves a more factual record than the idealized Deuteronomic tradition, and probably was inserted into the Deuteronomic material at a very late date.

Read
Judg.
1–2:5

The separate tradition preserved in Num. 13 and 21:1–3 also omits any reference to Joshua, and records an invasion from the south under the leadership of Moses. In preparation for the attack, Moses sent out spies who penetrated as far north as Hebron and brought back glowing reports of the agricultural productivity of the land. A battle with the people of Arad resulted in the destruction of that site. There is no tradition of settlement or of further invasion from the south.

Read
Numbers 13,
21:1–3

Despite the fact that archaeological and biblical sources are inadequate for any detailed or precise formulation of how the invasion was accomplished, a number of hypotheses have been developed. One analysis finds three separate waves of invasion: one from the south by the Calebites and Kenizzites, both part of Judah; one encompassing Jericho and its environs by the Joseph tribes, led by Joshua; and a third in the Galilee area.[9] Another theory suggests that there were two Hebrew invasions separated by 200 years: a northern invasion under Joshua during the fourteenth century in which the Ephraimite hills were seized (perhaps to be related to the Habiru problem of the El Amarna correspondence) and a southern invasion around 1200 B.C. involving the tribes of Judah, Levi and Simeon, as well as Kenites and Calebites and perhaps the Reubenites, with Reuben finally migrating to the area northeast of the Dead Sea.[10] Still another suggestion is that, prior to the thirteenth century, a number of Hebrews of the Leah tribes had united in an amphictyony centered in Shechem and that the Joseph tribes, under Joshua, invaded in the thirteenth century. The earlier occupation may have been a peaceful one, in contrast to the devastation wrought by Joshua's forces. The Shechem covenant (Josh. 24) marked the union of the Leah group and the newcomers.[11] The recital of further hypotheses could add but little to this discussion. No single view can be embraced with full confidence. Perhaps it will be enough to say that in the light of present evidence, the entrance of the Hebrews into Canaan was marked in some instances by bloodshed and destruction and in others by peaceful settlement among Canaanite occupants; and, although the thirteenth-century date best fits the

[8] Compare Judg. 1:10–15, 20 and Josh. 15:13–19; Judg. 1:21 and Josh. 15:63; Judg. 1:27–28 and Josh. 17:11–13; Judg. 1:29 and Josh. 6:10.

[9] W. O. E. Oesterley and T. H. Robinson, *An Introduction to the Books of the Old Testament,* Living Age Books (New York: Meridian Books, Inc., 1958), pp. 71–74.

[10] T. J. Meek, *Hebrew Origins,* chap. 1.

[11] M. Newman, *op. cit.,* pp. 103–108.

invasion, it is likely that movement into the land by Hebrew people had been going on for at least 200 years.

THE JUDGES

The Hebrews were established in Canaan. Their status in the eyes of the Canaanites, how they organized their communities, what patterns of living they developed, and how they worshiped is not known. Some may have lived in tents (Judg. 4:17; 5:24) or caves (Judg. 6:2) ; others adopted the cultural patterns of settled society.

On the basis of archaeological study, it is surmised that three kinds of Hebrew settlements were developed.[12] Villages were built on abandoned tells or in previously unoccupied areas. Where Canaanite cities had been destroyed, new dwellings were constructed amid the ruins. In some instances, by mutual agreement, Hebrews settled more or less peacefully among the Canaanites (Josh. 9:3–7) . By comparison with Canaanite dwellings, Hebrew houses were poorly built. In new villages little attention was given to town planning and homes were constructed wherever the owner desired. Defensive walls were relatively weak and crudely composed, revealing limited mastery of structural engineering principles. Hebrew pottery, in contrast to well levigated, well fired Canaanite ware, appears quite poorly made. Some Hebrews ventured into Canaanite agricultural and commercial pursuits, others continued to raise flocks and herds (I Sam. 17:15, 34; 25:2) . Despite efforts of a conservative element, fiercely loyal to old tribal ways, Canaanite cultural patterns were gradually assimilated. The unsettled nature of the times is revealed by the numerous destroyed layers from the thirteenth to eleventh centuries found in some excavations.

Literary information about this period is limited to the book of Judges, the third volume of the Deuteronomic history, which presents events within a somewhat stereotyped theological framework. When this theological structure is removed, a collection of early traditions reveals the chaos of the times. Numerous enemies threatened the loosely organized tribal structure; moral problems beset some communities; lack of organization afflicted all.

The book of Judges is usually divided into three parts: Chapters 1:1–2:5 which was previously discussed; Chapters 2:6–16:31, containing traditions of the judges; and Chapters 17–21, a collection of tribal legends. The second section, most important for reconstruction of Hebrew life, reports that in time of crisis, leadership came from "judges" (Hebrew: *shophet*) , men best described as governors[13] or military heroes, rather than as those who preside over law cases. These leaders were men of power and authority, individuals empowered by God to deliver the people—charismatic personalities.[14] Apart from

[12] G. E. Wright, *Biblical Archaeology*, pp. 89 ff.

[13] E. Kraeling, *Bible Atlas*, p. 145.

[14] "Charismatic," a term derived from the Greek *charisma* meaning "gift," refers to the gift of divine power enabling the judges to accomplish what others could not do. References to specific acts of divine possession may have been added by editors.

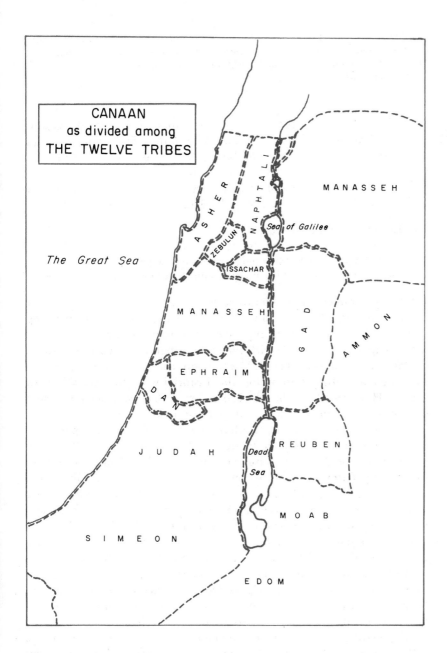

CANAAN
as divided among
THE TWELVE TRIBES

Abimelech's abortive attempt to succeed his father (Judg. 9), no dynastic system appears to have developed, and the role of the judge when not delivering the people is not defined, although perhaps, as local leaders and chiefs, they did preside at the settling of disputes. Long terms of office ascribed to these men may reflect a protracted military struggle, an on-going office of protector-of-the-people conferred for life, or an artificial term of office designed by an editor. Attempts to formulate a chronology of leadership have proven fruitless, for the total of terms of office is 410 years—a period much too long for the interval between the invasion and the establishment of the monarchy. Events probably fall between the twelfth and the eleventh

JUG FROM THE LATE BRONZE AGE PROBABLY IMPORTED TO PALESTINE FROM CYPRUS. *White decorative stripes have been added to the rich chocolate-brown background. Such vessels would be in use among the Canaanites when the Hebrews entered the land.*

centuries.[15] Leaders represent only the tribes of Judah, Benjamin, Ephraim, Naphtali, Manasseh, Gilead, Zebulun and Dan. Enemies included Syrians (possibly), Moabites, Ammonites, Amalakites, Philistines, Canaanites, Midianites and Sidonians.

The Deuteronomic theology-of-history formula is summarized in Judg. 2:11–19, and reiterated in Judg. 3:12–15; 4:1–3; 6:1–2:

    a. Israel sins and is punished.

    b. Israel cries to Yahweh for help.

    c. Yahweh sends a deliverer, a judge, who saves the people.

    d. Once rescued, the people sin again, and the whole process is repeated.

When this framework is removed, stories devoid of the theological concerns of the editors remain. The age of the stories and how long they circulated prior to being recorded cannot be determined, but they do appear to coincide with the archaeological evidence of turmoil during the settlement period,[16] although such evidence cannot be construed as substantiation for the historicity of the narratives in Judges. However, the archaeological evidence does warn against casual dismissal of the stories as being without historical content.

Read Judg. 3:1–11

After a report of Joshua's death (Judg. 2:6–10) [17] which appears to have been written as an introduction to the narrative that follows, the gap between the death of Joshua and the time of the judges is bridged by an explanation that the reason all the enemy were not eliminated was to test Israel, and by an accounting of the adventures of Othniel who was introduced in Joshua 15:16 ff. The enemy is Cushanrishathaim, king of Aram-naharaim, usually translated "king of Mesopotamia." The name of the monarch is, as yet, unknown to scholars, and it has been proposed that it is artificial, meaning "Cushan of double-wickedness,[18] or that it represents a tribe.[19] It is possible that a place in Syria listed by Rameses III as Qusana–ruma represents the area from which the enemy came,[20] although Edom and Aram have also been suggested.[21] The story is so vague that it is often treated as a transitional legend, designed to introduce the traditions of the judges.

Read Judg. 3:13, 15b–29

The story of Ehud the left-handed, recording deliverance from Moabites, represents a cherished memory extolling Ehud's trickery and murder of Eglon, an account to be recited on occasions when Hebrew-

---

[15] A possible chronology is outlined by J. Myers, "Judges," *The Interpreter's Bible,* II, p. 682.

[16] Wright, *Biblical Archaeology,* pp. 89 ff.

[17] Previously reported in Josh. 24:29, and Judg. 1:1.

[18] John Bright, *A History of Israel,* pp. 156 f.

[19] Cf. Hab. 3:7; W. F. Albright, *Archaeology and the Religion of Israel,* p. 205, n. 49.

[20] Albright, *loc. cit.*

[21] Kraeling, *op. cit.,* p. 150.

Moabite hostilities were recalled. The narrative suggests a time when land on the eastern side of the Jordan north of the Arnon River, held by the Benjaminites, was seized by the Moabites. Eglon was murdered at Gilgal which seems to have been located a few miles west of the Jordan, and with Ephraimite assistance, the Moabites were pushed back across the Jordan. The location of the "sculptured stones" and Seirah (v. 26) are unknown. Possibly Jericho is the "city of palms" (cf. Deut. 34:3).

The story of Shamgar appears to have been added after the Deuteronomists completed their work, for not only is the Deuteronomic formula missing, but the record of the battle of Taanach which follows begins with the death of Ehud (4:1). On the other hand, a rest period of eighty years (3:30), double that given elsewhere (3:11, 5:31, 8:28) may indicate that the Deuteronomists simply listed Shamgar without expanding his story. The title "son of Anath" perhaps refers to the hero's village of Beth Anath (location unknown) or to his warrior role, for Anath was a goddess of love and war. Only Shamgar is depicted as an enemy of the Philistines.

Read
Judg.
3:31

The battle of Taanach has been recorded in two accounts: one in prose (ch. 4), the other in poetry (ch. 5). Of the two, the poetic form is undoubtedly older,[22] representing a victory song from a cultic celebration of Yahweh's military triumphs, or, perhaps, a unit of folk literature, such as a minstrel's song recalling victory over the Canaanites. As early Hebrew poetry coming from a time close to the events described (possibly eleventh century), the poem is of great literary importance, for it permits penetration into the period of oral preservation of tradition.

Read
Judg.
4–5

The original poem begins in Judg. 5:4, the first two verses having been added later to provide a setting. The opening verses describe a theophany in terms of storm and earthquake as Yahweh comes from Seir in the mountains of Edom. The reference to Sinai, often treated as a late addition, may reflect the tradition that Sinai was in Edom. Troublous days are related in Verses 6 to 8. (The relationship of Shamgar ben Anath to the judge of the same name is not known.) Verse 8a defies accurate translation and Verses 9 and 10 are asides by the minstrels, expressing respect for the volunteer warriors. Deborah and Barak, Hebrew heroes, are called to lead against the foe, and tribal responses to the challenge are recorded. It is quite clear that whatever amphictyonic links may have existed were not compelling enough to make all groups participate. Ephraim, Machir (Manasseh), Zebulun and Naphtali joined the followers of Deborah and Barak. Reuben, Dan (at this time still on the seacoast) and Asher did not come.

Read
Judg. 5

In the battle fought at Taanach, near Megiddo, a tremendous rainstorm, interpreted by the Hebrews as an act of Yahweh, transformed the brook Kishon into a raging torrent. Canaanite chariots were trapped in the heavy mud and the tide of battle turned to favor

---

[22] Archaic Hebraisms, parallels to Canaanite poetry, interpretive additions by copyists are briefly discussed by Jacob Myers, "Exegesis of Judges," *The Interpreter's Bible*, II, 717 ff.

A DYE VAT, NOW RESTING ON ITS SIDE, FROM TELL BEIT MIRSIM. *The vat was carved out of a single block of limestone. The thread or cloth was dipped into the dye through the center opening and then the excess dye was carefully squeezed out and any run-off was caught in the outer trough and channeled back into the vat. The value placed on dyed cloth is evident from the remarks of Sisera's mother (Judg. 5:30).*

Deborah and Barak. Meroz, an unknown group or location, is cursed for failure to help, and Jael, a Kenite woman, is blessed for the murder of the Canaanite general, Sisera, who sought sanctuary in her tent. As if death at the hand of a woman were not degrading enough, the singers added a taunt song, mocking the fruitless wait of Sisera's mother. Her pitiful attempts to reassure herself of her son's safety close the poem. The closing statement, a wish that all Yahweh's enemies might suffer Sisera's fate (v. 31), may have been added later.

The theological convictions are clear. Yahweh was the god of a specific people. Their wars were his wars and Yahweh fought for his own. Others had their own gods and enjoyed a similar relationship.[23] Social relationships are also revealed. Individual tribes were free to decide whether or not to participate in specific battles, but it was expected that they would rally when the war-cry was sounded. This, together with lack of reference to the tribes of Simeon, Judah and Gad and the listing of the people of Meroz as though they belonged to the tribal federation, raises questions about the patterns of relationship between the tribes. Were they really united by amphictyonic bonds?

23 Cf. references to Hebrews as "people of Yahweh" in vs. 11 with Num. 21:29 where Moabites are called "people of Chemosh." As Yahweh fought for Israel so Chemosh fought for Moab (see ref. to Moabite Stone in Part Five).

How many and what tribes settled the land? Does the amphictyonic pattern truly reflect eleventh-century relationships? For these questions there are no sure anwers.

The prose version of the battle differs in significant details. Only two tribes, Zebulun and Naphtali, participate in the battle, there is no condemnation of tribes not involved, and Sisera's death is described differently. New details appear: the name of Deborah's husband, Lappidoth, the strength of Canaanite forces and the mustering place of the Hebrews at Mount Tabor. Behind the prose account, there may be an ancient oral tradition, but specific details must be treated with caution.

Read Judg. 4

Two traditions lie behind the story of Gideon, one using the name Gideon for the hero, the other using Jerubbaal. Just as the Hebrews had swarmed into the land held by the Canaanites, so desert people— Midianites, Amalakites, and people of the east—came with their camels[24] and possessions, threatening Hebrew holdings. Two etymological legends open the account, one explaining how the name "Yahweh-Shalom" (Yahweh is peace) came to be given to a spot in Ophrah (location unknown) and one explaining how the names Jerubbaal (Ba'al fights) and Gideon (the smiter) could represent the same individual.[25] Gideon, a shrewd warrior, experienced divine possession; unwilling to rely upon this alone he put Yahweh's promise of assistance to a material test. With a small band of warriors chosen for alertness and courage, he routed the enemy in a pre-dawn attack. The war-cry "A sword for Yahweh and for Gideon" signified divine support and sanction for the holy war. During the pursuit of the fleeing enemy, tribesmen participated from Naphtali, Asher, Manasseh and even from the touchy Ephraimites who had to be appeased by flattery. When Gideon paused in his attempt to capture the fleeing Midianite rulers, Zebah and Zalmunnah, and sought food from the people of Succoth, the townsmen were uncertain of Gideon's ability to capture the men and refused him, saying:

Read Judg. 6–8

> Is the palm of Zebah and Zalmunnah in your hand that we should give bread to your army?

This literal translation brings out a meaning that may reflect the custom of removing the hands of the slain to facilitate rapid tallying of the dead.[26] Once the kings were captured, the Succothites experienced the vengeance of Gideon. Gideon's grateful followers sought to make him king, but he chose a monetary reward.

Abimelech, son of Jerubbaal (Gideon), was more ambitious than his father. By murdering his brothers, with the exception of Jotham, and thus eliminating any potential rivalry, he had himself proclaimed king at Shechem. Jotham's evaluation of Abimilech's regal ability is expressed in Jotham's fable. Within three years, Abimelech's rule was

Read Judg. 9

[24] The camel had recently been domesticated and now, used in warfare by the invading Midianites, was tantamount to the introduction of a new weapon against which no adequate defense had been invented.

[25] Judg. 6:25–32 reflects a struggle against Ba'alism not found elsewhere in Judges.

[26] Note the removal of the heads of Midianite leaders as a proof of death (Judg. 7:25).

Read
Judg.
10:1–5

Read
Judg. 10:17–
12:7

Read
Judg.
12:8–13:1

contested by the men of Shechem and Abimelech was killed. No Deuteronomic editing is found in this account, and it may be that it was added after the Deuteronomic work was completed. On the other hand, perhaps the moral in 9:56 f. was enough to satisfy the Deuteronomists.

Tola, an Issacharite judge from Ephraim, and Jair from Gilead are listed without reference to enemies or battles. Once again it has been surmised that these names were derived from special sources and added after the Deuteronomic editing.

Two traditions are merged in the story of Jephthah, the Gileadite, one dealing with struggles against the Ammonites, and the other treating Moabite problems (11:12–28). Jephthah, the son of a harlot and a refugee with a warrior band, is elected leader of Gilead by people and elders in a time of crisis, a custom known in other Near Eastern cultures. Vows are recited before Yahweh at Mizpah in Gilead (location unknown), but only later is divine seizure mentioned (11:29), perhaps a note added by a later editor wishing to demonstrate Jephthah's charismatic qualities. To insure Yahweh's support, Jephthah promised to sacrifice whoever came out of his tent upon his victorious return, knowing full well that it would be someone of his family. Human sacrifice does not receive too much attention in the Bible but is noted at II Kings 3:27, suggesting that the custom prevailed for a long time. Sacrifices such as that promised by Jephthah usually came in moments of extreme desperation and were designed to rouse the deity to furious action.[27]

The ritual of bewailing of virginity that develops out of the death of Jephthah's daughter is not mentioned elsewhere in the Bible, and the account of the sacrificial death of the young woman may be associated with a fertility ritual adopted into Hebrew religious practice (cf. Ezek. 8:14). Possibly it is an adaptation of a custom similar to Anat's weeping for the dead Ba'al, which incorporates an Hebraic aetiological legend. The remaining portion of the Jephthah story reflects intertribal conflict and provides interesting insight into dialectical variations among the groups (12:6). Only in 12:7 does Jephthah finally receive the title "judge."

Three leaders are mentioned between the end of the Jephthah cycle and the introduction of the Samson stories. No information concerning the social or political situation is given, but with Samson the Philistine issue is introduced. Like many other heroes, Samson had a miraculous birth: his mother, hitherto barren, was informed by a divine messenger that she was to conceive,[28] the child was to be a Nazirite, living under a vow of consecration.[29] As a grown man, Samson's particular gift was his superhuman strength, and the secret of his magnificent strength lay in his Nazirite relationships to Yahweh, symbolized by his long hair. When he revealed this secret to his Philistine bride, Delilah, he was betrayed to his enemies. Samson's story is important for what it portrays of Hebrew-Philistine relation-

[27] Cf. II Kings 3:27.

[28] Judg. 13:2–14; cf. I Sam. 1; Matt. 1:20; Luke 1:11–13, 26–31.

[29] The root *nzr* means "to keep apart"; hence, a Nazirite is one set apart by a vow. Cf. Num. 6:1–21.

ships. Despite the tendency to maintain separate national identities, there was intermarriage of the *sadiqa* type, in which the wife remained with her parents and the husband paid periodic visits.[30] Rivalry between Hebrews and Philistines was keen and some skirmishes did occur, but there was no open warfare. It is interesting that no language problem appears to have existed; Hebrews and Philistines were able to communicate without difficulty.

The story of Micah of Mount Ephraim follows. Having robbed his mother, in terror of the curse she uttered against the thief, he confessed his crime and was forgiven. Part of the restored silver was utilized to make an image, or perhaps two images, for Micah's house shrine. What was portrayed is not indicated, but apparently the shrine was dedicated to Yahweh. For a time, one of his sons served as priest, but a Levite from Bethlehem was later employed. The status of the Levite as one of the family of Judah is puzzling, for the term "Levite" may indicate a priestly order or a tribal relationship. Here the term appears to relate to the priestly function. When the tribe of Dan was compelled by the pressure of surrounding peoples (principally the Philistines) to abandon the land held along the seacoast and to migrate northward, the priest and the images were stolen from Micah and taken along with the Danites. The slaughter of the unsuspecting people of Laish and the occupation of their city by the Danites concludes the story. Micah of Ephraim, with his personal shrine, priest and images, perhaps gives some insight into individual family worship practices.

Read Judg. 17–18

The lawlessness of the period (reflected in the intertribal hostility, justice by the imposition of the will of the stronger upon the weaker, and the continuing destruction and occupancy of Canaanite cities) is succinctly summarized by an editor: "In those days there was no king in Israel; every man did what was right in his own eyes."

A second story involving a Levite records the homosexuality of the men of Gibeah and the brutal sexual abuse and murder of the Levite's concubine. The seizure of maidens during the vintage festival, a stratagem by which the Hebrews avoided the specifications of a hastily made vow, may reflect an annual ritual, which is here given an historical setting.

Read Judg. 19–21

The period of the judges was a time of social, political and moral unrest. Law, which can only have significance if means of enforcement are available, appears to have been pretty much a hit-and-miss matter. The bonds uniting the Hebrew tribes are not clearly revealed: some situations evoked a co-operative spirit; others met with indifference or intertribal hostility. The newly won land was not held without difficulty: from without, Moabites and Ammonites pressed in; within the land were Canaanite citadels that had not been conquered; from the seacoast, the Philistines exerted expansive pressures eastward and northward. The socio-political structure of Hebrew society as reflected in the book of Judges simply could not cope with the situation. Something or someone had to unify the tribes, control the enemy, establish law and develop the nation. It was time for a king.

[30] Cf. W. R. Smith, *Kinship and Marriage in Early Arabia*, S. A. Cook (ed.) (London: A. & C. Black, 1903), pp. 93 f.

The Monarchy

THE Deuteronomic history of Israel continues with the stories of Samuel and Saul which form the records of the beginnings of Hebrew kingship. Some sources are designated, such as "The Book of the Acts of Solomon" (I Kings 11:41), "The Chronicles of the Kings of Israel" (I Kings 14:19, 15:31, 16:5) and "The Chronicles of the Kings of Judah" (I Kings 14:29, 15:7, 22:45), but multiple traditions may be discerned in contradictions and doublets. There are three separate descriptions of the origin of the monarchy, two favorably disposed toward kingship and the third hostile (compare I Sam. 7–8, 9–10, 11). Saul's death is reported twice (I Sam. 31, II Sam. 1), and there are other indications of composite authorship.[1] Some scholars attempt to analyze sources according to Pentateuchal patterns, developing a documentary hypothesis. A simpler and sounder solution is recognition of the principle of progressive interpretation by which the earliest source in Samuel was expanded by those who, without altering the words of the earlier tradition, added other points of view and new interpretive material, thus altering the major thrust of the earlier writing. The final stage in this process is the editing by Deuteronomists.

The earliest source in I Samuel begins in Chapter 4 with the account of the continuing struggle between powerful Philistine city-states and Hebrew communities. There seems to be little reason to question the historicity of this information. Indeed, as the early source is read, the impression grows that an objective witness, someone personally familiar with events described, produced the record. Once the Hebrew kingdom came into being, royal records, from which some of the material may have been drawn, would be made. The early source in Samuel is one of the best and earliest examples of accurate historical writing known to us, and it forms the core of what was to become the record of the Hebrew kings.

The first three chapters of Samuel are late additions explaining how the extraordinary role that the prophet Samuel played in Hebrew history could be traced to his miraculous birth, the consecration of his life to Yahweh's service, and to the divine summons and commission.

Read
I Sam.
1–3

---

[1] E.g., the saying "Is Saul among the prophets?" (I Sam. 10:11; 19:24); David's flight to Achish of Gath (I Sam. 21:11–16; 27:1 ff.); the Ziphite treason (I Sam. 23:19–28; 26:1 ff.); David's sparing of Saul's life (I Sam. 24; 26); Yahweh's rejection of Saul (I Sam. 13:7–15; 15).

CHART IX

Years B.C.	Archaeological Period	Palestine	Egypt	Mesopotamia

Last quarter twelfth century to middle of ninth century	Iron Age	Time of Samuel the seer-prophet
		Philistines battle the Hebrews
		  the battle of Aphek
		  the loss of the Ark and the return of the Ark
		  the destruction of Shiloh
		The Ammonites attack and are beaten by Saul
		  Saul is crowned king, the beginning of the kingdom.
		  David enters Saul's court
		  Saul battles Philistines
		  David becomes an outlaw
		  Saul and Jonathan are killed
		Ishba'al becomes king in Israel
		David becomes king in Judah
		David unites Israel and Judah
		David conquers Jerusalem
		David brings the Ark to Jerusalem
		David extends the boundaries of the kingdom
		  Absalom revolts and is killed
		  Adonijah revolts and is killed
		Solomon becomes co-regent until David's death
		  Solomon builds the temple and palace
		  Jeroboam revolts and is exiled
		  The saga of the nation, the Davidic history and law codes are written down
		Solomon dies
		Jeroboam returns from exile
		The kingdom splits in two
			Egypt is too weak from the war with the Sea People and the loss of Palestine to exercise much authority.
			
			Egypt begins to grow in strength
				Assyrian expansion begins under Tiglath Pileser I (ca. 1116–1078); campaigns in Anatolia and Phoenicia
				
				Later, Assyrian power declines Phoenicia begins to expand by sea

The psalm or prayer of Hannah in Chapter 2 is, in reality, a royal psalm composed to honor the king and may be as late as the post-Exilic era (note references to the messianic king in Verse 10) and, apart from Verse 5, has little to do with joy in the birth of a child. Later this song was to serve as a prototype for the Magnificat (Luke 1:46–55). Interesting worship customs are reflected in the opening chapters: the father performs the ritual on behalf of the family (I Sam. 1:4, 21) and the priest appears to be little more than the keeper of the shrine, receiving payment by sharing in the offerings (I Sam. 2:13 ff.). The vocational summons that came to Samuel from Yahweh occurred in the temple during sleeping hours, suggesting a rite of incubation.[2]

Read I Sam. 4–7:2

The earliest account begins with the report of the battle of Aphek, a strategically located Hebrew city at the edge of Philistine territory that had been captured by Joshua (cf. Josh. 12:18). Ebenezer, the locale of

[2] An incubation rite is one in which a worshiper sleeps in a shrine or other holy place to receive a message from the god of the shrine through a dream or vision.

the Hebrew encampment, has not been discovered. The Hebrews, defeated in the first skirmish, sent to Shiloh for the sacred ark[3] of Yahweh Saba'oth ("Yahweh militant" or "Yahweh of hosts"). The presence of this sacred emblem brought a moment of panic to the Philistines and a surge of confidence to the Hebrews.[4] Despite the presence of the ark, the Hebrews were defeated and the ark captured and placed as a trophy of war in the temple of Dagon at Ashdod.[5] A plague attributed to the ark encouraged the Philistines to return it to the Hebrews and it was sent to Beth Shemesh and deposited in a field belonging to Joshua of Beth Shemesh. The Hebrews made no attempt to move it into the city; instead they sacrificed before it in the field. A later writer explained that the Levitical priests attended the ark in the field (6:15).[6] The death of seventy men (possibly from the plague) was explained on the basis of the holiness of the ark, for holiness could benefit or injure. Ultimately, the ark was sent to Kireath-Jearim, and remained in the possession of a certain Abinadab until David removed it to Jerusalem. The Old Testament does not explain why the ark was not returned to Shiloh, but archaeological excavation of Shiloh has revealed that the city was destroyed about this time, and it has been suggested that perhaps the Philistines, continuing their forays, had sacked it.

Suddenly the ark stories cease and a cycle of traditions pertaining to the kingship begins. The amount of reliable data in the ark traditions has been questioned, but they constitute all of the literature that we possess describing a period that has received but meagre assistance from archaeological studies so far.

It has been noted that three different accounts tell of Saul's assumption of the kingship. The one best fitting the cultural context and presumed to be earliest is in Chapter 11:1–11, 15, recording the siege of Jabesh-Gilead in Transjordan by the Ammonites under Nahash. Unable to cope with the powerful enemy and hopeful of preventing destruction of the city, the Jabesh-Gileadites offered to surrender themselves and enter into a covenant of slavery (11:1). Nahash agreed, demanding that, as a symbol of servitude, the right eyes of the inhabitants be gouged out. In the period of grace before the sealing of this humiliating and painful contract the story reached Saul and, in violent anger experienced under divine seizure (thus designating his

Read
I Sam.
11:1–11,
15

---

[3] The term "ark" is an anglicized word from the Latin *arca,* a "chest" or "box," used in the Vulgate to translate the Hebrew word *'aron.* No exact description of the ark is given in the Samuel section, but the D writer stated later that it was made of acacia wood and contained the two tablets of the decalogue (Deut. 10:1–5), and the P writer, who labelled it "ark of testimony," described it later still in detail (Exod. 25:10–21; 37:1–9). That it had cultic significance is clear from Psalm 132:8. For further details, see "Ark of the Covenant," *The Interpreter's Dictionary of the Bible* and the bibliography listed there.

[4] Progressive interpretation can be discerned in I Sam. 4:8 where the words "woe to us" of vs. 7 are expanded by an account of Yahweh's feats in Egypt. The names "Phineas" and "Hophni" in vss. 11 and 17 are details added by a scribe who failed to alter the Hebrew syntax to make it conform to his changes.

[5] Cf. Moabite inscription, p. 167 where sacred items of Yahweh are brought before Chemosh.

[6] Other additions can be found in 6:17 f., an explanation of the symbolism of the great stone, and also in 7:2.

charismatic role), Saul summoned the tribes on the threat of violent retaliation and delivered the beleaguered city. Saul's military prowess led to his coronation at the Yahweh shrine of Gilgal.

Read
I Sam.
9–10:16

A different tradition describes Samuel's selection of Saul. Searching for lost asses, Saul consulted Samuel, who is described as a seer or clairvoyant. Having been informed by Yahweh that Saul was the divine choice for savior of the people, Samuel anointed God's man in a private ceremony.[7] After leaving Samuel, Saul met a band of ecstatic prophets and experienced divine seizure, demonstrating, thereby, charisma. Saul's selection is part of a divine plan. This tradition, generally believed to be later than the one discussed previously, may contain a solid historical core in the report of Saul's seizures. The description of the ecstatic prophets of Gibeath-elohim is probably accurate and contributes to the study of early Hebrew prophecy. Perhaps this story comes from a prophetic circle desirous of emphasizing the role played by one of their profession in the selection and anointing of the king.

Read
I Sam.
8; 10:17–24;
12:1–5

Another account expressing a completely different point of view states that, in their desire to be like other nations, the people demanded a king. Samuel's speech, reflecting an era familiar with the harshness of monarchic despotism under Solomon and his successors, warns of the dangers. Selection was by sacred lot, and Saul, hiding in the baggage, was chosen. Here, the writer's attitude is that acceptance of a human ruler was tantamount to rejecting Yahweh as king (8:7). Those preserving this tradition believed in a theocratic state and looked back to the old independent tribal structure (idealized in their thinking) as the time when reliance upon divine leadership was customary. The way of kingship was the way of Canaan.

Read
I Sam.
7:5–17;
10:25–27;
11:12–14

Several small units of traditions were added. Chapter 7:5–17 is an etymological legend explaining how Ebenezer got its name. Chapters 10:25–27 and 11:12–14 record how resistance to Saul's leadership was quashed when he won the battle of Jabesh-Gilead. An interesting reference to the use of shrines as repositories for records (10:25) may point to the sources of the sanctuary legends utilized by Bible editors.

Read
I Sam.
13–14

Saul's story which began in Chapter 11 is picked up again in Chapter 13. How much has been lost from the early account can be seen by the sudden introduction of Saul's son, Jonathan, as a young warrior (13:2). No traditions of Saul's marriage and home life remain, and even the details of his age and length of reign have been lost (13:1). The Philistine struggle continued, interrupted by a note designed to prepare the reader for the fall of the house of Saul (13:7b–15a; cf. 10:8). Once Saul and Jonathan had only 600 men under their command, but a later editor heightened the odds, listing Philistine forces as 30,000 chariots and 6,000 horsemen (13:5), unlikely numbers for the hill country of Michmash, and dramatized the inequality of arms, suggesting that within the entire Hebrew army only Jonathan and Saul possessed weapons of war (13:22)!

When an earthquake put the Philistine camp in an uproar (14:15),

---

[7] The Hebrew verb "to anoint" (*mashah*) is the root from which the word "messiah," meaning "anointed one" is derived. The king is, therefore, an "anointed one," a messiah.

Saul sought an oracle from the sacred ark[8] but received no answer. To ensure divine support for an attack, Saul vowed that none of his men would eat that day until the Philistines were routed. Unwittingly Jonathan violated the oath (14:27).

In the evening Saul's exhausted and hungry men began to kill sheep and cattle. Killing for food had ritual significance. The blood, which in Hebrew thought was believed to contain the life power, had to be poured out, signifying its return to the deity. Hungry Hebrew soldiers ignored this ritual. A huge stone was rolled into place and animals were slain at this spot, presumably with the blood being poured on or beside the rock (14:33 f.). The text says "Saul built an altar, to Yahweh." Whether or not the stone itself served as the altar, or whether Saul built a separate altar for burnt offerings, cannot be determined. The writer of this account, unlike the writer in 13:8 and following verses, finds nothing objectionable in what might be termed Saul's priestly role.

When Saul again sought an oracle from Yahweh, and again received no response, he surmised that the deity had been offended and vowed that the guilty party would die. Again, the concept of corporate personality is demonstrated: the actions of one individual affected the well-being of the entire group. Sacred lots, named, according to a tradition preserved in the LXX, "Urim" and "Thummin" were consulted. What techniques were used are not known, but Jonathan was identified as the offender (14:42). Saul's vow to kill the guilty party was not fulfilled, for the troops voted against the killing of the popular prince. What is implied in the note that Jonathan was "ransomed" is not clear and perhaps someone died in his place. Deuteronomic editors close this portion of Saul's story with a summary of his activities and a few words about his family.

The next cycle of stories describes the decline of Saul's power and the rise of the Davidic line. The account of Saul's failure to destroy everything and everybody in the Amalakite war, thereby offending Yahweh (ch. 15), makes the transition from the previous material. The story of the divine choice and secret anointing of David (16:1–13) is late.[9]

Read
I Sam.
15–16:13

The earliest tradition of David's coming to Saul's court begins in I Sam. 16:14–23. A mental illness, diagnosed as an evil spirit sent by God, troubled Saul. Music soothed him, and David, a skilled musician, was brought to play the lyre. As a member of the royal household, David won Saul's affection (16:21), became a bosom friend of Jonathan (18:3 ff.), and married Saul's daughter Michal (18:20 ff.). Participating in the military forays against the Philistines, David excelled as a warrior and became, to the women of Israel, a popular hero and the subject of a chant:

Read
I Sam.
16:14–25:44

[8] The presence of the ark at Michmash contradicts the tradition that it remained at Kireath-Jearim until David had it removed to Jerusalem (II Sam. 6:2 ff.). W. R. Arnold, *Ephod and Ark*, Harvard Theological Studies, III (Cambridge: Harvard University Press, 1917), has suggested that there may have been more than one ark. However, in view of the fact that the LXX reads "ephod" rather than "ark" at this point, the question must be left open.

[9] Note in vs. 11 the motif of the hidden hero.

Saul has slain his thousands,
But David his ten thousands.

I Sam. 18:7

Such repute evoked jealous hostility from Saul who recognized in David a potential rival for the kingship. One tradition suggests that David's marriage to Michal was sanctioned by Saul because the king saw a way to get rid of David by demanding a marriage price[10] of 100 Philistine foreskins (18:25 ff.). A later editor explained that David presented 200 foreskins, not the required one hundred. Thwarted in his attempt to eliminate his rival, Saul sought to kill David on the night of the wedding but Michal's clever ruse saved David's life (19:11–17). David, with the band of guerrilla warriors, fled to the wilderness (23:6–15).

A later and completely different record of the development of David's warrior reputation and early relations with Saul, preserved in Chapter 17, tells of the slaying of the Philistine giant, Goliath. But even here, two traditions are merged. In one David is described as leaving Saul's court to do battle (17:1–12, 32–54); in the other David had not yet met Saul but brought provender for his brothers in Saul's army. Troubled by Goliath's taunts, David killed the giant with a

A SLINGSTONE AND SLING. *The stone in the photograph is about the size of a tennis ball. The pouch and thongs are modern replicas patterned after slings shown in ancient inscriptions and drawings. The stone was placed in the pouch, and then, suspended by the two thongs which were held in one hand, was whirled rapidly about the head. When one thong was released the stone left the pouch and hurtled toward its target. For a reference to the accuracy of certain slingers see Judg. 20:16.*

[10] The Hebrew term *mohar*, "marriage price," refers to the sum paid by the groom to the father of the bride. The bride became the property of the groom, bringing with her into marriage her own possessions, and probably in the case of Michal, personal servants. The *mohar* was by way of compensation. Marriage was not a matter of religious observance, but a civil contract. Cf. DeVaux, *Ancient Israel*, pp. 24–38.

ASSYRIAN WARRIORS HURLING STONES. *The soldiers carry extra ammunition in their left hands. The carving is from a wall decoration in the palace of Sennacherib at Nineveh (early seventh century).*

stone from his sling.[11] Only then was he introduced to Saul (17:12–30, 55–58; 18:1–2; 17:31 is a transitional verse). Another popular folk tale credits one of David's soldiers, Elhanan, with killing Goliath (II Sam. 21:19), leading some scholars to speculate that perhaps the hero David usurped a title of "giant killer" rightfully belonging to another.

Traditions blackening Saul and enhancing David's reputation expand the story of David's marriage into Saul's family (18:10–19) and the tradition of Jonathan's affection for David (19:1–10; 20:1–42).[12] The approval and protection of David by the prophets is recounted in 19:18–24. Saul's reputation suffers further in the story of the flight of David's parents to Moab (22:1–5). Even the expanded accounts of David's wilderness adventures and his merciful action in saving Saul's life[13] magnify David's heroic stature (23:15–24:22). The section closes with an editorial report of Samuel's death (25:1).

[11] The ancient sling must not be confused with the modern "slingshot" (see illustration). Sling stones found in Palestinian excavations vary from the size of a golfball to something larger than a tennis ball.

[12] Here two traditions seem to have been combined, the second expanding the details of the first (20:1–17, 24–34; and 20:18–23, 35–42).

[13] This particular account probably circulated orally for it appears in a different setting in I Sam. 26:1–25. Both stories may rest on sound historical memory.

The early tradition continues in Chapter 25 with the story of Nabal ("fool"—see 25:25). David, with his armed guerrillas, guaranteed protection from plunder if material support for himself and his men was promised (25:21). Nabal refused to pay and David prepared to raid his holdings. By taking goods to David's camp, Nabal's wife, Abigail, saved the situation (25:23 ff.). Abigail's presentation speech has been expanded by later writers (verses 28–31 were probably additions). Upon learning of his wife's action Nabal suffered a paralytic stroke and soon died; David married Abigail. Meanwhile, Saul gave Michal, David's first wife, to another man, Palti. David acquired still another wife, Ahinoam (25:43 f.).

Saul continued his pursuit of David. At one point David could have killed the king, but fear of the taboo of killing Yahweh's anointed prevented him (ch. 26). David's speech to Saul on this occasion reflects the belief that Yahweh could only be worshiped within his own territory (26:19), indicating that religious belief of this period was monolatrous rather than monotheistic.[14]

**Read
I Sam.
27; 28:1–2;
29; 30**

Convinced that Saul would not cease in the attempt to destroy him, David joined the Philistines. His adventures are recorded in Chapters 27; 28:1–2; 29; 30. His Philistine allies believed he raided Judaean towns (in reality he was plundering desert tribal groups) and gave him the city of Ziklag (location unknown). Meanwhile David courted the Hebrews, sharing booty with Judaean cities. A tense moment came when the Philistines prepared to attack the Hebrews at Mount Gilboa and included David in the forces. Fortunately, certain Philistine leaders distrusted him and insisted that he be sent back to Ziklag (ch. 29). Meanwhile Ziklag had been raided by the Amalakites and the inhabitants, including David's two wives, had been led away as captives. David pursued and rescued his people (ch. 30).

The end of Saul's leadership in the Hebrew kingdom was at hand and the tragic decline of the first monarch in Israel is movingly portrayed in his desperate search for supernatural guidance (ch. 28:3–25, where Samuel's death is reported once again). Rejected by Yahweh, unable to receive an oracle through regular channels or communication with the deity (28:6), Saul turned to a necromancer—one who consorted with the dead. The prophet Samuel was raised (visible only to the medium) and Israel's defeat and Saul's death were foretold. The story, probably more interpretive than factual, indicates belief in the continued existence of the individual in Sheol, the place of the dead, but the nature of this existence is not clear.

The battle of Mount Gilboa is briefly reported (ch. 31). Saul's sons were killed, and Saul, to prevent capture and torture, committed suicide. His decapitated body and the bodies of his sons were nailed to the wall of the city of Beth Shan as a final token of Philistine derision

---

14 Distinctions in concepts of deity need to be kept in mind. Monotheism means belief in one god and denial of the reality or existence of any other. Monolatry is the belief in and worship of one god without denial of the reality or existence of other gods—a concept prevalent among the Hebrews until after the Exile (cf. Deut. 32:8; Jer. 5:19). Henotheism, which ascribes power to several gods in turn by virtue of one absorbing the other, should not be confused with monolatry. For further discussion, cf. Meek, *op. cit.*, pp. 204 ff.

and defilement. Saul's head was sent throughout the Philistine kingdom as a proof of the monarch's death. The people of Jabesh–Gilead,
remembering perhaps their earlier deliverance by Saul, rescued the
bodies and provided proper burial for the members of the royal
family. Thus Saul's regal career ended as it had begun, with the
people of Jabesh–Gilead.

A slightly different report of Saul's death is put in the mouth of the
Amalakite courier who informs David of the death and presents Saul's
crown and personal amulet as verification. David's lament, which the
editor notes is taken from the Book of the Upright (Jashar) —a work
unfortunately lost to us—is generally conceded to be one of the oldest
fragments of Hebrew literature in the Bible, and there seems to be no
reason to question its authenticity as a Davidic song. The poem
displays strong emotion, particularly concerning Jonathan's death
(II Sam. 1:25b–26).

**Read
II Sam. 1**

The figure of Saul never emerges clearly from the limited information provided by the early tradition. There is no record of his early
years or of his family life, and he is introduced as a grown man of
immense stature, a well-known figure who tilled his family estates.
There can be no question of his leadership ability, for time and again
he united the Hebrew people to fight against superior armies and
weapons, and led them to victory. Long after he had been succeeded
by David there remained a group fearlessly loyal to his memory.
Clearly Saul was given to violent emotional expression. His vehement
response to the news of the siege of Jabesh–Gilead, his violent anger
against the priests of Nob, his moods of deep depression and his
brooding hatred of David, provide some insight into the intensity of
his feelings. His devotion to Yahweh never waned, and when he realized that he had been abandoned by his god, he emerges as a most
tragic figure, desperately seeking some means to restore relationships.

The powers inherent in the kingship did not, apparently, encourage
him to exploit the people. His capital city of Gibeah, a few miles north
of Jerusalem, has been excavated (assuming Tell el-Ful is Gibeah),[15]
and a fortress often identified as Saul's palace appears to have been
little more than a large two-story dwelling constructed on the foundations and outline of an earlier Philistine building. The structure was
about 115 by 170 feet, and the largest room about 14 by 23 feet.
Pottery found in the ruins was similar to that in common use in Saul's
day. The usual household equipment—spinning whorls for making
yarn, grinding querns to produce flour, storage jars for oil, wine and
grain, a game board, some sling-stones, and two bronze arrowheads—
would seem to indicate, in the absence of other evidence, that Saul's
monarchical headquarters were simple indeed.

15 Cf. Paul W. Lapp, "Tell el-Ful," *BA*, XXVIII (1965), 2–10.

11
David

**Read
II Sam.
2–4**

THE way was open for David to assume the throne: Jonathan, the natural successor, was dead; David had won recognition as a popular hero and a military expert, and had gained the loyalty of the southern cities of the Hebrew nation by sharing booty with them. His marriage to Michal, Saul's daughter, might also have been significant for it related David to the royal household.[1]

David's first move was to Hebron where he was anointed king over "the house of Judah" (II Sam. 2:2 f.). The groups forming "the house" are not indicated, but Martin Noth has suggested that a six-tribe confederation consisting of Judah, Caleb, Othniel, Cain, Jerahmeel and Simeon might have been involved.[2] Apparently the Philistines were unconcerned, for they counted David as an ally. David now began to woo the northern groups. A letter to Jabesh–Gilead commended the people for providing proper burial for Saul and Jonathan, offered David's support and reminded them that David was now king (II Sam. 2:5–7).

But the northern tribes had taken other action. Abner, Saul's commander-in-chief, had Saul's fourth son, Ishbaal, appointed king in Israel.[3] No mention of Ishbaal has been made prior to this time, and nothing is known of him apart from a note appended by a Deuteronomic redactor to the effect that he was forty years old at this time (II Sam. 2:10–11).

A curious episode interrupts the narrative to explain the hostility between Abner, commander of the army of Ishbaal, and Joab, commander of David's forces. Twelve men from each of the armies

[1] Cf. J. Morgenstern, "David and Jonathan," *Journal of Biblical Literature,* LXXVIII (1959), 322–324.

[2] M. Noth, *The History of Israel,* p. 182.

[3] The name *"Ish-bosheth,"* "man of shame," is the work of a redactor who contributed to the downgrading of Saul by reacting against the Canaanite name Ishbaal, "man of Ba'al," or perhaps, as Dr. Albright has suggested, "Ba'al exists" (cf. *Archaeology and the Religion of Israel,* pp. 113, 207 n. 62). The older form of the name is preserved in I Chron. 8:33. It should not be assumed that in naming a child after the god Ba'al, Saul had compromised his faith in Yahweh. There is no evidence to suggest that Saul was other than a devout Yahweh worshipper, and his son's name may simply reflect the use of a popular name of the period; it seems to indicate that there was, at this period, no open conflict between Ba'alism and Yahwism.

engaged in a contest in which combatants paired off, each placed one hand upon the head of the adversary and with the free hand sought to thrust him through with a sword. The significance of this strange match is not known, although a relief from Tel Halaf depicts men in this very position.[4] Abner's men were defeated and Abner and those who remained fled. In the pursuit, Asahel, a brother of Joab, followed Abner and was killed by the more experienced warrior. The battle marked the beginning of a protracted struggle between Ishbaal and David in which "David grew stronger and stronger, while the house of Saul became weaker and weaker" (II Sam. 3:1). Later, a literal-minded editor inserted an isolated fragment about David's family, portraying David's growth in strength in terms of his six wives and six sons (II Sam. 3:2–3).

Now problems developed within Ishbaal's household. Abner took one of Saul's concubines for himself and inasmuch as the taking of a king's widow could be construed as seeking to take the place of the dead king, Ishbaal questioned Abner's intentions. Angered by the accusation (which may have been justified), Abner offered to bring Israel under David's control if David would enter into a covenant with him. What Abner was to gain is not stated, unless it would be a guarantee of safety and security and position with David. David accepted but demanded the return of his wife Michal, Saul's daughter.[5] Once this action, a token of good intention, had been taken, Abner began to undermine Ishbaal's position among the northern tribesmen. Subsequently twenty northern leaders and Abner participated in a feast as David's guests to plan strategy for bringing Israel under Davidic rule.[6]

But David had failed to consider Joab. As redeemer-of-blood[7] for the death of his brother, he killed Abner, placing David in the embarrassing position of having to retain his friendship with Joab and hold the loyalty of the northern tribesmen with whom he had broken bread. The compromise was effected by David's denial of any part in Abner's death, by his public lamentation in which he composed a dirge for Abner, and by the participation of Joab in the mourning rites. The dirge (II Sam. 3:31–34), like that for Saul and Jonathan, may be a Davidic composition.

The report of Abner's death in the northern kingdom was accepted as a sign of impending doom. Ishbaal was murdered by two military leaders who removed his head and brought it to David, seeking his

---

[4] *Journal of the Palestine Oriental Society,* XXI (1948). It has been suggested that the contest was a form of "belt-wrestling" in which combatants fought to the death. Cf. G. Cornfeld, *Adam to Daniel* (New York: The Macmillan Company, 1961), p. 273.

[5] Noth, *op. cit.,* pp. 184 f., believes that the marriage of David to Michal did not take place until this time and that the account of the marriage in Saul's lifetime is a late tradition.

[6] The significance of a meal shared was that of peaceful relationships, for a man did not break bread with an enemy. Participation in a meal signified that a bond of peace existed between the participants so that Abner departed "in peace." Cf. in English, "companion" (*com-panos*—with bread).

[7] See p. 88, n. 18.

favor (II Sam. 4:4–11). Although he had gained politically through this event, David could not afford to express approval. The two were promptly executed (II Sam. 4:12).[8]

Read
II Sam. 5
All opposition was now removed and David entered into a covenant with the northern tribes and was anointed king at Hebron (II Sam. 5:1–3). His role as "shepherd" of Yahweh's people was carefully delineated, and it is possible that the covenant took the form of a written contract agreed to by both parties, sworn to before Yahweh, and deposited in the Hebron sanctuary. Through this event the tribes of the north and of the south, first brought together through a national emergency under Saul, accepted the concept of nationhood. Undoubtedly the nation was weak and, without continuing crises, could easily have disintegrated through national suspicions and jealousies. Apparently David recognized the uneasy nature of the bond and took steps to consolidate the kingdom. The neutral Jebusite city of Jerusalem, which had remained free of Hebraic control up to that time, was taken, and this strong fortified hill-city strategically located near the border between the north and south, became the capital.

At this point a number of isolated fragments have been inserted into the narrative. At II Sam. 5:4–5 a Deuteronomic editor added a note about David's age and the time spent in Hebron. Another insertion at 5:8b relates how a proverb came into being. In 5:11–12 a brief statement about David's palace appears, and verses 13–14 give details about his expanding harem as David cemented good relationships with the Jebusites by marrying some of the townswomen.

Philistine reaction to David's assumption of the combined thrones of Israel and Judah was not delayed, for verse 17 records that the Philistines attacked upon hearing the report of the anointing at Hebron. David met and defeated his former allies in the valley of Rephaim, west of Jerusalem. Other battles with the Philistines are reported (cf. 18:1), but it would seem that from this time on they posed no real threat to the Davidic empire.

Read
II Sam.
6–8
Having achieved political union and having made Jerusalem the capital, David now sought to make this city the center for the national cult of Yahweh. The sacred ark was brought into the city with great rejoicing (ch. 6). The reference in 6:19 to raisin cakes, usually associated with the worship of foreign deities or with the fertility cult,[9] may indicate an adoption of features of Canaanite religious practice by the Yahweh cult. Ritual sacrifices associated with the moving of the ark were performed by David. No special shrine or temple was constructed for the ark, making it necessary for a writer to explain why David failed to build a temple for Yahweh although he constructed a palace for himself (ch. 7).

Two isolated fragments of Davidic history comprise Chapter 8. The first summarizes David's military campaigns (8:2–14): he subdues Moabites, Edomites and Ammonites, making these areas subject states controlled by garrisons. Despite the absence of references to the

---

[8] At 4:4 the account is interrupted by a legend associated with Meribaal (changed to Mephibosheth by a later editor).

[9] Cf. Hos. 3:1.

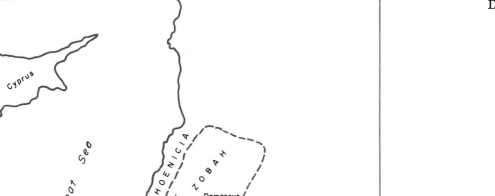

conquest of other Canaanite city-states such as Jerusalem, it can be safely assumed that they were brought under control, for it is quite clear that David intended to develop a kingdom free of conflicting elements. The second historical note lists the officials of David's court (8:15–18). Joab was commander-in-chief of the army, but a certain Benaiah is said to have been in charge of the mercenaries made up of Cretans (Cherethites) and Philistines (Pelethites). In addition to a court recorder and a secretary, two priests are named, and David's sons are also said to be priests. A similar list of officials is given in II Sam. 20:23–26 with the role of chief of forced labor added, implying that David initiated the *corvée*. Such lists demonstrate that the old "chief-tain-type" kingship represented by Saul belonged to the past; kingship now involved administration of a large unified central state and military control of subject areas. Gone forever was the time when it could be said "everyone did what was right in his own sight."

Read
II Sam.
21:1–14; 9

Quite suddenly, the early narrative introduces Saul's grandson Meribaal (ch. 9), and here it is best to follow the suggestion made by a number of scholars and insert II Sam. 21:1–14 into the text before the discussion of Chapter 9. Not only do these verses provide a setting for the discussion in Chapter 9, but in their present position they stand as an isolated fragment.[10]

A famine in David's kingdom was attributed to the death of the Gibeonites at the hand of Saul (II Sam. 21:1).[11] There is no record of Saul's action and precisely what crime is referred to is not clear. Perhaps it was thought that the killing of the Gibeonites was a violation of the covenant of peace recorded in Joshua (ch. 9), for the writer takes pains to point out that the Gibeonites were not Hebrews. It is also pointed out that Saul acted out of zeal for the kingdom. In view of these statements, it would appear that the writer is attempting to demonstrate that David's subsequent actions were more a matter of political expediency than anything else, for David agreed to atone for the death of the Gibeonites by giving seven of Saul's sons, any one of whom might have been considered a contender for the throne, to the Gibeonites for hanging. On the other hand, the Semitic belief that physical disasters, such as famine, could be accounted for by acts which offended the deity might have been involved. In this instance the violation of a covenant of peace could be interpreted as the cause of a famine that would continue until the breach was rectified.

The mountain of Yahweh where the men were hanged was probably the high place of Gibeon, a Canaanite shrine used for Yahweh worship. Saul's concubine, Rizpah, protected the bodies from attacks by carrion birds. The bones of Saul and Jonathan were eventually exhumed and, together with the remains of the seven sons, were interred in the tomb of the family of Kish.

One descendant of Saul, Meribaal, the son of Jonathan, was spared, perhaps because of the friendship which had existed between David and Jonathan, but perhaps also because as a cripple or deformed person he could not be considered a rival for the throne. It is possible that David hoped to win support from those who still believed in the Saulite kingship and resented the assumption of the throne by David. Thus, Meribaal entered David's household.

Read
II Sam.
10–12

Chapter 10 of II Samuel makes it clear that David did not hold his newly conquered territories without effort. The death of a king who had signed a treaty with David brought to the throne a successor who resented Hebrew control and who planned rebellion. Thanks to the military skill of Joab, the Hebrews defeated the rebels. Suddenly the story of the rebellion is interrupted, and the reader is informed of what was taking place at the court at this same time. The account of the armies in the field is taken up again in chapter 12:26–31.

[10] Bentzen, *op. cit.*, II, 94; Pfeiffer, *op. cit.*, p. 353.

[11] The account of the plague in chap. 24 would seem to belong in this same context, and the plague story may come from the same early tradition to which chap. 9 belongs.

From what may be personal records or personal knowledge of the court life of David, the writer of the early materials provides a glimpse into family relationships in the royal household. Whatever prowess David may have shown as a military leader was utterly lacking in his leadership within his family. His own ruthlessness, in taking whatever he desired, is partially revealed in the story of the acquisition of the kingship, and is fully portrayed in the story of Bathsheba. What David was in himself was reflected in the character of his family.

The Bathsheba story is told simply, without theological interpretation. As king, David had Bathsheba brought into his harem while her husband Uriah, a Hittite mercenary, was fighting in David's army. When she became pregnant David had Uriah returned home in the hope that he would spend at least one night with Bathsheba so that he could be said to be father of the child. Uriah did not go to his home. As a soldier he observed the taboo that required sexual abstinence.[12] David managed to get him drunk in the hope that Uriah might stagger home, but the soldier did not break the taboo. It was clear that Uriah must die, and Uriah carried his own death warrant back to Joab, who could be trusted to do whatever David requested. Uriah was sent to one of the more dangerous battle areas and, at a crucial moment, Joab withdrew support so that Bathsheba's husband and those with him perished.

At this point theological judgment is introduced with the appearance of the prophet Nathan (II Sam. 11:27b–12:1). The king's role as guardian of the national safety and of individual freedom is reflected in the parable Nathan related to David. A powerful, rich man fulfilled the nomadic rule of hospitality by offering the very best of provender to a guest, not by drawing from his own flocks but by stealing a lamb from a poor and weaker neighbor. In righteous anger David demanded the name of the rich man, declaring that such an act was worthy of the death penalty (12:5). Nathan's response was "You are the man" (vss. 9b to 12 are a later addition). While David was not to suffer the penalty he had pronounced, the child of the unlawful relationship with Bathsheba was to die. David's reaction to the pronouncement of doom for his child reflects his pragmatic approach to religion. While the child lived David fasted hoping that Yahweh would be persuaded to alter the child's fortune. When the child died, rather than performing the customary mourning rites David returned to the normal pattern of life (12:20–23). A footnote to the story announces the birth of Solomon and the pet name given by Nathan to the new prince—Jedidiah or "Beloved of Yahweh" (12:24 f.).

Subsequent chapters recount the decaying family relationships within David's household. Amnon, one of David's sons, raped his half-sister Tamar and was killed by Tamar's brother, Absalom. To escape punishment Absalom fled and David, while mourning for Amnon,

Read II Sam. 13–20

[12] The reasoning behind this taboo is not clear. It is possible that it was believed that association with women before battle might make a man "effeminate in battle" (cf. G. B. Caird, *The Interpreter's Bible*, II, 997). It is more probable that, because the war was a "holy war" (note the reference to the ark in vs. 11), the taboos were rules of ritual purity to enable a man to be sanctified for battle. For other taboos see Deut. 23:9–14.

longed to see Absalom (13:37–39). Joab knew David's mind and arranged for a "wise woman," possibly a representative of the wisdom school, to present a problem to the king. Once again the accessibility of David to the common people demonstrates the role of the king as defender of human rights. Like Nathan, the woman posed a problem involving Semitic justice, and once again David in his response judged himself. David recognized Joab's role in this plot and sent Joab to bring Absalom back from exile. Two years later Absalom was fully readmitted to the royal household (ch. 14).

Absalom began to undermine David by suggesting that David was neglecting his duty of safeguarding the rights of his subjects. Within four years he had won enough people to his way of thinking, including David's counselor, Ahithophel, that he dared to be crowned king at the shrine in Hebron (15:1–12). David fled, leaving ten concubines to care for the palace, Zadok and Abiathar to care for the ark, and Hushai to act as spy.

The problems of that hectic period were further complicated by Meribaal, son of Jonathan, who thought that the state of disorder provided opportunity for seizure of the throne (16:1–14). The attitude of Shimei makes it clear that then was a faction still loyal to Saul that Meribaal might count upon for support. Meribaal's plans never developed; Absalom took over the palace and erected his personal tent upon the roof, proclaiming to all that he had usurped his father's throne and was master of the royal concubines. The taking of the royal concubines constituted a proclamation of kingship, and there is some evidence in the Bible that a new king inherited his predecessor's harem.[13] Then Absalom made the error that cost him the kingdom. Relying upon the advice of David's spy, Hushai, and rejecting the counsel of Ahithophel, he failed to press his advantage by attacking David when the royal forces were still unorganized (ch. 17). Meanwhile David mustered his army and Absalom was defeated and killed in the battle of the forest of Ephraim (ch. 18). David's mourning for Absalom was so intense that Joab warned the king that he was making a bad impression upon those who had fought to retain his kingdom and that military victory was a time for rejoicing (19:1–15). In a spirit of magnanimity David forgave those who had opposed him, including Meribaal, and rewarded the faithful with the exception of Joab who had rebuked him. Joab was replaced as commander by Amasa. The spirit of distrust between north and south was not diminished and the sense of being separate peoples was still prevalent (cf. 19:41–43).

The interpretation of Sheba's rebellion (ch. 20) presents something of a problem. Despite David's generosity in forgiving his enemies, a number of persons from the southern kingdom of Judah were not sure of David's attitude toward them because they had supported Absalom. David urged the Judaeans to welcome him as king (19:11 ff.). Whether it was caused by jealousy over this action, or perhaps by the

13 Cf. II Sam. 12:8 where Nathan says David inherited Saul's concubines. See also the situations involved in II Sam. 3:7 f. and I Kings 2:13–22. On the other hand, there are protests made against incest: cf. Gen. 35:22 and 49:3–4; Lev. 18:8; Deut. 27:20. When David finally recovered his harem he set the women apart, probably because they had been violated by Absalom, cf. II Sam. 20:3 ff.

belief of a rebellious group of Israelites that there was still a chance to break away from Davidic rule, is not clear, but Sheba led the northern tribes in rebellion. His war cry was a call for independence: "We have no portion in David, and we have no inheritance in the son of Jesse, every man to his tents, O Israel." David commissioned his new commander, Amasa, to rally Judaean troops, but he was so slow in executing this responsibility that David turned again to Joab and his mercenaries. Joab murdered Amasa and pursued Sheba to the far northern city of Abel. Here Sheba died at the hand of his own people who decided that it was better that one man should die than the whole town suffer, and for a time the rebellious mood of Israel was quiet.

Now the Philistines attacked, on the assumption that the trouble within the Hebrew kingdom had weakened David's power. David participated in one battle but he had neither the strength nor the stamina for warfare. His men sent him back to Jerusalem and carried on without him (21:15–22). A further summary of the Philistine battles and a list of warriors who participated is given in 23:8–39.

Read II Sam. 21

At this point, two intrusions interrupt the narrative. The first, Chapter 22, is a psalm identical to Ps. 18. According to the superscription (vs. 1), David sang this song on being saved from Saul. However, the psalm appears to be a national hymn of thanksgiving from dire distress used in some cultic celebration. The poem reflects the time when the temple had been erected (vs. 7) and when the Davidic line had been established (vs. 50–51), so it comes from a later period than David's time. The second intrusion consists of the first seventeen verses of Chapter 23 in which an oracle pertaining to the kingship is attributed to David, giving David the status of an inspired person. This passage is from a later time.

Read II Sam. 22–23

The Davidic story continues in I Kings. The opening verses demonstrate that the Hebrew monarchy was like that in surrounding cultures wherein the life and health of the nation was reflected in the physical well-being of the ruler. Not only was it important that the king be a person of strength and beauty,[14] but he had to be a man of sexual vigor and potency, for the reproductive power of the monarch symbolized the blessings of fertility for the land and flocks. Because David was impotent, Abishag, the young Shunamite maiden was brought to court in the hope that she might stimulate him sexually.[15] When she was unable to arouse him, David's kingdom was threatened.

Read I Kings 1–2:12

Adonijah, David's son, was aware of the monarch's impotency and chose this moment to seek the throne, enlisting the help of Joab and Abiathar, the priest (1:8). An enthronement feast was held at the shrine at En-rogal near Jerusalem, to which David's sons (except Solomon) and those who could be counted upon for support were invited. The omission of Solomon from the invited guests would

---

[14] Cf. I Sam. 9:2; 10:23; 16:12; 17:42; II Sam. 14:25; I Kings 1:6.

[15] It has been argued that sexual concepts should not be read into this story (cf. Cyrus Gordon, *Introduction to Old Testament Times,* p. 167). The very fact that the writer of this account found it necessary to note that David did not have sexual relationships with Abishag (cf. vs. 4) signifies that this information was important for the understanding of the story itself and for what followed. Cf. N. Snaith in *The Interpreter's Bible,* III, 19 f.

indicate that Adonijah was aware of the political aspirations of Bathsheba and her son. Nathan, the prophet, reported the coup to Bathsheba, and together they plotted the means whereby Solomon could become king. They convinced the aged king that he had promised the crown to Solomon (a promise not noted before) and, revealing Adonijah's plans, persuaded David to have Solomon crowned coregent. Riding upon the royal she-mule and accompanied by the priest Zadok and the prophet Nathan, Solomon went to Gihon, close to the city of Jerusalem, and was anointed king. In triumph he returned to Jerusalem, and Adonijah, hearing the news, knew his cause was lost. In fear of reprisal, Adonijah sought sanctuary in the shrine at En-rogal, clinging to the horns of the altar.[16] Solomon spared Adonijah's life, asking only a promise of loyalty (1:53). Without further difficulty, Solomon joined his father upon the throne of the Hebrew kingdom.

The last days of David are recorded in the first twelve verses of I Kings, Chapter 2. The failing monarch required promises from Solomon that both Joab and Shimei would be put to death, and that the family of Barzillai, the Gileadite, would be rewarded because of the aid it had given to David when Absalom had revolted. Much has been written on these verses by scholars, with some arguing that the passages are to be treated as a late addition,[17] with others justifying David's wish on the basis of the Hebraic belief in the importance of the practice of blood revenge,[18] and with still others using the passages to reveal the vindictiveness of the ailing king who, having failed to settle his own accounts, passed the responsibility on to his son.[19] The accounts seem to be designed to remove the stigma attached to Solomon for the way in which he brought about consolidation of the empire by the removal of potential rivals. The stories protect Solomon's reputation and explain the deaths of Shimei and Joab as the fulfillment of a deathbed wish of David.

Thus the record of David's reign closes. The identity of the author of the early account has been debated many times. It is recorded that David had a scribe and a recorder in his court (II Sam. 8:16 f., 20:23 f.); perhaps it can be assumed that it would be the function of these officers to record the royal transactions and to prepare a daily chronicle or what might be called a "history" of royal events. Such documents might have provided the basic materials for the historian of the Davidic account. Whether or not personal memoirs were also employed cannot be known. Many scholars are convinced that the writer was someone close to the court, and both Abiathar, David's priest, and Ahimaaz, Solomon's son-in-law, have been suggested. Whoever the writer was, the tragic decline of David's career, beginning with his association with Bathsheba, was sketched with artistic skill.

[16] Hebrew altars had four horns (probably symbolic ox horns), one mounted at each corner of the altar. By clinging to these horns an individual could claim sanctuary, because the spilling of blood in an act of vengeance would violate the holy place.

[17] Cf. R. H. Pfeiffer, *Introduction to the Old Testament*, p. 368.

[18] Cf. J. A. Montgomery and H. S. Gehman, *The Book of Kings*, International Critical Commentary (New York: Charles Scribners, 1951), pp. 88 ff.

[19] Cf. N. K. Gottwald, *A Light to the Nations*, p. 200.

David is never permitted to become, as idealized personalities often do, someone removed, unreal, and too good to be true. He is introduced as a young court musician whose winsome personality soon made him a favorite and won for him the friendship of Jonathan. As they participated in military forays, David's skill as a warrior brought him fame and popularity. At what point David realized that he might become king is not revealed by the biographer. As a refugee among the Philistines and as a chief of an outlaw band, he had the opportunity to test his ability to lead and administer. When Saul and Jonathan were both dead, David was a natural contender for the throne, and it is at this point that the biographer reveals how well David had learned to manipulate men and situations to his own advantage. Even a tragedy, such as the death of Abner, could be converted into a step toward power.

Another aspect of David's personality—his utter ruthlessness in achieving his ends—is disclosed in the story of the murder of Uriah. Some hint of this side of David's character was foreshadowed in his callous attitude toward Nabal, and if it is true that the aged king asked Solomon to kill Joab and Shimei, a vindictive trait is exposed. The closing years of his reign could not have been particularly happy ones for David. Family tragedies, such as the rape of Tamar, the murder of Amnon, and the rebellion of Absalom, must have burdened the king. Finally, he appears as a confused old man, physically enfeebled, impotent and no longer an adequate symbol of the vigor of the nation. To save his crown and perhaps himself from Adonijah, he was compelled to share his throne with his son Solomon. Whereas Saul emerged as a tragic figure, the last pictures of David are of a pathetic hero.

12
Solomon

Read
I Kings
2:13–11:43

UNDER Solomon, national and religious self-consciousness, encouraged by the king and the temple priesthood, resulted in the production of a great body of literature, of which the Davidic record was but a part. Unfortunately, no biographical data like that pertaining to David have come to us from the reign of Solomon, nor from those rulers that succeeded him. Instead, a history developed by the Deuteronomists is all that remains. The compilers acknowledge some of their sources, including "The Book of the Acts of Solomon" (I Kings 11:41), "The Book of the Chronicles of the Kings of Israel" (I Kings 14:19), and "The Book of the Chronicles of the Kings of Judah" (I Kings 14:29), but it is difficult to determine what material may have come from these sources, and it is impossible to know what principles guided the Deuteronomists in their selection of data. Within the stories pertaining to Solomon's reign numerous Deuteronomic additions can be recognized[1] and, when these are removed, a sketchy literary picture of the monarch's career remains, an account which appears to be relatively correct. Archaeological evidence has helped to fill in other details.

Following David's death Solomon acted quickly to strengthen his position. Those who might have presented a challenge to his rule (I Kings 2:13–46) were eliminated. Adonijah requested Abishag, the young woman who had been David's last concubine, as a wife. It has been noted previously that such a request was tantamount to seeking to take the place of the dead monarch, as Solomon's response clearly indicates:

> Ask for him the kingdom also; for he is my elder brother and on his side are Abiathar the priest and Joab the son of Zeruiah.
>
> I Kings 2:22

This request brought about Adonijah's murder. Abiathar was spared and sent to Anathoth, perhaps because he was a priest.[2] When Joab learned of Solomon's pogrom he fled to a shrine, but even as he clung to the horns of the altar, Solomon's executioner, Benaiah, murdered

---

[1] Cf. I Kings 3:3, 6b–7a, 14; 5:3–5; 6:11–13; 8:9, 14–61; 9:1–9; 11:1b–2, 3b, 4b–6, 11–13, 41–43.

[2] Vs. 27 is a midrash or commentary explaining the significance of Solomon's action.

him. Shimei, whose loyalty to the family of Saul had never wavered, was finally killed when he violated parole. For his services Benaiah was made commander-in-chief of the army. The editors summarize the discussion of the strategic murders with the statement "So the kingdom was established in the hand of Solomon."

Solomon's biographer appears to have been impressed with certain facets of Solomon's career—his marriages, his wisdom, his wealth, his buildings, and his international business dealings. Of Solomon's 700 wives and 300 concubines (I Kings 11:3a), only Pharaoh's daughter is singled out for specific mention. This marriage demonstrates the wealth and power of the Hebrew monarchy, for Pharaoh's daughters did not ordinarily marry outside of their own family, and perhaps indicates the weakness of the Egyptian kingdom at this time.[3] This strategic marriage provided a basis for trade relationships (10:29) and gained for Solomon's empire the city of Gezer as a wedding payment (9:16). How important the marriage was in Solomon's eyes is perhaps demonstrated by the fact that of all his wives only Pharaoh's daughter appears to have had a special apartment built for her within the royal palace (7:8; 9:24).

Solomon's wisdom, extolled by the editor of Kings, became the symbol of all wisdom for later Hebrew history. Not only were portions of the book of Proverbs ascribed to him, but Ecclesiastes, the Song of Songs and the Wisdom of Solomon were composed in his name. None of these writings are believed to be the work of the Hebrew monarch. According to I Kings 4:29–34 Solomon is supposed to have composed proverbs and songs, but the specific themes which are said to be the subject of these compositions are scarcely mentioned in the writings bearing Solomon's name.

Solomon may have composed wise sayings, but it is more likely that his reputation for wisdom rests upon a different and somewhat more significant base.[4] Within the courts of the ancient Near East, the wise man held an office of special honor. Jeremiah put wise men of Babylon in the same category as princes (Jer. 50:35). The high standing of the wise man is reflected in Egyptian literature, for Amen-em-opet was controller of the land,[5] and the "councils of Duauf," which probably come from the fourteenth century, link wisdom with the scribe along with the comment that every court office lay open to such a person. It is possible that Solomon's reputation for wisdom stems from the establishment of a wisdom school *par excellence* within the royal court, rather than from his own personal contribution to wisdom literature. In a kingdom so young and in a court so recently organized, the establishment of such a school with an international reputation was

3 Cf. I Kings 11:19 f. where the pharaoh's sister-in-law is given to Hadad, a prince of Edom. Cf. John Wilson, *The Culture of Ancient Egypt* (Chicago: University of Chicago Press, 1961), pp. 253 f., where it is noted that Rameses II, who had a huge family, married one son to the daughter of a Syrian sea captain.

4 That monarchs did compose wisdom sayings can be demonstrated in "The Instructions for King Meri-ka-re" which a twenty-second century B.C. Pharaoh prepared for his son and in the "Instructions of King Amen-em-het" prepared for Amen-em-het's son in the twentieth century B.C.; *ANET*, pp. 414 ff.

5 Cf. "The Instruction of Amen-em-opet," *ANET*, pp. 421 f.

worthy of record. How much support subsequent monarchs gave to the wisdom school cannot be ascertained, but the caption above Chapter 25 of Proverbs indicating that the material was copied by "Hezekiah's men" may have reference to royal patronage. If this interpretation of the scanty references is correct, Solomon's fame as a wise man is, perhaps, justified.

Perhaps the king's most important role for his biographers was as the builder of the temple of Yahweh. Construction details are set forth in I Kings 6, and the manufacture of the accoutrements is recorded in I Kings 7:9–50. From his sources the editor drew information concerning the trade agreements between Solomon and Hiram, King of Tyre. Twenty Galilean cities, plus Hebrew grain and oil, were exchanged for timber and gold (5:1, 6–12; 9:10–14). Labor was recruited through the *corvée* or forced labor policy.

By modern standards the temple was small—ninety by thirty feet and forty-five feet in height.[6] The building was modeled after Phoenician-Canaanite temples (see the sketch of the Tainat temple) and was divided into three sections. The porch or *ulam* served as an entrance hall. Two bronze, free-standing pillars named Jachin and Boaz stood "within" this area.[7] Through "folding doors" entrance was gained to

KING AHIRAM *of* BYBLOS *is pictured seated in his throne chair with its guardian cherubim. The carving is from a side panel of the royal sarcophagus.*

---

6 The unit of measurement used in the Bible is the cubit, which is the distance between the elbow and fingertip. While cubit measurements differed, 18 inches is assumed to be equal to a cubit for convenience. Cf. R. B. Y. Scott in *BA*, XXII (1959), 22 ff.

7 The significance of the names is not known. For a discussion of various theories, cf. John Gray, *I & II Kings*, The Old Testament Library (Philadelphia: The Westminster Press, 1963), pp. 174 ff.

the central chamber or *hekal,* a room about sixty feet long decorated with pomegranates, lilies and palms. Here were numerous cult objects, such as the incense altar, the table of shew bread, the ten golden candlesticks (five on the right and five on the left), basins, cups, goblets, etc. Beyond this room was "the most holy place" or the "holy of holies" or *debir.* This cubical room, thirty by thirty by thirty feet, was probably a raised section approached by stairs (although stairs are not mentioned). In this room the sacred ark was placed between two guardian cherubim. Here was the dwelling place of the deity. The appearance of the cherubim is not known. They may have resembled the winged beasts with bearded human faces that acted as guardians in Mesopotamian cities, or the winged sphinx-like figures found in the carved ivories at Megiddo or depicted in the portrait of the king of Byblos.[8] A three-story complex of rooms was constructed against the side and back walls of the temple, but just how these rooms were used is not indicated. It is possible that they were for storage.

The temple should not be thought of in terms of a modern church or synagogue. For the most part the people of the land continued to worship at local shrines. The temple was the royal chapel, the center of the national cult of Yahweh. The public did not enter the building, although presumably certain rituals performed within the *hekal* could be witnessed through the open doors. Public ceremonies were associated with the altar for burnt offerings in the open courtyard before the temple proper. It is clear from Babylonian temple records and from the responsibilities of the priestly class as set forth in Lev. 5, 6, 13, 15, that temples were as much administrative centers for the nation as

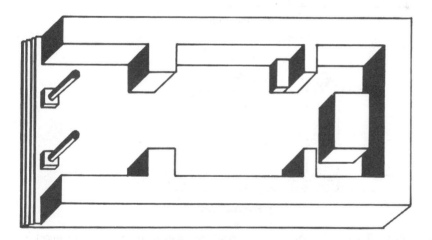

THE TAINAT SHRINE. *An isometric drawing of the eighth or ninth century shrine found at Tainat (ancient Hattina) between Aleppo and Antioch in Syria. The drawing is based on the sketch appearing in* The Biblical Archaeologist, *IV (1941), 21. The shrine was built next to the royal palace. Two free-standing pillars stood in the porch area and a raised pediment occupied the inner room.*

[8] Cf. Wm. F. Albright, "What Were the Cherubim?" *The Biblical Archaeologist Reader,* ed. by G. E. Wright and D. N. Freedman (Chicago: Quadrangle Books, Inc., 1961), pp. 95 ff. (also in an Anchor paperback edition).

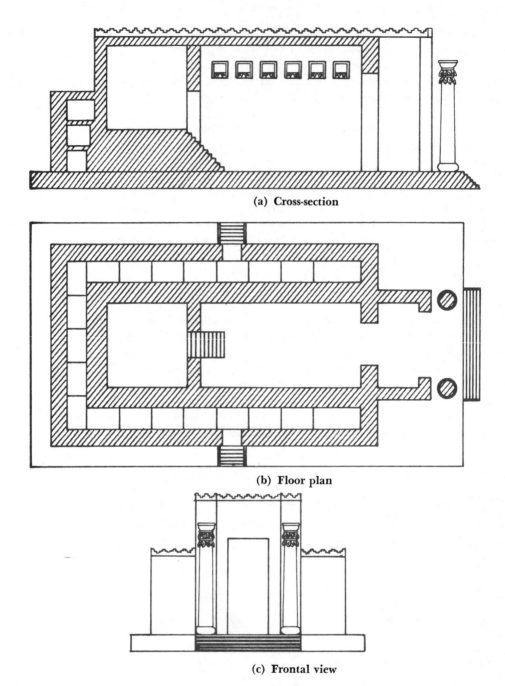

(a) Cross-section

(b) Floor plan

(c) Frontal view

HYPOTHETICAL RECONSTRUCTION OF SOLOMON'S TEMPLE. *All reconstructions of temples are, of necessity, hypothetical. The particular floor plan shown here (b) suggests that the two free-standing pillars named "Jachin" and "Boaz" stood in front of the temple proper, although it would have been just as feasible to place them within the porch or* ulam *as in the Tainat shrine. The cross-section (a) portrays the innermost room or* debir *(described as a perfect cube in I Kings 6:20) with a floor level above that of the rest of the temple. The* debir *might just as well have been on the same level as the rest of the building and the roof in this part of the building may have been lower. The recessed windows are styled after stone frames found in the excavation at Ramat Rahel, Israel. The crenelations on the roof are based on remnants of structures found at Megiddo and utilized in the Stevens reconstruction of the temple (cf. G. E. Wright,* Biblical Archaeology, *p. 139), but no one knows if such battlements were used on shrines. The capitals are styled after one found at Megiddo. The temple faced the east.*

places of worship. Present-day responsibilities of departments of health, sanitation and social welfare were included in the duties of the priesthood. The fact that Solomon acted as a priest and that he was able to depose Abiathar and appoint individuals of his own choice suggests a bureaucratic administrative pattern (cf. 4:1–2, 5).

How ritual for temple services developed is not known. Possibly certain rites from local Hebrew and Canaanite shrines were adopted. Festivals accompanying seasonal changes found in Canaanite worship may have become part of the Hebrew agricultural interpretation of religion. The structural design of the temple, planned by Phoenician artisans, was most likely designed to accommodate rituals familiar to Phoenicians and Canaanites,[9] for the Hebrews had had no such building prior to this time. It also seems likely that, having been in the land for more than a century, the Hebrews had developed religious rituals associated with their own sacred symbols. Such a psalm as 24:7–12 may have been sung in a ritual in which the ark was taken into the temple. In addition to the temple for Yahweh, Solomon built shrines for other deities (11:7).

Solomon's palace was a major building operation, requiring thirteen years to complete, as compared to seven for the temple. Standing near the temple, the royal complex must have somewhat overshadowed the building designed for the deity. A construction program of this magnitude required money, some of which Solomon raised by taxation (4:7–19) and some of which came from business profits. Horses were imported and resold at a profit to other nations (10:28).[10] Simultaneously a strong force of war-chariots and cavalrymen were developed for national security (10:26 and following verses; compare with 4:28), and these forces were stationed throughout the empire in strategically located chariot cities. The excavation of Megiddo has uncovered a stable of five units, each capable of sheltering thirty horses, which was at one time dated in the time of Solomon but is now believed to come from the ninth century.[11] It has been suggested that the House of the Forest of Lebanon (7:2–5) may have been a stable for horses and chariots although the biblical description does not provide support for this idea. Additional evidence of Solomon's business activities has been discovered in the Negeb, east of the Arabah, where ancient copper mines and primitive smelters that may belong to his time have been found.[12] Ezion-geber, at the head of the Gulf of Aqabah, was a fortified storehouse and a port which gave Solomon access to the Arabian peninsula, African cities on the Red and Arabian Seas,[13] and possibly

[9] The temple may have been dedicated at the New Year with the coming of the fall rain. Cf. J. Gray, *op. cit.*, pp. 192 f. The "bronze sea" may have represented the cosmic ocean, important in the New Year rites, cf. Gray, *ibid.*, pp. 176 ff.

[10] The text at this point is defective. If, as the RSV translation indicates, Solomon imported horses from Egypt and Kue (believed to be Cilicia in Asia Minor) and sold them to the Hittites and north Syrians, one wonders why the Hittites had to buy through Solomon when they might have purchased the animals directly.

[11] Y. Yadin, "New Light on Solomon's Megiddo," *BA*, XXIII (1960), 62 ff.

[12] It has been argued recently that no metallurgic work was done during the time of the Hebrew monarchy and that the material evidence has to be credited to the Edomites and dated in the eleventh century (cf. Beno Rothenberg and Alexandru Lupu, "Excavations at Timna," *Museum Haaretz Bulletin*, No. 9, June 1967.

[13] Nelson Glueck, "Ezion-geber," *BA*, XXVIII (1956), 70–87.

"SOLOMON'S PILLARS." *The massive stone outcroppings pictured above are in the Negeb about sixteen miles north of the ancient port city of Ezion-Geber on the Gulf of Aqabah. They have been called "Solomon's pillars" because some scholars believe that copper was mined here in Solomon's time. Smelting furnaces and heaps of slag have been found nearby. The aridity of the area, the burning heat of the summer sun, the distance from central Palestine and the problem of transporting food and equipment necessary for sustaining life in this barren area must have resulted in a high mortality rate.*

also to India if "Ophir" (I Kings 9:28) can be equated with Suppara, India.[14]

In spite of the mobile army, Solomon was unable to control all parts of the extensive Hebrew kingdom. An Edomite rebellion which appears to have taken place early in his reign is recorded in I Kings 11:14–25. A certain Hadad, exiled in David's time, returned when Solomon became king and became an adversary.[15] Unfortunately the text breaks off in the middle of Verse 25. Some scholars suggest that Verses 23 and 24 should be treated as intrusions into the text, and that the difficult Verse 25 should follow after Verse 22 and read in conclusion that Hadad reigned over "Edom" (as certain manuscripts have it). In any event Solomon appears to have retained his hold on Ezion-geber (I Kings 9:26 ff.).

Another rebellion was led by Jeroboam, an Ephraimite, whom

---

[14] Jack Finegan, *Light From the Ancient Past*, p. 182 and works cited there.

[15] When a monarch died the decrees issued against individuals were, apparently, rendered null and void, permitting exiles to return home.

Solomon had placed in charge of one section of the *corvée* (I Kings 11:26 ff.). When Solomon sought to kill him, Jeroboam took refuge with Shishak, king of Egypt. Despite good relations of trade and marriage with Egypt, extradition rights were apparently not observed.

A figure as colorful as Solomon would naturally attract legends. Folktales developed about his wealth (10:14–25), trade (10:11–12), and international reputation for wisdom (3:16–28; 10:1–10). The final touch was added by Deuteronomists who are responsible for the account as we have it. Stern judgment was passed upon Solomon for his numerous wives who led him to worship other deities beside Yahweh. At the same time, the speeches placed in Solomon's mouth reflect Deuteronomic convictions about the significance of the Hebrew religion and contain interpretations of history that follow the Deuteronomic point of view.

13
J and the Law

IT has been noted that Solomon's time was marked by great literary activity and, if one can generalize from the Gezer Calendar, literacy may have been widespread.[1] In addition to the material pertaining to the monarchy, the so-called "J" materials came into being. J should not be treated as history, in the modern sense, but rather as a religious saga recounting myths, legends and folktales. How much of J was in written form, gathered and combined prior to this time, cannot be determined. Some legends were probably preserved in oral form as tribal recitations. Certain stories appear to be Hebraized Canaanite shrine legends, for they refer to Canaanite cult objects[2] and some designations suggest shrine deities.[3] Some stories, such as the flood story, can be traced back to Babylonian and Sumerian accounts and were perhaps drawn from Canaanite versions of these stories. A few passages, such as Gen. 4:23—the song of Lamech—come from specific tribal groups. This is to say that the J writer did not originate the material but compiled, edited and reworked sources into a great schematic framework. Three major themes appear to have been combined:

1. Legends and myths pertaining to human beginnings, containing aetiological materials explaining why certain aspects of life are the way they are.
2. Patriarchal narratives demonstrating that Yahweh, the creator of the heavens and earth and all that is within them, was the same deity who miraculously led the fathers of the Hebrew nation and prepared the Hebrew people for their glorious role, rejecting other neighboring groups which became subsidiaries of the Solomonic kingdom (such as the legends about Esau/Edom).
3. The Mosaic tradition leading up to the invasion of Palestine.

Within this framework, a pattern can be discerned consisting of a series of waves, with each peak symbolizing a new beginning in

---

[1] The Gezer Calendar, found in 1908 during the excavation of Gezer and usually described as a schoolboy's "exercise tablet," is an inscription in soft limestone in late Iron I script listing agricultural activities or seasons. The pattern is reminiscent of "Thirty days hath September. . . ."

[2] Cf. Gen. 12:6; 13:18; 18:1, where references are made to "terebinths."

[3] Cf. "El-roi," the god of Beer-lahai-roi, Gen. 16:13 f.; "El Olam," god of Beer-sheba, Gen. 21:33.

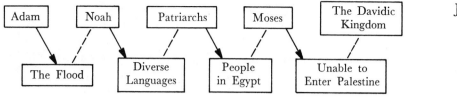

Yahweh's relationships with man and each trough representing the miscarriage of the experiment.

Man is introduced as Yahweh's gardener in Eden, but is expelled when he attempts to become like the deity. Yahweh expunged this poor beginning with the flood and preserved only a righteous remnant, Noah, as the foundation for a new beginning. When Noah's descendants attempted to invade the realm of the divine, Yahweh limited mankind's powers by creating non-co-operating language groups. From one group Yahweh chose Abraham, and when the patriarch's descendants became enslaved in Egypt, a new beginning was made in the Exodus under Moses. Because the people sinned in the desert, they could not enter Palestine. Another new beginning, of which J was a part, is to be seen in the Davidic kingdom, firmly established in J's time in the promised land. If J saw signs portending failure in Solomon's reign, he gives no clear indication in his writings.

Another pattern appears in J's implication that Yahweh's efforts to work with mankind in general were unsuccessful, so the deity singled out a specific group to be identified as his own people.

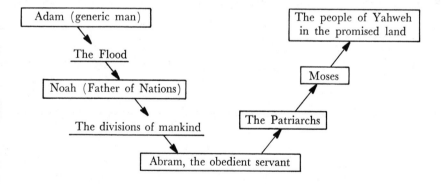

It is J's concern to indicate that what had occurred in history, in the creation of the Hebrew nation, in the development of wealth and power as experienced under David and Solomon, did not "just happen" but came about through the intervention of Yahweh in human affairs. The present status of the nation could only be appreciated through a theologized version of past tradition. Furthermore, emphasis upon what Yahweh had done in the past dramatized what the relationship of the people to Yahweh in the present should be, for Yahweh was continuing to do in the present what he had done in the past.

There can be little doubt that the writer was a Judaean, a learned master of magnificent prose characterized by the direct simplicity of the folktale, the adroit use of adjectives, and the sophisticated wisdom of one who has insight into national destiny. J was proud of the Hebrew kingdom and at times exhibited a spirit of superiority as he looked upon the pre-Hebrew inhabitants of Palestine whom he called "Canaanites" (Gen. 24:3, 37), or revealed his feelings about the Bedouins ("Ishmaelites," Gen. 16:12). At times he appears to have moved toward universalism, but he actually never abandoned the nationalistic, particularistic point of view. Yahweh was the creator of all, but Yahweh was Israel's god and Israel was Yahweh's people. All the nations of all the world will secure blessing—but through Abraham (Gen. 12:3b).

While there is absolutely no hint provided as to authorship, it is perhaps not amiss to suggest that the writer was associated with the Temple and that this great saga was used when rites of renewal and rebirth would quite properly call for a recital or dramatization of the creation account,[4] perhaps at great religious festivals such as the New Year. Some parts of the narrative may have been used for other festal occasions, such as rites of enthronement in which the allegiance of the nation was pledged to the monarch in the form of a covenant ceremony, blessed and protected by Yahweh.[5] It is doubtful that the saga was set apart for priestly perusal, but any suggestions as to how it may have been used are hypothetical.

Only a few clues enable scholars to suggest the reign of Solomon as the time of writing. In the first place the Deuteronomic material presumes a knowledge of J so that if the setting of Deuteronomy in the seventh century is correct then J must have been written before that time. In the second place, Gen. 27:40, which deals with Hebrew-Edomite relations suggests by the phrase "and you shall serve your brother" that Edom had been subdued, and according to II Sam. 8 this occurred during the reign of David. The subsequent part of the verse suggests that Edom had broken free from this bondage, and it has been suggested that this may have taken place in Solomon's reign when Hadad led a rebellion (I Kings 11:14–25). The only other times when an Edomitic revolt is noted are in the ninth century during the reign of Jehoshaphat when, according to I Kings 22:47, Edom was ruled by a deputy (cf., however, II Chron. 20), or during the reign of Jehoram (second half of the ninth century) when Edom won freedom (II Kings 8:20), thus giving a ninth century date for J. Because there is no hint of the division of the Hebrew kingdom into independent northern and southern units, it would seem that J should be dated in the tenth century. The physical abundance depicted in the "blessing of Jacob" (Gen. 49) and the twelve-tribe pattern also seem to reflect Solomon's era.

The following list of passages indicates those forming the core of the

---

4 Cf. Part Seven, chap. 23, the references to the Akitu festival.

5 Prior to the construction of the temple such a ritual may have been performed at Shechem in the temple of Ba'al-berith (Judg. 8:33; 9:4), or El-berith, "the covenant god" (Judg. 9:46).

J saga. To read these passages without reference to the material which was later added to expand and amplify the stories is difficult, for the gaps that appear in the development of the theme are sometimes due to the incorporation of significant themes in the sections treated as additions. For example, in the Moses cycle the persecution of the Hebrews is introduced in Exod. 1:8–13, and Moses suddenly appears in 2:11–23a. Whatever stories may have been included in the early strand of tradition are gone, and at a later time the story of Moses as the hero of the Exodus was expanded by a story of the miraculous deliverance of Moses from the hostility of Pharaoh as a child (just as J has him escape as an adult in 2:15), modeled after the story of Sargon of Agade. At the same time, it is possible from the outline below to see how the writer developed his theme from creation to the time when the Hebrews were about to enter Canaan. Almost every documentary analysis is in agreement on the bulk of what is to be included in the various collections, but each scholar finds some passages that do not fit the schema. J materials listed below represent generally accepted passages. Those marked with an asterisk are, according to personal analysis, probably not J. The parenthetical remarks, also marked with an asterisk, indicate where this writer believes they belong.[6]

———— PASSAGES BELONGING TO J ————

Beginnings

Gen. 2:4b–3:24.	Creation myth.
Gen. 4:1–16.	Why the blacksmith bears a trade-mark.
Gen. 4:17a.	The birth of Enoch (the account of Cain as a city dweller in 4:17b contradicts 4:1–16 and hence represents a different tradition).
Gen. 4:18–26.	The beginnings of nomadism (note 4:26b where the beginning of Yahwism is indicated in spite of Gen. 4:1–16).
Gen. 5:29.	Noah is blessed for the gift of wine (cf. Gen. 9:18–27).
Gen. 6:1–4.	The sons of God and the daughters of men.

The Noah Cycle

Gen. 6:5–8.	God's decision to destroy men by flood.
Gen. 7:1–5, 7–10, 12, 16b, 22–23; 8:2b–3a, 6–12, 13b.	Noah and the flood.
Gen. 8:20–22.	Noah's offering.
Gen. 9:18–27.	Noah's vineyard and drunkenness.
Gen. 10:8–19, 21, 24–30.	The descendants of Noah.

The Diffusion of Tongues

Gen. 11:1–9.	The tower of Babel.

[6] Some analyses are similar to those proposed by F. V. Winnett, *The Mosaic Tradition* (Toronto: University of Toronto Press, 1949).

The Abram (Abraham)–Isaac Cycle

Gen. 11:28–30.	Remnants of the Abram (Abraham) genealogy.
Gen. 12:1–4a.	The summons to leave home.
Gen. 12:6–9.	Abram in Canaan.
Gen. 12:10–20.	Abram and Sarai in Egypt.
Gen. 13:1–5, 6a, 7–11a, 12b–18.	Abram and Lot.
Gen. 16:1–2, 4–8, 11–14.	Abram's son Ishmael.
Gen. 18:1–16, 20–19:28.	The destruction of Sodom and Gomorrah.
Gen. 19:30–38.	The ancestry of Moab and Ammon.
Gen. 21:1–2a, 7.	The birth of Isaac.
Gen. 21:33.	Abraham at Beer-sheba.
*Gen. 22:15–18, 20–24.	Renewal of promise to Abraham (*15–18 appears to be a post-D redaction; 20–24 come from an unknown source).
Gen. 24:1–67.	Isaac takes Rebekah as wife.
Gen. 25:1–6, 11b.	Abraham's other children (because this account comes as an intrusion in the J account it is often treated as a late addition).
Gen. 26:1–3a, 6–33.	Isaac and Rebekah in Gerar (note the repetition of the Abraham legends. Cf. Gen. 26:1–5 and Gen. 12:1–4; Gen. 26:6–11 and Gen. 12:10–20).

The Jacob Cycle

Gen. 25:21–26a.	The birth of Esau and Jacob.
Gen. 25:27–34.	Esau sells his birthright.
Gen. 27:1–45.	By deception Jacob obtains Esau's blessing (two accounts are blended; the earliest is: 27:1–10, 17, 18a, 20, 24–27a, 29b–32, 35–39a, 40a, 41–45).
Gen. 28:10–22.	Jacob at Bethel (The full account is probably an expansion of the J material).
Gen. 29:1–30.	Jacob marries.
Gen. 29:31–35.	The birth of Reuben, Simeon, Levi, and Judah.
Gen. 30:1–43.	Jacob and Laban (conflation of J and E materials. Probably J = 30:9–16, 22, 24b, 25, 27, 29–43).
Gen. 31:1, 3, 21a, 44, 46, 48 and parts of 51–53a.	Jacob's flight. The covenant with Laban.
Gen. 32:3–12, 22.	Jacob prepares to meet Esau.
Gen. 33:1–17.	Jacob meets Esau.
Gen. 34:3, 5, 7, 11–13, 18, 19, 25–26, 30–31.	The defeat of Shechem.
Gen. 35:21–22a.	Reuben and Bilhah.
Gen. 38:1–30.	Tamar and Judah.

The Joseph Cycle

(overlaps Jacob cycle)

Gen. 30:22–24.	The birth of Joseph (a conflation of J and E).
Gen. 37:3–36.	Joseph and his brothers. (The original "J" mate-

rial has been expanded. Probably J = Verses 3–4, 12–18, 21, 23, 25–27, 28b, 31–35).

Gen. 39:1–23.	Joseph and Potiphar's wife.
Gen. 42.	Joseph and his brothers. (An expanded J story. J = 42:2, 5–7, 26–28, 38.)
Gen. 43.	Joseph and the second visit of his brothers.
Gen. 44–45:4.	Joseph reveals his true identity.
Gen. 45:9–14, 19, 21–24, 28; 46:28–34.	Jacob comes to Joseph.
Gen. 47:1–26.	Jacob settles in Egypt.
Gen. 47:29–31; 48:2b, 9b–10a, 13–14, 17–19.	Jacob's blessing.
*Gen. 49:1–27.	Poetic form of blessing (*from an early non-J source).
Gen. 50:1–11, 14.	The death and burial of Jacob.
Exod. 1:6.	The death of Joseph.

The Moses Cycle

Exod. 1:8–12.	The persecution of the Hebrews.
Exod. 2:11–23a.	Moses' flight to Midian.
Exod. 3:2–4a, 5, 7–8a, 16, 18; 4:1–16, 19–20a, 22–23.	Moses is told to save the Hebrews.
Exod. 4:24–26.	Yahweh tries to kill Moses.
Exod. 4:29–31.	Moses convinces the Hebrews.
Exod. 5:3, 5–23; 6:1.	Moses and Pharaoh (references to Aaron are redactional).
Exod. 7:14–15a, 16–17a, 18, 21a, 23–25.	Nile waters are turned to blood.
Exod. 8:1–4, 8–15a.	The swarm of frogs.
Exod. 8:20–32.	The swarm of flies.
Exod. 9:1–7.	The death of the cattle.
Exod. 9:13, 17–18, 23b–24, 25b–29a, 33–34.	The hailstorm (9:14–16, 19–21, 29b–32 are redactions possibly added by the compiler of JE).
Exod. 10:1, 3–11, 13b, 14b–19.	The plague of locusts (10:2 is a redaction).
Exod. 10:24–26, 28–29.	Pharaoh accedes to Moses' demands.
Exod. 11:4–8; 12:29–30.	Death of Egyptian firstborn.
*Exod. 12:21–27.	Passover rite (*late redaction).
*Exod. 13:3–16.	Firstfruit ritual (*late redaction).
Exod. 13:21–22.	Yahweh leads his people.
Exod. 14:5–7, 10–14.	Pharaoh's pursuit.
Exod. 14:19b–20, 24–25, 27b, 30–31.	Yahweh saves his people.
Exod. 15:22–25, 27.	Wilderness wanderings.
Exod. 16:4–5.	Yahweh gives his people daily bread.
Exod. 17:1b–2, 7.	The people thirst.
Exod. 19:2.	At Sinai (2b may be E).

142

*Exod. 19:3b–9.	Covenant terms (*a late redaction, probably Exilic) .
Exod. 19:18, 20a, 21.	Yahweh on Sinai.
*Exod. 24:1–2, 9–11.	The Covenant meal (*a late redaction extending the idea of Exod. 18:12–E) .
Exod. 32:9–14.	Moses intercedes for the people.
*Exod. 32:25–34.	Punishment (*verses 30–34 are the work of R^je) .
Exod. 33:12–23.	The glory of Yahweh.
*Exod. 34:1–28.	The tablets of law, including the "ritual decalogue" (*possibly a D source reworked by R^p) .
Num. 10:29–32.†	Moses with Hobab (here Hobab is Moses' brother-in-law. Cf. Judg. 4:11) .
Num. 10:35–6.	The Song of the Ark (an old poem used by J) .
Num. 11:4–15, 18–23, 31–35.	Quails for food.
Num. 12:16; 13:17b–20, 22–24, 26b, 28, 30–32.	Spying out Canaan.
Num. 14:1, 3–4, 11–12, 31–32, 39–45.	The failure of the first attack.
*Num. 16:1a, 12–15, 25–26, 27b–34.	Revolt of Dathan and Abiram (*J reworked in the spirit of D) .
Num. 20:1b.	Death of Miriam.
Num. 20:2a, 3.	Lack of water.
Num. 21:1–3.	The struggle at Hormah.
Num. 21:14–18, 27–30.	Early poems probably preserved in J.
Num. 22:2–3a, 5–7, 17–18, 22–35a.	Balaam and his ass.
Num. 24:3–9, 15–19.	Balaam's oracles.
Num. 25:1–5.	Israel yoked to Ba'al of Pe'or.
Num. 32:34–39, 41–42.	J's summary of holdings of Gad, Reuben and Manasseh.

† The J material in Numbers is so interwoven with the material that was added to expand the account that it is impossible to separate J with any certainty. The material attributed to J must be accepted as conjectural.

THE J SAGA

Read Gen. 2:4b–3:24

Just when or how the J creation myth (Gen. 2:4b–3:24) originated is not known. Because scholars believe that various older myths can be traced within the story, it is not likely that the J writers invented the story.[7] As it stands in its present form, the myth describes God in anthropomorphic terms planting a pleasure park, molding man from

[7] For example, vs. 8 is repeated in vs. 9, vss. 10–14 interrupt the sequence and vs. 24 appears to conclude a section. Vss. 3:17c, 19ab and 3:18, 19c, reflect a combination of differing conclusions, the first referring to an agricultural community, the second to a Bedouin way of life. Man is expelled from the garden in 3:23 and again in 3:24, etc.

clay as a potter might do, and blowing into man's nostrils his own breath, animating the earth that was man so that man began to breathe.[8] This creature was to be a gardener and was forbidden to eat of the tree of moral knowledge on threat of immediate death (2:16 f.). Perceiving the loneliness of man, Yahweh decided to create a helper and continued to mold creatures out of clay, bringing each in turn to the man. Man named each creature (thus J explains how creatures received their specific designations) but found none that was really suited to his needs. Then God caused man to sleep and extracted a rib (perhaps J's explanation of our "floating ribs") and modeled a new creation from this part of man. When man awoke and saw this new creature, he cried "At last! This is it!" (Perhaps J implies that this is the experience of every man who falls in love.) In man's recognition that woman is "bone of my bone" and "flesh of my flesh" and in the observation of Verse 24, J implies that man is incomplete until he finds the one who represents his missing part! J's delight in punning is apparent, for the new creature is called *ishshah* (woman) because she was taken from *ish* (man).[9] Man, therefore, rejected the animal kingdom in favor of the creature made from himself—woman—and perhaps J intended to provoke a smile, for in this instance woman was "born" of man.

At this point the serpent is introduced, a creature made to be a helper but rejected by man. Wiser or more cunning than the other creatures, the serpent scoffed at the prohibition pertaining to the tree of knowledge of good and evil, pointing out that eating the fruit would not bring death but would result in possession of knowledge restricted to divine beings. Thus tempted, the woman and man ate and, as the serpent had promised, found that they did not die but possessed moral knowledge. The new knowledge brought awareness of nudity and so men, unlike animals, require artificial clothing—first of leaves, then of animal skins. In guilty awareness of the violation of God's command, the couple attempted to hide. Yahweh, walking in the garden, could not find them and called them forth, and all three participants in the misdemeanor were punished. The sentences explain phenomena of life—why the serpent crawls upon its belly, why men kill snakes, why snakes bite men, why women experience pain in childbirth and yet continue to have children, why men toil so hard for a living, and why nature seems to thwart man's best efforts. Now, lest man should eat of the other tree—the tree of immortality—and become like a god, the man and his wife were expelled from the garden and prevented from re-entering by the guardian cherubim and the sword of lightning.

The motifs within this story are very familiar. The mortality of

[8] The breath should not be interpreted as "soul" but rather as the vitalizing principle in life: plants, animals, and men. In the mind of the J writer, man is simply animated earth, and he distinguishes between body and life rather than between body and soul. Cf. von Rad, *Genesis,* trans. by John H. Marks (Philadelphia: Westminster Press, 1961), p. 75.

[9] The term translated "man" elsewhere in this story is *adam* and here again J has a pun for *adam* (mankind) is made from *adamah* (the reddish mother earth).

THE SERPENT SE-TA. *The serpent is portrayed with a pair of human legs in the fifteenth century* B.C. *Egyptian Papyrus of Ani, the so-called "Book of the Dead."*

man, the kinship of man and animal, the separation of man and animal,[10] and the similarity of man to the gods except that man does not possess immortality are all themes within the Gilgamesh Epic. While other pre-Exilic Hebrew literature known to us ignores this story and while some scholars have argued that it should not be included within the J material,[11] there is elsewhere in J (the Tower of Babel story) the theme of man seeking to enter the realm of the divine, and the Psalmists have picked up the theme of man's mortality and sub-divine status (compare Ps. 8:5; 49:20). Centuries later, Christian theologians interpreted the story in terms of man's "fall" from a pure state and although the story does tell of the expulsion of Adam from paradise (see Rom. 5), its central theme is the ascent of man through moral knowledge to a level of awareness akin to that possessed by the deity.

Read Gen. 4:1–16

The story of Cain and Abel, sons of Adam and Eve, is a legend relating to a specific group of people, revealing the author's belief that animal offerings (symbolic of the herdsman) are superior to agricultural offerings (symbolic of the farmer).[12] The account is aetiological, explaining why the roving blacksmiths (one meaning of the name Cain is "smith") are able to roam from place to place with no strong tribe to guarantee safety and, possibly, explaining how a peculiar mark, which may have been the symbol of the smith's trade, came into being. In its present setting the story forms part of the pattern of deepening evil that culminated in the flood. In a sense, Cain and Abel are "everyman"—brothers separated by jealousy and misunderstanding that leads to violence. J indicates that man having acquired moral knowledge had not achieved moral responsibility.

Read Gen. 6:1–4

Of the stories pertaining to human beginnings, perhaps that telling of the intermarriage of divine beings and "the daughters of men" is most perplexing. Divine-human marriages were common in the mythologies of the Near East and quite often the children were mighty warriors, so perhaps J was drawing on one of these themes.[13] Perhaps he saw in the story another example of man's arrogance and an attempt to achieve divinity; but God limited human life to a maximum of 120 years. It is also possible that J is attacking Canaanite cult prostitution in which the hierodules, both male and female, played the role of the deities who met with worshipers in sacred copulation rites. J notes that such relationships were the prelude to the flood. In any

[10] Cf. the separation of Enkidu from the animals in the Gilgamesh Epic, Tablet 1.

[11] Cf. Pfeiffer, *op. cit.*, p. 160.

[12] A similar rivalry is found in the Sumerian story of Dumuzi and Enkimdu; cf. *ANET*, p. 41.

[13] Cf. Gilgamesh Epic where Gilgamesh is the child of a goddess and a human father and is a great fighter, Hercules in Greek mythology, etc.

case, we have only a truncated myth, and J's purpose in recounting it is not clear.

The source of the flood story can be traced to Mesopotamia and the eleventh tablet of the Gilgamesh Epic, which in turn rests upon an older Sumerian flood legend.[14] It is unlikely that such a story would develop within Palestine where the Jordan flows below sea level. The obvious marks of literary borrowing and the discovery of a fragment of the Gilgamesh Epic at Megiddo from the fourteenth-century level[15] suggests that the story was known in Canaan prior to the Hebrew invasion, and would have come into the J material from Canaanite sources.

Read the
Noah
Cycle

Certain noteworthy differences between the Mesopotamian versions and the J account can be discerned. When the Hebrews borrowed the story, they related it to their own deity, Yahweh, discarding the polytheistic pattern of the Gilgamesh account. Furthermore, the flood in the Hebrew story came as a judgment resulting from Yahweh's regret that he had made man because of the latter's continued evil action, while in Gilgamesh mankind was to be destroyed by vote of the gods with no real reason provided.[16] Finally, the hero of the Gilgamesh flood story, Utnapishtim, is rewarded with immortality for himself and his wife, while Noah and his family die as all mortals must. What the Hebrew writers borrowed they transformed in the light of their own theological convictions.

During the excavation of ancient Ur and nearby Al 'Ubaid, Sir Leonard Woolley uncovered evidence of what he interpreted as a major flood which occurred in the middle of the fourth millennium, and which covered an existing culture with a deposit of sediment to depths varying from eight to eleven feet.[17] Similar deposits were found in other Mesopotamian sites, but these were from different periods. It has been argued that the Mesopotamian and biblical flood traditions may have their origin in a flood of unprecedented proportions. Woolley's interpretation of the evidence has been challenged and there are those who argue that what Woolley and others interpreted as river sediment is, in fact, a great layer of sand deposited by the dreaded *idyah*, a dust storm which occurs in the spring and summer in Mesopotamia, and which may lay down a thick layer of sand particles to form what is known as an "aeolian formation." The aeolian formation is quite different from river sediment. But this

[14] Cf. A. Parrot, *The Flood and Noah's Ark*, E. Hudson (trans.) (New York: Philosophical Library, 1955) ; A. Heidel, *The Gilgamesh Epic and Old Testament Parallels* (Chicago: University of Chicago Press, a Phoenix Book, 1946 and 1963) .

[15] D. J. Wiseman, *Illustrations from Biblical Archaeology* (Grand Rapids, Michigan: W. B. Eerdmans, 1958) , p. 13.

[16] In the so-called "Atrahasis Epic," the noise made by man disturbed the gods and brought on the flood. Cf. E. A. Speiser's translation of "Atrahasis" in *ANET*, p. 104.

[17] Woolley's thesis is presented in L. Woolley, *Ur of the Chaldees* (Harmondsworth, Middlesex: Penguin Books, 1950) , chap. 1, and A. Parrot, *The Flood and Noah's Ark*, pp. 13 ff. The challenge is published in Martin A. Beek, *Atlas of Mesopotamia*, H. H. Rowley (ed.) , D. R. Welsh (trans.) (London: Thomas Nelson and Sons, 1962) , p. 12, and the rebuttal is by M. E. Mallowan, "Noah's Flood Reconsidered," *Iraq*, XXVI (1964) , pp. 62–82.

re-interpretation cannot be accepted as final, as the rebuttal from sup-porters of the Woolley hypothesis has demonstrated. We can only conclude that Mesopotamian floods did occur, that there is ample literary evidence of the disaster they brought to some settled areas, and that it is quite possible that the flood traditions rest in an actual ex-perience or series of experiences of the destruction wrought by these high waters.

Read Gen. 11:1–9 The tower of Babel story can be related to the ziggurats or temple towers of Mesopotamia. These huge, man-made mountains of sun-dried brick, faced with kiln-baked brick often in beautiful enamels, rose several hundred feet above the flat plains of Mesopotamia. Used in the worship of the various deities to whom they were consecrated, they seemed to J a fitting symbol of man's arrogant pride. Selecting the ziggurat at Babylon dedicated to Bel-Marduk, J describes the great building project as an attempt of man to invade heaven, which, in Near Eastern thought, was believed to be just above the zenith of the firmament. To thwart human ambitions, Yahweh caused men to speak in different languages, and because men who cannot speak together cannot work together, the project failed. This, J explained, was why mankind, descended from a common ancestor, Noah, spoke different languages. Once again J's delight in puns is demonstrated for God confused (*balel*) man's speech at Babel, or as Dr. Moffatt's translation aptly puts it, the place "was called Babylonia" for there God "made a babble of the languages."

Read the Abraham Cycle The patriarchal narratives begin with the story of Abraham and tell of a promise made by Yahweh that a great nation would come from Abraham's offspring (which J believed was fulfilled in his time). Placed as it is, following three failures of man to fulfill divine expecta-tions (Adam, Noah, Babel), the Abrahamic cycle represents a new beginning, a new creation by Yahweh, centered not in mankind in general but in one individual who responds to a divine call and through whom mankind in general may receive blessing. The thrust of the story, as indicated by its location, is in the concept of election, the special choice by Yahweh of a man, and hence a people, through whom the divine intention might be realized. It is possible that the remnant motif, which plays a large role in later thought, finds its beginning here, for it is in the faithful one that Yahweh puts his trust and builds for the future.[18] Where the Abraham tradition originated is not known, but most likely it came from tribal families among the Hebrews with a tradition of Mesopotamian origins. The two names for the patriarch, Abram and Abraham, may reflect separate cycles. The identification of the two names is preserved in a late priestly tradition (See Gen. 17:5).

Like other Hebrew heroes, Abraham went to Egypt[19] and returned, rich in material wealth, to spend some time in the Negeb (Gen.

[18] Cf. G. A. Danell, "The Idea of God's People in the Bible" in *The Root of the Vine* (Westminster: Dacre Press, 1953), pp. 23–36.

[19] Nomadic peoples frequently entered Egypt; cf. Papyrus Anastasi VI, "The Report of a Frontier Official," *ANET*, p. 259.

13:1–2). If there is any remnant of historical truth within this account, the Negeb journeys would seem to fit best into the period between the twenty-first and nineteenth centuries, a period during which, according to the great explorer and archaeologist Dr. Nelson Glueck, numerous settlements dotted the Negeb.[20] Moving northward into Palestine, the families of Abraham and Lot separated. Lot went to Sodom to become the paternal ancestor of the Ammonites and Edomites.[21] Abraham, after being promised the area subsequently occupied by the Davidic-Solomonic kingdoms, settled at Hebron where he is said to have founded the shrine (Gen. 13:18). Abraham became the patriarchal ancestor of the Ishmaelites, of Isaac and the tribes descended from him, and of various other unknown tribal groups.

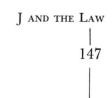

The Isaac stories repeat many of the motifs found in the Abrahamic cycle, so it would appear that the J writer had cycles of very similar material pertaining to the patriarchs, and he combined them by making one figure the ancestor of the other. The election motif is touched with the element of the miraculous, for when Abraham's hope for posterity has faded, Isaac is born. Isaac became the paternal ancestor of the Edomites (Esau) and the Israelites (Jacob), and from Jacob came the majority of the tribes forming the Hebrew nation.

Read the Isaac Cycle

The familar motif of an old woman bearing offspring after many years of barrenness through the gracious intervention of Yahweh appears again, this time associated with Rebekah (compare Sarah: Gen. 11:30; 16:1; Rachel: Gen. 29:31; 30:22). Rivalry between Edom and Israel, symbolized by the twins Esau and Jacob, began in the womb and the results of that struggle were predetermined by Yahweh. Like Ishmael, the first-born of Abraham, Esau, the first-born of Isaac, did not enjoy the preferential status usually associated with primogeniture (see Gen. 43:33), and this loss of stature is explained by Esau's sale of his birthright, an action that parallels an incident recorded in Nuzi texts. J does not condemn Jacob's deception of Isaac to obtain Esau's blessing, possibly because what took place was actually in accord with Yahweh's prediction and was, therefore, a fulfillment of Yahweh's will. On the other hand, there is little condemnation of trickery in J, for it was assumed that a clever person would resort to such tactics.

Read the Jacob Cycle

J's literary artistry is clearly demonstrated in depicting the rugged, hungry hunter selling his birthright for a bowl of lentils; in the picture of the bewildered, blind father seeking to assuage Esau's bitter disappointment with a second blessing; and in the interplay of characters: father, mother and sons. His delight in the play on words appears when Jacob (*Ya'akob*) grabs his brother's heel (*'akeb*). The differences between the two boys, foreshadowing distinctive way of life for their descendants, is emphasized by the separateness of their habits, interests, food, attitudes and associations. Esau is the hunter, the man

[20] Nelson Glueck, *Rivers in the Desert*, pp. 68 ff.

[21] According to this tradition Sodom would appear to be to the north of the Dead Sea for Abraham and Lot are pictured standing between Ai and Bethel, and Lot went eastward from this spot.

of the steppes; Jacob symbolizes the established farmer or herdsman, the businessman, the man given to the settled life.

Jacob's Bethel vision is undoubtedly linked to the concept of the Mesopotamian ziggurat with its stairway between heaven and earth. Even Jacob's assertion that this was the "gate of heaven" is reminiscent of the name Babylon (*Bab-ilu,* "gate of gods"), a city with a great ziggurat. The story links Jacob with the important cult center at Bethel and provides an aetiological basis for the massebah that must have stood there. Archaeological research has disclosed that the city was standing during the Middle Bronze period, and it is possible that the name "Bethel" ("House of El") symbolizes its importance as a Canaanite sanctuary.[22] Cult legends associating the place with the patriarchs sanctified it as a Yahweh shrine, which it was to become. What is most significant in the episode is the divine assurance of fulfillment of the election promise given to Abraham, by which J clearly keeps before the reader the line of succession for the chosen people.

Haran again becomes the center of patriarchal action in the marriage sequence when Jacob is bested by his uncle Laban. Once again J's literary skill is revealed. The communal watering hole which could not be utilized until all owners were present, was opened by a young man determined to prove himself before an attractive young woman. The substitution of Leah, the older and presumably the less comely daughter, for Rachel on the wedding night, becomes a test of Jacob's love for Rachel and, ironically enough, provides the offspring from which came the tribal groups that produced the great Hebrew leaders Moses and David.

Jacob's methods of increasing his flocks rested on beliefs in magic. Finally, financially secure, he left Laban to return to his homeland where, despite his fears, he was warmly welcomed by Esau.

The story of Judah and Tamar, which has no particular relationship to the Jacob cycle, preserves an independent tradition of the way in which the Judah tribe was saved from extinction by a wily widow. The responsibility for continuing the line of a married man who died without offspring rested with the next of kin, according to a custom known as "levirate" (husband's brother) marriage (cf. Deut. 25:5 ff.).

Read the Joseph Cycle

The Joseph traditions reflect dependency upon older Egyptian stories. The story of Potiphar's wife is like the Egyptian "Tale of the Two Brothers,"[23] and the account of the seven lean years may be related to the "Tradition of the Seven Lean Years in Egypt" found in the Egyptian sources.[24]

Read the Moses Cycle

The election motif is continued in the Moses cycle but, with the deliverance of the Hebrews from Egypt, it takes on the new emphasis of salvation-history, a theological interpretation greatly expanded by later writers. The real character of Moses cannot be ascertained from J or from the expansion of his story by subsequent editors. All that

[22] G. von Rad, *Genesis,* p. 281, suggests there may have been a god named "Bethel."

[23] Cf. John A. Wilson, "The Story of the Two Brothers," *ANET,* pp. 23 ff.

[24] John A. Wilson, "The Tradition of the Seven Lean Years in Egypt," *ANET,* pp. 31 f.

remains is an interpretation of this great leader by those who wrote long after Moses had died. The participation in building Pithom and Raamses may rest upon sound historical memory. Pictures of slaves, including Syrians, making bricks have been found in the fifteenth-century tomb painting depicting the building of the temple of Amun at Karnak (cf. Exod. 5:6 ff.).

Moses is introduced as an adult, a murderer compelled to flee because his act was witnessed by a Hebrew. The sneering rebuke of the witness may reflect a lost J tradition of Moses' involvement with the royal family of Egypt or may simply imply that Moses was setting himself above others. The flight to the desert brought Moses into the family of Reuel, the Midianite. At the burning bush (note the absence of any mention of the sacred mountain), Moses was summoned by Yahweh to deliver the people from Egypt. The strange record of Yahweh's attempt to kill Moses and the rescue by the action of Zipporah, Moses' Midianite wife, is related to the origin of the rite of circumcision, possibly suggesting that Israel learned the custom from the Midianites.[25] The reluctant pharaoh, finally persuaded by dramatic acts, released the Hebrews. Passages making a definite link between the Exodus and Passover and Firstfruits are often associated with the J source but may also be treated as later additions.

Yahweh's presence with the fleeing Hebrews was symbolized by pillars of cloud and fire. Just how the pursuing Egyptians were halted is not clear, except that their chariots became mired in the sea. After wandering in the wilderness, the complaining people reached Mount Sinai where, according to tradition, covenant terms and law were given. The account concludes with the abortive attempts to enter Palestine and the apostasy of the people.

THE ROLE OF MOSES

As we shall see, subsequent writers expanded the role of Moses, exalting him as the founder of law, religious faith and the nation Israel. There can be little doubt that Moses played an important role in bringing at least some of the tribes into a unity centered in the worship of Yahweh and in leading his followers away from Egypt to the outskirts of Palestine. The idealization of his savior role by later generations points back to some kind of charismatic greatness. Historically, almost nothing can be known of him for certain; there remains only the impact of his personality, amplified generation by generation as men looked backward with reverent awe to their founder. To argue that Moses was a monotheist and to attempt to trace specific laws to him pushes the evidence too far.

Moses' significance lay not only in what he represented to those who knew him, but in what he symbolized to generations who never saw him and for whom the interpretation was more important than the historical fact. The legal materials attributed to Moses and often

[25] For a summary of different interpretations cf. J. C. Rylaarsdam, "Exegesis: Exodus," *The Interpreter's Bible*, I, 882.

included in J appear to represent settled culture rather than rules for persons living at the edge of agricultural communities; for example, the parts of the ritual decalogue (Exod. 34:10–26) referring to the wheat harvest, ingathering festivals and firstfruit rites.

MONARCHY AND LAW

The successful management of any organization of people must proceed according to rules, and the government of a nation requires law that provides means to prevent anarchy and to guarantee justice to the people. No royal edicts and no promulgations by legal councils are found in the Bible. Nor have any law codes from ancient Palestine been found to date. Yet Saul, and more particularly David and Solomon, must have had some legal precedents to govern the land. The role of the king as arbitrator in difficult cases is hinted at in Nathan's parable (II Sam. 12), in the case of the woman of Tekoa (II Sam. 14) and in Absalom's contentions (II Sam. 15:1–5). It seems probable that Hebrew administrative policy and law was built upon existing Canaanite precedents, although no such codes are known to us.

Many laws are contained within the Pentateuch but just when and how these laws developed is a moot question. A basic principle to be remembered in the study of the history of law is that legal rulings do not precede the conditions they seek to control. Law develops out of situations, not before them. Therefore, laws pertaining to problems of settled culture cannot be of Mosaic origin but, being in existence in Canaan when the Hebrews entered the land, were adopted and adapted. To argue that Moses prescribed for conditions which the Hebrews would encounter upon entering the land ignores the variations that occur in the laws ascribed to Moses, and the disarrangement of the laws indicates that the legal prescriptions developed over a period of time and were not uttered at one moment. As Johs. Pederson has put it: "When everything authoritative is Mosaic, then every generation will naturally lend to the time of Moses its own manner of living and thinking."[26]

The discovery of Oriental codes much older than those of the Bible, yet prescribing laws similar to those found within the Bible, has helped scholars to understand better the nature of Hebrew law. The Imperial law code of King Hammurabi of Babylon, coming from the end of the eighteenth and the beginning of the seventeenth centuries, was discovered by the French in 1901–02. Hammurabi's laws were not an original creation but reveal development, for it can be demonstrated that the Hammurabi code is related to the law code of King Lipit-Ishtar of the city of Eshnunna who lived in the nineteenth century B.C. Behind Lipit-Ishtar's law code, it can be assumed that older formulations of law stand, extending back into Sumerian times.[27]

Both the Hammurabi code and the Lipit-Ishtar code indicate that

[26] J. Pedersen, *Israel, Its Life and Culture* (Copenhagen: Povl Branner, 1926), I–II, 18.

[27] Cf. T. J. Meek, *Hebrew Origins*, chap. 2.

the laws had divine sanction. The stele upon which the Hammurabi laws were inscribed depicts, in a relief, the monarch receiving authority to enact law from Shamash, the sun god and patron of justice. In like manner King Lipit-Ishtar, in the prologue to his law code, indicates that he was summoned by the god Enlil to establish justice in the land which he proceeded to do in accordance with the divine command.[28] Just how the laws were supposed to have been imparted to the monarchs is not revealed, but the point was that the directions or laws for the guidance of human affairs were given by the gods and therefore were superior to the intentions and desires of any single human being. In the same way, the Hebrew people declared that their laws came from Yahweh and were to be obeyed.

Within the Old Testament two different kinds of law are to be found. The first, known as casuistic law, presents the ruling in a conditional formula beginning "If a man . . ." or "When a man . . ." etc. (cf. Exod. 22:1 f., 10 f.). This pattern of presentation is found in codes throughout the ancient Near East and in the Bible probably reflects laws current among the pre-Hebrew inhabitants of the land.[29] The other form of law, called apodictic law, sets the ruling in a terse statement of prohibition or command: "You must not . . ." or "You shall not . . ." or "You shall . . ." (cf. Exod. 23:18, 19). While apodictic law is found in other ancient law codes, it does appear in far greater measure in the Old Testament than elsewhere. It is therefore proper to suggest, as many scholars have done, that these laws, particularly those involving the name of Yahweh, represent original Hebrew law,[30] although it is impossible to know just when these laws may have originated.

Within the Bible one of the oldest collections of law is embodied in what is known as "The Covenant Code," which has been given a literary setting in the midst of a covenant ceremony involving Moses and Yahweh (cf. Exod. 20:22–23:33). Quite obviously, the editors sought to give divine sanctions to these laws. As these laws reflect festivals relating to an agricultural economy, they cannot be earlier than the Hebrew invasion of Palestine and most probably reflect an ancient Canaanite code which was Hebraized. Such laws of the harvest festival as the law of the firstfruits (Exod. 22:29b–30), the law of the Sabbath (Exod. 23:12), the festival laws related to the feasts of the unleavened bread, the firstfruits and the ingathering (Exod. 23:15–19a) are listed with other early rulings such as the prohibition against boiling a kid in its mother's milk (Exod. 23:19b).[31] How many other laws belong to a very early period is a matter of debate,

---

[28] Cf. *ANET*, p. 159.

[29] The similarity between Hebrew law and the Hammurabi code has been commented upon many times. Cf. T. J. Meek in the footnotes to the translation of the Hammurabi code in *ANET*, pp. 164–180.

[30] Wm. F. Albright, *From Stone Age to Christianity*, pp. 267 f., goes too far in insisting that apodictic laws are unique in Israel. Cf. T. J. Meek, *Hebrew Origins*, pp. 72 f., for a modification of this concept.

[31] This law is often understood as a protest against a Canaanite practice recorded in the Ras es-Shamra texts. Cf. Cyrus Gordon, "Canaanite Mythology" in *Mythologies of the Ancient World*, S. N. Kramer (ed.) (Chicago: Quadrangle Books Inc., 1961), p. 186.

_____ CHART X _____

Punishment in Hammurabi's Code	Punishment in The Covenant Code
HOUSEBREAKING	
Thief is put to death.	Exod. 22:2–3. If the thief is injured or killed during darkness there is no blood guilt on his killer.
GIVING FALSE TESTIMONY	
In murder cases: death penalty. In sorcery cases: ordeal by water. In property cases: according to the individual case.	Exod. 23:1–3. Perjury prohibited and no penalty given.
THEFT OF AN ANIMAL	
Restitution 10– to 30–fold	Exod. 22:1. Restitution 2– or 4– or 5–fold.
THEFT OF A PERSON	
Thief is put to death.	Exod. 21:16. Thief is put to death.
A SON STRIKES HIS FATHER	
The son loses his hand.	Exod. 21:15. The son is put to death.
PERSONAL INJURY	
The *lex talionis* (law of retaliation) is invoked among equals; fines are paid when a noble strikes a freeman or slave.	Exod. 21:20–27. The *lex talionis* is invoked among equals; freedom is granted to a slave permanently injured.
INJURY CAUSING MISCARRIAGE	
A fine is paid for the death of the fetus. If the woman dies, restitution is made in silver, but if she is a noblewoman the killer's daughter is put to death.	Exod. 21:22. A fine is paid. If physical injury occurs to the mother the *lex talionis* is invoked.
GORING BY AN OX	
No penalty unless the ox was known to be a gorer and then reparations are paid.	Exod. 21:28–32. If an ox known to be a gorer kills a man, the ox and its owner are killed. If a slave is gored the ox is killed and reparations paid.

for the setting in which they now appear is late and reflects the work of editing.

It is possible to surmise the probable sources of Hebrew law and to suggest that codification began during the period of the early monarchy, although it is impossible to determine which laws may have come from that time. The process appears to have involved the adoption of certain Canaanite civil and agricultural laws which probably reflected the effects of Egyptian control and the proximity of

Mesopotamian culture; the modification of Canaanite jurisprudence by tribal traditions (cf. Judg. 19–20); the role of king as interpreter and enforcer of law; and contributions from prophetic and priestly circles. Some form of national code must have developed, and there can be little doubt that it is preserved in part in the Bible.

The abundance of religious law designed to guide the professional in the various responsibilities of the priesthood, may have originated in guidance-giving oracles. The placing of all law within the framework of a God-given code reflects the conviction that the nation—including its coming-into-being, its organization and administration and the status of every individual within it—was, so to speak, under Yahweh.

The Divided Kingdom

14

The History of the Kingdoms

THE record of Solomon's greatness fails to indicate the seething bitterness and resentment that must have been developing among the people. Only when Rehoboam appeared for succession rites were the feelings expressed by those who bore with smoldering anger the heavy burdens of Solomon's despotism. The northern and southern peoples were kept from full union by geographical factors, by the northern people's basic distrust of the Davidic monarchy with its center in Jerusalem (a southern city despite its proximity to the north-south border), by resentment to Solomon's extravagant excesses and the resultant heavy taxation, and possibly even by different religious or theological outlooks indicated by the support of the schism by the prophet Ahijah (I Kings 11:29 and following verses). Judah appears to have accepted Rehoboam without question, but when the young prince went to Shechem to be anointed king and received the approbation of the people, he was confronted with a demand for a policy statement. The request reveals the severity of Solomon's rule:

Read II Kings 12

> Your father made our yoke heavy. Now therefore lighten the hard
>   service of your father and his heavy yoke and we will serve you.
>   (12:4)

Rehoboam turned to his advisors for counsel: the elder statesmen recommended compliance while the younger men advocated a "get-tough" policy. Rehoboam accepted the latter. His arrogant and harsh rejection provoked immediate response: withdrawal from the United Kingdom. The rebel cry was an old one (cf. II Sam. 20:1):

> What portion have we in David? We have no inheritance in the son
>   of Jesse. To your tents, O Israel! Look now to your own house
>   David. (12:16)

Jeroboam, the exiled taskmaster who had recently returned from Egypt, became the first king of Israel. Rehoboam ruled Judah. Gone forever was the United Kingdom; and in the eighth century Israel disappeared altogether from history.

INTERNATIONAL DEVELOPMENTS

As the southern kingdom reaffirmed its loyalty to the Davidic line by retaining Solomon's rash offspring as monarch and the northern

CHART XI. EVENTS TO THE FALL OF ISRAEL

Judaean Prophet	Judaean King	Date	Israelite King	Israelite Prophet	Events in Palestine	Events in Assyria	Events Elsewhere
Shemaiah	Rehoboam (922–915)	922	Jeroboam I (922–901)		Shishak invades		
	Abijam (915–913)	915					
	Asa (913–873)	913					
		901	Nadab (901–900)				
		900	Baasha (900–877)			Beginning of program of expansion under Ashurnasirpal (883–859)	
		877	Elah (877–876)				
		876	Zimri (876)	Jehu			
			Omri (876–869)				
	Jehoshaphat (873–849)	873					
		869	Ahab (869–850)	Elijah	Coalition against Assyria		
		850	Ahaziah (850–849)				Battle of Qarqar (853)
	Jehoram (849–842)	849	Jehoram (849–842)	Elisha			
	Ahaziah (842)	842	Jehu (842–815)		Jehu pays tribute to Assyria		
	Athaliah (842–837)						
	Joash (837–800)	837					
		815	Jehoahaz (815–801)				
		801	Jehoash (801–786)				
	Amaziah (800–783)	800					
		786	Jeroboam II (786–746)	Amos			
	Uzziah (788–742)	783			Uzziah pays tribute to Assyria		
		746	Zechariah (746–745)				

Prophets	Kings of Judah		Kings of Israel		Events	Assyria	World Events
Isaiah	Jotham (742–735)	745	Shallum (745) Menahem (745–738)		Menahem pays tribute to Tiglath Pileser III		Tiglath Pileser III defeats Syria and Damascus (732)
Micah	Ahaz (735–715)	742 738 737 735	Pekahiah (738–737) Pekah (737–732)		Syro-Ephraimitic war (734)		Philistia, Edom, Judah and Moab revolt
		731	Hoshea (731–721) (last King of Israel)	Hosea			
		721			Fall of Samaria to Shalmaneser V and Sargon II	Sargon is King of Assyria	
	Hezekiah (715–687)	715			Judah joins in revolt (714) Philistia and Ashdod besieged (711)		Marduk-apal-iddin siezes the throne of Babylon
						Sargon murdered (705) and Sennacherib is king	
						Sennacherib banishes Marduk-apal-iddin	XXV Egyptian Dynasty (Ethiopian) (716–663)
					Sennacherib invades Judah; Judah pays tribute (701)		

159

kingdom asserted independence, two great powers destined for significant roles in Palestinian affairs were preparing for expansion of empire. Egypt, which had been quiescent during the period of the United Kingdom, was conquered by a Libyan prince named Sheshonk —or Shishak as the Bible prefers to call him—and the twenty-second Egyptian dynasty was established. Five years after Solomon's death, Sheshonk's armies invaded Palestine. I Kings 14:25 records only the plundering of the Temple treasury, but II Chronicles 12:4 suggests wider desolation, a detail substantiated by Sheshonk's account found at Karnak which records the sacking of towns in southern Galilee, and by a fragment of what may have been an Egyptian victory stele bearing Sheshonk's name discovered at Megiddo. Fortunately for the Hebrew kingdoms, Sheshonk appears to have been satisfied with the booty from the single raid, for he made no effort to control Palestine. Toward the close of the eighth century, Egypt was conquered by an Ethiopian monarch, Pi-ankh, and in the seventh century, when the Assyrians embarked upon world conquest, Egypt was invaded, first by Esarhaddon in 671, and again by Ashurbanipal in 667.

At first, the gradual growth of Assyria did not directly affect Palestine. Tiglath Pileser I (1114–1076) pushed Assyrian control to the Mediterranean but not southward into Hebrew territory. In the ninth century, Ashurnasirpal II (883–859) developed the Assyrian war machine to a peak of strength and from this time onward Assyrian politics influenced Palestine. In 853, according to an inscription of Shalmaneser III (858–824), Ahab of Israel suffered defeat and paid tribute after he had joined a coalition of twelve Syrian kings to contest Assyrian expansion at Qarqar. Shalmaneser, after neglecting Syria for a few years, began a systematic plundering of the area. That Israel paid tribute is clear from the black obelisk of Shalmaneser III on which Jehu is portrayed prostrate before Shalmanesar, and a list of the booty paid to Assyria is given. One eighth century inscription records tribute taken from Menahem of Samaria by Tiglath Pileser III (747–727) (cf. II Kings 15:19), while another refers to payments made by "Azriau of Iuda," possibly Azariah or Uzziah of Judah, suggesting that both Hebrew kingdoms contributed to the growing wealth of Assyria. In 722, the son of Tiglath Pileser III, Shalmaneser V (726–722), attacked Israel but died before the final victory which was accomplished by his successor, Sargon II (721–705). According to his report, Sargon led away 27,290 inhabitants from Samaria to be enlisted in his army. Conquered peoples from other areas were moved into Israel so that revolt of the thoroughly mixed population became unlikely. The kingdom of Israel had come to an end and the northern Hebrew nation was part of the Assyrian kingdom. By payment of heavy taxes Judah avoided the fate of Israel, but Assyrian influence in Judaean affairs was strong.

During the period of the two Hebrew kingdoms, in addition to pressure from Egypt and Assyria, Israel had other border problems. When the northern kingdom separated from the south, the Philistines attempted to regain lost territories, the Aramaeans of Damascus created trouble on the northern frontier, and the powerful city-state of

KING ASHURNASIRPAL II OF ASSYRIA *and an attendant in a winged costume participate in a religious ritual. The low relief, carved in gypseous alabaster, is from the ancient Assyrian city of Calah (Nimrud) excavated by Austin Henry Layard from 1845 to 1848 and by M. E. L. Mallowan from 1949 to 1961. Ashurnasirpal's inscriptions boast of the ruthless treatment of captive peoples and of the terror inspired by Assyrian military tactics.*

Tyre, with whom Israel ultimately formed an alliance through marriage, proved to be a persistent menace. Judah, always open to Egypt on the southern boundary and now weakened by the loss of Israel, was threatened by Edom, Moab and Philistia.

Against this background of Near Eastern history the internal history of the Hebrew kingdoms must be studied. For this history we are dependent upon accounts in Kings and Chronicles and limited information coming from archaeological research. The Deuteronomic editors of Kings may have drawn upon official court records, but their work betrays theological and Judaean bias. Each monarch is judged on the basis of his adherence to the principles of southern Yahwism and his opposition to Ba'alism and other religions. Consequently no Israel-

161

ite king is commended and only two Judaeans, Hezekiah and Josiah, are fully approved, although six others receive modified approbation. When the editorial evaluation is removed, there remains an outline of successive rulers with brief comments on significant events of their reigns.

Writing in the fourth century, the Chroniclers utilized an edition of Kings similar to the one we possess but did not hesitate to supplement the narratives. Some additions appear to have historical validity; others reflect theological convictions. Historical data in Kings and Chronicles must be accepted cautiously, and most additional material in Chronicles remains *sub judice,* except where sustained by archaeological or other confirming evidence.

The outline below presents, in parallel columns, the history of Judah and Israel up to the time of the collapse of Israel (722/721). The dates in the center column are approximations and, because biblical chronology is not fixed, variations of two to five years may be assumed in some instances. Asterisks indicate a change of dynasty.

Judah		Israel
Read I Kings 12–14 Rehoboam, son of Solomon, having lost Israel, Ammon and Moab, was determined to regain these territories. Dissuaded by Shemaiah's prophetic warnings, he strengthened Judaean fortifications, but his efforts failed to prevent invasion by Sheshonk of Egypt. Judaean villages were destroyed, Jerusalem entered, and the Temple plundered. The raid must have affected Judaean military strength adversely, and the intermittent warfare with Israel attempting to fix the Israel-Judah border continued to drain the national resources.	922*	Jeroboam had won a kingdom without headquarters or government. His immediate task was the development of administrative patterns. Shechem became the capital and was fortified. To offset the attraction of the Jerusalem temple, royal sanctuaries were dedicated in the border cities of Dan and Bethel. Within these shrines golden calves, symbols of Yahweh, or perhaps pedestals upon which the invisible deity stood, were placed, and festal observances paralleling those of Jerusalem were instituted. Chapters 13–14 of I Kings which condemn Jeroboam are largely
Read I Kings 15 Abijah or Abijam, Rehoboam's son and successor, may have pushed Judaean borders as far north as Bethel (II Chron. 13), but he was unable to retain control of this important Israelite city.	915	homiletic. Chapter 13, a legend about an unknown prophet, comes from the post-Josiah period (cf. 13:2). The story of the illness of Jeroboam's son may have an historical core (I Kings 14:1–6, 12, 17) that was expanded
Asa, the next king, is commended by the editors for his efforts to subdue the fertility cults. During his reign, border warfare with Israel continued.	913	by later writers. What result the Sheshonk invasion had is not known, but the economy must have suffered.

Judah

When Baasha began to build Ramah to sever Judah's northern trade route, Asa bribed Ben Hadad of Syria to move the Syrian armies to Israel's northern frontier. Baasha's men withdrew from Ramah and Asa stole the building materials and constructed fortresses at Mizpah (possibly Tell en-Nasbeh) **and** Gibeah just north of Jerusalem. The Chroniclers record a battle between Judah and the Cushites or Ethiopians (II Chron. 14:9 ff.) but this has not been verified.

Israel

901 **Nadab,** Jeroboam's son who reigned less than two years, was murdered with all members of Jeroboam's family
900* by **Baasha** of the house of Issachar. Baasha fought with the Philistines, moved the capital from Shechem to Tirzah and attempted to curtail Judah's trade by building a fort at Ramah. Asa's strategy (bribing the Syrians to attack on the north) compelled Baasha to abandon his building project and move his men to deal with
877 the Syrians. **Elah,** Baasha's son and successor, and all members of Baasha's family were
876* murdered by **Zimri,** a chariot commander who had the support of the prophet Jehu. Seven days later Israelite soldiers battling the Philistines elected their field commander

**Read
I Kings 16**

AN ARTIST'S RECONSTRUCTION OF TELL EN-NASBEH. *Tell en-Nasbeh, excavated between 1926 and 1935 by Dr. William F. Badè of the Pacific School of Religion, is believed to be the site of ancient Mizpah, the city fortified by King Asa of Judah. The massive walls were thirteen to twenty feet thick and probably forty feet high. The single, strongly fortified gate had a paved, drained forecourt with benches where the elders of the city might have sat to render judgment (cf. Amos 5:15; Ruth 4:11; Prov. 31:23).*

Judah		Israel
	876*	**Omri** to the kingship. Omri swiftly moved the army to Tirzah, and Zimri, doomed without military support, committed suicide by firing the royal citadel. Another contender for the throne, a certain Tibni, was eliminated. Omri purchased the hill of Samaria and constructed a new capital city. Although Omri's dynasty is dismissed in a few words by the Deuteronomic editors, perhaps because he was not a Hebrew, his family ruled for three generations and long after the dynasty had ceased Assyrian annalists referred to Israel as "the house of Omri." The Moabite Stone records that Omri expanded Israel's borders to include northern Moab.
It was not until **Jehoshaphat,** Asa's son, became king that peace was established between the two Hebrew kingdoms and cooperative attacks on mutual enemies were undertaken. Jehoshaphat's son, Jehoram, married Athaliah, daughter of Ahab of Israel (II Kings 8:26), thus linking the Divided Kingdom through royal marriage. The Judaeans joined the Israelites in the Syrian-Israelite war (I Kings 22:2f.) and later,	873	
	869	Omri's son **Ahab,** who married

A MODEL OF A SECTION OF MEGIDDO IN THE TIME OF AHAB. *The low structures on the right, just inside the city wall, are stables capable of housing 450 horses. The open area in front of the stables represents an exercise or parade ground. The large pit to the right and outside of the stable area marks the entrance to an underground passage leading to a spring, the water supply for the city. In the background, the impressive structure with the tower is a model of the governor's palace with a private walled court, and the size and magnificence of this building testifies to the affluence of Ahab's day. The circular structure outside of the courtyard is a storage pit for grain. The outline of walls and buildings in the foreground represents structures from the older Canaanite layers of habitation that archaeologists found beneath the ninth century levels.*

Judah	Israel
when the Moabites rebelled, southern soldiers assisted Israel (II Kings 3:7 ff.) .	Jezebel, a Tyrian princess, receives much more attention for Jezebel brought to Israel the worship of the Tyrian Ba'al, Melkart. Under royal sponsorship the cult flourished, coming into dramatic conflict with Yahwism championed by the prophetic school of Elijah. War flared between Israel and Syria and, after the defeat of Ben Hadad, Ahab entered into trade agreements with his former enemies and participated in a coalition with Syria and other small nations to halt the westward development of Assyria. According to the records of Shalmaneser V, Ahab contributed 2,000 chariots and 10,000 soldiers. The Assyrians claimed victory at Qarqar. Because the Israelite town of Ramoth-gilead had not been included in the peace settlement of the Syrian-Israelite war, Ahab began a

**Read
I Kings 20**

A MANGER FROM THE MEGIDDO STABLES. *The holes in the upright pillars were for tethering the horses.*

Read I Kings 22	Judah		Israel
			new anti-Syrian campaign with the assistance of Jehoshaphat of Judah. Ahab died in battle
Read II Kings 1		850	and **Ahaziah**, his son, became king. Injuries suffered in a fall rendered the king powerless to control a revolt by the Moabites; after his death, his
Read II Kings 3, 8	Jehoshaphat was succeeded by his son **Jehoram**, son-in-law of Ahab, and during his reign Edom broke free of Judaean control (II Kings 8:20–22).	849 849	brother, **Jehoram**, continued the war with Moab. Aided by Jehoshaphat of Judah and the Edomites, Jehoram was at first victorious, but Mesha of Moab turned the tide of battle and Moab became an independent kingdom (cf. II Kings 3 and The Moabite Stone). Elijah, the prophet, died during this period and Elisha, his disciple, became "father" or "chief" of the pro-
Read II Kings 9–10 Read II Kings 11	When Jehoram's son **Ahaziah**, king of Judah, was killed by Jehu of Israel, his mother **Athaliah** ascended the throne to become the first and only Hebrew woman to reign. Eligible heirs, with the exception of Joash or Jehoash, the infant son of Ahaziah, were murdered. Joash was concealed in the temple by his aunt, the wife of the chief priest (II Chron. 22:11). Athaliah was not tolerated for long. She was an usurper, standing outside of the Davidic line, and she encouraged Baalism.	842 *842 842*	phetic guild. While Jehoram and Ahaziah of Judah were engaged in battle with the Syrians, Elisha anointed **Jehu** king of Israel, thus engendering civil war. Ahaziah of Judah and Jehoram of Israel were killed at Jezreel, and a reign of terror began in which the family of Ahab, including Jezebel, was eliminated and the followers of Ba'al persecuted. Weakened by internal intrigue, Israel was helpless before the power of the Aramaean Kingdom of Hazael, and large amounts of territory were lost in the Transjordan area.
Read II Kings 12–13	**Joash** was seven years old when he was crowned king in a secret ceremony and, in the uprising that followed, Athaliah was murdered. As Jehu persecuted Baal worshippers in Israel, Joash attacked them in Judah. Joash was murdered by his servants and his son, **Amaziah**,	*837 815 801	**Jehoahaz**, son of Jehu, inherited a nation reduced to impotency by the Aramaeans. **Jehoash**, his son and successor, a more successful warrior, was able to recapture some of the
Read II Kings 14	ascended the throne. Territory lost to Edom was repossessed and the Edomite mountain fortress of Sela (Petra) was	800	lost land, for King Adadnirari III of Assyria broke the power of Damascus in 800. Jehoash attacked Judah, invaded

166

Judah	Israel
invaded. In war with Israel Amaziah was defeated and Jehoash's army looted the holy temple. Like his father before him, Amaziah died at the hands of his servants. **Azariah** or **Uzziah,** son of Amaziah, **783** fought the Edomites when he came to the throne and Judah gained control of the important Red Sea port of Elath (Ezion-geber). Unfortunately, Azariah	Jerusalem and looted the temple. During this period Elisha, who appears to have been a friend of the king, died (II Kings 13:14ff.). **786** **Jeroboam II,** son of Jehoash, was perhaps the most successful warrior king since David, for under his rule Israel gained mastery over Syria and Moab to control an area approximating that embraced at the time of the

Read
II Kings
15

I (am) Mesha, son of Chemosh [. . .], king of Moab, the Dibonite—my father (had) reigned over Moab thirty years, and I reigned after my father,—(who) made this high place for Chemosh in Qarhoh [. . .] because he saved me from all the kings and caused me to triumph over all my adversaries. As for Omri, (5) king of Israel, he humbled Moab many years (lit., days), for Chemosh was angry at his land. And his son followed him and he also said, "I will humble Moab." In my time he spoke (thus), but I have triumphed over him and over his house, while Israel hath perished for ever! (Now) Omri had occupied the land of Medeba, and (Israel) had dwelt there in his time and half the time of his son (Ahab), forty years; but Chemosh dwelt there in my time.

And I built Baal-meon, making a reservoir in it, and I built (10) Qaryaten. Now the men of Gad had always dwelt in the land of Ataroth, and the king of Israel had built Ataroth for them; but I fought against the town and took it and slew all the people of the town as satiation (intoxication) for Chemosh and Moab. And I brought back from there Arel (or Oriel), its chieftain, dragging him before Chemosh in Kerioth, and I settled there men of Sharon and men of Maharith. And Chemosh said to me, "Go, take Nebo from Israel!" (15) So I went by night and fought against it from the break of dawn until noon, taking it and slaying all, seven thousand men, boys, women, girls and maid-servants, for I had devoted them to destruction for (the god) Ashtar-Chemosh. And I took from there the [. . .] of Yahweh, dragging them before Chemosh. And the king of Israel had built Jahaz, and he dwelt there while he was fighting against me, but Chemosh drove him out before me. And (20) I took from Moab two hundred men, all first class (warriors), and set them against Jahaz and took it in order to attach it to (the district of) Dibon.

THE MOABITE STONE, *which dates from the ninth century* B.C., *was discovered at the site of ancient Dibon in 1868 by the Rev. F. A. Klein, a German missionary. Fortunately a squeeze or impression was made by pressing soft, moist, paper-pulp tightly against the inscription and permitting it to dry before removal, thus giving a precise copy, for shortly afterward the stone was smashed by bedouin who hoped to get a better price by disposing of the pieces individually. Some parts were lost but the remainder were acquired for the Louvre by Charles Clermont-Ganneau, the French orientalist. With the aid of the squeeze, it was possible to restore the original text.*

The stone is black basalt and is three feet ten inches high, two feet wide, and fourteen inches thick. There are thirty-four lines of script of a dialect closely resembling Hebrew. The account, written in the first person singular, supplements the biblical history of Israel from the time of Omri to Ahaziah. Like the Hebrews the Moabites attributed military success or failure to their god. The first twenty lines are reproduced above.

Judah	Israel
contracted leprosy (attributed by the Chroniclers to a cultic violation) and was compelled to live in isolation, and his son Jotham governed as regent (cf. II Kings 15:1–7; II Chron. 26). In the year that Azariah died the prophet Isaiah began his work.	Davidic empire (minus, of course, Judah, Edom and Philistia). Fortunately, Jeroboam was not troubled by the Assyrians and his reign, marked by prosperity and wealth, provides a social background against which some of the prophetic

JEHU PAYS TRIBUTE. *In 1846 during the excavation of the ancient city of Calah, Austin Henry Layard discovered a four-sided pillar or obelisk of black limestone, six and one half feet high. Five panels of bas reliefs extended around the pillar with an accompanying cuneiform description of the reliefs. The pillar commemorated the achievements of Shalmaneser III during the thirty-five years of his reign. In the top panels pictured above, Jehu or his representative is pictured kneeling before Shalmaneser, and the second panel at the top shows a group of Israelites bearing tribute. Some features of Israelite dress can be discerned: they wore soft caps, sleeveless fringed tunics, and had rounded beards. The taller, armed figures are Assyrians. The inscription pertaining to Jehu reads: "The tribute of Jehu, son of Omri: I received silver, gold, a golden bowl, a golden vase, golden goblets, golden pitchers, tin, a scepter for the king, and staves." Identifying Jehu as a "son of Omri" must be understood as "successor to Omri" and also as a sign of the importance of Omri's reign. The lower panels represent tribute from other parts of the Assyrian empire.*

Judah		Israel	THE HISTORY OF THE KINGDOMS

utterances of Amos and Hosea must be understood.

746 **Zechariah,** son of Jeroboam, reigned less than one year and

745* was murdered by **Shallum,** who was promptly killed by

745* **Menahem.** To prevent conquest by Assyria, Menahem voluntarily submitted to Tiglath Pileser III (Pul) and paid heavy tribute, a detail confirmed in an Assyrian text.

Jotham was regent for eight years before gaining the crown. Little is known of his reign except that the Temple was repaired (II Kings 15:33ff.) and, according to the Chronicler, war was waged with Ammon (II Chron. 27:5ff.) . **Ahaz,** son of Jotham, refused to join an anti-Assyria coalition and, in the so-called Syro-Ephraimitic war, Judah was attacked by King Rezin of Syria and and King Pekah of Israel. About the same time Edomites and

742

735

738 Shortly after **Pekahiah,** son of Menahem, became king, he was murdered by his captain,

737* **Pekah.** At this time participation in a political alliance against Assyria cost Israel the loss of towns in northern Galilee and Gilead. Pekah's murderer and successor **Hoshea** seized the moment of

732* the death of Tiglath Pileser III and the ascension of Shalmaneser V to the Assyrian throne as the time to

Read II Kings 16–17

ANCIENT SELA. *The massive stone outcropping rising 950 feet above the floor of the valley at Petra and known today as Umm el-Biyerah ("mother of cisterns") because of the numerous cisterns carved in its surface, is believed to be the site of ancient Sela. The approach to the summit is by a narrow trail which winds up the steep sides to the acropolis. If this is the site of Sela, the Hebrew conquest of the unapproachable site was an amazing feat. Here Amaziah defeated the Edomites (II Kings 14:7), and if the account in II Chron. 25:11 ff. is accurate, it is here that 10,000 Edomites died after being hurled from "the top of the rock."*

Judah

Philistines united against Judah (II Chron. 28:1–21). The pressure was too much and Ahaz called on Tiglath Pileser for help. Judah paid huge indemnities for this aid and Assyrian deities were introduced into the temple of Yahweh. During this period, Edom recaptured the seaport of Elath. Ahaz' international policies were vigorously opposed by the prophet Isaiah, but there can be little doubt that Ahaz' refusal to participate in the anti-Assyria pact and his voluntary surrender of sovereignty saved Judah from Israel's fate (II Kings 16:7ff.). Judah became a vassal to Assyria, the mightiest empire the Near Eastern world had known.

Israel

throw off the Assyrian yoke. Counting on help from Egypt, Hoshea refused to pay tribute to Assyria. Shalmaneser attacked Samaria but died while the siege was still in process, leaving the subjugation of Israel to his successor, Sargon II (722).

721 When Samaria fell in 721 and all Israel capitulated, great numbers of the people (according to Sargon, 27,290) were deported to the Assyrian province of Guzanu and to the region south of Lake Urmia. From other parts of the far-flung Assyrian empire, emigrants were brought to Israel. Israel's history as an independent nation had terminated. Sargon divided the territory into small provinces. Revolts were abortive. Among those Israelites who remained in the land, the worship of Yahweh continued, but homage was paid to the gods of Assyria.

BROADLY speaking, E can be said to include the literature which remains in the Pentateuch after P and D (easily identified) and J sources are removed, although in numerous passages it is difficult to distinguish between J and E.[1] Distinctiveness of grammar, style and vocabulary, not always apparent in English translations, provide the basis for the identification of E material. Some of the more obvious features include labeling the sacred mountain Horeb rather than Sinai as in J, the identification of pre-Hebrew inhabitants of Palestine as Amorites, not Canaanites as in J, and naming Moses' father-in-law Jethro rather than Reuel. As we noted, E does not use the name "Yahweh" for the deity until it is revealed on Mount Horeb (Exod. 3:15).

Because of E's fragmentary nature, it is impossible to make more than the most general comments about the writer's moral and theological concerns. At times E appears to exhibit greater concern than J with the moral implications of traditions, so that when Abraham pretends that Sarah is his sister, E points out that she was, in reality, a half-sister (Gen. 20).[2] E makes it clear that Sarah did not cohabit with Abimelech. On the other hand, E seems untroubled by Aaron's lie. (When challenged by Moses in the golden calf episode, Aaron implied that the molten metal just happened to flow into the calf pattern, whereas the E editor has stipulated that Aaron fashioned the statue; cf. Exod. 32:4 and 24.) Some cruder anthropomorphisms of J are avoided in E and God's will is revealed through dreams (Gen. 15:1; 20:3; 28:12) or messengers (Gen. 21:17; 22:11), but E does not hesitate to state that God wrote laws with his own finger (Exod. 31:18b). E's interest in ritual has led to the suggestion that perhaps the writer was a priest,[3] for he mentions the prohibition against eating the ischial sinew (Gen. 32:32), and refers to oil libations poured out on masseboth (standing pillars) (Gen. 28:18; 35:14) and to tithing

[1] It has been argued that E does not represent a separate source but at best the results of re-editing J. Cf. P. Volz and W. Rudolph, *Der Elohist als Erzähler. Ein Irrweg der Pentateuchkritik?*, Beiheft, Zeitschrift für die Alttestamentliche Wissenschaft *(BZAW)* LXIII, Giessen, 1933; and W. Rudolph, *Der 'Elohist' von Exodus bis Josua, BZAW*, LXVIII, Berlin, 1938.

[2] Marriage with half-sisters was later prohibited (cf. Lev. 18:9, 11; 20:17 and II Sam. 13:13).

[3] R. H. Pfeiffer, *Introduction to the Old Testament*, p. 173.

(Gen. 28:22). At the same time a reforming interest is also apparent. For example, the story of Abraham's near-sacrifice of his son may be a sermonic parable directed against child sacrifice (Gen. 22). The condemnation of the golden calf, a cult symbol in the royal shrines at Bethel and Dan, constitutes a very bold protest (Exod. 32).[4]

It is generally agreed, despite slender evidence, that E is a product of the northern kingdom.[5] There is more information about Jacob and Joseph, more emphasis on northern shrines of Bethel and Shechem, and less data pertaining to Abraham and Hebron than in J. The use of the Israelite designation of Horeb as the sacred mountain, which appears also in the Elijah cycle (I Kings 19:8), also points to a northern provenance for E.

E is often given a date in the eighth century B.C., usually during the reign of Jeroboam II (c. 786–746), a prosperous time reflected in the lack of mention of struggle and difficulty in E, or in the ninth century in the time of Jehu (842–815) when pro-Yahwist parties were in control. On the other hand, there is no reason why the writing could not have been produced in the tenth century during the reign of Jeroboam I, immediately following the separation of the two kingdoms. If writings like J and E were a product of the national cult and were used in ritual, it would seem natural that when the royal shrines were erected at Bethel and Dan, E was compiled from the same or similar sources as J. The literature, as we are able to extract it from the Torah, is probably best understood as a product of the developing cult or as the result of a process of progressive interpretation by which the relationship of the northern kingdom to Yahweh continued to be expressed and expanded.

It has been argued that E lacks J's dramatic simplicity of style and this may be so, but one cannot avoid noting the tense, moving portrayal of the Abraham-Isaac episode of Gen. 22, and the excellent characterizations in the Joseph cycle that reflect the work of a master raconteur. E's objective is that of J: the proclamation of Yahweh's purposes for his people, promised in the past, expressed through salvation history, being realized in the present and giving promise for the future.

How E came to be combined with J can only be conjectured. When Israel collapsed before Assyria in the eighth century, it is possible that priests from Bethel fled across the border, seeking sanctuary in Jerusalem and bringing with them sacred traditions of their shrine and nation. Why the writings were merged cannot be known. It can only be said that in the editing preference appears to have been given to J materials. No E creation story has survived, although it is possible that the use of the term "Elohim," together with "Yahweh," in Gen. 2:4b–3:24 signifies a fusion of J and E primeval myths.[6]

---

4 *Ibid.*, p. 170, Pfeiffer believed the golden calf episode to be post-Exilic.

5 S. Mowinckel has argued that E belongs to Judah. Cf. "Der Ursprung der Bil' amsage," *Zeitschrift für die Alttestamentliche Wissenschaft*, XLVIII (1930), 233 ff.

6 Cf. Weiser, *op. cit.*, p. 103.

The Abraham Cycle

*Gen. 15:1–3, 5 f., 11, 12a, 13–14, 16.	Often ascribed to E, but note the name "Yahweh" which was not yet revealed. The material appears to be late, reflecting D influence.
Gen. 20:1–17.	Abraham and Sarah in Gerar.
Gen. 21:8–21.	The Hagar story.
Gen. 21:22–32, 34.	Abraham and Abimelech at Beer-sheba.
Gen. 22:1–13, 19.	Abraham and child sacrifice.

The Jacob Cycle

Gen. 28:11–12, 17–18, 19b–21a, 22.	Jacob's dream.
Gen. 30:1–8.	Jacob and Laban (a conflation of J and E).
Gen. 30:26, 28; 31:2, 4–17, 19–20, 21b–43, 45, 46b, 49–50, 53b–55.	Jacob leaves Laban.
Gen. 32:1–2.	Jacob at Mahanaim.
Gen. 32:13–21.	Jacob and Esau.
Gen. 32:23–32.	Jacob wrestles with God and Jacob becomes Israel.
Gen. 33:18–20.	Jacob at Shechem.
Gen. 35:1–8.	Jacob at Bethel.
Gen. 35:16–20.	Birth of Benjamin and death of Rachel.

The Joseph Cycle

Gen. 30:22–24.	The birth of Joseph (a conflation of J and E).
Gen. 37:5, 9–11, 19–20, 22, 24, 28a, 29–30, 36.	Joseph is sold into slavery.
Gen. 40:1–23.	Joseph interprets dreams.
Gen. 41:1–45, 47–57.	Joseph and Pharoah.
Gen. 42.	Joseph and his brothers. (A conflation of J and E. E material may include 42:1, 3–4, 8–25, 29–37.)
Gen. 45:5–8, 15–18, 20, 25–27; 46:1–5.	Jacob comes to Joseph.
Gen. 48:1–2a, 7–9a, 10b–12, 15–16, 20–22.	Jacob's blessing.
Gen. 50:15–26.	Deaths of Jacob and Joseph.

The Moses Cycle

Exod. 1:15–2:10.	Moses' infancy stories.
Exod. 3:1, 4b, 6, 9–15, 19–22.	Moses encounters Yahweh.
Exod. 4:17–18.	Moses leaves Jethro.
Exod. 4:20b–21.	A warning about Pharaoh.
Exod. 4:27–28.	Moses and Aaron.
Exod. 5:1–2, 4.	Moses and Aaron before Pharaoh.

* Asterisks mark passages usually assigned to E but which, according to personal analysis, may not be E.

Exod. 7:15b, 17b, 20b; 9:22–23a, 25a, 35a; 10:12; 13a, 14a, 20–23, 27; 11:1–3.	E materials pertaining to the plagues.
Exod. 12:31–42a; 13:17–19; 14:15– 19a, 21–23, 26– 27a, 28–29.	The Exodus.
Exod. 15:20 f.	Miriam's song (vss. 1–18 are a separate expansion).
Exod. 16–18.	Basically a conflation of J and E, so combined that any separation is conjectural. (Possible E material = 17:3–6, 8–16, 18:1–27.)
Exod. 19.	May contain J–E material at 19:1–3a, 18. The remainder has been overwritten by a redactor.
Exod. 20:1–23:19.	Whether or not E contains legal material has been debated. Many scholars place these two law codes in E.
Exod. 20:1–20.	The ethical decalogue.
Exod. 20:22–23:19.	The Covenant Code (based on an old Canaanite civil code). 23:20–33 is by Rʲᵉ or Rᵈ.
Exod. 24:12–14, 18b; 31:18b.	Moses receives stone tablets of law from God.
Exod. 32:1–8, 15–24, 35.	The Golden Calf.
Exod. 33:4–6.	Discarding of ornaments.
Exod. 33:7–11.	The Tent of Meeting.
Num. 11:1–3.	Complaints at Taberah.
Num. 11:16–17.	The seventy elders.
Num. 11:24–30.	Eldad and Medad.
Num. 12:1–15.	Rebellion of Aaron and Miriam.
Num. 13–14.	Sending out spies. The E material is closely interwoven with J and P and the following list of E passages is conjectural: 13:17b–20, 22–24, 26b, 28, 30–32; 14:1, 3–4, 11–25, 31–32, 39–45.
Num. 16:1b, 2a, 12–15, 25–26, 27b–34.	Dathan and Abiram rebel (E mixed with J and re-edited).
Num. 20:1b.	Death of Miriam.
Num. 20:4–13.	Water problems.
Num. 20:14–21.	Problems with Edomites (contains both J and E).
Num. 21:4–9.	The brazen serpent (late addition to J?).
Num. 21:21–25.	The battle with Sihon of the Amorites.
Num. 21:33–35.	The battle with Og of Bashan.
Num. 22:3b–4, 8–16, 19–21, 35b–41; 23:1–30; 24:1–2, 10–14, 20–25.	Oracles of Balaam (interwoven with J).
Num. 25:1–5.	Worship at Ba'al Peor (some J?).
Num. 32:1–5, 16–17, 20–27, 34–41.	Reuben and Gad settle in Transjordan.

The E tradition, insofar as it can be isolated, commences with a number of variations of the J tradition. The story of Sarah in the court of Abimelech displays E's striking sensitivity to Sarah's situation. By divine intervention, both Sarah and Abimelech are protected from guilt and sin, thus shielding the woman who was to be mother of the heir of the divine promise from any possible taint. E does not err anachronistically, as does J in Gen. 26, by linking Abimelech of Gerar to the Philistines. A different reason and setting is provided for the expulsion of Hagar (cf. J in Gen. 16), and Sarah's envy and personal enmity is replaced by a mother's jealous desire to protect her son's inheritance. Abraham's participation in the expulsion is due to the revelation that this was part of God's plan for the future. Ishmael's salvation and future is, according to E, the result of divine mercy and intervention.

Read the Abraham Cycle

The near-sacrifice of Isaac is the most moving story in E's Abrahamic cycle. The concept of a God who would demand so barbaric and traumatic an ordeal for both father and son can only be characterized as sub-human, unless the author, who has in other Abrahamic stories revealed sensitivity to the human predicament, had some purpose that would justify the harshness of the characterization. Such a purpose becomes clear when the story is recognized as a parable designed to teach that Israel's god did not want or demand child sacrifice, but, on the contrary, required a substitution.

Human sacrifice has been noted earlier in discussion of the *herem* and the Jephthah story in Judges. It is clear that child sacrifice was practiced in Judah (II Kings 16:3; 21:6; 23:10; Jer. 19:5) and in Moab (II Kings 3:27) and elsewhere (II Kings 17:31). Regulations governing firstfruit rituals in which, by offering a part, the ownership of the whole by the deity was recognized, required that the firstborn child be sacrificed. Exod. 22:29, part of the so-called "Covenant Code," states that the firstborn child be "given" to the deity just as the firstborn animal was given. Subsequent legislation contained a redemption clause providing for the replacement of the child by an animal (Exod. 13:12–15). It is possible that the E story, in which Abraham, the father of the people, dramatized the deity's demand for the substitutionary practice, stood between Exod. 22:29 and the later legislation as one of the factors bringing about cultic reform and the abandonment of the human sacrifice. The primacy of this interpretation has been challenged by those who believe that the story signifies exactly what it portrays—a test of Abraham's faith and the recognition that Israel's existence was due to the mercy of God, with the anti-human sacrifice element being secondary.[7]

The Jacob cycle begins with the dream of a stairway between heaven and earth, reflecting the cosmology of the era and calling to

Read the Jacob Cycle

---

[7] G. von Rad, *Genesis*, pp. 239 ff.

SYNAGOGUE FLOOR AT BETH ALPHA. *The mosiac floor of the sixth century* A.D. *synagogue found at Beth Alpha depicts an artist's concept of the near-sacrifice of Isaac by Abraham. The patriarch stands at the right with the sacrificial knife in his right hand, and with the left hand holds Isaac close to the altar with its leaping flames. Isaac's name appears to the left of the boy's head, and Abraham's name is to the left of his head. At the far left, two servants stand with the ass. Above Abraham's head, the hand of God is seen breaking through the sky-line and the accompanying Hebrew words read "lay not," the initial words of the deity's command to halt the sacrifice. Below the hand is a ram tied to a tree and the Hebrew words here are "Here is a ram."*

mind the ziggurats of Mesopotamia with the stairways or ramps uniting the topmost levels with earth and providing a means for divine-human encounter. Some additions to the J cycle suggest that E represents little more than a variant tradition. Other portions are more significant. Jacob's contest with God and the subsequent change of name (Gen. 32:23–32) is most significant, for a name change signifies change in destiny and status. Jacob's refusal to release the deity until a blessing was given is reminiscent of folk tales in which a deity or other non-human power was held until some gift was given.[8] It has been suggested that the deity represents the god of the land to be possessed (El Shaddai) and that the story symbolizes divine sanction for the Jacob tribe to wrest the land from its earlier inhabitants, the Canaanites.[9] It is significant that when Jacob arrives at Shechem he raises an altar to "El, the God of Israel" (33:18–20) and a second altar at Bethel (35:1–8).

Read the Joseph Cycle

The Joseph story presents slight variants to J. Joseph is rescued from a pit where he was placed by his hostile brothers and is taken to Egypt

[8] *Ibid.* p. 316.

[9] G. A. Danell, *Studies in the Name Israel in the Old Testament* (Upsala: Appelbergs Boktryckeriaktiebolag, 1946), p. 18.

and sold there by Midianites, not sold by his brothers to Ishmaelites as in J. Divine protection and guidance enabled Joseph to rise from the status of a prisoner to that of Vizier in the royal court. Ultimately, all the Jacob tribes came to Egypt to enjoy the privileges afforded by Joseph's office.

E's Moses tradition parallels J's with some significant additions. E's reasons for the persecution of the Hebrews and the story of the miraculous preservation of the child destined to be savior of the people set the stage for the Exodus. According to E, the name "Yahweh" was unknown to the Hebrews prior to the revelation to Moses and this suggests that the cult of Yahweh which united the northern tribes was a relatively late development.[10] E introduced the "rod of God" by which miracles were wrought, assigned Aaron a more significant role as wonder-worker and heightened the account of the plagues.

Read the Moses Cycle

The relationship of the Decalogue to the traditions of the sacred mountain is, as Martin Noth has pointed out, at best a tenuous one,[11] and it cannot be determined for certain whether the commandments should be assigned to E or to some separate cultic source. In their present form, some laws reflect settled culture (see Exod. 20:17) but do not provide a basis to justify questioning the antiquity of all, despite the impossibility of giving a date to any. The laws constitute a minimum expression of cultic and social responsibilities of Yahwism.

The Covenant Code or "book of the Covenant," as the section is sometimes called, appears to be a self-contained legal collection inserted into the Mosaic tradition. As noted previously, the forms and contents are much like law codes found elsewhere in the Near East. The code could just as easily be ascribed to J as to E and probably represents Hebrew borrowing of established Canaanite law with Hebrew legal additions.[12]

The condemnation of the cult of the golden calf, placed in Moses' mouth, is perhaps the most startling E tradition,[13] for the cult was under royal aegis. The story of the brazen serpent preserved by E is an aetiological cult legend explaining the seraph-serpent symbol in Hebrew worship (see II Kings 18:4).

---

[10] M. Noth, *Exodus,* The Old Testament Library, J. S. Bowden (trans.) (Philadelphia: The Westminster Press, 1962), p. 43.

[11] *Ibid.,* p. 160.

[12] *Ibid.,* pp. 109–194 for detailed study.

[13] Noth assigns the tradition to J. *Ibid.,* p. 243 f.

16
Prophecy and the Earliest Prophets

DURING the eighth century, utterances of a class of men known as "prophets" were recorded in Israel and Judah. The Hebrew prophetic movement appears to have begun during the early years of the occupancy of Canaan and may owe something to the Canaanites and other people, among whom "inspired" persons engaged in activities similar to those recorded of the Hebrew prophets.[1] From Mari, an ancient Babylonian caravan city, has come the account of a "man of (the god) Dagon" who, when seized by the deity, delivered oracles to the king. His statements were authenticated with the claim "the god Dagon sent me." Other Mesopotamian texts refer to *baru* (priests)[2] studying such omens as the configurations in animal entrails, patterns in bird flights, or designs created by oil on water to secure messages.[3] An eleventh century papyrus from Egypt relates the adventures of Wen-Amon, an Egyptian official sent to the Phoenician port-city of Byblos. During his stay, a boy from the town of Dor was possessed by the god, but no oracles were uttered. The account implies that some form of cataleptic seizure was involved.[4] Frenzied actions on the part of the prophets of Ba'al and Asherah are reported in the Bible (I Kings 18:19; Jer. 2:1; 23:3).

THE NATURE OF PROPHECY

Divine possession is recorded in the Bible: Gideon is said to have been "clothed" with God's spirit (Judg. 6:34); Yahweh's spirit came suddenly upon Saul, transforming him (I Sam. 10:6 ff.) and provoking great fury in him (I Sam. 11:6); ecstatic frenzy is also recorded of Saul (I Sam. 19:18–24), but whether or not Saul's actions can be considered

---

[1] Martin Noth, "History and the Word of God in the Old Testament," *Bulletin of the John Rylands Library*, XXXII (1949–50), 194 ff.

[2] The word *baru* signifies "to see" and refers to a *seer* who reveals information not "seeable" by ordinary men. He obtained visions by employing divinatory techniques. (Cf. Ezek. 21:21 where the Babylonian monarch uses similar methods.)

[3] Cf. J. Lindblom, *Prophecy in Ancient Israel* (Oxford: Basil Blackwell, 1962), pp. 85 ff.; A. Johnson, *The Cultic Prophet in Ancient Israel* (Cardiff: University of Wales Press, 1944), p. 12.

[4] *ANET*, pp. 258.

178

typical of the prophets is debatable. On the other hand, apparently some prophetic behavior was so extreme that a prophet could be classified as a madman (cf. II Kings 9:11; Jer. 29:26).

It is not impossible that Hebrew tribes had their own "inspired" seers before they came into Canaan. Arab tribal religion uses such persons, who appear to be counterparts to those found in pre-Islamic ancient Near Eastern and biblical sources. Seers or *kahins* give divinations obtained through trances, dreams, and ecstatic experiences and at times the oracles are spoken in rhythmic prose. Dervishes, experiencing religious ecstasy induced by convulsive dancing or drugs or music or special exercises or some combination of these, are able to interpret dreams, disclose the future, and "see" events occurring in distant places.[5] Despite the fact that the evidence is of recent date and that persons among whom the studies have been made are adherents of Islam which began in the seventh century A.D., the actions described in ancient Near Eastern sources and in the Old Testament are so nearly parallel[6] that it is not unreasonable to suggest that these groups have retained and kept alive very ancient patterns. On this basis, it might be said that Hebrew tribes on entering Canaan might have included those who obtained oracles and practiced divination and clairvoyance and that Hebrew prophecy could best be understood as indigenous rather than acquired or adopted. That the prophetic movement underwent change and development will be clear from the evidence to be presented.

Three biblical terms designate a prophet: *ro'eh, hozeh* and *nabi.* The earliest is *ro'eh* or "seer." Samuel is called a *ro'eh* (I Sam. 9:9), and an editorial note explains that the *ro'eh* was later called a "prophet," or *nabi.* Samuel's role in this particular account is that of a clairvoyant, but Samuel performed also as a priest and participated in Hebrew politics. The term *ro'eh* is used of Zadok, a priest in David's time (II Sam. 15:27), and it is possible that some priests were clairvoyant. The word *ro'eh* contains no hint of ecstatic behavior but suggests that divine disclosure came through some form of trance. If as some have suggested, signs and omens were employed, then the *ro'eh* is best understood as a counterpart of the Babylonian *baru.*

Hozeh, which also means "seer," is derived from the root *hazah,* "to see." In II Sam. 24:11 we are told that the prophet Gad, who is called David's *hozeh,* obtained messages from Yahweh but no hint is given about how the message came. In II Kings 17:13 the term *hozeh* is used with "prophet" to designate those by whom Yahweh had warned his people. The prophet Amos is called a *hozeh,* perhaps in derision (Amos 7:12). Isa. 29:10 refers to covering seers' heads so they could

---

[5] J. Pedersen, "The Role Played by Inspired Persons Among the Israelites and the Arabs," *Studies in the Old Testament Prophecy,* H. H. Rowley (ed.) (Edinburgh: T. & T. Clark, 1946), pp. 127–142; Lindblom, *op. cit.,* pp. 6 ff.

[6] For the use of music by prophets, cf. I Sam. 10:5 f.; Exod. 15:20 f.; I Chron. 25:1 ff. Ezekiel denounces prophets for false visions and divinations (Ezek. 13:7), and prophetic dream oracles are condemned in Jer. 23:25 ff. Cf. Jer. 27:9; 29:8 f. For the cultic dance, cf. II Sam. 6:5, 14. Cf. W. Eichrodt, *Theology of the Old Testament,* The Old Testament Library, J. A. Baker (trans.) (Philadelphia: The Westminster Press, 1961), pp. 310 ff.

not obtain messages. Studies of the words *hozeh* and *ro'eh* have failed to demonstrate any marked difference in meaning, and most English translations render both by "seer."

The distinctive word for prophet in Hebrew is *nabi* (plural, *nebh-iim* or *nebiim*), derived from the Akkadian root *nabu* which is not found in Hebrew and which means "to call," "to speak," "to proclaim," "to name." The prophet is, therefore, "a speaker" or "a spokesman" or one who "calls out" or "proclaims." If the passive form is adopted, he is "one who is called" by the deity. The LXX term is *prophetes,* derived from *pro* meaning "for" or "in behalf of" and *phemi* "to speak."[7] Aaron is appointed *nabi* to Moses and the context makes it clear that Aaron is to be the spokesman (Exod. 7:1), or as Exod. 4:16 indicates, "the mouthpiece" when Moses acts as a god. Similarly, the *nabi* was a spokesman for God, uttering as oracles given divine words. The term *nabi* is also used for non-Yahweh prophets and so-called "false-prophets."

A fourth term, "a man of God" (*'ish 'elohim*) or "the man of God" (*'ish ha-'elohim*), is used to designate holy or inspired persons. Samuel is labeled "man of God" (I Sam. 9:6–10) and so is Shemaiah who warned Rehoboam against attacking Israel (I Kings 12:22–24). Both Elijah (I Kings 17:18–24; II Kings 1:10–13) and Elisha (II Kings 4:7, 9) are given the title. The Chronicler, perhaps to pay distinct respect to the inspired leaders of the past who play an important role in his interpretation of history, titled Moses (I Chron. 23:14; II Chron. 30:16, cf. Ezra 3:2) and David (II Chron. 8:14, cf. Neh. 12:24, 36) men of God, along with certain inspired persons (cf. II Chron. 11:2; 25:7 f.).

It would seem that the Hebrew writers did not employ the terms in such a manner that clear distinctions can be drawn between men of God, seers and prophets. All were, perhaps, in a sense, men of God as they were believed to be inspired of God. Prophets "saw" visions to obtain oracles, and so did seers. Differences in status or means of acquiring oracles are not clearly set forth (note the parallelism in Isa. 29:10; 30:10). The eighth century prophets and their successors in the seventh and sixth centuries are set apart because their oracles have been preserved and we are enabled to study their words. It is probable that other oracles of equal significance may have been uttered by other inspired persons. For these reasons, no attempt will be made to develop any distinctions among these categories.

Often the prophet seems to stand alone and apart from the rest of society, but there is evidence to indicate that he may also have been part of a school or guild. Samuel is said to have been head of a group of prophets (I Sam. 19:20), Elijah had a disciple, Elisha, and a school of prophets (II Kings 2); Isaiah had disciples or pupils (Isa. 8:16),[8] and Jeremiah had a personal scribe, Baruch. It is clear that strong, dynamic, charismatic personalities tended to draw about them those who hoped to share the charisma or who hoped to learn methods and techniques of prophecy. The chief personality or leader was called

---

[7] Lindblom, *op. cit.* p. 1, prefers to interpret *pro* as "forth"; thus, a prophet is a "forth-teller."

[8] The Hebrew term means "those who are taught."

"father" (cf. I Sam. 10:12; II Kings 2:12; 6:21; 13:14) which in this
context simply means "head man" or "master" (II Kings 2:3 ff.; 6:5).
The disciples were called "sons of the prophet" (cf. II Kings 2:3; 6:1),
not implying physical descent but rather the embodiment of the spirit
of "the father."

The relationship between prophet and priest and prophet and
cultus is not clear. At one time it was customary to find in Hebrew
religion a tension between prophet and priest or cult.[9] At present it is
more common to find scholars suggesting that prophets may have been
a part of the cultus, associated with priests in cultic ritual. As we shall
see, anti-cultic pronouncements of the eighth century prophets appear
to give support to the first hypothesis, but there is a considerable
amount of evidence to lend credence to the second. The prophets
encountered by Saul were from the shrine at Gibeath-elohim, "the hill
of the gods" (I Sam. 10:5). The prophet Samuel was trained by the
priest Eli and performed as a priest. As we shall see, Ezekiel, the
prophet, had priestly interests. Isaiah received his summons to prophesy within the temple precincts. Aubrey Johnson has proposed that
prophets and priests worked side by side in Yahweh shrines and in the
Jerusalem temple, and he concludes that when the prophets criticized,
they stood within the cultus seeking to correct abuses.[10]

The role of the prophets as set forth in the prophetic writings is to
proclaim Yahweh's word or, as the term *nabi* implies, to act as
Yahweh's spokesmen. During the past half century, prophetic utterances have been subjected to form critical analysis, and it has been
demonstrated that oracular forms stem from cultic, legal, heraldic and
other sociocultural sources. Some utterances, such as those of Amos,
may be associated with festal occasions like the New Year observance.
Judgment pronouncements reflect forms used in law court statements
or in proclamations by a royal messenger. Some salvation oracles
employ patterns used in lamentation rituals or in minstrelsy. The
results of form critical studies should not be used to anchor the
prophets in any of the groups from which they borrowed their literary
forms, but rather to demonstrate the versatility of the spokesmen for
God who were capable of employing many well-known literary patterns to communicate their message.

It is often pointed out that prophets demonstrate extensive knowledge of Hebrew traditions. This is true, but the prophets are not
confined by past history. Woven through the prophetic works are
references to major themes of the salvation history of the nation: election or choice of the people by God, the Exodus or the saving-preserva-
tion of the people, the covenant bonds, the occupation of Canaan with
divine help, and the Davidic line with its messianic-kingship overtones. But, as we shall see, the prophets also turned away from traditions: Amos reversed the popular concept of "Yahweh's day" and
Jeremiah proposed a new covenant to replace the old.

The prophets also challenged current practices. Cultic ritual, with

[9] Cf. W. F. Badè, *The Old Testament in the Light of Today* (Boston, New York:
Houghton Mifflin Company, 1915), pp. 134 f., 158, 184; W. R. Smith, *The Old
Testament in the Jewish Church* (London: A & C Black, 1895), pp. 278 ff.

[10] A. Johnson, *The Cultic Prophet in Ancient Israel.*

its emphasis upon what a man does in ritual, is played down, and
moral themes, concerned with what a man is in human associations,
are emphasized.[11]

Thus, the prophets should not be universally categorized as anti-
cultic preachers, as upholders of past traditions, as predictors of the
future or as moralists. They are best recognized as charismatic personalities, men under the compulsion of an experience that causes them to
utter, despite opposition, challenge, mockery and imprisonment, the
words they believed to be Yahweh's words given to them, words representing Yahweh's will, Yahweh's intentions, Yahweh's purposes, and
Yahweh's action. Their concern was with their own immediate present. If the understanding and interpretation of that immediate present demanded recollections from the past or indications of what the
future might hold, then past and future were utilized. If the best and
most meaningful presentation called for dramatic enactment, utilizing
legal or mourning or folksong modes of utterance, then these forms
were used. To resist the demands of God or to flee from their assigned
role was impossible. One could only respond to what Yahweh required
and suffer the consequences in the conviction that Yahweh would
prove the utterance to be true.

How Yahweh's word came is not known. Rites of incubation, in
which the individual slept in a holy place and received a message in
dreams or visions, were practiced in the Near East. When Daniel (or
Dan'el) in the Ugaritic story of Aqht desired a son, he spent seven
days and nights in the sanctuary until he received a revelation.[12]
Incubation rites were not unknown to the Hebrews,[13] but there is no
clear evidence that prophetic messages were received through this
technique. Nevertheless visions were experienced, for Isaiah's prophetic summons came in a vision in the temple area, and visionary
patterns appear in the prophecies of Amos, Jeremiah, Ezekiel and
others.[14]

Free association rites are known to have been utilized by seers. The
whole mind and personality of the seer is focused upon a single item,
or problem; all else is blanked out in what might best be described as
a trance state. A train of thought is begun leading to an answer to the
problem or to an oracle. There is, as we shall see, some indication that
the prophets may have utilized some form of this technique, acquiring
oracles from concentration on a pot of boiling water (Jer. 1:13 f.) or
on a man testing a wall (Amos 7:7 f.).

Some prophetic oracles reflect personal experiences either social or
introspective. Some of Hosea's proclamations grew out of his unfortunate marriage and some of Jeremiah's out of vilification by his countrymen. On the other hand, certain of Jeremiah's and Isaiah's experiences

---

[11] Moral concern was widespread in the Near East, and is found in the Prologue
of Hammurabi's code (cf. *ANET*, p. 164), and in the Canaanite story of Aqht from
Ugarit (cf. *ANET*, pp. 149 ff.). Moral-ethical issues become the burden of anyone
sensitive to suffering and to hardships imposed by man upon man.

[12] *ANET*, pp. 149 f.

[13] Cf. Jacob at Bethel (Gen. 28:11 ff.) and Solomon at Gibeon (I Kings 3:4 ff.).

[14] Cf. S. Mowinckel, *The Old Testament as the Word of God*, pp. 25 f.

were personal and inward, suggesting that they developed out of inward listening or concentration that produced mental images, mental communication culminating in what might be termed an "ineffable experience" (cf. Jer. 20:7–9).[15]

Perhaps it is best to generalize and describe prophetic experiences as many and varied. Lack of detailed information in the Bible prevents, in the light of present knowledge, real precision in analysis.

THE EARLIEST PROPHETS

Ideally, prophecy is traced in Hebrew tradition to key figures of the past. Abraham (Gen. 20:7), Aaron (Exod. 7:1), and Moses (Deut. 34:10) are called "prophets" and Miriam (Exod. 15:20) and Deborah (Judg. 4:4) are prophetesses.[16] These designations mark the respect and veneration of later generations and reflect the tendency to characterize national heroes as inspired persons. Apart from Aaron little information is given of the prophetic roles of these people: Abraham interceded for Abimelech, and Moses spoke intimately with Yahweh (becoming for the Deuteronomist the symbol of the ideal prophet who was to come, Deut. 18:18), Miriam sang a victory song, and Deborah "judged" and gave advice.

Actually, the earliest information about the prophetic movement is found in the early source in Samuel, in parts of Judges, and in J and E. It is possible that some persons who are not described as *nebhiim* but who reflect prophetic activities may rightfully belong among the prophets. For example, Balaam (Num. 22–24), a non-Hebrew spokesman for Yahweh, utters oracles obtained in visions under the influence of Yahweh's spirit.[17]

Samuel, trained as a priest by Eli, officiated at sacrificial rites (I Sam. 7:9), judged Israel (7:15), performed as a seer (9:1–12) and had an itinerant ministry (9:12; 10:8). Whether Samuel could be said to precede an era of specialization or whether Samuel was called a *nabi* in his own day can be debated. There is no doubt that his dynamic social, political and religious influence prefigures later prophetic interests. He sent Saul to the prophetic group at Gibeath-elohim where music was used, possibly to inspire ecstatic responses (see I Sam. 10:5, 10), and Samuel headed a group that provoked extreme reactions in Saul (I Sam. 19:23 ff.).

During the reign of David, two prophets were active in the life of the court: Nathan and Gad.[18] Nathan's challenge to David in the

---

[15] The term "mystical" is avoided because of the difficulty in defining the word precisely.

[16] Cf. B. D. Napier, *Prophets in Perspective* (New York: Abingdon Press, 1963), pp. 58 ff. for a discussion of these "prophets."

[17] Cf. A. Guillaume, *Prophecy and Divination Among the Hebrews and Other Semites* (New York: Harper and Brothers, 1938), pp. 133 f.

[18] Ahitophel, who counsels Absalom, is not usually classified among the prophets, yet cf. II Sam. 16:23. Cf. Wm. McKane, *Prophets and Wise Men*, Studies in Biblical Theology No. 44 (Napierville: Alec R. Allenson, Inc., 1965) for detailed analysis.

parable of the ewe lamb represents coherent thought without any
aspects of ecstatic behavior (II Sam. 12). He confronts the monarch as
Yahweh's spokesman and with divine power, for he is able to lift the
death penalty that David had unwittingly invoked upon himself and
transfer it to the unborn child. During the palace uprising he cooperated with Zadok the priest in bringing Solomon to the throne. The
Chronicler refers to the "Book of Nathan" (II Chron. 9:29). Gad's
activities are reported only twice in David's career (I Sam. 22:3 ff.;
II Sam. 24). The Chronicler mentions "The Chronicles of Gad, the
seer" (I Chron. 29:29), but what these may have contained cannot be
known. It is quite clear that these men played no small role in the
royal court and enjoyed positions of some status.

At the time of the division of the kingdom, the dramatic action of
Ahijah the prophet may have been partially responsible for Jeroboam's revolt (I Kings 11:29–39). Much later, the prophet, now blind
and disenchanted with Jeroboam's lack of enthusiasm for Yahwism,
opposed the king, pronouncing imminent death for Jeroboam's ailing
son and predicting the forthcoming doom of Jeroboam's house. During
this same period Rehoboam refrained from attacking Israel on the
advice of the prophet Shemaiah (I Kings 12:21–24). An embellish-
ment of Shemaiah's role is given in II Chron. 12:5 ff. and reference is
made to a book which the prophet is supposed to have written
(12:15). Later, Baasha of Israel is condemned and the end of his line
predicted by the prophet Jehu in terms very much like those used by
Ahijah to Jeroboam's wife (I Kings 16:1 ff.).

It becomes clear that the courts of the Hebrew kings employed
prophets to secure guidance and advice from Yahweh. It is also plain
that prophets such as Ahijah (and perhaps Jehu), not intimately
connected with the court, were consulted at moments of critical
importance. There can be little doubt that, from Samuel's time
through the beginning years of the divided kingdom, Yahweh's
prophets were instrumental in keeping ethical and religious responsibilities before the king, proclaiming both the will of Yahweh and the
judgment of Yahweh when violations occurred.

As the kingdom of Israel moved more and more toward Canaanite
religion, prophets emulating Ahijah's dramatic approach stood against
king and cult to present Yahweh's claims. As Jehu promised, Baasha's
dynasty soon ended and out of the confusion that followed, Omri
emerged as victor and monarch. During the reign of his son Ahab,
prophets of Yahweh again became involved in national politics. One
was an unknown prophet who promised Ahab victory over the Syrians
**Read
I Kings 20** of Damascus. The account reveals the current belief of both Syrians
and Hebrews that the battles involved national deities (cf. vss. 23 ff.).
A second prophetic figure reinforced the promise of success. A third
predicted Ahab's fate because the Syrian monarch was spared. A
strange note in this last story suggests that prophets were not recognized when their eyes were bandaged or covered. Whether or not some
mark or symbol was worn on the forehead or whether the trance state
**Read
I Kings 22** was revealed in the eyes cannot be known. Of a fourth prophet,
Micaiah, Ahab rather petulantly complained, "I hate him, for he never
prophesies good concerning me, only evil." With the help of Jehosha-

ISRAELITE STRUCTURE FROM HAZOR. *Two rows of standing pillars from the time of Ahab were unearthed in the excavation at Hazor. The pillars supported the roof of what was probably a large public building. Hazor had been the Canaanite city where a coalition of forces opposing the invading Hebrews under Joshua met defeat (Josh. 11:1–15; 12:19). Later Solomon fortified the city, and when the kingdom was divided Hazor came under Israelite control. In the time of Ahab it was a thriving city but in the eighth century it was captured by Tiglath Pileser III.*

phat of Judah, Ahab determined to take back Ramoth-gilead, then in the possession of Syria. Four hundred yes-men prophets told the king what he yearned to hear: that he would conquer.[19] One, Zedekiah, donned horned headgear and dramatized the manner in which the Syrians would be pushed about. Micaiah, after a mocking mimicry of the 400, foretold doom and held to his prediction despite physical abuse by Zedekiah and imprisonment with a bread and water diet. What happened to him when his prophecy was fulfilled is not told, for Ahab, despite elaborate precautions, was killed.

Much more is told of Elijah and his disciple Elisha, both of whom championed the cause of Yahweh in Ahab's reign. Elijah came from Tishbe, a community in Gilead on the eastern side of the Jordan, and apart from this note no further information about his background is given. Numerous legends grew up about him, many tinged with the miraculous. His story begins abruptly with the announcement of a drought caused by Yahweh—an announcement that actually sets the

Read
I Kings 17–
19; 21;
II Kings
1–2

[19] Both truth and falsehood were believed to come from Yahweh.

185

stage for the struggle between those who proclaimed Ba'al as the fertility and rain deity and those who saw Yahweh as the life-power behind the nation. The drought narrative is interrupted by two anecdotes: the first tells of two magical vessels, a pot of oil that never ran dry and a jar of meal that was never empty, and the second of the resuscitation of a dead child. The drought is terminated by a contest in which Elijah, Yahweh's sole representative, is pitted against 450 prophets of Ba'al and 400 prophets of Asherah all under the patronage of Jezebel and the royal court.[20] The ritual of the followers of Ba'al is reminiscent of the actions of El as reported in the Ras es-Shamra texts. When El, the father god, learned of Ba'al's demise, he donned sack-cloth, sprinkled ashes on his head and gashed himself in mourning rites. Similarly the worshipers of Ba'al gashed themselves and per-formed the limping mourning dance at Carmel. Elijah's mocking words, spoken when the sun at the zenith was burning down upon those crying to the dead rain god for answer, reflect the death of Ba'al, for Ba'al was on a journey to the realm of Mot, the god of death and sterility: he was "asleep."[21] Elijah, in a rite reminiscent of sympa-thetic magic,[22] used water to produce water and the climax of the story is the coming of the thunderclouds and the torrents of rain.

It is probable that the rituals were part of the New Year festival. The Canaanite New Year began in the fall with the sowing of grain and the ritual resurrection of Ba'al and the coming of the autumnal rains.[23] It is possible that Elijah's ritual may have represented in part the Hebrew cultic ritual for the New Year which also began in the fall and was marked with the coming of rain. The contest itself dramati-cally demonstrated the impossibility of simultaneously retaining Yah-weh as a national deity and Ba'al as the fertilizing or life-sustaining god, the activator of the land and therefore its rightful owner.[24] Elijah's point was that Yahweh was Israel's god, responsible for all aspects of national well-being, including the bringing of fertilizing rain, and was, therefore, owner of the land. Arguments concerning the fire from heaven (which was apparently lightning), suggestions that Elijah may have poured naphtha rather than water on the altar, or allegations that someone assisted Elijah and secretly lit the fire are fruitless and completely miss the thrust of the account. The story symbolizes a power struggle, a point clearly made by Elijah: "If

[20] There is no way of determining whether or not these persons were followers of Ba'al Melkart of Tyre, Ba'al of Carmel, or some other Ba'al. Nor can it be known if a Yahweh shrine had previously stood on Carmel.

[21] "Sleep" is often used as a synonym for death, cf. I Kings 1:21; 2:10; Ps. 13:3; Jer. 51:39, 57; Dan. 12:2.

[22] Sympathetic or homeopathic magic operates on the assumption that "like produces like" and that by acting out that which is desired, or by employing objects similar to that which is to be affected, certain desired results will follow. Distinction should be made between a rite believed to be automatically effective and one that petitions a god that something *may* happen. Cf. James G. Frazer, *The New Golden Bough*, ed. T. H. Gaster (New York: Criterion Press, 1959), pp. 7 ff. and in particu-lar Gaster's note on p. 128.

[23] Cf. DeVaux, *Ancient Israel*, p. 190.

[24] It is possible that Carmel represented a border territory recovered by Israel from Tyre and the issue was over control of this particular segment of land. Cf. Eichrodt, *Theology of the Old Testament*, pp. 314 f.

Yahweh is God, follow him; but if Ba'al, then follow him" (I Kings 18:21). For Elijah there was no choice: his name, which meant "Yahweh is my God," testified to his commitment. The validity of his belief was demonstrated in the rain contest which discredited the prophets and priests of Ba'al and Asherah. Elijah struck when he had the advantage and a blood purge followed, provoking Jezebel to a threat of reprisal.

In many ways Elijah is made to appear as a second Moses. He fled to the wilderness to escape the monarch's wrath, and in the desert God protected him. At Horeb, the holy mountain for Israel, he encountered Yahweh. Violent natural phenomena were often interpreted as manifestations of the deity, particularly in the southern tradition, J, but for Elijah, Yahweh was in none of these. In intimate person-to-person, voice-to-voice relationships, following or coming out of an eerie quietness,[25] Yahweh spoke to Elijah. Elijah was commissioned to anoint two Yahweh followers for their roles as defenders of the faith: Jehu, who was to become king, and Elisha, who was to succeed Elijah; and one non-Hebrew: Hazael, king of Syria. The anointing of Elisha appears to have been accomplished when the prophet's mantle fell upon the young disciple. Jehu and Hazael were said to have each been anointed secretly by Elisha following Elijah's death.

Elijah had other encounters with Israel's royal family. Ahab's greed, stimulated and encouraged by the ruthless Jezebel, resulted in the false accusation and death of Naboth, whose vineyard Ahab coveted.[26] Like Nathan in David's time, Elijah confronted Ahab with his crime and pronounced the sentence of doom marking the end of Ahab's line. Ahab's subsequent humiliation of himself led Elijah, like Nathan, to recall the curse of Yahweh and transfer it to the son, Ahaziah.

When Ahaziah suffered the crippling fall that ultimately caused his death, he sent messengers to inquire of Ba'al-zebub, the healing god of flies at Ekron, to ask if he would recover.[27] The messengers were intercepted by the champion of Yahwism, and Elijah demonstrated that there was no need to go to Philistia for oracles, for life and healing were with Yahweh.

According to tradition, Elijah did not die but was miraculously transported to heaven in a chariot of fire.[28] The sole witness to this event was Elisha, his disciple and successor, and it is probably through Elisha and the prophetic society that he inherited that the stories of Elijah were preserved.[29] The impact of Elijah's legendary career was to touch later generations for whom he became a messianic figure, the

[25] Not to be confused with conscience.

[26] Naboth's refusal to sell or exchange his vineyard reflects the significance of land inheritance in ancient Israel. Cf. De Vaux, op. cit., pp. 53 ff., 166 f., J. Pedersen, Israel, I–II, 89 ff.

[27] It has been proposed that the name of the god of Ekron has been deliberately distorted and that it should read Ba'al-zebul on the analogy of the title "Zebul Ba'al" ("Lord Ba'al") found in the Ras es-Shamra texts.

[28] His translation places him in the cult of humans who become like gods (cf. Utnapishtim in the Gilgamesh Epic).

[29] The letter attributed to Elijah in II Chron. 21:12 ff. in which Jehoram of Judah is condemned for apostasy is probably the work of the Chronicler.

Read
II Kings
2–9; 13

forerunner of the Day of Yahweh (Malachi 4:5) or the one who was to calm the wrath of God and to be instrumental in the restoration of the tribes of Jacob (Ecclesiasticus or Sirach, ch. 48) or the messianic herald (Luke 1:17).[30]

Elisha is depicted as a wealthy peasant, the owner of twelve yoke of oxen which he sacrificed in a farewell feast on his departure from home to follow Elijah (I Kings 19:19 ff.). The editors make it clear that he is the divine choice as successor to Elijah and that he inherits Elijah's charisma. Elisha stories may have been gathered from several sources and combined. Some accounts are doublets echoing aspects of Elijah's career, and in view of the close association of the two men this is not surprising. In II Kings 4:1–37 the tales of the magical jar of oil and the raising of the dead boy duplicate Elijah's feats with some added details. Other Elisha adventures have far greater emphasis upon the miraculous and the magical than anything found in the Elijah cycle and may come from prophetic dervishes grouped around individual shrines, each claiming its own miraculous heritage from the prophet.[31] These stories refer to the transmission of prophetic power from Elijah to Elisha, the magic mantle by which the Jordan is divided, the cleansing of the spring at Jericho, and the cursing of the boys at Bethel. Other legends tell of Elisha's purification of poisoned food (4:38 f.), feeding of 100 prophets at Gilgal (4:42 f.), and causing an iron axe-head to float (6:1–7). Even after death Elisha's magical powers were effective, for the power in his bones revived the dead (13:21 f.).

References to his role in ninth century history are few. He fulfilled Elijah's commission to Hazael (8:7–15) and Jehu (9:1–6). His clairvoyant powers enabled him to envision the hardship Hazael would bring to Israel. In the Moabite campaign when Jehoram of Israel and Jehoshaphat of Judah determined to recover control of Moab, Elisha was consulted (3:4–27). It is possible that his associations with Naaman the leper (ch. 5), with the Aramaeans (6:8–23) and with Hazael (8:7–15) reflect the unusual status of this prophet and suggest a recognition of his clairvoyant and prophetic powers in both Israel and Syria.

For the next century there are no references to prophetic activity in either Israel or Judah. Israel felt the pressure of the Aramaeans and the growing power of Assyria. Judah lost territory to Edom. Tension developed into war between the once united kingdoms. Relatively speaking, from the best evidence available, the century appears to have been marked by prosperity. When prophetic activity is next recorded, it is in the collected utterances of the prophets themselves—the so-called "writing prophets"—an older term used by those who believed that the prophets wrote the books that bear their names. It is now apparent that behind the prophetic writings as we now have them are older, smaller, independent units of material, consisting of autobio-

---

[30] The New Testament indicates the prevalence of belief in Elijah redivivus (cf. Matt. 11:14, 16:14, 17:10 ff.; John 1:21).

[31] John Gray, *I & II Kings*, The Old Testament Library (Philadelphia: The Westminster Press, 1963), p. 416.

graphical narratives, biographical prose often containing authentic sayings, and collections of utterances or oracles. At times autobiographical and biographical materials are parallel, presenting the same information with varying details or emphases. In addition, prophetic writings have been expanded by later hands and incorporate materials from different periods, some of which can be readily recognized and, at times, dated and some which form the basis of scholarly debate as to genuineness.

17

Amos and Hosea

NORTHERN prophecy was revived by two prophets whose oracles are included in the biblical collection often referred to as "The Minor Prophets," a reference to the length rather than the importance of their utterances. Amos was a Judaean who believed he was commissioned by Yahweh to address his words to Israel, but Hosea was a native Israelite. With these two men the custom of recording oracles appears to have begun, for if the words of their prophetic predecessors were preserved in written form they have long since been lost to us. Within a few years prophets sharing similar concerns with Amos and Hosea were active in Judah and their words too, were preserved.

AMOS

Read
II Kings
15 and
Amos 1–9

The earliest collection of prophetic oracles are those of Amos who prophesied at Bethel in Israel. Like his predecessors, he stood in judgment of moral and ethical evil but, unlike them, he did not limit himself to single issues or to individual situations, but dealt with the decline of Yahwism and human behavior in all levels of society. Of his background and lineage nothing is known, and the references to his presence "among" the shepherds (*noqedim*) of Tekoa (1:1) and his claims to be a herdsman (tender of oxen)[1] and a dresser of sycamore fig trees (7:14) do not tell us whether he owned flocks or herds and groves or cared for the possessions of others, or whether, as some have suggested on the basis of the term *noqedim,* he tended Temple flocks.[2] Tekoa was located on a hilltop about 2,800 feet above sea level and ten miles south of Jerusalem. Only scrub growth and grass grow on these rugged slopes and eastward the land drops away rapidly to the wilderness of the Dead Sea. According to II Chronicles 11:6, Rehoboam fortified Tekoa; and Jeremiah referred to it as a relay station for distress signals (Jer. 6:1). Amos' work with sycamore figs must have necessitated travel to the Shephelah and coastal regions where these trees grew (cf. I Kings 10:27; II Chron. 9:27 f.). Whatever his social

---

[1] Possibly a copyist's error and the term should be "shepherd." Cf. LXX and J. Morgenstern, "Amos Studies—I," *Hebrew Union College Annual,* XI (1936), 35.

[2] I. Engnell, *Studies in Divine Kingship in the Ancient Near East* (Upsala: Appelbergs Boktryckeriaktiebolag, 1943), p. 87.

and economic status, he is not to be thought of as an uninformed yokel invading the sophisticated world of Bethel. His utterances, couched in excellent Hebrew, reflect knowledge of historical traditions (2:9 ff.; 9:7), geography (note the numerous cities he mentions), patterns of cause and effect (3:3 ff.), and Israelite cult practices. His vivid imagery, drawn from nature, suggests an intelligent observer capable of relating his insights and experiences in powerful terminology. Perhaps the very simplicity of his life caused him to be shocked at the extravagances of the rich and the terrible poverty and helplessness of those who were the prey of the powerful. The luxury of summer and winter palaces as opposed to the hovels of the poor, the greedy demand of the very rich contrasted with the cry for justice and equity of the underprivileged drove him to harsh pronouncements against powerful, smug, content men and women, priests and king.

Precisely when Amos prophesied is not specified. The editorial superscription places him in the time of Uzziah of Judah (783–742) and Jeroboam II of Israel (786–742), an age of affluence and security. According to 7:10 he was in Bethel during Jeroboam's reign. Some effort has been made to discover the date implied in the enigmatic reference to "two years before the earthquake" and what appear to be references to an earthquake within the text (4:11; 6:11; 8:8; 9:1–5). Dr. Julian Morgenstern's studies have led him to date this catastrophe on New Year's Day, 749 B.C., so that Amos' visit to Bethel took place exactly two years earlier, on New Year's Day in 751 B.C.[3] On that occasion, Dr. Morgenstern believes, Amos made a single prophetic speech. Other scholars argue for a series of oracular utterances over a wider period of time, and some suggest that Amos may have spoken at several shrines—Samaria (3:9–12; 4:1 ff.), Gilgal (4:4; 5:4), and Carmel (1:2; 9:3).[4] Some prefer a more general date of around 750 B.C. Other references within the book have been explored as clues for dating. An eclipse of the sun seems to be mentioned in 5:8 and 8:9, and such an eclipse is known to have taken place in June, 763. Amos records the names of two Aramaean kings, Hazael and Ben Hadad, but only approximate dates are available for these monarchs. Hazael's reign is roughly between 842 and 806, and Ben Hadad's between 860 and 740 B.C. Either Morgenstern's precise date of New Year's Day 751, or the general date of 750 B.C. may be accepted.[5]

There can be no doubt that Amos believed himself commissioned by Yahweh to proclaim a message (7:14), but his apparent disassociation with the title "prophet" and with the prophetic movement—"I am no *nabi'*, nor a son of a *nabi'*"—has been a problem to scholars. It has been suggested that Amos was at Bethel for some time working with the temple staff. Amaziah's advice that he go to Judah and earn his keep implies that he was doing just that at Bethel. Amos' refusal to be identified with any specific prophetic group, no matter where

---

[3] J. Morgenstern, "Amos Studies," pp. 123–140.

[4] John D. Watts, *Vision and Prophecy in Amos* (Grand Rapids: W. B. Eerdmans, 1958), p. 18; R. S. Cripps, *A Critical and Exegetical Commentary on the Book of Amos* (London: Society for Promoting Christian Knowledge, 1929), p. 12.

[5] Cripps, *op. cit.*, pp. 34–41, argues for 742–741 B.C.

located, was, perhaps, a rejection of the implication that he prophesied for remuneration.[6] Other solutions propose a re-translation
of the verse to read "I *was* no prophet, nor a prophet's son . . .
and Yahweh said to me . . ." suggesting that Amos' prophetic activity
began in response to a divine call,[7] or "Am I not a prophet? a son of a
prophet? . . . and Yahweh said to me . . ."[8] implying that Amos was
defending his prophetic status. That Amos did not oppose prophecy as
such is clear from 3:8 and 7:15.

**Read
Amos 7–9**

How Amos received his summons to prophesy is not recorded but
probably the five visions preserved in autobiographical prose form,
together with poetic oracles in Chapters 7, 8 and 9, are involved, for
the superscription 1:1 mentions the words which Amos "saw" (*hazah*).
Whether or not these visions came during service as a cult ministrant
at Bethel cannot be determined. If 1:2, a passage often treated as
editorial, is by Amos and the prophet is protesting that true Yahwism
is centered in Jerusalem—"Yahweh roars from Zion and utters his
voice from Jerusalem"—it may be that Amos received his call in
Jerusalem.

There is a progression within the visionary series leading to a
powerful prediction of doom. The opening vision, the horde of locusts
(7:1–3), occurs in the spring at a critical moment so far as the crops
were concerned. It is not clear whether Amos actually saw a swarm of
insects and, in concentrating upon them, interpreted their significance
symbolically, or whether his vision was of an hallucinatory type in
which the locusts were products of his imagination. He was convinced
that the locusts came as divine punishment, and the prophet called
upon Yahweh to remit the penalty, and the calamity was averted.
Amos' role as lone intercessor for the people is similar to that of
Abraham in the J account of the destruction of Sodom and Gomorrah
(Gen. 18:22 ff.).

The second vision of destructive fire (7:4–6) may reflect the drought
or aridity of summer during which the earth was seared, or may refer
to supernatural fire such as lightning, or may indicate a scorched earth
policy practiced by an enemy. Again, Amos intervened and the
penalty did not come. In the third vision (7:7–9), a man testing a wall
for perpendicularity is seen to be Yahweh testing the nation. This time
Amos did not intervene for there was a note of finality in Yahweh's
words "never again": the holy places of Israel and the royal palaces are
doomed. The fourth vision (8:1–3) occurs in the late summer when
the last fruit had been gathered, and the proximity of divine judgment
is suggested. In the final vision (9:1–4), Yahweh is standing upon the
altar at Bethel ready to strike.

If, as some have suggested, Amos' visions are associated with the
New Year festival which would occur in the fall of the year at the time
of the autumnal equinox and just prior to the commencement of the
rainy season, the visions and words would have had particular signifi-

---

[6] J. Lindblom, *Prophecy in Ancient Israel*, pp. 183 ff.

[7] Cripps, *op. cit.*, pp. 232 f. See also H. H. Rowley, "Was Amos a Nabi?" *Festschrift
Otto Eissfeldt*, ed. J. Fück (Halle: Niemeyer, 1947), pp. 191 ff.

[8] N. H. Snaith, *Amos, Hosea, and Micah* (London: Epworth Press, 1956), p. 43.

cance. Although it cannot be proven conclusively that a New Year ritual was enacted in Israel and while no detail of the cultic rite is set forth in the Old Testament, there are indications that on the basis of analogy with known Babylonian rites such a festival may have occurred. Part of this festival would have included a prophetic oracle of the future, a prediction of the national destiny for the coming year, a forecast of the Day of Yahweh. Obviously, it was hoped and expected that the prediction would be of blessing. Amos, led by his visions, was compelled to pronounce doom, and gave as a reason for Yahweh's destructive intent religious and social misbehavior within the nation. In the setting of the New Year festival, the pronouncement of dread judgment could only have a disruptive effect; even without this setting, the oracles would be disturbing.

OUTLINE OF CONTENTS

The book of Amos can be conveniently divided into four sections:

a. Chapters 1–2, oracles against foreign nations climaxed with an indictment of Israel.
b. Chapters 3–6, denouncement of Israel.
c. Chapters 7–9:10, visions of doom.
d. Chapters 9:11–15, the closing oracle of hope.

Within this broad outline smaller units may be isolated: the biographical section at 7:10–17 and the doxologies at 4:13; 5:8–9; 9:5–6.

The extent to which the book reflects the actual words of Amos has been a matter of some scholarly debate. The authenticity of the anti-Philistine oracle (1:6–8) has been challenged because the Philistine city of Gath, destroyed in 711 by Sargon II,[9] is not mentioned and the reference to the "remnant of the Philistines" may reflect the Exile period. However, in predicting the doom of Philistia, the reference to the remnant would be most apropos, and if the record in II Chron. 26:6 is correct, Gath had suffered at least partial demolition by Uzziah of Judah. The oracle against Tyre (1:9–10) has been questioned because it is almost an exact replica of that against Philistia and, so far as it is known, the Israelites were at this time on good terms with Tyre. What "covenant of brotherhood" (treaty) Tyre is supposed to have violated is unknown. The oracle against Edom may refer to the Edomitic refusal to give sanctuary to the Judaeans during the Babylonian invasion and would therefore come from the Exile; it could also refer to some situation in Amos' day with which we are unacquainted.

Whether or not Amos would have lashed out against Judah (2:4–5) is debatable. He might wish to warn his countrymen of their danger, so that the oracle could have been added by the prophet at a later time. He may have listed Judah in his denunciations because he believed Judah had merited inclusion. Certain characteristics of style, reflecting the Deuteronomists, have led to the suggestion that this

[9] *ANET*, p. 286.

oracle was added at a much later date by those interested in adapting Amos' words to the southern kingdom.[10]

The account of Amos' clash with Amaziah, priest of Bethel (7:10–17), is a descriptive incident in a biographical prose style which may contain Amos' words but refers to the prophet in the third person, indicating that the account was not composed by him.

The final chapter, the oracle of hope (9:11–15) which stands in sharp contradiction to the harsh message of doom found elsewhere in the book, may be the work of Amos but fits best into the time of, and is stylistically close to, similar oracles found in Deutero-Isaiah. The reference to the fallen "booth of David," which might be interpreted as a Judaean's reaction to the separation of the Israelite kingship from the Davidic line, is better recognized as an Exilic lament over the fall of Judah. The hope for the re-inhabitation of ruined cities (9:14) also reflects the mood and spirit of the Exile.

Read Amos 1–2

Chapters 1–2. Amos' denunciatory oracles, whether delivered in a single address or given on a succession of days, are ordered to tease his listeners into a state of unreadiness for his verbal attack on Israel. The oracles against Damascus (1:3–5), Ammon (1:13–15) and Moab (2:1–3), perhaps delivered with vehemence as the prophet faced toward these nations, would receive enthusiastic response, for the Israelites had little affection for these long-time enemies. If the disputed oracles against Philistia (1:6–8), Tyre (1:9–10), Edom (1:11–12) and Judah (2:4–5) are added, the response may have been even greater. The Syrians are cursed for cruelty in the seizure of Gilead, the Ammonites for viciousness in their land grab in the Transjordan, and the Moabites for the desecration of the dead (a crime not condemned by the editors of Kings when practiced by Josiah, as in II Kings 23:16 ff.).

The prophet next lashed out at the northern kingdom and Israel is admonished for judicial dishonesty, apostasy and willful violation of religious obligations. Justice was perverted and those in the right ("righteous") in a legal suit were judged guilty by officials so greedy for gain that they would accept almost any sort of bribe. The poor had become the pawns of the wealthy. The apostate people practiced sacred prostitution at cult shrines, drinking wine purchased with monies from unjust fines. All that Yahweh had done to bring the nation to its present affluence had been forgotten. Nazirites, men under a religious vow of abstinence (see Num. 6:2–8), were compelled to drink wine, and prophets were forbidden to speak Yahweh's word. Yahweh's verdict promised doom from which there would be no refuge, and should a man escape, those possessions he held so dear would be lost to him (2:13–16).

---

[10] For discussion of Deuteronomic characteristics, cf. S. R. Driver, *The Books of Joel and Amos* (Cambridge: Cambridge University Press, 1934), pp. 119–121.

A literary pattern or form has been recognized in these oracles:[11]

a. the affirmation: "Thus says Yahweh . . ." by which the prophet authenticates the oracle.
b. the opening formula: "For three transgressions . . . and for four I will not revoke the punishment. . . ." The numerical progression is a literary device found also in Canaanite literature signifying no specific number, but rather "much" or "many."
c. the listing of specific evils, introduced by "because."
d. the punishment, commencing with "so . . ." or, in the case of Israel, "behold. . . ."

The denouncement of Israel (Chapters 3–6). Having introduced his major theme, Amos expanded his case against Israel. Once again a literary pattern can be discerned:[12]

Read
Amos
3–6

a. opening formula: "Hear this word" (3:1; 4:1; 5:1).
b. the naming of the group addressed.
c. the indictment.
d. the judgment, introduced by "therefore."
e. the signature, "says Yahweh."

The pattern here is not as neat as a literary analyst might desire, for a secondary pattern appears in 4:4–13 where a series of complaints introduced by "I gave," "I withheld," "I smote," "I slew," etc., concluding with "Yet you did not return to me," and signed with "says Yahweh," serve to expand the statement found in 4:4–5. Another pattern occurs in Chapters 5 and 6 with a collection of oracles introduced by "woe."[13] The relationship between these patterns is not clear. They may represent oracles delivered at different times or may simply be stylistic variations employed by the prophet to accent oracles of diverse nature.

Although Amos tends to ignore secondary causes, he is convinced that events do not occur without reason and argues that when a

A RED BURNISHED JUGLET FROM THE IRON AGE. *Some Iron Age artifacts are made with rounded bases which required stands to keep them upright. This practical, flat-bottomed juglet is typical of items used in average households —perhaps to hold milk or water or grape juice or oil. The burnishing, which is a smoothing of the clay before firing with a bone or stick or even with the potter's wet hands, produces a smoother, harder and shinier surface less impervious to liquids and often quite decorative.*

[11] It is possible that this literary pattern is drawn from the law courts. Here Yahweh is judge, pronouncing doom. Other lawsuit oracles portray Yahweh as a contender in a legal suit (cf. Micah 6:1 ff.; Isa. 2:1 ff.; 3:12 ff.; Jer. 2:4 ff.).

[12] Another law court pattern with slight variation of form.

[13] Oracles of reproach and admonition.

prophet is compelled to speak it is because Yahweh has given an oracle
(3:3–8). The threat of punishment for Israel results from Yahweh's
close identification with these people (3:2), for they alone, of all
peoples of the earth have had close, intimate associations with the
deity (note the use of the verb "to know" in much the same sense that
J has used it to portray personal bonds of kinship or belonging or
perhaps in a covenantal sense).[14] In this claim Amos sets forth the
concept of election, the free choice of Israel by Yahweh, a theme
greatly expanded and developed by subsequent prophets. Because
these ties have been violated, Israel must suffer: the pampered women
of Samaria, like prize cows from the fertile area of Bashan to the east
of Lake Galilee, greedily demand more and more from their avaricious
husbands (4:1). They are promised enslavement, with the victorious
enemy dragging them with war hooks through breached walls. The
religious activities by which the people sought to please Yahweh
provoked only scorn from the prophet, for the festal and cultic
activities obscured Yahweh's real nature and activity (4:4–5). Famine
(v. 6), drought (v. 7–8), crop failure (v. 9), disease (v. 10) and
earthquake (possibly v. 11) went unrecognized as warnings from
Yahweh. The complaint "yet you did not return to me . . ." may
imply that the people continued to devote themselves to Ba'al, attributing these natural disasters to the fertility god. Amos was now
prepared to present Yahweh: "Prepare to meet your God, O Israel!"

Verse 4:13, together with 5:8 and 9:5–6, has been interpreted as a
"liturgical appendage," added, possibly, when the book of Amos was
employed in liturgy. The similarity of thought and style to the work of
II Isaiah suggests an Exilic provenance. On the other hand, the
passages may represent a cultic hymn from Amos' day,[15] and although
5:8 and 9:5–6 do cut across the thought patterns of the sections of
which they are a part, 4:13 is not out of place as part of the presentation of Yahweh in his true colors.

The introduction of Yahweh continued with an ironical funereal
lament for Israel written in "qinah" or limping meter, possibly
because a limping walk or dance accompanied the dirge.[16] The will of
Yahweh had been declared; Israel's fate was assured; the nation was as
if dead. Still, a conditional element appears in the next verses, a
promise that if Israel would seek Yahweh the nation would live or
escape destruction. Worship at Bethel and Gilgal in Israel and at Beer-
sheba in Judah is rejected, for Yahweh was not to be found in these
places. Presumably not only the place but the method of seeking
Yahweh was wrong, and in expounding this concept Amos castigates
the people for social injustice and moral indifference, providing an
intimate picture of Israelite business ethics and practice. The accusa-

---

[14] Cf. H. B. Huffman, "The Treaty Background of Hebrew Yāda'," *BASOR,*
(1966), 31–37.

[15] Cf. J. D. W. Watts, "An Old Hymn Preserved in the book of Amos," *Journal of
Near Eastern Studies,* XV (1956), 33–39.

[16] Structured after the mourning songs sung by professional wailers at funerals.
The word *qinah* refers to verse in which the second line is shorter or contains fewer
stresses than the first, producing a "limping" effect. The usual metrical arrangement
which is 3:2 is prominent in the book of Lamentations.

tions are climaxed with a plea to "seek good" which is what Yahweh demands.

The thrust of Amos' condemnation is against the division of life into compartments. He argues for unity. What a man does in the market place, in the law court, in his dealings with others cannot be walled off from worship. Yahweh is a God of all people; therefore the dealings of man with man are directly related to the dealings of God with man. His is a cry for the recognition of man's moral responsibility before God.

THE DAY OF YAHWEH

The "woe" oracles begin in 5:18 and introduce the "Day of Yahweh" concept. The precise meaning of this term is not known. It may have had a futuristic significance pointing to a "day" that was to come. It is quite clear that "that day" was, in the hopes of the public, to be a time of joy and blessing. Amos spoke of doom from which there was no escape. It is also possible that "Yahweh's Day" was New Year's Day, the time of new beginnings, of purgation of past sins and evils, and the day when Yahweh, personified by the cultic symbol, the ark, or by the king, was enthroned. Each New Year's Day was Yahweh's Day when it was expected that the new and hoped for future would begin. The prophetic oracle would announce the nature of that day. The people looked for a favorable oracle, but Amos spoke of judgment.

The condemnation of cultic rites introduced in 4:4 f. and 5:4 f. is picked up again with new vehemence. It has been argued that Amos was not opposed to cultic ritual *per se* but condemned the mind set of the people by which responsibility to Yahweh was performed perfunctorily and without relationship to daily life and society. If we take Amos' words as they stand, there seems to be little doubt that he condemned the entire religious pattern—feasts, sacrifices, ritual music, offerings, tithes—everything. Yahweh refused to accept gifts or listen to prayers or to judge the nation by these. Yahweh heeded only the cries of the oppressed and mistreated which stood between the religiosity of the people and their God. If Amos was not actually opposed to the cult, then it is clear that he set ethical and moral behavior before observance of cultic rites, what man did in his relationships to his fellow man above that which the men of Israel performed in religious duties. It is possible that he was implying that the latter were not efficacious without the former. His closing cry is, perhaps, a summation of his message:

> "But let justice roll down like waters
> and righteousness like an everflowing stream."
>
> Amos 5:24

The prose verse that follows (5:25), perhaps expanded by later editors with the addition of verses 26–27, may provide further insight into Amos' attitude toward ritual: "Did you bring to me sacrifices and offerings the forty years in the wilderness, O house of Israel?" Amos

appears as a conservative, in the best sense of this term, resenting
elements of Canaanite worship that had become part of Yahwism, and
the reference to the nomadic ideal dramatizes this conflict. In nomadic
tribal society, responsibility for human welfare within the group rested
with each member. It was the duty of each to care for others because
the group was a totality, bound by *hesed*—the unwritten bond of
loyalty uniting those who belong together.[17] Yahweh was bound to
the group by this intimate tie in such a way that injustice and social
disorder within the group demanded that divine power be exercised to
correct the wrong. City life and Ba'alism had brought new concepts. Canaanite life was business-centered: the religion was one of
fertility, growth, productivity and increase, and ethics were, apparently, adapted to these concepts. Yahwism had absorbed the patterns
of Ba'alism. When the nation prospered and the rich became richer,
all was well. Good crops, large flocks and herds and good business
were symbols of divine approval and blessing. What happened to the
individual within this pattern was secondary. There was a general
pervasive feeling of well-being, security and contentment within the
nation. Against this mood of smug complacency Amos launched his
next "woe" (6:1–7), climaxing his attack with the promise of destruction with Yahweh as enemy rather than protector (6:11–14). The
attack is expanded in 8:4–14 and 9:2–4.

AMOS' RELIGIOUS CONCEPTS

Amos' beliefs concerning Yahweh and divine-human relationships
were similar to those held by the J compilers. Yahweh the creator, the
"God of hosts" (Amos never speaks of Yahweh as "God of Israel"),
possessed power over nature and nations. Despite the universalistic
emphasis, Yahweh's particular concern was Israel, the chosen or
elected people. Like J and E, Amos emphasized Yahweh's action in
history in bringing the Hebrews to nationhood and greatness, and
pointed out that the continuance of power and security rested in
Yahweh.

But the election idea had become to the people a guarantee of
divine security,[18] and under this protective cloak moral and ethical

[17] There is no single English word by which to translate *hesed* although perhaps
"loyalty" comes as close as any. For a comprehensive study see Nelson Glueck, *Hesed
in the Bible,* trans. by A. Gottschalk (Cincinnati: The Hebrew Union College Press,
1967), and in the same volume the introductory essay, "Recent Studies in *Hesed,*" by
Gerald A. Larue.

[18] The "covenant" is not mentioned by Amos or any other eighth century prophet
(Hos. 8:1 may be an exception). It may be argued that the covenant is a late
development—originated by J and E and endorsed by Hosea—cf. W. A. Irwin, *The
Old Testament: Keystone of Human Culture* (New York: Henry Schuman, 1952),
pp. 191 ff.; or developed by the Deuteronomists (R. H. Pfeiffer, "The Transmission of
the Book of the Covenant," *Harvard Theological Review,* XXIV (1931), 99, n. 1 and
Introduction to the Old Testament, p. 52; or that it is implied in prophetic writings,
e.g., James Muilenburg, "The History of the Religion of Israel," *The Interpreter's
Bible,* I, 299; W. Eichrodt, *Theology of the Old Testament,* trans. by J. A. Baker
(Philadelphia: Westminster Press, 1961), p. 51. For detailed discussion see G. E.
Mendenhall, "Covenant," *The Interpreter's Dictionary of the Bible* (Nashville:
Abingdon Press, 1962). Substitute terms may have been used to designate the cove-
nant, cf. Huffman, *op. cit.*

abuses developed without restraint. Their God was too small. They limited his interests and powers to subservience to their own personal concerns. Amos sought to expand their concepts. Yahweh was the God who had been involved in the salvation history of the people. The welfare of all was his concern. He could not be limited by popular religious sentiment. Yahweh, who, according to J, had in time past visited judgment upon sinful mankind (Eden, the Flood, Sodom and Gomorrah), now, according to Amos, had judged those whom he had chosen and was about to execute judgment by destruction. The close and deep relationship between Yahweh and Israel (implied by the verb "to know") had been destroyed. The possibility of the survival of a remnant, an idea previously introduced by J (cf. Noah), is only touched upon by Amos (5:15).[19]

The "Day of Yahweh," popularly accepted as a day of darkness for Israel's enemies (already implied in Amos' oracles against foreign nations), was to include the destruction of Israel. The reason for destruction was not lack of ritual observance—there was plenty of that—but the abundance of social evil. Election, according to Amos, implied social responsibilities: justice, mercy, decency; and the smoke of sacrifice could not obscure the evil deed, nor the chanting of hymns obliterate the cry of the wronged. Amos' religious concepts embraced ethics and morals.

Whether or not Amos was a monotheist is a debatable question. It is quite possible that Amos' statement recorded at 9:7 may have come as a distinct shock to his listeners:

> "Are you not like the Ethiopians to me,
> O people of Israel?" says Yahweh.
> "Did I not bring up Israel from the land
> of Egypt, and the Philistines from
> Caphtor and the Syrians from Kir?"

Israel and Judah accepted Yahweh as their deity. When the kingdom separated, Jeroboam I had demonstrated, in the erection of two shrines to Yahweh, that Yahweh was equally the god of Israel and Judah. The quarrel was not Yahweh on one side against the other, but Yahweh with a separation within the family of those who worshiped him. Heretofore, there has been no indication that the Hebrew people conceived of Yahweh as planning the welfare and destinies of other peoples. In fact there is substantial evidence, both prior and subsequent to Amos, that other gods were believed to be responsible for the welfare of the peoples where they were worshiped. Amos moved Hebrew theological speculation from local to international levels. His claim in 9:7, echoed in 6:14 and in the pronouncements of Chapters 1 and 2, that Yahweh was active in the affairs of other peoples has been interpreted as monotheism. Monotheism may be defined loosely as belief in a supreme god, but to be precise, the definition needs to include the rejection or denial of the reality or existence of other gods. Such a denial does not occur in Hebrew literature until the Exile, so that Amos' concept of God is best labeled "monolatry," the worship

---

[19] It is possible that Amos saw Judah continuing as the "chosen people." The idea is more fully developed by other prophets.

of one god without a denial of the existence of other gods. The other gods may not be worshiped or believed to be part of the divine hierarchy as in henotheism,[20] but their reality is not contested. To some, such precise definitions are scholarly hair-splitting, but without them the varieties of religious expression within Israel cannot be discerned.

Amos' utterances resulted from deep personal religious experiences which were not, apparently, shared by everyone. His oracles, prefaced or terminated by "Yahweh says," are to be compared to those of a herald or messenger who speaks what he has been given to say, words, which, as we have noted, burn within demanding utterance. For Amos and for his listeners, the words were the words of God.[21]

What happened to Amos after his Bethel visit and who preserved his oracles are questions without answers. Amos may have had disciples who recorded and pondered his words.[22] He may have written them down himself.[23] It cannot be assumed that two years later when the earthquake came someone remembered Amos' words; human memory is not that good. The preservation of his words must have occurred at the time of, or soon after, their utterance. If these words were part of the cultic New Year, they may have been officially recorded. Certainly the Assyrian conquest must have given them the authority necessary for their ultimate preservation. Amos drops out of known history after the Bethel appearance. The puzzling tale in I Kings 13:1-11 (cf. II Kings 23:16-18) may be, as Wellhausen suggested, a reference to Amos that was displaced from the reign of Jeroboam II to the reign of Jeroboam I. If this is so, Amos was killed by a lion on his return from Judah. The story, edited in its present form by Deuteronomists, may represent an ancient tale, but whether it is to be associated with Amos is questionable.

HOSEA

**Read II
Kings 15;
Hosea 1–14**

Hosea, the only northern prophet whose oracles have survived, is usually dated after Amos. The superscription to his writings is confusing, for it mentions Jeroboam II of Israel (786–746) and four Judaean kings, Uzziah (783–742), Jotham (742–735), Ahaz (735–715) and Hezekiah (715–687). As there is no hint of the fall of Israel, the book is dated prior to 722/21. It would appear, therefore, that the Judaean editors erred in listing Hezekiah, unless it is assumed that, despite the lack of any specific reference to the fall of Israel (cf. however, 13:16), the restoration oracles imply that Israel has been conquered and the people exiled (cf. 11:11; 14:7). Chapter 1:4, promising punishment of Jehu's house, indicates that Hosea's prophetic work began in the time

---

[20] Cf. *Supra,* n. 14, chap. 10.

[21] Cf. R. B. Y. Scott, *The Relevance of the Prophets,* pp. 84 ff. for a discussion of the prophetic word.

[22] R. B. Y. Scott, *op. cit.,* p. 72, suggests that Amos' disciples initiated the practice of preserving in written form their master's oracles.

[23] C. Kuhl, *The Prophets of Israel* (London: Oliver and Boyd, 1960), p. 60, thinks Amos recorded his oracles after having returned home.

of Jeroboam, for Jehu's dynasty ended less than a year after Jeroboam's death when Shallum murdered Zechariah. Because Hosea 6:8 and 12:11 allude to Gilead as part of Israel, it is probable that the area had not yet been annexed by Assyria (cf. II Kings 15:29); therefore, this material was written before 735. Chapters 5:8–10, 13 may reflect the so-called Syro-Ephraimitic war (cf. II Kings 15:37). Within the text are reflections of the confused, hectic power struggle that followed Jeroboam's death, when leaders came to power not because of charismatic qualities but by intrigue and murder (cf. 7:7; 8:4, 10; 10:3).

External events are also reflected. Assyria, always a menacing power, was directly affecting Israelite politics (7:11; 8:9; 9:3, 6; 10:6; 12:1). The precise length of Hosea's ministry must remain uncertain, but from the evidence, it would appear that he was most active between 746 and 735, although a date extending beyond the collapse of Israel cannot be ruled out.

The general prosperity noted in Amos' time continued and with the same inequities, but it was not only social injustice that troubled Hosea; the psychic illness of the nation, the infidelity and apostasy, the hollowness of the relationships between Yahweh and his people stirred him far more. If the central stress of Amos' writings can be said to be a concern for justice and ethics (Amos 5:24), the major emphasis of Hosea's work is on the steadfast, reliable, continuing loyalty and love (*ḥesed*) of Yahweh for his wayward, unfaithful people (Hos. 6:6)—an emphasis that appears to have deep roots in the prophet's bitter marital experiences. Hosea's image of Israel as an unfaithful wife who forsakes Yahweh for Ba'al is adopted by subsequent prophets.

The book of Hosea can be divided into two segments: a short introductory section (chs. 1–3) concerned with the prophet's marriage to Gomer, and their three children—Jezreel, Not-pitied and Not-my-people—and a larger collection of oracles (chs. 4–14) dealing with Israel.[24] There is no clear-cut grouping of materials within the second part and in some places there is a confusion of ideas. Some statements are little more than mutilated fragments requiring textual emendations for intelligible translation.[25] For these reasons the book of Hosea has often been labeled "disorderly," and there have been those who have suggested that perhaps there is a reflection of a disturbed, disorderly personality in the work. It is more probable that because Hosea's work was preserved in Judah after the fall of Israel—possibly having been taken there by disciples fleeing Assyrian armies—the lack of order and the poor text might reflect the confused historical situation, rather than the man. Some additions have been made to the original text, the most obvious of which are aimed at Judah, seeking to exempt that kingdom from the prophetic indictment (cf. 1:7; 4:15; 6:11; 11:12). Other additions include 1:10–2:1 which may have been

---

24 Yehezkel Kaufmann, *The Religion of Israel,* trans. and abridged by Moshe Greenberg (Chicago: University of Chicago Press, 1960), pp. 368 f. postulates two different writers, a ninth century prophet for chs. 1–3 and Hosea for the remainder.

25 Fragmented portions include 2:2–5, 16–17; 4:4–19; 8:1–3; 9:11b; 10:8–10; 12:7–10, 11–13. For details consult any analytical commentary.

added during the Exile when hopes of restoration were strong,[26] and 14:9 which is in the style of wisdom literature (cf. Proverbs). Passages that have been challenged but which must remain *sub judice* include 2:18, 21–23, and 14:5–7.

Despite the disturbed condition of the text, much of Hosea's descriptive skill can be discerned. At times he employs a direct style as when he scoffs at those seeking oracles from wooden idols, "their staff gives them oracles" (4:12); or in his rejection of the golden calf symbol, "a workman made it, it is not God" (8:5); or as he mocks the stupidity of a ritual act, "Men kiss calves!" (13:2). On other occasions he uses metaphors: "Ephraim is a cake not turned" (that is, half-baked! 7:8), and like "a wild ass wandering alone" or "like a dove, silly and without sense" (7:11). With striking imagery he portrays the manner of Israel's folly, "For they sow the wind, and they shall reap the whirlwind" (8:7). The power of the prophet's message rests in no small part in his magnificent figures of speech.

Chapters 1–3. Practically all that we know of Hosea's personal life comes from these chapters, but numerous problems have been raised concerning proper interpretation. The opening oracles, in biographical prose, state that in response to Yahweh's command to marry a "wife of harlotry" Hosea married Gomer, daughter of Diblaim (unknown). Three children were born and to each the prophet gave a symbolic name: Jezreel, a son, called after the place where Jehu's dynasty came to power (II Kings 10:11), served as a warning that Yahweh was going to punish Jehu's line; *Lo'-ruhamah* or "Not-pitied," a daughter, signified that Yahweh had no more pity for his people; and *Lo'-ammi* or "Not-my-people," a son, symbolized the broken relationships between Yahweh and Israel.

By modern western ethical standards and in view of the condemnation of harlotry throughout Hosea's writings, the divine command to marry a "wife of harlotry" has seemed incredible to many writers. Some have treated the account as allegory—without foundation in fact, but designed to teach—but this thesis has had no supporters in recent years.[27] There is no hint of allegorical interpretation in the account; the name "Gomer" has no real symbolic significance,[28] and allegorical interpretation tends to destroy the power of the symbol. Others have suggested that Yahweh's command is to be understood in a proleptic sense, in which the writer looked back over what had taken place viewing Gomer in the light of what she had become. According to this interpretation, Gomer was not a harlot at the time of marriage.[29] A contradictory argument suggests that it was only after the marriage that the prophet realized what Gomer really was.[30] In his

[26] For a defense of the authenticity of this passage, see John Mauchline, "Hosea," *The Interpreter's Bible*, VI, 573 ff.

[27] For a history of this interpretation, cf. O. Eissfeldt, *The Old Testament, an Introduction*, trans. by P. R. Ackroyd (New York: Harper and Row, 1965), p. 389.

[28] For discussion of the name "Gomer," cf. Mauchline, *op. cit.*, p. 569.

[29] George A. Smith, *The Book of the Twelve Prophets*, The Expositors' Bible (New York: Hodder and Stoughton, n.d.), I, 232 ff.

[30] Weiser, *op. cit.*, p. 234.

awareness that he had married a harlot, Hosea understood how
Yahweh felt about Israel. Still others believe that Hosea deliberately
married a harlot because he believed he had been ordered to do so[31]
or because a sublimated sex drive drove him to take a woman from a
social level he abhorred.[32] Gomer has been classified as a worshiper of
Ba'al participating as a cult prostitute in sexual rituals,[33] and she has
been defended as an innocent woman, the victim of "slanderous
insinuations" of modern critics, with the references to "adultery"
signifying spiritual apostasy.[34]

Nor have the children been spared. Some think all three were
Hosea's and that only later, after the birth of the third, was Gomer's
adultery recognized by the prophet;[35] others think that the first child,
Jezreel, was Hosea's and the two whose names symbolize rejection were
children of adultery.[36] Hosea begged the children to plead with their
mother to change her ways but to no avail, and the prophet divorced
her with terms used for disestablishment of marriage, "she is not my
wife and I am not her husband."[37]

In Chapter 3, an autobiographical section, the prophet states, "And
Yahweh said to me, 'Go again, love a woman who is beloved of a
paramour[38] and is an adultress' ", or, in another translation, "And
again Yahweh said to me, 'Go love a woman who is beloved of a
paramour and is an adultress' "—the text can support either. Much
debate centers in the identification of this woman. Is she Gomer whom
Hosea again takes as his wife by paying the marriage price, placing her
on probation because of his conviction that Yahweh still loves Israel
despite the apostasy of the people?[39] Is this story a legendary or
allegorical addition?[40] Is the story an autobiographical duplicate of
the biography given in the first chapter, with differences explained by
different time of writing and perhaps a different mind set?[41]

It has been argued that the symbolism of the marriage demands that
Gomer be the woman in both stories and that they must be seen in
sequence: as Hosea loved Gomer, so Yahweh loved Israel; as Gomer

[31] Fleming James, *Personalities of the Old Testament* (New York: Charles
Scribner's Sons, 1939), p. 233.

[32] W. O. E. Oesterly and T. H. Robinson, *An Introduction to the Books of the
Old Testament*, pp. 351 f.

[33] Leroy Waterman, "Hosea, Chapters 1–3 in Retrospect and Prospect," *Journal of
Near Eastern Studies*, XIV (1955), 100–109.

[34] Pfeiffer, *Introduction to the Old Testament*, p. 568.

[35] J. P. Hyatt, *Prophetic Religion* (New York: Abingdon-Cokesbury Press, 1947),
p. 42.

[36] George A. F. Knight, *Hosea*, The Torch Bible Commentaries (London: S.C.M.
Press, 1960), pp. 44 f.

[37] For forms of divorce, cf. DeVaux, *Ancient Israel*, pp. 34 f.

[38] The phrase "beloved of a paramour" may have cultic significance. Cf. A. D.
Tushingham, "A Reconsideration of Hosea, Chapters 1–3," *Journal of Near Eastern
Studies*, XII (1953), 150–153. The mention of "raisin cakes," a cultic food,
strengthens the argument (cf. Jer. 7:18).

[39] J. A. Bewer, *The Prophets*, Harper's Annotated Bible (New York: Harper and
Brothers, 1949), pp. 491 f.

[40] Cf. Norman H. Snaith, *Mercy and Sacrifice. A Study of the Book of Hosea*
(London: S.C.M. Press, 1950).

[41] Lindblom, *op. cit.*, pp. 165 ff.

became a harlot and sought other men, so Israel became apostate in the pursuit of Ba'al; as Hosea divorced Gomer, so Yahweh abandoned Israel; but as Hosea discovered his love for Gomer, so he recognized that Yahweh still loved Israel and would receive the nation back or, in another interpretation, as Hosea recognized Yahweh's continuing love for Israel, he took Gomer back.[42]

With equally rational arguments it is proposed that Chapters 1 and 3 are parallel accounts: Hosea was ordered by Yahweh to love a woman who had a predisposition to harlotry; according to marriage patterns, he purchased the woman but, knowing of her ways, he placed her on probation, prohibiting at first all sexual relationships; later, having become the mother of his child Jezreel, she was found to be an adultress, as the names of the two younger children make clear, and was divorced, symbolizing Yahweh's rejection of his people and the punishment that was to come.[43] According to this interpretation there is no forgiveness and restoration in Hosea.

Quite obviously one can become lost in diverse opinions and theories. Actually, only the barest outline of Hosea's marriage can be discerned; the details are hypotheses and no single hypothesis completely satisfies. What is significant is the impact upon the prophet of his experience with the harlotrous woman, whether she was Gomer or another, for Hosea's oracles are interspersed with references to the adultery and harlotry of Israel as symbols of apostasy.[44] Of equal importance is Hosea's recognition of the tenaciousness of love, and Yahweh's love for his people is described in terms of a compassion and loyalty that will not let go despite the disloyalty of the people. The degree to which Hosea identified his own experience with that of Yahweh is quite clear in Chapter 2 where the opening remarks are apparently addressed to Hosea's children, but as the statement expands, Gomer becomes Israel and Hosea's complaint becomes Yahweh's indictment. Returns from the worship of Ba'al listed as bread, water, wool, flax, oil and drink, were gifts of Yahweh, unrecognized by the wayward woman or nation. Only by punishment could the nation be brought to an awakening, after which the honeymoon days of the desert, when Yahweh and Israel were alone following the flight from Egypt, could be relived. The extent to which Canaanite forms and terminology had been taken into popular Yahwism is clear from 2:16 where the prophet indicates that Yahweh is called "My Ba'al." The oracle of hope in 2:19 looks to a new marriage relationship for the old had been violated and terminated by divorce.

Chapters 4–14. Attempts to organize the materials in these chapters usually result in a listing of topics touched upon by the prophet.[45] There is no order and one idea stumbles over the next. Authenticating statements such as "Thus says Yahweh" or "says Yahweh" which neatly

[42] Hyatt, *op. cit.*, pp. 42 f., Bewer, *op. cit.* p. 492.

[43] Lindblom, *op. cit.*, pp. 167 f.

[44] Exceeded only by Ezekiel, chaps. 16 and 23.

[45] Mauchline, *op. cit.*, pp. 557 f. discusses the possibility that the oracles were given at a New Year festival.

open and close Amos' pronouncements are absent here, and one oracle merges into the next. Echoes of literary forms employed by Hosea remain. For example, the opening oracle of Chapter 4 uses a law court pattern and begins with Yahweh's statement of complaint (4:1–2). In 4:2 a heraldic or messenger style is introduced in which the prophet, as God's messenger, repeats the words of condemnation and punishment (see also 5:1 ff.; 5:8 ff.; 8:1 ff.). Unfortunately, the recognition of forms does not help us very much.

What are far more important are the underlying themes that provide the basis for the prophet's indictments: election, the history of apostasy, Yahweh's loyal love and compassion, and the threat of punishment tempered with the possibility of redemption. Election, the miracle of God's choice of Israel, runs like a leitmotif through Hosea's oracles, underlying all other themes and appearing uniquely in varied similes, now as love of a father for a son (11:1), now as care employed in cultivating a vineyard (9:10). The illustrations are strong and warm. Israel is a wayward youth testing Yahweh's love by rebellion, forgetful of the patience and love given by Yahweh during the tender growing years. Israel is like grapes growing in the wilderness (9:10), becoming a lush vineyard under Yahweh's care (10:1). Israel is a favorite heifer spared hard labor by a kind master (10:11). Each image reveals the special place the nation held in Yahweh's love and each picture is darkened by Israel's behavior.

The national history is sketched (possibly on the basis of the E tradition), and despite its foundation in Yahweh's election, the record is stained by greed, indifference and apostasy (12:2–14; 13:5 f.) and the relegating of Yahweh to a subordinate role in Israel's religion (4:17; 5:4; 7:15). Yahweh, ready to punish but moved by the compelling power of election ties, withheld his anger (11:8 ff.). But the time for compassion had passed and punishment was at hand. In a series of startling descriptions, the prophet portrays Yahweh as the enemy, as a lurking lion or leopard or bear (5:14; 13:7 f.), as a moth and dry rot (5:12), as the slayer of children (9:16) and as the destructive east wind (13:15).

As election was the basis for expressions of relationship between Yahweh and Israel, apostasy, or harlotry as Hosea prefers to call it, formed the basis for estrangement and social evils. There can be no question that Hosea believed that as Yahweh's influence became second to that of Ba'al, moral and ethical standards declined. It has often been noted that Hosea's list of social evils (4:1–2) parallels the prohibitions in Yahweh's decalogue. Religion or "knowledge of God" could not guide when priests and prophets (the ordinary channels for

A SEAL IMPRESSION FROM THE HANDLE OF A TAX JAR. *Taxes were collected in kind and that portion of grain or oil or other produce destined for the royal coffers was stored in large jars bearing the royal insignia: a handle stamped with the winged symbol and the name of the tax district. This seal reads "Belonging to the King" in the top line and "Hebron" in the second. It comes from the eighth or seventh centuries.*

trasmitting Yahweh's will) were incapable (4:4–6). The perfunctory "turning to Yahweh" was a mockery (5:4; 6:1–4; 7:14; 8:2, 3a, 13). It was to Ba'al and wooden idols that men turned for guidance, and to participation in the sexual rites and sacrifices at the high places for religious expression (4:12–14a). Even kings betrayed their calling, were drunken on feast days (7:5), and were little more than non-charismatic individuals of short tenure (7:7; 8:4; 10:7), who in confusion sought alliances with Egypt or Assyria (5:13; 7:11; 12:1), ignoring Yahweh, the one source of national salvation and deliverance (7:10; 13:4).

The national way of life pictured by Hosea is Canaanite. The waves of emphasis on sexual rituals, idol worship, and meaningless cultic rites, and the frantic search for meaning and security that rise and fall throughout the book, leave the impression of a nation gone mad, whirling aimlessly and precariously on the brink of disaster. The picture is extreme, echoing the prophet's emotions.

Hosea's portrayal of Yahweh is more anthropopathic than anthropomorphic.[46] Yahweh's love is like that of a husband for a wife or a parent for a child. His anger grows from outrage and frustration as he struggles with Israel's fate (7:13; 11:8 ff.) calling for return and reconciliation (14:1 ff.). Harsh, destructive punishment is promised, tempered with the hope of future restoration (14:4 ff.). Despite the anthropopathisms, Hosea never demeans Yahweh: Yahweh is God, reacting on a divine plane, "For I am God not man, the Holy One in your midst, and I will not destroy" (11:9). The term "Holy One," used for the first time in the Bible, marks the separation between the divine and the common, between the sacred and the profane. Yahweh is "other" than man, separated by majesty, purity and power.[47] For Hosea, the deity is the saving God of Israel, "I am Yahweh, your God from the land of Egypt, you know no God but me and besides me there is no savior" (13:4). Attempts to maintain national safety and welfare through Ba'al or by human means were doomed, for Yahweh controlled the forces of nature and the life-power of Israel. Yahweh requested not sacrifice but fidelity, not empty forms but a religion of meaning, "For I desire *hesed*, not sacrifice, knowledge of God rather than burnt offerings" (6:6). Following the punishment, Yahweh would bring about a new Exodus and once again lead his people into deep, meaningful relationships. The old bond was canceled; a new relationship would have to emerge.

[46] "Anthropopathism" means the attributing of human feelings and emotions to the deity as opposed to "anthropomorphism" which refers to the depiction of the deity in human form as in the J creation story.

[47] For discussions of the concept of holiness, see J. Pedersen, *Israel, Its Life and Culture*, III–IV, 264 ff.; L. Köhler, *Old Testament Theology*, A. S. Todd (trans.) (Philadelphia: The Westminster Press, 1958), pp. 51 ff.; W. Eichrodt, *Theology of the Old Testament*, pp. 270 ff.; Th. C. Vriezen, *An Outline of Old Testament Theology* (Oxford: Basil Blackwell, 1958), pp. 149 ff. A more detailed treatment is found in M. Eliade, *The Sacred and the Profane* (New York: Harcourt, Brace and Company, 1959).

18

Isaiah and Micah

OF the two Judaean prophets who were active in the eighth century, there can be little doubt that Isaiah was the more powerful. He lived in the capital city of Jerusalem and was brought into immediate association with the Temple, with the royal family and with national and international policies. Nevertheless, Micah, who dwelt in the Shephelah was not out of touch with the political activities of the era, for Judah was a small country and, despite the limited means of communication, information was rapidly disseminated. Because of the bulk of Isaiah's work (amplified by later additions) it is listed among that of the Major Prophets, but the smaller book of Micah's words is classified with the Minor Prophets.

ISAIAH OF JERUSALEM

The book of Isaiah, which at first glance appears to be the work of one individual, the eighth century prophet, Isaiah of Jerusalem, is considered by most scholars to be composite. The book can be divided into three parts:

a. Chapters 1–39 contain, with numerous additions, oracles of Isaiah of Jerusalem, called First (I) or Proto-Isaiah.
b. Chapters 40–55 record the words of a sixth century prophet living in exile in Babylon, called Deutero-Isaiah or Second (II) Isaiah.
c. Chapters 56–66 from the post-Exilic period are a continuation of the work of Deutero-Isaiah, probably by his disciples, and perhaps containing some of the Babylonian prophet's sayings. This section is called Trito-Isaiah or Third (III) Isaiah.

Questions about the integrity of the book of Isaiah can be said to have begun when Abraham Ibn Ezra, a Jewish scholar of Spain (d. 1197), remarked in a commentary that Isaiah's name at the head of the book was no more guarantee of authorship than Samuel's name at the head of the two books bearing his name. In the eighteenth century, analytical study by J. C. Doederlein (1775) and J. G. Eichhorn (1782) drew clear distinctions between I and II Isaiah. Subsequent research strengthened their arguments. The basis for the division is as follows:

1. There is no indication within the book of Isaiah that the contents are to be taken as the work of a single author, and there are reasons to doubt the integrity of the book.

2. There are striking stylistic variations and differences in vocabulary. Not only does Isaiah 40–55 form a unity of thought and emphasis centered in the restoration from Babylonian captivity, but the style of writing differs from I Isaiah. Isaiah of Jerusalem used brief, emphatic diction so familiar in eighth century prophetic oracles. His vocabulary is limited and his utterances are designed for delivery to specific audiences. Deutero-Isaiah's work is more uniform and lyrical in style, more hymnic in quality, and more extensive in vocabulary.

3. There are differences in historical interest: I Isaiah is concerned with Assyria as the dominant power. The kings with whom he associated are those of the last half of the eighth century, and the setting of his work is this period. In II Isaiah the Babylonian Exile is the background for the proclamation of deliverance, and the prophet is concerned with interpreting the Exilic experience. The dominant nation is Babylon. Interest is focused on a new rising power, Persia, and the monarch Cyrus is named and recognized as a deliverer of the people (Isa. 45:1). Such detailed information could not have been known to Isaiah of Jerusalem, for the Persian nation did not come into existence until after the eighth century.

4. There is a difference in theological content. Isaiah of Jerusalem preached doom, the proximity of punishment, and the remnant concept. Isaiah of Babylon announced that the punishment was past, suffering was over, and deliverance was at hand.

5. Differences between II and III Isaiah will be discussed later, but there is reasonable evidence to demonstrate that Trito-Isaiah, despite similarity of style, is later than Deutero-Isaiah.

From the start the results of analytical study were challenged by competent scholars, including the nineteenth century German exegete Franz Delitzsch, and the controversy has continued in diminishing intensity to the present time.[1] Different historical situations reflected in the writings are explained by the argument that the literature is revealed and that the prophet spoke not his own words but God's; and if Isaiah, 200 years before the time of Cyrus, was able to predict the deliverer's coming and he does come, then the verification of the words proves that they are God's and that God is a God of history. Differences in style are dismissed by the suggestion that in dealing with future events the prophet, freed of the present, employed a different mode of expression. Appeals are also made to tradition. Ben Sira's writings were much closer to Isaiah's time (second century B.C.) than those of present-day scholars and no mention of a division is made in his work (Ecclesiasticus 48:20 ff.). Nor did the first century A.D. Jewish historian Josephus (Antiquities: XI: 1:1 f.), who suggests that Cyrus freed the Jews because he read the prophecy of Isaiah, recognize more than one Isaiah. The Isaiah scroll from the Qumran community on the Dead Sea, the earliest Hebrew text of Isaiah, makes no division between Chapters 1–39 and 40–66, and this document is dated first

---

[1] For a defense of the unity of Isaiah cf. Oswald Allis, *The Unity of Isaiah* (London: Tyndale Press, 1950); E. J. Young, *Studies in Isaiah* (Grand Rapids: Eerdmans, 1954) and *Who Wrote Isaiah?* (Grand Rapids: Eerdmans, 1958).

methodology for literary analysis set forth in the chapter "How Do We
Read?" is accepted.

How and why materials from authors separated by centuries should
have been combined is not known, and the history of the text is both
confused and complex. II Chron. 32:32 implies that Isaiah's work, in
part at least, may have been included in the lost "Book of the Kings of
Judah and Israel." If II Chron. 36:22 and Ezra 1:1–2 refer to
II Isaiah's prophecy of the return from Exile (cf. Isa. 44:28; 45:1–3)
rather than Jeremiah's more general comment (Jer. 29:10), then,
perhaps, Deutero-Isaiah was at one time attached to the book of
Jeremiah. By the second century B.C., as Ben Sira's references demonstrate, the book of Isaiah had taken its present form.

Isaiah of Jerusalem spoke of disciples (8:16) and the biographical
sections of the book undoubtedly came from these followers. It has
been proposed that there was an Isaianic school or guild responsible
for the additions to the original work. This attractive proposition
presents difficulties, for it suggests a line of disciples extending over
two centuries, not mentioned in biblical sources, and coming into
prominence only at the close of the Babylonian captivity. On the other
hand, there can be little doubt that Isaiah's words and those of other
eighth century prophets were studied and restudied, particularly during the Exile. In the Exilic period, when words of doom must have
assumed new and deeper significance because they were fulfilled, those
students or disciples who pored over these oracles perhaps were led to
new insight, understanding and hope. Out of their insight could have
come Deutero-Isaiah with its message of redemption, utilizing some
Isaianic terms ("Holy one of Israel") and developing ideas drawn
from Isaiah of Jerusalem. The message, appended to the great prophet's work, completed the pattern of doom and hope of a remnant with
the joyous announcement that what was promised was about to be
fulfilled. Beyond such speculation we cannot go at present.[2]

LITERARY ANALYSIS OF THE TEXT

The complexity of Isaiah 1–39 makes possible a variety of literary
analyses. There is general agreement that Isaiah 1–39 is composed of
smaller collections of prophetic oracles, autobiographical and biographical materials representing Isaiah's work or reports on his work
by disciples, and non-Isaianic writings. Some sections may be dated by
content or superscriptions (cf. 6:1; 7:1; 14:28; 20:1). Some non-
Isaianic materials are readily recognized because they contradict sayings
of Isaiah to which they have been appended or because they portray

[2] For specific comment on the "Isaianic School," cf. A. Bentzen, *Introduction to
the Old Testament* (Copenhagen: G. E. C. Gads Forlag, 1949), II, 114; R. H.
Kennett, *The Composition of the Book of Isaiah in the Light of History and
Archaeology*, The Schweich Lectures, 1909 (London: Henry Frowde, 1910), p. 40;
Sidney Smith, *Isaiah, Chapters XL–LV* (London: Oxford University Press, 1944),
p. 75.

idealistic, eschatological pictures of the restoration of Judah, indicating that they come from the Exilic or post-Exilic period. Some material is also separated on the basis of style, a method that is far from reliable. Following the detailed literary analysis below, the text will be discussed in terms of historical periods (so far as they can be determined) out of which various portions have come.

Broadly speaking, six major divisions may be identified in Isaiah 1–39:

I. Chapters 1–12, oracles dealing primarily with Judah and Jerusalem.
II. Chapters 13–23, oracles directed against foreign nations.
III. Chapters 24–27, the so-called "Little Apocalypse of Isaiah."
IV. Chapters 28–33, a miscellaneous collection of sayings.
V. Chapters 34–35, oracles of judgment and restoration.
VI. Chapters 36–39, material on Hezekiah's revolt against Sennacherib paralleling II Kings 18–20.

Within this broad outline, smaller collections can be recognized. Non-Isaianic materials are in italics.

I. Chapters 1–12 Oracles concerning Judah and Jerusalem.
1. 1:1–2:4—a collection of oracles on Judah's sin terminating with an eschatological restoration oracle.[3]
   a. *1:1 An editorial superscription* designed to introduce Isaiah's collected works.
   b. 1:2–4 Israel's estrangement from Yahweh.
   c. 1:5–9 Desolation during war.
   d. 1:10–17 Prophetic torah (instruction) in the laws of Yahweh.
   e. 1:18–20 An appeal and warning.
   f. 1:21–25 A diatribe in the form of a funeral dirge over Jerusalem.
   g. *1:26, 27 Fragmentary restoration oracles.*
   h. 1:28–31 An oracle of judgment.
   i. *2:1–4 An eschatological restoration oracle* also found in Micah 4:1–3, suggesting that it may be part of a cultic hymn on the Day of Yahweh used in New Year rites and inserted by editors of Isaiah's and Micah's work. Read Isaiah 2:12 for a contrasting concept of the "day." On the other hand, the oracle may come from the Exile when hopes for restoration were strong. The text is better preserved in Micah.
2. 2:5–4:6 Oracles of condemnation and threat.
   a. 2:5 An exhortation.
   b. 2:6–21 A diatribe against divination and idolatry with the threat of judgment on Yahweh's day. Something of a refrain appears in 2:10, 19, and 21.
   c. *2:22 An interpolation, not found in the LXX.*
   d. 3:1–15 The threat of loss of leaders with anarchy to follow. Verse 15 contains one of the few "signatures" to Isaiah's oracles.

[3] Eschatological oracles deal with the end of an age or the end of time and appear to be closely linked to the Day of Yahweh concept. They are often introduced by the phrase "in that day" and may be constructive—pointing to restoration of devastated areas or the realization of paradisaical hopes through an act of God—or destructive, looking to a day of violence, judgment, wrath and punishment. The Greek word *eschaton* means "the last thing," and "eschatology" is a doctrine of last things.

e. 3:16–4:1 Condemnation of the women of Jerusalem. The prose expansion in *verses 18–23 containing a catalogue of female accessories is probably the work of a later writer.*

f. *4:2–6 An eschatological restoration oracle* from the late Exilic or early post-Exilic period.

3. 5 and 9:8–11:9 A collection of oracles, linked by the refrain "For all this his anger is not turned away and his hand is stretched out still" (5:25; 9:12, 17, 21; 10:4), and interrupted by biographical materials (Chapters 6 and following).

   a. 5:1–7 The song of the vineyard.

   b. 5:8–24; 10:1–2 A pattern of seven "woes" against individual sins.

   c. 5:25; 9:8–21; 10:3–4 Oracles against Israel.

   d. 5:26–30; 10:5–9 Assyria, rod of Yahweh's anger against Israel.

   e. *10:10–11 Warning oracle* directed against Jerusalem—probably a late addition.

   f. 10:12–19 Oracle warning Assyria of the danger of arrogance.

   g. 10:20–23 Oracles on the remnant of Israel.

   h. 10:24–27 Oracle of hope for Judah.

   i. 10:28–32 Descriptive oracle of the approach of Assyrian soldiers.

   j. 10:33–34 Oracle on Yahweh's devastation.

   k. *11:1–9 An eschatological ode with messianic overtones terminating the collection.*

   l. *11:10–16 A post-Exilic addition, also eschatological.*

4. 6:1–9:7 Autobiographical and biographical materials, comprising the earliest materials in the book.

   a. 6 The prophet's vision and commission to prophesy. The text of the final verse is corrupt.

   b. 7:1–9 Material from the Syro-Ephraimitic crisis.

   c. 7:10–17 The Immanuel oracle.

   d. 7:18–23 Four pictures of devastation: 18–19, 20, 21–22, 23–25.

   e. 8:1–4 Oracle on the fall of Damascus and Samaria.

   f. 8:5–8, 9–10 Oracles of threat and protection. *Verses 9 and 10 may be non-Isaianic additions.*

   g. 8:11–15, 16–22 Autobiographical notes.

   h. 9:1 Oracle of hope for the restoration of Israel.

   i. *9:2–7 Messianic oracle.* If this is by Isaiah, as some scholars now suggest, it appears to celebrate the birth of a royal prince of the Davidic line. The chronology of the kings of this period is difficult, but it could hardly be Ahaz' son, Hezekiah, despite the fact that his name—meaning "Yahweh is my strength"—fits nicely. If it is an enthronement song,[4] Verse 6 would have to be interpreted symbolically, signifying the beginning of the king's role as representative or "son" of Yahweh.[5] If this is an enthronement song it may have been written on the occasion of Hezekiah's accession.

5. 12 *Two psalms, 1–2 and 3–6, reflecting hope and joy in restoration appended to close this section,* are from the Exilic and post-Exilic periods.

[4] Cf. Margaret B. Crook, "A Suggested Occasion for Isaiah 9:2–7 and 11:1–9," *Journal of Biblical Literature*, LXVIII (1949), 213–224, who argues that this is a coronation song from the enthronement of Jehoash, the boy king (II Kings. 11:21).

[5] For brief comment, cf. R. B. Y. Scott, "Isaiah," *The Interpreter's Bible*, V, 231 f. In the enthronement ritual the king may have been given a new name and thus, in a sense, have been "reborn." Cf. Azariah ("Yahweh is my helper") changed to Uzziah ("Yahweh is my strength"). Cf. E. Leslie, *Isaiah* (New York: Abingdon Press, 1963), p. 22.

II. Chapters 13–23   Oracles against foreign nations.

1. *13:1–14:23   Oracles against Babylon from the late Exilic period.*
2. 14:24–27, 28–32   Oracles against Assyria and Philistia.
3. *15–16   Oracles against Moab.* These were used in part by Jeremiah (48:28–38). If these oracles are by Isaiah, there is no clue concerning the time or occasion when they were given.
4. 17   Oracles reflecting the Syro-Ephraimitic war.
   a. 1–3   Against Damascus.
   b. 4–6   An eschatological oracle concerning Israel.
   c. 7–8, 9   Two eschatological oracles.
   d. 10–11   Oracle of condemnation.
   e. 12–14   Oracle of judgment with no specific group mentioned.
5. 18   Oracle on Ethiopia-Egypt at the time of the fall of Ashdod. *Verse 7 is not part of the original oracle.*
6. 19   Oracles on Egypt.
   a. 1–4   Threat of anarchy.
   b. 5–10   The failure of the Nile.
   c. 11–15   Lack of leadership.
   d. 16–17   Eschatological oracle.
   e. *18, 19–22   Late eschatological oracle.* It is unlikely that it refers to the establishment of a temple at Heliopolis in the second century B.C.[6] More probably the Elephantine temple of the sixth century is meant.[7]
   f. *23–25   A late eschatological oracle.*
7. 20   A biographical section on the failure of the conspiracy against Assyria and the fall of Ashdod.
8. *21   Sixth century oracles on Babylon, Dumah and Arabia.*
9. 22   Oracles on Sennacherib's attack on Jerusalem.
   a. 1–4   The valley of vision.
   b. 5–11   The day of tumult (8b–11 in prose).
   c. 12–13   The reaction of the people.
   d. 15–25   A domestic issue.
10. 23   Oracles against Tyre (*13, 15, 17–18 are late additions*).

III. *Chapters 24–27   The little apocalypse—from the post-Exilic period.*

IV. Chapters 28–33   Miscellaneous oracles.

1. 28–31   The Assyrian Cycle.
   a. 28:1–4   The fall of Israel.
   b. 28:5–6   Eschatological oracle.
   c. 28:7–13   Oracle on the word of Yahweh.
   d. 28:14–19   Oracle against necromancy.
   e. 28:20–22   An oracle of destruction.
   f. 28:23–29   An oracle on farming.
   g. 29:1–5c, 6   An oracle on the destruction of Jerusalem. (*Verses 5ab, 7–8 are a later addition reversing Isaiah's words.*)
   h. 29:9–19   An oracle on the blindness of the people. (*Verses 11–12 are a prose expansion.*)
   i. 29:13–14   An oracle on emptiness of worship.
   j. 29:15–16   An oracle on politics (Verse 16 seems to stand apart).
   k. *29:17–24   Two late oracles of restoration 1–21, 22–24.*
   l. 30:1–7   Two oracles against Egyptian alliances: 1–5, 6–7.
   m. 30:8–11   An oracle to record for future testimony.

---

6 Josephus, *Wars:* 7:10:3.

7 Cf. article "Elephantine Papyrus" in *The Interpreter's Dictionary of the Bible.*

n. 30:12–14   An oracle on lack of trust.
o. 30:15–17   An oracle against Egyptian alliances.
p. *30:18–26   Restoration oracle—late.*
q. 30:27–28   Theophanic oracle.
r. 30:29–33   A salvation oracle.
s. 31:1–5   An oracle against Assyrian alliances. *Vs. 5 is a late addition reversing the thought of the preceding verses.*
t. *31:6–7   A late eschatological oracle.*
u. 31:8–9   An anti-Assyrian salvation oracle.
v. *32:1–8   A messianic oracle—late.*
w. 32:9–14   An oracle against the women.
x. *32:15–20   A late restoration oracle.*
y. *33   A wisdom psalm.*

V. Chapters 34–35   Post-Exilic restoration oracles.
VI. Chapters 36–39   Biographical material on Hezekiah's revolt. The material in this section is the same as that found in II Kings 18:13 to 19:37 with one exception: II Kings 18:14–16 which describes Hezekiah's heavy payments to Assyria and his willing capitulation to Sennacherib.

It is possible to conjecture how these collections may have developed. The earliest collection of materials, the biographical and auto-biographical materials in Chapters 6 to 9, may have been gathered by Isaiah and his disciples. Another early section, Chapters 28 to 31, is composed of oracles that the prophet may have gathered. With Chapters 6 to 9 as a nucleus, other oracular materials from small collections were added to form the larger unit, Chapters 1–12. These basic materials were expanded over a long period of time by the addition of new materials, in some instances in fairly large units and in other cases in single oracles or statements. The final composition appears to have taken from some time before the second century B.C.

ISAIAH, THE MAN

Despite many oracles and the biographical material, it is surprising to realize how little we actually know about Isaiah. It is clear that he is a Jerusalemite, one who loves the city (cf. 8:18; 28:16), yet one who looks with unclouded vision recognizing evils that infest it. There is no indication that the prophet traveled to other places, and it has been surmised that perhaps he lived all his life in the environs of Jerusalem.

Like Hosea, his contemporary in Israel, he was married, but unlike the Israelite prophet, he gives no hint of marital discord. Like Hosea, Isaiah gives his children symbolic names. Unlike Amos, Isaiah encounters no difficulty when he goes to the temple, and the experience that was to affect his whole life took place within the temple precincts. Nor did Isaiah encounter hostility from those in authority, for the prophet appears to be on intimate terms with both Ahaz and Hezekiah. Because of his participation in national affairs, he has been called "the statesman prophet," but such a label restricts rather than explains the prophet's interests. The role of the prophet as a charismatic speaker for Yahweh included many responsibilities and embraced many issues, including politics.

The social evils of the day were to Isaiah, as to Amos, an offense against Yahweh, and the empty forms of religion that led men to ignore the plight of others were treated as a mockery. Those appointed to lead continually proved their ineptness, and Isaiah's condemnations of princes, priests, prophets and judges echo the feelings of Amos about these same persons, and his scorn for the women of Jerusalem is as virulent as was Amos'. Possibly the best way to understand and know the prophet is to read his oracles in historical context.

ISAIAH AND THE HISTORY OF THE PERIOD

Read II
Kings 15–20;
II Chron.
26–32

Isaiah's oracles are so intricately related to happenings of his era, that the history of the period must be understood. The following outline is drawn from accounts in II Kings, supplemented by information from Chronicles and Assyrian king records.[8]

Because there was no outside power strong enough or interested enough to provide any real threat, Israel and Judah prospered in the eighth century. King Adad-nirari III of Assyria in 805 took tribute from Damascus, but Israel, a few miles to the south of the Aramaean capital, was unaffected. A succession of weak rulers reduced the Assyrian threat. Jeroboam II (786–746) expanded his kingdom into the Transjordan area and worked in economic harmony with Phoenician cities. Prosperity and social inequalities graphically pictured by Amos brought hardship and suffering for the underprivileged. Parallel economic growth took place in Judah in Uzziah's time (783–742). Edom was recaptured; trade with Arabia developed through the Red Sea; two cities of Philistia, Gath and Ashdod, became vassals (II Chron. 26:6 f.), and despite the absence of a prophetic record comparable to the book of Amos, conditions condemned by Isaiah when he begins his prophetic work at the King's death suggest that the situation in Judah and Israel was the same.

746. Jeroboam II died and a period of decline in Israel began. Lack of stability in Israelite leadership, resulting in the assassination of four kings within twenty years, produced a national policy that fluctuated between pro-Egyptian and pro-Assyrian alliances. A sense of aimlessness or lack of direction, clearly reflected in Hosea, made Israel an easy target when Assyrian forces began to move westward and southward.

745. Tiglath Pileser III (called "Pul" in II Kings 15:19 after "Pulu," the name under which he controlled Babylon) became ruler of Assyria and began an expansionist program. Up to this time, Assyria had periodically raided northern Syria for bounty and to maintain open channels for exploitation of minerals, timber and trade. Assyria's new program included conquest and rule. In addition to subduing Mesopotamian neighbors in the immediate vicinity of Assyria, Tiglath

---

[8] Cf. *ANET*, pp. 281–288; David D. Luckenbill, *The Annals of Sennacherib* (Chicago: University of Chicago Press, 1924).

Pileser began subjugation of the west, starting in 743. A coalition of small nations, led by Azriau of Iuda, undoubtedly Uzziah (Azariah) of Judah, opposed him. The Assyrian account, taken from slabs found at Calah, has many lacunae, but it is clear that Tiglath Pileser subdued his opposition. The records list tribute received from frightened rulers of smaller kingdoms, including Rezin of Damascus and Menahem of Samaria.[9]

742. Uzziah died and Jotham became king. Because of his father's long illness, Jotham had administrative experience as regent of Judah and was able to give Judah governmental stability that is in complete contrast with the situation in Israel. Uzziah's military program was continued and the Chronicler reports a Judaean victory over Ammonites who paid tribute for three years.

ISAIAH'S VISION AND COMMISSIONING

Isaiah's commissioning as a prophet which came in a vision in the year of Uzziah's death is recorded in autobiographical form. The elements of the prophet's report of this event are complex but leave no doubt about the overwhelming quality of the experience that was to determine the course of his life and condition his awareness of the majestic splendor of Yahweh's exalted sanctity or "otherness." It is possible to interpret Isaiah's vision in terms of an inward experience coming out of meditation.[10] On the other hand, it seems more probable that the experience is related to a very concrete cultic observance, possibly the New Year festival.

Dr. Julian Morgenstern has theorized that Solomon's temple, oriented with portals facing east enabled the first rays of the rising sun to penetrate the holy of holies at the time of the autumnal equinox.[11] Seraphim, the six-winged creatures that chanted an antiphonal hymn of Yahweh's holiness, are often described as "mythical" figures but no mythology concerning them is known. The term "seraphim" is derived from a Hebrew verb meaning "burn," so that seraphim have been called "burning ones." The word seraph is also associated with serpents in the story of the seraph serpents of the wilderness wanderings (Num. 21:6 ff.; Deut. 8:15) and the seraph snakes mentioned in two of Isaiah's oracles (Isaiah 14:29; 30:6). It is possible that in Isaiah's vision the bronze seraph serpent, a Canaanite symbol later destroyed by Hezekiah (II Kings 18:3 ff.) despite the sanctuary tale that legitimatized its presence (Num. 21:6 ff.), entered Isaiah's

Read Isa. 6; II Kings 15; II Chron. 26

---

[9] For the text of Tiglath Pileser's annals, cf. *ANET*, pp. 282 ff.

[10] F. James, *op. cit.*, p. 248.

[11] For a discussion of Dr. Morgenstern's thesis that the kings of Judah enacted a New Year death-and-resurrection ritual borrowed from Canaan, in which the king represented the deity, cf. Julian Morgenstern, *The Fire Upon the Altar* (Chicago: Quadrangle Books, 1963), and "The King-god Among the Western Semites and the Meaning of Epiphanes," *Vetus Testamentum*, X (1960), 138–197; XIII (1963), 321–323. For a discussion of the Isaiah theophany in the light of this hypothesis, cf. "Biblical Theophanies," *Zeitschrift für Assyriologie*, XXVIII (1913), 36–39, and *The Fire Upon the Altar*, pp. 28–30.

A NINTH CENTURY ASSYRIAN PANEL *in low relief from the royal palace at Calah showing an attendant in a costume with four wings and a bird headdress participating in a ritual (fertility?) involving a tree (of life?). It is possible that the Hebrew New Year ritual employed costumed altar attendants.*

experience as the early morning sunlight played upon it. It has been suggested that the sun's rays entering the inner cella of the temple may have struck the gold-plated olivewood cherubim, making it seem as though they burned with fire, providing the source of Isaiah's imagery.[12] It is possible also that the seraphim were temple ministrants or altar attendants in winged costumes with specific choral and purification responsibilities in the New Year rites.

[12] H. Buck, *People of the Lord* (New York: The Macmillan Company, 1966), p. 226.

Isaiah's cry of woe is a cry of awakening as he discovered that ritual purification alone did not make a people holy or acceptable to Yahweh. The gulf between sacred and profane was not one of ritual impurity but of moral or inner uncleanliness. Isaiah's term "the Holy One of Israel" (1:4; 5:19, 24) implies that Yahweh, as the God of a particular people, demanded ethical and ritual purity of those who were close to him, for ethical and moral impurity made it impossible for the Holy Yahweh to draw near to his people.

When the purification rite was completed, the prophet responded to Yahweh's call for a messenger. The scene is a (heavenly) court where a messenger is dispatched by a monarch. The message was not reassuring, for the prophet was to aid in bringing destructive judgment on the people—he was to preach a message that men would not heed; indeed, they would turn away and because of failure to heed would be destroyed.[13] Some find this interpretation too harsh and suggest that the commission reflected Isaiah's intention to preach whether or not the people heard.[14] It has also been argued that the passage was written after the prophet had been at work and represents his evaluation of his work.[15] Isaiah's response contains a note of incredulity: "how long?" The response is as harsh as the commission: until all is desolate. The final verse (13) is problematic, for although Isaiah did believe that a remnant would return (cf. 7:3) the 10 per cent figure appears a much too precise qualification. The verse is generally taken to be an expansion of Isaiah's work by a later hand.[16] The final phrase, absent in the LXX, is meaningless.

What Isaiah's next moves were cannot be known, but there is **Read Isa.** something of a tacit agreement among scholars that the bulk of **1–5; 10–12** Chapters 1 through 5 and 10 through 12 contains the earliest oracles, possibly spoken during the ten years following the temple experience. One small section (1:4–9) seems to fit best into the setting of Sennacherib's invasion in 701. The remaining oracles consist of scathing denunciations of contemporary Judaean society, demonstrating that Isaiah, like Amos and Hosea in Israel, looked with a jaundiced eye upon the attitudes and living patterns of his countrymen. Some themes and thought patterns expressed by the prophet will be developed below, but as Professor Napier has pointed out, no analysis can substitute for personal reading of Isaiah's powerful words.[17]

The reproach oracle that introduces the book of Isaiah utilizes a courtroom setting in which Yahweh, as plaintiff, complains that his people do not know him. How do they not know him? Sacrifices, rituals, festivals honoring Yahweh abounded, but these rites were tangible evidence of lack of knowledge, for they expressed the popular belief that Yahweh could be pleased and pacified by cultic ceremonies (1:10–15). Yahweh's demands, set forth in prophetic torah (instruc-

---

13 Lindblom, *op. cit.*, pp. 186 f., Leslie, *op. cit.* pp. 24 f.

14 Hyatt, *op. cit.*, p. 34.

15 Bewer, *The Prophets*, p. 27.

16 Cf. Scott, *The Interpreter's Bible*, V, 212.

17 B. Davie Napier, *Song of the Vineyard* (New York: Harper and Brothers, 1962), p. 223.

tion), called for justice and fidelity—moral concerns and loyalty to Yahweh. The people were so ignorant of their deity that they did not know that his requirements were primarily moral and ethical. Leaders were evil (1:21–23) and idolatry was everywhere (2:6–8), while Yahweh's judgment hovered, dark and threatening but ignored, above the nation (2:9 ff.). When judgment came, anarchy would triumph, princes and leaders would fall, arrogant women would be humbled (3:16 f.) and the finest soldiers would be destroyed (3:25 f.). Like a series of hammer blows, Isaiah's words struck at greed, pride and indifference, pounding out a promise of chaos, confusion and destruction. But his words of appeal went unheeded (1:18 ff.) as his initial vision had promised they would.

In Chapter 5 the prophet assumes a minstrel's role and sings a song that has often been called "daring" because it employed a fertility or agricultural motif, a theme prominent in the cult of Ba'al. It is important that the real point of the song be recognized, for this is a song of social and religious concern. Israel, the vineyard of God, failed to produce anything but wild grapes (a symbol of the social evils of the day). Like a wise landowner, Yahweh prepared to uproot and destroy the vineyard. The seven-fold woe oracles that follow (interrupted by Chapters 6–9) are confessions of evils, for Isaiah documented his challenges to popular mores and popular religion. These were uneasy, troubled days with threats to national security on all sides. Isaiah argued that the greatest threat was within, in the prosperity that fostered greed and ruthlessness and injustice, in religion that was outward rather than inward.

738. Tiglath Pileser III was now receiving tribute from subject states, including Syria and Israel. A deportation policy quickly quenched potential revolutions, for leaders were promptly moved to distant parts of the Assyrian empire. In a new environment without the supporting sentiment of their own people, the leaders' rebellious inclinations were rendered ineffective.

735. Pekah of Israel and Rezin of Damascus, believing that the time was ripe to break free of Assyria, urged Jotham of Judah to join in revolt. Jotham refused and, as the two northern kings prepared to compel him to cooperate, Jotham died, passing the problem to his son and successor, Ahaz. Ahaz continued his father's non-participation policy and Rezin and Pekah attacked Judah, thus beginning the Syro-Ephraimitic war. (Cf. II Chron. 28:1–15 for an extensive, though

BRONZE BRACELETS. *Isaiah's denunciation of the haughty women of Jerusalem pictured them "mincing along . . . tinkling with their feet" (Isa. 3:16). The tinkling sound was produced by metal anklets and a mincing walk could only increase the clinking. Either Isaiah or a follower added an expanded list of contemporary feminine finery and included bracelets in the collection (Isa. 3:19). The bronze bracelets pictured above are typical of those found on the wrists of skeletons coming from Isaiah's time. Larger and heavier bronze bands of similar design are often found on the legs and are the anklets which became symbols of vanity to Isaiah. Bracelets, gold bracelets in particular, were prized gifts and apparently played a rather important role in wooing a young woman (Gen. 24:22, 30, 47; Ezek. 16:11).*

ASSYRIAN ARCHERS. *The carving is from the limestone wall panels of King Sennacherib's palace at Nineveh (early seventh century).*

probably exaggerated, account.) Edomite and Philistine attacks upon Judah added to the confusion. In desperation Ahaz, despite Isaiah's counsel, sought aid from Tiglath Pileser, offering a handsome bribe. The Assyrians needed little persuasion and the northern coalition was destroyed. By 734 the northern and eastern sections of Israel, including Galilee and the Transjordan area of Gilead, had become Assyrian provinces (II Kings 15:29). The pressure on Judah's Mediterranean flank was eased as Philistia too became an Assyrian province.

Isaiah opposed Ahaz' plan to seek aid from Assyria, but to no avail. Chapter 7, which is usually divided into three parts (vss. 1–9, 10–17, and 18–25), records in biographical prose the prophet's advice. The first section comes out of the early period of the war when Syrians and

Read Isa. 7–8; 10

Ephraimites moved on Jerusalem. Isaiah attempted to assure Ahaz that the efforts of Pekah and Rezin would fail, that they would be overcome, and that Judah's wisest policy was quiet trust in Yahweh. The presence of Isaiah's son, Shear-jashub, whose name meant "a remnant shall return," symbolized Isaiah's words of warning and threats of doom prior to the encounter with the king. The name should not be taken as a sign of hope, for a remnant may be only the tattered evidence of what once was, as Amos preached (Amos 3:12; cf. Isa. 17:6).

The second section introduces the sign "Immanuel," meaning "God is with us," by which Isaiah hoped to persuade the vacillating king that the best security was found in trust in Yahweh, not in alliances with Assyria. The prophet referred to an unidentified[18] young woman (Hebrew: 'almah) who was about to bear a child that would be named ."Immanuel," signifying Yahweh's support of his people. By the time the child would be weaned, the prophet promised, the military threat from Syria and Israel would be past, the two nations destroyed, and Judah would enjoy great prosperity. This interpretation, which seems to fit the historical situation best, has been challenged.

The word 'almah refers to a young woman old enough to bear a child and does not in itself indicate whether a girl is a virgin or married. The LXX translators employed the Greek word parthenos, which means "virgin," although the term neanis, which corresponds better to 'almah, was available. When the Christian Church began its mission in the Greek-speaking world and the Gospel of Matthew was written, predictions of Jesus' birth were sought in the LXX version of Jewish scripture; thus, in Matt. 1:18–23, the citation from Isaiah 7:14 is from the LXX, not the Hebrew text. It is argued by some Christian scholars that the sign was far more wondrous than the birth of any child and pointed ahead to the birth of a Messiah, a deliverer—a promise fulfilled in Jesus. Still others, recognizing that the announcement of a deliverer who would come 700 years later would be of little comfort to Ahaz in his crisis, find a double meaning in the sign Immanuel: an immediate significance relating to the young woman of Ahaz' day and a futuristic one foretelling the coming of Jesus.[19] However, it should be pointed out that within the Hebrew text there is no indication that the child would perform messianic functions; the baby is a sign or signal of Yahweh's intention to save the nation if they would rely on their deity.

The chapter closes with four oracles promising invasion and destruction without any indication of the victim (7:18–25).

Chapter 8 opens with the promise of the birth of a child who would bear the unwieldly name Maher-shalal-hashbaz, meaning "the spoil speeds, the prey hastens," to signify the speedy demise of Rezin and Pekah. The mother is called "prophetess" and is usually assumed to be the prophet's wife. The oracle reiterates what Isaiah had said in

---

18 Kuhl, *The Prophets of Ancient Israel* (London: Oliver and Boyd, 1960), p. 78, identifies her as the prophet's wife.

19 It is also suggested that the LXX translation of the term reflects an additional revelation. Cf. Kissane, *The Book of Isaiah,* 2nd ed. (Dublin: Browne and Nolin, 1960), I, 89.

7:10–17 that Ahaz had nothing to fear for his enemies would perish. 8:5–8 appears to have been spoken after Ahaz had rejected Isaiah's advice and had turned to Tiglath Pileser for help. Isaiah predicted that Assyrian influence would sweep into Judah like an overwhelming flood. The autobiographical oracles that follow reveal that Yahweh reassured his prophet in his ministry and that Isaiah, perhaps in disappointment, perhaps to demonstrate that his words would come to pass, entrusted his teachings to his disciples for preservation. It is possible that oracles warning Assyria of pride in accomplishment come from this period (ch. 10).

732. Damascus fell and Rezin was killed by the Assyrians. A cer- Read Isa. 17 tain Hoshea ben Elah may have saved Israel from destruction by murdering Pekah, seizing the throne, then immediately surrendering and paying huge tribute to Tiglath Pileser. Isaiah's oracles against Damascus fit well into this period (ch. 17). Note the utter destruction in the eschatological oracles (17:4–6).

In purchasing Assyrian aid Judah became a subject nation, paying regular stipends to Tiglath Pileser. Subservience had religious over-tones. It was clear to the Assyrians that Yahweh was not powerful enough to protect his people. As Judah had become a vassal nation and Ahaz a puppet king, so Yahweh was a subject deity. A great bronze Assyrian altar was placed in the Temple of Yahweh, a symbol of the dominance of Ashur, chief god of Assyria, over Yahweh. The extent to which enthusiasm for the introduction and cultivation of new facets of religion was carried is indicated in Isaiah 2:6–8, 20; 8:19 f., and by Ahaz' sacrifice of a son to the god Moloch (II Kings 16:3 f.).

727. Tiglath Pileser died and Shalmaneser V became ruler of Assyria.

724. Hoshea of Israel stopped paying taxes to Assyria. What prompted this action is not clear, but perhaps it was an effort to break free taken in cooperation with several other Palestinian communities. Shalmaneser wasted no time. Israel was invaded and Hoshea was seized. The powerful capital city of Samaria refused to capitulate and a three-year siege began.

722. Samaria fell to Shalmaneser between spring and autumn, 722, or just before the king died (December, 722) according to one account, or, according to another, to Shalmaneser's successor, Sargon II, in late December, 722 or early spring of 721.[20] The Assyrian policy of deportation was followed: 20 per cent of the population was removed,[21] and people from other conquered territories imported. The remnant Israelites became the Samaritans with whom the Ju-daeans were to enter into controversy in the post-Exilic period.[22]

It is possible that Hoshea's brash refusal to pay taxes led Isaiah to Read Isa. 28:1–4, 7–29 prophesy the downfall of Samaria. The remaining verses in which the prophet turns on Jerusalem, warning that their priests and prophets

---

[20] For a concise discussion of this problem, see J. Finegan, *op. cit.,* pp. 208–210.

[21] This deportation forms the beginning point for numerous legends of the "ten lost tribes of Israel."

[22] For an excellent summary of Samaritan history, cf. article, "Samaritans," in *The Interpreter's Dictionary of the Bible.*

who should be spokesmen for Yahweh were bringing a similar fate to Judah, come from the same period. The mocking laughter of his listeners, who say they have a covenant with death (Hebrew: *maweth*) or perhaps with the Canaanite god of death (Mot) so that when disaster comes death will pass them by, leads the prophet to promise doom.

Read Isa. 14:28–31

715. Ahaz died and was succeeded by Hezekiah who at first followed the policy of paying tribute regularly to Sargon II, despite many enticements to revolt. During this same year, an Ethiopian king, Pi-ankh, unified Egypt and established the 25th dynasty, bringing new strength and vigor to Egypt and placing the nation once again in a position of power in the international scene. The oracle appearing in Isa. 14:28–31 appears to have been given at this time.[23]

Read Isa. 9:2–7; 11:1–9

If Chapters 9:2–7 and 11:1–9 are the work of Isaiah, as some scholars maintain, they may have been written on the occasion of Hezekiah's coronation. The darkness and uncertainty of the times is reflected in the opening verse of Chapter 9 and a deep longing for better days marks both poems. The significance of the Davidic line (so important to Isaiah) and the need for charismatic leadership is clearly expressed (11:2). Chapter 11 draws a picture of ideal peace: a harmony and balance of relationships among people and in nature, and living conditions that were both safe and secure. The king as the messiah ("anointed one"), chosen and appointed by Yahweh, was the hope of the nation. Unfortunately for the Judaeans, the dream was not realized: Hezekiah was something less than the ideal king (9:6) and the pressure of external powers could not be ignored.

714. The throne of Ashdod was seized by an adventurer named Iatna or Imani and invitations were dispatched to kings in Philistia, Edom, Judah and Moab (all Assyrian vassals) to cooperate in a rebellion against Sargon. Hezekiah was eager to join, but Isaiah walked about Jerusalem naked, dramatizing the disastrous fate participation would bring (Isa. 20). Whether through Isaiah's influence or other factors, Hezekiah did not join the rebels, and when, in 712, the rebels were defeated by Sargon, Judah was spared.[24] But Hezekiah did not cease planning for independence. The defences of Jerusalem were strengthened and the Siloam tunnel was dug to bring water from the spring Gihon into the city so that fresh water would be available in time of siege. Religious reforms were introduced. The Assyrian altar was removed from Yahweh's temple, and Canaanite cult objects were destroyed, including the serpent symbol (Nehushtan) which a sanctuary legend explained as having come from the time of Moses (II Kings 18:3 ff., cf. Num. 21:6).

Read Isa. 30:1–17; 31:1–4; 18:1–6

705. Sargon was murdered by his son and successor Sennacherib. In that same year, Marduk-apal-iddin, who earlier had attempted to claim the throne of Babylon (Merodoch-baladan in the Bible, cf. Isa.

[23] For a different date for this oracle, cf. Eissfeldt, *op. cit.*, pp. 305, 313, and Bewer, *The Prophets*, p. 44, who favor 726 B.C. at the death of Tiglath Pileser. Ahaz' death is often dated in 725 B.C.; cf. Oesterley and Robinson, *op. cit.*, p. 249.

[24] Fragments of Sargon's victory stele were discovered in the excavation of Ashdod; cf. D. N. Freedman, "The Second Season at Ancient Ashdod," *BA*, XXVI (1963), 138.

A HEBREW IRON PLOW POINT. *Isa. 28:23 ff. provides considerable information about Hebrew agriculture. For plowing, the Hebrew farmer used an iron plow point with a collar into which a wooden shaft was thrust. Such a plow harnessed to an ox would cut a furrow rather than turn the earth as modern plows do. The term "plowshare" commonly used in English translations (I Sam. 13:20 f.; Isa. 2:14) is a misnomer for it denotes a plow with a blade. It is not difficult to imagine a sword being beaten into a plow point (Isa. 2:14; Mic. 4:3) or vice versa (Joel 3:10).*

39:1–8; II Kings 20:12–19), once again claimed kingship and encouraged Hezekiah to join in the anti-Assyrian movement. Sennacherib marched on Babylon, was welcomed by the populace, and Marduk-apal-iddin was banished to Chaldea. Meanwhile, Egypt had become involved with Judah in an anti-Assyrian plot. When Isaiah learned of this secret agreement (Isa. 29:15), he denounced the plan (30:1–5, 6–7, 8–14, 15–17; 31:1–3, 4, and 18:1–6?) for he realized that Egypt, despite its new strength, could not muster military power to defeat Sennacherib. Deaf to Isaiah's pleas, Judah entered alliances with Ammon, Moab, Edom and Philistia (all Assyrian vassals) and began attacks on cities in Philistia that refused to participate (II Kings 18:8).

701. Sennacherib invaded Palestine. Phoenician cities capitulated and paid tribute. The Egyptians were routed and Judah alone remained to face the Assyrians. Sennacherib dispatched three officials to demand surrender (II Kings 18–19; Isa. 36–37).[25] When Hezekiah refused, Judah was invaded. Sennacherib's annals report that 46 walled cities fell and 200,150 inhabitants were taken captive.[26] Hezekiah was shut up in his royal city like a caged bird. Isaiah

Read Isa. 1:7–9; 36–37

[25] H. W. F. Saggs, *The Greatness That Was Babylon* (New York: Hawthorn Books, Inc., 1962), p. 109, says that the report of the discussion between Hezekiah's representatives and the officer of Assyria is like the discussion between peoples barricaded within the city of Babylon and Assyrian officials in 732–1, reported in a letter.

[26] This figure has been interpreted as the total population of the villages overrun. The number has also been reduced to 2,150. Cf. Gray, *op. cit.* pp. 613 f.

described the isolated city as a lonely watchtower in a cucumber patch (1:8). The stricken city was so badly bruised and battered (1:5–6) that Hezekiah had no alternative but to capitulate and pay tribute (II Kings 18:14 ff.). According to Sennacherib's record, 30 talents of gold, 800 talents of silver and much more in other precious items were included in the ransom.[27] The city of Jerusalem was spared. The account of deliverance preserved in II Kings 19 and Isaiah 37 attributing the saving of the city to divine intervention by the angel of Yahweh with no report of surrender or payment of tribute, may reflect a later situation.[28]

**Read Isa.
22; 29:1–6;
30:27–28**

Other Isaianic material may come from this period. Chapter 22 may reflect rejoicing at the withdrawal of Sennacherib's army. Isaiah was appalled at the devil-may-care, live-today attitude of the people, who celebrated rather than mourned for what had happened to the rest of the land (22:13). The oracles on the downfall of Jerusalem may also come from this period (Isa. 29:1–5c, 6; 30:27–28).

So terrible was the effect of the Assyrian invasion that Judah never again mustered strength or courage to challenge Assyrian authority. Hezekiah remained upon the throne but his territorial powers were limited to Jerusalem and its environs. Sennacherib divided the remainder of Judah among loyal Philistine rulers who began to rebuild devastated areas. How and when the Davidic kings regained control over lost Judaean territory is not known. Nor is there information about the fate of Isaiah and his disciples during these dark years. It can be assumed that they lived long enough beyond the end of the eighth century to assemble collections of Isaiah's oracles. A legend, preserved in the Apocrypha, tells of the martyrdom of Isaiah by King Manasseh in the seventh century, but there is no way to determine whether there is any factual basis for the account.

MAJOR EMPHASES IN ISAIAH

The study of Isaiah's writings makes it possible to suggest that there were certain major underlying beliefs that gave order and pattern to all that the prophet said and did. Foremost among these would be his concept of God. If one single label were to be used to characterize Isaiah, it would have to be "prophet of faith" for at the heart of his interpretation of international relationships was constant and unwavering faith in Yahweh's ability and desire to protect Judah. In his confrontation with Ahaz, there appears a note of irritation and

[27] *ANET*, p. 288.

[28] For discussion of the possibility of a second Assyrian assault about 688, cf. Bright, *op. cit.* pp. 282–287. The miraculous deliverance is often explained in terms of a plague. Herodotus (*History* II, 141) records an Egyptian account of the defeat of Sennacherib's army at the borders of Egypt in which mice are said to have gnawed the archer's bowstrings during the night. Some scholars arguing that mice and plague often go together suggest that pestilence might lie behind Herodotus' account and possibly also the Biblical story. However, there is no relationship between the two events. Cf. E. A. Leslie, *Isaiah* (New York: Abingdon Press, 1963), pp. 95 f.

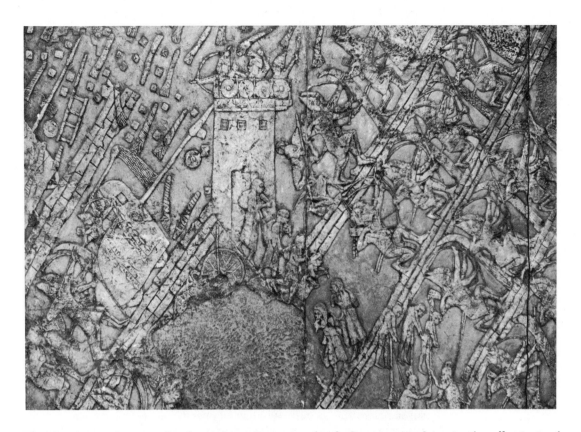

THE ASSYRIANS BESEIGE A JUDAEAN CITY. *Because artists had not mastered perspective all aspects of the battle appear on one plane. A wheeled battering ram assaults the walls on one side as refugees pour out the opposite side. Something of Assyrian terror tactics are portrayed in the lower right hand panel which pictures captured Judaeans impaled on stakes and displayed where they would have a demoralizing effect on the people within the beseiged city.*

impatience with the monarch's uncertainty and unwillingness to trust the national deity (7:13). For the prophet there could be no doubt or hesitation. He was equally sure in his proclamation of Yahweh's distaste of religion that lost itself in ritual and ceremony but disregarded the plight of the underprivileged and condoned exploitation by the rich and powerful. His epithet for Yahweh, "the Holy One of Israel," which may have come from some cultic source, but may just as well have been coined by the prophet,[29] conveys not only transcendence and otherness but, in its setting in Isaiah's vision, moral and ethical purity. Yahweh was not just "the Holy One" as Hosea had said, but "the Holy One *of Israel*," belonging to Israel in a unique and peculiar way. To be one with their deity, the people had to possess the kind of purity that Yahweh demanded—ritual and ethical cleanliness. No other people stood in this kind of relationship to Yahweh; through Isaiah, the election concept is portrayed in new terms. The fact that Yahweh could call Assyria the "rod" of his anger would imply that Yahweh's power extended beyond Palestine and controlled other peo-

[29] Cf. Helmer Ringgren, *The Prophetical Conception of Holiness* (Uppsala: Almqvist & Wicksells Boktryckeri, 1948), p. 27.

ples. Like Amos, Isaiah's concepts approach monotheism and universalism but never achieve them, for the existence of other gods is not challenged and Isaiah's concerns were local and nationalistic in religion and politics. World affairs were important insofar as they affected his beloved homeland.

Isaiah's words reveal his deep love and hope for Jerusalem. Here was the capital of the kingdom, the seat of the Davidic dynasty, and here was the very dwelling place of Yahweh. Repeatedly the prophet's deep concern for the city is revealed as it is singled out time and again for attack. Isaiah's realistic assessment of the people's conduct compels him to foresee doom for the city, with Yahweh himself as the enemy:

> So Yahweh of hosts will come down to fight against (not "upon")
> Mount Zion, and on its hill.
>
> Isa. 31:4. Vs. 5 is a non-Isaianic addition.

The remnant has often been isolated as an important theme in Isaiah's teaching, but the meaning of the term is not clear. Sheldon Blank has argued that a "mere" remnant is meant, not one that will represent the essence of the nation or signify the choice of a select few, but simply a remnant that manages to escape[30] (cf. Isaiah 17:6; 30:14). An opposite point of view is held by those who find in the remnant Isaiah's disciples and others faithful to Yahweh's commands.[31] The position taken throughout our discussion has favored the first point of view simply because there does not seem to be any evidence to substantiate the second. Whatever hopes Isaiah may have had for the future are not made explicit, unless it be that his word, bound up in his disciples, would prove true. The so-called messianic oracles may come from the time of Isaiah, but there is no reason to assert that they must be Isaiah's work, while, in view of the rest of the prophet's teachings, there is reason for doubt: the door must be left open.[32]

MICAH

The last collection of prophetic oracles from the eighth century are from Micah, the prophet of the Shephelah. According to the editorial superscription, he was active during the reigns of Jotham, Ahaz and Hezekiah (742–687 B.C.), and although it must be admitted that a prophetic ministry of this length is not impossible, most of the datable material comes from the time of Ahaz and Hezekiah. One hundred years later, the prophet Jeremiah quoted Micah 3:12 noting that the oracle was given in Hezekiah's time (Jer. 26:18). Micah was, therefore, a contemporary of Amos, Hosea and Isaiah, but echoes of themes found in Amos and Isaiah are not indications that Micah knew or was influenced by either of these men.

---

[30] S. H. Blank, "The Current Misinterpretations of Isaiah's She'ar Yashub," *The Journal of Biblical Literature*, LXVII (1948), 213. See also Kennett, *op. cit.*, p. 11.

[31] Cf. Pfeiffer, *op. cit.*, p. 437 and J. M. P. Smith, *The Prophet and His Problems* (New York: Charles Scribner's Sons, 1914), pp. 182 f.

[32] Cf. Scott, *op. cit.*, pp. 231 f. and 247 ff. for a valuable treatment.

Micah's home town of Moresheth (1:1) or Moresheth-gath (1:14) has not been located and it is possible that it was one of the "daughter" villages of the city of Gath, the old Philistine site located in the Shephelah which had come under Judaean control.[33] The area was rich in grain, olives, figs and grapes. Micah has been called "rustic," "rural," and his words have been labeled "course," but there is no reason to think that Gath and its environs were any more "backward" or "rural" than Jerusalem which was also surrounded by agricultural communities. Micah's writing reveals skill in imagery and sharpness in delineation of evils and disasters, and his statement of Yahweh's demands in religion is one of the best-known sections of prophetic literature (6:8). The importance of Micah's work is demonstrated by Jeremiah's reference to it and by the serious study it received during the Exile.

The Book of Micah may be divided into four parts (non-Micah materials are italicized).

I. Chapters 1–3 containing Micah's oracles against the evils of Samaria and Jerusalem.
   a. Chapter 1 contains a theophany and ends with a lament for the fallen nation. 1:2–9 may belong to 722 B.C., the period just prior to the fall of Samaria when Assyrian armies threatened to overrun both nations. 1:10–16, the dirge over the desolation befalling Judaean cities may reflect Sennacherib's ravaging of the country in 701.
   b. Chapter 2 opens with a woe oracle reminiscent of Isaiah 5:2 ff. condemning greedy, powerful land owners so covetous that they were unable to sleep, and scolding listeners for refusal to acknowledge the validity of the prophet's words. *2:12–13 is a restoration oracle from the Exilic period.*
   c. Chapter 3 may be part of an autobiographical collection (cf. 3:1a) of scathing pronouncements against prominent citizens who betray justice and prophets who give oracles of "peace" when they are paid and pronounce curses when they are not.
II. Chapters 4–5 contain eschatological and late material.
   a. Chapter 4 is composed of non-Micah material.
      4:1–4 parallels Isaiah 2:2–4.
      4:5–13 contains oracles from the Exilic period (note the mention of Babylon in 4:10).
   b. Chapter 5 contains both genuine and intrusive material.
      5:1 portrays a siege, possibly in 701.
      5:2–4 is a messianic oracle of the Exilic period.
      5:5–6 conveys no meaning or guidance for a time setting.
      5:7–9 is a late oracle dealing with the remnant.
      5:10–15 is a threat oracle, probably by Micah.
III. Chapters 6:1–7:7 consist of oracles by Micah.
   a. 6:1–8 is an oracle portraying Yahweh's wishes for his people.
   b. 6:9–16 contains oracles of condemnation, possibly from 701.
   c. 7:1–7 is a lament on social immorality.
IV. Chapter *7:8–20* is made up of words of hope and comfort from the Exilic period.

---

[33] For attempts at identification, cf. articles in the *Interpreter's Dictionary of the Bible:* "Moresheth" (Tell ej-Judeideh), "Micah" (Tell en-Menshiyeh).

There are few teachings in Micah that haven't appeared in the
works of the other eighth century prophets. The most significant new
statement by the prophet deals with true religion (6:1–8). Here, a
courtroom setting is pictured with Yahweh and the people stating
their cases as hills and mountains sit in judgment. Yahweh makes his
complaint (6:3), asking why his people have turned from him and
recalling election history and warm associations of the past (6:4–5).
The people retort, "What does Yahweh want?" "How do we come to
him?" and efforts to appease the deity are cited: animal and oil
offerings, even human sacrifice. The judgment is given:

> He has shown you, O man, what is good!
> And what does Yahweh require of you
> But to do justice (*mishpat*), to love kindness (*ḥesed*)
> and to walk in humility with your God (6:8).

Although some scholars have argued that these verses come from the
post-Exilic period, most accept them as the work of Micah.[34]

[34] R. E. Wolfe, "Micah: Introduction and Exegesis," *The Interpreter's Bible*, VI,
938.

PART
SIX

The Last 100 Years of Judah

19

From Manasseh to
the Deuteronomic Reform

WHEN Hezekiah died (687), his son Manasseh, still a young boy, was enthroned.[1] The folly of adhering to a policy of antagonism toward Assyria was apparent, and Manasseh pledged loyalty to his overlords. Shortly afterward (680), Sennacherib was murdered by his sons and one of them, Esarhaddon, formerly governor of Babylon, became king of the Assyrian Empire. To prevent challenge from his brothers or the army, Esarhaddon, through good military tactics and favorable omens, was soon in complete control of the empire.

Read II Kings 21–35; II Chron. 33–36

In 675 Tarqu, an Ethiopian pharaoh (cf. II Kings 19:9—Tirakah), joined the king of Tyre in an anti-Assyrian alliance. By 671 Esarhaddon had invaded Egypt, routed Tarqu's forces and laid claim to the title "King of Upper and Lower Egypt"—a title more high sounding than factual. When Esarhaddon had left, Tarqu, with numerous local princes, laid claim to Lower Egypt. Once again Esarhaddon marched on Egypt but died *en route* (669).

Esarhaddon had planned carefully the future of his kingdom, and, in accordance with an agreement, two sons came to power, Shamash-shum-ukin as crown prince of Babylon and Ashurbanipal as ruler of Assyria. Migrating Scythians and Cimmerians[2] on the northern border of the empire, powerful Median tribes to the east, and restless Chaldeans in the lower Euphrates region kept the two kings busy protecting their inheritance. Meanwhile, Tarqu went unpunished for insurrection. Ashurbanipal finally marched on Egypt, recruiting on the way from vassal kingdoms, including Judah. Egypt once again became part of the Assyrian Empire.

[1] In addition to materials in II Kings and II Chronicles important information has been drawn from Assyrian and Babylonian annals, cf. *ANET* (appropriate sections); D. D. Luckenbill, *Ancient Records of Assyria and Babylonia* (Chicago: University of Chicago Press, 1927), II; L. Waterman, *Royal Correspondence of the Assyrian Empire* (Ann Arbor: University of Michigan Press, 1930–36), 4 vols.; D. J. Wiseman, *Chronicles of the Chaldaean Kings (625–556 B.C.)* (London: The British Museum, 1956). For a broad treatment of the history of the period, cf. Saggs, *op. cit.*, and in less detail, Bright, *op. cit.*, pp. 288–319; Noth, *op. cit.*, pp. 253–289.

[2] Scythians and Cimmerians, Indo-Europeans from the Black Sea area, began to move toward Asia Minor during the eighth century. The Cimmerians are called "Gomer" in the Bible (cf. Ezek. 38:6). For a brief archaeological history, cf. A. L. Mongait, *Archaeology in the U.S.S.R.*, trans. by M. W. Thompson (Baltimore: Penguin Books, 1961), pp. 152–163. For a more detailed discussion, cf. T. T. Rice, *The Scythians*, Ancient People and Places Series (New York: Frederick A. Praeger, 1958).

—— CHART XII ——

Date	Judaean King	Prophet	Events in Palestine	Events in Assyria	Events in Babylon	Events in Egypt
687	Manasseh (687–640)		Assyrian influence at a peak			
				680: Sennacherib murdered; Esarhaddon becomes king		675: Egypt and Tyre in alliance against Assyria
						671: Egypt invaded
			Manasseh pays taxes to Assyria	669: Esarhaddon dies; Ashurbanipal becomes king (669–626)	Shamash-shum-ukin becomes crown prince	Egypt invaded again
					Shamash-shum-ukin rebels against Assyria	Psammetichus rebels against Assyria (XXVI Dynasty 663–525)
640	Amon (640–638)		Continued subjugation to Assyria Amon murdered	Ashurbanipal dies	Nabopolassar becomes king of Babylon	
638	Josiah (638–609)	Zephaniah	626: Scythian invasion, Josiah seizes Bethel	Sin-shar-ukin becomes king		
			621: Deuteronomic reform instituted			

Date	Kings of Judah	Prophets	Judah	Assyria	Babylon	Egypt
609	Jehoahaz (Shallum) Jehoiakim (Eliakim, 609–598)	Nahum Jeremiah	Josiah challenges Necho and is killed Jehoiakim pledges allegiance to Babylon	612: Nineveh sacked, Assyria collapses Nabopolassar overthrows Assyrians		609: Necho challenges Babylon
						Egypt defeated at Carchemish
		Habakkuk	Jehoiakim rebels Jehoiakim dies		605: Nebuchadrezzar defeats Egypt 604: Nebuchadrezzar becomes king 601: Egypt and Babylon battle to a stalemate Nebuchadrezzar moves on Jerusalem	
598	Jehoiachin (598–597)	Ezekiel	Jerusalem falls, people enslaved		Jehoiachin of Judah taken captive to Babylon Revolt in Babylon	
597	Zedekiah (597–586)		Judah joins in revolt by western nations 586: Jerusalem destroyed Judah a vassal state		More Judaeans moved to Babylon	Some Judaeans flee to Egypt

233

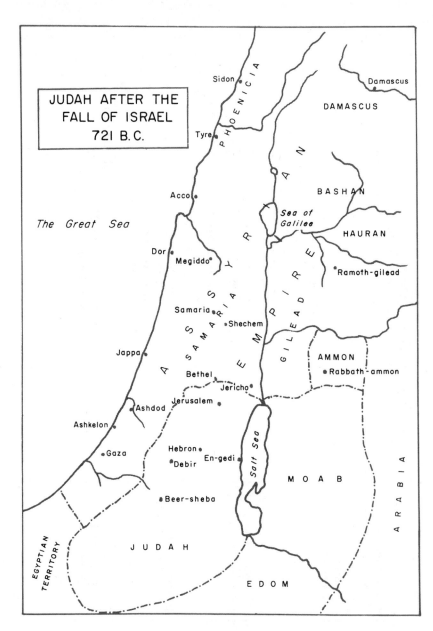

JUDAH AFTER THE
FALL OF ISRAEL
721 B.C.

New problems were to trouble the empire. The Elamite kingdom on the eastern side of the lower Euphrates was being weakened by an invasion of Iranian peoples, later known as Persians. Shamash-shum-ukin of Babylon allied with Chaldeans and Elamites against Ashurbanipal. In Egypt a new rebellion led by Psammetichus, a former Assyrian favorite who had replaced Tarqu, weakened Assyrian power. Attacks by Arab tribes aided the Babylonian cause. Ashurbanipal attacked Babylon. Shamash-shum-ukin committed suicide during the siege and Ashurbanipal placed a puppet ruler in charge. Arabs and Elamites were overcome and the leaders were viciously punished.

Throughout this troubled time, Manasseh of Judah remained loyal

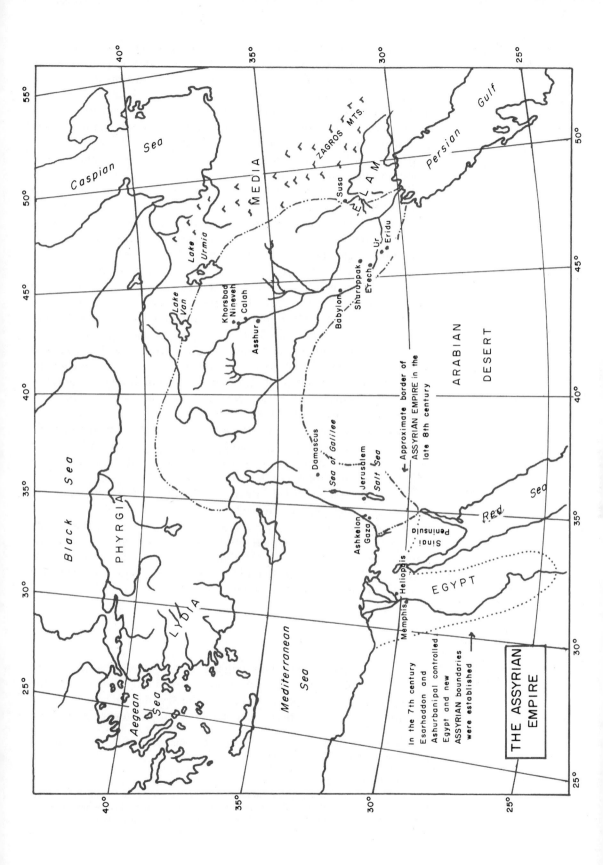

THE ASSYRIAN
EMPIRE

Caspian Sea

Black Sea

Aegean Sea

Mediterranean Sea

Red Sea

Persian Gulf

ZAGROS MTS.

MEDIA

ELAM

PHYRGIA

LYDIA

ARABIAN DESERT

EGYPT

Sinai Peninsula

Lake Urmia

Lake Van

Khorsbad
Nineveh
Calah
Asshur

Babylon
Shuruppak
Erech
Ur
Eridu

Susa

Damascus
Sea of Galilee
Jerusalem
Salt Sea

Ashkelon
Gaza

Memphis
Heliopolis

← Approximate border of
ASSYRIAN EMPIRE in the
late 8th century

In the 7th century
Esarhaddon and
Ashurbanipal controlled
Egypt and new
ASSYRIAN boundaries
were established →

to Ashurbanipal. If the note in II Chronicles 33:11 ff. is accurate, Manasseh was taken as a prisoner to Babylon and humilated, perhaps for some minor security infraction, but there is no mention of this event and no record of any trouble with Manasseh in Assyrian records.[3] The only references are to payment of tribute[4] and cooperation in warfare.[5] According to Assyrian custom, subject nations were bound by an agreement and an oath sworn before the great gods of Assyria; violation of the contract incurred divine wrath and punishment.[6] Subject nations also worshiped Assyrian deities, and Ashurbanipal erected altars to Ashur in conquered areas.[7] In Judah, with full cooperation from Manasseh, Assyrian worship flourished, together with cultic rites (including child sacrifice) that had not been operative since before Hezekiah's reform. No prophetic utterances and very little other reference to the worship of Yahweh have come from Manasseh's long reign. It is possible that pro-Assyrianism and anti-Yahwism went hand-in-hand. The report of Manasseh's return to Yahweh in II Chron. 33:15 ff. seems incongruous and stands in sharp contrast to the Deuteronomist's accusation that Manasseh's evils caused Yahweh to punish his people by exile (II Kings 21:10 ff.).

Manasseh died in 640 and was succeeded by Amon, his son, who continued his father's policy of cooperation with Assyria during the two years of his reign. Amon's murder by servants brought eight-year-old Josiah to kingship. It is not recorded who influenced Josiah's early life, but the king became an enthusiastic supporter of Yahwism. Ashurbanipal's annals do not go beyond 639 and hence there are no Assyrian records concerning relationships with Josiah. Information about Assyrian affairs from commercial records and state documents indicate that the disintegration of the empire had begun.

When Ashurbanipal died in 626, the Chaldean Nabopolassar seized the throne of Babylon and formed alliances with Median tribes. In the same year a movement of peoples out of the north, including Cimmerians and Scythians, pressed southward to threaten Assyrian holdings in Syria and Palestine. Herodotus (I, 103–106) says that the Scythians swept through Palestine, but there is no archaeological evidence of such a movement, so far.

ZEPHANIAH

**Read
Zephaniah**

The long period of prophetic silence in the seventh century was broken by Zephaniah. In the past, some scholars sought to identify the vision of destruction in Ch. 2:4–15 with the Scythian movement of 626 recorded by Herodotus. Because Zephaniah's prophecies are placed in a

---

[3] Punishment similar to that mentioned in Chronicles is described in Ashurbanipal's records, cf. *ANET*, p. 288, item viii.

[4] *ANET*, p. 300.

[5] *ANET*, pp. 291, 294.

[6] *ANET*, p. 294. Assyrian punishment included a wide assortment of torture, harassment, and humiliation for leaders. So terrifying and impressive was Assyria's war record that the coming of their armies struck fear into their enemies.

[7] *ANET*, p. 294.

universal context, there are those who argue that it is reading too much into his words to identify the Scythians as a menace to the whole Near Eastern world. Nevertheless, 626 is not an improbable date for Zephaniah's utterances. In 2:13 the prophet anticipates the destruction of Nineveh which took place in 612, so that his oracles must predate this event. Zephaniah's condemnations of evils in Jerusalem and Judah reveal no knowledge of the reform movement instituted by Josiah in 621 (see below) and portray the very social and religious evils that Josiah sought to change. It is clear that a time prior to 621 must be postulated, and 626 is probably as close as one can come to the year or years of the prophet's activity.

No hint of the prophet's personality is given in his words. It has been suggested that he may have belonged to the temple cult[8] but this cannot be known for sure. The prophet's lineage, carried back four generations to a certain Hezekiah in the superscription, has been interpreted as an indication of royal blood, but Hezekiah is not an uncommon name (cf. I Chron. 3:23; Ezra 2:16). Nor can the name Cushi be interpreted as anything more than a proper name, despite the generic significance of "Ethiopian" or "man of Cush."

Zephaniah's major emphasis is eschatological, not in the sense of "that day" found in the eighth century prophets where Israel or Judah was singled out for destruction, but in a new, universal sense, in which man and beast, fish and plant are swept away (1:2). Nevertheless, within the universal setting, it is Judah and Jerusalem that are the foci of the prophet's and Yahweh's concern. Indictment of apostasy, familiar from eighth century prophetic literature, appears again with a specific condemnation of the worship of Milcom, god of the Ammonites, Ba'al of Canaan, the host of the heavens (cf. 1:4–6), and of those who affect foreign attire and rites. The prophet also indicts those who deny Yahweh's action in human affairs (1:12). Like his eighth century predecessors, he calls for repentance (2:1–3, cf. Isa. 1:18 f.; Amos 5:15; Hosea 14:1).

A literary arrangement familiar from previous analyses of prophetic writings occurs in Zephaniah. Following the indictment of the nation, the prophetic attack moves to foreign nations (2:4–15), and after a brief interruption in which Jerusalem is again condemned (3:1–7), the book closes with oracles of restoration and promise. The oracles against foreign nations predict the doom of Philistia, then Egypt and Assyria. (The Moab oracles are late, 2:8–11.) In the day of Assyria's greatness, Zephaniah saw the weakening of the nation and its ultimate destruction. The Jerusalem oracles condemn officials, prophets and priests (3:1–7).

For the most part the prophet concentrates less on specific evils than upon devastating judgment. The opening oracle, describing the "sweeping away" of all life, is expanded in fierce and terrible images of destruction. There is no hint given of the direction from which the trouble would come, and no mention is made of the instrument of Yahweh's anger. What effect Zephaniah's words had upon the people

---

[8] Bentzen, *op. cit.,* II, 153.

and upon King Josiah cannot be known, but it is not impossible that the prophet helped to spur the reform movement that was to occur a short time later. Attempts to include oracles of restoration and healing in the collection of authentic pronouncements of Zephaniah are not convincing, for not only do these additions remove the force of the prophetic promise of destruction, but they reflect the mood, setting and hopes of the late Exilic period.

The book may be analyzed as follows:

I. 1:1–2:3 Fierce judgment as follows:
   1:1 Superscription (late editorial addition).
   1:2–6 An oracle of judgment.
   1:8–13 An oracle of judgment on Jerusalem (cf. 1:13 and Amos 5:11).
   1:7, 14–18 An oracle of judgment (cf. 1:15 and Amos 5:18 f.).
   2:1–3 A call to repentance.
II. 2:4–15 Judgment on foreign nations.
   2:4–6 An oracle against Philistia.
   2:7 An oracle of restoration from the Exilic period.
   2:8–11 An oracle of vengeance from the Exilic period.
   2:12 An oracle against Ethiopia.
   2:13–15 An oracle against Assyria.
III. 3:1–7 An oracle against Jerusalem.
IV. *Restoration oracles from the Exile, including a deliverance song (3:14–15).*

THE DEUTERONOMIC ERA

In Judah, young Josiah began to challenge Assyrian control. A section of the Assyrian province in what had been the kingdom of Israel which included the city of Bethel was seized. Some foreign religious influences were removed. In Jersualem, in 621 Yahweh's temple was refurbished, and during the process a scroll of the law, purporting to be a covenant made between Yahweh and his people in the time of Moses, was found and taken to the King. Josiah's frightened concern that no one had ever kept the agreement and the observation of a Passover unlike any kept since the time of the Judges (II Kings 23:22) suggest that the scroll contained new regulations. The general consensus of scholars is that the bulk of the seventh century scroll is contained in our present book of Deuteronomy. Determined to fulfill the requirements of this Mosaic covenant and encouraged by the promise of the prophetess Huldah that he would die in peace (II Kings 22:20), Josiah instituted a reform-by-violence movement and a sincere effort was made in Judah to perform the will of Yahweh.

DEUTERONOMY

The book of Deuteronomy purports to contain the words of Moses, spoken in a farewell address just before the invasion of Canaan. The setting of the oration is the eastern side of the Jordan River. The general tone of the book is a combination of the homiletic and legal-

istic. It contains a brief history of events from the experiences at
Horeb to the conquests on the eastern side of the Jordan, lists
numerous laws together with exhortations to hear and obey, promises
blessings if the rulings are obeyed and curses if they are violated, and
concludes with the death and burial of Moses.

The Mosaic authorship has been successfully contested on several
bases. Moses died before the Hebrews entered Canaan (ch. 34), but
there is evidence that Deuteronomy was written in Palestine, for the
writer speaks of the Transjordan area as "the other side of the Jordan,"
a term that would only be used by someone within Canaan (1:1–15;
3:8; 4:46). The concluding chapter tells of Moses' death and burial
(ch. 34). The use of the aetiological formula "to this day" indicates
that the writer lived after Moses' time (3:14; 10:8; 34:6) and Moses is
referred to in the third person (ch. 27). There is good evidence that
the book is a composite post-Mosaic compilation.

From very early times, scholars recognized the relationship of Deuteronomy to the scroll found in the Temple of Yahweh in 621,[9] but it
was not until the nineteenth century that DeWette identified Deuteronomy as the book upon which the Josianic reforms were based. The
identification rests upon the following arguments:

a. The centralization of worship in the temple in Jerusalem, the destruction of other Yahweh shrines, the defiling of non-Yahweh holy places,
and the removal of cultic paraphernalia associated with non-Yahwistic
religions (II Kings 23) were all actions fulfilling Deuteronomic legislation calling for a central Yahweh shrine (Deut. 12:1–14), and for prohibition of worship of astral deities (Deut. 17:3) or use of Canaanite
symbols (Deut. 16:21 f.) or any toleration of non-Yahweh religious rites
(Deut. 18:10 f.) or shrines (Deut. 12:3).

b. The celebration of the Passover in the temple in Jerusalm (II Kings
23:21–23) rather than in the homes of the people conformed with the
command in Deut. 16:1–8.[10] The novelty of this arrangement is revealed
in II Kings 23:22.

c. The notation in II Kings 23:9 that priests from the vacated shrines did
not go to Jerusalem to serve in the temple shows knowledge of the provision in Deut. 18:6–8.

The date, place of origin and authorship of Deuteronomy have
been the subject of much inquiry and debate. The terminal date for
Deuteronomy is 621 because Josiah's reform of that year was founded
on it. Another theory argues that a Jerusalem priest, deeply affected by
prophetic preaching, sought to heal the breach between prophet and
priest and composed Deuteronomy during the seventh century.[11] It
has also been suggested that Deuteronomy is a seventh century work of
Levites and aristocracy.[12] A completely different hypothesis, one that
has gained a large following, surmises that Deuteronomy originated in
the northern kingdom of Israel, possibly at the old amphictyonic

---

[9] For example, Jerome, *Commentary on Ezekiel* at 1:1 made the identification in
the fifth century A.D.

[10] For a brief history of the Passover, cf. De Vaux, *Ancient Israel*, pp. 454 ff.

[11] Pfeiffer, *op. cit.*, p. 179.

[12] Kuhl, *The Old Testament*, pp. 84 f.

shrine at Shechem; that its time of origin was in the century or so
preceding the Josianic reforms; and that its preservation and introduction in Judah was the work of conservative, rural, Levitical priests.[13]
Arguments that the book must have come from the late Exilic[14] or
post-Exilic period[15] have not been persuasive. Nor have the theories
that the bulk of Deuteronomy originated in Solomon's time[16] or in
Samuel's day[17] found many supporters.

II Kings 22:8–10 describes two readings of the entire scroll of
Deuteronomy in a single day, and it has been suggested that the
original scroll may have contained a somewhat smaller legal *corpus*
than our present book of Deuteronomy. There are indications that
different collections of materials have been brought together or that
additions may have been made from time to time. For example, the
requirement that sacrifice be made in a single place is repeated (cf.
12:5–7 and 12:11–12) and so are the rules for slaughtering for food
(cf. 12:15–17 and 12:20–25). A small collection of cultic regulations
(16:21–17:7) interrupts the discussion of the duties of officials (cf.
16:20 and 17:8 ff.). There are four separate introductory statements
(cf. 1:1; 4:44 f.; 6:1; 12:1) and two introductory units (1:1–4:40 and
4:45–5:31; 4:41–43 is from P). There are two concluding speeches,
28:1–69 and 29:1–30:20, and in the second there is clear indication of
knowledge of the Exile (cf. 30:1 ff.). There are sudden shifts in
person, from the second person plural (cf. 12:1–12) to the second
person singular (cf. 12:13–31).[18]

Attempts have been made to discover the original core of Deuteronomy and to trace the various editions through which it may have gone,
but it seems simpler and perhaps more accurate to recognize the
principle of progressive or continuing interpretation at work: additions were made to the central core of material, at times embodying
total units and at other times taking the form of minute details as in
the P contributions. Each addition gave a slightly different emphasis
to the total work or to some sensitive point. It can still be maintained
that D drew from older sources and interpreted and supplemented the
material. The relationship between D and the Covenant Code of E
clearly illustrates this point. Exod. 21:2–11 prescribes for the freedom
of the male slave after six years of servitude; Deut. 15:12–18 reinterpreted this law, making provision for the liberation of the female slave
and adding a characteristic Deuteronomic humanitarian touch: that
the owner should not send his former slave away empty-handed, but

[13] G. von Rad, *Studies in Deuteronomy*, Studies in Biblical Theology, 9 (Napierville: Alex R. Allenson, Inc., 1953).

[14] R. H. Kennett, *Deuteronomy and the Decalogue* (Cambridge: Cambridge University Press, 1920).

[15] G. Hölscher, "Komposition und Ursprung des Deuteronomiums," *Zeitschrift für
die Alttestamentliche Wissenschaft*, XI (1922), 161–255.

[16] A. C. Welch, *The Code of Deuteronomy* (London: James Clarke and Co.,
1924).

[17] E. Robertson, *The Old Testament Problem* (Manchester: Manchester University Press, 1950).

[18] This shift can be seen in the King James and Rheims-Douai Versions where the
archaic pronoun "thou" is used for the second person singular.

should provide a liberal supply of food to sustain him as he entered his new life of freedom. Similarly, in expanding the law providing for the return of strayed animals (Exod. 23:4), the Deuteronomist placed the responsibility for the care and feeding of the animal upon the finder until the rightful owner was located (Deut. 22:1–3).[19] Chapters 12–26, 28 are usually identified as the core of the book, and in this section there is a close relationship to the E material. The general setting is provided by Chapters 1–11 which places the entire book into a hortatory or sermonic framework. A more detailed analysis follows.

I. Chapters 1:1–4:43 A survey of the past and a statement of the people's duty.
> 1:1–5 An introduction fixing the time and place of the farewell address.
> 1:6–3:29 A recapitulation of past history.
> 4:1–40 Concerning obedience to ordinances and statutes.
> 4:41–43 A detail added by the P writers.

II. Chapters 4:44–11:32 A statement of the nature of Israel's duty.
> 4:44–49 An introduction giving the setting of the statement.
> 5:1–33 A summary of the covenant including the decalogue.
> 6:1–11:32 The requirements for life in Canaan.
>> 6:4 is the *Sh'ma:* "Hear, O Israel. . . ."
>> 10:12 reflects Micah.

III. Chapters 12–26, 28 The rules for life in Canaan.
> 12–14 Statutes and ordinances.
> 15:1–16:17 Legislation for the year of release.
> 16:18–18:22 Rules for leaders.
> 19:1–26:19 Further legislation.
> 28 Blessings and curses.

IV. Chapter 27 A composite chapter providing for a covenant rite to be instituted at Shechem. Note the mention of Mounts Ebal and Gerizim.
> 27:1–8 The establishment of the law and altar at Shechem.
> 27:9–10 The call to hear and obey.
> 27:11–26 The ritual of blessings and curses.

V. Chapters 29–30 Threats and promises. 30:1–5 refers to the Exile.

VI. Chapter 31 The writing of the law and the commissioning of Joshua.

VII. Chapter 32 The song of Moses (verses 48.52 are from P).

VIII. Chapter 33 The blessing by Moses.

IX. Chapter 34 Moses' death and burial.

The opening section of Deuteronomy, a recitation of the acts of Yahweh, encompasses the wilderness wanderings from the time of the revelation at the sacred mountain, named Horeb as in E, to the distribution of the conquered land on the eastern side of the Jordan. The abortive attempt to enter Palestine through the Shephelah was due to lack of trust in, and reliance upon, Yahweh, according to the Deuteronomists. This faltering in faith made it impossible for Moses

Read
1:1–4:40

[19] The "humanistic" elements introduced by the Deuteronomists are discussed by M. Weinfeld, "The Origin of the Humanism in Deuteronomy," *Journal of Biblical Literature,* LXXX (1961), 241–247. Weinfeld suggests that the source of the new morality is to be found in the wisdom schools. For a listing of parallel laws in E and D, cf. S. R. Driver, *A Critical and Exegetical Commentary on Deuteronomy,* The International Critical Commentary (New York: Charles Scribner's Sons, 1895), pp. iv–vii.

and his generation to enter the promised land. Accordingly the D writer described a wilderness journey that led from Horeb to Kadesh-Barnea, to the Gulf of Aqabah, and then, circumscribing Edom, northward to the Transjordan region. Moses was able to see the land that Israel was to inhabit from the top of Pisgah, but he could not enter. The section closes with a sermonic address calling for obedience to the prescriptions of the covenant.

Read
4:44–11:32

The second section consists of a collection of homilies on the significance of the covenant which serves as a preface to the full statement of the law. The decalogue, given by God to the people at Horeb, is almost identical with that of Exodus 20 but while there is repetition, there is excitement and promise too. The emphasis throughout the presentation is upon hearing, remembering and obeying on the one hand, and on Yahweh's love, promises and ability to fulfill his promises on the other. Israel is charged with responsibility for total annihilation of all the inhabitants of Canaan (7:16, 23 f.). The section concludes with a covenant charge offering blessings or curses (11:26 ff.).

Read
12–26; 28

The third section sets forth the laws or terms of the covenant, answering, in effect, the question: What does it mean to be the people of Yahweh? The answer is given in rules containing self-justifying reasons that called for total commitment to the worship of Yahweh and intolerance of apostasy, and set forth prescriptions for ceremonial observances, prohibition of certain rituals associated with other religions, responsibilities of leaders, and laws respecting food, social behavior, festal observances. The rulings reveal that in the mind of the Deuteronomists the conquest of Canaan was a holy war.[20] Among the ceremonial instructions are ritual guides for presenting firstfruits and tithes (ch. 26). The closing chapter, listing blessings and curses, contains an expanded commentary on what may have been an older collection of six blessings (28:3–6) and six curses (28:16–19). If this expanded version represents what was read to Josiah of Judah, the monarch's frantic response can be understood. What is most unnerving about the vivid portrayals in the curses is the knowledge that these horrors represent accurately conditions within a city during siege—conditions which were experienced, in part at least, during the siege of Jerusalem by Nebuchadrezzar a quarter of a century later.

Read
27; 29–34

Chapter 27, a separate dodecalogue of curses in ritual form, is an intrusion in the central collection from another hand. Chapters 29–31, in sermonic style reviewing the acts of Yahweh in the past and calling for commitment to Yahweh's ways, may be homilies delivered during the ritual observances. The "song of Moses" (ch. 32) has been identified through form analysis as a ninth century poem dealing with the covenant tradition in the form of a lawsuit.[21] Of particular interest is the expression of the election tradition (32:8–9) which says that when "Elyon" divided mankind into nations, Yahweh received Israel or Jacob as his portion. If "Elyon," a Canaanite appellation for the high

[20] von Rad, *Studies in Deuteronomy*, pp. 45 ff.

[21] G. E. Wright, "The Lawsuit of God: A Form-Critical Study of Deuteronomy 32," *Israel's Prophetic Heritage* (New York: Harper and Brothers, 1962), pp. 26–67.

PLOWING WITH A COW AND DONKEY YOKED TOGETHER—A VIOLATION OF DEUT.
22:10. *The reason for the Deuteronomic prohibition, which is one of
several rulings against mixing materials, seed or animals, is not understood.*

god El, is taken to be a substitute name for Yahweh,[22] then Yahweh
chose Israel out of all the peoples when the earth was divided among
the hierarchy of deities. On the other hand, if Elyon represents the
chief god of the Canaanite pantheon, then Yahweh received Israel as
his patrimony. The first interpretation is generally preferred. Chapter
33, Moses' blessing, is an old poem added to the Deuteronomic collection. The period represented in the poem appears to be marked with
prosperity for both Israel and Judah and may come from somewhere
between the tenth and eighth centuries. It is reminiscent of Jacob's
blessing in Gen. 49 (J). The final chapter tells of Moses' death and
burial.

THE MAJOR TEACHINGS OF D

Despite the fact that older material, including the Covenant Code
from E, was used by the Deuteronomists and that the place of origin
may have been the amphictyonic center at Shechem, Deuteronomy has
been preserved as a Judaean document, a product of the seventh
century. The fall of Israel foreseen by the prophets, whose warnings
that apostasy, ignorance of Yahweh's law and man's inhumanity to his
fellow, would not go unpunished, had not been heeded, and the fact
that a multitude of shrines, feasts and festivals had not saved Israel

[22] *Ibid.*, p. 28, n. 7.

was a matter of deep concern. The patterns of faith and conduct that had, according to the prophets, brought about Israel's downfall were prevalent in seventh century Judah. Deuteronomy was, therefore, an attempt to resolve tension between cult and conduct, between ritual behavior and moral action. In Deuteronomy the demand is not one over against the other, but both; not an assertion that God demands ritual and moral purity, but an affirmation that Yahweh was the source of both. Here the cult is exalted as the divinely instituted means of mediation between God and man, for in and through the cult the divine enters the world of men to purify, cleanse, bless, and enable men to find their way through the confusion of the world. For the first time in biblical literature, we encounter a fully developed statement of the significance of the cult and of cultic and moral law. The law (Torah) was God-given at Horeb as a means of accomplishing a divine-human fellowship, and this fellowship was bound into the sacred agreement—the covenant. The wider problem of Israel's relationship to the rest of mankind was not solved; indeed, it is barely touched upon. What was essential was the achievement of a full understanding of God-man relationships within the family of Yahweh. The following points appear to have been central:

**Read
6:4–15;
13:6–11**

1. Deuteronomy proclaimed the uniqueness of Yahweh, insisting that there was no other god like him, that he alone was Israel's deity, a god that could not be represented by any form or symbol and a god intolerant of the worship of any other god. The cultic confession of faith in 6:4 is often interpreted as an expression of monotheism when translated "Hear, O Israel, Yahweh our God is one Yahweh," but the statement may be translated equally well as "Yahweh our God, Yahweh is one" or "Yahweh is our God, Yahweh alone." In view of the prohibition of worshiping other gods that follows, it would appear that the last translation best represents the interpretation of the period, and proclaims monolatry rather than monotheism.

**Read 6:4–9,
20–25; 11:18–20**

2. Deuteronomy provided legislation to enable the people to "know" their deity and understand his will for them. Through the prophets, Yahweh had complained that the people did not "know" him, referring to personal, inner knowledge, growing out of communication on deep intimate levels. To compel the people to know Yahweh, the Deuteronomists outlined a program of massive education, designed to keep before the community the traditions, commandments, and basis of the Yahweh-Israel relationship. Instruction in the covenant was to begin in the home. Phylacteries and mezuzoth were to serve as visual reminders, and cultic observance and public adherence to covenantal rules would educate through communal participation.

**Read
12:2–31**

3. Deuteronomy centralized the cults by introducing the law of the central shrine. This law is related to the proclamation of Yahweh's uniqueness, for royal Yahweh-shrines in the northern and southern kingdoms had demonstrated the division among Yahweh's people and had made possible the introduction of Canaanite interpretations whereby Yahweh's individual manifestations in different cult centers could degenerate into the worship of the deity as the "Yahweh of a specific shrine," as opposed to the "Yahweh of another shrine." By concentrating all festal observances, all community worship, in one place, an otherwise uncontrollable unity and cohesiveness could be maintained.

The shrine was to be located in a place chosen by Yahweh and to seventh century Judaeans this could only mean Jerusalem, although the city is not named and there is reason to believe that possibly Shechem or Bethel was intended in the earliest form of the law.[23] Only Yahweh's name (Heb. *shem*) was to dwell in the shrine, giving rise to what has been called "name (*shem*) theology"[24]—a decided move away from the anthropomorphic concept of a god residing in the shrine.

The cultic and economic problems raised by limiting Yahweh's altars to one were anticipated and provided for. Every act of killing was, in a sense, a sacrificial rite[25] and required that the blood, the life-principle, be poured out at an altar as an offering to the deity. If there was to be but one altar, how could one kill for food? The D writers answered: as you would kill a wild animal, remembering always to pour out the life-blood on the ground (12:15 f., 21–25).

Tithes were customarily brought in kind to the local sanctuary, but with the single altar in Jerusalem, a genuine hardship could be placed on those who lived far away. The Deuteronomists met this problem by providing that tithes could be sold locally and the money taken to Jerusalem and spent for representative offerings (14:22–29).

Local altars were places of refuge where, in the event of homicide, the killer might take refuge from the next-of-kin (*go'el*)[26] of the victim until the accidental nature of the case could be determined. To compensate for the loss of local sanctuaries, cities of refuge, strategically located, were to be set apart.

Read
19:1–10

The closing down of local shrines would deprive priests in charge of their means of livelihood, and Deuteronomic legislation provided that rural priests might minister at the central shrine should they desire to do so. As individuals without inheritance, the Levites were commended to the care of the people, together with widows, orphans and strangers. Provision was made for a rightful share of offerings. The priests cooperated with judges in courts of law, possibly seeking oracles (17:8–13), and were responsible as health officers for the proper diagnosis of leprosy (24:8).[27]

Read 18:1–8;
26:12 ff.

4. Deuteronomy interpreted the concept of election in terms of the idea of a holy people. The miracle of Yahweh's choice of Israel as his own people was an act of love, as the prophets, in particular Hosea, had said. But Yahweh was holy, a god of ritual and moral sanctity as Isaiah had taught. Anything belonging to or associated with another god was anathema to Yahweh. Holiness involved separation and to be a holy people Israel had to avoid contact with whatever was detestable to Yahweh. Election brought with it the loyal "covenant" love (*ḥesed*) of Yahweh that could be trusted and relied upon. It also brought Yahweh's jealousy, that could tolerate no association with that which belonged to other gods. Fidelity on the part of Israel reaped the rich reward of blessings from Yahweh; apostasy brought vindictive punishment.

Read 7:6 ff.;
14:2; 26:19;
28:9

5. The Deuteronomists placed stress on practical goodness, kindness and thoughtfulness in human relationships and in dealing with animals.[28] These rulings are scattered throughout the book.

Read Ch. 24

[23] Cf. De Vaux, *op. cit.*, pp. 338 f.

[24] von Rad, *Studies in Deuteronomy*, pp. 38 ff.

[25] De Vaux, *op. cit.*, p. 338.

[26] Cf. De Vaux, *op. cit.*, pp. 21 f., 160, 166 f.

[27] For additional duties, cf. 21:5; 31:9 ff., 25.

[28] Cf. M. Weinfeld, *op. cit.*

Read 12:32

6. Deuteronomy introduced an interpretation of history, often called a "theology of history," which was based on the belief that faithfulness to Yahweh guaranteed Yahweh's protection and blessing, and infidelity caused Yahweh to withdraw his sustaining life-power. On the basis of this thesis it could be argued that any hardship or misfortune pointed back to an offending act. Should one fail to find such an act in one's own conduct, one could look to one's ancestors, for Yahweh could visit punishment for sin of the parents on children and grandchildren (5:9 f., cf. 8:19 f., 11:22–28; 12:28–31). In the light of this teaching it was possible to explain the suffering of the innocent and retain faith in the justice of Yahweh (yet cf. Deut. 24:16).

7. Deuteronomy provided for its own canonization, warning against any alteration in its provisions. The document was designed as a standard for faith, as a binding set of rules in covenantal form calling for one people bound by law to one god.

Apart from the homiletical framework, it is clear that the book was related to a cultic ceremony, and this cultic setting gave the work the characteristic of immediacy or constant relevance. Each enactment of the covenant ritual was an act of renewal in which the past became alive in the present, and participants shared in a ceremony through which the community of Yahweh's followers was regularly brought into being (cf. Deut. 5:3).

THE IMPACT OF DEUTERONOMY

Read II Kings
23:4–27;
II Chron.
34:33–35:27

The record in II Kings and the slightly different version in II Chronicles leave no doubt that Josiah acted immediately in accordance with Deuteronomic provisions. Shrines outside of Jerusalem were destroyed and desecrated (II Kings 23:15 ff.). Cultic implements and images were broken and burned and the houses of cult prostitutes were torn down until, at last, the only shrine left in the land was the temple of Yahweh in Jerusalem. Passover was observed in accordance with the new law, and all ritual worship was performed at the temple.

What the reactions to the infringement on local religious life might have been are not recorded, but some local priests eschewed the privilege of serving in the Jerusalem temple. What hardships were wrought on the people cannot be known, but as we shall see, there are hints in Jeremiah of resentment against Deuteronomic law. Ultimately, Jeremiah appears to have found the legislation inadequate, and this led him to propose a covenant of the heart. The Deuteronomists were impressed with what Josiah did and, because he acted in accordance with the covenant requirements, all of his accomplishments receive approbation.

There can be no doubt that Deuteronomy played a part in Josiah's break with Assyria. The first move, the refurbishing of the temple which led to the discovery of Deuteronomy, was in itself an act of rebellion. Then, strengthened by the assurance of divine approval and encouraged by Huldah's prediction of a peaceful demise, Josiah took bolder steps away from Assyrian control. The Judaean kingdom was extended by the seizure of surrounding cities and lands. In each locale the demolition of sacred shrines demonstrated the new power of Jerusalem, the capital city with its solitary Yahweh temple. It is possible that Josiah's death at the hands of Necho resulted from his conviction that, as a man under divine protection, he could not be stopped or injured.

How long support for Deuteronomy continued cannot be determined, but from Jeremiah, as we shall see, there is some evidence that enthusiasm was cooling. Perhaps so long as Josiah was alive and neo-nationalism was stressed from the throne and the temple, Deuteronomic law was generally observed. When Josiah died, a king of a different temperament, Jehoiakim, was soon to become ruler, and Deuteronomic principles do not appear to have received the same support. Traditional evils which the Deuteronomists had hoped to eliminate were once again engaged in openly.

Perhaps by its very nature Deuteronomy was marked for limited success. Events were soon to shake the foundations of the neat theological analysis, "Obey Yahweh and prosper, disobey and suffer punishment," and new questions demanding new answers were raised. Even the Deuteronomic historians were compelled to recognize that the principle had not worked for Josiah and his reform, and thus they blamed the failure to receive blessings upon the accumulated evils of Manasseh's reign (II Kings 23:26). Furthermore, sweeping reforms introduced by fiat and carried out by force require constant vigilance and long enforcement to become custom. Josiah had neither the time nor the strength. On the other hand the Deuteronomic reform did not fail. Deuteronomic historians continued to write well into the Exilic period, interpreting history in accordance with their theology, and both the Deuteronomic historical interpretation and the Book of Deuteronomy were to become part of the official canon of the Judaeans, the Jews.

20

From the Fall of Nineveh
to the Fall of Judah

FOR three years Ashurbanipal's successor held the Assyrian throne and at his death Sin-shar-ishkin became king. In the summer of 612, Nabopolassar, a Chaldean leader, aided by Medes and northern nomads, attacked, looted and destroyed Nineveh, an event that marked the crumbling of the last vestiges of power in Assyria and established the foundations for the Neo-Babylonian Empire. There is some evidence that the defeat of Nineveh was the occasion of rejoicing in Judah, although the Assyrians established a new capital at Harran. Within a few years Harran was conquered by the Medes.

NAHUM

**Read
Nahum**

The reaction of at least one individual to the fall of Nineveh is preserved in a poem echoing sheer mocking joy in the defeat of Assyria. The book of the prophet Nahum falls into two parts: Chapter 1 contains an incomplete poem in an alphabetic acrostic form,[1] and Chapters 2 and 3 are concerned with Nineveh. Attempts have been made to read out of this short poem something of the writer's status and personality, but there is really no way of learning much about the man for, in his jubilant mood, he treats only one theme—Nineveh. His words form a triumphant shout of praise to Yahweh that the enemy has fallen. His native village of Elkosh (1:1) has not been located.[2] The prophet may have been a Judaean who reacted with intense pleasure at the news of Nineveh's defeat or he may have been a descendant of the exiles of Israel living in a village near enough to Nineveh to enable him to witness the siege, thus accounting for the graphic descriptions in his poem. He may have been a cult prophet in Jerusalem.

The two chapters dealing with the siege (chs. 2–3) appear to have been written near the time of the battle. The reference to the sack of

---

[1] The acrostic form ends with the fourteenth letter of the Hebrew alphabet which contains twenty-two consonants.

[2] Proposed sites include the village Elkese in Galilee, suggested by Jerome in the fifth century A.D., and the village of Elkush, north of Nineveh where the prophet's tomb is shown, and it has also been pointed out that the name of the Galilean town of Capernaum means "village of Nahum."

ASSYRIAN SOLDIERS FLAYING CAPTIVES. *Nahum's bitter attitude toward the Assyrians may have been engendered in part by the knowledge of the cruel treatment given to prisoners and conquered peoples by Assyrian warriors. The portrayal is from one of the wall panels of Sennacherib's palace at Nineveh (early seventh century).*

Thebes (3:8) guarantees a date after 663, the date of Ashurbanipal's successful attack. The context of the poem suggests a date close to 612.

The opening chapter is a separate work which employs theophanic imagery (1:3b–5) and depicts Yahweh as an avenger (1:2–3, 9–11), a wrathful deity (1:6), a refuge for his people (1:7–8), and a deliverer (1:12–13). While it cannot be determined for certain, it seems that someone other than Nahum wrote this chapter. The litergical or hymnic quality of this section has led to the suggestion that the first chapter was combined with the last two to form a liturgy for use in the New Year festival in the autumn of 612 after the fall of Nineveh.[3]

The last chapters employ forceful, descriptive terminology to create a compact, vivid word picture of the confusion and horror during the Babylonian attack. In Nahum's thought, God acts against an enemy who has earned punishment and wrath. The closing, mocking verses, indicate that the battle was over and the quietness of death and desolation had descended upon the city and its leaders. All who

[3] P. Humbert, "Le Problème du livre de Nahoum," *Revue de Histoire et Philosophie Religiouse,* XII (1932), 1–15.

suffered the cruelty of Assyrian tyranny clap their hands in rejoicing (3:18–19).

It has also been proposed that the book was developed to propagandize, to encourage a strong stand against Assyria and to extend hopes for the restoration of the nation of Judah.[4] It seems better and simpler to recognize the book of Nahum as consisting of genuine oracles by the prophet concerning the fall of Nineveh, to which an introductory poem was added to adapt the total work to liturgical usage.[5]

THE GROWTH OF NEO-BABYLONIAN POWER

Not all of the old Assyrian empire bowed to Babylon. A young Assyrian prince was made king and an invitation was sent to Pharaoh Necho of Egypt to join in stopping the growth of the new Babylonian empire. As Necho moved northward to join his allies, Josiah, perhaps in an attempt to protect Judah from both Assyrian and Egyptian control, attempted to stop him and was killed in the battle of Megiddo. Necho proceeded into Syria and Josiah's son Shallum, or Jehoahaz (possibly his throne name), took the throne, supported by the free men of Judah. Within three months he was deposed by Necho and taken as a hostage to Egypt. His brother Eliakim was appointed king and his name changed to Jehoiakim.[6]

The Babylonian army, led by Nabopolassar's son Nebuchadrezzar (the Nebuchadnezzar of the Bible), defeated the Assyrians and Egyptians at Carchemish in 605. Fleeing Egyptians were pursued to their own borders and only saved from invasion by the death of Nabopolassar which necessitated Nebuchadrezzar's return to Babylon. He was crowned king in April, 604.

In Judah, Jehoiakim, having promised allegiance to Babylon, retained the crown. He was an unpopular ruler and Jeremiah makes reference to his extravagance in building a new summer palace at Bethhaccerem (Ramat Rahel), a hill site a few miles south of Jerusalem.[7] Jeremiah also refers to the brutal and tyrannical role that Jehoiakim played, thus suggesting that he was anything but esteemed.

The Egyptian-Babylonian power struggle had not been completely settled and in 601 the two nations met again. Apparently the battle was a stalemate, and Nebuchadrezzar returned to Babylon to strengthen his forces. Possibly the failure of Nebuchadrezzar to win a decisive victory encouraged Jehoiakim to make a fatal error and rebel against Babylon. At the time, Nebuchadrezzar was engaged in a frontier struggle and it was not until late in 598 that Babylonian

---

[4] A. Halder, *Studies in the Book of Nahum* (Upsala: Lundequistska, 1946).

[5] Lindblom, *op. cit.*, p. 253.

[6] As previously noted, the change of name may indicate the assumption of a "throne name." It may also symbolize the right of the conquering ruler "to name" his appointees as a symbol of his power in bringing the individual into being as a king.

[7] Jer. 22:13–19, cf. Y. Aharoni, "Excavations at Ramat Rahel," *BA*, XXIV (1961), p. 118.

armies moved on Jerusalem. During that same month Jehoiakim died,
passing his problems to his 18-year-old son Jehoiachin.[8] The siege of
Jerusalem began on December 18, 598 and the city was taken on
March 16, 597.[9] The temple was looted and Jehoiachin and leading
citizens and artisans were taken as prisoners to Babylon. Jehoiachin's
uncle Mattaniah, whose name was changed to Zedekiah, was appointed king over a nation once again suffering from the ravages of
war. Nebuchadrezzar had not only attacked Jerusalem, but Jehoiakim's new summer palace and the cities of Debir and Lachish all bear
archaeological witness to Babylonian demolition.

HABAKKUK

The new threat to Judaean security in the rise of Babylonian power,
the evil of Jehoiakim's rule, and the faltering of the Josianic reform
produced turmoil in the mind of the prophet Habakkuk whose cry, "O
Yahweh, how long?" introduces his collected oracles. Nothing is
known of the man beyond the editorial note that he was a prophet
(1:1). Many scholars have surmised that he may have been a Jerusalem cult prophet, for the notations in Chapter 3 suggest that his
words may have been used in the temple liturgy.[10] A legend preserved
in Bel and the Dragon[11] seems to be void of historical content.
Habakkuk is not a Hebrew name and may be derived from an Assyrian word for a plant or herb (hambakuku).

It is difficult to date with certainty the time of the oracles. The only
real clue is the reference in 1:6 to the Chaldeans as the instrument of
Yahweh's judgment, and even this passage has been given different
interpretations. The German scholar B. Duhm argued that "Chaldean" should be changed to read "Kittim," a term originally used
with reference to the people of Cyprus but later applied to the Greeks
and Romans. Duhm believed that Habakkuk was written in the late
fourth century in the time of Alexander the Great.[12] A first century
B.C. scroll of Habakkuk, containing only the first two chapters and an
interpretive commentary[13] found at Qumran, reads "Chaldeans" in
1:6 but employs the word "Kittim" when applying it to their own day.
It is clear that in the Qumran literary tradition the original meaning
was "Chaldean." If those who suffer at the hands of the Chaldeans are
Assyrians, as some have suggested, the book is to be dated in 625 when

[8] For a completely different ordering of events, cf. II Chron. 36:5 ff.

[9] For a succinct analysis of dating, cf. J. Finegan, op. cit., p. 222.

[10] P. Humbert, Problèmes du livre d'Habacuc (Neûchatel: Secrétariat de l'Université, 1944) puts the liturgy in the years 602–610.

[11] See below, Part Nine, chap. 30.

[12] B. Duhm, Das Buch Habakuk (Tubingen: J. C. B. Mohr, 1906), pp. 4–30.

[13] This form of commentary called pesher (because this Hebrew term signifying
"this means" introduced the commentaries) was not concerned with the prophet's
meaning for his own time, but only with the prophetic significance of the words
for the commentator's own day. For a translation of the Habakkuk commentary, cf.
T. H. Gaster, The Dead Sea Scriptures in English Translation (New York: Doubleday Anchor Book, 1956), pp. 246–256.

Nabopolassar revolted, or near 612 when Nineveh fell.[14] On the other hand, if it is Judah that is to suffer at the hands of the Babylonians and if some of the references in Chapter 2:9 ff. can be related to the actions of Jehoiakim, then a date between 609 and 598 B.C. is preferable. The latter interpretation seems to fit the situation best, and if the prophet's anticipation of a Babylonian attack was prompted by Jehoiakim's efforts to achieve independence, then a date after 601 seems most appropriate. The fact that the Egyptians are not mentioned may indicate that the oracles are from 598.

Two titles (1:1, 3:1) divide the book. The first two chapters include oracular statements; the last chapter, entitled "a prayer of Habakkuk," is a hymn. For clearer analysis the book can be divided as follows:

1. 1:1–2:5   The prophet's dialogue with Yahweh.
2. 2:6–20   Oracles of woe.
3. 3:1–16   A theophanic hymn of praise to Yahweh for past victories.
4. 3:17–19   A statement of trust.

**Read
1:1–2:5**

The first section opens with a query to Yahweh (1:2–4), in whose control lay the destiny of Judah. The Josianic reform had led to genuine efforts to observe Yahweh's will as revealed in Deuteronomy, but Josiah had died in battle and his successor, Jehoiakim, was a tyrant. Now, the emphasis on the observance of law (*torah*) had slackened and the ancient problem of the perversion of justice and the oppression of the righteous by the wicked was as acute as it had ever been. The cry, "Violence," which was an appeal to Yahweh to deliver, went unheeded. How long, asked Habakkuk, could a righteous deity tolerate this situation?

Yahweh's answer (1:5–11) was that the instrument of justice was to be the Chaldeans, despite the fact that they did not recognize Yahweh's role in their conquest (1:11). It seems clear that the Babylonians were on the march.

The answer shocked the prophet. How could a pure and holy deity use a people as ruthless and unrighteous as the Chaldeans to punish Judah, a people that, despite their evil ways, were more righteous than the Babylonians? How long would Yahweh permit the Chaldeans to enslave people (1:12–17)? The prophet went to a tower to "see" how Yahweh would reply.

The answer came in the form of a command and a statement of reassurance (2:2–5). The prophet was ordered to inscribe on a tablet, in letters large enough so that a fleeing man could read it without stopping his flight, the message that the end was at hand. The just or righteous, he was assured, would "live by his faith" or "faithfulness." The meaning of this statement is not clear. Does it mean that the righteous man would, could or should live with steadfast, unyielding, moral courage, knowing that he is right—small comfort if the enemy kills without discrimination—or does it mean that the righteous man should live in the faith that Yahweh would deliver him from the

---

[14] Weiser, *op. cit.,* p. 262.

enemy because of his faithfulness to Yahweh's way?[15] The prophet introduced the problem of theodicy,[16] the righteousness of Yahweh, which was to be discussed over and over again by subsequent writers.

Read 2:6–20

The woe oracles seem to be directed against specific individuals. The person indicated in the first oracle (2:6–8) cannot be identified, but the reference to plunder may indicate the Babylonians. The second (2:9–11) and third (2:12–14) fit what we know of Jehoiakim, whose construction of a summer palace placed heavy burdens on his countrymen.[17] The remaining oracles condemn drunkenness and idolatry, and a liturgical statement closes the section.

Read 3:1–19

Whether or not the hymn and statement of trust are the work of Habakkuk cannot be determined. This chapter is missing in the Qumran scroll, but this fact, in itself, proves nothing. The chapter stands apart from the rest of the book in its hymnic quality, and although it has been interpreted as the answer to the question posed in 2:1–3,[18] in reality only the statement of trust (3:17–19) is applicable. The liturgical notations "according to Shigionoth"[19] (3:1), "Selah"[20] (3:3; 9:13) and the final word to the "choirmaster"[21] suggest that a hymn and confession of trust (3:17–19) borrowed from cultic ritual have been added to Habakkuk's work to adapt it to liturgical usage. The imagery of the hymn is reminiscent of a lost myth of a battle between Yahweh and the sea, similar to that of the struggle between Ba'al and Yam (3:12–15). The theophany is like that in Judg. 5 (cf. 3:3 ff.), but is more elaborate and introduces new mythological motifs. It has been suggested that the chapter is the product of the seventh century, that it employs archaizing techniques, and that it is the work of one writer, possibly Habakkuk the prophet.[22]

THE LAST DAYS OF JUDAH

Zedekiah's rule was a tenuous one. Jehoiachin, the king in exile, was treated as a royal hostage and Babylonian tablets recording the allotment of provender to the monarch (listed as "Yaukin of Yahud") and his family have been found, confirming the note in II Kings

[15] For a re-interpretation and a re-application of Habakkuk 2:4 in a New Testament, Christian context by the apostle Paul, cf. Galatians 3:11; Romans 1:17. For the interpretation of the Qumran community, cf. Gaster, *The Dead Sea Scriptures*, p. 253; James Alvin Sanders, "Habakkuk in *Qumran*, Paul, and the Old Testament," *Journal of Religion*, XXXIX (1959), 232–244.

[16] The word "theodicy" is made up of two Greek words *theos*, god, and *dike*, justice. The postulate of a righteous, all-powerful deity raises the question of the presence of evil in the world, and/or the reason why evil seems to be more powerful than good or why the evil triumph over the righteous.

[17] Cf. Jer. 22:13–17.

[18] Weiser, *op. cit.*, p. 262.

[19] The word "Shigionoth" cannot be translated. It may refer to an instrument, to the time in the service for a song, or to the tune or mood of the music.

[20] "Selah" indicates an interlude, perhaps for instruments or cymbals.

[21] The "choirmaster" seems to have been the chief of the musicians.

[22] Wm. F. Albright, "The Psalm of Habakkuk" in *Studies in Old Testament Prophecy*, H. H. Rowley (ed.) (Edinburgh: T & T Clark, 1950), pp. 1–18.

25:29 f. Moreover, Jehoiachin retained his holdings in Judah, for storage jars bearing the stamped seal of "Eliakim, steward of Jehoiachin" have been found, indicating that financial returns from Judah holdings were garnered in the name of the absentee king.[23] The portrait of Zedekiah preserved in Jeremiah's words depicts him as a vacillating, rather weak ruler not fitted for the delicate responsibilities of his age. Whatever his character may have been, he failed to recognize and appreciate, as Jeremiah apparently did, the master statesmanship and military skill of Nebuchadrezzar.

A revolt in Babylon, perhaps led by certain elements of the army, may have caused Zedekiah to believe that Nebuchadrezzar's power was crumbling, and it would appear that the Jerusalem prophet Hannaniah furthered this hope (cf. Jer. 28:1 ff.). It is possible that some of the exiles were restless, for Jeremiah wrote them a letter urging them to be good citizens (Jer. 29). A cooperative plan of revolt was developed by small nations, including Edom, Moab, Ammon, Tyre and Sidon, and Zedekiah was urged to ally himself with them (Jer. 27). Zedekiah refused but later that same year (594), the Pharaoh Hophra of Egypt attacked Philistia in an attempt to regain control of territory important for trade and shipping and Zedekiah joined this rebellion. Once again Nebuchadrezzar moved on Jerusalem and, after an eighteen-month siege beginning in late December, 588 or January, 587, took the city in August, 586.[24] These were disastrous months for Judah. Babylonian armies ravaged nearby cities, including Debir and Lachish.[25] From the excavation of Lachish, twenty-one ostraca[26] have been recovered consisting of correspondence between a scout or soldier in charge of an outpost and an officer within the city, written about the time the siege of Jerusalem was about to begin.[27] Some letters are so indistinct and fragmentary that their meaning is obscure, but others are quite clear. They speak of those who hinder and weaken and they invoke the name of Yahweh and refer to "fire-signals" by which information was relayed. Shortly afterward the Babylonian armies destroyed Lachish and other Judaean cities. The siege of Jerusalem is related briefly in II Kings 25:1–21 (cf. Jer. 39:1–10). The city was without food and when the Babylonians finally entered, Zedekiah and his soldiers fled. Zedekiah was captured and brought for judgment before Nebuchadrezzar who was in Syria. His fate was worse than death. His family was murdered one by one before him, and then Zedekiah was blinded so that the last sight he would remember would be the destruction of his loved ones. In chains he was led to Babylon. The city of Jerusalem was utterly destroyed: the temple of Solomon was pulled down, the walls of the city were demolished and buildings were set afire.

23 Cf. Wright, *Biblical Archaeology*, p. 181.

24 For dates one year earlier, cf. Wright, *op. cit.*, p. 180.

25 The fires of Lachish were so fierce that mud-brick walls were baked a bright red.

26 Ostraca are pottery sherds which have been written upon. It was a common practice to use pieces of broken pottery in this manner.

27 H. Torczyner, *The Lachish Letters* (*Lachish I*) (London: Oxford University Press, 1938).

Once again Babylonian soldiers took into captivity what remained of skilled or talented leadership, leaving only the poor and the under-privileged. So great was the devastation of Jerusalem that governmental headquarters were moved to Mizpah, probably Tell en-Nasbeh a few miles north and west. A certain Gedaliah was placed in charge of Judah.[28] Little by little, as Babylonian soldiers withdrew, refugees returned, including Judaean soldiers. Encouraged by the king of Ammon, one of these men, named Ishmael, murdered Gedaliah. Pursued by angry Judaean warriors, Ishmael went to Ammon. In fear of reprisal from Babylon, many Judaeans fled to Egypt, compelling Jeremiah and his scribe to accompany them. The tattered remnant predicted by the prophets remained in Judah. In Babylon, another remnant of the educated, informed and talented kept alive faith in Yahweh and the fierce nationalism that was to be the rebirth of the people of Judah, the Jews.

JEREMIAH

Some insight into the last tumultuous trouble-ridden days of Judah comes from the book bearing the name of the prophet Jeremiah. According to the editorial superscription (1:1) Jeremiah was the son of Hilkiah, a priest of the village of Anathoth a few miles northeast of Jerusalem.[29] Unlike Isaiah and Hosea, Jeremiah remained unmarried (16:2). The superscription notes that he received his summons to prophesy in the thirteenth year of Josiah (cf. 25:3) or about 627/626 B.C., leading to the hypothesis that he may have been born about 650 or, in view of the prophet's complaint that he was too young for prophetic responsibilities (1:6), between 650 and 640.[30] Many scholars have proposed that his first oracles, which dealt with an enemy from the north (1:11–19), are to be associated with the movement of the Scythians, but others, including J. P. Hyatt, have argued that the foe from the north is to be identified as Neo-Babylonian,[31] and that the thirteenth year of Josiah was the date of Jeremiah's birth, for Jeremiah speaks of Yahweh consecrating him while he was still in the womb (1:5).[32] Because, to the best of our knowledge, the Scythian threat was not realized and the Neo-Babylonian one was, it is attractive to accept the latter theory. However, references to Jeremiah's wrestling with his call from Yahweh can hardly be considered pre-

[28] A clay seal found at Lachish read "Property of Gedaliah who is over the house" and may have belonged to the new governor.

[29] There is no reason to suspect that Hilkiah of Anathoth was the priest of the same name who discovered the Deuteronomic scroll, nor can it be assumed that he was a priest of Ba'al, nor that he was descended from Abiathur, the priest banished by King Solomon to Anathoth (I Kings 2:26), as some have suggested.

[30] It should be remembered that Josiah was only eight years old when he became king.

[31] J. P. Hyatt, "Jeremiah," *The Interpreter's Bible*, V, 797.

[32] *Ibid.*, p. 779. For a completely different solution in which the "foe from the north" is interpreted mythologically, cf. A. C. Welch, *Jeremiah, His Time and His Work* (Oxford: Oxford University Press, 1928).

natal and the implications of the superscription (and 25:3) should not be ignored. The superscription goes on to say that Jeremiah continued to prophesy until the eleventh year of Zedekiah (587), but events subsequent to this date appear in Chapters 40–44, a separate source. Jeremiah's prophetic ministry extends over a period of more than forty years.

Passages recording Jeremiah's personal response to his work, his loneliness and sense of frustration, and the vituperative attitude of his countrymen tend to create in the reader a feeling of genuine intimacy and empathy beyond that experienced with other biblical writers. Jeremiah's sensitivity to nature, his allusions to village life, and his changing moods are recorded in poetry charged with emotional power and illuminated by vivid imagery (cf. 4:20–21, 29; 6:24; 8:18). His deep religious awareness, his sense of personal relationship with Yahweh, his outcries and protests yet his constant yielding to what he understood to be divine will reveal the emotional depth of his experiences. He appears as one upon whom the waning fortunes of the nation, the callous indifference to community welfare of Jehoiakim, and the apostasy of the people laid a heavy burden and produced emotions akin to physical torment (4:19 f.). Yet, when Babylonians removed the leading citizenry, Jeremiah rose above his personal situation to direct words of wisdom and guidance to those being led by false hopes to anticipate an early return to Judah (ch. 29).

Despite his loneliness, Jeremiah had at least one disciple, Baruch, son of Neriah, who copied the prophet's oracles and delivered them to King Jehoiakim (ch. 36). It is possible that the bulk of the record of Jeremiah rests upon Baruch's work.

Traditionally the entire fifty-two chapters of Jeremiah have been attributed to the prophet, but it is clear that such a thesis is no longer tenable. There is a considerable difference between the Hebrew and the LXX texts, not only in the order of the contents but in length. The LXX version is shorter, omitting numerous individual verses but adding others, raising a question as to whether passages were dropped from the LXX tradition or added to the Hebrew. Chapter 52 of Jeremiah parallels II Kings 24:18–25:21 and is a summary of events from 598 to 566, from the same source as II Kings. Chapters 50 and 51 come from a period after the destruction of Jerusalem but before the death of Nebuchadrezzar in 562 and represent the time when the captive Judaeans, or Jews as they came to be called, dreamed of the overthrow of Babylon by an enemy vaguely defined as a foe from the north or, at times, as the Medes. Certain eschatological and restoration oracles represent the thinking of the people of the Exile and are, therefore, additions to Jeremiah's work: 3:14–18; 4:23–26; 12:14–17; 16:14–15; 23:1–4, 5–6, 7–8; 25:30–38; 30:8–9, 10–11, 16–17, 18–22, 22–24; 31:1, 7–9, 10–14, 23–25, 27–28, 35–37, 38–40. Numerous passages in Chapters 26–45 relating Jeremiah's activities in the third person may represent Baruch's memoirs. Therefore, the book is composite, containing genuine Jeremiac sayings, Baruch's contributions and later additions.

Chapter 36, which tells of a scroll dictated by Jeremiah to Baruch for

INCENSE ALTARS *from the Early Iron Age
found at Megiddo, perhaps similar to those
used in Jeremiah's time to burn incense to
Ba'al (cf. Jer. 1:16; 7:9; 11:12 f.; etc.)*

presentation to King Jehoiakim, is usually taken as the starting point
for study of the literary tradition. The king destroyed this scroll but
Jeremiah immediately dictated another containing the same material
and numerous additions (36:32). The contents appear to have been
the accumulated oracles of the prophet, including those denouncing
"Israel and Judah" and foreign nations (36:2). Some attempts have
been made to isolate this scroll from the total work assigned to
Jeremiah, but results have not been particularly satisfactory.[33] The
bases for selections are that the material must represent oracles from
626 to 605 and that they must be composed of indictments and threats.
The choice of oracles is generally limited to Chapters 1 to 25. Just how
helpful such lists are is not clear. The problem is complicated by the
Deuteronomic style which appears in varying degrees in Jeremiah's
work, for it is not clear to what extent Jeremiah may have adopted or
employed a Deuteronomic style (which could have become popular
after 621), or to what degree his work has been edited by Deuteron-

[33] Hyatt, *Interpreter's Bible*, p. 787, lists 1:4–14, 17; 2:1–37; 3:1–5, 19–25; 4:1–8,
11–22, 27–31; 5:1–17, 20–31; 6:1–30 and possibly 8:4–9:1. Eissfeldt, *op. cit.*, p. 351
selects the following: 1:2, 4–10, 11–17, (19) ; 3:6–13; 7:1–8:3; 11: (1) , 6–14; 13:1–14;
16:1–13; 17:19–27; 18:1–12; 19:1–2; 10, 11a; 22:1–5; 25.

omists, or to what extent his scribe, Baruch, may have utilized Deuteronomic patterns. It seems wiser to begin with an analysis of the entire content of the book and to proceed from there on an historical basis, so far as possible.

The book of Jeremiah may be divided into seven parts:

I. Ch. 1   The prophet's vocational summons.
II. Chs. 2–25   Oracles against his own people.
III. Chs. 26–29   Biographical material.
IV. Chs. 30–33   Prophetic oracles.
V. Chs. 34–45   Biographical material.
VI. Chs. 46–51   Oracles against foreign nations (in the LXX these follow Chapter 25).
VII. Ch. 52   An historical appendix paralleling II Kings 24:18–25:21.

A more detailed breakdown follows (non-Jeremiac material is italicized):

I. The Vocational Summons: Chapter 1.
   1:1–3   Editorial superscription.
   1:4–10   The call to be a prophet.
   1:11–12   The vision of the almond rod.
   1:13–19   The vision of the boiling pot.
II. Oracles against his own people: Chapters 2–25.
   2:1–3:5   Oracles against Judah.
   3:6–13   Oracles on apostasy of Judah which reflect D styling.
   3:14–18   Restoration oracles loosely combined.
   3:19–20   A lament.
   3:21–24   Indictment in form of situation (21–23) and response (24–25).
   4:1–6:30   The foe from the north (*5:18–19 may be a late Deuteronomic expansion*).
   7:1–8:3   The temple sermon (colored by D styling).
   8:4–9:11   Concerning Judah and Jerusalem.
   9:12–16   An expansion by Deuteronomists.
   9:17–19   A funeral dirge.
   9:20–22   Laments.
   9:23–24   An isolated oracle.
   9:25–26   A late addition.
   10:1–16   Late material in the style of II Isaiah (6–8, 10 are not in the LXX and 11 is an Aramaic intrusion).
   10:17–25   The destruction of Jerusalem (*Verse 25 is a psalm fragment, cf. Ps. 79:6 f.*).
   11:1–17   Jeremiah and Deuteronomy (Deuteronomic styling).
   11:18–12:13   The persecution of Jeremiah (Verse 13 is an isolated fragment).
   12:14–17   A late restoration oracle.
   13:1–14   Symbols and parables.
   13:15–15:21   Oracles of disaster.
   16:1–9   The loneliness of Jeremiah.
   16:10–18   A Deuteronomic expansion.
   16:19–21   Fragments.
   17:1–18   A mixture: *1–4 is not in the LXX, 5–8 is hymnic, 9 f. and 11 are wisdom sayings,* 12–13 is a fragment on the temple and 14–18 is a monologue.

JEREMIAH AND JOSIAH

626. Jeremiah's commission to prophesy came at a moment of dramatic restlessness in the Near East when the death of Ashurbanipal, the Chaldean-Medean power bloc and the migrations of Cimmerians and Scythians caused concern for national safety in Judah. Jeremiah's record of his summons by Yahweh conveys his conviction that he was chosen, predestined for his prophetic role before he was born, and that the call to prophesy came before he felt he was old enough for the task. The expression of inadequacy is reminiscent of Moses' protestations (cf. Exod. 3:9 ff., E), but like Moses, Jeremiah was assured that Yahweh's strength would sustain him.[34] The words which he was to

Read Ch. 1

[34] William L. Holladay, "Jeremiah and Moses: Further Observations," *Journal of Biblical Literature,* LXXXV (1966), 17–27.

utter were Yahweh's words, charged with divine power, capable of building up, should the pronouncement be favorable, or destroying kingdoms, should the oracle be destructive. The same theological conviction we have seen in other prophetic writings undergirds this statement, for whatever happened for weal or woe could be traced to Yahweh and the deity's reaction to Judah's fidelity or apostasy. Although Jeremiah was commissioned as a prophet to "the nations," his real mission was to Judah.

The first visions are associated with everyday objects transformed in the prophet's mind to symbols. The branch of the almond tree, *shaqed* in Hebrew, becomes *shoqed* or "watching" to the prophet and brings a promise that Yahweh was watching over his word. A boiling pot tipped toward the south becomes a warning that hordes of enemies would pour out of the north into Judah. If the reference is to the Scythian-Cimmerian movement, then Jeremiah was wrong; if it has a longer time significance then the Neo-Babylonians proved him to be right; or if these oracles are to be dated fifteen or twenty years later, as Hyatt has proposed, then Jeremiah was correct.

Read 2:1–3:20 Oracles condemning Judah for apostasy may be associated with the early period of Jeremiah's prophetic ministry and reflect the socio-religious situation prior to Josiah's reform. The impression of Hosea's marriage symbolism upon the young prophet is discernible in 2:2. In 2:4 the familiar law court setting is employed with Yahweh, the plaintiff, presenting the issue (2:5), reciting the history of the case (2:6–9), presenting the uniqueness of the violation (2:10–13), appealing to the precedent of Israel (2:14–15), warning against present policy (2:16–19), and, finally, drawing upon Isaiah's vineyard parable and Hosea's imagery, presenting a long summation in which the arguments of the defendant are refuted. A prose summary, possibly prepared by Baruch, places this kind of condemnation in the reign of Josiah. Yahweh's lament over the apostasy of the nation follows (3:19–20).

Read 3:21–4:4 An indictment (21) followed by a recital of penitence (22) may be derived, in part, from some liturgy utilized at a Yahweh shrine or may be Jeremiah's idealization of what the people's attitude should be. The setting is the autumn, the time of the New Year, when mourning for the dead Ba'al and rites of purgation were observed. Yahweh's call (22a) evokes a penitent response, a promise of return, a rejection of the way of Ba'al (22–23) and a confession of the sin of apostasy (24–25). Yahweh's rejoinder is a demand for a radical change of attitude and commitment (4:4), upon which potential blessings rest (4:1–2).

Read 4:5–6:30 The collection of fragments of war oracles may be associated with the Scythian threat and reveal something of the physical and mental suffering of the prophet as he envisions the disasters. So complete is the devastation pictured by the prophet that the earth is returned to its primeval emptiness (4:23 ff.). Chapter 5 introduces a literary pattern of statements and responses. Yahweh comments upon the impossibility of finding a faithful follower (5:1–3). The prophet responds that they are discussing only the poor, but when he looks among the rich and

A COSMETIC MORTAR. *The cosmetic mortar pictured here is from the time of Jeremiah and was found at Tell en-Nasbeh which is believed to be the biblical city of Mizpah (Jer. 40:6 ff.). Cosmetic mortars were usually made from limestone or marble and were from three to four inches in diameter. Fragments of green malachite ore were placed in the mortar and ground to a fine powder with a pestle, then oil was added to make a paste and the green eyeshadow called* kohl *or* kuhl *was applied to the eyelids. A black cosmetic preparation for eyebrows, eyelashes and for outlining the eyes was made by grinding antimony to powder and adding oil. It was the use of these products that Jeremiah had in mind when he described Jerusalem as a harlot enlarging her eyes with paint (Jer. 4:30). A reddish colored cosmetic mixture was made by using iron oxide as a base.*

powerful he discovers only infidelity (5:4 f.). The result is condemnation by Yahweh and the threat of complete destruction.

JEREMIAH AND DEUTERONOMY

Read Chs. 11–12

The most important socio-religious event of Josiah's reign was the discovery of the Deuteronomic scroll, but it is difficult to assign passages in Jeremiah to this subject with any certainty. Chapter 11 may be a Deuteronomic essay inserted in Jeremiah's work to make the prophet appear as a supporter of the code.[35] It is possible that it contains an historical kernel.[36] On the other hand, if Jeremiah did support Deuteronomy, it is not impossible that he used D language in urging its support and in proclaiming its contents.[37] It has also been argued that Jeremiah is not referring to the D covenant code but to the Sinai covenant.[38] The first five verses echo the curse of Deut. 27:26 as well as the familiar Deuteronomic recitation of the past. Verses 6–13 tell of Jeremiah's commission to support the code and of the failure of his mission. Verses 14–17 refer to Yahweh's rejection of his people. The monologue which follows (18–20) portrays the hostility of those refusing the message and, in 21–23, the opponents are identified as men of Anathoth, Jeremiah's birthplace, where Deuteronomic legislation would affect the future of the Yahweh shrine (or any other) and the priesthood.

A second monologue raises the problem of theodicy[39] (12:1) and mentions the rejection of the prophet by his own family. Yahweh's response to the query about theodicy is Yahweh's promise of the destruction of the nation and the abandonment of his temple. With-

---

[35] J. M. Meyers, "The Book of Jeremiah," *Old Testament Commentary*, ed. H. C. Alleman and E. F. Flack (Philadelphia: The Muhlenberg Press, 1948), pp. 712 f.

[36] E. Leslie, *Jeremiah* (New York: Abingdon Press, 1954), pp. 82 ff.

[37] C. H. Cornill, *Das Buch Jeremia* (Leipzig: B. Tauchnitz, 1905), p. 144; J. Skinner, *Prophecy and Religion* (Cambridge: University Press, 1955), pp. 102 ff. For a detailed analysis, cf. H. H. Rowley, "The Prophet Jeremiah and the Book of Deuteronomy" in *Studies in Old Testament Prophecy* (ed. H. H. Rowley) (Edinburgh: T & T Clark 1950), pp. 157–174.

[38] J. P. Hyatt, *The Interpreter's Bible*, V, 906.

[39] Martin Buber, *The Prophetic Faith* (New York: Harper and Brothers, 1949), pp. 170 f. places this question in 609 after the death of Josiah.

out Yahweh the nation could have no inner strength; indeed, Yahweh's sword was to be turned against his chosen people (12:12). On the basis of these chapters it could be argued that Jeremiah supported the Deuteronomic reform with enthusiasm, that he encountered bitter opposition in his home community when he attempted to preach there, and that his efforts to bring about the reform were unavailing (cf. Jer. 15:16 f.).

Other passages may be selected to reflect another response. For example, Jeremiah 8:8 ff. may refer to the prophet's rejection of D as a false work by the scribes, or this passage may be interpreted as a reflection of Jeremiah's attitude after his work on behalf of the code failed. Whatever Jeremiah's original response to D may have been,[40] if 31:31 ff. is by the prophet as most scholars believe, it is quite clear that Jeremiah became convinced that the formalizing of religion in a covenantal code or in a rigid credal statement was inadequate. He returned to the emphasis of his prophetic predecessors and stressed a religion of inner commitment rather than outer observance. The covenant of the future would be inscribed on the human heart rather than on tablets of stone, and knowledge of God would not be knowledge about Yahweh acquired through teaching but inner, personal knowledge gained through experience.

JEREMIAH AND THE DEATH OF JOSIAH

Read 22:10–12; 8:14–15

609. The death of the king and the capture of Jehoahaz seems to have been the occasion for the remarks in 22:10–12. Jeremiah correctly ascertained that Jehoahaz would never return to the throne of Judah. The words of despair in 8:14 f may also be from this period.

JEREMIAH AND JEHOIAKIM

Read Chs. 7, 26

Soon after Jehoiakim became king, Jeremiah prophesied the destruction of the temple of Yahweh, the symbol of national unity and security. His words, preserved in the so-called "temple sermon" (ch. 7), provoked a violent response and a threat of death. Indeed, in Baruch's record (ch. 26) we are told that a fellow prophet, Uriah, fled to Egypt after preaching much the same message, only to be extradited and executed. Jeremiah escaped a similar sentence through protection by the politically powerful Ahikam, son of Shaphan, the royal secretary (cf. Jer. 26:24; II Kings 22:8 ff.). The rejection of Deuteronomic cultic rules is clear from Jeremiah's words about families participating in the worship of the queen of heaven (7:18) and in child sacrifice (7:31).

---

[40] It should be noted that Jer. 3:1 is based on Deut. 24: 1–4.

A second sermon is reported, probably by Baruch, in what is often referred to as the "Tophet sermon." The breaking of the clay flask was a ritual act carrying with it symbolic meaning and divine power.[41] For this prophetic act Jeremiah was beaten and placed in stocks by Pashhur, a temple official. Whatever discouragement the prophet may have experienced in punishment and public disgrace did not prevent him from continuing to make his message heard. In December, 604, during a public fast, a scroll prepared earlier was read to the people in the temple precincts, then read to the princes, before being delivered to the king. As Jehoiakim listened to the words, with derisive contempt he burned the scroll, piece by piece, showing utter disdain for anything Jeremiah might have to say. The prophet immediately reproduced the scroll in an expanded form, providing, as we have noted previously, what may be the nucleus of the present book of Jeremiah.

Read 19–20:6; 36:9–32

Jehoiakim's building program, his indifference to the plight of the poor, his use of violence and his greed were, in part, the bases for Jeremiah's hostility to the king. The ruler's death in 598 produced little sorrow in the prophet.

Read 22:13–23; 45

Outside of Judah the Near Eastern world was in turmoil. Necho's abortive efforts to halt Nebuchadrezzar at Carchemish convinced Jeremiah that the Neo-Babylonian Empire was destined to become the dominant world power. Any attempt at retaliation by Egypt, he prophesied, would fail. During the time of his struggles with Jehoiakim, he turned his attention to the surrounding nations and pronounced a series of doom oracles. A summary list of the nations against which he hurled his condemnations is given in 25:17 ff., perhaps by Baruch. Statements against these nations are found in Chapters 46–49. It is probable that the basic material in these oracles is by Jeremiah, but there can be little doubt that his work was expanded by later hands. The oracle against Egypt predicts the failure to meet Nebuchadrezzar's threat of world domination and the words against Philistia are made to foretell an attack by Necho.

Read Ch. 25; Chs. 46–47

How much of the oracle against Moab can be accepted as Jeremiah's work is hard to determine. It is possible that this pronouncement may have been given in 602 when Jehoiakim rebelled against Nebuchadrezzar and suffered attack by Moabites, Ammonites, Syrians and Chaldeans (II Kings 24:2 ff.). Another possible date is in the time of Zedekiah (cf. Jeremiah 27:1–11). The oracle contains a remarkable roster of Moabite communities. The Ammonite oracle, less vehement in character, is no less positive in its prediction of destruction, and the words directed against Edom contain condemnations and promises of desolation. The oracles against Damascus (49:23–27) are probably not by Jeremiah, for Damascus had ceased to be a problem since the Assyrian conquest. It is possible that there is a genuine core of Jeremiah's words in the condemnation of the Arabs (49:28–33).

Read Chs. 48–49

[41] In Egypt, during the twelfth or thirteenth dynasties, the execration of enemies involved the inscribing of names or places on bowls and smashing them. Cf. *ANET*, pp. 328 f.

Jeremiah and Jehoiachin

Read 13:18–19; 22:24–30

The brief reign of Jehoiachin receives only passing mention by Jeremiah. Even as the young king took control of the kingdom, the Babylonians were occupying the surrounding country. There could be no doubt that Jeremiah's prophecies of the fall of the city were to be fulfilled. As Jehoiachin (or Coniah) was taken into exile, Jeremiah predicted that none of his descendants would occupy the throne of Judah.

Jeremiah and Zedekiah

Read Ch. 24

Much of the recorded work of Jeremiah relates to Zedekiah's time. Immediately after Nebuchadrezzar's hosts had departed, taking with them the cream of Judah's artisans and leaders, Jeremiah expressed his lack of confidence in Zedekiah's ability to save the nation from ultimate destruction. On the other hand he saw in the exiles the hope of the future, and introduced into biblical thought an idea that was to be expanded by subsequent writers—that the true Israel was to be found among these exiles (24:4–7).

Read Chs. 27–29

Apparently some of Jeremiah's countrymen had not been impressed by Babylonian power, possibly because the city and the temple were not destroyed in the first siege. Jeremiah had no such illusions and warned against false confidence in Judah's ability to evade Nebuchadrezzar's yoke. Oracles by the prophet Hananiah, predicting a triumphant return of the people and plunder seized by Babylon, provoked Jeremiah to a dramatic portrayal of servitude in which he donned a neck-yoke. Messages sent to the exiles promising restoration and return were countered by Jeremiah in a letter wisely advising the captives to prepare calmly and intelligently for a lengthy absence from Judah and to seek their personal welfare in the prosperity of Babylon.[42] Jeremiah's

Read Chs. 34; 37–40

letter suggests that the exiled Judaeans lived in their own community, owned their own homes, cultivated their own gardens and apparently experienced no major suffering or inconvenience. (Yet, cf. Psalm 137.)

When Zedekiah's folly brought about the return of Nebuchadrezzar's army, Zedekiah, in a desperate effort to win Yahweh's favor and support, declared the release of all Hebrew slaves in accord with Deuteronomy 15. The covenantal requirement was no sooner announced than it was violated, and the newly freed slaves were taken back into bondage. The armies of Babylon arrived. During a lull in the siege, Jeremiah attempted to visit his home in Anathoth but was arrested as a deserter and imprisoned in a cistern empty of water but not of miry sediment. When he was rescued from this cell and brought before Zedekiah, he advised surrender to Babylon—counsel that the monarch rejected. After the fall of the city when the second deportation took place, Jeremiah was permitted to remain in Judah.

[42] Apparently Jeremiah's advice was heeded and a colony of Jewish scholars remained in Babylon for over 1,000 years.

After the murder of Gedaliah, there were those who determined that **Read 40–44** the only way to be safe from punishment by Nebuchadrezzar was to seek refuge in Egypt. Jeremiah sought to dissuade them, but they were determined to flee, and when they departed they took with them Jeremiah and his scribe, Baruch. In Egypt, Jeremiah is reported to have prophesied the fall of Egypt to Nebuchadrezzar.

JEREMIAH'S CONFESSIONS

A number of monologues in which Jeremiah reveals his inner emotions and personal communications with Yahweh are labeled "Confessions." They include: 11:18–23; 12:1–6; 15:10–12, 15–21; 17:9–10, 14–18; 18:18–23; 20:7–12, 14–18.

The youthful naiveté with which the prophet entered his career, the resultant suffering at the hands of his opponents (including his own family), his loneliness and isolation from the ordinary joys of his countrymen, and his frustration and cries for vengeance, depict the inner turmoil of the prophet. His experiences, which caused him real physical pain, grew out of a commitment to Yahweh which both delighted him (15:16) and isolated him from pleasures of society. Doubts about Yahweh's constant support (15:18b) were answered with the guarantee of fortifying strength (15:19 ff.). As he became the subject of mockery and ridicule, he determined never to utter the oracles of Yahweh again, only to find that the fire of Yahweh's demands burned within him, compelling him to cry out his words of doom against his will, so demanding was the power of his experience of the divine (20:7 ff.). Fluctuating moods, anger, demands for vengeance, coupled with moments of strength and assurance, mark him as the most human of men, an individual torn between destiny, duty, a committed life, and the pressures of an unsympathetic, hostile audience.[43]

HEAD OF A GODDESS. *Figurines of clay, often called "Astarte figurines," have been found by archaeologists at many sites in Palestine in material remains coming from the period of the divided kingdom (Iron II). The face or front of the head was formed by pressing soft clay into a carefully prepared mold. The back of the head was roughly shaped by hand. The body consisted of a solid pillar of clay, flared at the base so it could stand alone. Usually the breasts were prominent and the arms, formed of strips of rolled clay, are flattened at the end to form hands which may merge into the body beneath the the breasts or cup or support the breasts as though offering them to an infant. Such representations are called* dea nutrix *or "the nurse goddess," symbolizing the mother who feeds her children. It is quite possible that these figurines are representations of the "queen of heaven" favored by the women of Jerusalem in Jeremiah's time (Jer. 7:16–20; 44:16–19).*

[43] Martin Buber, *The Prophetic Faith*, p. 182, points out that the sufferings of the prophet are symbolic of the suffering of the nation throughout its history.

JEREMIAH'S CONCEPT OF GOD

From the confessions it is easy to ascertain that Jeremiah believed Yahweh to be a god of judgment and justice, reliable and sure, concerned with the people's ethical behavior and obedience. Other passages reveal that Jeremiah emphasized the election tradition. Drawing upon Hosea, he glorified the wilderness tradition as the time when the people were faithful to their deity and argued that infidelity developed with the settlement in Canaan. What is new in Jeremiah's teaching is the reference to the covenant which was not specifically mentioned by his prophetic predecessors, but which, under Deuteronomic influence, was brought into central focus (11:3 ff.). Judah was the chosen of Yahweh, linked not only by ties of obedience and love, but by the binding, contractual force of the covenant.

Like earlier prophets, Jeremiah emphasized moral conduct and condemned the cult (6:20), but he went much further in his mockery of those who accepted the existence of the temple as a symbol of divine protection. The centralization of the cult under Deuteronomic influence no doubt contributed to this idea, and Jeremiah's prediction that the temple would become a ruin like the shrine at Shiloh was more than religious heresy and bordered upon treason. Jeremiah's argument was that Yahweh could not be protector of his people when they had forsaken him and that the very symbol of his protective role had become meaningless and would be removed because of national apostasy (ch. 7). Ritual was secondary; obedience was primary. Complete commitment to Yahweh and national security went hand in hand, as did unfaithfulness and disaster.

Yahweh's interest and power was not limited to Judah. He was creator of the world, and all human authority, all world leadership, all history was under his control (27:5 ff.; 31:35 ff.). Yahweh was god of nature, but was concerned with moral behavior (5:25 f.). Nor was the worship of Yahweh restricted to Judah or Jerusalem; Jeremiah taught that those in exile should pray to Yahweh on behalf of their captors, in the assurance that their prayers would be heard (29:7). This teaching moves beyond the monolatrous statements of Deuteronomy toward monotheism, encouraging belief in the possibility of worshiping Yahweh in any spot on the face of Yahweh's earth, and although the first full statement of monotheism was to come over half a century later, Jeremiah's expanded concepts provide the basis for such beliefs.

The theme of Yahweh's redemptive love developed by Hosea is expanded by Jeremiah. The national debacle foreseen by the prophets had become a reality and the war-weary Judaeans looked toward the future. Jeremiah did not extend hope for a quick return from exile but gave the exiles a new identity as the seed of the new Israel. As Yahweh in anger had sent them away, so Yahweh in love would restore them. A new god-people relationship would be established (24:4 ff.) and a new covenant of the heart formed (31:31 ff.), a concept that would be of great significance to those in exile and unable to perform covenant rituals. So confident was Jeremiah of Yahweh's redeeming love and of the future of the people, that at the height of the Babylonian siege he purchased a plot of ground in Anathoth from a cousin (32:6–15). Yahweh was not only god of the past, but lord of the future.

PART
SEVEN

The Exile

21

Life and Literature
of the Early Period

THE Exilic period falls into two parts: the years between 597 and 586 and the years after 586 up to 538 or 537. The mood and mind set of the people of Judah during the first period seems to have been one of continuing hope. In the second period, from the meagre sources available, despondency and humble acceptance of their tragic conditions appears to have characterized the remnant in Judah. Up until 586, so long as the temple—the symbol of Yahweh's power—was intact, and so long as Jerusalem itself, perhaps somewhat battered by the Babylonian siege, was still standing, a "business as usual" atmosphere seems to have prevailed. Jeremiah's preaching indicates that oppression of the poor, exploitation, apostasy—those evils which the prophet said provoked Yahweh to anger—were unchecked. There is no evidence of serious concern about further danger to national welfare.

When Babylonian forces returned in 587, some Judaeans fled to Egypt (II Kings 25:25 f.; Jer. 42 f.) and settled at Tahpanhes, or Daphnae, a border fortress in northern Egypt believed to be located at modern Tell Defneh. Concerning the fate of these migrants we know nothing, but from a later period we have knowledge of a Jewish military colony at Elephantine, the town guarding the southern Egyptian border near the first cataract of the Nile. Fifth century papyri from this site mention a Jewish temple dedicated to Yahweh (spelled *Yahu* or *Yaho*) and possibly to two other deities, although the evidence is not clear.[1] It is possible that the colony was founded between 598 and 587[2] and may have included Jews fleeing Judah prior to the fall of Jerusalem. Some Jews sought sanctuary in Moab, Ammon and Edom (Jer. 40:11), but no information is available about these refugees.

Jewish captives in Babylon no doubt suffered hardships, but Jeremiah's letter implies that they lived in a village where they could build private dwellings and cultivate the soil. No restrictions seem to have been placed on marriage or worship (Jer. 29). Hope was strong for a speedy return to Jerusalem, and so long as the temple remained, it

[1] Cf. E. G. Kraeling, "New Light on the Elephantine Colony," *BA*, XV (1952), 50–67; reprinted in *The Biblical Archaeologist Reader*, pp. 128 ff.; H. H. Rowley, "Papyri from Elephantine," *DOTT*, pp. 256 ff.; W. F. Albright, *Archaeology and the Religion of Israel*, pp. 168–175.

[2] Cf. John Bright, *A History of Israel*, p. 327. For a date between 569 and 525, cf. E. G. Kraeling, "New Light on the Elephantine Colony," p. 65.

—— CHART XIII ——

Date	Judaean King	Jewish Writer	Events in Palestine	Events in Persia	Events in Babylon	Events in Egypt
585	Jehoiachin in Exile	Lamentations Ezekiel	Gedaliah assassinated Palestine governed as a Babylonian province	585: Astyages succeeds Cyaxeres as King of Medes	Babylonians under pressure from Medes, Armenians, Tyrians and Egyptians	570: Pharaoh Apries (589–569) battles the Greeks 568: Nebuchadrezzar invades Egypt
562		Job Deuteronomists P writers			562: Nebuchadrezzar dies. Amel-Marduk releases Jehoiachin from prison 560: Amel-Marduk dies. In the struggle for the throne Nabonidus becomes king 552–545: Bel-shar-user is regent of Babylon, Nabonidus remains in the desert	
559		Holiness Code		559: Cyrus becomes king of Anshan 550: Cyrus controls the Median-Persian empire		
538		II Isaiah		539–538: Cyrus takes control of Babylon	Babylon taken over by Cyrus of Persia	

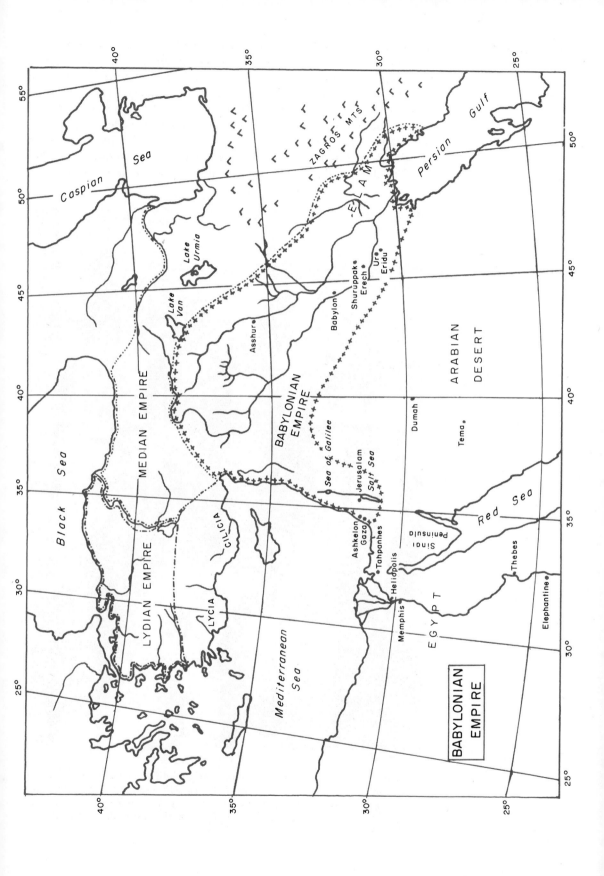

BABYLONIAN EMPIRE

must have been assumed that Yahweh had punished his people but had not forsaken them. More information about this period comes from Ezekiel whose prophetic work extends from the first deportation into the period following the destruction of Jerusalem.

What impression the magnificent city of Babylon made upon the exiles can only be imagined. Nebuchadrezzar had made Babylon into one of the most beautiful cities in the world. This great metropolis straddled the Euphrates and was surrounded by a moat and huge walls 85 feet thick with massive reinforcing towers. Eight gates led into

THE ISHTAR GATE OF ANCIENT BABYLON. *An artist's reconstruction, depicting a royal procession moving along Marduk's way, through the Ishtar gate, and turning into the courtyard of Nebuchadrezzar's palace which lies behind the lush growth of the famous hanging gardens. In the distance, the ziggurat of Marduk can be seen.*

THE ZIGGURAT OF MARDUK IN ANCIENT BABYLON. *An artist's reconstruction of the ziggurat E-temen-an-ki with the shrine of Marduk before it. A bridge linked the two parts of Babylon which were separated by the Euphrates river. To lessen the pressure of the flow of the water the piers of the bridge were boat shaped.*

the city, the most important being the double gate of Ishtar with a blue facade adorned with alternating rows of yellow and white bulls and dragons. Through the Ishtar gate a broad, paved, processional street known as "Marduk's Way" passed between high walls, past Nebuchadrezzar's palace and the famous "hanging gardens" to the ziggurat of Marduk, the national god. This tremendous brick structure named *E-temen-an-ki*, "the House of the Foundation of Heaven and Earth," was 300 feet square at the base and rose in eight successive stages to a height of 300 feet. Temples dedicated to various gods and goddesses abounded. Beyond the city were lush orchards, groves and gardens, fed by an intricate canal system, from which supplies of fruits and vegetables were obtained. Domesticated animals, fish, wild fowl and game provided a varied diet. From east and west, north and south, came caravans with goods for trade and barter. In festal seasons, sacred statuary from shrines in nearby cities was brought to Babylon by boat and land vehicles. Truly Babylon was, as her residents believed, at the "center" of the world. The magnificent splendor of the city must have impressed the Jews, and as we shall see, there is some evidence that Babylonian religious concepts also made an impression on the exiles.

Some Judaeans were held as hostages within the city proper and among these were Jehoiachin, the exiled king, and his family. Tablets discovered in the excavation of the city and dated between 595 and 570 include lists of rations paid in oil and barley from the royal storehouses to captives and skilled artisans from Egypt, Ashkelon, Phoenicia, Syria, Asia Minor and Iran. Specifically mentioned were "Yaukin, king of the land of Yahud" (Jehoiachin of Judah), his five sons, and eight other Judaeans. It is important to note that Jehoiachin was still called "King of Judah." Royal estates in Judah were managed, at least up until 586, by "Eliakim, steward of Jehoiachin," whose seal impressions have been found in excavations at Debir and Beth Shemesh.

The immediate impact of the news of the fall of Jerusalem upon the exiles must have produced shock and horror. But, as we shall see from the literature, there developed a new hope for restoration, a new discovery of the meaning of election and covenant, and a new sense of destiny, which grew in strength and excitement until something of a triumphant climax is reached in the writings of Deutero-Isaiah. Not all exiles responded to the new concepts and some of Isaiah's words castigate these blind, unresponsive ones, but as it is impossible today to read, unmoved, the stirring, inspiring words preserved from those times, it is quite reasonable to imagine that there must have been those roused to peaks of hope and encouragement as they contemplated the future.

EZEKIEL

Among the elite of Judaean society deported by Nebuchadrezzar in 597 was Ezekiel, a son in the priestly family of Buzi (1:3). The Jews were settled on the Kabari canal, or the "river Chebar" as it is called in Ezek. 1:1, which tapped the Euphrates' waters for agricultural and navigational purposes. The initial verses of the Book of Ezekiel, written in autobiographical form, speak of the thirtieth year, but no guidance is given as to the significance of this period which could refer to the thirtieth year of the prophet's life, to the time when the oracles were recorded some thirty years after his first vision, or to the thirtieth year of the Exile. The vocational summons which came in the fifth year of Jehoiachin has been dated July 21, 592.[3]

Innumerable problems are associated with the Book of Ezekiel. The prophet stipulates that he is among the exiles, but his words in Chapters 1 to 24 are addressed to Jews in Jerusalem. May one assume that he was permitted to break his exile and return to Jerusalem—and

---

[3] H. G. May, "Ezekiel," *The Interpreter's Bible*, VI, 68, discusses the dating problems arising out of autumnal and vernal calendars. All dates in this section follow May's chronology.

there is no evidence that this was possible—or did he send his oracles back to the Jerusalemites by courier? For some, his intimate knowledge of events in Jerusalem suggests that he was in that city, for his words had devastating effects upon some hearers there (cf. 11:13–14). Consequently, it has been proposed that Ezekiel prophesied in Palestine and that the Babylonian setting is the result of editing; or that he was exiled to Babylon, received his call there, and then returned to Palestine; or that he spoke in Babylon for the benefit of his hearers there, having received detailed information about events in Palestine by courier or by clairvoyance.[4] No clear solution is possible and scholars are divided between a Babylonian and a Palestinian provenance. We will assume that Ezekiel remained in Babylon and that references to his visits to Jerusalem are visionary experiences, perhaps supplemented by his personal memories of the city and by news received from informants from Palestine.

The integrity of the book has been challenged, with one scholar limiting authentic Ezekiel passages to some 170 verses,[5] and others accepting almost the whole book as genuine[6] or attempting to identify larger sections containing an Ezekiel core.[7] The book has been classified as a third century, pseudonymous story about a priest in the time of Manasseh, which was later edited to provide the Babylonian setting—in which case there would have been no such person as Ezekiel.[8] It has also been dated in the time of Manasseh and identified as a northern Israelite work, later edited by someone from Judah and given a Babylonian setting.[9] Most scholars accept a sixth century date but recognize that the book was carefully edited, perhaps by the prophet's disciples, so that it is, therefore, very difficult to isolate genuine Ezekiel materials.[10] Because of the complexity of this problem, we shall make no attempt to identify genuine Ezekiel passages. The book will be accepted as "Ezekielan" (Ezekiel and his disciples) except where study of the text has made it clear to most scholars that we are dealing with non-Ezekiel intrusions.

The book is usually divided into four major parts:

I. Chapter 1–24   Prophecies against Jerusalem and Judah delivered prior to 587.

[4] For a discussion of the history of the debate over locale, cf. Eissfeldt, op. cit., pp. 367 ff., and May, Interpreter's Bible, VI, 51 f.

[5] G. Hölscher, Hesekiel der Dichter und das Buch (Giessen: A. Töpelmann, 1924).

[6] C. G. Howie, The Date and Composition of Ezekiel, Journal of Biblical Literature Monograph Series, IV (Philadelphia: Society of Biblical Literature, 1950).

[7] H. G. May, Interpreter's Bible, VI, 50, lists the following passages believed to incorporate genuine Ezekiel material which cannot be isolated: 5:5–17; 7:1–27; 10:1–22; 12:21–28; 13:1–23; 17:11–21; 20:45–49; 21:1–7; 22:1–31; 23:31–35; 24:6–24; 26:1–6; 27:9b–25a; 27; 28:1–10; 29:1–5; 30:1–26; 31:10–18; 32:17–32; 33:30–33; 37:1–14; 42:13, 14; 43:6–12, 18–27; 44:1–2, 6–31; 45:10–25.

[8] C. C. Torrey, Pseudo-Ezekiel and the Original Prophecy (New Haven: Yale University Press, 1930).

[9] James Smith, The Book of the Prophet Ezekiel (New York: The Macmillan Co., 1931).

[10] For a discussion of the textual history, cf. Eissfeldt, op. cit., pp. 372 ff., Weiser, op. cit., pp. 224 ff.

EZEKIEL'S CALL

Read Chs. 1–3

Yahweh's summons to Ezekiel came as a vision which combines imagery much like that used by Isaiah of Jerusalem (Isa. 6) with an inner conviction not unlike that of Jeremiah (Jer. 1:5) of being chosen or destined for the prophetic role. The theophany out of the north[11] is usually associated with an approaching storm transmogrified in Ezekiel's mind into the chariot of Yahweh.[12] The imagery, which strikes the modern mind as strange and weird,[13] may have developed out of the prophet's recollections of the enthronement of Yahweh in the Judaean New Year ritual,[14] with some influence coming from the Babylonian setting.[15] The concept of the deity enthroned upon the cherubim[16] calls to mind the sacred ark and is in keeping with the use of winged figures, often animals with human faces, as symbolic guardians at the entrances to buildings or on throne chairs.[17]

[11] In Canaanite mythology, the pantheon was located in the north and this concept entered Hebrew-Jewish thought. Cf. Ps. 48:2 where Yahweh's abode on Mount Zion is located in the far north.

[12] Cf. Ps. 6:48; 104:3, where Yahweh is said to ride the clouds as a chariot. Ba'al also rode the clouds, cf. Gaster, *Thespis*, pp. 89, 122, and passages cited there.

[13] This imagery prompted an attempt at a Freudian analysis of Ezekiel, cf. E. C. Broome, "Ezekiel's Abnormal Personality," *Journal of Biblical Literature*, LXV (1946), 277–292. For a refutation see C. G. Howie, *op. cit.*, pp. 69 ff.

[14] Cf. May, *The Interpreter's Bible*, VI, 69 for a brief statement and bibliography.

[15] Cf. Oesterley and Robinson, *op. cit.*, p. 274.

[16] The four living creatures are identified as cherubim in Ezek. 11:22.

[17] Cf. the mythological cherubim in the J story of the garden of Eden (Gen. 3:24).

Like other prophets, Ezekiel was commissioned to bring unpleasant information and announce the forthcoming annihilation of Jerusalem. The description of the prophet eating a scroll (2:8–3:3), symbolizing the absorption of the message (cf. Jer. 15:16), interrupts the commissioning narrative which, as many scholars have pointed out, should include a statement of the reception Ezekiel might expect from his countrymen. As Yahweh's watchman, the prophetic responsibility included the burdensome knowledge that with him rested the safety and salvation of those to whom he was sent.

ORACLES OF JUDGMENT

In five dramatic acts, the prophet depicted the siege and destruction of Jerusalem and prolonged punishment for Israel and Judah. It should be remembered that symbolic acts depicted reality, and what the prophet did was as good as accomplished, so to speak, as an act of Yahweh, even though the event had not yet taken place. Jerusalem would fall by siege and sword, and famine and pestilence would take their toll. Those who escaped death would testify that Yahweh had indeed kept his promise of destructon (6:10). Here we find no nationalistic idealization of the city and the temple like that characterizing Isaiah's work. Ezekiel saw no hope for the city or the temple: both would perish.

Read Chs. 4–7

Nor did Ezekiel envision a brief period of punishment: the Exile would fall by siege and sword, and famine and pestilence would take reading in the LXX, the prophet lay on his left side portraying the period of Israel's punishment, and he lay for forty days on his right side to portray Judaean punishment. Subtracting 190 years (days), the LXX reading, from 721, the date of the fall of Israel, would give a date of 531 for the time of the termination of that punishment. The forty years (days) of Judah might be symbolic, signifying one generation or simply a long time. Using 586, the date of the fall of Jerusalem, and subtracting the forty years (days) the Exile should have ended in 546, a date reasonably close to the historical termination.

Perhaps Ezekiel's background as a member of a priest's family heightened his sensitivity to the separation of the holy and the profane. For the prophet the profanation of the religion, the temple and the land was the underlying cause of that which had happened and was about to happen. He envisioned the idolatry practiced in the temple precincts in Jerusalem, the destruction of the wicked and the departure of the glory (kabod) of Yahweh. The opening vision, dated September 7, 591, reports the miraculous transportation of the prophet to Jerusalem where he witnessed cultic rites of the god Tammuz,[18] sun worship and the adoration of idols. Such apostasy was more than Yahweh's holiness could tolerate, and Ezekiel watched the withdrawal of Yahweh's glory (kabod). Without the divine presence, Jerusalem

Read Chs. 8–11

---

[18] Tammuz was a Sumerian deity. According to the Epic of Gilgamesh, he was one of the lovers of Ishtar, the fertility goddess. Wailing rites were associated with her rejection of him, or perhaps with Tammuz' role in the nature cycle.

AN ALTAR FROM MEGIDDO. *A horned Canaanite incense altar just over two and a half feet high was found at Megiddo. Such altars were used by the Judaeans and were symbols of apostasy to Ezekiel who predicted their destruction (Ezk. 6:4, 6) and to Jeremiah who said that there were as many incense altars in Jerusalem as there were streets (Jer. 11:13).*

had no strength and could not stand. It was clear that those presently exiled in Babylon had been given sanctuary from the final holocaust and that any hope for the future rested with them.

Read Ch. 12   Having been brought back to Babylon, the prophet dramatized the Exile to assure the skeptics that Jerusalem's end was at hand. The surviving remnant would testify to the evil that brought about the downfall and to the fact that Yahweh, rather than being defeated by another god, had, in his anger, willed the destruction of his own people.

Read Chs. 13–19   There were those who would not accept the harsh realities of Ezekiel's teaching and who refused to believe that Jerusalem would fall or that the Exile would be prolonged. Jeremiah had faced these same attitudes and had been compelled to write a letter to prepare the exiles for a long absence from Judah. So Ezekiel, in uttering oracles on the fall of Jerusalem, included a scornful denunciation of false prophets whose utterances were words of their own composing, expressions given in the futile hope that somehow Yahweh would bring them to fruition. The true prophet spoke Yahweh's words, and Yahweh's words were of doom.

So great was Jerusalem's evil that, on the basis of corporate personality, the combined weight of the righteousness of Noah, Daniel and Job, if they were present, could not save the people. Noah is, of course, the survivor of the flood; Daniel may be the hero of the Canaanite myths of Aqht or an unknown prototype of the hero of the biblical book of Daniel; and Job was a righteous sufferer whose story became the basis for the book of Job. This evaluation of Jerusalem's ills may have been added in the post-Exilic period.

The prophet reiterated Israel's history in Chapter 16, recalling Yahweh's protective care of the unwanted offspring of mixed parentage; the covenant bond described in marriage terms; and the harlotry of the nation by which Yahweh was betrayed. Judah's evil was greater than that of Sodom and Gomorrah. Punishment had to follow. Ezekiel did not rest his prophecy in a negative future. He peered beyond and saw forgiveness, restoration and the formulation of an everlasting covenant.

The eagle allegory in Chapter 17 may be an expansion of Ezekiel's rejection of Egypt as a protective haven for fleeing Judaeans. The exposition of the principle of individual responsibility in Chapter 18 may not be by Ezekiel.[19] The problem of theodicy, which assumed great importance in the Exilic period, is met by the argument that the wicked perish and the righteous survive; each man suffers for his own sins. If one who was righteous throughout his life should perish, perhaps it could be concluded that a sudden reversal of behavior patterns had condemned him. In the same manner, the sparing of an evil man could be explained by a last minute repentance. The idea of corporate personality is utterly rejected: suffering could not be explained by reference to another's sin; each man paid his own penalty.

In another recital of the nation's apostasy there is no idealization of the desert wanderings as in the writings of the eighth century prophets. Yahweh's ordinances were violated from the beginning. After each violation Yahweh hoped for repentance and change in the next stage of Israel's pilgrimage, and each time the hope proved vain. Once again, hope was projected into the future, when dispersed peoples would return, purged of their rebellious elements.

Read Chs. 20–24

Oracle after oracle hammered home the prediction of the fall of Jerusalem; the oracles on Yahweh's sword which did not distinguish between the righteous and the wicked, on Jerusalem's blood-guilt (21), on the burning away of the dross (22:17–22), on Samaria and Jerusalem, on the unfaithful wives of Yahweh (23), on the boiling pot (24:1–14), and finally on the death of Ezekiel's wife (24:15–24). The section closes with word of the fall of Jerusalem (24:25–27).

Read Chs. 25–32

Pronouncements against foreign nations follow. It is very difficult to determine which words actually belong to Ezekiel. Chapter 25 condemning Ammon, Edom and the Philistines is often labeled non-Ezekiel.[20] Just as Psalm 137 recalls the delight of the Edomites at Jerusalem's fall, so Ezekiel 25 recalls the glee of Judah's neighbors.[21] Oracles against Tyre and Sidon are suspect (26–28), but could be expansions of Ezekiel's sayings. Tyre yielded to Nebuchadrezzar about 572 after a thirteen-year siege. The obscure allusion to the king of Tyre in the garden of Eden reflects a tradition similar to that preserved in J.

19 May, *Interpreter's Bible*, VI, 49.
20 Cf. May, *op. cit.*, pp. 200 ff. for details.
21 See also Lam. 4:21.

Read Chs.
33–39

In the first of two anti-Egyptian oracles (29:1–16, 17–21) the image of Egypt as a great dragon recalls a mythological pattern, lost to us, in which Yahweh battled the dragon of the deep.[22] Egypt, Ezekiel believed, would be destroyed by Nebuchadrezzar (30:10 ff.). The section closes with a dirge on the descent of Egypt to the netherworld.

For Ezekiel the exile was an interim stage between the destruction of the old Israel and birth of the new. Chapter 33, a transition chapter, leads to oracles promising rebirth and restoration. In 33:1–9, which is linked to 3:16 ff., the prophet is depicted as a watchman, and 33:10–20, which is linked to Chapter 18, discusses individual responsibility. The announcement that Jerusalem had fallen (33:21 f.) was followed by a denunciation of rulers or shepherds of Jerusalem (34:1–10) whose mistreatment of the flock they were supposed to lead is contrasted with the role of Yahweh, the master shepherd or, perhaps, the "good" shepherd (34:11 ff.).

Oracles of judgment against foreign nations and promises for the future of Judah precede the vision of dry bones (37:1–14). The exiled people were the dry bones, without hope and convinced that they were dead now that the city of Jerusalem had been destroyed (37:11). But the Exile was not to be the end. By Yahweh's command, the miracle of renewal begins and bones are activated; new life is breathed into them and the vision of a new future in their own land is given. That future included the rebirth of the united kingdom of Israel and Judah under a Davidic monarch, a new sanctuary and an eternal covenant. The new ideal which plays so large a part in Ezekiel's subsequent oracles begins to take form. The temple and old city were gone. Ezekiel looked to the new city and the new temple. The Davidic line was still alive in the family of Jehoiachin, and in it Ezekiel saw the leadership of the future. The old covenant had been violated (perhaps terminated) and Ezekiel envisioned new relationships bound by a covenant that could never fail.

Oracles on Gog and Magog picture a climactic battle against Israel. The foe cannot be identified with certainty. Gog may refer to King Gyges of Lydia in Asia Minor who was known as Gugu from Akkadian records, to a Babylonian deity Gaga, to an Armenian people called Gaga, or to some mythological foe. Magog has been said to represent the Scythians. Meshach may refer to Mushku or classical Phrygia in Asia Minor. Tabal may be Tabal of Urartu in the Lake Van area. Gomer may be the Cimmerians.[23] All identifications are tentative. These enemies are symbols of people in power as the prophet writes. Their failure to overcome restored Israel will enable Yahweh to demonstrate his power and holiness. Whether this battle was meant to symbolize the close of a time of tribulation and the inauguration of a new era of peace and prosperity is not clear, but it does serve to provide the setting for the introduction of the vision of the new temple and the new Jerusalem.

[22] Cf. Isaiah 27:1; 51:9–10; Job 38:8–11.
[23] Cf. Saggs, *op. cit.*, pp. 116 f., 223.

Details of the temple appearing in Chapters 40 to 42 do not parallel in every detail the description of Solomon's temple in II Kings 6 f. The temple stood at the center of the new theocratic state. Ministrants were to be Levitical priests of Zadokite lineage. Now Yahweh's glory (*kabod*) returned (43:1–5), symbolizing the restoration of covenant relationships. The picture is idyllic, and paradisiac aspects are emphasized by references to sacred trees and waters reminiscent of the J story of Eden. Springing from beneath the temple was a river with purifying waters so potent that the saline Great (Dead) Sea could be made to sustain marine life and give nourishment to trees whose fruits would never fail and whose leaves would heal (47:1–12). The book closes with the division of land among the tribes and the announcement of a new name for Jerusalem: "Yahweh-shammah," meaning "Yahweh is there."

Read Chs. 40–48

CENTRAL THEMES

1. Perhaps the stress on the importance of the cult reflects Ezekiel's priestly background. The harshest condemnations are directed against apostasy and acts which profaned the temple. In the idealized future state, a purified people observe the rules for holiness, and sacrifices are made in the correct manner. Ritual and moral laws are viewed as divine gifts enabling man to know how to live (20:11 ff.), and the uniqueness of Yahweh's people is to be expressed through the cult and the law.

2. As one commissioned to preach judgment of the past and present, Ezekiel saw himself as a watchman responsible for the safety of the exiles. By keeping before the people the basis for punishment and by exposing the spirit of lawlessness that had characterized their relationships to Yahweh from the bondage in Egypt to the Exile in Babylon, the prophet hoped to warn them away from any continuation of this attitude. Like II Isaiah Ezekiel found his listeners unwilling to take his teachings seriously.

3. A definite change in emphasis can be discerned in Ezekiel's teachings. Up until the fall of Jerusalem in 586, his message was of doom. After the destruction of the temple and the city, he stressed the holy community, the ideal nation and the glorious future that was part of Yahweh's plan. It was in the future state that the election formula would find complete fulfillment: "You shall be my people, I will be your God" (cf. 11:20; 14:11; 36:28; 37:23, 27).

4. The Exile was an interim stage, between the termination of old relationships and the beginning of new associations. In one sense the new age would be a restoration of the old, with a new Exodus and a new everlasting covenant, with the kingdom restored under the Davidic kingship.

5. The use of the concept of the divine *kabod*, which is, in essence, identical to Yahweh,[24] enabled the prophet to depict the deity without

[24] Cf. Jacob, *Theology of the Old Testament*, p. 81.

employing gross anthropomorphisms and, simultaneously, to move away from the idea that Yahweh's name (*shem*) rather than the real presence was in the temple.[25]

6. The concept of individual responsibility, if it is really Ezekiel's, is not new for it is implicit in J, in Abraham's query when the destruction of Sodom and Gomorrah was under discussion: "Will you really destroy the righteous with the wicked?" (Gen. 18:23), and in David's confession of responsibility for evil (II Sam. 24:17). It is also stated as a law in Deut. 24:16. Pragmatically, it was obviously untenable, for there were those who had escaped death despite the fact that they were more evil than some who had died. These were spared, it was argued, as examples of the wickedness of the Jerusalemites (12:16), to demonstrate the justice of the complete destruction of the city (14:21–23).

On the other hand, the concept has another significance. It marks the cancellation of old debts. What happened to those who escaped did not depend upon what their ancestors had done, but upon what each individual did. The nation with its corporate identity had perished, the individual Jew remained. Participation in the new tomorrow rested upon individual response to Yahweh's promises.

7. Restoration would come, not because the people deserved it, but because Yahweh's reputation had been besmirched (36:22). The restoration of the people, the punishment of mocking neighbors and the crushing of the great powers would demonstrate that Yahweh had not been defeated, but had acted deliberately against his people. Restoration of Israel vindicated Yahweh.

LAMENTATIONS

The effect on Jewish morale of the downfall of the capital city and the destruction of the temple which had symbolized Yahweh's enduring patience and love for nearly 400 years must have been devastating. Only a small collection of five poems, written over a considerable period of time, provides any insight into the shock, horror and grief of the people.

Ancient tradition assigns the authorship of Lamentations to Jeremiah. A prefatory comment in the LXX says the poems are by Jeremiah, possibly on the basis of II Chron. 35:25,[26] but modern scholars reject this hypothesis for several reasons. There is no indication in the Hebrew version that Jeremiah was the author, and ideas presented within the poems contradict Jeremiah's teachings. For example, it is highly unlikely that Jeremiah, out of his personal experiences of Yahweh, would state that prophets did not receive visions (Lam. 2:9); nor would the prophet accept the argument that the sins of the past were responsible for the destruction (Lam. 5:7), for he consistently preached that the apostasy of the day would engender divine wrath. The plaintive reminiscence of the hope for deliverance

---

25 Cf. Vriezen, *An Outline of Old Testament Theology*, p. 247.

26 The third century preface reads: "And it came to pass, after Israel was taken captive and Jerusalem made desolate that Jeremiah sat weeping and lamented with this lamentation, saying. . . ."

by Egypt (Lam. 4:17) contradicts Jeremiah's dismissal of the possibility of aid from the south. The authors or author remain unknown.

Four poems (chs. 1–4) employ an artificial alphabetical acrostic structure in which a sequence of the twenty-two letters of the Hebrew alphabet is followed in the opening word of each stanza.[27] The fifth imitates the structure using twenty-two lines without the alphabetical scheme. The first three chapters, with minor exceptions, employ three lines to each stanza;[28] the fourth poem has two lines and the fifth has one per stanza.[29] Despite formal structuring, the poems convey genuine pathos and deep emotional stress. It has been suggested that the alphabetic form was designed for mnemonic reasons, or perhaps, to indicate that the author's feelings and suffering ran the emotional gamut from *aleph* to *tau,* or in present-day speech, "from A to Z." Attempts have been made to discover some chronological sequence for the poems on the basis of content. Chapters 2 and 4, often attributed to a single writer, are sometimes considered to be earliest because they appear to be very close to the actual time of the fall of Jerusalem. Some scholars date Chapter 1 to the post-Exilic period when the temple was rebuilt;[30] others label it the earliest of the poems.[31] A more likely suggestion is that all of the poems reflect the Exilic period and, despite their independence and individuality, may reflect the work of one author (or perhaps two) writing over a considerable period of time.[32]

The opening word of the collection, "how" (Heb. *'ekah*), gives the Hebrew title to the book[33] and introduces the dirge form of the poem.[34] The desolate city is portrayed as a widow, not dead but alone, forsaken, weeping in the night when none can see. The contrast between the glories of the past introduced in the first verse and the present state portrayed in subsequent verses conveys to the reader the desolation of the city. There is a forthright recognition that Jerusalem's sin caused the downfall, and the imagery of the adulterous woman (1:8–9) is reminiscent of Hosea.

Read Ch. 1

The dirge terminates in Verse 11, and an individual lament, written in the first person singular, portrays the city speaking and explaining the tragedy that occurred. Verse 17 returns to the third person singular form and describes Yahweh as the commander of Jerusalem's enemies. The closing verses, a confession of guilt written in the first person singular, portray the unfaithful wife in the days of distress calling for help to her lovers (other gods?) to no avail. The poem closes with an

[27] Poems (chapters) 2, 3, 4 make slight variations, placing the seventeenth letter (*pe*) before the sixteenth letter (*'ayin*).

[28] 1:7 and 2:19 have four lines each.

[29] The poetic structure is clearly depicted in the translation by N. K. Gottwald in *Studies in the Book of Lamentations,* Studies in Biblical Theology, 14 (London: S.C.M. Press, 1954), pp. 7–18; or the translation of T. J. Meek in *The Complete Bible, An American Translation* (Chicago: University of Chicago Press, 1939).

[30] R. H. Pfeiffer, *Introduction to the Old Testament,* p. 723.

[31] Weiser, *op. cit.,* p. 306, citing Rudolph.

[32] N. K. Gottwald, "Lamentations," *The Interpreter's Dictionary of the Bible.*

[33] The title "Lamentations" is from the Vulgate translation of the LXX "Threni."

[34] Cf. the dirges in II Sam. 1:19; Jer. 9:16 ff., noting the use of the word "how."

expression of grief and anguish. Because there is a suggestion in the poem that Jerusalem was not completely destroyed, it is possible that these verses were written after 597 but before the collapse of the nation in 586.

Read Ch. 2 The first ten verses of Chapter 2 describe Yahweh as the enemy, bending his divine bow against his own people, pouring out anger without restraint, scorning the sacred temple and altar and satisfied only when the city lay in ruins. For the stunned, shocked elders and maidens sitting in silence in sackcloth and dust, the event is simply incomprehensible. The people are dazed, bewildered and numbed by the horror of the event.

In his own words, as a witness, the writer takes up the description (vss. 11–22). Children die of starvation in their mothers' arms. Cannibalism is practiced. The dead lie in the streets. Nothing remains but a broken people in a ruined city through whose smouldering ruins rings the mocking laughter and remarks of enemies and tormentors. Yahweh fulfilled his threats of punishment (2:17) despite the false omens of hope given by some prophets. But the real cry of anguish to Yahweh is in the partially expressed question "Oh Yahweh, how could you act without pity or mercy?"—a cry of theodicy stemming from the writer's emotional response to the death of loved ones (2:22) and the terrible results of the siege.

Read Ch. 3 The first thirty-nine verses of the third poem are in the form of an individual lament in which the nation is the speaker,[35] personified as a man who has experienced Yahweh's anger. Some of the imagery suggests that the poet had Jeremiah in mind as he described the city's misadventures. The city experienced divine wrath, was stoned and broken, encircled without hope of escape, torn to pieces, pierced by arrows and ultimately become the laughingstock of enemies. In Verse 21 the mood of the poem changes and the writer affirms the constant loyalty of Yahweh.

Verses 40–47 are part of a national lament written in the first person plural and they call for a return to Yahweh even as they confess that sins had not yet been forgiven (vs. 42). The closing verses (48–66) return to the first person singular and express the sufferer's complaints, words of assurance (55 ff.) and a prayer against enemies (61 ff.).

Read Ch. 4 The fourth poem, which has affinities with the second, begins as a lament in the third person singular, shifts in verses 17 to 20 to the first person plural and ends with a statement of hope for the exiles and a promise of punishment for Edom. The immediacy of the horrors described suggest that the poem was written shortly after the siege, but there is a reflective note that implies that the event is past and the poet is thinking back on what took place. The writer recalls the scattered stones of the temple, the leading citizens transformed into living scarecrows, children crying for food and, once again, cannibalism. The people looked in vain for help from Egypt (4:17) and, when the city fell, there were none who escaped (4:19). The closing

---

[35] Cf. Gottwald, *Studies in the Book of Lamentations*, pp. 37–41. For an opposing point of view, cf. T. J. Meek, "Lamentations," *The Interpreter's Bible*, VI, 23.

words express the belief that the time of punishment is over and the Exile ended (4:22).

The last poem is a national lament setting the predicament of the **Read Ch. 5** people before Yahweh, calling the deity to witness what the nation had become. There is no admission of guilt, only the argument that the fathers (perhaps the leaders) had sinned and the punishment fell upon those who suffered the onslaughts of the Babylonians. Even the cry "we have sinned" (5:16) may reflect the totality of the group through time, and point back to the nation through history rather than signify a recognition of responsibility by the present sufferers. The social evils of war are depicted throughout the poem, and the miserable plight of the exiles is revealed. The poem closes with a statement of praise of Yahweh and a questioning cry reminding Yahweh of the people's need and seeking restoration of relationships.

THEODICY

In depicting the horrors of the fall of Jerusalem, the poems raise the problem of theodicy. There is an acknowledgment of sin, but there is also the recurring note of incredulity that Yahweh could have brought such horrendous punishment upon his own people. There is the recognition that an angry Yahweh was himself the enemy and that both good and evil come from Yahweh (3:38), but there is also a note of impatience arising out of the conviction that the punishment had taken place, Yahweh had demonstrated his just anger, so how long must punishment continue? The final request asks that Yahweh assert himself on behalf of his people.

CULTIC USE

After the temple was destroyed again in A.D. 70 by the forces of the Roman general, Titus, the book of Lamentations was liturgically used on the ninth day of the Jewish month Ab (July–August) to commemorate both the Roman and Babylonian destructions. How far back the liturgical use of Lamentations can be traced is debatable, but Zechariah 8:18–19 suggests fasts associated with the siege and destruction of Jerusalem (cf. II Kings 25:1–4; Jer. 39:2) and Zechariah 7:3 ff. implies a long practice of the custom, dating back to the Exile. A Sumerian poem of similar nature, bewailing the fate of the city of Ur,[36] written during the early part of the second millennium bears striking affinities to the Hebrew poem.[37] It is possible that the Sumerian poem was used in a commemorative ritual, so that the Jewish poet may have composed his laments according to a custom

[36] Cf. *ANET*, pp. 455–463 for the translation by S. N. Kramer.

[37] For similarities and differences and an excellent discussion of the significance of this kind of writing, see T. H. Gaster, *Festivals of the Jewish Year* (N.Y.: William Sloane Associates, 1953), pp. 200 ff.

well established and well known in the Near East. It is reasonable to suggest that the poems of Lamentations were employed in a commemorative liturgy during the Exile, with the first person singular portions recited by a leader representing the corporate group or the city and other portions spoken by the congregation.

22

Literature of the Middle Period

ABOUT thirty years are embraced in the period which we are labeling for convenience "The Middle Period" of the Exile and which extends roughly from about 585 to 555. During these years a considerable body of literature was produced by the exiles: new additions were made to the prophetic oracles, the Deuteronomic history was brought to a close, the initial stages of the editing of the P source were undertaken and, if our dating is correct, the magnificent Wisdom writing which wrestles with the problem of theodicy, the book of Job, was composed.

JOB

In its present form, the book of Job records the sad adventures of a good and righteous man, stricken by God, and comforted by friends whose comments set forth the attitudes toward sin, suffering, righteousness and divine justice which were current in the writer's day. The prose prologue introduces the reader to Job, presenting him as one whose every act was kind, good and just, as a man of faith whose blamelessness and righteousness were affirmed by God. Indeed, it was God's boast of Job's upright behavior that prompted "the Satan,"[1] a member of the court of heaven,[2] to raise the question of the reason for Job's piety. Was it not because Job was blessed with every good thing that he was righteous? Would not Job, once robbed of possessions and later of health, reveal his true nature and curse God? The stage is set. Job has lost sons, daughters and possessions and is suffering personal bodily affliction. The reader is invited to discover the answer to the

---

[1] The title "Satan" is derived from a root meaning "to obstruct" or "to oppose" and has the sense of "one who plays the adversary" (cf. Num. 22:22; I Sam. 29:4; Ps. 109:6). The Satan or "the adversary" in the book of Job is not to be thought of as an anti-God demonic figure or even as an evil being, but as a member of the court of heaven who was given permission by God to test Job's righteousness or to play the adversary. He is subordinate to God and acts only in accord with the orders of God. For a discussion of Satan, cf. E. Jacobs, *Theology of the Old Testament*, pp. 70 ff., and the article "Satan" in *The Interpreter's Dictionary of the Bible*.

[2] For a discussion of the "court of heaven," cf. James F. Ross, "The Prophet as Yahweh's Messenger," *Israel's Prophetic Heritage*, ed. B. W. Anderson and W. Harrelson (New York: Harper and Brothers, 1962), pp. 102 ff.

question: will Job curse God? But the author is really dealing with more significant questions concerned with theodicy and how a righteous man can live in the face of adversity (cf. Habakkuk). In the poetic section following the prologue, each of Job's friends presents a position to which Job responds, and out of these statements the writer of Job skillfully develops his theme. As we shall see presently, this mode of presenting the problem of theodicy and struggling with the meaning of existence was popular among wisdom writers of Egypt and Mesopotamia prior to the development of the Hebrew nation.

Earlier it was suggested that Wisdom Schools may have been introduced into Hebrew society during Solomon's age,[3] perhaps in imitation of court patterns of surrounding nations. Wisdom writings are characterized by an appeal to human experience and common sense, tending to rest the reasonableness of an argument upon the logic of that which may generally be observed to occur in life and avoiding appeals to theological or nationalistic beliefs.[4] Such writings tend to be universal in appeal, for they touch upon problems of human experience that transcend political or theological boundaries, expressing provenance only by references to local deities or settings. The problem of the suffering of the innocent or righteous has preoccupied thinkers in every culture postulating righteous or moral gods in control of human destiny and where the assumption is made that there is some sort of relationship between sin and suffering and between righteousness and blessing. Many writings on this theme, some much older than Job and some bearing striking affinities to Job, have been found among Egyptian and Mesopotamian documents.

The Egyptian essay recording a "Dispute over Suicide" between a man and his soul was noted earlier in the discussion of the First Intermediary Period (2200–1900 B.C.).[5] Shortly afterward, during the early second millennium, "The Protests of the Eloquent Peasant" was composed, employing a prose prologue and epilogue to frame nine "semipoetic" discourses through which a peasant, deprived of his rights, successfully argues his case before the chief steward.[6] If the author of Job was acquainted with these or similar stories from Egypt, and it is quite possible that he was, there is no evidence of literary borrowing.

From Mesopotamia has come a poem dedicated to "the lord of wisdom" which treats of a righteous sufferer often called "the Babylonian Job."[7] Forsaken by the whole pantheon of gods, unable to secure an omen, considered a social outcast by friends and family, deprived of property, responsibility and respect, unable to bring about change by exorcism and magic, and accepting the theological dictum that human fortunes are determined by the gods, the unfortunate

[3] Cf. *supra*, "The Solomonic Kingship."

[4] For further discussion see the section on "Wisdom Writings," chap. 28.

[5] Cf. supra "Before There Was an Israel." For the text, see *ANET*, pp. 405 f., *DOTT*, pp. 162 ff.

[6] Cf. *ANET*, pp. 407–410.

[7] Cf. *ANET*, pp. 434–438, W. G. Lambert, *Babylonian Wisdom Literature* (Oxford: The Clarendon Press, 1960), pp. 21–62.

individual pours out his sad tale. In this lament the sufferer refused to equate sin with suffering, and, as he rehearsed his past good deeds, reflected that man cannot really know the will of the gods, and he goes so far as to suggest that what seems pleasing to man might be judged an offense by the gods. The stubborn faith that the gods would prove themselves merciful which seems to sustain the sufferer appears only once. Ultimately, deliverance came through Marduk, the lord of wisdom, to whom the poem is dedicated. In another Babylonian poem, a satirical dialogue between master and servant, a somewhat pessimistic mood of religious skepticism prevails as the master seeks to discover some action that might have a beneficial end, only to learn from the servant that death alone is the answer.[8] Still another poem, in acrostic form, deals with human misery in a polite dialogue between a sufferer and a friend.[9] The advice of the friend, often poorly preserved in the existing texts, is not out of harmony with what Job's friends recommend, and the sufferer's retorts touch on issues and reveal attitudes not unlike those of Job. It is obvious that the presentation of the problem of theodicy in conversational form and the portrayal of attitudes and ideas similar to those in Job were popular in Mesopotamia, but at no point is it possible to demonstrate direct borrowing by the author of Job.[10]

While it cannot be proven conclusively, it is usually argued on the basis of the setting, that the story of Job is Edomitic in origin. The opening verse locates Job in Uz, which may have been anywhere between Damascus and Edom in the desert area east of Palestine.[11] Job's friends may have come from southeastern Palestine.[12] Attempts to date the book precisely by clues found within have not been successful and suggestions have ranged from the patriarchal to post-Exilic periods.[13] It now appears that to a pre-Exilic prose story poetic dialogues were added so skillfully that the relationship between the two parts is much closer than appears on the surface.[14] It is generally held that the prose prologue and epilogue, reflecting folktale style and the smoothness of a tale often repeated, circulated independently. Here the deity is known by the familiar titles Elohim and Yahweh. The dialogue portions are quite distinctive in style and content and use the terms El, Eloah, Elohim and Shaddai in reference to the deity. Some portions of the dialogue appear to be intrusive. A new figure, Elihu, is introduced without warning, accompanied by a literary style change (chs. 32–37). A hymn on wisdom interrupts a Joban soliloquy and presents ideas not in harmony with those of Job and his friends

---

[8] Cf. *ANET*, pp. 347 ff., Lambert, *op. cit.*, pp. 139–149.

[9] Cf. *ANET*, pp. 438 ff., Lambert, *op. cit.*, pp. 63–91.

[10] For a more extensive analysis of Egyptian and Babylonian poems in terms of their relationship to Job, see the introduction to the study of Job by S. Terrien in the *Interpreter's Bible*, III, 878–884; or M. H. Pope, *Job*, The Anchor Bible (Garden City, N.Y.: Doubleday and Co., Inc., 1965), pp. l–lxvi.

[11] Cf. Pope, *op. cit.*, pp. 3–5.

[12] *Ibid.*, p. 24.

[13] For a discussion of dates, cf. *ibid.*, pp. xxx–xxxvii, Terrien, *op. cit.*, pp. 888–890.

[14] For a detailed analysis, cf. Terrien, *op. cit.*, pp. 884–888.

(ch. 28). It would appear that the book of Job, like so many other biblical writings, was subjected to continuing or progressive interpretation after the original writer had completed his work. Careful analysis of the text suggests that Job was probably composed during the sixth century[15] by a writer who utilized a well-known prose folktale, possibly of Edomitic origin, and added poetic dialogue, perhaps of his own composition.[16]

The following literary analysis readjusts the third cycle of speeches (chs. 22–26) in accordance with the convincing suggestion of S. Terrien.[17]

I. The Prologue   Chs. 1:1–2:13.
    a. Scene 1, on earth: 1:1–5.
    b. Scene 2, in heaven: 1:6–12.
    c. Scene 3, on earth: 1:13–22.
    d. Scene 4, in heaven: 2:1–6.
    e. Scene 5, on earth: 2:7–13.
II. Dialogue   Chs. 3–42.

a. *First Cycle,* chs. 3–14.	b. *Second Cycle,* chs. 15–21.
Job speaks: 3.	————
Eliphaz speaks: 4–5.	Eliphaz speaks: 15.
Job responds: 6–7.	Job responds: 16–17.
Bildad speaks: 8.	Bildad speaks: 18.
Job responds: 9–10.	Job responds: 19.
Zophar speaks: 11.	Zophar speaks: 20.
Job responds: 12–14.	Job responds: 21.
c. *Third Cycle,* chs. 22–31.	*Terrien's Reconstruction.*
Eliphaz speaks: 22.	Eliphaz speaks: 22.
Job responds: 23–24.	Job responds: 23–24:17, 25.
Bildad speaks: 25.	Bildad speaks: 25:1–6; 26:5–14.
Job responds: 26.	Job responds: 26:1–4; 27:1–12.
Job continues: 27.	Zophar speaks: 24:18–24; 27:13–25.
Wisdom poem: 28.	Job . . .?
Job speaks: 29–31.	

    d. *The Elihu Interruption:* chs. 32–37.
    Prologue: 32:1–5.
    Elihu's First Speech: 32:6–33:33.
    Elihu's Second Speech: 34.
    Elihu's Third Speech: 35.
    Elihu's Fourth Speech: 36–37.
    e. *The Divine Encounter:* chs. 38–42.
    The Divine Summons: 38:1–3.
    God speaks: 38:4–40:2.
    Job responds. 40:3–5.
    God speaks: 40:6–41:34.
    Job responds: 42:1–6.
III. Epilogue: Ch. 42:7–17.

[15] The large number of Aramaisms suggest a late date and may reflect the influence of the Babylonian environment. There are stylistic relationships to Deutero-Isaiah.

[16] Terrien, *op. cit.,* pp. 884–888.

[17] *Ibid.,* p. 888.

The prologue poses the question of whether or not Job's piety and faithfulness to God depend upon the benefits he enjoys. The only way for the heavenly court to ascertain the answer to this query is to test Job. It should be noted that there is no question of Job's righteousness and goodness, for the author makes this a precondition for the story (1:1), a fact acknowledged by God (1:8; 2:3) and not questioned by the Satan. Even after being afflicted, Job remained righteous (1:22; 2:10). It is clear that the writer is informing his readers that no correlation is to be made between Job's suffering and sin, and the reader knows what Job, his wife and his three comforters cannot possibly know: the real reason for Job's misfortunes.

Read the Prologue

The prologue may have been drawn from an ancient story of a righteous sufferer (cf. Ezek. 14:14). Whether or not the author identified himself with Job and portrayed his own unfortunate situation or whether he had in mind someone like Jeremiah through whom he proposed to deal with the universal problem of the suffering of the righteous cannot be determined for sure. What is more likely is that Job was meant to be a symbol of the nation Israel and that the shattering of Job's health and holdings represented the eclipse of Judah. That Judah was not without sin could not be denied, but there had been a Deuteronomic reform, and a genuine effort had been made to fulfill the divine will. The parallel would be clear to the people of the Exile.

Job's opening remarks present his problem: the meaninglessness of his present state and the belief that in his case death was preferable to suffering. The first response by Eliphaz is a gentle argument, urging patience and trust in God and introducing the conviction that sin and suffering are related. Eliphaz' words rest, in part, upon an eerie nocturnal vision by which it was revealed to him that no man could be righteous before God, and on the basis of this he reminded Job that even the most pure fall short of divine perfection, so vast is the gulf between the sacred and the profane. He urged Job to turn to God in faith and submission. Job's response, calling attention to his impossible situation and raising the question as to why God should be so concerned with human affairs and with Job in particular, provoked Bildad, the second friend, to a much more forceful argument. Shocked into anger by Job's words, Bildad implied that Job's children must have sinned and stated that, if Job were really righteous, God would deliver him. Bildad's position was grounded in tradition.

Read the First Cycle

Job's answer gets to the heart of the problem (9:15–24). He is not guilty, there is no reasonable answer, tradition notwithstanding, for his suffering; his punishment is without cause. It should be remembered that, according to the prologue, Job is right! God, he argues, makes no distinction between right and wrong and both the innocent and the guilty are destroyed. Here and elsewhere Job's presentation reflects the Exilic situation. When the destruction came, righteous and wicked suffered alike. Jeremiah's advice to make the best of the Exilic situation gives no answer to the problem of why God brought this suffering (cf. Jer. 29:4–9 and Job 9:27 ff.). A man accused cannot possibly justify himself to his accuser and Job called on God to meet in frank and fair discussion, preferably before an impartial umpire to explain why Job, the innocent one, suffered (10:1 ff.).

Zophar, the last speaker, responded with vehemence and blindly accused Job of evils deserving even greater punishment. He called for penitence. Once again echoes of the Exilic situation appear in Job's response (12:17–21), but these are so broadly stated that it is possible to interpret the words as a general rather than particularistic statement. Job continued to call for a confrontation with God.

Read the Second Cycle

Eliphaz, having abandoned the role of the understanding counselor, attacked *ad hominem,* implying irreverence (15:11–13). Job rejected the comfort of patent answers and, in words that portray national affliction (16:11–17), argued that he had a witness in heaven to speak in his behalf (16:19). What is meant by this claim is not clear.[18] Bildad's words contribute nothing particularly new to the discussion, but Job's response again contains references that justify the interpretation of Job as representing the nation (19:10–12). Job expressed belief in a *go'el,* a redeemer or vindicator (19:25), whose identity is not given and who has been the subject of much scholarly speculation. Unfortunately, the text in this section is hopelessly corrupt and how Job may have expanded this concept in the succeeding verses cannot be known.[19] Zophar's indignant speech reiterates theological clichés about the temporality of the joys of the wicked and the terrors that are sure to follow. Job's appeal to evidence is in the tradition of the wisdom school. He finds the wicked to be happy and content, and even as they deny God they enjoy prosperity.

Read the Third Cycle

Eliphaz' accusations are, in the light of the prologue, absurd, and his advice has become repetitious (ch. 22). Job continues to seek a confrontation with God and to maintain innocence (23:5 ff.). According to Terrien's analysis, Bildad's statement is contained in 25:1–6 and 26:5–14 and Job's response is in 26:1–4 and 27:1–12. Zophar's final speech (24:18–24; 27:13–25) repeats previous points. In a magnificent final presentation, Job summed up his position, maintaining the injustice of his suffering and expressing his confidence in the justice of God.

Read Ch. 28

The wisdom poem stands apart from the theme of the book and is perhaps an ancient hymn to wisdom which some later editor inserted. The poem contends that man is unable to find wisdom in experience or tradition and that the only way to wisdom is through God.

Read Chs. 29–31

Job's words in these chapters form a soliloquy which ignores the earlier dialogue and even the presence of the three friends. The nostalgic reminiscences of better days, the inner search for any possible misdemeanor that may have offended the deity and the insistence upon his innocence summarize Job's position in both the prologue and the dialogues.

Read Chs. 32–37

The Elihu speeches, abruptly introduced with a brief prose statement (32:1–5), are supposed to represent the words of a younger man. Elihu is indignant at the failure of the older men to beat back Job's

18 Cf. Terrien, *op. cit.,* pp. 1025 ff. for a detailed discussion.
19 Cf. *Ibid.,* pp. 1051–1056 for discussion.

arguments, but Elihu is not much more effective. In part his speeches repeat earlier arguments, but he does go beyond the earlier speakers in extolling the divine majestic power and glory of a God so exalted that he is beyond human comprehension and so transcendent that men like Job who are "wise in their own conceit" are ignored (37:24).

The theophany comes in a whirlwind so that no form of God can be discerned, and the divine response consists of a flow of demanding questions impossible for Job to answer, so that the gap between divine and human understanding is emphasized. Job, awed by the manifestation and overwhelmed by the barrage of questions, appears to be ready to drop the whole issue (40:3–5), but God refuses to let the matter rest and again challenges Job with questions beyond Job's comprehension. Job's response is one of submission in which he expresses willingness to accept that which he cannot understand, recognizing his human role as something small, insignificant and perhaps unworthy before God. He has no further questions for the problems are too large for him. He has one comfort, the God whom he knew only through tradition, he now knows through personal experience.

Read Chs. 38–42:6

The blunt prose of the epilogue comes as a shock after the lofty theological discussion of the poetic section. The author picks up the theme of the prologue: Job has been tested and has proven that God's estimate of him was correct, for he had not cursed God. Without further ado his health and fortune are restored, and it is made clear that the counselors did not know what they were talking about.

Read the Epilogue

THE PURPOSE OF JOB

The obvious question raised in the prologue was "Will the righteous Job, once deprived of the good things of life, abandon and curse his God?" The equally obvious answer of the book is "He did not." Job's only outcry was for justice, for if rewards in this life rest on righteousness, then something was wrong in Job's case. His outcry raised a second question, "Why, if God is just and in control of life, and why, if righteousness is rewarded and wrongdoing punished, does the righteous Job suffer horrendous misfortunes?" It is clear that traditional answers were inadequate. The responses of Job's friends failed to answer the questions and ultimately God declared they were inaccurate (42:7–8). Thus neither Eliphaz' arguments that no man could achieve perfection and that the punishment was a chastening for Job's own good, nor Bildad's appeal to the tradition that suffering is rooted in human fallibility, nor Zophar's horrified response that Job's challenging the justice of his suffering was akin to blasphemy, nor Elihu's thesis that God leads man to the brink of death only to rescue him so that man might in grateful humility relate his experiences to others (33:19–33) have any foundation other than in human speculation. It seems probable, therefore, that, in addition to reflecting on the general theme of theodicy so common among ancient wisdom writers, this author was expressing his belief that theological arguments about the relationship between sin and suffering were of no avail, for it is impossible for those on earth to know (as only the reader of the prologue could know) what went on in heaven.[20] Thus the book had a satirical thrust, akin to that of the Babylonian dialogue between master and servant. If the setting is the Exile, and if Job is not simply an individual but symbolizes the nation, then the writer has moved away from the explanations of suffering and the Exile of the book of Ezekiel to recommend an acceptance of that which even the inquiring Job with his quest for solutions was unable to understand.

The third question implied in the book is "What does the righteous one do in such a situation?" Obviously, it is useless to rail and demand answers. One can only submit and continue to trust, holding firm to the belief that justice will be done. At this point something of Ezekiel's dreams for the future enter, for the author implies that the suffering will end and Job (the nation?) will be restored. The presumptuousness of a demand for answers is clearly shown in Job's response to God's questions—submission and trust—and it is this attitude that the writer commends to both the individual sufferer and to the nation in exile. The predicament of the exiled people cries out for answer; Job advises trust, patience, submission and unrelenting faith that God would ultimately set matters right.

Finally, the poet has depicted Job as one whose righteousness did not rest upon material rewards, but in faith and love of God.[21] Job knows, with the unshakable conviction of one who has been faithful regardless of what his friends said, that he is righteous. In this conviction he did not hesitate to challenge prevalent beliefs. His challenge is not to God but to popular theology. His faith rests upon the firm belief that somewhere there is an answer that has evaded man and can only come from God. The answer is not given but, in a sense, Job's faith is vindicated. The reasons for his condition lie beyond human comprehension so that the righteous man and the righteous nation must in moments of dark despair live in trust, or, in Habakkuk's words, "live by his faithfulness."

CONTINUING INTERPRETATION IN THE PROPHETS

Read the additions under discussion

Even as Ezekiel and Job wrestled with the problems of suffering and restoration, other Jews searched for words of hope and guidance in the oracles of the prophets who had predicted the downfall of Israel and Judah. Predictions of doom had been fulfilled; were there other clues that might reveal what Yahweh had in store for his people? It is possible that Hosea's teachings about Yahweh's grace and mercy stimulated hope, and there were those who in the renewed study of Hosea's words added new insights and new promises. Commentaries on the

---

[20] Cf. Gerald A. Larue, "The Book of Job on the Futility of Theological Discussion," *The Personalist* (Los Angeles: The University of Southern California, 1964) XLV, 72–79.

[21] Cf. Yehezkel Kaufmann, *The Religion of Israel*, p. 335.

names of Hosea's children, those symbols of Yahweh's rejection of his people (Hos. 1:4–9), were composed. One was affixed to the verses introducing the children (Hos. 1:10–2:1), softening their harshness by the prediction of the restoration of the united kingdom, and the promise that the people would be recognized as "sons of the living God." Another (2:21–23) looked to the days when Yahweh would pity "Not-pitied," accept "Not-my-people" as his own, would bring blessing out of Jezreel and restore the covenant relationships.

Prophecies of hope and restoration were appended to the works of other eighth century writers. The last five verses of Amos (9:11–15) envision the restoration of the Davidic kingship (represented in Jehoiachin in exile), the rebuilding of ruined cities and a bounteous future marked by peace and security. To Isaiah's doom oracles were added restoration oracles. Some additions reveal deep and intimate appreciation of Isaiah's style and may represent contributions by the prophet's disciples or school, if such a group can be postulated for the Exilic period.[22] Some of Isaiah's harsh predictions are reversed as in the oracles of restoration of 4:2–6 (4:2 cf. 2:13; 4:3 cf. 2:6–8; 4:4 cf. 3:16, 17, 24; 4:6 cf. 2:12 ff.).

If, as some scholars believe, Isaiah 9:2–7 and 11:1–9 are not by Isaiah of Jerusalem, they may be from the Exilic period. The author of the first poem proclaimed that light was breaking into the darkness of the Exile. He rejoiced in the birth of a child in the royal family, perhaps the prince Zerubbabel who was to play an important role in the post-Exilic period. The exalted names given to the child express the exalted hopes of the writer. Chapter 11:1–9 portrays the ideal king who, like David, would establish the united kingdom of Israel and Judah. He envisions a time of perfect peace under a charismatic ruler of the Davidic line. These poems fit well into the Exilic period when dreams were dreamed of an ideal future, an ideal Davidic kingship and future glory for the Jews.

Some additions to Isaiah recognized the threatening power of the Median empire on Babylon's eastern flank and anticipated the fall of the Babylonian kingdom (Isaiah 13–14; 21). Other oracles commented on the fall of Moab (15–16), overcome by some unnamed disaster which could have been anything from attacks by desert tribes[23] to an invasion by Babylonians.[24] Some passages employ vivid imagery in visualizing punishment for the enemy and rise to sublime heights in idealizing the future (chs. 34–35). Additions to Isaiah were not all made at one time. Chapters 34 and 35 are so close in parts to Deutero-Isaiah, in both style and content, that some scholars have proposed that they should be included in that work.

At least one Exilic poem exalting the restored Zion was added to two prophetic collections and appears in Isaiah 2:2–4 and Micah

[22] For the literary structure of these oracles, cf. R. B. Y. Scott, "The Literary Structure of Isaiah's Oracles," in *Studies in Old Testament Prophecy*, ed. H. H. Rowley (Edinburgh: T. & T. Clark, 1957), pp. 175 ff.

[23] Wm. F. Albright, "The Biblical Period," in *The Jews, Their History, Culture and Religion*, ed. L. Finkelstein (New York: Harper and Brothers, 1949), p. 44.

[24] Josephus, *Antiquity of the Jews:* 10:9:7.

4:1–3. Other additions to Micah prophesy the regrouping of the scattered people (2:12–13), the coming of a messianic leader like David (5:2–4, 7) and Yahweh's forgiveness of his people (7:8–20). More recent prophetic pronouncements were also studied. An addition predicting restoration was added to Jeremiah's oracles (Jer. 3:15–18) in which the fact that the ark of the covenant was forever lost is apparent. One composite appendage (Jer. 10:1–16), parts of which are similar in style and content to Deutero-Isaiah, warns against forsaking Yahweh for idols made by artisans. The myth of the return of David which later becomes a basis for messianism is found in an eschatological oracle (30:8–9). Other restoration sayings appear in 31:7–14. An oracle on the fall of Moab, not unlike that found in the additions to Isaiah, may be from the Exile (ch. 48), and other pronouncements of punishment on foreign nations appear to be from the same period (49–51:58).

THE DEUTERONOMISTS

The Deuteronomic history concludes with the release of Jehoiachin and his family from prison by Amel-Marduk, Nebuchadrezzar's successor, probably about 651 (II Kings 25:27–30). As they contemplated the future, the Deuteronomists echoed the hope previously expressed by Jeremiah and Ezekiel: that the destruction of Jerusalem and the temple would not nullify the divine promise to David of an eternal kingship (II Sam. 7:8–16). The promise is reiterated in Yahweh's address to Solomon in terms that clearly reflect the Exilic setting (I Kings 9:3–9).

In evaluating the past, the Deuteronomists drew upon the Deuteronomic code. The holy war concept of Joshua rests on Deut. 6:19; 7:1 ff. The theological framework of Judges reflects the Deuteronomic conviction that disobedience to Yahweh resulted in disaster while obedience guaranteed blessing. Judgment was passed on the rulers of Israel and Judah in the light of Judaean theology and adherence to the Deuteronomic code. Northern kings were automatically condemned because the establishment of Yahweh shrines at Dan and Bethel violated the law of the central shrine. Southern monarchs were judged on their efforts to eradicate Ba'alism and their adherence to the Deuteronomic code, which most of them had never known.

From time to time some hint of the Deuteronomists' hopes for the future can be discerned: the Exodus from Egypt foreshadowed a new exodus from Babylon, and Yahweh's gracious response to the outcries of his disobedient people in the period of the Judges gave hope that the deity would once again respond to his people's prayers (Deut. 29–30). The emphasis on courage in the face of great odds (Deut. 7:17 ff.) could only have strengthened Jewish faith in the future. Finally, the fact that the Davidic line was still represented in Jehoiachin, who was receiving royal recognition in Babylon, may well have fed Jewish hopes, despite the condemnation of II Kings 24:9.

In addition to completing the history of the nations, Deuteronomic editors made additions to the work of Jeremiah. Some portions of Jeremiah are so expressive of the theology of D that they can be recognized as units added by Deuteronomists. For example, Jer. 5:18–19 reflects the Exilic setting and the D interpretation of history, and the same can be said for 16:10–13 and 22:8–9. It is clear from these additions and from the closing verses in II Kings 25 that the literary activity of the D writers was not terminated by the fall of Jerusalem, and many scholars have suggested that the Deuteronomic history underwent its final revision during the Exile and assumed a form approximating that which we have today.

THE HOLINESS CODE

During this period of creative productivity, another body of writings, cultic and ethical in nature, took form as the so-called Holiness or H code of Leviticus 17–26. This material takes its title from the repeated emphasis on Yahweh's holiness, best summarized in Lev. 19:2: "You shall be holy, for I, Yahweh your god, am holy" (see also 20:7, 8, 26; 21:6, 8, 15, 23; 22:9, 16, 32, and implications elsewhere).

Read Lev. 17–26

Parallels in language, style and content to Ezekiel (cf. Lev. 17:15 with Ezek. 44:31; Lev. 18:8 and 20:11 with Ezek. 22:10, etc.) and the presupposition in Lev. 17:1–9 of the central shrine called for in Deuteronomy, have led many scholars to place H in the Exile, close to the time when Ezekiel was written. Much of the material may have come from an earlier date, but the editing reflects the Exilic period. In its present form, the code parallels Deuteronomy in the hortatory tone that creeps in from time to time (cf. 19:33 f.), and like Deuteronomy, H is said to have been given by Yahweh to Moses at Sinai, and the closing has the familiar pattern of blessings and curses.

The code is concerned with ritual purity for laity and priests. If Israel was to be the people of Yahweh, care had to be taken not to violate Yahweh's holiness. Numerous apodictic laws and some casuistic rulings seem to be loosely strung together, and despite attempts to isolate small collections or units, no real pattern of sources has been found. The contents are as follows:

1. Chapter 17 is concerned with laws of killing for food and sacrifice. As noted above, reference to the central altar suggests acceptance of the Deuteronomic law, but the holiness code is stricter, eliminating the special provisions found in D for slaughter for food when one lives away from the central shrine.[25]

2. Chapter 18 sets forth in apodictic form principles governing sexual relations.

3. Chapter 19 consists of general religious and ethical precepts for daily life for the entire community. The presentation is apodictic in form and rather complex in order.

---

[25] Attempts to analyze this change are fraught with complexities. The H code may be reverting to a primitive sacrificial law. There is no recognition of any practical difficulties. For further discussion, cf. M. Noth, *Leviticus,* The Old Testament Library, trans. by J. E. Anderson (Philadelphia: Westminster Press, 1965), pp. 129 f., N. Micklen, "Leviticus," *The Interpreter's Bible,* II, 87–90.

4. Chapter 20 corresponds closely to Chapter 18, providing rules for sexual behavior and other general regulations. Provision is made for the death penalty.

5. Chapter 21 provides for the ritual purity or holiness of the priesthood. Aaron symbolizes the high priest and his sons the general priesthood.

6. Chapter 22, written in impersonal casuistic style, is concerned with holy things, cultic offerings and gifts.

7. Chapter 23 presents the festal calendar (cf. Deut. 16) covering the Sabbath, feasts of unleavened bread, Firstfruits, pentecost, atonement and ingathering or booths.[26]

8. Chapter 24 is composite, dealing with the role of the high priest (24:1-9), and providing a legal example for the punishment of blasphemy by a foreigner (24:10-23).

9. Chapter 25 discusses the Sabbatical year and the year of Jubilee.

10. Chapter 26 consists of blessings and curses. The Holiness Code was incorporated into the Torah, but just when this was done cannot be determined. Some of the laws are not uniquely Israelite but represent the broad general basis of law in the Near East;[27] others represent laws specifically designed for the Jewish community.

THE PRIESTLY SOURCE

Another collection of writings, largely cultic in emphasis, was also begun during the Exile. Drawing upon ancient priestly lore, possibly contained in written sources brought to Babylon by priests but more probably stored in the memories of those who had been responsible for rituals and tradition, and colored to some degree by the Babylonian setting, these materials were compiled over a long period of time and were ultimately added to the other materials represented by J, E, D and H, partially, no doubt, as a continuing interpretation of the history of the people and the meaning of that history. Because the final compilation was not completed until after the Exile, the discussion of this material will be reserved until later.

[26] The history of these observances is complicated. Cf. Martin Noth, *Leviticus*, pp. 165–176; Micklem, *op. cit.*, pp. 110 ff.; Hans-Joachim Kraus, *Worship in Israel*, trans. by Geoffrey Buswell (Richmond, Virginia: John Knox Press, 1966), pp. 26 ff.

[27] For example, laws concerning sexual relationships with near relatives (Lev. 18:6 ff.) are similar to those of Hammurabi's code, 154–158; cf. *ANET*, pp. 172 f.

23

Life and Literature
of the Late Period

ONE of the greatest writings of the Exile was produced near the end of the time of captivity during the period we are calling "The Late Period of the Exile" (*ca.* 555 to 538) . The unknown prophet of Babylon whose work was affixed to that of Isaiah of Jerusalem was a proclaimer of a new vision of Yahweh and his relationship to his people, and was a keen observer of developing events and of contemporary society. To understand his work, patterns of international relations during the Exilic period must be considered together with some aspects of the festal life of Nebuchadrezzar's Babylon.

THE LAST DAYS OF THE NEO-BABYLONIAN EMPIRE

Nebuchadrezzar died in 562. During his reign he maintained control of his vast empire with difficulty. A rival, King Cyaxeres of Media, began to build a powerful state with its capital at Ecbatana. Median tribes were subdued, Armenians overcome and the new Median empire pushed into Asia Minor, only to be stopped by the Lydians. During this period, Nebuchadrezzar was campaigning in the west, attempting to quiet unrest that had developed, perhaps augmented by the efforts of the Egyptian Pharaoh Apries or Hophra (589–569) . After a thirteen year siege, Tyre became a Babylonian possession with semi-independence (cf. Ezek. 29:17–20) . Meanwhile, Pharaoh Apries was defeated by the Greeks at Cyrene (570) . In 568, perhaps to prove to the Egyptians the folly of pressing into Asia, Nebuchadrezzar invaded Egypt.

When Nebuchadrezzar died in 562, his long rule was followed by a period of social upheaval and in seven years four different monarchs sat on the Babylonian throne. Amel-Marduk (562–560), a son of Nebuchadrezzar, died a violent death and is believed to be the Evil-merodoch of II Kings 25:27–30 who released King Jehoiakim from prison. Nergal-shar-usar (cf. Jer. 39:3, 13: possibly Nergal-sharezer) , a brother-in-law, ruled four years (560–556) and just prior to his death suffered defeat in a battle with the Medes. His infant son Labashi-marduk was scarcely crowned when Nabonidus or Nabu-na'id, who was not of the same family, seized the throne in a rebellion supported by chief officials of state. Nabonidus' mother was a high-priestess of the moon god Sin and his father was a nobleman, and Nabonidus came into conflict with the priests of Marduk, perhaps through his efforts to make Sin the chief god of the empire. A famine attributed to royal impiety, together with spiraling inflation, produced tension within the empire. Nabonidus moved to the desert oasis of Teima (southeast of Edom) and from this center established military and trade posts throughout the desert as far as Yatrib (later Medina) near the Red Sea. In Babylon, his son Bel-shar-usur (Belshazzar in Daniel) ruled as regent from 552–545. The absence of the monarch created serious religious problems, particularly for the annual Akitu or New Year festival. Finally the monarch returned to Babylon, perhaps to lead his forces against Elamite raiders in southern Babylonia. But new forces were at work that were to deprive him of his crown and terminate the Neo-Babylonian empire.

THE AKITU FESTIVAL

The most important religious celebration of Babylon and one that provides a background for understanding II Isaiah was the Akitu festival[1] observed annually from the first to twelfth of *Nisanu* (Hebrew *Nisan:* March–April). The festal origins may lie in Sumerian times; the rites continued to be observed into the Persian-Greek period. The chief figure in the cult during the Neo-Babylonian era was Marduk, god of Babylon and supreme deity in the empire. His temple, called Esagila ("House of the Uplifted Head"), stood near the great ziggurat.

Rituals of preparation occupied the first days and included lustration rites, the carving of images of wood, which were then overlaid with gold and ornamented with jewels and semi-precious stones (Isa. 40:18–20; 41:7), and prayers for blessing. The temple was ceremonially cleansed and wiped down with the body of a sacrificed sheep and with oils.

The recitation of the Enuma Elish,[2] the creation myth of Babylon, was also part of the ritual. This myth relates the story of the birth of the gods, the battle between Marduk, champion of order, and Tiamat, symbol of chaos, and the creation of man in a god-ordered universe. Opening verses describe a time when there was neither heaven nor earth but only the watery abyss ruled by Apsu, symbol of fresh water, and his consort Tiamat, the sea. Out of the first principle, water, came heavenly beings, created in pairs. With the arrival of many offspring came noise so upsetting that Apsu and Tiamat planned to kill their grandchildren. The plot, overheard by the wise

[1] For detailed discussion see S. A. Pallis, *The Babylonian Akitu Festival* (Copenhagen: Andr. Fred. Host & Son, 1926).

[2] Like the Hebrew titles for biblical books, the Babylonian creation myth was known by the opening words *enuma elish* meaning "When on high." The myth may be read in *ANET*, pp. 60 ff., or A. Heidel, *The Babylonian Genesis* (Chicago: University of Chicago Press, 1963), now in a Phoenix paperback edition.

earth god Ea, was foiled with the killing of Apsu. But Tiamat was still alive. Mustering her creative powers, she formed frightful monsters and over this array placed one of her children, Kingu, pinning on his breast the tablets of destiny, symbolic of control of the future. The stage was now set for a dramatic, cosmic encounter of gods.

When none among the gods of order was able to stand up to Tiamat and Kingu, Marduk, son of Ea and his wife Damkina, entered the arena having been promised supreme kingship should he defeat the enemy. Kingu was overcome and the tablets of destiny became the property of Marduk. Tiamat was killed and split in two, like an oyster. With one half of the dead goddess, Marduk formed the arch of the heavens and with the other half, the earth. In the realm above he set Anu the sky god, in the realm below Ea, the earth god, and between the two the air god, Enlil. Other gods were given abodes in the heavens and the stars were formed in their likeness, with constellations to mark the passage of time. The sun, moon and stars were heavenly bodies with special courses to run.

Marduk was acknowledged as king by the other gods. To serve the needs of the deities, Marduk created man, moulding the human form out of clay mingled with the blood of the dead Kingu. A shrine was built to Marduk where the gods might visit and pay homage, and his city was called *Bab-ilu* or Babylon, "gate of gods."

On the days of the Akitu festival following the recitation of the Enuma Elish the king was ritually deposed, deprived of symbols of office and compelled to make a negative confession before Marduk. Subsequently he was restored to office in a ceremony in which his face was slapped until the tears ran, a symbol that Marduk was friendly. A human scapegoat, usually a condemned prisoner, was paraded through the streets.[3] Scapegoat rituals are communal purgation rites in which the sins of the community are placed upon the victim. The expulsion and destruction of the scapegoat rendered the community cleansed of taint and ready to begin the new year.[4]

The next day the god Nabu (Nebo in Isa. 46:1) arrived from Borsippa, then, subsequently, the other gods. For a time Marduk disappeared later to reappear, suggesting some form of a death-resurrection emphasis. On the eleventh day, at the divine assembly held in the chamber of destiny, the fate of the nation for the coming year was determined, possibly by sacred oracles or by magic. To ensure fertility, a sacred marriage was performed. On the final day, at a great banquet accompanied by much sacrificing, the unity of the nation was cemented in commensality rites enjoyed by gods, king, priests and people. On this day the king took the right hand of the god, perhaps in a ritual in which the god was led to his throne but certainly as a symbol of divine favor and blessing (cf. Isa. 45:1). At the close of the ritual, the various gods returned to their own cities.

---

[3] T. H. Gaster, p. 555, note 456, in J. G. Frazer, *The New Golden Bough*, T. H. Gaster, ed. (New York: Criterion Books, 1959).

[4] *Ibid.*, "Scapegoats," p. 554. See also T. H. Gaster, *Festivals of the Jewish Year* (New York: William Sloane Associates, 1953), pp. 141 ff.

King Cyaxeres of Media died in 585 and was succeeded by his son Astyages (585–550). Among the formerly migratory Aryan groups that composed part of the empire was the tribe from Parsua, the land west of Lake Urmia, now settled in the area east of the Persian Gulf called Parsa, after their former homeland. By the middle of the seventh century, tribal holdings had expanded and incorporated the Anshan area north of the gulf. At the beginning of the sixth century, King Cambyses I, known as "King of Anshan," a petty prince within the Median Empire, married the daughter of the emperor, King Astyages, and the son born of this union was Cyrus, destined to become "the Great."

Cyrus became king of Anshan in 559, and Astyages, cognizant of Cyrus' intention to revolt, prepared to attack. A rebellion within his army frustrated Astyages' plans, and by 550 Cyrus was in control of the Persian-Mede empire and was beginning a series of brilliant military maneuvers. Nabonidus, fearful of Cyrus' power, entered into alliances with Croesus of Lydia in Asia Minor (560–546) and with Amasis of Egypt (569–525). Cyrus moved across northern Mesopotamia, removed Syria from Babylonian control, and disregarding the usual military practice whereby hostilities ceased during the winter months, attacked Croesus in his winter palace at Sardis and made Lydia part of his kingdom. The Babylonian-Egyptian pact was dissolved. Cyrus conquered Afghanistan and prepared to move on Babylonia.

Babylon was ready for Cyrus. Fifth columnists had been at work spreading pro-Persian propaganda.[5] Babylonians, irritated by Nabonidus' long absence in the desert and troubled by the monarch's religious deviations, were willing to heed reports about the liberal-minded Persian. It is not impossible that the subversive work reached into the Jewish community.[6] The Persians entered Babylon without battle. According to the Cyrus cylinder,[7] Cyrus came at the invitation of Marduk who, angry with Nabonidus, searched for a righteous man and pronounced the name of Cyrus, commanding the Persian king to assume control of the land (cf. Isa. 45:4).[8] Cyrus records that his army strolled toward Babylon, weapons sheathed, welcomed by the entire countryside. Upon taking control of the city, he forbade plunder by his troops, began a program of urban renewal, permitted captive peoples to return home, restored sanctuaries and returned sacred implements to their respective shrines. Cyrus speaks of himself as a wor-

---

[5] Saggs, *op. cit.*, p. 152.

[6] Morton Smith, "II Isaiah and the Persians," *Journal of the American Oriental Society*, LXXXIII (1963), 415 ff.

[7] The Cyrus cylinder is a small barrel-shaped clay cylinder upon which the monarch had inscribed the report of his conquest. Cf. *ANET*, pp. 315 f.; *DOTT*, pp. 92 ff.

[8] M. Smith, *op. cit.*, speculates that Persian subversives may have suggested to the Babylonians that Cyrus was chosen by Marduk, and suggested to the Jews that he was chosen by Yahweh.

shiper of Bel-Marduk.[9] Whether or not he was a follower of the prophet Zoroaster cannot be known for sure, but some parts of II Isaiah have been compared with the religious documents of Zoroastrian faith, known as the Gathas, and parallels suggesting dependence have been noted,[10] but the evidence is still *sub judice*.

ZOROASTRIAN RELIGION

The date of Zoroaster's birth is not known and dates accepted by scholars vary from the pre-Exilic through the Exilic periods.[11] According to tradition, he was born in eastern Iran, perhaps near Lake Urmia. Legends concerning his early childhood relate miraculous escapes from enemies who wished to destroy him. The account of his spiritual pilgrimage tells how he was led by Vohu Manah (Good Thought) to an assemblage of spirits and was instructed by Ahura Mazda (also called Ormazd or Hormuzd) in a true or pure religion. His initial efforts to reach his countrymen were unsuccessful, but he eventually converted King Vishtaspa, chief of a small tribal federation. With royal support, the influence of the religion spread and attempts were made to convert neighboring groups by force through a series of holy wars. In one of these wars, Zoroaster died.

His teachings centered in a cosmic dualism in which Ahura Mazda, the all-knowing creator and sustainer of the world of good, was pitted against the powers of evil symbolized by Angra Mainyu, the epitome of evil. Here truth struggled with the lie and light battled darkness. Ethical values were attributed to the opposing forces by the prophet, so that right and wrong tended to have black and white characteristics. Man, endowed with free choice, is involved in the cosmic struggle and must choose between the sides. Within this cosmic bipolarity, Zoroaster envisioned history moving toward an ultimate goal. In the final epoch of time, truth and goodness would triumph. Then, in the eschaton, a savior would come to renew all existence and resurrect the dead, uniting the body and soul.

At death, man's soul approached the "Bridge of Separation" over which the righteous were able to pass to paradise but where the evil were turned back for punishment. At the end of time, after the resurrection, every man would be tested in a flood of molten metal. For the righteous the final test would be as entering a warm bath, but for the evil the fiery test would mean complete extinction. As one possessing free will, the individual could not be judged as a member of a group; nor could he be burdened with the sins of his ancestors. Each man, by personal choice and action, determined his own ultimate fate.

[9] The term Bel, a form of Ba'al, was used in conjunction with the proper name, Marduk.

[10] M. Smith, *op. cit.*, pp. 418 ff.

[11] For a discussion of dates, cf. Jack Finegan, *Archaeology of World Religions* (Princeton, New Jersey: Princeton University Press, 1952), pp. 77 ff.; R. C. Zaehner, *The Dawn & Twilight of Zoroastrianism* (London: Weidenfeld and Nicolson, 1961), pp. 33 ff.

The eschatological hopes promised rewards beyond man's wildest dreams or punishment that signified complete extermination.

When Cyrus seized control of the Median empire during the sixth century and founded his own royal Achaemenid line,[12] the house of Vishtaspa, Zoroaster's patron, was terminated. Without royal support Zoroastrianism had to struggle for existence. What impact this religion may have had on Cyrus is not known. The Cyrus cylinder speaks of allegiance to Marduk, and Jewish records indicate that Cyrus spoke of being commissioned by Yahweh to build the Jewish temple (II Chron. 36:22 ff.; Ezra 1:1-4). Possibly Cyrus diplomatically employed the name of whatever god was in popular use in the part of the empire with which he was dealing.[13] At present there is no way of knowing what god Cambyses II, son of Cyrus who ruled from 529 to 522, may have worshiped. Not until Darius I, the Great (521-486), the Achaemenid prince who rescued the throne of Persia from a usurper named Gaumata is there any tangible evidence of allegiance to Ahura Mazda and the religion of Zoroaster. On the other hand, the pervasive influence of the great teacher and his followers should not be underestimated, and it is not impossible that some of the expressions of the cosmological motifs in II Isaiah owe something to the teachings of Zoroaster.

THE WRITINGS OF DEUTERO-ISAIAH

Reasons for the separation of Isaiah 40-55 from the work of Isaiah of Jerusalem have been stated, but the criteria for dating these chapters in the closing days of the Exile have only been touched upon. To begin, there echoes throughout II Isaiah complaints of abandonment, forsakenness and loneliness similar to those more fully expressed in Lamentations, Ezekiel and Job (cf. Isa. 40:2, 27; 42:24 f.; 43:27 f.), coupled with promises of forgiveness and fulfillment (40:11; 41:8-10, 14-16; 43:1-7, 10-13). The period into which these statements fit best is the Exile. Further evidence for dating is obtained from the allusion to the destruction of Jerusalem and the temple (44:26-28). It is clear that the Assyrian oppression is long past (52:4) and, despite the fact that there is no mention of the Exile as such, the announcement of the proximity of Babylon's fall (43:14; 47:1-3; 48:14, 20), the naming of Cyrus of Persia as the deliverer (44:28; 45:1) and less direct references to him (41:1-4, 25; 48:14-15) point to a time of writing somewhere between June, 546 when Cyrus began to threaten Babylonian supremacy and 538 when Babylon came under Persian control.

No mention of Cyrus is found in Chapters 49-55 and it has been suggested that Chapters 40-48 were composed before Cyrus took Babylon when the prophet's hopes for the captive Jews were highest and that Chapters 49-55 represent writings from 538 when Cyrus failed

---

[12] Named after an ancestor "Hakhamanish" or, in the Greek form, "Achaemenes."
[13] Jack Finegan, *Archaeology of World Religions*, p. 94.

to fulfill the prophetic hope that he would become a Yahweh worshiper. On the other hand, the pattern may reflect editorial organization in which two collections of materials are represented: one of hymns and oracles about Yahweh and Israel and the fall of Babylon and the other centered in the new Jerusalem, Mount Zion and the mission of Yahweh's people. But even so broad a division may be oversimplification, as many themes overlap and are found in both sections.

Attempts to develop a structural outline have not been particularly successful, but significant studies have been made of the literary forms, stylistic characteristics and the use of illustrative materials in II Isaiah.[14] Small units have been isolated, including consolation words (40:1–2; 43:1–2), mocking themes (44:9–11), diatribes (48:1–11), heraldic pronouncements (40:9–11). Four hymns on the "servant of Yahweh" theme were recognized by B. Duhm in 1892 and since that time have been the subject of much study. The usual listing of these songs is 42:1–4; 49:1–6; 50:4–9; and 52:13–53:12, although some scholars would expand the first and third to 42:1–7 and 50:1–9 or consider 42:5–7 and 50:10–11 separate hymns. These poems will be considered separately. Themes of comfort, joy, thanksgiving for release from anxiety, promise for the future in the light of impending deliverance and salvation, and paeans of praise to Yahweh as creator, redeemer and savior, are threaded through the entire work, and despite the seeming disorder of the work, there is a flow of ideas linked by these recurring stresses. No attempt will be made to analyze the literary structure of Deutero-Isaiah for little more than a listing of components would result.

The introductory chapter of Deutero-Isaiah touches upon major themes developed within the rest of the work and presents what may be a summary description of the divine commissioning of the prophet. The opening verses employ the familiar heraldic motif in which a messenger is dispatched by the king or the assembled court (of heaven) to proclaim a royal edict. The message announced the termination of the period of servitude and forgiveness for sin, which, in accordance with Jeremiah's prediction, had been a double punishment (Jer. 16:18). The message was designed as the beginning of Yahweh's comforting acts on behalf of his people and called for the preparation of a royal highway[15] over which Yahweh would return to Jerusalem just as Marduk entered his city of Babylon on the level, paved, processional way. This theophany would mark the return of Yahweh's glory (kabod) which Ezekiel had seen depart (Ezek. 9:3–10:22) and would, Jeremiah assumed, signal the restoration of covenant relationships.

The summons to "cry" may be part of Deutero-Isaiah's prophetic call. In view of the numerous passages echoing aspects of the Akitu

Read Ch. 40

[14] J. Muilenburg, "Isaiah 40–66: Introduction and Exegesis," *The Interpreter's Bible*, V, 384–393.

[15] Possibly the prophet had in mind the King's highway linking Aqabah and Damascus. Cf. *supra* Part Two, chap. 5, "The Land."

ritual, it is quite possible that the experience of divine commissioning may have come during the New Year festival. Deutero-Isaiah's response to the order to "cry" reflects something of the mood of Job: the frailty of human existence and the passive acknowledgment that Yahweh's will would be done. In striking contrast is the dynamic nature of the order to bring good news to Jerusalem, to present Yahweh with a cry reminiscent of Amos 4:12 as both majestic conqueror and tender ministrant to his flock (40:10–11).

The emphases on the creative role of Yahweh and on the revealing of future destiny are best understood against the background of the Akitu festival. Unlike Marduk who annually sought guidance for the creation ritual from the assembled gods, Yahweh needed no advisor. Passages mocking the stupidity of idol worship (40:18–20, which should be read with 41:7) reflect preparatory rites of the opening of the Akitu festival when images were carved.[16] The dramatic contrast between man-made objects of adoration and the transcendent Yahweh illustrates the superiority of Israel's God, the true creator.

To those Jews who, like the exiles referred to by Ezekiel, believed themselves cut off from Yahweh, the prophet announced Yahweh's constancy and succor and called for an awakening to Yahweh's greatness. Jews were warned not to succumb to the rich ritual of Babylonian religion. Sustaining power promised for the weak and feeble introduces the theme of renewal of national life and strength and the promise of a new future. In effect, the prophet is announcing the long-awaited Day of Yahweh.

Read Ch. 41 The theme of Yahweh's control of history is now picked up, and in presenting the amazing exploits of Cyrus, described as "one from the east," an eschatological hope is unfolded promising a paradise as a demonstration of Yahweh's power. Once again Babylonian theology is challenged. Now the setting is the chamber of destiny where, in the Akitu ritual, the fate of the nation for the coming year was decided. Yahweh called for evidence that Babylonian predictions had ever been accurate, and it is argued that Yahweh determined Cyrus' mission and foretold his success. Just when or where the prediction was made cannot be ascertained, and the corrupt state of 41:27 only adds to the confusion. For the first time the servant motif is introduced (41:8–10). There can be no doubt that in this passage the servant is Israel, the chosen offspring of Abraham. Election began with Jacob.

Read Chs. 42–44 The initial verses of Chapter 42 reintroduce the servant concept but without indicating whether the prophet is referring to Israel, to some individual or group within Israel, to Cyrus of Persia, or to someone else. This servant was to bring justice to the world. Subsequent verses expand the theme, leading up to a mighty hymn of praise, eschatological in its promises. The problem of the "servant," which will be discussed later, grows out of passages that fail to identify what group or individual is meant. Several interpretations are possible. The significance of election to Deutero-Isaiah's message lies in the emphasis on the constancy of Yahweh's love for his people upon which the argument for future hope rests (ch. 43). It is possible that some echo of Zoro-

---

16 Cf. *ANET*, p. 331.

astrian theology appears in 43:2, but the ideas here are so broad that they could just as easily apply to the Exodus tradition.

In Chapter 45, for the first time, Cyrus of Persia is specifically named, and Deutero-Isaiah arguing from the premise of a universal deity draws a neat syllogism to prove that it is Yahweh who directs Cyrus' destiny, whether Cyrus knows it or not! Indirect references to the Akitu festival appear in 45:20 ff. where guess-work predictions arrived at in the assembly of the gods are compared with the accuracy of Yahweh's pronouncements, and in 46:1 f., where one can almost picture the processional. Scorn for those who worship immobile and mute statues, obviously a reference to Babylonians, serves to introduce Yahweh who is beyond representation, whose will is made known and whose purposes come to pass. Here II Isaiah makes one of several clear-cut statements of monotheism (46:9). **Read Chs. 45–47**

Having promised the deliverance of the exiled people (46:13) Deutero-Isaiah now pronounces the doom of Babylon and mocks the inability of soothsayers and astrologers to deliver the nation (cf. Isa. 3:16 and 47:3).

Within the message of hope and redemption, a solemn warning is issued to exiles drawn to Babylonian religion (48:5) or with serious doubts about the prophet's message. The exultant cry of promise draws on the tradition of the Exodus from Egypt, promising that what Yahweh did in the past he would do again (48:20–22). The servant theme in Chapter 49 is far from clear. The servant, chosen in the womb and predestined for his task, is to bring Israel back to Yahweh (49:1–5). This servant will be a light to the nations (49:6). If the prophet is continuing the servant theme in Verse 7, then the servant-redeemer is despised and abhorred. Could a member of the captive royal family be meant here, or is this a group within the exiled people, or is the reference to the exiled people personified as an individual? **Read Chs. 48–51:8**

The arguments of those who said that Yahweh had forgotten his people (49:14 ff.) or had, as Hosea had phrased it, divorced Israel (50:1 ff.) are denied. II Isaiah's appeal is to tradition, and the promise of redemption is renewed (51:1 ff.).

The prophet now calls upon Yahweh to redeem as in the past, beginning his hymn with "Awake, awake" (51:9–11). Yahweh's response is a promise of release, and similar cries "rouse yourself, rouse yourself" (51:17) and "awake, awake" (52:1) are directed toward Jerusalem to encourage the people to rise to the challenge of the new tomorrow. **Read Chs. 51:9–54:17**

Within this section is the portrait of the suffering servant, a motif of redemptive suffering drawn from the Akitu rites where the human scapegoat bore the sins of many to bring new purification to the nation (52:13–53:12). In Deutero-Isaiah's use of this concept, the servant suffers and is cut off from the land of the living like the Akitu victim, but unlike the Babylonian scapegoat, the servant is promised that he will witness the fruits of his suffering (53:10 f.) and will share the booty of the rich and powerful (53:12). Chapter 54 is a comfort hymn contrasting the state of abject misery with the promised good fortune.

The final chapter continues the words of promise and urges repen- **Read Ch. 55** tance, for the time of Yahweh's inbreaking is at hand and the exiles must be prepared. The word of Yahweh had been spoken, the time for fulfillment had come.

DEUTERO-ISAIAH'S CONCEPT OF GOD

As we have noted, for the first time in Hebrew literature a full statement of monotheism is set forth. Yahweh alone is God; there is no other anywhere; all other gods are false (44:6, 8; 45:18; 46:9). This new theology placed everything under the control of one supreme deity, from creation through past history, from the present into the future. Nor is there any recognition of divine or semi-divine anti-god forces. Yahweh alone created weal and woe (45:7). The monotheistic presentation is given striking force by contrast with Babylonian beliefs.

Babylonian gods, fashioned by men out of common elements (40:19–20; 41:7; 44:9–20; 46:6), were completely helpless, most apparently so when rocking and swaying on the backs of animals in the festal processions (45:20; 46:1–2), or in their inability to move or respond to communicants' needs (46:6–7). Yahweh was not a created deity, but was the creator and, as Job had made clear, was above and beyond his creation, so transcendent as to defy confinement in descriptions or images (40:22–25). Nevertheless, Deutero-Isaiah argued, Yahweh revealed himself, not only in creation, but in history and through his spokesmen, the prophets.

The Akitu ritual traced creation to Marduk; Deutero-Isaiah announced it as a primal act of Yahweh (40:26; 42:5; 44:24; 45:7, 18; 48:13). Marduk's creation was a complicated affair; Deutero-Isaiah's was relatively simple as the prophet drew in part on the J tradition (42:5) but also incorporated ideas that point to the concepts found in the Priestly source (cf. Gen. 1:1–2:4a).

In the Akitu ritual an assembly of gods determined the shape of things to come for the year ahead; Deutero-Isaiah argued that the future, like the past and present, was in Yahweh's hands. Babylonian techniques for discerning events were unnecessary (40:13) for Yahweh had revealed his will in summoning the prophet to explain current happenings as acts of Yahweh. The validation of the future rested in the accuracy of past predictions. As Yahweh had chosen Israel (Jacob) while still in the womb and had delivered the people from Egypt to lead them to the promised land, so Yahweh called them again, and using the great Persian warrior Cyrus, would deliver them again to the promised land.

The majesty of the hymns of praise to Yahweh and the lyrical quality of the songs of joy are apparent in English translations. The prophet's words take wings as he conveys his understanding of Yahweh and Yahweh's plans for his people. If Job stood humbled and perhaps perplexed before the majesty of Yahweh, Deutero-Isaiah was triumphant and lifted for this was Israel's god, whose power and glory could not be overshadowed, even by the attempts of the Babylonians with their lofty ziggurats, numerous temples and elaborate rituals.

The holiness of Yahweh, so important in Ezekiel and the H code, is reflected in the repetitive use of the term "Holy One of Israel" (41:14, 16, 20; 43:3, 14, 15; 45:11; 47:4; 48:17) borrowed from the writings of Isaiah of Jerusalem. The unique relationship of Yahweh to Israel is implied, but the words seem to have lost the sense of making a sharp delineation between the sacred and the profane and have become a simple substitutionary label for Yahweh.

Perhaps a term holding far more meaning for the exiles when applied to Yahweh was "Redeemer" (*go'el*) which appears over and over again (41:14; 43:14; 47:4; 48:17; 49:7, 26; 54:5, 8). The depth of the covenant relationship as conceived by Deutero-Isaiah is revealed in this familial term usually applied to next of kin. The redemption motif was already present in the Exodus tradition and is clearly reflected in the cultic prayer recited at the Firstfruits festival (Deut. 26:5 ff.), but through the trauma of the exile in Babylon, the theme of deliverance was given a deeper and more intimate meaning, warmer in tone, closer in feeling, contrasting strangely with the vision of the transcendent deity.

YAHWEH AND HISTORY

The validation of Deutero-Isaiah's hope for restoration rested, in part, in his interpretation of history as the product of acts of Yahweh. The universalistic emphasis implied in monotheism is not completely abandoned as the prophet develops the theme of history, but it is certainly tempered by the concept of election which develops a strong particularism. The God of the whole word is Israel's God. Past history, for II Isaiah, is Israel's history (41:8–9; 51:2, etc.). Present history consists of events related to Israel's welfare (44:26–28; 45:1–4). The idealized future is predominantly centered in the exaltation of Israel (41:14 ff.; 42:14 ff.; 43:3 ff.; 47; 48:14). The newly redeemed nation is summoned to a new role following the new exodus,[17] to become Yahweh's servant, the proclaimer of Yahweh's will, a light to the nations.[18] Once again the theme is not completely new, for in J it had been announced that nations would be blessed through Abraham (Gen. 12:3).

THE SERVANT OF YAHWEH

Of all the themes developed by Deutero-Isaiah, the one that has produced the greatest amount of scholarly theorizing is that of the servant of the Lord. In the many passages where the servant is clearly

[17] For a discussion of Exodus typology, cf. B. Anderson, "Exodus Typology in Second Isaiah," *Israel's Prophetic Heritage,* B. W. Anderson and W. Harrelson (eds.) (New York: Harper and Brothers, 1962), pp. 177–195.

[18] It is possible that the prophet meant that Israel, being highly exalted, would be a light or beacon to the nations. Cf. P. A. H. deBoer, "Deutero-Isaiah's Message," *Oudtestamentische Studiën,* XI (1956), 80 ff.

identified as Israel, no problem exists, but when no clear identification is made numerous hypotheses may be developed. The greatest amount of study has been concentrated upon the four servant poems: 42:1–4; 49:1–6; 50:4–9; 52:13–53:12.

Some have argued that the servant is to be understood as an individual, and identifications have included: Moses, King Uzziah, King Josiah, Jeremiah and Ezekiel among II Isaiah's predecessors; Jehoiachin, Zerubbabel the descendant of Jehoiachin, Cyrus and the prophet himself among his contemporaries; and in a futuristic sense, a messianic figure, including the Christian designation of Jesus of Nazareth.[19] Others have supported a collective interpretation and, in the light of the concept of corporate personality, such a point of view is feasible. Among the groups suggested are a prophetic order, ideal Israel and a pious remnant.[20]

Perhaps some clue to the problem can be found by comparing descriptions of the servant in the four poems with references outside of the poems to Israel as the servant. For example:

  a. Both are formed in the womb by Yahweh, 49:1, 5; cf. 44:2, 24.
  b. Both are chosen by Yahweh, 42:1, cf. 41:8 f.; 43:10; 44:1; etc.
  c. Both are sustained by Yahweh, 42:1; cf. 41:10.
  d. Both are to be a light to the nations, 49:6; cf. 42:6.
  e. In both Yahweh is glorified, 49:3; cf. 44:23.

On the other hand there are differences. Whereas the prophet speaks of rebellious, discouraged Israel (40:27; 41:8–10; 48:4), he finds the anonymous servant to be undismayed and faithful (42:4; 50:5–9). Furthermore, whereas Israel is to be redeemed (43:1–7), the servant is to be the instrument of redemption (49:5).

No single argument for a corporate group or for an individual will satisfy all critics, and therefore, for the purpose of this book, it will be assumed that Deutero-Isaiah, in speaking to his own generation of the servant of Yahweh, had Israel in mind. If the servant poems are not discussed out of context, and it can be assumed that the prophet was unvarying in his references to the servant, then on the basis of identifications of Israel as the servant outside the four poems it should be assumed that the servant in the poems is Israel also. Nor was it unusual for the writers in Israel to personify the group in a single individual, for Abraham and Jacob are sometimes individuals and sometimes symbols of the nation that developed from them. Nor are the varying characteristics of the servant inconsistent with the differing roles of the servant and the changing moods of the prophet. As he viewed his people, he saw attitudes like those encountered by Ezekiel and reflected in Lamentations and Job. As he contemplated the potential of the captives, he moved away from negative evaluation, and as he interpreted their plight, he developed a theology of redemp-

19 Isaiah 53 was often interpreted as typifying the passion of Jesus by New Testament writers. For a listing of passages see C. M. Dodd, *According to the Scriptures* (New York: Charles Scribner's Sons, 1953), pp. 88 ff.

20 For a detailed study, cf. C. R. North, *The Suffering Servant in Deutero-Isaiah*, (Oxford: Oxford University Press, 1956), and *Isaiah 40–55* (London: S.C.M. Press, 1952), also available in a Torch paperback.

tive suffering. His imagery was drawn from past history, present circumstance, and future hope. Thus the servant could be viewed as the instrument of justice and a light to the nations in the first two poems, and as a sufferer and one whose suffering would redeem in the last two.

It is in the concept of redemptive suffering that the poet-prophet introduces a new theological understanding of the Exile. The event was not a meaningless stroke of ill fortune; nor was it to be understood only as punishment for sin—although he would not argue that point. The meaning went deeper. Israel was the scapegoat for the whole world, just as the poor stumbling sufferer in the Akitu festival was for Babylon. On Israel's head were the sins of the nations, and out of Israel's suffering would come redemption, salvation, a new beginning and a new world.

The future role of the servant was that of Yahweh's prophetic servant, to proclaim and make known the divine will to all peoples, to bring knowledge of Yahweh's will to the world, to introduce the new creation. The triumphant servant would see the fruits of his suffering. The hope is ideal and eschatological; the instrument was to be Israel, the servant of Yahweh.

The Persian Period

24

Life and Literature
of the Early Period

ONLY limited information is available concerning the Jews in the Persian period. Apart from Biblical sources and a few Persian inscriptions, contributions coming from archaeological studies or literary documents from other parts of the Near East have been, at best, peripheral. Nevertheless it is possible to gain some insight into the historical situations that produced the biblical literature of this period and to reconstruct in broad general outline some aspects of Jewish life and thought.

The Persian conquest brought dramatic changes in governmental policies to that part of the world once controlled by Babylon. Cyrus' liberal attitude toward his subjects, his respect for local tradition and custom—both religious and cultural—and his willingness to permit flexibility within his empire, appear to have won for the Achaemenid ruler generous cooperation from his people. A workable government, not without its bureaucratic structure, put minimal social pressures on the populace.

Read II Chron. 36:22–23; Ezra 1:1–6

Cyrus' policy enabling captive peoples to return to their homelands encouraged Jews to journey to Palestine. In the book of Ezra, compiled in the fourth century B.C., the royal edict affecting the exiles has been preserved in two versions: one in Hebrew, the language of Judah (Ezra 1:2–4), and the other in Aramaic, a sister tongue which had become the business language for the western part of the Persian empire (Ezra 6:3–5). It is possible, as many scholars have suggested, that the Aramaic version is the original account, and perhaps the Hebrew version rests on the spoken announcement of the herald who proclaimed it.[1] In any case, the decrees are in basic agreement in that both record permission to rebuild the temple, and although the privilege of returning to Palestine is mentioned only in the Hebrew version, perhaps it is implied in the Aramaic.

Within the fifth Persian satrapy[2] Cyrus had created the province of Judah, extending from a line north of Hebron and just south of Bethzur to the area north of Jerusalem, a distance of about twenty-five miles. This land appears to have been removed from an administrative

---

[1] R. A. Bowman, "Ezra: Exegesis," *The Interpreter's Bible*, III, 571.

[2] A satrapy was a Persian administrative unit ruled by a satrap or governor.

_____ CHART XIV _____

Events in Palestine	Prophet	Events in the Persian Empire	Events in Greece
The province of Judah is created and Jews return from Exile	III Isaiah	Invasions on Persia's northern frontiers	
Conflict with Palestinians; Sheshbazzar is governor		530: Cyrus is killed 529: Cambyses II is king	
Zerubbabel is governor; Temple is rebuilt	Haggai Zechariah	522: Cambyses commits suicide 521: Darius I becomes king	
Samaritan-Jewish conflict			Persian- Greek wars
		490: Darius defeated by Greeks at Marathon	
Nabateans move into Edom; Edomites move into southern Palestine	Malachi Obadiah	486: Xerxes becomes king and destroys Babylon 465: Artaxerxes becomes king 460: Egypt is aided by Greeks, and rebels but is reconquered in 455	
Wall built around Jerusalem	Nehemiah Ezra		
Correspondence with Jews of Elephantine	Jonah	424: Darius II becomes king	
Ruth is written		404: Egypt wins independence	
The Chronicler is at work; the Torah is completed; the Psalms are compiled		358: Artaxerxes III is king 335: Darius III becomes king	Philip of Macedon is uniting Greece
			333: Alexander defeats Darius at Issus
			322: Alexander takes Tyre

district with headquarters in Samaria. A certain Shesh-bazzar (Ezra 1:8; 5:14), who, if he is to be identified with Shenazzar of I Chronicles 3:18 (a tenuous hypothesis),[3] may have been the son of the exiled King Jehoiachin and therefore a prince of the Davidic line, was appointed governor. The narrative in Ezra 3:1–4:4, which implies that Zerubbabel was the first governor, has confused the issue, leading some scholars to the conviction that Shesh-bazzar and Zerubbabel were one and the same person, and that Shesh-bazzar was the governor's Baby-

[3] Cf. John Bright, *A History of Israel*, p. 343 where the identification is supported, and M. Noth, *The History of Israel*, p. 309, where the theory is dismissed.

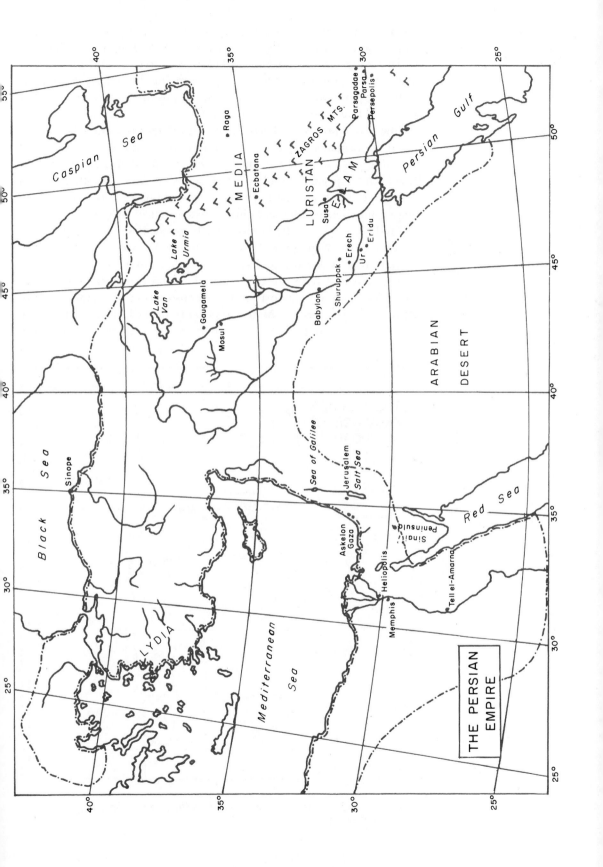

THE PERSIAN EMPIRE

vincing argument.[4] Without entering into the arguments, it seems simplest and best in the light of the evidence to recognize Shesh-bazzar as the first governor and Zerubbabel as his successor and to acknowledge Cyrus' political acumen in encouraging loyalty by giving the returning Jews one of their own people, possibly a member of their own royal family, as their first governor.

How many Jews went from Babylon to Palestine cannot be known, but it is estimated that their numbers were limited. Among those returning was the governor, Shesh-bazzar, Zerubbabel the prince of the Davidic line, Joshua the high priest, some Levitical priests, followers of Deutero-Isaiah and perhaps the prophet himself, and others whose longing for their childhood home matched that of the writer of Psalm 137. Others were to follow. How much financial support or material aid may have been given by Cyrus cannot be ascertained, but the Persian ruler is known to have given grants of money to assist in resettlement and both the Cyrus cylinder[5] and the edict preserved in Ezra 6:3–5 mention support for the reconstruction of shrines and the return of sacred vessels. Many Jews born in exile and comfortably settled in Babylon preferred to remain where they were despite the

Read Ezra 1:6–11

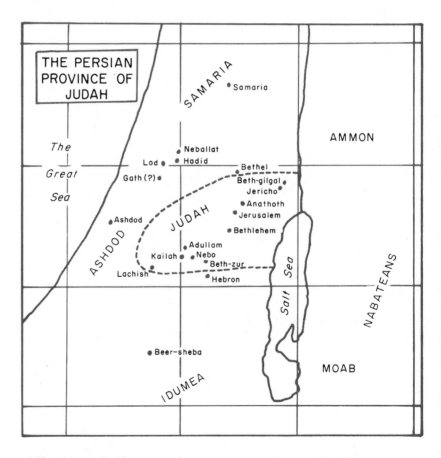

THE PERSIAN PROVINCE OF JUDAH

---

[4] Cf. article on Sheshbazzar in *The Interpreter's Dictionary of the Bible.*
[5] Cf. *ANET,* pp. 315 f.

predictions of future glory for Palestine by Ezekiel and Deutero-Isaiah.

What emotions the Jews experienced as they entered Jerusalem, with its tumbled stones serving as a grim reminder of the devastation of half a century earlier, have not been recorded. In contrast with the splendors of Babylon, the scene must have been shocking: ruins of the sacred altar, the demolished temple, the fallen walls and broken dwellings covered with drifted soil and overgrown with weeds. Perhaps there was a small village, a cluster of homes built by those who had not been exiled. All of this must have seemed a far cry from what may have been anticipated from the words of the Exilic prophets.

With considerable energy the newcomers began to build homes and lay the foundation for a new temple. According to Ezra 3 the altar was built, almost at once, and the offering of sacrifices begun. But work did not proceed without difficulty. Crop failure placed severe economic strains upon the community. Animosity and jealousy between the exiles and the descendants of those who had remained in the land hindered progress. The permanent residents appear to have greeted the Babylonian Jews with something less than enthusiasm (cf. Ezra 4:4 f.), possibly because of claims relating to repossession of family land or because of other economic reasons. On the other hand, it is not impossible that some exiles contributed to the tension. Raised and educated in the environment of sophisticated Babylon, with differing outlooks and customs, and persuaded by the prophets of the Exile that they had been cleansed by suffering to be the seed of the new Israel and the hope of the future, they may have been somewhat patronizing to their rural cousins. When local people sought to participate in the rebuilding program, their offers were haughtily refused (Ezra 4:3). There is some evidence that the followers of Deutero-Isaiah did not favor a policy of separation and, in keeping with the monotheistic emphasis of the great prophet, argued that all who came to the one God in the faith of Judaism would be accepted (Isa. 56).

Read Ezra 3–4:5

Samaritan Jews appear to have added to the problem of relationships, perhaps because they resented the establishment of a separate province of Judah out of territory they had considered to be within their jurisdiction. Consequently, they did all they could to hinder progress. The tension between Samaritan and Jew, which may have had its roots back in the suspicion that appears to have always existed between the north and the south even in the time of the united kingdom, did not lessen, but grew into a breach that was never to be healed. It is not surprising to find that the work of the temple ground to a halt while the exiles concentrated on social and economic problems.

Meanwhile, Cyrus seems to have paid little heed to the Jewish settlement. Nomadic invaders from Central Asia drove him to press for expansion of his kingdom on the northeastern borders. In 530, in a frontier battle, Cyrus was killed. His tomb, long ago plundered, is a simple structure of square cut stones built on a raised platform with six tiers of stairs. Plutarch, who lived between A.D. 46 and 120, recorded an inscription which was supposed to be on the tomb: "O man, whoever you are and from wherever you come, for I know you will

CARVED FIGURES ALONG THE STAIRWAY TO THE APADANA (HALL OF PILLARS) AT PERSEPOLIS. *The two outer figures with the fluted headdress are Persians, and the central figure with the domed headdress, short skirt and trousers, is an Elamite. Their rather rigid position with the spear held on the left toe may indicate some sort of salute. Darius the Great constructed this magnificent city, and Alexander the Great demolished it.*

come, I am Cyrus and I won for the Persians this empire. Therefore, do not begrudge me this little earth which covers my body" (*Life of Alexander:* vi. xxix. 5).

News of Cyrus' death reached Babylon late in 530 and his son Cambyses II (529–522) who had been reigning as king of Babylon ever since Cyrus captured that city, now became "King of the lands" and "King of kings," officially beginning his first year in Nisanu (March–April) in 529. Almost immediately the new monarch began the invasion of Egypt, and, with the conquest of this territory in 525, ruled the greatest empire the world had ever known. So far as it is possible to tell, Cambyses II continued Cyrus' policy of non-interference with the religious and social customs of his people.

When Cambyses, perhaps mentally and emotionally ill, committed suicide, a pretender, Gaumata the Magian, posed as Cambyses' brother (who had been murdered) and claimed the throne. Simultaneously, various provinces (conquered areas) seized this moment to attempt to gain independence. Gaumata, the usurper, was overcome by Darius I, the Great (521–486), an Achaemenid prince who recorded his achievement and his version of events leading up to his victory in the Behistun rock inscription carved into a high cliff above the main highway between Ecbatana (the capital city) and Babylon. A relief panel shows Darius with one foot on the neck of the prostrate Gaumata, behind whom are the captured leaders who attempted to

defect. What is more significant, perhaps, is the figure of the winged
disc with a human head, the symbol of Ahura Mazda, god of the
Zoroastrian faith. With Darius, Zoroastrianism became the religion of
the Persian court. There is no evidence of any official change in attitude toward the beliefs of the different groups constituting the empire,
but, as we shall see, there is ample evidence that some Persian concepts
made a lasting impression on Jewish religious thought.

The disrupting events associated with the death of Cambyses seem
to have been interpreted by two prophets, Haggai and Zechariah, as
signaling the collapse of the Persian empire and the time for the
establishment of the ideal state envisioned by the Exilic prophets.
With the fanatical zeal of those who have but one theme by which all
else is interpreted, they convinced Zerubbabel, who was by this time
governor of Judah, and Joshua, the high priest, and indeed, the whole
populace, that once Yahweh's temple was completed, Zerubbabel
would be crowned king of the new kingdom of the Jews which would
soon be established. But before turning to their persuasive message
preserved in their collected oracles we will consider the final portion of
the composite book of Isaiah, Chapters 56–66, which belong in the
period just before the time of Haggai and Zechariah.

TRITO-ISAIAH

The last eleven chapters of Isaiah, which, at times, reveal a close
affinity to the words of Deutero-Isaiah, appear to have been recorded
in the early post-Exilic period, possibly, in part, by Deutero-Isaiah's
disciples, and possibly, in part, by the great prophet himself. It is clear
that the temple was still in ruins (64:11) and that initial steps toward
rebuilding, perhaps the laying of foundations, had been taken (66:1).
Much work remained, including the repair of city streets (58:12) and
walls (60:10), and no significant restoration appears to have been
done in the outlying villages (61:4). It is clear that the provenance of
the writings is Judah.

No real unity or singleness of theme exists in these chapters, and
because smaller collections of poems can be recognized it is doubtful
that the work should be attributed to a single writer. Three poems of
promise in Chapters 60–62, and similar poems in 57:14–19 and 66:6–16
are alike in theme and structure, and so strongly resemble the work of
Deutero-Isaiah, particularly the servant songs, that it is reasonable to
suppose they may be the work of the great Jewish prophet of Babylon.
Attacks on leaders in 56:19–57:13 seem to be by a different hand with
no relationship to the foregoing passages. Broadly speaking, Trito-
Isaiah appears to be the work of several different authors, all deeply
affected by Deutero-Isaiah, using many of the same characteristic
expressions of their master, and employing a variety of literary types,
including laments and oracles of promise and condemnation, to convey
their messages. The chapters read as though the enthusiastic hopes of
Deutero-Isaiah were being reinterpreted in a new and different set-

ting, illustrating once again the pattern of continuing or progressive interpretation.[6]

Read Isa. 56:1–8

The immanence of the in-breaking of Yahweh into human affairs to fulfill the Exilic predictions of a new kingdom is expressed in the opening words of Trito-Isaiah, in particular in the word "soon." After stressing the importance of Sabbath observance and ethical behavior the prophetic writer, in a universalistic spirit akin to that of Deutero-Isaiah (cf. 44:5; 49:6), welcomed into the cultic community those eunuchs (excluded by Deuteronomic law, cf. Deut. 23:1) and foreigners (excluded by Ezekiel, cf. Ezek. 44:9) willing to accept Jewish covenant responsibilities and beliefs. Universalism is carried further in the statement that Yahweh's temple and the privilege of sacrificing upon the holy altar would be open to all who accepted the Jewish faith. Such a claim invalidated any attempt to exclude any group of Jews from the cultic community and perhaps may be interpreted as placing responsibility for proselytism upon the Jews who recognized themselves as central figures in the new kingdom.

Read Isa. 56:9–57:13

The next three oracles form a unity and include a diatribe against corrupt leaders (56:9–12), a lament over the plight of the righteous and a complaint about leaders (57:1–6), and a closing diatribe accompanied by a threat (57:7–13). The expressions of complaint in the first poem sound much like those of Jeremiah (cf. Jer. 2:20 ff.) or Ezekiel (cf. Ezek. 16:23 ff.) and appear to reflect conditions prior to the destruction of Jerusalem. On the other hand, there is no reason to suppose that the practices condemned by the earlier prophets automatically ceased in Judah with the Exile. In its present setting, the poem provides a fitting answer to those who ask why Yahweh delayed the establishment of the new kingdom. The prophet responded that ancient evils had not been eliminated, perhaps imitating and drawing upon an older oracle from the time of Jeremiah. The second poem laments the fate of the righteous whose deaths went unnoticed while the coming of the kingdom was delayed and the followers of non-Jewish cultic rites mocked. The final poem continues the theme of apostasy and concludes with the familiar threat of punishment for the wicked and reward for the righteous.

Read Isa. 57:14–21

The next oracle of promise with its hymnic addition (vss. 19–21) is so close in style and theme to Deutero-Isaiah that it might well be the work of that prophet who had returned to Jerusalem (cf. vss. 16 f. and Isa. 54:7 f.). The poem gives reassurance of Yahweh's forgiveness and intention to restore.

Read Isa. 58:1–59:15a

As we shall see, there is evidence in Zechariah (ch. 7) that, after the destruction of the temple, those left in Judah observed regular fasting rites as they periodically commemorated this event and mourned their loss. Isaiah 58:1–3 suggests that some questioned the validity of the fast inasmuch as Yahweh seemed to pay no attention to it. The prophet's answer laid bare the emptiness of mere outward ritual performance. Like earlier prophets, he demanded a change in ethical and moral conduct, not only as a witness to sincerity in the observance

[6] Cf. R. H. Pfeiffer, *Introduction to the Old Testament,* p. 480.

of the fast, but as a fulfillment of what Yahweh demanded of men before the kingdom would be established. Concern for the poor and oppressed is in the tradition of earlier prophecy. The stirring predictions provide clues as to the time of writing, for there is no indication that the temple has been rebuilt, and 58:12 implies that much restorative work was yet to be done. Oracles on the Sabbath (58:13–14) and on falsehood and unrighteousness (59:1–8) are followed by a penitential prayer of confession (59:9–15a) in which the community admits guilt and sin.

The next section contains two isolated fragments (59:15b–20, and 59:21) which may have been added to the preceding material for liturgical purposes. The confessions of guilt recited by the cultic community were followed by a statement of Yahweh's act of purgation (which had been experienced in the Exile). The promise of the new eternal covenant in Verse 21 (cf. Jer. 31:31–34) provides a triumphant and comforting conclusion to the liturgy.

Read Isa. 59:15b–21

The three poems of consolation and praise in Chapters 60–62 so closely resemble the writings of Deutero-Isaiah, that they may, like 57:14–21, be the work of the prophet from Babylon, supposing, as it has been suggested, that he accompanied those returned to Palestine. Otherwise, the poems are the work of a disciple whose style and vocabulary were deeply affected by his teacher.

Read Isa. 60–62

The opening call to witness a theophany, the revelation of the divine glory (*kabod*), suggests the rising of the sun, and perhaps the occasion is the New Year festival and the prophet is proclaiming the dawning of the Day of Yahweh. The approach of that day, when the promises of restoration would be fulfilled, can be seen in the return of the exiled people; perhaps new groups were arriving from different parts of the Persian empire to swell the numbers of those who first responded to the opportunity to return. From this immediate evidence the prophet moved into speculations about the future when more people would come, when the city wall would be rebuilt by foreigners (60:10), when the temple would be restored (60:13–14) and when the triumphant role of the Jew as the victor rather than the vanquished would be realized. The joy, prosperity and peace of the new-Jerusalem-to-come could only be appreciated by contrast with the present surroundings of the speaker (60:15 ff.), and his visions of the future were marked by supernatural glories to be experienced in an earthly paradise. As a messenger of Yahweh the King, the prophet stated his commission (61:1–3) and then recited the message heralding restoration, prosperity, peace and an ideal human community. Following the triumphant proclamation is an exultant song of joy (61:10–11).

In his jubilant revelation of what he had envisioned and in his effort to convey the magnificent transformation he sees taking place, the prophet gropes for terms to express the newness of what he sees. Jerusalem receives a new title: "the Zion of the Holy One of Israel" (60:14), with walls named "Salvation" and gates called "Praise" (60:18). The people are called "oaks of righteousness" and "the planting of Yahweh" (61:3). In contrast to the divorce imagery in Hosea the land is called "married" and the people "my delight is in her" (62:4). In fulfillment of Ezekiel's visions the people would be known as "the holy people," "redeemed of Yahweh," and Jerusalem as "sought out" (62:12). The revelation of Yahweh as "light" is to his chosen people and to the world. In recompense for the double cup of suffering experienced by Israel, the reward would also be doubled and witnessed by the nations (62:2). The oracle closes with a stirring call to rebuild Jerusalem in preparation for the coming of the exiles.

Read Isa. 63:1–6

A little poem (63:1–6) in dialogue form introduces Yahweh as judge of nations, and stresses that Yahweh alone would act as judge and executioner, rewarding or punishing as he deemed fit. The portrayal of Yahweh as god of avenging justice with garments stained with blood from the wrathful trampling of peoples is both terrifying and horrifying.

Read Isa. 63:7–65:25

The words of reassurance for Israel which follow the judgment poem take the form of a recitation of the past expressions of Yahweh's loyal love for his people (ch. 63). The people respond with a prayer for the realization of the theophany promised by the prophets (ch. 64). Something of the desperate situation of the people is revealed in the closing cry of the prayer beseeching Yahweh to act on behalf of his people.

Yahweh's response (65:1–25) presents the plight of a deity who almost begs his people for recognition only to be rejected, provoked and affronted. Thus it was, the poem explains, that the decision was made to punish but leave a remnant as the seed of the future. The faithful remnant were to be inheritors of the divine promise in the restored, redeemed community.

Read Isa. 66

The final chapter in the Trito-Isaiah collection has been widely discussed among scholars.[7] Some believe the chapter is composite, a collection of small oracular units with no binding unity. Others find larger units. It has been suggested that the setting is Babylonian, Egyptian or Judaean. Some think there is a rejection of the temple in the opening verses while others find only a rejection of corrupted attitudes and worship patterns.

There is no reason why the whole chapter could not have come from Judah in the post-Exilic period, perhaps from a slightly later time than the rest of Trito-Isaiah, when the rebuilding of the temple was underway. In contrast to the enthusiasm which we shall find expressed by Haggai and Zechariah, the writer of the opening verses believed that Yahweh did not need or want a temple, and that the building and rituals would only serve as food for man's pride. Moreover, there is a rejection of the promise implicit in Haggai's prediction that once the temple was restored the fortunes of the exiles would improve (cf. Hag. 1:2 ff.). Verse 3, directed against the cult and perhaps against syncretistic cult practices, seems to be intrusive, the work of a different hand. The announcement of the theophany, the divine judgment, and the restoration of the people (vss. 6 ff.) conforms to the ideas of other contributors to Trito-Isaiah, in stressing the event as an act of Yahweh, echatological in nature, designed to introduce with startling suddenness the golden age (cf. vss. 12–16). Verse 17, which picks up the

---

[7] For an excellent summary, cf. J. Muilenburg, "Isaiah, Chapters 40–66," *The Interpreter's Bible,* V, 757–60.

theme of Verse 3 and is perhaps by the same writer, also appears to be intrusive. The final oracles (18–21, 22–23) convey hope for the future, and in 22 and 23 the idea of a new creation, involving not only Judah and Jerusalem, but the entire world presses universal restoration to the uttermost. Apparently some editor, who believed that a note of judgment on apostates was needed, affixed the rather gruesome picture of the privilege of the redeemed to witness the eternal affliction by worm and fire of the bodies of sinners.

MAJOR CONCEPTS IN TRITO-ISAIAH

The contributors to Trito-Isaiah followed the teachings of Deutero-Isaiah in recognizing Yahweh as the sole deity beside whom there could be no other. The continuing violation of the covenant law by those who paid homage to false gods or who contaminated the cultic rites placed these individuals outside of the community of the redeemed. It was in the loyal remnant, swollen by others who accepted the covenant faith, that Yahweh placed the hope for the new tomorrow. In the past he had chosen Abraham and those who would descend from him; now he had chosen the new remnant. As old relationships were disestablished through apostasy, the new relationship would be safeguarded through a new act of Yahweh, more magnificent than anything ever before witnessed. As their forefathers had seen the dawning of an age of hope that had materialized into an empire only to be destroyed through sin, this new people could also see the breaking of a new age that offered greater and more wonderful possibilities than anything in the past. As the old kingdom came through a series of mighty acts of Yahweh, the new kingdom would be established, not through anything the people might do, but as a mighty creative act of Yahweh ushered in by a theophany and developing within the context of immediate history.

The words of these prophets were directed to Jews raised in exile and now united with the descendants of those who had remained in Palestine. For at least one contributor to III Isaiah there was room for all within the new kingdom, as well as for those who were yet to come. The only criterion for fitness to participate in the coming joys was fidelity to the covenant with the accompanying practice of mercy, understanding, compassion and human brotherhood.

HAGGAI

Apart from the designation "Haggai the prophet," little is told about this prophet. No record of his family or his prophetic call has been preserved, and even the analysis of his name, which is related to the word for "festival," has produced nothing more than the suggestion that he may have been born on a feast day.

His oracles, which because they refer to the prophet in the third person appear to have been gathered by an editor, provide us with a rather precise chronology, indicating that all were given within a four-month period between August and December, 520 B.C., which falls in the second year of Darius I. Unfortunately, some slight disarrangement appears to have occurred in these oracles and although four addresses are listed, some scholars think there are really five. Verse 1:15a seems to stand alone. By linking it with 2:15–19, the following sequence is obtained:

> 1:1–14, the first oracle.
> 1:15a; 2:15–19, the second oracle.
> 1:15b–2:9, the third oracle.
> 2:10–14, the fourth oracle.
> 2:20–23, the fifth oracle.

Read Hag. 1:1–14

The first oracle delivered in August, 520 at the time of the new moon festival (cf. Num. 28:11–15), explained that the famine afflicting the community had come as a punishment from Yahweh because the temple had not been built. The pronouncement stirred leaders and people to action. When just over three weeks had passed since the first oracle was given and the people were at work and the economic outlook had improved, Haggai was led to promise that from this time onward Yahweh would bless his people.

Read Hag. 1:15a; 2:15–19

Read Hag. 2:1–9

Nearly one month later the prophet was confronted by some older men who looked at what had been accomplished and complained that the present building could never measure up to Solomon's temple (cf. Ezra 3:10–13). Haggai replied that ultimately the glory of the second temple would outshine that of the first, for Yahweh would cause the nations to shower it with treasures.

Read Hag. 2:10–14

The precise meaning of the fourth oracle, delivered early in 519, is not clear. Literally, it appears to be concerned with a liturgical issue about the power of contamination possessed by clean and unclean objects. Many scholars think a much broader problem is involved: whether the Samaritans or people who had remained in the land and who now wished to participate in rebuilding the temple, being unclean or unpurged by exile, would contaminate the work—a socio-theological rather than purely liturgical issue (cf. Ezra 4:1–3). The priests' response, which is apparently in agreement with Haggai's, reveal how far this prophet was removed from the speaker whose words were preserved in Isa. 56:3 ff.

Read Hag. 2:20–23

The final oracle goes much further in its promises for the future than anything previously uttered and predicts the overthrow of Persia and the establishment of a new kingdom with Zerubbabel as king—a prophecy that failed to be realized. Doubtless the disturbed state of affairs in the Persian empire prompted Haggai to interpret events as signs of Yahweh's action on behalf of the Jews.

ZECHARIAH

Zechariah prophesied in the same period as the prophet Haggai, and the first eight chapters of Zechariah's work reveal the pressure of problems and issues similar to those found in Haggai's oracles. Chapters 9–14 belong in a different and later context, as we shall see, and represent the work of another person. These later chapters are often labeled Deutero-Zechariah (Chapters 1–8 are, therefore, Proto-Zechariah) and will be considered separately.

Like Haggai, Zechariah is mentioned in Ezra 5:1 and 6:14 where he is called a prophet, but in Nehemiah 12:16 he is listed among the priests. It is quite possible that, like Ezekiel who appears to have had great influence upon him, he was both. Because he is called "the prophet Zechariah" and is referred to in the third person, his work, like that of Haggai, was compiled by an editor. The edited work may be divided into three major sections, with several subsections:

I. Introduction, the initial address, November, 520, Ch. 1:1–6.
II. A. Eight Visions, all received in February, 519, Chs. 1:7–6:8.
      1:7–17, a vision of reconstruction.
      1:18–21, the four horns and the four blacksmiths.
      2:1–5, the man with the measuring line, and a word to Jews in Babylon (6–10).
      3:1–10, a vision of Joshua and the Satan.
      4:1–14, a vision of a seven-branched lampstand and two olive trees.
      5:1–14, a vision of a flying scroll.
      5:5–11, a vision of a woman in an ephah.
      6:1–8, a vision of the four horsemen.
  B. A truncated historical appendix, Ch. 6:9–15.
III. Closing oracles from December, 518, Chs. 7–8.

Shortly after Haggai had answered those who were making disparaging remarks about the new temple, Zechariah received his call to prophesy. No details of the commissioning of the prophet are given, but the message included a call for moral change and a warning drawn from past history. Yahweh's promise to return indicates that Ezekiel's prediction was not yet fulfilled (cf. Ezek. 43).

Read Zech. 1:1–16

In the first nocturnal vision of the three patroling angels and of the angel of Yahweh riding a red horse, a response is given to the inquiry about how long it would be before the new Israel was a reality. The answer was that Yahweh had returned to Jerusalem guaranteeing the rebuilding of the city and future prosperity.

Read Zech. 1:8–17

The vision of the four horns and four smiths predicted the destruction of Israel's conquerors. The four horns may symbolize the four corners of the earth.

Read Zech. 1:18–21

It is possible that Zerubbabel planned to rebuild the wall around Jerusalem. In the vision of a man with a measuring line (an inversion of the message of Amos 7:7 ff.), the prophet rejected this idea and promised divine protection for the city. Like Haggai, Zechariah appears to have believed that the building program ought to be concentrated in the temple.

Read Zech. 2:1–5

The proximity of the Day of Yahweh and the idealized Jewish kingdom led the prophet to urge those remaining in Babylon to come to Jerusalem.

Read Zech. 2:6–13

The scene of the next vision is the same court of heaven described in the prologue of Job. The Satan, the prosecutor, stood at the right

Read Zech. 3:1–10

hand of Yahweh, the judge. Before them was Joshua, the high priest, whose filthy clothes symbolized guilt and impurity—whether his own or the nation's is not indicated. It is possible that Joshua had been charged as unfit to perform priestly functions and was exonerated through the prophetic vision, or, perhaps, the vision provides a stylized picture of the rite of investiture of the high priest in which Joshua divests himself, symbolically, of his old character or perhaps of impurity and dons new robes representing his new office. The charge, given by Yahweh's angel, lists the high priest's duties.

The use of the term "Branch" for Zerubbabel (3:8) is related to Isa. 11:1 and Jer. 23:5 where the branch of the Davidic line is described as the ideal king. For the first time a term that has clear messianic overtones is applied to a living person in the post-Exilic age. The prophet was convinced that the new age was at hand. The identity of the "stone" set before Joshua is unclear.

Read Zech. 4:1-14

Verses 6b–10a interrupt the thought in Chapter 4 and therefore will be considered separately. The symbolism of this vision is confusing. The oddly formed lampstand represents the all-seeing eyes of Yahweh (vs. 10). The olive trees are Zerubbabel and Joshua divinely anointed for special responsibilities.

Verses 6b–10a, beginning with "This is the word of Yahweh" and ending with "the hand of Zerubbabel" constitute a promise that Zerubbabel would complete the building of the temple. Perhaps this verse is a further reply to the skeptics who troubled Haggai.

Read Zech. 5:1-4, 5-11

The next two visions are concerned with sin. The scroll announced doom for perjurers and thieves. The woman signified sin and for Zechariah the proper depository for sin was Babylon (Shinar)!

Read Zech. 6:1-8

The visions end as they began, with those who patrol the earth.

Read Zech. 6:9-15

The historical appendix records the crowning of the "Branch." Despite the fact that Joshua's name appears in Verse 11, the subsequent verses clearly refer to Zerubbabel, while the priest who stands by the throne in Verse 13 is Joshua. It is possible, as numerous scholars have suggested, that Zerubbabel's name originally stood in Verse 11, but was altered to Joshua by someone who, after Zerubbabel failed to fulfill prophetic expectations, desired to center hope for future messianic leadership in the high priesthood.

Read Zech. Chs. 7-8

In 518 a deputation from Bethel asked whether the annual mourning rite for the old temple should be continued because the new temple was nearly completed. Zechariah's response comes as a harsh rebuff, for he denied that the fasts had any significance at all, and like his eighth century predecessors, he stressed the importance of the moral life. His concluding remarks looked to the new Israel and the exalted position of the Jew.

MAJOR EMPHASES IN HAGGAI AND ZECHARIAH

Like Haggai, Zechariah provides important information about the struggle of the Jews to form a new state after the Exile and about problems associated with the construction of the second Temple. There can be little doubt that the two prophets were instrumental in bringing the temple to completion. With the new temple, Jewish religion was given a center for worship, an altar for sacrifice and a headquarters for administration and interpretation. In Babylon, Jewish scholars were to continue wrestling with the implications of the faith for centuries, but it was always to Jerusalem that the faithful looked as the center of the religion.

The effect of the teachings of the Exilic prophets, particularly Ezekiel, is readily recognizable, and belief was strong that fulfillment of Exilic prophecies of the ideal kingdom was at hand. With Haggai and Zechariah the concept of leadership begins to acquire overtones that later become messianic and eschatological, but it was not until the hopes for the future failed and the possibility of an earthly king ruling an ideal kingdom faded that messianic and eschatological themes developed. Zechariah and Haggai are really not concerned with eschatological (end of time) ideas, but rather with the new tomorrow that was so close that it was to follow the completion of the temple, a new day that was imminent in Zerubbabel, the "servant of Yahweh" (Hag. 2:23; Zech. 3:8), "Yahweh's signet" (Hag. 2:23), "the Branch" and the "Rod" (Zech. 3:8; 6:12 f.) of the root of David. The political ends and the national triumph to be experienced under Zerubbabel came not through the monarch but through mighty acts of Yahweh, and it was the conviction that this new day was at hand that give these prophetic oracles their sense of urgency and immediacy, reflections of the enthusiasm and driving power of the two prophets.

Zechariah's visions show how far advanced the development of angelology was in Jewish thought. Not only is there a court of heaven with the Satan, the accuser, familiar from the Joban prologue, but angelic horsemen and angelic interpreters are added. At this point, apart from the Satan, the angelic functionaries are anonymous and without titles.

Zechariah and Haggai give no indication of a change in the way in which the "word of Yahweh" was experienced, but they appear to have had experiences much like the early prophets (cf. Zech. 7:8; Hag. 1:2, 7, etc.). Like their predecessors, they believed that Yahweh revealed his intentions to his servants, the prophets.

A new answer is given to the problem of theodicy. Yahweh was about to act to reward the righteous, not in the distant future but immediately—a prediction that failed. There was no argument with the teachings of the Exilic prophets that the Exile was punishment for sin, a purging, and that a new community would arise. Haggai and Zechariah were convinced they were part of the ideal Israel.

THE COMPLETION OF THE TEMPLE

Whatever dreams Haggai and Zechariah may have entertained for the collapse of Persia were dispelled when, by 519, it became clear that Darius had put down all rebellions and was in control of a tightly consolidated empire. Although Darius made no effort to interrupt the building of the Jewish temple, the satrap Tattenai, governor of the "province beyond the river," attempted to intimidate the builders and

Read Ezra 5:3–6:22

dispatched a letter of inquiry to verify the Jewish claim of official permission to build. The letter went to the summer capital of the empire at Ecbatana and a search of the archives produced Cyrus' edict (Ezra 6:3–5), completely vindicating Jewish claims. Indeed, Darius went further and presented items for sacrifice and ordered Tattenai's province to provide a subsidy for the Jews.

In the spring of 515 the new temple, now the second temple, was completed. The dedication service (Ezra 6:17) did not reach the elaborate proportions of Solomon's (cf. I Kings 8:5), but these were difficult days for the Jews and the kingdom was much smaller. With the temple came renewed interest in liturgy and worship patterns which ultimately was to result in the compilation of a book of Psalms, as we shall see.

Hopes for the ideal kingdom under Zerubbabel faded, and the Jewish prince disappears from history, perhaps, as some have suggested, removed from office by the Persian king. It was one thing to rebuild a place for worship, but quite another to become the symbol of divine overthrow of the existing government. How the Jewish community was affected by the failure of the prophetic hopes is not recorded. In the absence of a king, the role of the high priest in the temple assumed greater significance as the community, which saw itself as a people of Yahweh, looked to this office for leadership. Meanwhile the political affairs of Judah were administered by a governor appointed by the Persians, although it is possible that the Jewish state was incorporated in a larger district with headquarters at Samaria.

INTERNATIONAL DEVELOPMENTS

Under Darius the empire prospered. From all parts exotic products flowed into central cities. Beautiful new buildings were erected. Communication was facilitated with road improvements, a canal was dug linking the Nile and the Red Sea, and better protection was provided for caravans. Banking and commerce were encouraged and a coinage system was developed for the empire.

Meanwhile, development and expansion were taking place in the Aegean world. Greek mercenaries had fought both for Cambyses and against him in the war with Egypt. Greek power had now become a threat to be reckoned with on Persia's western front. Finally, Darius engaged in war with the Greeks, suffering bitter defeat at Marathon in 490. When Darius died in 486, the Greek-Persian struggle was inherited by his son, Xerxes.

Xerxes, or Khshayarsha (485–465), who is probably the King Ahasuerus mentioned in Esther 4:6, had a troubled reign. A revolt in Egypt was followed by another in Babylon, and on this great city Xerxes released his anger, pulling down portions of the city wall and demolishing Esagila, the shrine of Marduk. The war with Greece went badly and Xerxes was forced to withdraw from Europe. In 465 he was assassinated.

In 460, Egypt, supported by Greece, revolted against Artaxerxes I

A TRIBUTE BEARER. *A stone relief from Persepolis depicting a tribute bearer. The rosette pattern at the top of the relief was a popular motif in Persian art.*

Longimanus (465–424), son of and successor to Xerxes, and it was not until 455 that Egypt again came under Persian rule. Darius II, son of Artaxerxes I by a Babylonian concubine, came to power following a civil war marked by numerous assassinations, and he reigned during a tumultuous time in Persian history. Satraps rebelled and weakened the empire. Fortunately for the Persians, the Greeks were embroiled in their own Peloponnesian war and were far too busy to take advantage of Persia's weakness.

Artaxerxes II Mnemon (404–359), the next monarch, struggled through civil war, intrigues, assassinations, and a revolt by which Egypt gained her long-sought independence. When Artaxerxes III (358–338) assumed the throne, his able but ruthless approach brought the loss of provinces by rebellion to a halt and made possible the repossession of some areas previously lost. When provinces along the Mediterranean revolted, the Persian army, greatly strengthened by Greek mercenaries, attacked and destroyed a number of coastal towns, including Sidon, and opened the way for an attack on Egypt. About this same time, Philip of Macedon was uniting Greece, and now Greek

A CARVING IN A DOORWAY AT PERSEPOLIS *portrays Darius the Great with the famous Persian short sword killing a winged monster. Whether or not there was cultic significance to this scene is not known, but perhaps it is meant to symbolize Darius' defeat of demonic forces.*

armies, strengthened by Macedonian forces, were poised for world conquest.

Artaxerxes III was murdered by a certain Bagoas, a eunuch, who exterminated most of the Achaemenid line before passing the kingship to Darius III Codommanus (335–331) because, as an imperfect man, Bagoas could not rule. Darius reconquered Egypt but was unable to withstand the tremendous military power of the new Greek-Macedonian forces led by Alexander the Great. Now the Hellenization of the Near East, already well under way, was to be greatly accelerated, as we will see in the next section on the Greeks. During the years of Persian rule, walls were erected around the city of Jerusalem, largely through the efforts of Nehemiah. Some information about Jewish life in Egypt comes from the Elephantine papyri, which were written during the reigns of Artaxerxes I and his son Darius II (423–405).

MALACHI

The book titled "Malachi" is the last in the prophetic collection known as "The Twelve," or Dodecapropheton (see Chart I). Despite the opening words, the author is unknown, and the superscription was appended by an editor who believed the words "my messenger" (*mal'akhi*) in 3:1 were a clue to the personal name of the prophet. The term translated "burden" or "oracle" (*massa'*) in 1:1 appears also in Zechariah 9–14 and it has been suggested that the four chapters of Malachi which are a unity, were at one time gathered in a larger collection incorporating the chapters now appended to the work of Zechariah.

There are indications within Malachi that suggest it was a product of the first half of the fifth century, possibly from the time of Artaxerxes I. The temple had been rebuilt (3:1, 10) and Judah was under a governor (1:8). Complaints about poverty, poor harvests and locust plagues (3:6 ff.) which, according to Haggai, ought to have ceased with the completion of the temple, and inferences of disappointment because of the delay in the coming of the ideal kingdom (2:17 ff.), point to a period after 515. The discussion of "mixed marriages," which were ultimately forbidden by Ezra, suggests that his legislation had not yet been passed.

Malachi's oracles are given in response to a series of questions, perhaps representing the give-and-take situation of the street orator. It appears that there were those who questioned current theological dogma, and in a manner similar to that employed by the wisdom school, argued from experience that prophetic utterances had been inaccurate.

The book appears to begin in the middle of a discussion. The prophet has been asked, "What evidence is there that Yahweh loves his people?" His response drew upon history, past and present. In the choice of Jacob and the rejection of Esau, Yahweh had expressed his love (election). When the Babylonians came, Edom had escaped the devastation that came to Judah by quietly submitting to Nebuchadrezzar and rejoicing in the fall of Jerusalem (cf. Ps. 137:7; Lam. 4:21 f.). Now Edom was under pressure from the Nabataeans, a people that had formerly lived by preying on caravans and was now moving toward a settled mode of life.[8] The Edomites, forced out of their homeland, migrated into the territory south of the Persian province of Judah, becoming the people known in later times as Idumeans. The Edomites were, according to Malachi, confident that they would recover, just as the Jews were recovering, but the prophet declares that their efforts would fail. The immediate and future problems confronting the Edomites were, for the prophet, evidence that Yahweh hated the descendants of Esau, just as the reestablishment of the Jews demonstrated divine love.

The priests, accused of despising Yahweh, asked "What have we done?" The prophet's response is an attack on the official cult and on the careless attitudes toward rules of purification and sacrifice, which reveal not only the priests' indifference to liturgical responsibilities but deliberate attempts to defraud Yahweh (cf. 1:14). The prophet described the functions of the priesthood: to guard divine knowledge and to instruct the people in Yahweh's way (2:7).

*Read Mal.
1:1–5*

*Read Mal.
1:6–2:9*

[8] Cf. article on "Petra" in *The Biblical World*, C. F. Pfeiffer (ed.) (Grand Rapids, Michigan: Baker Book House, 1966), pp. 443 ff.

Read Mal.
2:10–16
When the prophet condemned those who divorced their Jewish wives to marry aliens, the offenders argued that because all mankind was created by one God, all were children of one father, so that it didn't matter whether a woman was a Jewess or an alien (cf. Isa. 56:3 ff.). The prophet replied that divorce in itself was a violation of a covenant made before Yahweh, and marriage to one who worshiped another deity was violation of the Yahweh-Israel covenant.

Read Mal.
2:17–3:5
Those whom the prophet accused of wearying Yahweh asked "How?" The prophet described their mockery of Yahweh's righteousness (2:17), and responded to the issue about theodicy with the belief, current in his time, that the Day of Yahweh was at hand.

Read Mal.
3:6–12
Yahweh's call for the people to return was meaningless to those who believed they were fulfilling the law. But nonpayment of tithes and offerings robbed Yahweh, and the people were subsequently robbed as Yahweh failed to pour out material blessings.

Read Mal.
3:13–15
Those who challenged the accusation that they had spoken against Yahweh, were reminded of discouraging remarks about the futility of serving Yahweh.

Read Mal.
3:16–4:3
The prophet's demand for reform prompted some to pay heed to his words, and the prophet issued a stern warning about the Day of Yahweh.

Read Mal.
4:4–6
Because Malachi was placed at the end of the collection known as "The Twelve," it was necessary to add a note to close the total collection. The three-verse colophon reminding the reader to observe Mosaic law included an interpretation of Mal. 3:1, in which the messenger who would prepare Yahweh's way is identified as Elijah. According to II Kings 2:11, Elijah did not die but was miraculously transported to heaven in a whirlwind and was, therefore, capable of being sent back to earth to herald the Day of Yahweh.[9]

The book of Malachi is primarily concerned with the disintegration of cultic ritual and morals. The fact that the emphasis appears to fall more upon ritual underscores the importance of the temple and its cultus in the prophet's thinking as well as the impact of the teachings of Ezekiel, Haggai and Zechariah.

OBADIAH

The Nabataean displacement of Edomites prompted another Judaean, Obadiah, to express his feelings. The bitter memories of Edomitic behavior during the Babylonian conquest are revealed in the stinging words of what can best be identified as a hymn of hatred.

The bulk of Obadiah is generally placed in the first half of the fifth century. References to the sacking of Jerusalem (vss. 1 ff.) and to the same disruption of the Edomites mentioned in Malachi suggest the post-Exilic period. The intense nationalism is characteristic of other writings from fifth century Judah. The similarity between vss. 1–9 and

---

[9] Elijah subsequently became the forerunner of the Messiah, and in the New Testament both John the Baptizer (Luke 1:17; Matt. 11:14; 17:12 f.) and Jesus (Mark 8:28; Matt. 16:14; Luke 9:19) were identified as Elijah.

Jer. 49:7–22 has led some scholars to suggest that both prophets adapted a pre-Exilic and anti-Edom hymn to their own use.[10] The late R. H. Pfeiffer dated the last three verses of the poem in the fourth century,[11] but they can just as easily be placed in the fifth century and attributed to Obadiah.

The first nine verses of this poem mock the Edomites for the failure of their sources for security—remoteness, alliances, national strength. Now they have suffered a fate not unlike that which had come upon Judah in 586. According to Obadiah, the Nabataean attack was divine punishment for the role of the Edomites during the Babylonian conquest. Like other post-Exilic writers of this period, Obadiah believed that the Day of Yahweh was near when all aliens would suffer the wrathful punishment of the deity and only Judah would be saved to take possession of and rule in the new expanded kingdom. The fact that this poem was preserved probably indicates that it represented more than the view of a single individual and portrayed what was a rather common interpretation of events.

[10] R. H. Pfeiffer, *Introduction to the Old Testament*, p. 585; J. A. Thompson, "The Book of Obadiah: Introduction," *The Interpreter's Bible*, VI, 858.

[11] R. H. Pfeiffer, *Introduction to the Old Testament*, p. 586.

25

Life and Literature
of the Late Period

THE next major project facing the people of Jerusalem was the rebuilding of the wall of the city. Zechariah's dramatic claim that Yahweh would protect the city with a wall of fire (Zech. 2:5) was an inspiring ideal, but in real life a city without a physical wall was open to any wild animal or band of marauders that cared to enter by day or night and, in the event of war, offered no protection from the enemy. As in the days of the erection of the second temple, dynamic and determined leadership was needed to accomplish the rebuilding. Such leadership was found in Nehemiah.

THE WORK OF EZRA AND NEHEMIAH

For information about Nehemiah and his biblical contemporary, Ezra, we are dependent upon the fourth century work of the Chronicler. Although the records were compiled some time after the reported events occurred, there is reason to believe that the Chronicler incorporated accurate "personal diary" material into the narrative. Neh. 1:1–7:73a, the so-called "Nehemiah Memoirs" (and perhaps 13:4–31), have been accepted by scholars without serious challenge as based on genuine autobiographical data from Nehemiah. On the other hand, the so-called "Ezra Memoirs" (Ezra 7–10; Neh. 7:73b–10) have been questioned. If genuine Ezra material is contained in these chapters, it has been so completely overwritten by the Chronicler that attempts to extract the original work are fruitless.

Chronological difficulties confront those who attempt to unravel the sequence of events of this period. Biblical tradition places Ezra before Nehemiah. Ezra, a priest and scribe from Babylon, led a group of exiles to Jerusalem (Ezra 7:1–5). The events recorded in Ezra 7–10 are dated in the seventh year of Artaxerxes (cf. 7:7 f.), and Nehemiah's work is placed in the twentieth year (cf. Neh. 1:1; 2:1). If Artaxerxes I Longimanus (464–424) is meant, then the first date would be 458/7 and the second, 445/4. If Artaxerxes II Mnemon (404–358) was the king, the dates would be 398/7 and 385/4.

There is reason to suppose that Nehemiah preceded Ezra. Ezra, as an expert in the law of Yahweh, left Babylon with the expressed purpose of interpreting that law to the Jerusalemites (Ezra 7:10), but there is no record of Ezra reading the law to the people until Nehemiah arrived, thirteen years later (Neh. 8:1–8). Why did he wait so long? It can be argued that the event reported in Nehemiah refers to a second reading, a repetition of an earlier ceremony, but the text does not indicate this. Ezra's prayer refers to the wall of Jerusalem (Ezra 9:9) which was not erected until Nehemiah's time, although it has been suggested that a low wall previously built around the city had been destroyed and that it was this wall that Nehemiah rebuilt (cf. Ezra 4:23 f.; Neh. 1:3).[1] But there is additional evidence. The census list compiled by Nehemiah (Neh. 7:1–73a) fails to include those who returned to Jerusalem with Ezra, whose names are given in Ezra 8:1–20, and there is no indication from the names mentioned in Neh. 1–7 that the Ezra group participated in the rebuilding of the wall. Nehemiah made efforts to increase the sparse population of Jerusalem (Neh. 7:4; 11:1–2), but Ezra seems to have worked in a flourishing city (Ezra 9:4; 10:1). Finally, it seems strange that Artaxerxes would have appointed two officials to Judah, giving each about the same amount of authority and status; and what is more strange is that these two officials, both committed to the welfare of Jerusalem and Judah, appear to have ignored one another within the limited confines of Jerusalem.[2]

A number of solutions have been proposed for the sequence problem. One that is widely accepted suggests that Nehemiah came under Artaxerxes I Longimanus (465–424) or in 445/4, and that Ezra came under Artaxerxes II Mnemon (404–358), or in 398/7. It has also been suggested that the Chronicler simply reversed the dates and that Nehemiah came in the seventh year of Artaxerxes I or in 458/7, and Ezra in the twentieth year, or 445/4. It is possible that the seventh year in Ezra 7:7 should read the "thirty-seventh year," or 428/7.[3] It must be admitted that the dating issue is still unresolved. The accumulated evidence indicates that Nehemiah preceded Ezra, and we shall proceed on that premise without attempting to provide precise dates for Ezra, although placing him in the reign of Artaxerxes II in 398/7 seems, at this moment, to be the best solution.[4]

Some help for dating Nehemiah's visit is found in the mention of his principal opponent Sanballat (Neh. 2:10, 19; 41:7), governor of Samaria, and Sanballat's sons in the Elephantine papyrus dated in 408[5] (discussed below). From the tone of the letter, it would appear that Sanballat was still governor of Samaria, but was somewhat aged, and that business arrangements were in the hands of his sons.

---

[1] R. A. Bowman, "Ezra: Exegesis," *The Interpreter's Bible*, III, 649 ff.

[2] Cf. *Ibid.*, pp. 562–563 for a more extensive list of sequence problems.

[3] Cf. *Ibid.*, pp. 563, 624; Jacob M. Myers, *Ezra-Nehemiah*, The Anchor Bible (Garden City, New York: Doubleday and Company, Inc., 1965), pp. xxxvi ff. for a more detailed development of arguments.

[4] Cf. Eissfeldt, *The Old Testament: An Introduction*, pp. 552 ff.

[5] Cf. *ANET*, p. 492; *DOTT*, pp. 260–265.

Therefore, it would appear that Nehemiah came to Judah in the twentieth year of Artaxerxes I Longimanus (465–424), or in 445/4.

Read Neh. 1:1–7:4

Nehemiah, a descendant of Jewish exiles in Babylon, lived in Susa, a Persian royal city, and was employed in the court of King Artaxerxes I as the royal cup-bearer, an office of considerable importance and responsibility insofar as the officeholder protected the king from potential poisoning. A delegation of Judaeans came with Nehemiah's brother, Hanani, to report on the sad condition of Jerusalem. When Artaxerxes was informed, he was most generous, and Nehemiah was given authority and aid to build a wall around Jerusalem. The jealous animosity of the officials in Samaria (possibly because once again they lost control of Judah), and in the Ammonite province ("across the river"), which had delayed other building programs in Jerusalem, proved to be undiminished. Sanballat of Samaria and Tobiah from the Transjordan province,[6] aided by Geshem from Arabia hinted that Nehemiah had anti-Persian motives, a suggestion that could have had serious consequences in the light of the rebellion of Persian provinces.

Under Nehemiah's leadership the walls were built,[7] but not without threats from Sanballat, Tobiah, the Arabians and probably opponents from Ashdod, which necessitated armed protection for the workers. Economic difficulties, similar to those mentioned in Malachi 3:5–15, added to the problems, and conditions became so severe that Nehemiah did not accept the stipends legitimately belonging to his office lest he place further burdens on the people. Social inequality and increasing pressures on the poor by the rich demanded corrective measures which Nehemiah was able to bring about. According to Neh. 6:15, the wall was completed within fifty-two days, but another tradition, preserved in Josephus (Antiquities, XI:v:8), reports that two years and four months were required.

Read Neh. 13:4–31

In 433, after serving twelve years as governor of Judah, Nehemiah returned to Persia. Within a year or two (the dates are not certain) he was reappointed to Judah. During his brief absence, Eliashib, probably the same man who was high priest (Neh. 3:1), had cleared a storage room within the temple precincts for the special use of Nehemiah's old enemy, Tobiah the Ammonite. Moreover, tithes due the Levites for temple service had not been paid and Sabbath laws had been completely relaxed. In short order Nehemiah had Tobiah ousted from the temple and instituted action to have tithes paid and Sabbath regulations observed. What appears to have disturbed the governor most was intermarriage between the Jews of Judah and their neigh-

Read Neh. 10

bors, and the resultant hybridization of the language. A document preserved in Nehemiah 10 but attributed by the Chronicler to Ezra (see Neh. 9) may be an accurate record of a formal agreement prepared

[6] Both Sanballat and Tobiah appear to have been Yahwists. Cf. J. Bright, *A History of Israel*, p. 366.

[7] The descriptions given in the book of Nehemiah are important for studies of the ancient city of Jerusalem. Cf. M. Burrows, "Nehemiah 3:1–28 as a Source for the Topography of Ancient Jerusalem," *Annual of the American Schools for Oriental Research*, XIV (1934), 115–140; M. Avi-Yonah, "The Walls of Nehemiah," *Israel Exploration Journal*, IV (1954), 239–248; K. Kenyon, "Excavations in Jerusalem 1961–1963," *BA*, XXVII (1964), 34–52.

by Nehemiah and forced on the Judaeans, by which the very reforms discussed in Nehemiah's Memoirs (Neh. 13:4–31) were instituted. The fact that the document is not included in the Memoirs may indicate, as M. Noth has suggested,[8] that it came to the Chronicler's hand as a separate source, perhaps from official files.

The information pertaining to Nehemiah's role as governor is scanty and the Chronicler passes over many years in silence. It is clear that when Nehemiah first came to Jerusalem, he followed a cautious but wise policy of investigation before action. As one committed to the preservation of the national identity of the Jews, he realized that only practices of exclusiveness and isolationism, insofar as they were possible within the framework of Persian government, would maintain Judah as a province and the Jews as a people. The wall about the city afforded security and protection, as well as a sense of identity. Because intermarriage tended to break down Jewish identity by introducing into the Jewish home, society and business, the dialects of the stronger and more affluent peoples around Judah, Nehemiah emphasized marriage among Jews and sought to preserve the national tongue. Casual indifference to Sabbath laws and tithes weakened the binding force of religion, and thus Nehemiah was in close agreement with those rehabilitated exiles who stressed cultic observance and frowned upon religious or family intermingling with non-Jews. As a governor, he seems to follow the pattern established by Zerubbabel, but without the overtones of kingship.[9]

EZRA

The story of Ezra is contained in the so-called "Ezra Memoirs" which begin in Ezra 7–10 and conclude in Neh. 7:73b–10:39. The genealogical table (Ezra 7:1–5) reveals that Ezra was of a priestly family and that he was a scribe and an expert in the law of Yahweh. As a member of the learned society in Babylon, he was undoubtedly skilled in legal interpretation as well as writing. It is possible that he held some official post within the Persian court.[10] His authority and mission, clearly outlined in the copy of the Aramaic letter in Ezra 7:12–26, permitted the return of more exiles and empowered Ezra to investigate Jewish cultic law and appoint officials. Funds for sacrifice and sacred vessels for worship were provided. According to the Chronicler, Ezra became involved in the problem of mixed marriages by priests and Levites almost immediately. Ezra's demands went much further than those of Nehemiah. Under Nehemiah, the people had agreed to avoid

Read Ezra 7:1–10:17

[8] Martin Noth, *A History of Israel,* p. 329.

[9] It is possible that Nehemiah, as cup-bearer to the king, was a eunuch and therefore would not have been acceptable as king, even if he had had such ambitions. Cf. "cup-bearer" in W. Corswant, *A Dictionary of Life in Bible Times* (New York: Oxford University Press, 1960); or in *The Interpreter's Dictionary of the Bible.*

[10] Cf. Myers *Ezra Nehemiah,* pp. 60–61 for a discussion of possible offices and for a different analysis; cf. Noth, *The History of Israel,* pp. 331 f.

further intermarriage by promising not to permit their children to marry outside of the Jewish inner community (Neh. 10). Ezra demanded divorce of wives and abandonment of children of intermarriage (Ezra 10:18 ff.).

On a New Year's Day, Ezra and his Levitical helpers read and interpreted the law to the assembled people of Jerusalem, probably reading in Hebrew and interpreting in Aramaic. Just what "law" was involved has been debated, and it cannot be known whether the reading included Deuteronomy, the Holiness Code, or all the revisions made by the priestly writers (P), which would suggest the completed Torah, or just some of the P revisions.[11] Subsequently, the people participated in the festival of booths.[12] The penitential prayer (9:5–37) placed in Ezra's mouth by the Chronicler reviews the history of the Jews, stresses election and salvation motifs, and terminates in a rite of covenant renewal (9:38). Possibly the prayer is a psalm borrowed from an older collection by the Chronicler, and the covenant pledge is simply a transition device to lead into Chapter 10.

Ezra's importance was in strengthening the unifying power of the faith that gave the Jew his identity. In providing the people with an understanding of their religious heritage and the requirements of cultic law, he made adherence to the faith and obedience to the law rest upon comprehension and appreciation as much as upon official decree.

THE JEWS OF ELEPHANTINE

From the Persian fortress known as Yeb on the island of Elephantine at the first cataract of the Nile have come a considerable number of private and public papyri written in Aramaic.[13] Some of these documents afford an intimate glance into the life of a colony of Jews who lived in this military outpost of the Perisan empire. Correspondence between the Jewish leaders in Yeb and Bagoas, the governor of Judah, reveal that when Cambyses invaded Egypt (525) the Elephantine Jews possessed a temple of Yahweh (spelled Yahu or Yaho) with five entrances of hewn stone, stone pillars, a cedar roof, doors hinged with bronze, utensils of gold and silver and an altar of sacrifice. This temple was destroyed in 410 at the instigation of the priests of the ram-headed god Khnum. In a letter to Bagoas requesting permission to rebuild the temple, reference was made to the sons of Sanballat, governor of Samaria, apparently the same official with whom Nehemiah had come into conflict. No written reply from Bagoas was found, but a record of his words as reported by an emissary grants permission to rebuild the temple with an altar for incense and meal offerings, but no mention is made of an altar for sacrifice. The temple was restored and remained in use until it was again destroyed, probably by Pharaoh Nepherites I (399–393).

11 Cf. Bowman, *op. cit.*, pp. 773 f.

12 Neh. 8:13–18; cf. Lev. 23:39 ff. and note the variations.

13 See *ANET*, pp. 491 ff. for selected documents.

Some evidence of religious syncretism appears in a "treasurer's report" of temple contributors recording funds collected for Yahweh, Eshembethel and Anat-bethel or Anat-Yahu. There is also reference to "the gods." The element "Bethel" in two of the names appears as a divine name in Aramaean contexts between the seventh and fourth centuries, and the name Anat is the name of a Canaanite goddess in the Ugaritic pantheon. No information about beliefs concerning these deities has been found. Clearly, these Elephantine Jews were not governed by Deuteronomic regulations calling for a single sanctuary in Jerusalem and demanding worship of Yahweh alone.

In addition to providing information about the theological deviations of this particular group of Jews, the Elephantine materials have aided in fixing Nehemiah's chronology. The mention of the sons of Sanballat in a document written in 410, assuming that Sanballat is the same individual mentioned in Nehemiah's memoirs, places Nehemiah in the reign of Artaxerxes I and dates his visit to Jerusalem in 445/4.

RUTH

There were those who disagreed with the teachings that tended to divide the Jewish community by denigrating marriages between Jews and non-Jews, and by seeking to isolate Jewish life and religion from immediate intercourse with the non-Jewish world. Reaction against the particularists was not expressed through polemics or forthright statements of opposition so far as we can tell, but rather through short stories or *novellen* as they are labeled by form critics. This literature of response quietly communicated its points of view and taught its lessons.

One such story, the book of Ruth, is set in the period of the Judges. **Read Ruth** From the opening sentence, which is in classical story-telling style, the narrative is a model of excellence. The opening six verses set the stage for all that is to follow, recording the migration of a Hebrew family from Bethlehem in time of famine, the marriage of the two Hebrew sons to Moabite women, and the death of the male members of the group. The remainder of Chapter 1 records the return to Bethlehem of Naomi, the bereaved wife and mother, with Ruth, her Moabite daughter-in-law. The magic of the narrator's art is clearly seen in Ruth's statement in 1:16–17, which has been recognized as one of the most beautiful expressions of human affection and relationship. In the second chapter the meeting of Ruth and Boaz, a relative of the dead Hebrew males, is explained and in the next two chapters Ruth wins Boaz' love and marries him. The male child born from this marriage is received as the child of Naomi and as the one through whom the name of Ruth's deceased father-in-law, and hence her dead husband, would be carried on. According to an appendage, the child was the grandfather of King David.

It is widely recognized that the genealogical details in 4:17b–22 are secondary, and are probably drawn from the same source as the Davidic lineage in I Chron. 2:4–15. The story, without the appendage,

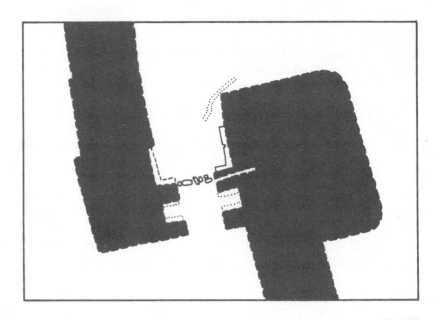

A SKETCH OF THE GATE AREA OF TELL EN-NASBEH. *The city gate was the business area of the city. All communication with the outside world passed through it and on the benches outside of the gate the elders sat as they reached decisions. The gate area of Tell en-Nasbeh was paved and provided with a drain to aid in drying the area after a rain. The gates, probably made of timber, pivoted in stone sockets, and when closed rested against a low line of stones placed across the threshold. A slot, which possibly accommodated an iron bar, was found in the main tower and it is assumed that at night this bar was pulled into place to reinforce the upper portions of the closed gate. The small rooms within the gate were guardrooms. The overlapping walls and massive tower gave the defenders a decided advantage over attackers who would be exposed on both sides when they rushed the gate.*

It was to the elders at the gate that Boaz took the problems involved in his marriage to Ruth (Ruth 4:1 ff.). Other references to the gate as a place of business, judgment and gossip are Deut. 22:24 f.; 25:7 ff.; Amos 5:10, 12, 15; Ps. 69:12.

may have originated in the pre-Exilic period, perhaps in the time of the Judges, circulating in oral form before being written down. As such, the story is an idyll, recording the friendship of two women, one Hebrew and the other Moabite, who have lost their husbands and relating how they managed to preserve the family name. The presence of Aramaisms and words associated with post-Exilic Judaism, plus the addition of the genealogy, suggest that the story was recorded in its present form in the post-Exilic period, possibly near the end of the fifth century.

Numerous suggestions have been made about the meaning of the story. It has been described as a tale told for enjoyment, and there can be no doubt about this evaluation. The fact that Ruth was a proselyte (1:16 f.) has led some scholars to suggest that the story teaches that foreign women could be blessed by Yahweh, and it must be agreed that this point is made in the account. The most common understanding of the purpose of the editor in formulating the story, as we have it, is that it constitutes a protest against the prohibition of marriages between Jews and non-Jews. At a time when the arguments were loudest, the quiet voice of the story-teller pointed out that David, the prototype of the ideal king, was descended from a mixed marriage. Surely if such a one as David had come from such a union, all mixed marriages could not be bad! To make this point, the unknown editor-teacher only had to identify the Boaz of the Ruth-Naomi story as the Boaz in David's ancestry, and to accomplish this it was only necessary to add a portion of David's genealogical table.[14]

The Levirate marriage, originally binding upon brothers in a family (Deut. 25:5–10),[15] was extended to include the next-of-kin, but the obligation in this case was not binding, as Ruth 4:3–6 reveals. Boaz became the *go'el*, the redeemer, when he acquired the family land and Ruth, declaring his intention to perpetuate the name of Ruth's dead husband and father-in-law.

JONAH

Like the book of Ruth, the story of Jonah is a *novelle* telling of a reluctant prophet, who demonstrated his unfitness for his task by attempting to flee from the responsibility of preaching impending doom and urging repentance upon the Assyrians of Nineveh. The hero, Jonah ben Amittai, is an eighth century prophet of the northern kingdom who was active during the reign of Jeroboam II (II Kings 14:25). The opening chapter of the book records Jonah's attempt to flee from Yahweh. In the second chapter Jonah is transported to Nineveh in the belly of a giant fish. The third chapter tells of Jonah's successful mission which, to his dismay, resulted in total repentance and the sparing of the city. In the final chapter the angry, sulking prophet is rebuked by God and shown the littleness of his attitude.

Read Jonah

Despite the pre-Exilic setting there is evidence that the story was written in the post-Exilic period.[16] The language, like that of Ruth, is characterized by Aramaisms and Hebrew vocabulary and style common in post-Exilic writings. Nineveh is described as though it were a great city of the past (3:3) and in exaggerated terms. The writer employs the universalistic spirit of Deutero-Isaiah which is not found in pre-Exilic literature. It is possible that some facets of the story may have been in circulation earlier, but this cannot be known for sure. In its present form, the writing appears to fit best into the post-Exilic

14 In a very cogent argument, it has been suggested that David really was of Moabite descent and that the book of Ruth was designed to explain the nature of that relationship and to demonstrate that David was truly an Israelite. Cf. Gillis Gerleman, *Ruth*, Biblicher Kommentar, Altes Testament, XVIII (Neukirchen Kreis Moers: Neukirchener Verlag, 1960), 5 ff. For a cultic explanation, cf. W. E. Staples, "The Book of Ruth," *American Journal of Semitic Languages and Literatures,* LIII (1937), 145–157.

15 In the story of Tamar and Judah, the father-in-law was involved; cf. Gen. 38.

16 Yehezkel Kaufmann, *The Religion of Israel,* pp. 282–286, maintains the eighth century date. For an Exilic dating, cf. W. Harrelson, *Interpreting the Old Testament,* pp. 359 ff.

period, about the end of the fifth or the early part of the fourth centuries.

Despite the use of an historical figure as the hero, the account is fiction, not history. The fictional nature can be recognized in the account of Nineveh's repentance, which included kings, nobles, the populace and animals—all fasting and wearing sackcloth (3:6–8)! The attempt of a man to flee a universal God by going to sea, and the delivery of that man by fish, cannot be accepted as anything but delightful, entertaining story-telling, designed to amuse even as it informed.

The unity of the work has been questioned, for 2:3–9 interrupts the normal flow from 2:1 to 2:10. The prayer-psalm fits Jonah's situation only in the most general way, and no reference is made to his plight in the fish's belly. It is possible that the writer of the story inserted the psalm, but it is more likely that a later editor added what he deemed to be an appropriate prayer.

As a good story-teller, the author's purpose was to hold his audience as he made his point. In reaction against those who waited with longing for Yahweh to establish the kingdom of the Jews and punish Israel's enemies, the author of Jonah called upon his countrymen to respond to the teachings of Deutero-Isaiah and his followers and to recognize their responsibility to their fellow men. Yahweh was a universal deity and was concerned about those ouside of the chosen people, wishing to extend divine compassion to all, including Israel's enemies. To dramatize the extent of Yahweh's concern, the writer chose Nineveh, conqueror and destroyer of the northern kingdom and hated oppressor of Judah—a safe choice since the power of both Assyria and Nineveh had been broken. Jonah represented Judah, called by Yahweh through Deutero-Isaiah to be a light to the nations, but refusing to be concerned about anything or anyone not Jewish and unhappy because Yahweh had not punished or destroyed their enemies. The author's missionary appeal is made without any zealousness for proselytizing, but rather out of compassion for mankind and in the conviction that Yahweh as a deity "slow to anger and abounding in *ḥesed*" (4:2) wished to forgive any who would repent. Repentance of those outside Judah could come only when the Jews accepted their responsibility for bearing witness of Yahweh's gracious and redeeming mercy beyond their own borders and outside of their own family.

26

The Great Documents
of the Persian Period

NOW the second temple stood within the walled city of Jerusalem. Cultic rites, conducted by the Levites, included sacrifice, offerings, prayers and songs. Through the work of Ezra, the people had acquired a new understanding of the law of Yahweh and the nature of the covenant. We can assume that temple literature included scrolls of prophetic oracles, the combined JE epic, the Deuteronomic history and probably a collection of hymns, prayers and liturgical data.

Nevertheless new material was needed. The history of the monarchy, which had started in Solomon's time and had been reworked by the Deuteronomist, had not been extended beyond the middle of the Exilic period. Now, in the Persian period, princes from the Davidic line had lost the privilege of government and the circumstances called for a new understanding and a new interpretation of the past. The author known as the Chronicler, whose writings include I and II Chronicles, Ezra and Nehemiah, accomplished the task of rewriting and up-dating the history.

As in Solomon's time the J writer had combined creation mythology and election and salvation traditions, and as in Jeroboam's day the E writer had done the same for the northern kingdom, now, in the light of the experiences of the Exile, a new interpretation of the combined JE sagas was needed. This need was met by the addition of the so-called P writings. The combined work was linked to the book of Deuteronomy to form the completed Torah.

The third literary effort in the period was necessitated by the completion of the temple and consisted of a collection of prayers and hymns or psalms designed for worship. The editor of the book of Psalms combined older collections, individual prayers and newer hymns into one massive unit for temple use, and this collection, together with some additions made shortly afterward, constitutes our present book of Psalms.

To these great literary works from the Persian period we will now turn, remembering that in every instance the writers or compilers made use of older materials. That which was added or omitted was part of an effort to keep relevant traditions that had meaning for the cult and the nation by concentrating on that which was seen to be central. In other words these writers in the Persian period engaged in the responsible task of continuing or progressive interpretation.

The Deuteronomic interpretation of the nation's past did not go beyond the middle of the Exilic period. Now, in the post-Exilic era, it was deemed necessary to extend that account and to review history from the point of view of more recent theological developments. It has been argued that the Chronicler had no intention of rewriting the history of Judah, but only wished to draw lessons in a homiletic or midrashic[1] fashion for the benefit of the community.[2] However, in a sense, all history writing is interpretation, and we have noted that the Deuteronomic history was an interpretation of events in the light of the Deuteronomist's "theology of history." The Chronicler continued this process from a somewhat different theological angle of vision.

It has been stated previously that the work of the Chronicler included I and II Chronicles and Ezra and Nehemiah. The arguments supporting this contention include the recognition of the flow of II Chron. 36:22–23 into Ezra 1:1–4 and the similarity of language, literary style, historical interest and theological outlook in the two books of Chronicles and Ezra-Nehemiah. In all documents the writer revealed his deep interest in that which pertained to the temple, the Levitical priesthood, temple singers and worship. There is a consistent emphasis on the importance of genealogies and statistics. Finally, the narratives provide a continuum despite the disrupted order of the Ezra-Nehemiah sequence, and present a unified statement of Jewish history up to the time of Ezra.[3] The uniformity of language, style and outlook suggests that the entire work is the product of a single writer, one steeped in Jewish history and cultic life, perhaps a priest or scribe. The affinities of style and outlook between the Ezra memoirs and the work of the Chronicler, first noted by C. C. Torrey,[4] have led a number of scholars, including W. F. Albright, to conclude that Ezra was the Chronicler.[5]

Whether or not one agrees that the Chronicler was Ezra there is growing accord among scholars that the writing is from the Persian period and that arguments for a date in the Greek period[6] can be

[1] The term "midrash" comes from a Hebrew root meaning "to search" or "to investigate"; therefore, the purpose of midrashic study was to seek out and reveal the inner meaning of biblical texts. Midrash dealing with legal texts of the Bible is called "Halachah"; midrash concerned with non-legal sections is labeled "Haggadah" and is homiletic. Chronicles belongs to the latter category.

[2] J. M. Myers, *I Chronicles*, The Anchor Bible (Garden City, New York: Doubleday & Company, Inc., 1965), p. xviii. See also G. von Rad, "The Levitical Sermon in I and II Chronicles" in *The Problem of the Hexateuch and Other Essays*, trans. E. W. T. Dicken (London: Oliver and Boyd, 1966), pp. 267 ff.

[3] For a detailed analysis of the unity of language and style, cf. S. R. Driver, *An Introduction to the Old Testament*, new edition, revised 1913 (New York: Charles Scribner's Sons, 1913), pp. 525 ff. (now in a Meridian paperback).

[4] C. C. Torrey, *Ezra Studies* (Chicago: University of Chicago Press, 1910), pp. 238 ff.

[5] W. F. Albright, *The Biblical Period*, p. 54.

[6] Pfeiffer, *Introduction to the Old Testament*, pp. 811 f.

maintained only with the greatest difficulty. The language of the book is Hebrew strongly influenced by Aramaic and with numerous Persian terms characteristic of the Persian period but which tended to die out during the Greek era. The Aramaic section of Ezra employs the same vocabulary, idioms and spelling forms as the Elephantine papyri and is, therefore, from the same time. Furthermore, the last Persian king mentioned is Darius II (423–405), and the Davidic genealogy in I Chron. 3:10–24 is traced up to the seventh generation from Jehoiachin (598/586); allowing twenty-five years for a generation, we arrive at a date roughly between 420 and 400. It would appear that the Chronicler wrote about 400 or shortly thereafter.[7]

Like other early historians, the Chronicler drew on sources[8] and some of these can be recognized. It is clear that he had before him copies of I and II Samuel and I and II Kings that were substantially the same as our present versions and that he did not hesitate to reproduce large portions of the earlier work.[9] He drew also from the "memoirs" of Ezra and Nehemiah and from a long list of official documents which he identifies: "The Books of the Kings of Judah and Israel" (II Chron. 16:11; 25:26; 32:32) or "The Books of the Kings of Israel and Judah" (II Chron. 27:7; 35:27; 36:8), "The Book of the Kings of Israel" (II Chron. 20:34), and a source titled "The Midrash of the Book of Kings" (II Chron. 24:27). He used prophetic material now lost to us but attributed to Samuel (I Chron, 29:29), Gad (I Chron. 29:29), Nathan (II Chron. 9:29), Iddo (II Chron. 9:29; 12:15; 13:22) and an unknown prophet (II Chron. 33:19). He was fascinated by what he could demonstrate by genealogical tables (cf. I Chron. 1–9). These varied traditions were woven into a connected narrative covering history from Adam to Ezra. The entire work can be simply outlined as follows:

I Chronicles
    Chapters 1–9, genealogical tables.
    Chapter 10, the death of Saul.
    Chapters 11–29, the Davidic period.
II Chronicles
    Chapters 1–9, the Solomonic period.
    Chapters 10–25, the Divided Kingdom up to Josiah's reform.
    Chapter 36, the Exile up to Cyrus' edict.
Ezra-Nehemiah, from Cyrus' edict to the restoration of the temple, city walls and Law.

The genealogical tables in the first section of I Chronicles provide tedious reading and may be drawn from a separate source. In their present position, they serve to introduce some of the Chronicler's dominant interests, including Judah, the Davidic line, and the temple. The lineage of the first three chapters leads directly to David. In the following chapters, the Chronicler moves back to pre-Davidic time to

Read I Chron. Chs. 1–9

---

[7] Cf. Myers, *I Chronicles*, pp. lxxxvii and W. A. L. Elmslie, "The First and Second Books of Chronicles," *The Interpreter's Bible*, III, 345 f.

[8] Cf. above, "The Problem of History," chap. 2.

[9] It should be remembered that there was no concern about plagiarism or copyrights at this time.

trace family lines from Judah (ch. 4). With the exception of Levi and Benjamin, the remaining members of the twelve-tribe federation are rather quickly dismissed. Levi receives special attention because of the Levitical priesthood which stemmed from this group. Levitical priests, the Chronicler notes, attended and protected the ark of Yahweh in the pre-temple period, and Levitical functionaries were officially appointed and installed by King David and the seer Samuel (9:22). The superiority of the Levites to the Korahite priesthood, which appears also in the "P" material, is carefully noted (9:17–34).[10] Moses, a Levite and the hero of the Deuteronomic history, is barely noted in passing and is called a "servant of God" (6:49). No reference is made to his leadership, for the Chronicler was interested in portraying David as the ideal leader. Benjaminite genealogy was important because it introduced Saul, the first king, whose reign served as a backdrop against which the entrance of David could be best understood (8:1–40; 9:35–44).

Read I Chron. Ch. 10

Saul's story begins in the midst of the final battle between the Israelite king and the Philistines and is taken from I Sam. 31. Because of a lack of interest in pursuing any details of the family of Saul, the Chronicler records that Saul's entire house was killed. It is now unnecessary for him to admit any challenge to David's rule by members of Saul's family. A theological judgment was added, explaining the unfitness of Saul to reign (vss. 13–14).

Read I Chron. Chs. 11–29

Nothing was drawn from the record in II Sam. 1–4 concerning David's mourning for Saul and Jonathan, and the Chronicler moved immediately to the account of David's crowning at Hebron and the conquest of Jerusalem (from II Sam. 5). The list of David's heroes in 11:10–41 is the same as II Sam. 23:8–29, but supplemental material in 11:42–12:40 comes from some unknown source. The Chronicler selected what he wished to use, combined different sources and altered the order of presentation as he saw fit.

In general, the account of the removal of the ark to Jerusalem follows that of II Sam. 5:11 ff., but the Chronicler stressed cultic problems and added new elements. Levites alone handled the ark, the entire nation participated in the act of moving the sacred symbol and Levitical choristers and musicians led the procession and guided the offerings, sacrifices and communal sharing of food. Psalm 105:1–15 is quoted as the official hymn for the ceremony. By comparison, the II Sam. ceremony appears crude and unorganized. The Chronicler's description is of a dramatic ceremonial, carefully planned and executed, and is perhaps based upon accurate, though somewhat idealized knowledge of temple ritual.

Succeeding chapters leading to Solomon's rule draw heavily upon the older history, and, in accordance with the Chronicler's intention of exalting David, omit significant details. No mention is made of

---

[10] Apparently at one time the Korahites challenged the authority and control of the temple cultus by Levites. The Chronicler, like the P editors (parts of Num. 16), supported the Levites and subordinated the Korahites by having David and Samuel state their role. For a succinct discussion, see "Korah" in *The Interpreter's Dictionary of the Bible*.

David's illicit relationships with Bathsheba nor of his part in the disposal of Uriah. There are no hints of such unhappy situations in the Davidic household as the rape of Tamar, the murder of Amnon, or Absalom's attempt to seize the throne. The sin of David in numbering Israel is recorded, but the Chronicler said that this was done at the instigation of Satan (21:1). For the first time the word "Satan" is used as a proper name without the definite article, and Satan's role is that of a tester or tempter of men, much like that ascribed to him in the prologue of Job. There is no suggestion that Satan is acting as the emissary of Yahweh, but on the other hand, there is no hint that he has assumed the role he was to occupy in later literature as the adversary of the deity.

According to the Chronicler, David selected the site, drew the plans, supervised the selection and preparation of materials, and organized the labor for the building of the temple, and by divine lot he established the orders of the priesthood (chs. 22–28). Every decision, every act is presented as though it was executed in an orderly manner and without problems. With pious solemnity, David is made to counsel his son Solomon and inform and bless the assembly (28:20–29:22). Solomon's ascent to the throne at David's death takes place smoothly. The Chronicler has succeeded in presenting as impeccable an account of the Davidic monarchy as is possible.

The story of the construction of the temple (chs. 1–7) follows the earlier account but with some interesting additions. Along with the ark, the tent of meeting is placed within the sanctuary (5:5). Levitical singers and musicians participate in the installation rites (5:12 f.) and Psalm 132:8–10 and the refrain "for his steadfast love endures for ever" which occurs over and over again in Psalm 136, are chanted (ch. 7). The unblemished history of the kingdom is continued and Solomon's career, like that of his father, appears perfect. The catalogue of sins in I Kings 11:1–8 is omitted.

Read II Chron. Chs. 1–9

Except for an almost complete ignoring of the northern kings, the Chronicler followed the Deuteronomic record in I and II Kings. New information is added, the most important details of which are listed below. Some additions are best understood when both the Deuteronomic history and the work of the Chronicler are consulted.

Read Chs. 10–25

a. A list of cities fortified by Rehoboam is given (II Chron. 11:5–12, cf. II Kings 12).

b. The Chronicler notes the flight of Levitical priests from Israel to Judah when Jeroboam I installed his own cult functionaries (11:13–17).

c. Details about the household of Rehoboam are provided (11:18–23).

d. There is more information about the Shishak invasion (II Chron. 12:5–8, cf. I Kings 14:25–28).

e. The battle between Israel and Judah in the time of Abijah is given in an extended version, and a long interpretive speech in which victory is explained by virtue of Judah's loyalty to Yahweh is attributed to Abijah (II Chron. 13:3–21, cf. I Kings 15:1–8).

f. The Asa tradition is enlarged by an account of the defeat of Ethiopian invaders. The Chronicler's interpretation of events is given through speeches by Azariah the prophet and in the condemnatory speech by a seer which follows the record of the struggle with Baasha of Israel (II Chron. 14–16, cf. I Kings 15:9–33).

g. The image of Jehoshaphat is heightened and the king is pictured as one to whom homage was paid by surrounding nations, and as an ideal spiritual leader who commissioned the Levites to take "the book of the law" to the communities of Judah (II Chron. 17–19, cf. I Kings 22).

h. The lengthy accounts of the prophets Elijah and Elisha in the Deuteronomic history are omitted by the Chronicler because these are northern prophets and Elijah appears in the post-Exilic history only as the writer of a letter condemning Jehoram for apostasy (21:12–15).

i. Uzziah's leprosy is explained as a punishment for the violation of a cultic taboo (26:17 ff.).

j. The story of King Hezekiah is expanded by a tradition which records the monarch's attempt to convert the northern kingdom to the true religion as expressed in Judah. Once again the role of the Levites is stressed (chs. 29–32).

k. The Chronicler was troubled by the long life of the wicked king Manasseh. According to theological dogma, he should have died early for his evil ways. The Chronicler explained the extensive life span by noting that Manasseh repented and was forgiven by Yahweh (33:1–13). The blame attached to Manasseh for the Exile in II Kings 21:10 ff. and Jer. 15:4 is nowhere apparent.

l. Josiah's reform is made to begin before the discovery of the law scroll.

The list could be extended, but most of the remaining material follows the outline of II Kings.

Read II Chron. Ch. 36

In the last chapter, the Chronicler follows the II Kings account and terminates the section with the edict of Cyrus providing for the restoration of the Jewish community.

Read Ezra–Nehemiah

Most of the material in Ezra-Nehemiah has been discussed.

The Chronicler had specific reasons for the omission of certain details of Judah's history. Wherever possible, he sought to build up the reputation of the Davidic line and therefore left out that which might deprecate the Judaic kingship. The same purpose seems to have determined what he chose to include and emphasize. His determination to concentrate upon Judah, Jerusalem, the temple and its cult, the Levites and the musicians explains why these themes appear over and over again in details added to the Deuteronomic history. The northern kingdom had forsaken Yahweh and had been destroyed. During the Persian period, Yahweh's community was where the Chronicler believed it had always been—in Judah with Jerusalem and the temple at its center. Because the Davidic line probably was no longer central in Jewish politics when the Chronicler wrote, he tied David and the Davidic line to the cultus, which was central. Thus, David became the embodiment of the ideal spiritual leader, and the people of Judah are portrayed as a worshiping community, bound to Yahweh by the covenant.

There is no doubt in the Chronicler's mind that something unique was at work among the Jews. Their religion was the true one and no other, including the Samaritan cult, was genuine. It was through this sense of exclusiveness, of being chosen and redeemed by Yahweh, that was so characteristic of the Persian period, that certain groups within

Judaism were to be able to maintain their identity despite the efforts of some to syncretize the faith in the dark days that were to come.

During the Persian period toward the close of the fifth and the beginning of the fourth centuries, the last major contribution was made to the Pentateuch. It has already been noted that the accumulation of priestly lore had been taking place in Babylon during the Exile. Now this process came to an end and the results were woven into the previously combined JE saga and into Deuteronomy.

In its final form, P gives an impression of homogeneity and, to some degree, appears to be a narrative paralleling JE. On the other hand, as we also noted earlier, in certain instances P seems to be no more than a series of small additions to the JE story which give the completed narrative an entirely new emphasis or coloration. In P, the process of progressive or continuing interpretation can be seen.

It is occasionally said that P is what remains when J, E and D are removed from the Torah, but the P editor had his own distinctive style, and the completed Torah reveals the fruits of his carefully worked out systematization and theological interpretation of the past. Broadly speaking, P can be distinguished from the other sources of the Pentateuch by an easily recognized characteristic language, literary style and theological outlook. Like J, P refers to the holy mountain as "Sinai," and, as in E, the name Yahweh is avoided until it is revealed to Moses. There is a strong emphasis on the gathered people of Israel as a "congregation" (see Leviticus). P avoids the covenant terminology of JE and D ("to cut a covenant") because the language was employed for both secular and divine agreements. In P, Yahweh "establishes" (Gen. 6:18; 9:9, 11; 17:7, etc.) or "grants" (Gen. 9:12; 17:2, etc.) covenants.[11]

P's style tends to be stiff and stilted in contrast with the flowing narrative form of J and E. As in D, once a phrase has been accepted it is used over and over again. This characteristic may be seen in the creation account in Gen. 1 in the repetitive use of "and God said," "and it was so," "and there was evening and there was morning," "and God saw that it was good." At the same time the repetition conveys to the listener or reader a sense of order, balance, dignity and weight, quite appropriate to the content. It is conceivable that the formal style of P reflects cultic settings and liturgical usage, where mnemonic devices and schematic arrangements might be expected, and where repetition served to reinforce the significance of traditional language. Genealogical tables are usually introduced by the stereotyped phrase "these are the generations of," but, as we shall see, these tables do more than give the priestly material a sense of orderly development; they are carefully designed to carry the reader from the universal to

---

11 W. Eichrodt, *Theology of the Old Testament*, p. 56.

the particular, from mankind in general to Israel in particular. The schematic, formalistic presentation, the noting of minute details and the recurring use of literary formulae that can be discerned readily in English translation aid the reader in separating the P source.

Insofar as possible, P moved away from depicting Yahweh anthropomorphically. There are notable exceptions: man is made in God's image (Gen. 1:26 f.; 5:1; 9:6) and after the six days of creation God rested (Gen. 2:2) and was refreshed (Exod. 31:17). P's emphasis is on the transcendence of God, and he stresses the distance between God and man and between the sacred and profane. Yahweh's revelation is through his glory (*kabod*) as in Ezekiel, but the *kabod* is veiled in a cloud (Exod. 24:15 ff.). Other theophanies or manifestations are drawn with minimal descriptions (Gen. 17:1 ff.; 35:9 ff.; Exod. 6:2 ff.). The transcendent deity is approached through the mediation of cultic ritual and cult functionaries. Cultic patterns are prominent, and even narrative portions relate to the cultus: the creation story leads to the establishment of the Sabbath (Gen. 2:2 f.), the flood account to the prohibition of eating flesh with its blood (Gen. 9:4), and the Abrahamic covenant to circumcision (Gen. 17:10 ff.). Clear-cut rules for sacrifice, for distinction between clean and unclean food and for festal observances, underscore the importance of the cult in maintaining the binding relationship between God and man. Consequently, the priests come into prominence as mediators. In the idealized portrayal of the desert period, the tent sanctuary of Yahweh is walled off from the people by priests and Levites who symbolically stand between God and the people (Num. 2). Yahweh speaks to Moses and Aaron, not to the people, and after the demise of these two heroes of the faith there is no further direct communication. Throughout P there is no hint of the reality of other gods, for between the final editing of P and the other contributions to the Torah were the experience of the Exile and the teachings of Deutero-Isaiah. No altar is recognized but that in Jerusalem. The image of the nation is that of a community of worshipers linked to Yahweh through the cult, its institutions and the clergy.

Within P there are clues that indicate that the final product was the result of editing and selection, perhaps done by one person. There are passages in disagreement, interruptions in continuity and isolated blocks of material. Num. 4:23 ff. states that the age for Levites to begin temple service is thirty years, but Num. 8:24 says twenty-five years. Aaron, as high priest, and only those of his descendants who succeeded him in office are anointed in Exod. 29:7, 29, and Lev. 4:3, 5, 16, recognizes only one anointed priest; but according to Exod. 28:41 and 30:30, Aaron and his sons are anointed implying that all Aaronic priests and not just the high priest were anointed. It would appear that traditions with slight differences were combined.

Distinct units of literature may be recognized within the opening chapters of Leviticus. The first seven chapters deal with sacrifice; Chapters 8 to 10 suddenly turn to the rituals at Sinai; Chapters 11 to 15 consider problems of cultic cleanliness and uncleanliness. The links between these units are weak, and it can be readily seen that small collections of priestly instructions have been combined;[12] there is also evidence of even smaller units within the collections. There have been some attempts to trace threads of sources running through P, but these efforts are far too detailed for discussion here and would not be particularly rewarding.[13]

Scholars usually place the time of the compilation of P in the post-Exilic period[14] for a number of reasons. In the writings of II Isaiah, Haggai, Zechariah and Malachi there is no presupposition of the teachings found in P. J and E knew of many cult places, and D sought the elimination of all but that in Jerusalem, but P assumes that the only cult center was at Jerusalem, and is, therefore, at the end of this line of development. On the other hand, some parts of P appear to be pre-Exilic. Certain cultic terms are the same as those found in the temple literature of Ugarit (twelfth to fourteenth centuries), and some of the ceremonial regulations may be drawn from pre-Exilic ritual. Therefore, P contains both pre-Exilic and post-Exilic literature which, merged with JED, constituted a reinterpretation of these previously combined writings.

The identity of the final editor or compiler is not known, but it can be assumed that he was a priest. Ezra has been put forth as a possible candidate, and it is suggested that P was the law that Ezra interpreted and imposed on the people. Unfortunately, these hypotheses cannot be confirmed.

STRUCTURE OF P

P gives the Pentateuch its chronological framework. Simply stated, the structure of P consists of a development from the general to the particular, from man in general to the chosen of Yahweh in particular, from Yahweh the creator of the world to Yahweh the God of the Jews. The theme may be diagramed in a number of ways. In the first sketch, God's narrowing interest is portrayed, beginning with the created heavens and earth, then moving to man (generic), narrowing to Noah and his son Shem (the father of Semites) and to a single family leading to Abraham. Finally, single sons are chosen, and ultimately Jacob, who becomes Israel. Within the family of Israel, Moses and Aaron are singled out as the greatest individuals.

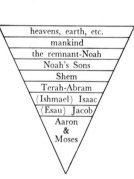

Another chart can be constructed from the genealogical tables.[15] Starting with Gen. 5 and the descendants of Adam, the first man, the line is traced through Seth to Noah. Noah's descendants are listed in

[12] For greater detail, cf. Martin Noth, *Leviticus*, The Old Testament Library, trans. J. E. Anderson (Philadelphia, Pennsylvania: The Westminster Press, 1965), pp. 9 ff.

[13] Cf. G. von Rad, "Die Priesterschrift," *Beiträge zur Wissenschaft von Alten Testament,* 1934.

[14] A notable exception is Yehezkel Kaufmann, *The Religion of Israel*, pp. 175 ff. Kaufmann dates P before D and puts the entire Torah in the pre-Exilic era. See also the last section of the article "Priests and Levites" in *The Interpreter's Dictionary of the Bible.*

[15] The underlined names indicate first-born sons.

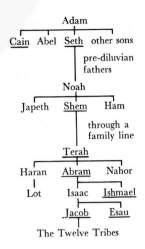

Adam

Cain Abel Seth other sons

pre-diluvian
fathers

Noah

Japeth Shem Ham

through a
family line

Terah

Haran Abram Nahor

Lot Isaac Ishmael

Jacob Esau

The Twelve Tribes

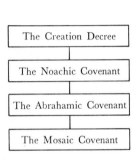

The Creation Decree
The Noachic Covenant
The Abrahamic Covenant
The Mosaic Covenant

Gen. 6:9–10 and Gen. 10. From Shem, the line is traced to Abram (Gen. 11:10 ff.) and with Abram a break with the locale of the past takes place and the lineage becomes Palestinian-centered. The chosen people do not descend from Ishmael, Abram's first-born by the Egyptian maid Hagar (Gen. 16:3, 15–16; 25:12 ff.), but from Isaac (Gen. 21:3–5; 25:19 ff.), and not from Esau, Isaac's firstborn (Gen. 36), but from Jacob (Gen. 35:22b–29). The rejection of the first-born can only be explained as God's free choice (election).

A third diagram, expressing the deepening relationship between Yahweh and his creatures, and beginning with mankind in general and ending with the Hebrews, centers in covenantal relationships. Having created mankind, God decreed that man should have plants for food and should exercise dominion over the animals. When man failed in his responsibilities, God began the human family anew in the chosen line of Noah and made a covenant promising that the new human line would never again perish by floods (Gen. 9:8 ff.). In Abraham, God narrowed his choice and made a new covenant embracing only the Abrahamic family and promising nationhood. The Mosaic covenant included only the descendants of Jacob and bound the twelve tribes to Yahweh. At Sinai the most important revelation was given, for here was given the cultic legislation that provided the continual link of the chosen people with Yahweh. The creation decree

BRONZES FROM PERSIA. *These items from Luristan in the Zagros mountains come from tombs dated between 600 and 1000* B.C. *The bit in the upper left hand corner indicates that the horse was used. The disc immediately below is a shield boss which was probably mounted in the center of the shield, and the indentation barely visible on the lower edge may have been made from the blow of an axe similar to the one shown in the lower right hand corner. The item in the center is a mace-head, a most formidable weapon. The epsilon-axe blade shown at the upper right was attached to a handle by rivets on the three inner tangs which have long since become oxidized and broken off.*

and the Noachic covenant are general, affecting all mankind. The Abrahamic and Mosaic covenants are particularistic.

The different divine names used by P signify a development in divine revelation. At first, P used the general designation "Elohim" for the deity. With Abraham, the name "El Shaddai" is introduced and used along with Elohim. The revelation of the personal name "Yahweh" at Sinai was reserved for the chosen people. The use of divine names by P, once again, provided the Jews with a sense of the uniqueness of their divine-human relationships.

The recognition of P's schematic arrangement of the Torah traditions reveals P's understanding of Yahweh's historic relationship to his people. In the final revelation given at Sinai, the significance of the cult in maintaining the binding covenant and in expressing the meaning of election is portrayed.

ELOHIM
(the general name)

EL SHADDAI
(used by Abraham)

YAHWEH
(the personal name)

—— THE P SOURCE ——————

From Creation to Noah

| Gen. 1:1–2:4a | Creation in seven days. |
| Gen. 5:1–28, 30–32 | Genealogical table from Adam to Noah. |

The Noah Cycle

Gen. 6:9–22
    7:6, 11, 13–16a, 17–21, 24;
    8:1–2a, 3b–5, 13a, 14–19
	} Noah and the flood.

Gen. 9:1–17	The Noachic covenant (the rainbow).
Gen. 9:28–29	The death of Noah.
Gen. 10:1–7, 20, 22–23, 31–32	Genealogy of the sons of Noah.

The Abraham Cycle

Gen. 11:10–27, 31–32	Genealogy from Shem to Abram.
Gen. 12:4b–6	Abram goes to Shechem.
Gen. 13:6a, 11b, 12a	Editorial expansions.
Gen. 16:3, 15–16	The birth of Ishmael.
Gen. 17:1–27	The Abrahamic covenant (circumcision).
Gen. 19:29	The rescue of Lot.

The Isaac Cycle

Gen. 21:1b, 2b–6	The birth of Isaac.
Gen. 23:1–20	The death and burial of Sarah.
Gen. 25:7–11a	The death and burial of Abraham.
Gen. 25:12–18	The Ishmaelites.
Gen. 25:19–20, 26b	Isaac's descendants.
Gen. 35:27–29	The death of Isaac.

The Jacob Cycle

Gen. 27:46–28:9	A wife for Jacob.
Gen. 31:18	Jacob leaves Laban.
Gen. 34:1–2, 4, 6, 8–10, 14–17, 20–24, 27–29	The rape of Dinah.
Gen. 35:9–15	Jacob at Bethel.

357

Gen. 35:22b–26	The sons of Jacob.
Gen. 49:28–33	The death of Jacob.
Gen. 50:12–13	The burial of Jacob.

The Esau Cycle

Gen. 26:34–35	The wives of Esau.
Gen. 36	The Esau genealogy.

The Joseph Cycle

Gen. 37:1–2	The identity of Joseph.
Gen. 46:6–27; 47:27–28	Israel in Egypt.
Gen. 48:3–6	The promise to Joseph.

The Moses Cycle

Exod. 1:1–5, 7, 13 f.; 2:23b–25	Israel in Egypt.
Exod. 6:2–13	The revelation of the divine name.
Exod. 6:14–25	Genealogical table.
Exod. 6:26–7:13, 19–20a, 21b–22; 8:5–7, 15b–19; 9:8–12, 35b; 11:9–10	Moses, Aaron and Pharaoh.
Exod. 12:1–20, 28, 43–51	The institution of the Passover.
Exod. 13:1–2	The law of the firstborn.
Exod. 13:20; 14:1–4, 8–9	Pursuit in the wilderness.
Exod. 24:3–8, 15–18a	The covenant ritual.
Exod. 25	The ark of testimony.
Exod. 26	The tabernacle.
Exod. 27	The altar.
Exod. 28–29	The priesthood.
Exod. 30–31:18a	The incense altar and other furnishings.
Exod. 34:29–35	Moses descends from Mt. Sinai.
Exod. 35–40	The building of cultic items.
Lev. 1:1–7:38	Rules governing making of offerings.
Lev. 8:1–36	The ordination of Aaronic priests.
Lev. 9:1–24	Aaron as high priest.
Lev. 10:1–3	The sin of Nadab and Abihu.
Lev. 10:4–11:47	Separation of clean and unclean.
Lev. 12	Laws of cleanliness pertaining to women.
Lev. 13–15	Laws of health and ritual cleanliness.
Lev. 16	The scapegoat and the atonement ritual.
Lev. 17–26	The "Holiness Code."
Lev. 27	Rules concerning vows and tithes.
Num. 1–4	Census taking.
Num. 5	Testing by the waters of bitterness.
Num. 6	Regulations covering the Nazirite.
Num. 7	Offerings at the tabernacle.
Num. 9	The purification of Levites.
Num. 8	Rules for Passover.

Num. 10:1–28, 33–34	The departure from Sinai.
Num. 13:1–17a, 21, 25–26a, 27	Spying out Canaan.
Num. 14:2, 5–10, 33–38	The forty-year sentence.
Num. 15	Laws concerning offerings.
Num. 16:2b–11, 16–24, 35–50	Korah's rebellion.
Num. 17–18	Aaronic and Levitical priests.
Num. 19	Purification rituals.
Num. 20:22–29	The death of Aaron.
Num. 21:10–13, 19–20, 31–32; 22:1	Israel in Moab.
Num. 25:6–18	Thwarting of intermarriage with Midianites.
Num. 26	Moses takes a census.
Num. 27:1–11	Inheritance laws.
Num. 27:12–23	Joshua is commissioned.
Num. 28–29	Festal offerings.
Num. 30	Rules governing vows.
Num. 31	Vengeance on Midian.
Num. 32:6–15, 18–19, 28–33	The settling of Reuben and Gad.
Num. 33	Recapitulation of Israel's journey.
Num. 34	The boundaries of the promised land.
Num. 35	Cities of refuge.
Num. 36	Inheritance rules.
Deut. 32:48–52; 34:1a, 7–9	Moses on Mount Nebo.

The priestly creation myth presupposes a pre-existent watery chaos out of which the cosmos was formed,[16] and thus from its opening reveals an affinity with the Babylonian *Enuma elish*. The order of creation parallels that of the Babylonian myth: the firmament, dry land, the luminaries and man.[17] In the Babylonian account, the gods rest and celebrate at the conclusion of their work, and in P, God rests and sanctifies the Sabbath. Although it is not possible to prove direct borrowing from the Babylonian myth by the Jewish writer, there can be no denying the close relationship between the accounts. Since Hebrew ancestry is traced to Mesopotamia through the patriarchs and as we have noted, the Babylonian Exile left deep imprints on Jewish thought, it is relatively easy to understand the common interpretation of the nature of the cosmos and to postulate a common source for the stories. It is usually conceded that the P account probably existed in the pre-Exilic period, although this idea is open to debate.

Read
Gen. 1:1–2:4a

[16] Older theological interpretations of the P story insisted that God created *ex nihilo*. For a discussion of this point, cf. E. A. Speiser, *Genesis*, pp. 12 f.; C. A. Simpson, "Genesis," *The Interpreter's Bible*, I, 466–7. However, cf. G. von Rad, *Genesis*, pp. 46 f.

[17] For a detailed discussion, cf. Alexander Heidel, *The Babylonian Genesis* (Chicago: The University of Chicago Press, 1951), now reprinted as a Phoenix paperback, pp. 129 f.

The differences between the P myth and the *Enuma elish* are as marked as the similarities, demonstrating a different handling of the basic material because of different theological convictions. The P account is monotheistic (despite the plural possessive form of 1:26[18] which may be addressed to the "court of heaven") and lacks the patterns of divine strife and social upheaval of the Babylonian myth. In P, God creates by fiat without battle,[19] although the term "created" in 1:1 (Heb: *bara'*) may be interpreted as implying "fashioning by cutting" and thus reflect the same division of the basic stuff of the cosmos as Marduk's splitting of Tiamat, and the Hebrew word for "deep," *tehom,* in 1:2 has affinities with Tiamat, the Babylonian symbol of chaos. The Jewish story is climaxed with the creation of the Sabbath (the final verse, 2:4a, should probably be placed at the beginning of the account).

There are striking differences between the J and P accounts in the order of creation, and these can readily be seen in the following chart:

P	J
light	heaven and earth
earth and seas	man
vegetation	a garden
luminaries	
fish and birds	animals and birds
land animals	woman
man and woman	
the Sabbath	

The primeval harmonious relationship between primordial man and animals found in J and in the Babylonian story of Gilgamesh[20] is reflected in P. The first man does not eat animals, but has a diet restricted to vegetable products (1:29), and only after the flood is man permitted to eat animal flesh (Gen. 9).

The cosmology of P was discussed earlier. The shell of the firmament (a hard substance) holds back the cosmic waters that would ordinarily flood the space between earth and sky. The lack of critical analysis of natural phenomena enabled the writer to envision day and night existing before the creation of the sun, moon and stars. Eight creative acts take place in six days. The pattern of "days" probably does not reflect great time periods, but perhaps refers to specific days during the New Year Festival on which symbolic rites were performed, just as in the Babylonian Akitu festival.

Read the Noah Cycle

Ten heroes span the period between the creation and the flood (Gen. 5).[21] Much of the P contribution to the already existing J story of the flood consists of small details pertaining to the structure of the

[18] Cf. Speiser, *Genesis,* p. 7 where, arguing from silence, it is said that because no other gods are mentioned, the translation must be interpreted in the singular ("in my likeness").

[19] The dragon battle motif did enter Jewish literature, cf. Ps. 74:12–17; Isa. 51:9–11.

[20] In Gilgamesh, Enkidu, a type of primitive man, lives and eats with animals.

[21] This is also true in the Gilgamesh epic.

ark, the age of Noah and similar minutiae. Other additions are more significant. For P, the flood comes as a punishment for wickedness, and Noah's role is clarified as the remnant in which hope is placed for the future. The emergence of land after the flood waters cease mirrors P's creation story, for, as in Gen. 1:2, the movement of the "spirit" or "wind" (Heb: *ru'ah*) causes the waters to subside and the earth to reappear (8:1) for the new beginning of the story of mankind. With the new start came new decrees to all living creatures to multiply (8:14–16), and to Noah, as a symbol of the new man, to include animal flesh in his diet. The relationship between man and animal that enabled them to live harmoniously in the microcosm of the ark was past. The Noachic covenant guaranteed that the earth would never again be covered by flood waters, and the symbol of that covenant, the rainbow, served two purposes: as a sign of the covenant for man, and as a reminder to God of his promise.

Most of P's contributions to the Abrahamic cycle are minor, but Chapter 17 is very important. God's relationship to Abraham is now set in covenantal form with the sign of the covenant being circumcision. Failure to be circumcised excluded the Jew from the holy community, and even Abraham, at the age of 99, was circumcised.

At the opening of the Isaac cycle, P noted that Abraham circumcised Isaac when the child was eight days old, in conformity with the Abrahamic covenant (17:9 ff., cf. 21:4). Details were added about Sarah's death and burial (Gen. 23). The conversation with the Hittites may accurately reflect polite forms of speech utilized in business transactions. P added extra details about the death and burial of Abraham.

P explained that Jacob's visit to Laban was to acquire a wife and to keep the family line clear of foreign ties, and was not, as J had suggested, to escape from Esau (cf. Gen. 27:43–45). Esau, in an effort to please his parents, also chose a wife among his kin-folk, from the Ishmaelitic line (28:8 f.). New details and genealogies were added to the Jacob account, and new information revealed about the burials in the cave purchased by Abraham was attached to the Joseph traditions (49:28–33; 50:12–13).[22]

P had a separate tradition of the revelation of the divine name to Moses and, as we have noted, introduces a new dispensation with this revelation. The patriarchal covenantal promise was about to be realized and the new covenant that would govern future relationships about to be given. Aaron, as the prototype of the high priest, is depicted as the interpreter of Moses and the agent of God (Exod. 6:28–7:1, 8–13). The tradition of the plagues is heightened, ritual acts are described and new details are provided for historical-cultic observance of the Passover (Exod. 12:1–20, 43–49).

The covenant ceremony (Exod. 24:3–8, 15–18) adds ritualistic details and blood sacrifice to the rather simple J ceremony and no doubt reflects some aspects of the annual covenantal recital observed

Read
Gen. 17

Read Gen.
22:1–20;
25:7–11a

Read Gen.
27:46–28:9

---

[22] The traditional location of this cave is beneath the Mosque of Abraham in modern Hebron. Sepulchral shrines within the Mosque commemorate the patriarchs and their wives. The foundation stones of the Mosque are Herodian (first century B.C.), indicating the long history of veneration of the spot.

in the temple. Following the covenant rituals, cultic ceremonies and equipment are discussed, and since for P the cult is the means of maintaining the relationship between Yahweh and his people, details of rites, costumes and accessories are provided by Yahweh. Each item utilized in temple ritual is given a divine origin. The tabernacle or tent of meeting, which in P becomes a fully developed sanctuary, is made of materials more easily obtained in a developed, settled society than in a wilderness setting.[23] When the ark of the covenant was built (and P's description indicates that it is a most ornate structure), the tablets of law were placed within it and the ark was set within the completed tabernacle in a spot corresponding to its location in the Solomonic temple. The primitive tent-sanctuary became, in P, an elaborate portable temple, the idealized magnificence of which was drawn from aspects of the completed temple.[24] To imagine the Hebrews carting a structure of this magnitude and complexity about the desert staggers the imagination. The details concerning the priests, priestly apparel and priestly responsibilities do not suggest a wilderness setting either. Indeed, it is possible that in the case of the high priest the various costumes result from a combination of older literary sources in P so that articles of dress come from different historical periods.[25]

The expansion of cultic and liturgical themes in the book of Leviticus is far too detailed for consideration here, but the analysis of the contents listed above suggests the main themes. In the midst of the discussion of the clean and unclean in the Holiness Code, one of the most significant statements of human relationship in the Bible is found: "You shall love your neighbor as yourself" (Lev. 19:18). Although the major thrust of P's writings is God-man relationships in a cultic setting, rules for human conduct punctuate the liturgical concerns or are related to ritual (cf. Lev. 6:1–7; 19:9–18).

One of the central cleansing rituals is that for the Day of Atonement[26] which provided for Aaron's (the high priest's) annual entry into the *debir*, the holy of holies of the tabernacle or temple. Rites of cleansing for the high priest and the priesthood prepared Aaron, followed by atonement rituals for the temple or tabernacle. Finally, the nation's sins were purged. The first ritual required the sacrifice of a bullock, which prepared the priest for entry into the presence of the deity. In the second rite, one of two goats chosen by lot was killed, and in the third the sins of the nation were confessed over the second goat and the sin-burdened animal taken into the wilderness to be destroyed, sins and all, by Azazel, presumably a wasteland demon.[27] The

23 Cf. Martin Noth, *Exodus*, The Old Testament Library, trans. by J. S. Bowden (Philadelphia: The Westminster Press, 1962), p. 202.

24 For a different point of view, see the article "Tabernacle" in *The Interpreter's Dictionary of the Bible*.

25 Cf. Martin Noth, *Exodus*, p. 220.

26 Cf. Lev. 23:27 f.; 25:9 where the title *yom ha-kippurim*, Day of Atonement, occurs.

27 For the identity of Azazel, see the article "Azazel" in *The Interpreter's Dictionary of the Bible*.

high priest then reentered the *hekal* or holy place to bathe and change clothing before returning to the altar in the courtyard to offer sacrifice. It is generally believed that the ritual is post-Exilic, for it is not mentioned in pre-Exilic literature,[28] and the impact of the Akitu festival can be recognized in the expulsion of the sin-bearer, here a goat rather than a man. The significance of the rite in providing a complete purging of sin for the nation and permitting an annual new beginning is not to be underestimated. In its present location, it forms a fitting prelude to the Holiness Code, which we have discussed earlier.

Details of camp organization are set forth by P (Num. chs. 2–3). The tabernacle is at the center and is surrounded by orders of Levites. The twelve tribes form a protective ring, with Judah in the favored position on the east, the side of the rising sun (see Chart). Other regulations, including those for testing the virtue of a wife by a jealous husband, and those for persons who become Nazirites, follow (Num. 5–6). Some regulations extend information previously provided (Num. 8, cf. Lev. 8). Provisions are made for a supplementary Passover to accommodate those defiled at the time of the regular observance (Num. 9). Ultimately, the Hebrews left Sinai and prepared for the invasion of Canaan, only to be sentenced to a forty-year desert sojourn because of lack of faith (Num. 14:26–38).

The seriousness of observing ritual law is exemplified in the story of the Sabbath-breaker (Num. 15:32–36), and perhaps also in the Korah tradition (Num. 16). Events leading to the arrival at the border of the promised land are sprinkled with further legislation strengthening the role of the Levites, guarding the sanctity of the theocracy envisioned by P, or governing human rights and relationships.

CHART XV. THE ORGANIZATION OF THE CAMP

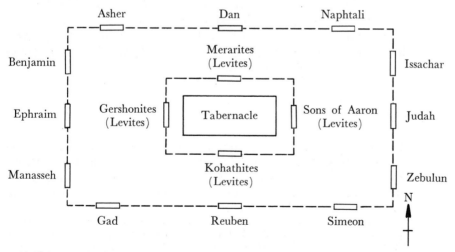

28 Cf. Martin Noth, *Leviticus,* The Old Testament Library, trans. by J. E. Anderson (Philadelphia: The Westminster Press, 1965), pp. 119 f.; N. Micklem, "Leviticus," *The Interpreter's Bible,* II, 77.

TORAH AND CULT

With the addition of P the Torah assumed its final form. Exactly when the point was reached after which no further changes or additions were made cannot be known, but it is not unreasonable to suggest that this occurred before the end of the Persian period (fourth century). Nor is it possible to determine the immediate use of the Torah in the temple cult. However, in time the Torah was given a lectionary form, so that a portion was designated for reading each Sabbath and the entire Torah would be read through in a three-year period. In this manner the theologized history of Israel was constantly recited to the worshipers, and the laws of the holy congregation or nation were made known and sacred festivals interpreted. Proper conduct of temple ritual was derived from the Torah, including everything from priestly responsibilities and dress to proper modes of offering and sacrificing.

It must be assumed, on the basis of the extensive library from the last century of the pre-Christian era and the first half century of the Christian era found at Qumran on the shores of the Dead Sea,[29] that copies of the Torah were reproduced in quantity for study in temple schools, as well as for private study.[30] The use of the Torah in the temple and the distribution of copies could only serve to freeze the traditions and to establish firmly temple traditions. On the other hand, study of the Law opened the way for discussions of the implications of Torah teachings at all levels of life. This is not to suggest that everyone followed the Law diligently, but rather that the Law tended to enter more and more into everyday life and at the same time played a central role in the cultus. It is, therefore, quite clear that the cultus was the central means of preservation and transmission of the history of the kingdom from the Solomonic period onward. The Yahweh festivals were times when the history was recited and perhaps mimed or dramatized in processionals or other rites in the pre-Exilic periods. In the post-Exilic period the "sacred history" was once again transmitted, primarily through the cult.

THE PSALMS

The third major literary compilation of this period was the collection of the Psalms, often labeled "The Hymnbook of the Second Temple." There can be little doubt that the poems were used in worship, and among scholars there is a growing acceptance of the thesis that,

---

[29] For details, consult one of the many books on the Dead Sea Scrolls such as M. Burrows, *The Dead Sea Scrolls* (New York: Viking Press, 1955); Géza Vermès, *Discovery in the Judean Desert* (New York: Desclee Company, 1956); T. H. Gaster, *The Dead Sea Scriptures* (Garden City, New York: Doubleday Anchor Books, 1956), etc.

[30] The persecution of Jews under Antiochus IV about 168 B.C., as recorded in I Macc. 1:54 ff., implies that many private individuals owned copies of the Law.

although many Psalms may be post-Exilic, some are of pre-Exilic origin.[31] The numerous authors listed in the superscriptions suggests the composite nature of the book, for one psalm is ascribed to Moses (Ps. 90), seventy-three to David (eighty-three in the LXX), twelve to Asaph, a choir leader (Pss. 50; 73–83), one to Ethan, a leader in the temple singers' guild (Ps. 89), ten to Korah (Pss. 42–49, 84, 85, 87), two to Solomon (Pss. 72, 127), one has a double title (Ps. 88), and fifty are undesignated.

The Hebrew title for the collection, *tehillim*, comes from a root meaning "to shout" (*hll*), so *tehillim* implies "raising the shout."[32] The familiar *hallel-u-yah*, generally translated "praise (ye) Yahweh," means "raise the (jubilant) shout: 'Yah(weh)'"[33] and helps to convey the idea of the psalms as "songs of praise"—an interpretation that fits some. The term "psalm" comes from the Greek word *psalmos*, which meant the twanging or sounding of chords on a musical instrument, and was the term used by the LXX translators for the Hebrew word *mizmor*, which seems to have signified a song or hymn sung to the accompaniment of a stringed instrument. The word "Psalter," which is often used to designate the collection comes from the Greek word *psalterion* meaning "a stringed instrument." These last titles imply that some psalms were sung and accompanied by instrumental music.

There is evidence of liturgical usage in some of the psalms. For example, the "Egyptian Hallel Psalms" (Pss. 113–118) are used at Passover, and the "Songs of Ascent" or "Songs of Going Up" (Pss. 120–134) may be pilgrim hymns. The division of the Psalter into five sections appears to be the work of the final editor who deliberately imitated the five-fold division of the Torah, ending each section with a doxology:[34]

I. Pss. 1–41 are called "Psalms of David," for most bear this title. The omission of the ascription in Ps. 10 is due to the division of a single psalm into two parts (now Pss. 9 and 10). The superscription of Ps. 33 is missing in the Hebrew but is found in the LXX. This collection is also known as "The Yahwistic Psalter" because the name Yahweh is ordinarily used for the deity.

II. Pss. 42–72 contain a second "Davidic" collection (Pss. 51–72), which ends in 72:20 with "The prayers of David, the son of Jesse, are ended." It is possible that at one time Pss. 51–72 preceded Pss. 42–50 and con-

[31] Cf. M. Dahood, *Psalms I*, The Anchor Bible (Garden City, New York: Doubleday and Company, Inc., 1966), pp. xxix-xxx.

[32] S. Mowinckel, *The Psalms in Israel's Worship*, trans. by D. R. Ap-Thomas (Oxford: Basil Blackwell, 1962), II, 218, Add. Note 1.

[33] Cf. Pius Drijvers, *The Psalms, Their Structure and Meaning* (New York: Herder and Herder, 1965), p. 55 for an interesting development of this idea.

[34] The divisions must have been made by the third century B.C. for they appear in the LXX. It should be noted that the numbering of the Psalms in the LXX differs slightly from the Hebrew because in the LXX Pss. 9 and 10 are united into a single poem, as are Pss. 114 and 115. Conversely, Pss. 116 and 147 are each divided into two parts. A completely different ordering of psalms is found in the Dead Sea Psalm scroll which contains canonical Psalms ranging from Psalm 93 through Psalm 150 plus several non-canonical hymns. Cf. J. A. Sanders, *The Dead Sea Psalms Scroll* (Ithaca, New York: Cornell University Press, 1966).

cluded the "Davidic" collection in the first division. This second collection is not uniform and Pss. 66, 67 and 71 lack superscriptions in the Hebrew versions and Ps. 72 is ascribed to Solomon in the LXX. Some repetitions occur in the second "Davidic" collection, for Ps. 53 reproduces Ps. 14, and Ps. 70 is the same as Ps. 40:13–17. Pss. 42–72 form part of "The Elohistic Psalter," which extends into the third division to Ps. 83 and uses the name "Elohim" for the deity about four times as often as "Yahweh."[35] The Korahite psalms (42–49) are included in this division. It should be noted that Ps. 43 was once part of Ps. 42 and therefore lacks a title.

III. Psalms 73–89 are largely Elohistic and include four Korahite psalms (84, 85, 87, 88), some Asaph psalms (73–83), a hymn of Ethan (89), and one psalm attributed to David (86).

IV. Psalms 90–106 are mainly songs of praise and do not lend themselves to the type of breakdown exhibited in the preceding sections.

V. Psalms 107–150 include the Egyptian Hallel (113–118), the Pilgrimage Psalms (120–134) and a "Davidic" collection (146–149). The final Psalm (150) is a doxology closing the entire collection.

The five-fold division may aid in understanding the way in which the Psalms were used in ritual. We have noted that the Chronicler placed emphasis on the use of music in the liturgy and on the role of the guilds of Levitical singers (cf. I Chron. 6:31 ff.; 25:1, 6; II Chron. 5:12 f.; Ezra 10:24; Neh. 12:47; 13:10) and probably the Psalms were part of the musical repertoire in the Persian period. Korahite Psalms may have been composed by the Korahite guild (II Chron. 20:19) and Asaph Psalms composed and sung by the Asaph guild (I Chron. 16:5, 7 f.). Just as the Torah appears to have been divided for reading through a three-year cycle, so the Psalms may have been divided for corresponding use. Genesis was begun on the first Sabbath and Psalm 1, which extols the law and the regular study of the Torah, would be an excellent accompaniment. The initial reading of each of the other books of the Torah begins on a Sabbath that corresponds to a division in the Psalter; the reading of Exodus begins on the forty-second Sabbath, Leviticus on the seventy-third, etc. The last four Psalms, which would fall due every three years, accommodate the difference between the solar and lunar calendars. How early this arrangement was developed cannot be known. At a much later date, it was used in worship in synagogues, but whether it can be pushed back into the ritual of the Persian period is debatable.

Superscriptions and notations within some of the Psalms appear to indicate liturgical usage, but it must be admitted that our understanding of the meaning of these instructions is most limited. For example, the words addressed "to the choirmaster" at the beginning of many songs (cf. Pss. 4, 5, 6, 8, 9) at times designate instruments: "for the flutes" (Ps. 5), "with stringed instruments" (Pss. 4, 6, 55, 61),[36] or the festal occasion when the song is to be used (Pss. 38, 70, 92, 100). Other instructions convey no meaning: "according to the Sheminith" (Pss. 6, 12), "according to the Gittith" (Pss. 8, 81, 84), and the label

---

[35] The Davidic Psalms (1–41, 51–72) and the Elohist Psalms (42–83) suggest different ways of dividing the Psalter than the present five-fold pattern and appear to represent older separate units or collections.

[36] Even here the allusions are obscure.

"A Shiggaion" (Ps. 7).[37] The word "Selah" appears to call for an interlude, perhaps an instrumental interruption. Analyses of these terms have not aided significantly in the understanding of the use of the psalms in worship, nor have they provided understanding of how singers and instrumentalists cooperated in making the most effective presentation of the poem.

The Psalms have been compared with hymnic poetry from Egypt,[38] Babylon,[39] Assyria[40] and Canaan.[41] Clearly, similar principles of rhythm and parallelism were employed in all Near Eastern poetry, and imagery resulting from a common cosmology or the correspondence of many everyday figures of speech tended to produce striking resemblances in poetic expression in the Near Eastern world. Nor can there be any doubt that the literature of Israel was affected by its neighbors. Ps. 104 employs the same theses and many of the same expressions as the Egyptian hymn to the sun of Akhenaton so that one is compelled to agree with J. H. Breasted and others that in some way Akhenaton's hymn was preserved and was employed by the author of Ps. 104.[42] Some scholars have found reminiscences of the cosmic battle reported in the *Enuma elish* in the Psalms (Pss. 24:1–2; 74:13–14; 93:3–4), or the reapplication of this ancient concept to new perils where enemies of Yahweh are described in terms of the powers of chaos.[43] Canaanite influence is, perhaps, more clearly discerned because of the dialectical proximity of Hebrew and Ugaritic,[44] but also in what appears to be the direct borrowing of Canaanite imagery by the Hebrews. For example, Ba'al is called "Rider of the clouds"[45] and Yahweh is described in the same way (Pss. 68:4; 104:3). The imagery in the Psalms acclaiming Yahweh's kingship (Pss. 47, 93, 96, 97, 98) is an adaption of the Canaanite proclamation of Ba'al as king.[46]

Despite the borrowing of motifs, imagery, terminology and the adaption of foreign hymnody, the Psalms are uniquely Hebrew and for our purposes must be interpreted primarily in terms of their rela-

---

[37] For a discussion of these terms see the article "Music" in *The Interpreter's Dictionary of the Bible.*

[38] A. M. Blackman, "The Psalms in the Light of Egyptian Research," *The Psalmists,* ed. D. C. Simpson (London: Oxford University Press, 1926).

[39] Geo. Widengren, *The Accadian and Hebrew Psalms of Lamentation as Religious Documents* (Stockholm: Bokförlags Aktiebolaget Thule, 1937).

[40] C. G. Cummings, *The Assyrian and Hebrew Hymns of Praise,* Columbia University Oriental Studies, XII (New York: Columbia University Press, 1934).

[41] J. H. Patton, *Canaanite Parallels in the Book of Psalms* (Baltimore: The Johns Hopkins Press, 1944).

[42] J. H. Breasted, *The Dawn of Conscience* (New York: Charles Scribner's Sons, 1933), pp. 308 f. For a comparison of the two hymns, see Breasted, *op. cit.,* pp. 281 ff.; Jack Finegan, *Light from the Ancient Past,* pp. 106 ff., *ANET,* pp. 309 ff.; and the discussion by Hugo Gressman, "The Development of Hebrew Psalmody," *The Psalmists,* D. C. Simpson (ed.) (London: Oxford University Press, 1926).

[43] N. H. Snaith, *Studies in the Psalter* (London: The Epworth Press, 1934), pp. 97–106; W. O. E. Oesterley, *A Fresh Approach to the Psalms,* The International Library of Christian Knowledge (New York: Charles Scribner's Sone, 1937), pp. 30 ff.

[44] Cf. Patton, *op. cit.,* p. 47.

[45] *Ibid.,* p. 20.

[46] Cf. John Gray, *Archaeology and the Old Testament World* (New York: Thomas Nelson and Sons, 1962), reprinted as a paperback by Harper and Row, 1965, pp. 105 ff. For a detailed study of Ugaritic influence, see M. Dahood, *Psalms I.*

tionship to the cult and the worshiping community within Israel. The Jewish cult did not accept all of the beliefs of their neighbors and what they adopted they adapted. No doubt in the very borrowing of foreign terms and imagery the concept of Yahweh and the nature of the religion of Israel must have been altered. For example, the concept of Yahweh as king is not a nomadic idea, and the fact that it was borrowed from the Canaanites and used in the Israelite cultus demonstrates a significant and fundamental change in theology and social outlook. We cannot know to what degree the Yahweh cult became Canaanitic in Israel with the establishment of the bull-calf cult at Dan and Bethel, but we can imagine from the prophetic protest, particularly Hosea 2:16; 4:14; 8:5, that much syncretism had occurred. On the other hand, although the Ugaritic myths contain numerous parallels to the Psalms in cultic terminology, the immense distance between Yahwism and Ba'alism, and the distinctive nature of the Hebrew-Jewish religion must be recognized on the basis of myth patterns. Therefore, despite the indications of outside influences, the Psalms must be approached in terms of their Hebrew-Jewish cultic setting.

Form criticism has provided the most penetrating study of the use of the Psalms in worship, and the contributions of the leading exponents of this method of study are worthy of note. Hermann Gunkel, who may be said to have been the first to apply form critical techniques to the Psalms observed that they could be classified according to types and that each type had its own specific function within temple ritual. Thus, a thanksgiving psalm would properly be used in a ritual or sacrifice of giving thanks. Gunkel assumed that psalms were ordinarily employed for public rather than private worship, although some may have originated in individual worship experiences.[47] Gunkel listed a number of different categories,[48] some of which are:

1. *Hymns,* designed for choral or solo praise of God, such as Pss. 8, 19, 29, 33, etc. A special category in this group was isolated and called "Songs of Zion" (Pss. 46, 48, 76, 84, 87).
2. *Enthronement Psalms,* celebrating the enthronement of Yahweh as king of the world and history (Pss. 47, 93, 97, 99).
3. *Public Laments,* reflecting some public calamity (Pss. 44, 74, 79, 80, etc.).
4. *Individual Laments,* voicing personal problems, illness, persecution (Pss. 3, 5, 6, 7, 13, etc.).
5. *Individual Thanksgiving Hymns,* in which reasons why thanks is given are recited (Pss. 30, 32, 34, etc.).
6. *Royal Psalms,* associated with the activities of the king in the cult (Pss. 2, 18, 20, 45, 132, etc.).
7. *Psalms of Confidence,* which are closely related to the individual laments (Pss. 4, 11, 16, 23, etc.).
8. *Wisdom Psalms,* reflecting the practicality of wisdom writers (Pss. 1, 37, 49, etc.).

[47] The use of "I" in the Psalms should be understood in the light of the concept of corporate personality, whereby a group can be symbolized in the first person singular. For example, note the fluidity of the "we" and "I" in Pss. 44, 60, 66, etc.

[48] Hermann Gunkel and Joachim Begrich, *Einleitung in die Psalmen,* Göttinger handkommentar zur Alten Testament (Gottingen: Vandenhoeck & Ruprecht, 1933).

A Hebrew oil juglet from the period of the divided kingdom. *These small vessels were usually dark grey or black in color and were baked in an oven in which the fire had been smothered thus forcing the carbon particles back into the clay and rendering it impervious to liquids. The decorative pattern was added by burnishing. Such juglets may have held perfumed oil used for cosmetic purposes (Amos 6:6; Song of Songs 1:3) or for healing (Isa. 1:6) or for honoring guests (Ps. 23:5).*

Sigmund Mowinckel, basing his research on Gunkel's work, studied the Psalms and the Israelite cultus in terms of parallels found in other Near Eastern cultures.[49] For the most part Mowinckel's categories are those of Gunkel, but a most important contribution was made in the theory of the enthronement festival. Mowinckel noted that in Pss. 47, 93, 95–100, Yahweh was referred to as "king" and argued that such terms as "Yahweh reigns" and "Yahweh is a great king above all gods" signified actual enthronement. In these Psalms he found motifs like those used in the Akitu festival: the creation of the world, the defeat of enemies and chaos and divine kingship. Mowinckel suggested that an annual festival of enthronement of Yahweh was observed in Israel in the pre-Exilic period, just as the Akitu festival was observed in Babylon. At the festival the enthronement Psalms were sung which included the cry, "Yahweh has become king." In the initial list of these Psalms were Pss. 8, 24, 29, 46, 48, 50 and 65, to which he later added Pss. 68, 75, 76, 82, 84, 85, 87 and 118, despite the omission of the cry "Yahweh reigns" in some. The enthronement festival, which marked the "Day of Yahweh," was a renewal rite when powers of chaos were overcome and included a processional in which the ark was carried to the temple for enshrinement as a symbol of Yahweh's presence. In this rite, the central themes of the Yahweh-Israel relationship were renewed and revitalized: election, covenant, promises to the Davidic line.

Artur Weiser is in general agreement with the Gunkel-Mowinckel analysis, but he replaces the enthronement festival with "the covenant festival," which, he says, included rites of covenant renewal, a recitation of sacred history and an emphasis on the necessity of obeying the law (cf. Josh. 24; Deut. 31:10–13; II Kings 23:1–3).[50] The festival commemorated the formation of the tribal confederacy as a covenanted people and cannot be reconstructed, but fragments of the liturgy are to be found in some of the Psalms such as Ps. 50.

Hans-Joachim Kraus has proposed a theory of a "royal Zion festival" held in Jerusalem on the first day of Tabernacles, during which the election of Jerusalem and the Davidic line were proclaimed and the ark brought into the city.[51] The festival's origin lay in the transportation of the ark to Jerusalem by David. Pilgrims from distant places

[49] S. Mowinckel, *The Psalms* Vols. I–II.

[50] Artur Weiser, *The Psalms,* The Old Testament Library, trans. H. Hartwell (Philadelphia: The Westminster Press, 1962).

[51] Hans-Joachim Kraus, *Worship in Israel,* trans. G. Buswell (Richmond, Virginia: John Knox Press, 1966), pp. 208 ff. For a more detailed statement, see his *Die Königsherrschaft Jahwes im Alten Testament* (Tübingen: Mohr, 1951).

came to Jerusalem and, as they stood outside the city, chanted such Psalms as 46, 48, 76, 87 and 122. In the processional of the ark, Psalms 95:1–6; 132:14–18 and 24:1–6 would be used, and at the sanctuary gates in the "entrance liturgy," Psalm 24:7–10 would be antiphonally chanted. The rite was climaxed with a "solemn act of adoration" before Yahweh. Kraus believes that Mowinckel's list of Enthronement Psalms is too inclusive for only Pss. 47, 93 and 96–99 refer to Yahweh as "king," and that the enthronement ritual is post-Exilic, reflecting the influence of Deutero-Isaiah and the Akitu festival.

No attempt will be made to treat the Psalms chronologically. Recent studies have rendered useless some aspects of former guides to dating.[52] The tendency to retain archaisms in liturgy and the use of uniform metrical patterns make identification of early and late materials very difficult. Only occasionally, as in Ps. 137, will internal evidence provide a guide to the period out of which the Psalm came. We will begin our study of the Psalms proper through the "Royal Zion Festival" outlined by Kraus, for not only does this festival offer the most promising approach to our understanding of the cultus, but it also enables us to relate specific Psalms to cultic ritual, and perhaps to gain some appreciation of the significance of the acts of worship. We shall then consider some specific categories of Psalms.

The festival, which was held in the seventh month at the Feast of Tabernacles, can best be understood in terms of the steps developed by Kraus:[53]

Read Pss. 42–43

a. Pilgrimage preparations. As the time for the festival drew near, worshipers, some coming from distant places, began their pilgrimages. Psalms 42–43 (which are really a single Psalm) express the longing of those who are far from Jerusalem. Memory of former festivals strengthened the anticipation of the one at hand, increased the sense of separation from Yahweh and produced fluctuating moods of despondency and anticipation.

Read Ps. 84

As the temple came into view, the pilgrims raised their songs of joy and longing. So intense was the mood that the pilgrims blessed cult officials who ministered in the temple and measured the joy of being in the courts against other pleasures.

Read Ps. 122

Kraus believes that the sentiment in Ps. 122 is anticipatory rather than realized. Two of the central themes of the festival appear in the praise of David and Jerusalem.

Read Ps. 46

b. The Pilgrims at the Gate: The Songs of Zion. "Songs of Zion" are referred to by Babylonian tormenters in Ps. 137 and therefore appear to be a special category of Psalms. In Ps. 46 Yahweh is praised for his control of nature's destructive forces, for his presence in Jerusalem which reassured his worshipers, for his action in history and for the sense of his near presence experienced by the pilgrims. The imagery of the streams of Jerusalem is Canaanitic, derived from the descriptions of the dwelling place of the Ugaritic father-god El at the source of the "two rivers."[54]

Read Ps. 48

Ps. 48 glorifies Mount Zion and employs Canaanite ideas. Mount Zion

[52] For example, the precise categories utilized by M. Buttenweiser, *The Psalms* (Chicago: University of Chicago Press, 1938) are no longer acceptable.

[53] Kraus, *Worship in Israel*, pp. 208 ff.

[54] *Ibid.*, p. 101. For references to the mythological "streams" from Jerusalem, cf. Ezek. 47:1; Joel 3:18; Zech. 14:8.

is, for the singers, the mountain of God (vs. 2), and is symbolic of Mt. Zaphon, the place of divine assembly located in the north in Canaanite mythology.[55] There can be little doubt, as Kraus has pointed out, that pre-Hebrew Canaanite mythological concepts associated with Jerusalem were transferred to the Hebrew cultus when David possessed the city and made it the center of Yahwistic religion. Verse 12 may refer to a processional. Statements extolling the security of Jerusalem (vss. 4–8) may grow out of pre-Exilic deliverances from such foes as Rezin and Pekah (Isa. 7:1–25) and Sennacherib (Isa. 24–27; 29:1–24; 36:1–37:38).

In Ps. 76 Zion is praised as the dwelling place of Yahweh, the God whose judgment is on behalf of his people and against their enemies. Other Psalms express the pride of those born in the holy city (Ps. 87), and offer prayers for the peace of Jerusalem (Ps. 122).

Read Pss. 76; 87; 122

c. The worshipers brought before Yahweh petitions for the King and temple similar to those found in Pss. 122:6 ff. and 84:9 f.

d. The festival proper began at the foot of Mount Zion with a processional, in which the ark was carried to the temple. The ritual included:

    i. An act of adoration and praise (Ps. 95:1–6), extolling Yahweh's name, reputation and activities in the sacred history (Ps. 99).

Read Ps. 95:1–6 and Ps. 99

    ii. The ascent of the hill, recalling David's role in bringing the ark to Jerusalem and reaffirming the Davidic covenant and the election of Jerusalem.

Read Ps. 132

    iii. The recitation of the "entrance Torah" at the gates of the courtyard. From the pilgrims rose the query, "Yahweh, who shall sojourn in thy tent? Who shall dwell on thy holy hill?" (15:1) and from the priests the response came in words recalling Yahweh's law and demanding individual personal examination of motives and actions by the worshipers. Only the righteous could enter through the "gates of righteousness" (cf. Ps. 118:19–20).

Read Pss. 15; 24:1–6

    iv. The entrance liturgy. Once again an antiphonal pattern can be discerned, with those bearing the ark demanding entrance for the "King of glory" and those within inquiring "Who is the king of glory?" (vss. 8a, 10a), to which a resounding response is given "Yahweh of hosts, he is the king of glory!" (vss. 8bc, 10bc).

Read Ps. 24:7–10

    v. An act of adoration. At this time the musicians, choristers and the entire company joined in a mighty paean (Ps. 150), and the wondrous acts of Yahweh were recited (Ps. 136).

Read Pss. 150; 136

    vi. The prayer for a theophany. Ps. 80, which may be one of the hymns preserved from the northern kingdom of Israel since it refers only to northern tribes, expresses the hope for a theophany through which the people will know that Yahweh is favorably disposed toward his people. The revelation of Yahweh (by what means we do not know) [56] in the cultic drama must have been a dramatic and traumatic moment. The apparent censure of cultic sacrifice was directed against those who believed Yahweh needed offerings for his sustenance and called for a proper spiritual attitude on the part of the giver. The worshiper was directed to look inwardly to evaluate his righteousness and worthiness to stand among the righteous in the courts of Yahweh.

Read Pss. 80; 50

    vii. The presentation of offerings and singing of hymns of thanksgiving. Yahweh was praised not only for his divine goodness but for the bless-

Read Ps. 65

---

[55] The Hebrew term *zaphon* is translated "north" in the Revised Standard Version. See, however, the translation in Dahood, *op. cit.*, p. 288 and cf. Isa. 14:13.

[56] Cf. Artur Weiser, *The Psalms*, pp. 394 f.

**Read Pss.
8; 134**

Read Ps. 121

ings of fertility, water and a good harvest, which ensured the physical life of the community.

viii. Nocturnal rituals. The ceremonies did not terminate at sunset and hymns of praise and adoration continued into the night.

ix. Departure hymns. When the time for the pilgrims to depart arrived, hymns of assurance were sung, promising Yahweh's protection and guidance.

The simplified outline of Kraus' argument provided here may give the impression that the schema is artificial, but in his detailed treatment of the festival, Kraus amply sustains his thesis. Of course there was opportunity within the festival period and at other times during the year for the individual to join in additional expressions of thanksgiving and praise or to seek help for problems. We will now consider some of the other categories of Psalms established by form critics.

INDIVIDUAL LAMENTS

Lament Psalms are by far the most numerous of all biblical Psalms. Individual laments should be thought of in terms of association with the cult, as suggested by the mention of the sanctuary and offerings and the implication that they were uttered in the presence of gathered worshipers. The pattern of these Psalms is well established:

1. The opening is usually an invocation or a cry for help to God in time of need.
2. The unhappy situation is explained.
3. Faith and trust in Yahweh are expressed.
4. Yahweh is petitioned to hear and save.
5. The motifs of enemies, the lowly situation of the petitioner, etc., are expressed.
6. The petitioner states his assurance of being heard or calls upon Yahweh to act.
7. Vows or promises of praise are given, or in instances where it would appear that the one who prays has received a favorable oracle or has had the petition answered, the vows are replaced by direct words of praise to Yahweh. At this point Lament Psalms approach Psalms of Praise which, in reiterating reasons why praise is given, often recall former unhappy situations (see below).

Among the many Individual Laments are Pss. 3, 6, 13, 17, 22, 26, 28, 31, 35, 38, 54, 55, 56, 57, 59, 64, 69, 70, 71, 86, 102, 109, 141 and 143. In these Psalms relief is sought from illness, persecution, mockery, failure, tormentors, rejection by friends, evil doers, reproach, shame, dishonor, loneliness and almost every other misfortune that could come to a man. The petitioners do not hesitate to call upon Yahweh to visit upon those who torment or persecute all manner of evil. The concluding promises of praise, should the requests be answered, in some of the Psalms of Lament should not be interpreted as bargaining, but rather as the recognition of a pattern of worship actually practiced.

These give thanks to Yahweh for deliverance from some unfortunate situation. The pattern in these Psalms is as follows:

1. A proclamation of praise and trust.
2. Recollection of the distress.
3. A report of the deliverance often mentioning the individual's cry and Yahweh's response.
4. The renewal of the vow of praise.
5. The statement of praise.

Some of the individual hymns are Pss. 9, 18, 30, 34, 40, 43, 92, 116. The troubles from which the individuals were delivered are similar to those listed under the Psalms of Lament. Perhaps such Psalms were recited before the gathered congregation as testimonials to the wondrous compassion and power of Yahweh on behalf of the individual.

COMMUNAL LAMENTS

These follow an outline similar to that given for individual laments. Yahweh is asked why enemies succeed, why the wicked prosper and the plea is made for deliverance as in former days. The innocence of the group is protested, and the vindictive nature of the enemy responsible for the unhappy situation is described. Some Psalms of communal lamentation are Pss. 10, 12, 44, 60, 74, 79, 80 and 83.

COMMUNAL THANKSGIVING PSALMS

These may be liturgies employed in major festal rites. Such Psalms honor Yahweh as creator of the world, as lord of history and for his mighty saving deeds. They call for joyful sacrifice and songs of praise to Yahweh for his gracious goodness, as they recall the dangers from which Yahweh delivered his people. Communal Psalms of Thanksgiving include Pss. 66, 67, 107, 113, 117, 118, 135 and 136.

ROYAL PSALMS

These are, as Gunkel indicated, associated with the activities of the king. Ordinarily they would be used in Jerusalem when the king participated in the cultus, either in sacrificial rites, or in seeking and receiving oracles, or perhaps at some ceremony in which the covenant between Yahweh and his people was renewed. The hymns include prayers offered by the monarch praising Yahweh or asking the deity for some benefit.

Ps. 2 is a coronation hymn. As we have seen, the death of a ruler and the accession of a new monarch were often times of rebellion by subject states or attack by enemies. This hymn promises the maintenance

Read Ps. 2

of order and reinforces the doctrines of the divine choice of Jerusalem and of the Davidic line.

Read Ps. 18

Ps. 18 is in part a royal hymn of praise to Yahweh for deliverance (vss. 1–30) and in part a statement of Yahweh's protection of the monarch. In the first section, a dramatic and well-detailed theophany is portrayed and the history of divine deliverance reviewed. The second part enables the king to declare before the entire community his dependence upon Yahweh for the power he has received.

Read Pss.
20; 21; 45

Ps. 20 is a prayer for the king recited in a cultic rite, possibly a coronation and Ps. 21 is prayer petitioning Yahweh on behalf of the ruler. These Psalms have also been interpreted as prayers uttered before (Ps. 20) and after (Ps. 21) battle. Ps. 45 is a cultic hymn sung at a royal wedding. Other Royal Psalms are 72, 101, 110 and 144.

WISDOM PSALMS

Teaching hymns which reflect the practical insights and counsel of the wise men of Israel found a place in the Hebrew cultus. They impart to the collection of Psalms a reminder of the way of religion in the life of the people. At times there is an expression of delight in the Torah, and again there is a study of the way of the righteous as opposed to the life of the unrighteous. The first Psalm in the Psalter belongs in this category. It contrasts two ways of life: righteousness and wickedness. It affirms simply that the way of the wicked fails while that of the righteous succeeds. It is clear that this particular "wisdom" writer did not wrestle with the problem of theodicy; rather the cultic setting where this Psalm was used affirmed the theological beliefs of the cult in the style and teaching mode of the wisdom school. Other Psalms in this category include 25, 32, 37, 49, 112 and 119.

Read Ps. 1

OTHER PSALMS AND THE CULTUS

It is impossible to discuss in detail all categories of Psalms recognized by form-critical studies. It is far more important to grasp what the form critics have made clear: that the Psalms are products of the temple cultus and that they must be understood in terms of their relationship to ritual and worship. Israel's heritage, interpreted as sacred history, was preserved and kept alive in the cult. Not only were worship rites based on events of the past, but in the Psalms the acts of Yahweh were recited. Unfortunately, it is not yet possible to place each Psalm in the festival or festivals where it was used, nor to recreate in any detail the activities of priests and people at any particular moment of the ritual.

The Hellenistic Era

27

The Early Hellenistic Period

THE Hellenistic period in Palestine technically begins with the defeat of the Persian empire by Alexander the Great (334–323). Greek influence had entered the Persian world much earlier, for Greek mercenaries fought in Persian armies and Greek traders introduced wares and ideas from the Hellenistic world. The period terminates with the conquest of Palestine in 63 by Pompey, the Roman. Our discussion will be divided into two major parts:

1. The Period of Hellenistic Rule.
2. The Period of Jewish Independence.

THE PERIOD OF HELLENISTIC RULE

Artaxerxes III Ochus (358–338) became king of Persia upon the death of his father Artaxerxes II, and secured his regime through a blood purge. Potential rivals in the rather large family of Artaxerxes II were eliminated.[1] Revolts in Phoenicia and Palestine, which may have involved Judah, were rudely put down. For ten years the port city of Sidon withstood Artaxerxes III before petitioning for peace, but Artaxerxes had the envoys murdered. It was clear to the Sidonians how Artaxerxes would treat them should they surrender and, rather than suffer the barbarous cruelties of the Persians, the Sidonians fired their city and thousands perished in the holocaust.[2] According to Josephus (*Antiquities* 11:7:1), Judah also experienced Artaxerxes' anger. Heavy fines were imposed and the temple was profaned. By 342, Artaxerxes had invaded Egypt to end that country's brief period of independence.

Artaxerxes was murdered by his son Arses (338–336), and Arses died by poison soon afterward. In 336, Darius III Codomannus (336–331) was crowned king, and in this same year Philip of Macedon, who had attempted to unify the Greeks, was murdered. Philip's twenty-year-old son, Alexander, who was to be called "the Great," became king

[1] Artaxerxes II had three sons by his queen Stateira and 115 by the 360 concubines officially assigned to him (one for each day of the civil year). Cf. A. T. Olmstead, *History of the Persian Empire* (Chicago: University of Chicago Press, 1948), p. 424, now issued as a Phoenix paperback.

[2] *Ibid.*, pp. 436 f.

CHART XVI

Events in Palestine	Jewish Writings	Events Elsewhere
	Esther	333: Alexander defeats Darius at Issus
Palestine controlled by Alexander	Joel Deutero-Zechariah	332–1: Tyre, Gaza, Palestine taken by Alexander
		323: Alexander dies and the Diodochoi rule
322: Ptolemy I controls Egypt and Palestine		
285: Palestine under Ptolemy II	Proverbs completed	LXX translated for Jews of Egypt
246: Ptolemy III		
221: Ptolemy IV	Ecclesiastes	
204: Ptolemy V	Song of Songs Tobit	200: Antiochus III defeats Ptolemy
198: Ptolemy loses Palestine to Antiochus III; Onias III is high priest		198: Antiochus defeats Ptolemy
		190: Romans defeat Antiochus
		187: Seleucis IV rules
175: Antiochus IV controls Judah; Onias goes to Egypt; Jason is high priest		175: Antiochus IV rules
171: Menelaus becomes high priest; Beginning of the Hasidim		Antiochus engages in the Parthian struggle
168: Seleucids defile Jewish altars Maccabean revolt begins	Daniel	
165: Judas Maccabeus rededicates altar		Antiochus V becomes king
164: Menelaus killed; Demetrius is high priest	Judith	Alexander Balas claims the Seleucid throne
161: Judas dies; Jonathan commands Jews		
153: Jonathan becomes high priest	I Esdras	Balas marries daughter of Ptolemy VI
150: Jonathan becomes governor	Baruch Letter of Jeremiah	
142: Jonathan murdered	Additions to Esther	
141: Simon creates a free state of Judah		Antiochus VII attacks Judah
138: The Jews defeat the Syrians		
135: John Hyrcanus rules Judah; Jews annex Idumea, Samaria, Perea, and destroy Samaritan temple; Sadducees, Pharisees, Essenes take form		
104: Aristobulus I rules Judah, annexes Galilee	Additions to Daniel	
104: Alexander Janneus rules Judah; Pharisees persecuted	I Maccabees	
78: Salome (Alexandra) rules; Sadducees persecuted	II Maccabees Wisdom of Solomon	
69: Aristobulus II becomes King and high priest Civil War breaks out		
64: Pompey creates the Roman province of Judaea		

and almost immediately was embroiled in the Persian-Greek power struggle which had begun in Philip's time.

The conquest of Persia was rapid. In 334, Alexander crossed the Hellespont and defeated Darius at the Granicus River. At Issus in North Syria, the Persians were beaten again in 333, and now Alexander controlled the western section of the Persian empire. Moving southward to possess Egypt, Alexander was detained seven months at the island of Tyre, which refused to capitulate until Alexander's men constructed a huge mole linking the mainland to the island and besieged the walls of the city. Gaza's resistance delayed the Greeks another two months, but the interior of Palestine yielded to hordes of Greek soldiers without struggle. In Egypt, Alexander, in accordance with Egyptian god-king political theology, was acknowledged as divine, the son of Zeus-Ammon. The city of Alexandria, which he founded, became a Greek center of learning and culture. In 331 Darius' forces were soundly defeated at the plain of Gaugamela. Alexander occupied Babylon, Susa and Persepolis without opposition, and then pursued the fleeing Darius to Ecbatana and on to Rhagae. Beyond Rhagae, Darius was murdered by his own disgruntled soldiers.

Alexander's aim was world conquest and unification. As cities succumbed to his military might, the process of Hellenization began. Literary and athletic contests were introduced, festivals were held and building programs begun. Greek language became the language of the empire and Greek culture flourished.

When Alexander died in Babylon in 323 at the age of 33, his empire crumbled, but under the Diodochoi ("successors"), who divided the territory, Greek culture continued. Alexander's general Perdiccas attempted to hold the empire together for Alexander's son, born soon after his father's death, but the greed of those who hungered for power was too great. Perdiccas was murdered in 321, and potential heirs to Alexander were killed soon after: his weak-minded half-brother Arrhedaeus in 317, his son in 311, and another son by a mistress in 309. Alexander's brilliant general Ptolemy I Lagos[3] (322–285) seized Egypt and established a dynasty that lasted until A.D. 30. Lysimachus became ruler of Thrace, and Seleucis I ruled Babylon, including Palestine. Antipater, who was succeeded by his son Cassander, got Macedonia and Greece; Antigonus took Phrygia; and Eumenes controlled the area south of the Black Sea.

It was an uneasy partition. Antigonus was greedy and, having brought about Eumenes' death, took over his territory. Ptolemy, who wanted Palestine as a buffer state, seized that area. Out of fear of Antigonus, a coalition was formed by the other Diodochoi, and in the battle of Ipsus in Phrygia in 301, Antigonus died. His holdings were divided and Alexander's empire was now in four parts: Lysimachus controlled Thrace and a portion of Asia Minor; Cassander held Macedon and Greece; Seleucis controlled an area extending from northern Palestine to the Indus River; and Ptolemy ruled over Egypt and central and southern Palestine.

---

[3] He was also called "Soter" (Savior).

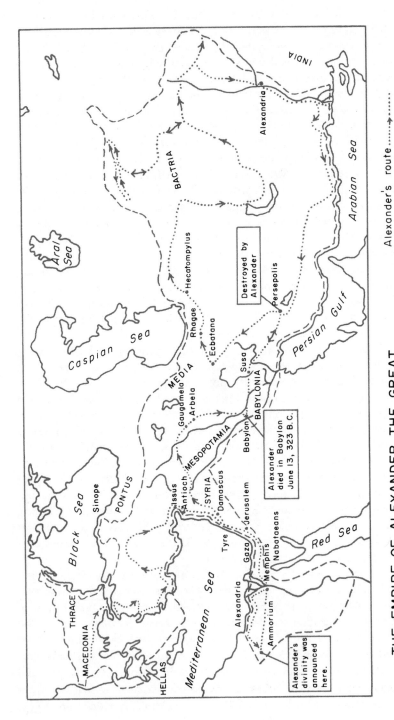

THE EMPIRE OF ALEXANDER THE GREAT

Alexander's route ·······→
Borders of Alexander's Kingdom ———

Aral Sea

Caspian Sea

Black Sea

Arabian Sea

Persian Gulf

Mediterranean Sea

Red Sea

INDIA

BACTRIA

MEDIA

MESOPOTAMIA

BABYLONIA

SYRIA

THRACE

MACEDONIA

PONTUS

HELLAS

Hecatompylus

Rhagae

Ecbatana

Susa

Persepolis

Gaugamela

Arbela

Antioch

Issus

Damascus

Tyre

Gaza

Jerusalem

Babylon

Sinope

Alexandria

Memphis

Ammorium

Nabataeans

Alexandria

Destroyed by Alexander

Alexander died in Babylon June 13, 323 B.C.

Alexander's divinity was announced here.

PALESTINIAN HISTORY IN LAMPS. *A sketch of the history of Palestine can be told with lamps recovered from excavations. The lamp in the upper right is from the Early Bronze Age and is simply a saucer in which oil (olive or animal) was poured and a wick, possibly of flax, was draped over the edge and set alight. Later, in the early part of the Middle Bronze Age the saucer was squared and wicks were laid in the corners of the dish. By the time of the Hyksos the saucer was folded inward on one side to form a channel for the wick, and by the time of the Hebrew invasion it had become the custom to elevate the spout and give the saucer a slight base (lamp in third tier). The Hebrews adopted this lamp but began to thicken the base (lamp at the rear on the bottom right platform). The six lamps in the foreground are from the Hellenistic period. The three on the left were made on a wheel and the spout was added. The three on the right (Delphiniform lamps) were made in two halves in molds and then brought together and sealed at the seam. By the Hellenistic period the open saucer lamps had been abandoned in favor of the closed lamp with a central opening through which oil was poured into the lamp and a spout in which the wick was placed.*

Palestine, the buffer state between Seleucis and Ptolemy, was to shuttle between Syria and Egypt. During the period of Egyptian control, a Jewish colony was established in Alexandria, which under Ptolemy I was becoming one of the greatest cultural and educational centers of the ancient world. Taxes in Judah were heavy, but the Jewish high priest was governor.

Ptolemy I was succeeded by Ptolemy II Philadelphus (285–246). The history of the Jews in this period is anything but clear, but it was under this monarch that the LXX was begun. During the reigns of Ptolemy II and Ptolemy III Euergetes (246–221), Egypt was strong financially and militarily. What burdens were placed upon the Jews in Palestine are not known, but perhaps the efforts of Ptolemy III to seize and hold parts of northern Palestine that had been under Seleucid control tended to make Palestine a military state subject to Near Eastern wartime controls. With Ptolemy IV Philopator (221–204),

Egyptian strength waned, although he was able to defeat the Seleucids at Raphia. When he died, his five-year-old son Ptolemy V was in no position to give adequate leadership for control of Palestine.

The Seleucid empire was now ruled by Antiochus III (223–187) who, like many before him, was called "the Great." Antiochus defeated Ptolemy at Gaza in 200 and again at Paneus in 198, and Palestine came under Seleucid control. Many Jews welcomed Antiochus as a deliverer. Antiochus, for his part, appears to have treated the Jews with respect, showing consideration for their religious traditions despite his enthusiasm for Greek culture, an enthusiasm shared by the strong pro-Greek party that had risen among the Jews.

In 187 Antiochus died. He had been defeated by Rome in the battle of Magnesia in 190 and had burdened his people with heavy taxation necessary to pay the indemnity demanded by Rome. The debt was inherited by his son Seleucis IV (187–175) who appointed a certain Heliodorus as collector. When Seleucis was murdered by Heliodorus, Antiochus IV (175–164) became king.

It is almost impossible to evaluate the significance of Antiochus IV from Jewish sources, so bitterly did Jewish writers react to him. He assumed the name "Epiphanes," which may be translated "the illustrious" or "the revealer" or "the revealed one." The Jews called him "Epimanes," which means "the cracked one" or "the mad one," so vigorously did he pursue the policy of Hellenization and so often did he violate Jewish sensitivities. Antiochus was an activist, determined to redeem the loss of military, economic and territorial prestige and power. His capital city, Antioch in Syria, was enlarged to accommodate Greeks seeking freedom from the growing pressures of Rome. A large community of Jews also lived there. New buildings were erected, new business was encouraged and Antioch became a center of commerce, wealth and culture. To strengthen political, religious and societal bonds, Antiochus encouraged Hellenic religion and culture, and it was at this point that he came into violent conflict with the separatist attitudes of the anti-Greek Jews of Judah. To meet the expenses of his program he laid heavy taxes upon his subjects.

Onias III, the Jewish high priest, was pro-Egyptian. When Antiochus became king, Onias retired to Leontopolis, Egypt, to found a Jewish colony. Antiochus sold the high priest's office to the highest bidder and Joshua, who preferred the Greek form of his name, "Jason," bought the post. Now the pro-Syrian, pro-Hellenistic Jason entered into a conspiracy with Antiochus to bring the Jews into conformity with Greek culture. Greek garb and food were common. A gymnasium was built in Jerusalem and young men attended, including priests who left their altar duties for discus throwing and other athletics. Many gymnasium activities were performed in the nude, and some Jews underwent surgery to remove the distinguishing mark of circumcision—an act which, to the orthodox, was tantamount to rejection of the covenant.[4]

In 171, a certain Menelaus offered more money for the high priest-

---

[4] The bulk of this information is drawn from I Maccabees, chap. 1.

hood and Antiochus accepted. Jason fled to Transjordan and Mene-laus robbed the temple treasury to pay his debt to the king. Now a new sect of Jews was formed from scribes and their followers, and these took the name "Hasidim," which means "pious" but which implies "loyalty." The Hasidim concentrated on the study of the Torah and observance of the Law, and when their religious customs were proscribed were among those who went passively to their death, rather than resist.

War broke out between Syria and Egypt, and Antiochus marched against his enemies in 170. His plans for conquest failed and a rumor arose that Antiochus had been killed in battle, prompting Jason to return from exile. But Antiochus was not dead. On his return from Egypt, he quelled a revolt inspired by Jason and looted the temple. A Phrygian named Philip was appointed governor of the Jews. In 168, Antiochus returned, for Jewish nationalistic pressures had not dimin-ished. This time Jerusalem was burned and its walls demolished. Thousands died in battle and many others were enslaved. Every ex-pression of Judaism was proscribed, including Sabbath worship, Torah study and circumcision, and the most excruciating punishments were devised for violators. Worst of all, on December 15, 168, an altar to the Olympian Zeus was built upon the Jewish altar of sacrifice and pigs' flesh was sacrificed. All Jewish temple worship ceased for this was "the abomination that made desolate" as the writer of the book of Daniel was to describe the act that contaminated the holy altar. The situation had become intolerable for the faithful Jews and, as we shall see, they were faced with a choice: succumb or do battle.

ESTHER

Read Esther

The book of Esther is a secular legend with its setting in Susa, the Persian capital. The story may have originated during the Persian period, although it probably was not reduced to the form in which we know it until the beginning of the Hellenistic era. Some scholars have attempted to discover references to Babylonian deities and rituals in the book, identifying Mordecai with Marduk, Esther with Ishtar, and other characters with minor, obscure deities.[5] Others have tried to relate the writing to Assyrian springtime rites, to Persian New Year observances,[6] to Greek wine festivals, to historical events such as the victory of the Jews over Nicanor in 161, or to other historical or cultic themes.

That Esther is not history, despite some accurate details about Per-sian government (cf. 1:14; 3:7), is clear from the numerous inconsist-encies and exaggerations. Ahasuerus is usually identified as Xerxes (Khshayarsha), who reigned between 485 and 465. A Persian admin-istrator named Marduka (Mordecai) is known from this period, but there is no indication that he was a Jew, although some Jewish parents

5 For a detailed discussion, cf. N. S. Doniach, *Purim and the Feast of Esther* (Philadelphia: The Jewish Publication Society of America, 1933), pp. 1–53.

6 For a strong defense of this hypothesis, cf. T. H. Gaster, *Purim and Hanukkah* (New York: Henry Schuman, 1950), pp. 12–18.

did give their children the name Mordecai, which honored the chief god of Babylon (cf. Ezra 2:2; Neh. 7:7). According to the Greek historian Herodotus, a contemporary, Xerxes' wife was Amestris, not Vashti or Esther. Nor do these names appear as the wives of other Persian monarchs. However, if Xerxes, like Artaxerxes II, had a concubine for each day of the year, Vashti or Esther may have been among them. Mordecai is supposed to have been one of the Jews that went into exile under Nebuchadrezzar, which would make him well over 100 years old when appointed to the court (2:5 f.). The extermination of 75,000 people by the Jews with Xerxes' permission seems unlikely (9:16). Certain exaggerations are so extreme that they must have been included to delight the audience. For example, the gallows are 50 cubits or about 75 feet high! Haman estimates he could raise 10,000 talents or about $18,000,000 by confiscating Jewish property—a sum estimated at more than one half of the annual income of the Persian empire. It seems best to recognize the story as a legend embodying, as most legends do, some accurate historical details.

The earliest references to the book of Esther are found in *Contra Apion* 1:8, the work of the Jewish historian, Josephus (A.D. 1). Josephus drew upon the LXX version of Esther, which includes the "additions to Esther" that we will consider later. The omission of any reference to Esther in the second century work known as Ecclesiasticus or Sirach, written by Jesus ben Sira, in which Jewish heroes are extolled, has led some scholars to date Esther after this time. Arguments from silence are never very convincing.

The tendency of the writer of Esther to refer to the events of the story as taking place in the distant past (1:1, 13; 10:2) and the expanded explanations (4:11; 8:8) suggest a time of recording long after the events described. The reference to the dispersed Jews best fits the Greek period (3:8). On the basis of this limited evidence, it would appear that the story was written in the early Greek period, a time when stories about Jewish successes in Persian royal circles would suffer least contradiction and a time when the spirit of Jewish independence appears to have been strong.

The book is completely secular[7] and contains no reference to the deity. It exalts a Jewish heroine who saves the people from persecution, and it delights in Jewish success and victory over the enemy. The writer possessed genuine narrative skill and developed his theme through a succession of dramatic climaxes, alternating tension with delightful humorous touches (cf. 1:21–22; 3:9; etc.). But the story is more than entertainment. It is a grim reminder to a people buffeted by great powers of the ever-present potential of persecution by a tyrant—not necessarily the king, but rather the power-hungry, attention-loving, minor official whose pomposity was so easily threatened by the non-conformist or the man of conviction. In the magnificent characterizations, the author provided his readers with a response to tyranny and oppression and exposed the transparent motives of the

---

[7] However, see the "Additions to Esther."

oppressor, and exalted the individual who remained faithful to his commitments and to himself. Later the book of Esther was linked to the festival of Purim.

JOEL

Read Joel

Joel is the work of an unknown prophet who conveys to his readers through dramatic imagery the immediacy of a frightful threat to national well-being, and the subsequent deliverance. The mood in the three chapters moves from concern, through terror, to desperate repentance and hope, to relief at salvation and exalted hopes for the future. The work appears to be a literary unity, the work of one writer. Because of the emphasis on Jerusalem and Judah, the author is, obviously, a Judaean.

At one time Joel was listed among the earliest prophetic writings, but this view has been abandoned. The text lacks themes prominent in eighth century prophetic books: kings, Canaanite religion, idolatry, apostasy. Nor are there references to Assyrians, Babylonians or Persians. The specific mention of the Greeks (3:6) and the indication that the temple is standing and the cult operating (1:9, 13, 16; 2:17) points to the early Hellenistic period. The imminent destruction of Tyre, Sidon and Philistia reflected in 3:4–8 suggests that Joel may have been written after Alexander the Great had begun the siege of Tyre.

The opening verses describe a plague of locusts sweeping over the land. It is usually assumed that subsequent passages describing the devastation of the land reflect the destructive activities of these insects. Such terms as "nation" in 1:6, "a great and powerful people" in 2:2 and the descriptions of the approaching hordes (2:4 ff.) are interpreted as symbols for the swarming locusts. But, if Joel is writing when Alexander's armies are moving through Palestine, it is possible that he is describing Greek armies. The initial swarm of locusts was, as in Amos, actually seen, but in the prophet's imagery the insects were symbolic of the waves of Greeks marching through the land. References to "the nation" and "the great and powerful people" were, therefore, historical. On this basis the book may be analyzed as follows:

1:1 The editorial superscription.
1:2–4 The initial vision of the swarm of locusts in which different kinds or stages of development of locusts are indicated.
1:5–14 The call to lamentation rites for the wasting of the land and the blending of locust imagery into a description of the invading enemy.
1:15–2:11 The interpretation of events as forewarnings of the Day of Yahweh, which is depicted as a day of gloom and destruction.
2:12–17 The nation is summoned to repentance rites in the hope that Yahweh will deliver the people.
2:18–29 Yahweh has saved his people. The Greeks did not destroy or plunder. There is promise of ample harvest and abundant blessing.
2:30–32 The second vision of the Day of Yahweh, now described as a day of salvation, blessing and restoration for the Jews and Judah.

3:1-3   The promise of judgment against Judah's oppressors.
3:4-8   The implication of the imminent fall of Tyre, Sidon and Philistia.
3:9-21 The third vision of the Day of Yahweh as a time of judgment for the people of the world, and a time of blessing for Judah.

Because a majority of scholars assume that the locusts represent a real plague[8] and that there is no reference to foreign invaders, the following analysis is provided:

1:1   The editorial superscription.
1:2-20   The plague of locusts and a drought.
2:1:11   The locusts as a warning of the Day of Yahweh.
2:12-17   The call for repentance.
2:18-27   The restoration of the land.
2:28-32   The signs of the Day of Yahweh.
3:1-16   Judgment on the nations.
3:17-21   Blessings on Judah.

For Joel, the locusts (or the Greeks) are signs of Yahweh's anger, and although there is no specification of evils, the nation is called to repent. As the danger passed, the penitential mood changed to thanksgiving. The concluding visions of the Day of Yahweh are quite distinct from the first (cf. 2:30-32; 3:9-21; and 1:5-2:11). In the first vision, judgment falls on Judah and the prospects are grim; in the last visions condemnation and threats are directed against Judah's enemies and hopes for the Jews are high. Clearly, the day of Yahweh concept was still strong in the Jewish community, and particularistic and nationalistic dreams for the future were undiminished. The last two visions of Yahweh's Day have an air of finality, as though the history of struggle for identity and the long hoped for period of blessing were to be realized. Once "that Day" had come, the future would be secure. This eschatological hope or idealistic doctrine of the end was soon to expand and develop new facets. The book reflects a liturgical framework which may have grown out of the close working relationship between the prophets and the cult.[9]

DEUTERO-ZECHARIAH

The second section of the book of Zechariah consists of two separate collections of oracles that defy precise dating: Chapters 9 to 11 and Chapters 12 to 14. At one time both collections were attributed to Jeremiah because in the New Testament the Gospel of Matthew (27:9-16) quotes part of Zechariah 11:12 f. and attributes the words to Jeremiah. Some scholars have argued for pre-Exilic dates. The first collection refers to both Judah and Ephraim and speaks of Egypt and Assyria, and it was assumed that the oracles must have come from the period of the divided Hebrew kingdoms. Chapters 12 to 14 were dated between 609 and 598, for they imply that Jerusalem was still

---

[8] J. A. Thompson, "The Book of Joel," *The Interpreter's Bible*, VI, 733 f., and "Joel's Locusts in the Light of Near East Parallels," *Journal of Near Eastern Studies*, XIV (1955), 52-55.

[9] Cf. T. H. Gaster, *Thespis*, pp. 44 ff.

standing but that Josiah, to whom it was assumed that 12:11 referred, was dead.[10] Most present-day scholarship places the time of writing in the early years of the Hellenistic period, although later dates have been proposed. The first eight verses are interpreted as a record of Alexander's campaign in Syria and Palestine in 332, and specific reference to the ramp built by Alexander's men in the siege of Tyre is found in 9:3 f. Furthermore, Greece is specifically mentioned in 9:13. We will accept the Hellenistic period as the time of writing but with reservations, for the evidence upon which the dating rests is far from conclusive.

The opening verses of the first collection pronounce judgment on Judah's neighbors: Aram or Syria with the cities of Hadrach, Damascus and Hamath; Phoenicia with Tyre and Sidon; and Philistia with four of the five confederated cities (Gath is omitted). Alexander's campaign had begun and the prophet interpreted the military activities of the Greeks as Yahweh's judgment and as a sign that the great Day of Yahweh was at hand. He envisioned the triumphant, victorious, messianic king entering the city of Jerusalem riding upon an ass, as Solomon had done after his coronation. So great was the royal authority that peace was established by fiat. Subsequent events include the release of captive Jews, the supremacy of the Jews over the Greeks and a dramatic theophany of Yahweh as the god of war protecting and exalting his people.

**Read Zech.
Ch. 9**

The two opening verses of Chapter 10 form an independent oracle condemning those who, in time of drought, sought aid from idols. The remaining verses appear to be from the early years of the Diodochoi, who are condemned as "shepherds." The restoration of the Jewish nation is predicted.

Read Ch. 10

The first verses of Chapter 11 appear to refer to the fall of the Diodochoi, but the remaining enigmatic verses provide no clue for intelligent interpretation.

Read Ch. 11

The second section, sometimes referred to as Trito-Zechariah, may also have been composed in the time of the Diodochoi. Yahweh's miraculous intervention, the defeat of Judah's oppressors and the establishment of the ideal kingdom, are foretold. Perhaps something of the low degree to which prophecy had sunk is implied in 13:4–6. The writer foretells a period of darkness for Yahweh's people after which the new kingdom will be established. The closing verses portray the pilgrims streaming toward Jerusalem for the New Year festival, and the worshipers include foreigners who recognize Yahweh as the supreme and only deity. Those who fail to come do not enjoy divine blessing.

**Read Chs.
12 to 14**

[10] For a different analysis, cf. Benedikt Otzen, *Studien über Deuterosacharja*, Acta Theologica Danica, VI (1964). Otzen dates chaps. 9 and 10 after Josiah's reign; chaps. 10, 11 and 12, which he finds to be Deuteronomic, in the period immediately preceding the Exile and in the earliest years of the Exile; and chap. 14 in the late post-Exilic period.

28
Wisdom Writings

EARLIER we discussed possible relationships of Hebrew wisdom to the court of Solomon and to wisdom writing in the ancient Near East. We also considered some characteristics of wisdom literature, but we have not examined the words of the wise as inspired utterances. To what degree the insights of the wise men were believed to be of divine origin is not known. Jer. 18:18 groups prophets, priests and wise men as recipients of divine instruction (cf. Jer. 8:8 ff.), but no clue is given as to how the insight was given. In the section of Proverbs believed to be the last addition to the entire work (chs. 1–9), wisdom is depicted as an hypostasis of Yahweh.[1] It is possible that Hebrew wisdom was not believed to be the result of intellectual speculation alone, but was related to, and perhaps derived from, divine Wisdom and was thus automatically linked to that which in the beginning gave order to primeval chaos and was the agent by which God created (cf. 3:19 f.; 8:22 ff.). If Wisdom was the ordering principle of the cosmos, then to receive insight from Wisdom was to acquire guidelines for living an ordered life in harmony with the cosmos. Some wisdom literature, in particular the first nine chapters of Proverbs, fits this interpretation, but it is impossible to read it back into earlier materials. Nor should wisdom be considered purely secular because it does not emphasize such central themes of prophecy or priestly teachings as the covenant, election, the cult, the role of Yahweh in history, Jerusalem, etc. Wisdom literature appears to rest in an acceptance of, and a profound respect for, a divine order which sustains the cosmos, but the writers do not presume to comment upon that order theologically.

The precepts of wisdom tended to be those verifiable by observation and were concerned with teaching man how to live.[2] The Hebrew

---

[1] The term "hypostasis" is borrowed from a Greek word which, in philosophy, had to do with "essence" or "identity" or "substance." Here it signifies an activity of Yahweh endowed with a distinct identity. Hypostasis moves beyond literary personification, which may be used for dramatic effect, to the recognition of individual identity. Wisdom is given a distinct personality and existence apart from, but still under, Yahweh. Whether or not Greek influence is involved in Prov. 1:20 ff.; 8; 9, is debatable, although the Greeks did hypostatize *logos* or "reason" and later *sophia* or "wisdom." For an excellent discussion, see R. B. Y. Scott, *Proverbs. Ecclesiastes,* The Anchor Bible (Garden City, New York: Doubleday & Company, Inc., 1965), pp. 69 ff.

[2] Cf. G. von Rad, *Old Testament Theology,* trans. D. M. G. Stalker (New York: Harper & Brothers, 1962), I, 418 ff.

word for wisdom (*hokmah*) is related to a root meaning "skill" or "care" and came to imply "skill in living." The wise man (*hakam*) was one who possessed knowledge about how a man might live skillfully or well—knowledge that could be imparted to others. The means of communication was sometimes a riddle but more often a proverb (Heb: *mashal*), which could be a poem of two balanced lines or a more extended writing akin to a parable. The concerns were largely those related to everyday life and the teachings, particularly in Proverbs, tend to be didactic and mundane. Whether or not the wisdom movement had any ties with the cult cannot be ascertained, but in the post-Exilic period wisdom writings show an increasing tendency to accord with accepted Jewish religious beliefs.

Wise men formed schools of instruction. Their words, spoken as a father (teacher) to a son (disciple), were copied and learned so that their followers would have precepts to guide and instruct in any situation in life.[3] Broadly speaking, wisdom teachings are practical as opposed to theoretical, individualistic rather than nationalistic, humanistic rather than theological. Religion is not neglected (cf. 1:7; 20:27), it simply isn't stressed. We will discuss some of these wisdom writings now, but will consider "The Wisdom of Solomon" later.

PROVERBS

The opening verse of Proverbs appears to attribute the entire book to Solomon, in accordance with the custom of attributing anonymous writings to ancient worthies, but it is clear from the contents that, like so many other books of the Bible, Proverbs is a composite work. Some words are assigned to Agur, son of Jakeh of the Ishamaelite tribe of Massa (Prov. 30:1, cf. Gen. 25:14), others to the mother of Lemuel, king of Massa (Prov. 31:1). Within the book, eight different collections can be identified, and within these larger units, smaller groupings have been found:

1. Chapters 1–9 are attributed to Solomon but appear to be the latest contribution to the book of Proverbs.
2. Chapters 10:1–22:16, also attributed to Solomon, appear to be the oldest collection of maxims and the original nucleus of the book.
3. Chapters 22:17–24:22, introduced in the LXX as "the words of the wise," are saying borrowed and adapted in part from the Wisdom of Amen-em-ope of Egypt.
4. Chapter 24:23–34 is a sub-collection titled "These also are the sayings of the wise."
5. Chapters 25–29 are labeled "The Proverbs of Solomon which the men of Hezekiah, king of Judah, copied."

[3] The story of Ahikar, a wisdom writing with an Assyrian setting, mentions this method and purpose of instruction (cf. Ahikar 1:15 ff.; 7:26; but see 4:21). Ahikar is the story of a vizier of the Assyrian court who is betrayed by an ungrateful nephew and who finally regains his position through his wisdom. A sixth century Aramaic version is known, but the tale may be much older. For a translation, see R. H. Charles (ed.), *The Apocrypha and Pseudepigrapha of the Old Testament* (Oxford: The Clarendon Press, 1913), II, 715–784.

6. Chapter 30 consists of "The words of Agur, son of Jakeh of Massa."
7. Chapter 31:1–9 is labeled "The words of Lemuel, king of Massa, which his mother taught him."
8. Chapter 31:10–31 is an alphabetic acrostic on the ideal wife.

Read Ch. 1–1:6 The first six verses of the first section form a one-sentence editorial introduction to the entire book of Proverbs. The opening verse, attributing the sayings to Solomon, cannot be taken seriously because of the composite nature of Proverbs, although some maxims may go back to Solomon's time. The subsequent verses designate the purpose of the collected wisdom sayings and the merits of possessing wisdom.

Read Chs. 1:7–9:18 The first verse of the next section (1:7), which is repeated in 9:10, stipulates that the basic premise of wisdom is reverence for Yahweh, which would include healthy respect for all expressions of Yahweh's will—moral, ethical and cultic. Here the writer sets forth a model of the ideal man. He is one who avoids evil company (1:10 ff.), complacency (1:32), contention (3:28 ff.), the adulteress (5:1 ff.; 6:23 ff.; 7:6 ff.; 9:13 ff.), debt (6:1 ff.), laziness (6:6 ff.), arrogance (8:13). On the positive side, the ideal is a careful individual, secure in time of calamity (1:26 ff.; 3:25 f.) because he is upright in his ways (2:6 ff.; 4:10 ff., 25 f.), discreet (2:11), reliable (6:1 ff.) and diligent (6:6 ff.). The recognition of the material rewards that come from adhering to the way of wisdom suggests that the writer was a comfortable, wealthy, respected citizen, who was somewhat out of sympathy with the wayward youth of his day (1:33; 3:9 f., 25 f.; 8:18, 20).

Read Chs. 10:1–22:16 The second unit is composed of short, pithy couplets almost all of which are set in antithetical parallelism. Each unit is complete and independent, although at times it appears that an editor made some effort to group sayings dealing with similar themes, such as the king (16:10, 12–15) or the fool (12:15–16; 18:6–7). Because of the simplicity of the poetic form, it is commonly agreed that this collection is the oldest in the book of Proverbs. The themes are diverse and include praise of integrity, discipline, diligence and condemnation of their opposites. Some sayings gain clarity from startling exaggerations (10:26; 11:22; 12:4; 15:7; 17:12; 18:9); others show acceptance of theological teaching similar to that of the Deuteronomists (10:3; 11:11; 12:7; 14:9; 16:3).

Read Chs. 22:17–24:22 The next precepts, drawn in part from the Wisdom of Amen-em-ope of Egypt (*ca.* 1000–600), are not attributed to Solomon and bear the simple title "Words of the wise." The literary structure is more complex than that found in the preceding collection, but it is possible that these sayings also belong to the pre-Exilic period. Only 22:17–23:11 are based on Amen-em-ope's instructions for court officials[4] and what the biblical writer borrowed was given a distinctive character by adaption to the Hebrew milieu.

Read Chs. 24:23–34 The few verses forming an appendage to the collection are concerned with justice and sloth. The passages in the next unit are in couplet form, like those of Chs. 10:1–22:16. They are said to have been **Read Chs. 25–29** copied by King Hezekiah's men, and it is quite possible that they are

4 Cf. *ANET*, p. 421.

pre-Exilic, as the numerous references to the monarchy would suggest. Some passages employ striking imagery (25:20, 21; 26:11, 17; 27:15–16).

The opening verses (1–4) of Chapter 30 are reminiscent of Yahweh's challenge to Job (Job 38:2–5). Perhaps a dialogue is represented here. A question is put to Ithiel and Ucal about the possibility of man knowing God (vss. 1b–4). These men respond that the fact that God's word is fulfilled, and that those who trust in him are protected, is knowledge enough (vss. 5–6). The last section (vss. 10–33) includes sayings using the familiar literary pattern of numeric progression, some of which are striking (vss. 18–19, 21–23), and two single-line proverbs (15a and 20).

Read Ch. 30

The words in the collection purporting to be the advice of a queen mother to an otherwise unknown King Lemuel deal with proper behavior for rulers.

Read Ch. 31:1–9

The closing section is an alphabetic acrostic since the initial letter of each of the twenty-two couplets begins with the successive of the twenty-two consonants of the Hebrew alphabet. The rather burdensome responsibilities of the wife of a successful businessman are enumerated.[5]

Read Ch. 31:10–31

ECCLESIASTES

Ecclesiastes, like Proverbs, is a product of the wisdom school, but is of a different temperament and outlook. Proverbs affirmed the accepted values of Jewish society; Ecclesiastes questions these same ambitions and goals. The author pretends to be Solomon (1:12 ff.), a claim accepted by the editor (1:1), but some passages indicate that the writer is a subject rather than a ruler (3:16; 4:1; 10:4–5). Although Solomon was only the second Hebrew monarch to rule from Jerusalem, the author speaks of the numerous Jerusalemite kings who preceded him (1:16; 2:9). The reference could be said to include Jebusite rulers but these are unknown in Hebrew-Jewish traditions. The language of the book is Hebrew with numerous Aramaisms suggesting the post-Exilic era. The author's spirit of individualism fits well into the early Greek period. Efforts to discover historical allusions within the text have not been particularly convincing. A reflection of the disturbed political conditions at the beginning of the Hellenistic period is found in 4:3 by some scholars, and others suggest that Ptolemy V is referred to in 10:16. The fragments of Ecclesiastes found at Qumran indicate that the book was known in the second century and, since there is no hint of the dramatic Jewish struggle for independence, a date prior to the second century is preferred. Therefore, the author was not Solomon, but a Jew of Jerusalem (although

[5] Margaret B. Crook, "The Marriageable Maiden of Prov. 30:10–31," *Journal of Near Eastern Studies*, XIII (1954), 137–140, has identified these verses as a memorandum from a training school for marriageable young women who would shortly be assuming positions of affluence in their communities. She rejects the thesis that the verses reveal actual domestic life.

SPINNING WHORLS. *Cloth making, which included the spinning of wool, goat hair, cotton or flax into yarn and the weaving of yarn or thread into cloth, was an important home industry in ancient Palestine. The last chapter of Proverbs includes spinning among the responsibilities of the busy housewife. The two objects pictured are spinning whorls: the larger is made of bone and the smaller of stone. A spindle, a shaft of wood or reed or ivory was thrust through the whorl, and when the spindle and whorl were spun the fibers fed to this combination were twisted into yarn or thread.*

Alexandria is also a possibility) living in the closing years of the fourth or the early decades of the third century.

Ecclesiastes appears to be a literary unity. A few passages, expressing beliefs that appear to be contrary to the major thrust of the book, have been labeled interpolations by some scholars and accepted as genuine by others (2:26; 3:17; 7:26b; 8:12 f.; 11:9b). The uniformity of language would caution against removal of these passages. This writer, like Job, believed in God and divine righteousness, but did not pretend to understand God's ways. The book concludes at 12:8 on the same note with which it opens; 12:9–10 is an appendix expressing appreciation for the author, written, perhaps, by a disciple; and 12:11–14 is an added ending, warning against taking Ecclesiastes too seriously and providing a succinct alternative as a guide for living.

The title of the book in Hebrew is *koheleth,* which appears to be related to the Hebrew word for an assembly or congregation (*qahal*), so that Koheleth is one who assembles people, perhaps the speaker. The term "Ecclesiastes" is from the LXX and refers to one who participates in an assembly. The English translation "Preacher" is unfortunate for it conveys the wrong image. Koheleth was a teacher, probably in a wisdom school. The book is a compendium of his teachings, not recorded in orderly literary fashion so that one idea leads logically to the next, but rather as a compilation of the teacher's speculations on the emptiness of life.

Ecclesiastes is intellectually linked to Job. Job demonstrated the futility of asking "Why?" of God. Koheleth accepts this. The intellectual struggle with orthodox theology was, for him, over. The question now was, "How does one live without theological or ultimate answers?"

Read Ecclesiastes

No summary or analysis of contents can be substituted for reading Koheleth. His basic premise is that life is meaningless.[6] Man's struggle to achieve a name, reputation, fame, fortune, pleasures, and even to acquire wisdom, is meaningless, ultimately counting for nothing. Nature is cyclic, season follows season and pattern follows pattern. There is no meaning to the cycle. Man can do nothing to change it; man can only conform to it. To make his point, Koheleth posed as Solomon, who, as king, was in a position to explore in depth the various ways by which man sought to give meaning to his life. The search for wisdom produced frustration (1:16 ff.); indulgence in pleasures and the acquisition of possessions were hollow. Koheleth learned, as Job had before him, that man is powerless before the cosmic order.

[6] The Hebrew word *hebel* is usually translated "vanity" and signified "breath" or "that which is transitory" or "empty." Here it means "empty of meaning."

There are predetermined times for everything and to these man can but yield. Ultimately, all creatures, great and small, wise and foolish, animal and human, share a common end and are made equal in the grave. What happens at death cannot be known (3:19 ff.).

In the face of Koheleth's experience and analysis of the futility of human ambitions, how should man live? Koheleth affirmed that wisdom was better than folly (2:13), friendship better than loneliness (4:9 ff.), keeping vows to God wiser than violating them (5:1 ff.), accepting one's lot and enjoying life to be preferred to constantly striving to better it (5:11 ff.). His response to the problem of theodicy is that one must enjoy pleasurable things when they are available, and when evil days come, accept these too (7:14). His advice was to press out of each moment of life as much enjoyment as possible (8:15–9:17), particularly in youth (11:9–12:1), because old age limits one's possibilities (12:1–8).

Koheleth has been called pessimistic, but his message comes through marked with realistic enjoyment of life (11:7). There is no bitterness in his denial of the validity of what he deems to be fruitless theological speculation (8:16 ff.) nor over-concern for that which cannot be changed (7:13). Like the writers in Proverbs, he frowns on laziness (10:18) and in the next breath extols the joys of bread, wine and money. He suggests a certain recklessness with possessions (11:1–2, 6) on the chance that good results will come of it. Like Job, he rejects the doctrine that the good are rewarded and the wicked punished and recognizes that sometimes it happens, sometimes it doesn't. Koheleth finds no ultimate meaning in life, only the meaning that each man gives to it in his commitment to full enjoyment of the brief span of years that are individually his.

SONG OF SONGS

Perhaps the most unusual book among the sacred literature of ancient Israel is this collection of poems which expresses so forthrightly in sensuous language the theme of passionate love. The title "The Song of Songs of Solomon," which means "the best of Solomon's songs," cannot be accepted as guaranteeing the work as one of King Solomon's compositions (cf. I Kings 4:32). The presence of Aramaisms and Persian and Greek loan words places the time of writing in the post-Exilic Hellenistic era, probably in the third century, although parts of the poems may be much earlier. We have appended the poems to the section on wisdom literature because it has been theorized that they were arranged and preserved by the wise men, thus explaining how the entire work was attributed to Solomon, the patron of Hebrew wisdom.

The poetry has been extolled for its beauty and elaborate imagery. Its symbols are sensuous. Its form is that of a collection of monologues and its point of view is secular. Numerous interpretations of the Song of Songs have been proposed:[7]

[7] For a detailed discussion, see T. J. Meek, "The Song of Songs," *The Interpreter's Bible*, V, 92 ff.

a. It has been labeled an allegory. Rabbi Akiba interpreted it as an allegory of God's love for his people, Israel. Later, Christians explained it as an expression of Christ's love for his Church.

b. Even as Akiba was giving his interpretation, young men of his day recognized the secular nature of the Song and sang it in the local wine shops.

c. It has been analyzed as a drama with two characters: Solomon and his bride; or with three characters: Solomon, the bride, and her shepherd lover to whom she remains faithful. The lack of proper divisions into acts and scenes tends to make any reconstruction along these lines appear forced or artificial to the western mind.

e. Comparison with Syrian wedding songs (called *wasf*) which are sung during a seven-day celebration in which the bride and groom are honored as king and queen and their beauty is extolled has led to the identification of the Song of Songs as an epithalamion. It has been pointed out in partial answer, that in the biblical song the bride is not called a queen.

f. Some scholars have found evidence of fertility cult ritual within the poems. (For example, 1:5 ff. is said to signify the death of fertility; 2:10 ff., rebirth; 3:1 ff. and 5:6 ff., the search for Tammuz.) It is quite possible that the Song originated in the fertility cult of Canaan, but because Yahwism rejected the idea of a hierarchy of gods with love affairs and divine marriages, the Song became secularized and was retained as a *wasf*. There are, obviously, antiphonal relationships between parts of the poem and these may hark back to a primitive cultic setting, but so far, any attempts to set these in a specific pattern or to explain the relationship between parts of the Song have been less than convincing.

It is best, perhaps, to accept this last hypothesis concerning the Song, for it explains how this literature with what appear to be secular erotic overtones came to be included in Jewish sacred literature: the Song originated in the sacred literature of Canaan. Therefore Rabbi Akiba was not wrong in stressing its cultic and religious significance even though by his interpretation he gave the Song a new meaning in Judaism, just as Christians were to give it still another meaning in Christianity. Nor were the young men wrong, for the amatory themes were not part of Jewish theology, but were prominent in secular life.

ECCLESIASTICUS (SIRACH)

Ecclesiasticus, the most extensive wisdom writing of the Hellenistic period, has been accepted as canonical by the Roman Catholic and Eastern Orthodox churches, but not by Jews and Protestants. It is the only wisdom document whose author is known. Jesus son of Sirach, to call him by the Greek form of his name, or Joshua or Jeshua ben Sira according to the Hebrew, was a Jew who conducted a wisdom school in Jerusalem. The Prologue to his work, written by his grandson, informs us that the grandson went to Egypt to translate his grandfather's work into Greek in the year 132, the thirty-eighth year of King Euergetes, who is assumed to be King Ptolemy VII Euergetes II Physcon who reigned from 170 to 117. Ben Sira must have been born before the beginning of the second century, and it is assumed that his school flourished during the early years of the second century, particularly at the time when Antiochus III controlled Palestine. His writings give no hint of the social pressures and problems associated with the reign of Antiochus IV, although it must be admitted that Ben Sira makes little reference to specific social and historical events. Chapter 50 refers to Simon, the high priest, in such warm, intimate terms that there can be little doubt that Ben Sira was present at the worship service he describes—probably the Day of Atonement. Josephus mentions two Simons who were high priests. The first, if he ever existed (there is considerable doubt about this), was Simon, son of Onias, or Simon I called Righteous, who would have to have lived about 300 (*Antiquities of the Jews* 12:2:5). Simon II, son of Jochanan (Greek: Onias), whose high priesthood is placed between 219 and 199, is believed to be the high priest observed by Ben Sira. Ecclesiasticus is, therefore, best dated about 180.

The title "Ecclesiasticus" is from the Latin translation and means "The Church's book," but the Hebrew title was, apparently "The Proverbs of Ben Sira" and the Greek "The Wisdom of Jesus, son of Sirach."[8] The book may be divided into two major parts: Chapters 1 to 23 and Chapters 24 to 50, with Chapter 51 forming an appendix. Like Proverbs, each section opens with a poem in praise of wisdom (1:1–20; 24), and like Proverbs, the entire book ends with an alphabetic acrostic (51:13–30). The bulk of Ecclesiasticus is wisdom sayings or groups of sayings covering a wide variety of subjects. At times Ben Sira expanded his comments into short essays. No particular order of presentation can be discerned and attempts at literary analysis usually end as topical lists. A broad outline of the book is as follows:

I. The Prologue, which consists of introductory remarks by Ben Sira's grandson. The Prologue stands outside of the chapter and verse divisions.

II. The First Book, Chapters 1 to 23.

    1:1–20, a hymn in praise of wisdom.

    1:22–16:23, instruction in wisdom, including a discussion of familial relationships (3:1–16) rules for daily living (4:20–6:4; 7:1–9:18, etc.) and the dangers of riches and greed (13:21–14:19).

    16:24–23:27, further instruction in wisdom, commencing with a discussion of the relationship of man to God and man to his environment (16:24–18:26).

III. The Second Book, Chapters 24 to 50.

    24:1–24, a poem in praise of wisdom, relating wisdom to the election of Israel.

    25:1–35:20, maxims for wise living.

    36:1–17, a prayer for the nation.

    36:18–38:23, maxims of a wife, friends, counselors and physicians.

    38:24–39:11, an essay on the scribe and the wise man.

    39:12–42:14, sayings on varied themes.

Read Ecclesiasticus

---

[8] Cf. R. H. Pfeiffer, *History of New Testament Times With an Introduction to the Apocrypha* (New York: Harper & Brothers, 1949), p. 352; G. H. Box and W. O. E. Oesterley, "The Book of Sirach" in the *Apocrypha and Pseudepigrapha of the Old Testament*, R. H. Charles, ed., I, 268 f.

42:15–43:33, in praise of God's creation.

44:1–50:24, in praise of famous men.

50:25–29, a conclusion, in which Ben Sira expresses dislike for either Idumeans or Nabataeans, Philistines and Samaritans.

51:1–12, an appendix in the form of a thanksgiving hymn.

51:13–20, an appendix in the form of an alphabetic acrostic relating Ben Sira's search for wisdom.

Ben Sira's themes, like those of other wisdom writers, tend to be universal rather than parochial. He warns his students against immoral associations with women but recognizes the merits of a good wife and a happy marriage (7:26 f.; 9:1 ff.; 25:16–26:28; 36:21 ff.; 37:11; 40:19; 42:12 f.). He encourages strict discipline in raising children (26:10–12; 30:1–13; 42:11), and inasmuch as no man can foretell the character of his children, his opinion on the size of families (16:1–3) appears to stand in sharp contrast to Psalm 127:3–5.

Some of Ben Sira's counsel was designed to guide students in proper social and political relationships. He instructs them in table manners, the role of the host and the guest (31:12–32:13). His comments on the merchant (26:29–27:3), the physician (38:1–15), and on lending money (29:1–7) are to aid his students in health and business matters, just as his admonitions to keep secrets (27:16) and to avoid slander (28:13 ff.) are guides for broader human relationships.

The lengthy statement in praise of famous men (44:1–50:24) is a concise review of biblical heroes. The darker side of David's life has been ignored and David is exalted for his military prowess and his contributions to Israel's religious heritage. Solomon's reputation as the father of wisdom is recognized, but he is condemned for his many wives. Only two other kings appear on the hero list: Hezekiah and Josiah, both of whom were praised in the Deuteronomic history for their religious reforms.

Ben Sira's attitudes to the religious practices of his day are closer to those of the writers of Proverbs than to Ecclesiastes. The beautiful description of the high priest Simon (50:1–12) reveals Ben Sira's deep appreciation of cultic ritual. He praised the Torah as a supreme gift from God (24:23). The personal religious attitudes and habits which he commended included moral and ethical behavior as well as ritual observances. Like the prophets before him he taught that atonement did not follow automatically upon the presentation of offerings (7:8 ff.; 35:12) but that God accepts the sacrifices of a righteous man (35:6 f.). Efforts to place Ben Sira in the tradition of the Sadducees force his teachings into patterns not yet established in his day,[9] despite the fact that he was rather vague about the afterlife, and expressed no belief in the resurrection of the dead (11:26–28; 38:16–23; 41:1–4, 10–11; 46:11–12; 48:5).[10]

---

[9] The Sadducees came into existence during the period of Jewish independence.

[10] The Sadducees did not believe in the resurrection of the dead; the Pharisees did. Cf. Josephus, *Antiquities* 13:5:9 and *Wars* 2:8:14 and in the New Testament, Matthew 22:23, Mark 12:18, Luke 20:27.

One of the most delightful stories to come out of the late Hellenistic period is that of Tobit, which relates how God solved two unhappy human dilemmas with a single angel.[11] The writing does not belong to the wisdom school, and the only justification for attaching it to the section on wisdom writing is that Tobit advises his son after the manner of the wisdom teachers. The tale is set in the eighth century in Nineveh and recounts the unfortunate blinding of a pious Jew, Tobit, and the desperate plight of the maiden Sarah whose seven bridegrooms had each been slain on their wedding night by the evil demon Asmodeus.

Read Tobit

There is ample evidence that the story is much later than its setting, and it fits best into the period between 200 and 180, or just before the period of Jewish independence. For example, in 14:5 Tobit speaks prophetically of events to come, but it is clear that he is describing the post-Exilic temple. He does not know of the beautification of this temple under the auspices of Herod the Great, which occurred in the Roman period (37–4), but idealistically envisions a future temple built by Jews of the dispersion on their return to Jerusalem.[12] The author confused the order of Assyrian monarchs, which would be unlikely for one contemporary with the events. Sennacherib was not the son of Shalmaneser as Tobit 1:15 indicates, but of Sargon. Nor were Nebuchadrezzar and Ahasuerus involved in the sacking of Nineveh, as noted in Tobit 14:15, but rather Nabopolassar and Cyaxeres.[13] According to II Kings 15:29, the tribe of Naphtali went into captivity in the time of Tiglath Pileser III, not in Shalmaneser's day as stated in Tobit 1:1. The reference to the Greek drachma (5:14) and to the book of Jonah (14:8) point to a Greek provenance, and because there is no hint of persecution of the Jews under Antiochus IV, a date between 200 and 180 is usually given to this story.

The place of writing has been the subject of much discussion and scholars have proposed Mesopotamia,[14] Egypt,[15] Judaea[16] and Antioch in Syria.[17] The Mesopotamian setting may be rejected on the grounds of the author's confusion of geographical details, such as the

[11] Tobit is accepted as canonical by the Roman Catholic and Eastern Orthodox Churches.

[12] It has been argued that chapters 13–14 were written after A.D. 70 and that the Roman destruction of the temple was in the writer's mind. Cf. F. Zimmerman, *The Book of Tobit*, Jewish Apocryphal Literature (New York: Harper & Brothers, 1958), pp. 24 ff.

[13] Tobit 14:15 is often treated as an interpolation.

[14] C. C. Torrey, *The Apocryphal Literature* (New Haven: Yale University Press, 1945), p. 85; L. H. Brockington, *A Critical Introduction to the Apocrypha* (London: Gerald Duckworth & Co., Ltd., 1961), pp. 36–39.

[15] D. C. Simpson, "Tobit," *The Apocrypha and Pseudepigrapha of the Old Testament*, I, 180.

[16] R. H. Pfeiffer, *History of New Testament Times with an Introduction to the Apocrypha*, p. 275.

[17] Zimmerman, *op. cit.*, pp. 15–21.

implications that Nineveh was a day's journey from the Tigris (6:1),[18] or that the trip from Ecbatana to Rages (or Rhagae) could be made in a single day.[19] The argument against Egypt is based on the fact that in Egypt sheep and camels were neither common nor in the possession of the ordinary citizen, as is implied in Tobit 9:2 and 10:10.[20] The choice of locale lies between Antioch and Jerusalem, with either city being a likely candidate.

Certain motifs in Tobit may have been borrowed from earlier writings. Tobit shows affinities with The Tale of the Grateful Dead, which relates how the hero of the story gave up his possessions to pay the debts of a dead man whose creditor refused to permit burial of the debtor's body. The story of Ahikar is known to the writer. He is familiar with the Story of the Dangerous Bride, in which a bride continues to lose bridegrooms to a monster on the wedding night until rescued by a hero.[21]

The author's purpose in telling the story, beyond the recounting of an interesting tale, is probably to encourage almsgiving and proper care for the dead and to teach that God sustains the righteous.[22] These may appear to be rather limited reasons, but in view of the development of Hellenized Judaism, a story designed to encourage adherence to traditional Jewish ways is of particular significance.

Tobit represents a Jew loyal to Jewish religious beliefs and practices even when banished and persecuted (1:3, 6–12; 2:8; etc.). No other writing of this period provides a more intimate expression of the warm bonds existing between husband and wife and parents and child in a Jewish household (2:11–3:6; 4:3–4). No other account demonstrates better that strict adherence to the tenets of Jewish religious legalism brought into human relationships principles of concern and compassion (1:17–20; 2:2–5). When Tobit enjoyed good fortune, he sought to share it. He lent money in simple trust. His precepts were uncluttered (4:7, 14; 12:7) and included the "Golden Rule" in its negative form (4:15).

The religious beliefs expressed throughout the story reveal the writer's reverence for the Torah and his strong faith in divine providence and the efficacy of prayer. Prayers did not go directly to the deity but, as the angel Raphael explained, were delivered to God by seven holy angels (12:15). The introduction of angelic intermediaries and the appellations used for God, depicting his majesty and glory (1:4; 12:12, 15; 13:6–7, 10–11, 15), acknowledge the transcendence of the deity and reveal how far Jewish theology had moved from the views of the J writer. References to the presence of God avoid any hint of anthropomorphism, and only the divine glory is mentioned (3:16; 12:15).

[18] Nineveh was on the east bank of the Tigris, and its location was known to Herodotus long after its destruction (Herodotus I:93; II:150).

[19] Pfeiffer notes that the trip takes nearly two weeks by camel (*History of New Testament Times*, p. 275.)

[20] Zimmerman, *op. cit.*, pp. 16 f.

[21] For a discussion of these and other similar parallels, cf. Pfeiffer, *History of New Testament Times*, pp. 264–271; Zimmerman, *op. cit.*, pp. 5–12.

[22] Brockington, *op. cit.*, p. 36.

Angels have appeared from time to time in Hebrew-Jewish literature (Gen. 22:11; 31:11; Exod. 3:3; Josh. 5:13–14; Judg. 13:3–5; I Kings 19:5; II Kings 19:35). Sometimes they are messengers of the deity; at other times they give protection (Ps. 91:11), support (Ps. 35:5–6) or succor (I Kings 19:5). In Tobit, angels are recognized as intercessors, and a specific angel, Raphael,[23] was assigned to a special task. Persian influence may lie behind the seven angels of Tobit (12:15), for Ahura Mazda was said to be attended by six archangels, forces for good. The demon Asmodeus may be the Iranian demon of anger or lust, "Aeshma daeva." It has also been suggested that his name is derived from a Hebrew root *shmd* meaning "to destroy," hence he would be "The Destroyer." The banishing of Asmodeus and the healing of Tobit's blindness with the heart, liver and gall of a fish involve magic. Magicians have been referred to earlier in biblical writings (Isa. 3:2–3; Ezek. 13:18–20; II Chron. 33:6), and magic is prohibited in the Torah (Exod. 22:18; Lev. 19:26, 31; 20:6, 27). There is no condemnation of magic in Tobit, and the rites of expulsion and healing were taught and approved by the angel Raphael.

[23] Raphael's role as a healer is reflected in his name, which is derived from a Hebrew root *rp'* meaning "to heal."

29

The Period of Jewish Independence

Read
I Macc.
Chs. 1–14

THE story of Jewish Independence recorded in I Maccabees reads like an adventure story. Jewish resistance to Antiochus' proscription of Judaism began in 168 at Modin, a village in the hill country twenty miles north of Jerusalem. Mattathias, an aged priest, not only refused to comply with a government edict to perform pagan sacrifice, but killed the Syrian official who delivered the order and a fellow Jew who was prepared to conform to the decree. With his sons Judas, Jonathan and Simon, the old man fled to the hills and organized an armed resistance party employing guerrilla tactics. At first the Jews were handicapped by their refusal to do battle on the Sabbath, but when Antiochus' soldiers killed nearly one thousand Hasidim on the Sabbath, Mattathias and the Hasidim who joined him agreed to fight on the holy day to preserve their lives.

Antiochus IV was engaged in a struggle with the Parthians, but dispatched a powerful army in 166 to put down the Jewish rebels. Mattathias had died, but his son Judas, who was called Maccabee,[1] defeated the Syrians. In 165, a second and stronger army was stopped by Judas, whose forces grew with each victory. Now Syrians and Jews signed a peace treaty which removed the hated restrictions on Jewish religious expression. Judas and his soldiers entered Jerusalem, cleansed the temple, and on the 25th of Chislev (December), three years to the day from the time Antiochus IV had desecrated the altar, reconsecrated the shrine and instituted worship services. The event has been commemorated ever since in the Feast of Dedication or the Festival of Hanukkah.

Antiochus died in 164 and his son Antiochus V Eupator became king. Judas attempted to seize the Acra in Jerusalem, the fortified high place held by a Syrian garrison. When he failed, Syrian reprisal was swift. The temple walls were razed and Menelaus, the high priest, executed. Antiochus V was killed by his cousin Demetrius I Soter in 162. Demetrius appointed a pro-Syrian, Alcimus, to the high priesthood. Judas continued to struggle against the Syrians until his death in 161. His brother Jonathan took command of the Jewish forces.

---

1 The meaning of the term Maccabee is not clear. It is usually taken to mean "the hammer." For a discussion of interpretations see S. Zeitlin and S. Tedesche, *The First Book of Maccabees,* Jewish Apocalyptical Series (New York: Harper & Brothers, 1950), Appendix B, pp. 250–252.

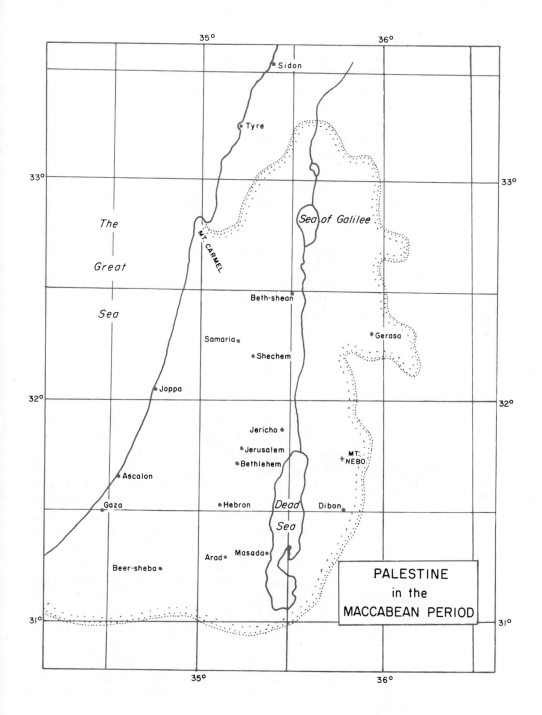

The Great Sea

Sidon

Tyre

MT. CARMEL

Sea of Galilee

Beth-shean

Samaria
Shechem

Gerasa

Joppa

Jericho
Jerusalem
Bethlehem

MT.
NEBO

Ascalon

Gaza

Hebron

Dibon

Dead Sea

Arad Masada

Beer-sheba

**PALESTINE
in the
MACCABEAN PERIOD**

Now a pretender, Alexander Balas, challenged Demetrius and sub-sequently became king. Jonathan threw in his lot with Balas and was rewarded with the high priesthood in 153, and with the governorship of Judah in 150. When Balas married Cleopatra, daughter of Ptolemy VI, in 150, the breach between Egypt and Syria was temporarily healed. In Egypt the Jews enjoyed particular benefits, and under Onias, son of Onias III, a Jewish temple was established at Leontopolis, a few miles from Memphis. Had the situation in Palestine been more normal, there is little doubt that there would have been much criticism of this violation of Deuteronomic law.[2]

Balas was next confronted with a legitimate heir to the throne, Demetrius II Nicator, son of Demetrius I. By 145, Balas had been murdered and Demetrius was king. Jonathan supported Demetrius, rescuing him with Jewish soldiers when his life was endangered by Balas' son Antiochus VI and Balas' former general Tryphon. At that desperate time Demetrius promised special favors to Jonathan which he failed to keep. Now Jonathan gave aid to Antiochus VI and Tryphon and, aided by his brother Simon, overcame Demetrius. Tryphon tricked Jonathan, imprisoned him and finally had him killed. Antiochus was murdered and Tryphon became king. Now Simon, Jonathan's brother, came to Jerusalem and by 142 had seized the Acra and had made Jerusalem a free city and the Jews an independent people. During these turbulent days several Jewish writings made their appearance, and a distinctive literary form known as apocalyptic writing came into being.

APOCALYPTICISM

The desperate plight of the Jews under Antiochus IV elicited a literary call for stubborn resistance to Greek culture and zealous loyalty to the traditional faith, in the conviction that God was about to act to bring in the long-awaited kingdom and to redeem his people. The roots of such thinking rested, in part, in Jewish sacred history, which proclaimed God's miraculous saving acts in the past in the story of the preservation of the righteous Noah, and the escape of Israel from Egypt; in part in Jewish theology, which extolled the justice of God, the punishment of the wicked and the rewarding of the righteous; and in part in Jewish particularism, by which election and covenant theory were woven throughout the Jewish interpretation of history to demonstrate the uniqueness of those chosen by God as his own. These Jewish beliefs were given new expression through influences coming from Iranian and Zoroastrian theology, including cosmic dualism and a concept of history that postulated a beginning, a series of time periods and a climactic ending of time. The catalyst was the persecution under Antiochus, which produced a failure of nerve, a despair of man's ability to effect the kingdom of God through his own efforts and a conviction that the situation could only get worse until God himself broke in to terminate the present evil age and inaugurate the ideal.

Literature of this kind is said to be "apocalyptic" or expressive of "apocalypticism," terms drawn from a Greek word meaning "to disclose" or "to reveal" or "to make manifest," and which signify the uncovering of information hidden from men. That which is revealed in apocalyptic literature consists of secrets of the future, knowledge

---

[2] Onias justified the Egyptian temple on the basis of Isaiah 19:19. The temple stood until A.D. 70.

possessed only by God and revealed to his elect. The mode of revelation is through visions marked by extreme, and at times almost grotesque imagery, or by cryptic numbers whose significance and meaning is interpreted by angels. The purpose of the apocalypticist is to encourage the faithful to endure persecution and hardship and to resist the forces of evil, in the conviction that the end of time is at hand. The fullest expressions of this form of writing are the book of Daniel in the Old Testament and the Revelation to John in the New Testament, although other examples are found in the Pseudepigrapha, including Enoch, The Testament of the Twelve Patriarchs, The Assumption of Moses and the Apocalypse of Baruch.

The fundamental theological problem confronting the apocalypticist is theodicy. The response postulates a cosmic dualism with a polarity of good and evil. The struggle between good and evil experienced in human life is a microcosmic manifestation of a macrocosmic phenomenon. The roots of good and evil were metaphysical and cosmological, for the divine order was in itself bipolar. Powers of evil and good may be personified as they are in Zorastrianism by Ahura Mazda and Ahriman, or as they were to become in Jewish thought in God and Satan (or some other), or they may be left unpersonified. There is a further postulation of an eschaton, an end of time, when the forces of evil will be finally and completely defeated by the power of good. Time is pictured as a straight line with a point of beginning (already present in Jewish thought), a series of time-periods, an ending (incipient in Judaism in the Day of Yahweh concept), and a

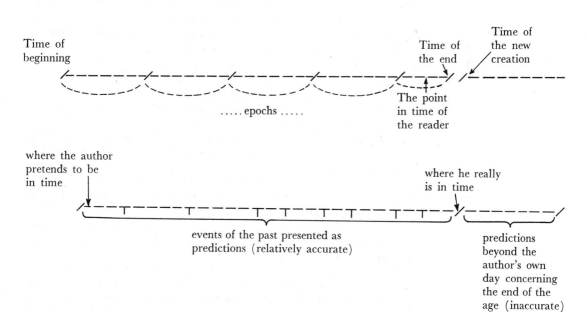

new beginning (implicit in the new beginnings in J). The reader is made to realize that he is standing at the threshold of the end of time, the destruction of the present evil world and the creation of a new world of righteousness. The writer speaks in the name of some ancient worthy and projects himself back in time to a specific historical setting and from that point "predicts" events that he knows have taken place as though they were "to come." Of course from his vantage point he can maintain relative accuracy, depending on his knowledge, in describing what has already occurred, but he colors his presentation with symbols, referring to nations as animals, or to rulers as "horns." When he attempts to go beyond his own day and unveil the shape of things to come, his predictions go awry, for history does not sustain his claims.[3]

Revelation comes through visions or dream-visions and interpretation is given by an angel (cf. Dan. 7:16; 8:15–18). The various apocalyptic writings so closely resemble one another that it is apparent that there was both borrowing of imagery and adherence to an accepted literary pattern. The visions are, therefore, more literary than experienced.

Because some motifs in apocalyptic writing are akin to those of prophecy, it is essential to distinguish between them:

1. The prophets, particularly the great figures of the eighth and seventh centuries, tended to be voices of doom in times of prosperity. Apocalyptic writing foretold deliverance in time of critical danger. The prophets dealt with the sins of prosperity; the apocalypticist was concerned with the evils and perplexity of adversity.

2. In prophetic utterances, there was almost always some conditional element: "If you return, you will be saved." Prophetic warnings were aimed at producing repentance and change. What happened depended upon man's response. In apocalyptic writing, the end is determined, and no matter what man does, events will occur as predicted.

3. The prophets structured their message within an historical context in the belief that God's salvation would be realized within and through history. The apocalypticist held that the whole universe was the battle ground and that the final victory lay outside of human history and would involve the destruction and re-creation of the universe.

4. With apocalypticism there came a movement away from the freedom and originality of prophecy to a dependence upon past prophecy and apocalyptic tradition. In prophecy, apart from the use of literary forms drawn from various local contexts, there appears to be no real literary dependence. The apocalypticist, on the other hand, depended on prophecy, assuming that all predictions must be fulfilled. The oracles of woe had been realized in the Exile, but the promises of restoration had never been adequately fulfilled. Daniel explained that the period of Exile was not yet completed, basing his argument on a reinterpretation of the seventy years mentioned in Jeremiah 25:11 f. and 29:10. Later, Daniel was re-interpreted by II Esdras (II Esdras 12:11–12).

5. The great prophets were known persons who wrote in their own names, who founded prophetic guilds, and who identified themselves with persons and events in their own times. The apocalypticists were pseudonymous, writing under pseudonymns and identifying themselves with historical settings outside of their own times.

---

[3] There are schools of theological interpretation that argue that these writings refer to that which is still to come. However, our stated task is to understand the literature, insofar as possible, in terms of the period out of which it came.

Other distinctions could be pressed, such as the dualism of apocalypticism and the stress upon individual salvation, but it is possible to push the distinctions too far. It should not be assumed that the analysis is designed to demonstrate the superiority of one form of religious expression over another; each had its own values and weaknesses. The apocalypticist made it possible for men to maintain belief in the righteousness of God when all historical evidence appeared to point to the opposite. He brought into an age of darkness and despair a shaft of light and hope that gave to the age an air of expectancy, of looking toward a golden age about to be realized. The conviction that righteousness would ultimately prevail and that men of faith would triumph produced courage to face adversity and suffering. Because the ethics of apocalypticism were not only concerned with what men did here and now but with what men would do in the coming kingdom, there tended to develop ethical concerns that had universalistic implications. At the same time, there was a moral narrowness, for righteousness meant doing that which placed a man on God's side, and the definition of that righteousness became more and more restrictive. The mechanistic concept of a predetermined future, which would come despite anything man might do, contained a potential for moral irresponsibility. The prophets declared that a good society could come as a by-product from good people, the apocalypticists held that the future was unconditional and the good society would come as an act of God. What is most significant is that apocalypticism faded when its promises failed. Fortunately for the Jews, all did not accept the apocalyptic way of thinking, as the Maccabean revolt demonstrates, for what happened in subsequent history certainly involved man.

DANIEL

Although Daniel is set in the time of Nebuchadrezzar of Babylon it clearly belongs to the time of Antiochus IV. Knowledge of the Babylonian-Persian period as revealed in the book is vague and, on occasion, inaccurate. The opening verse (1:1) states that Jehoiakim surrendered Jerusalem to Nebuchadrezzar, but as we have seen, Jehoiakim was dead before Nebuchadrezzar took the city. Belshazzar (Bel-shar-user) is identified as the son of Nebuchadrezzar and is called "king" (5:1), but we have seen that his father was Nabonidus and that, though he was a regent, he never became a king. King Darius is called a Mede, the son of Xerxes (Ahasuerus), in Daniel 9:1, although we know that he was a Persian and the father of Xerxes. As the story moves into the Greek period, it becomes more accurate. The writer knows of the desecration of Yahweh's altar by Antiochus IV in 168 (9:27; 11:31) but not of the restoration of worship by Judas Maccabeus three years later. The book must have been completed between 168 and 165, probably closer to 165. The presence of Persian and Greek loan-words lends support to the Hellenistic dating.

The book is written in Hebrew except for Chapters 2:4a to 7 which are in Aramaic. The presence of a sizable Aramaic section does not necessarily indicate composite authorship, for there are several links in ideas between the Hebrew and Aramaic portions. One conjecture is that the author may have composed the work during two different periods, drawing from older Aramaic sources for some motifs, but this explanation does not suggest any reason why the book could not have been written in one language. To date, no satisfactory solution has been proposed.[4]

The book falls into two sections: Chapters 1 to 6, which consist of stories about Daniel and his three friends, and Chapters 7 to 12, which outline four visions and the interpretations provided by angels. Who Daniel was is known only from this book, and the author models his hero on Joseph in Egypt. Whether or not Daniel is to be associated with the pre-Exilic righteous man in Ezekiel (14:14, 20; 28:3), or with the more remote Canaanite figure of the same name, cannot be known.[5] It is possible that a Daniel unknown outside of this book actually lived during the Exile and provided the basis for this account. In his loyalty to the prescriptions of the Torah, Daniel represents the Hasidim. He is called a "wise man" and symbolizes that segment of the wisdom movement that anchored wisdom in obedience to the Law.

Read Daniel Chs. 1–6

The first six chapters of the book of Daniel are fiction, set in the court of Babylon, and may be based on a Palestinian reworking of older folk tales. In their present form, they are designed to engender in the reader strength and courage in the face of the tyrannical oppression of Antiochus IV. For the four young men in the first chapter, loyalty to their beliefs is more important than life. Their refusal to eat non-kosher food is, no doubt, aimed at encouraging resistance among those under pressure from Antiochus to violate Jewish food laws (I Macc. 1:62 f.). In the second chapter, in which the Aramaic portion begins, Daniel interprets Nebuchadrezzar's dream, demonstrating that only Yahweh knows what the future holds and that the revealed wisdom of the Jew is superior to that of other peoples. The image in Nebuchadrezzar's dream introduces the epochs of world history which become progressively evil. The golden head represented the Babylonians and the silver breast and arms the Medians, who, probably because of the Exilic predictions of Isaiah 13–14, 21, the author of Daniel insists played an important role prior to the Persians. The Persians are the brazen belly and thighs, and the Alexandrian empire is represented by the iron legs. The feet and toes of mixed clay and iron are the separate kingdoms of the Diodochoi. The insecurity of the figure is such that God needed only to strike it with a stone to make it collapse. The writer is obviously teaching that the end was at hand and that Jews living in the Hellenistic era were near to the moment of divine intervention.

The reference to Nebuchadrezzar's image (ch. 4) may have served to remind Jews of a golden image of Apollo erected by Antiochus at

---

[4] See Eissfeldt, *The Old Testament, an Introduction*, p. 516, for several suggested solutions.

[5] The spelling of the name "Daniel" in the book of Daniel differs slightly from the spelling in Ezekiel and the Ugaritic texts; the latter are the same. Cf. G. R. Driver, *Canaanite Myths and Legends* (Edinburgh: T. and T. Clark, 1956), p. 8, n. 3.

Daphne. The courage of the young men in the fiery furnace was a model of resistance to stimulate fidelity to the ancestral faith.

On the basis of a fragmented manuscript found at Qumran and called "The Prayer of Nabonidus," it has been postulated that the story of Nebuchadrezzar's dream and madness may be drawn from an older story about Nabonidus.[6] For the second century Jews, the mad king must have called to mind Antiochus, whom they believed had gone mad with power, and the story reassured them that God would take care of this deranged monarch.

The account of Belshazzar's feast that announced the end of the Babylonian empire errs, as we have noted, in describing Bel-shar-user as a king and in ascribing the conquest of Babylon to Darius, wrongly called a Mede. The miraculous handwriting with the message "Mene, mene, takel and parsin" records weights: the min, the shekel and the half-mina, all possessing symbolic significance. The weights, as Daniel explains, meant that God had weighed or judged the Neo-Babylonians and had decided the empire was to end.

The final story in this section, the well-known tale of Daniel in the den of lions, is set in the fictional Median court of Darius. The testing of Daniel was like the testing of Jews by Antiochus, and the miraculous deliverance gave hope that God would soon act on behalf of his people. One must assume that the fact that salvation always came in the Daniel stories and that it did not come in real life was not missed by the Jewish readers, who took the message of the stories to be that loyalty to God was of supreme importance.

The author now introduces a series of visions revealing events to follow the fall of the Neo-Babylonian empire. For the Palestinian reader in Antiochus' day, it was clearly demonstrated that the time was at hand when God would act. Apocalyptic historiography, as we have noted, segmented history into periods but partitioned cosmic time into two ages—the present evil age and the glorious future. Events prior to Antiochus' day are placed in predictive form; that which lay beyond involved the kingdom of God.

Chapter 7 pictures the four empires as beasts. The lion-eagle was the Neo-Babylonians; the bear, the Medes; the leopard, the Persians; and the fourth beast with the iron teeth, the Macedonians. Now the symbol is changed, and the horns represent the successive rulers of Alexander's broken empire.[7] The single small horn, which utters blasphemy and plucks up the other three, was Antiochus. As anti-god, Antiochus defied the Most High and was destroyed. The radiant figure of the "Ancient of Days" (7:9 ff.) who sits in judgment and transcends history, is Yahweh. The whiteness of his hair and garments and the presence of fire reveal purity, mark the separation of the sacred from the profane and perhaps recall the Iranian imagery of the testing of

**Read Daniel
Ch. 7**

---

[6] D. N. Freedman, "The Prayer of Nabonidus," *BASOR* (1957), pp. 31 f.; M. Burrows, *More Light on the Dead Sea Scrolls* (New York: Viking Press, Inc., 1958), pp. 173, 400. For other parallels, see N. Porteus, *Daniel*, The Old Testament Library (Philadelphia: The Westminster Press, 1965), pp. 70 ff.

[7] Which rulers are meant is a matter of debate, cf. H. H. Rowley, *Darius the Mede and the Four World Empires of the Book of Daniel* (Cardiff: University of Wales Press Board, 1935), pp. 98 ff.

the good and evil in a stream of fire. The one "like a son of man" is not a messiah figure but the representation of the faithful Jews who would inherit the kingdom as Verses 18 and 27 indicate.[8] The cryptic numbers that give a clue to the time of judgment (7:25) are given in years,[9] and if the time is reckoned from the desecration of the temple by Antiochus IV, the author comes close to the time of re-dedication by Judas Maccabeus. The concept of a day of judgment in which the records of misdeeds were opened (7:10) is introduced for the first time.

Read Daniel Ch. 8

The second Hebrew portion of the book begins in Chapter 8, and there is a marked inferiority of quality and style of narrative. Possibly, as some scholars have suggested, the author prepared a separate collection of visions and appended these to the Aramaic section. The vision of the two-horned ram (the Medo-Persians), the single-horned he-goat (Alexander) and the four horns that sprout from the single horn (the Diodochoi) follow the same historical analysis as Chapter 7. The little horn that grew in power and desecrated the sanctuary is, of course, Antiochus IV. The interpreter of the vision is the angel Gabriel.[10] The number 2,300 refers to daily sacrifices offered every morning and evening. If the number referred to "days," the apocalypticist would be predicting that six and one-half years after the desecration of the temple, worship would be restored. If the number represents the number of sacrifices that would be missed, a three and one-quarter year period is in the writer's mind—a figure very close to the actual date of the re-institution of worship. Verse 26 explains why the predictions had not been known before: they were sealed for many days.

Read Daniel Ch. 9

Chapter 9 is an extension of the previous vision. Daniel sought to explain Jeremiah's prediction of seventy years of exile (Jer. 25:11–12; 29:10). Presumably, for all practical purposes, Jeremiah's words had been fulfilled when the Jews returned to Palestine in the Persian period. The seventy-year symbol was of little value to the author of Daniel, so he re-interpreted it under the instruction of Gabriel so that each year stood for a week of years, or seven years. The Exile was lengthened to 490 years, placing the end of the Exilic period in the future, somewhat distant from the author's immediate day. However, precise dating is ignored by the writer, and he brings the end of the Exile into his own time by the reference to the defiling of the temple (9:27).

Read Daniel Chs. 10–12

The last three chapters form a unit outlining the history of the Seleucid period through the reign of Antiochus IV and attempting to press into the hidden future. A second angelic figure is introduced,

8 Cf. A. Jeffrey, "Daniel," *The Interpreter's Bible*, VI, 460; S. Mowinckel, *He That Cometh* trans. G. W. Anderson (New York: Abingdon Press, 1954), pp. 348 ff.

9 The Hebrew term translated "time" is *'iddin*, which signifies a year, cf. Jeffery, *op. cit.*, p. 466.

10 The name "Gabriel" means "man of God." In the book of Enoch Gabriel is an intercessor and punisher of the wicked. In the New Testament, he announces the births of John the Baptizer (Luke 1:11–20) and Jesus (Luke 1:26–38).

Michael,[11] the patron angel of the Jews. Michael struggled against the Persians in what appears to be a celestial combat (10:11–12). Once again the apocalyptic interpretation of history brings the narrative to the writer's own day, to Antiochus Epiphanes, and to that one event that so horrified and shocked the writer that it came to be the turning point in his history—the profanation of the temple (11:31).

When the apocalypticist attempts to unveil the future, his predictions are wrong. He envisions an attack by Egypt that did not take place and other details are also in error.

The final chapter promises deliverance by the forces of Michael, then divine judgment. For the first time, the problem of theodicy is answered by pushing rewards and punishments beyond the grave, and for the first time, the concept of the resurrection of the dead is clearly presented. How much these concepts owe to Iranian religious thought cannot be determined for sure, for judgment in the afterlife had been accepted in Egypt for centuries.[12] Once again the reader is informed that this vital information, revealed centuries before, had been sealed until the "end of time" (12:4), implying that "now," in the days of Antiochus, it was made known because this was the end of time. A slight re-interpretation of the time of the end occurs in the interpolation at 12:11–12.

JUDITH

Read Judith

A stirring story of feminine intrigue and courage, written during the Maccabean struggle, recorded the deliverance of a besieged city through the beauty and wiles of Judith. The writing must be classified as fiction with an imaginary setting in the time of Assyrian world conquest. If the author knew precise historical details, he chose to ignore them, for he names the Babylonian monarch Nebuchadrezzar as king over the Assyrians at Nineveh, though the city had been destroyed seven years before Nebuchadrezzar was crowned (2:1 ff.; 4:2 ff.). There is no evidence that Nebuchadrezzar ever warred against the Medes or captured Ecbatana (1:7, 14). What is more surprising is that the author implies that the Jews were returning from captivity at the very time they were experiencing further deportations. The names of the Assyrian commander Holofernes and his general Bagoas may indicate that the writer had in mind a campaign against Phoenicia and the Jews waged in 353 in the time of Artaxerxes III Ochus (358–338), for the Persian commander's name was Holofernes and his general was Bagoas, a eunuch. But the exaggerations in the story can only be fictional. Holofernes moved a massive army 300 miles in three

---

11 Michael, whose name means "Who is like God?" appears in the War Scroll of the Qumran community as patron of the Jews, and in the New Testament as the contestant with the devil for Moses' body (Jude 9) and as the leader of the angelic hosts in the cosmic battle with the dragon (Rev. 12:7).

12 See the article "Resurrection" in *The Interpreter's Dictionary of the Bible* for a detailed discussion.

days (2:21)! Numbers are also exaggerated (cf. 1:4, 16; 2:5, 15; 7:2, 17). The town of Bethulia, which must have been close to Shechem (or perhaps was Shechem), has never been located.[13]

The literary style is somewhat heavy at times because of the insertion of long instructional speeches or prayers, a characteristic of Hellenistic writing. Nevertheless, there are excellent sequences and the reader is led through scenes of potential danger to the tense moment of the murder of Holofernes and Judith's escape in the fashion of a good spy story. As an ideal heroine Judith is beautiful and courageous, and as an example to Jewish women she is a model of pious and meticulous observance of the Law. Other characterizations are equally good.

The author did not write solely for entertainment, but as in other Jewish fiction, to instruct. As the ideal Jewess (the name "Judith" means "Jewess"), Judith demonstrated one of the ways in which loyal and religious women could aid the cause of freedom. She was a Maccabean counterpart of Jael (Judg. 4–5), using deception, intrigue, human weakness and in Judith's case, a touch of sensual enticement, to bring about the murder of an enemy general. She demonstrated the importance of active resistance to the enemy by the Hasidim.

The story has two parts. The first (chs. 1–7) describes the war of the Assyrians against the Jews, leading up to the siege of Bethulia. The second (chs. 8–16) tells of the deliverance by Judith. Once again Nebuchadrezzar is the model for the power-hungry Seleucid oppressor, and once again the Jews are the target. Standing in the way of Assyrian conquest is the legendary city of Bethulia, and against this tiny community the tremendous armed might of Assyria is mustered. Rather than using his armies to crush the city, Holofernes is persuaded to bring the people to their knees by cutting off the water supply.

In the second portion, Judith, a wealthy and beautiful widow, succeeds in penetrating the Assyrian camp. Using beauty and wisdom as her initial weapons, she manages to get Holofernes drunk, then murders him and returns with his head to Bethulia. The comment of the stunned Bagoas can only have been designed to provoke a chuckle (14:18). The Jewish victory and the dutiful performance of rites of thanksgiving and purification could only have produced a sigh of satisfaction among the Hasidim.

The theology of the book combines universalism (9:5 f., 12; 13:18) and particularism (4:12; 6:21; 10:1; 12:8; 13:7). The stress on piety tends to make obedience to the law the test of piety (cf. 11:12 ff.) and would suggest that the writer was a member of the Hasidim. He believes that God's help comes when man obeys the Law. There is no concern over the use of deceit or sensuousness in entrapping the enemy, nor is there any condemnation of Judith's murder of Holofernes. These were days of open warfare, and in dealing with the enemy, ethical considerations could be safely ignored. For this writer, loyalty and piety were equated.

---

[13] For a listing of possible sites, see the article "Bethulia" in *The Interpreter's Dictionary of the Bible*. Analyses of the name which means "virgin" or perhaps "house of God" have not been particularly helpful.

Judith has canonical status in Roman Catholic and Eastern Orthodox Bibles, but not in Jewish and Protestant versions.

I ESDRAS

I Esdras, or III Esdras according to Roman Catholic listings, is accepted as canonical only by the Eastern Orthodox Church. Its contents, with one major exception, are based on a version of II Chronicles 35–36, Ezra and Neh. 7:73–8:12. Apart from general comments and the consideration of the one unique story of the three guardsmen, we will pass by I Esdras without suggesting it be read or subjected to detailed analysis. For the specialist, a study of the textual variations between I Esdras, the LXX and the Masoretic text has value since I Esdras represents a different recension with certain omissions, additions and realignment of contents.[14] It may be broadly outlined as follows:

1. Chapters 1–2, the account of Josiah's celebration of the Passover, the fall of Jerusalem, the Exile, Cyrus' decree and the rebuilding of the temple. These chapters are the equivalent of II Chron. 35–36 and Ezra 1–4.
2. Chapters 3:1–5:6, the story of the three guardsmen.
3. Chapters 5:7–9:37, the return of the exiles under Zerubbabel, the rebuilding of the temple, and Ezra's arrival in Jerusalem, paralleling Ezra 2:1–9:36.
4. Chapter 9:38–55, Ezra reads the Law, paralleling Neh. 7:73–8:12.

The most acceptable date for I Esdras is the second century, preferably around 150. The dating is based on a study of the Greek style, two possible allusions to Daniel (cf. 4:40 and Dan. 2:37; 4:59 f. and Dan. 2:22 f.), and on the study of the relationship of I Esdras to the work of the Chronicler as we know it.

The most interesting addition to the traditions preserved by the editor is the story of the contest held in the court of King Darius by three young guards. Each extols what he believes to be the strongest thing in the world and the virtues of wine, the king, women and truth are presented. Some of the comments of the third speaker, who praises women and truth, are rather bold, but in fiction the incredible is seldom challenged. As a reward for the winning speech, the young man, who is certainly a Jew, requests that the promises to rebuild the temple and return the sacred vessels be kept.

**Read I Esdras
Chs. 3:1–5:6**

[14] For a brief discussion and bibliography, see R. H. Pfeiffer, *A History of New Testament Times*, pp. 236–250.

30

The Hasmonean Dynasty[1]

Read
I Macc.
Chs. 14–16

WITH Simon (141–135) a new era dawned for the Jews, and for the first time since the Babylonian conquest, they breathed the pure air of freedom. The atmosphere was charged with expectation. Simon seized the important port city of Gaza, providing Judah with a direct outlet to the Mediterranean world. Treaties were made with Rome and Sparta. Jewish coins were struck. Trade and industry increased and the arts were encouraged. A pro-Hellenistic, aristocratic, priestly group, later to be called the Sadducees, began to take form. The Hasidim tended to merge with other nationalists to become the nucleus of the religio-political party later called Pharisees.

In 138, Antiochus VII Sidetes was crowned king of Syria and attacked Judah, only to be soundly defeated near Modin by Jewish troops led by Simon's brothers, Judah and John. Three years later Ptolemy, Simon's son-in-law, murdered Simon and Judah and one of Simon's sons. John, later to be called Hyrcanus, rushed to Jerusalem and claimed the posts of governor and high priest. Antiochus VII seized this moment of internal disorder to attack Jerusalem. After a siege he won promises of large tribute payments, but when Antiochus was killed in 128 and Demetrius II Nicator once again became king of Syria, John Hyrcanus stopped payments to the Seleucids.

Under John Hyrcanus (135–105), Judaean territory was increased by the annexation of Idumea, Samaria and Perea. The Samaritan temple on Mount Gerizim, long an irritation to the Jews, was demolished. The Idumeans, descendants of the Edomites who had entered Judah in the early post-Exilic period, were compelled to become Jews and accept circumcision and obedience to the Torah. During Hyrcanus' reign, the characters of the Sadducee and Pharisee parties became clearly defined, and another group called the Essenes was formed.[2]

The Pharisees, whose name may have meant "separatists," were a group of religious lay leaders committed to the purification of Judaism

---

[1] The title "Hasmonean" is derived from the great grandfather of Mattathias, according to Josephus (*Antiquities* 16:7:1) but it has been argued that it may designate "princes" or "dignitaries," implying that the men of this line were "princes of Israel." Cf. S. Tedesche and S. Zeitlin, *The First Book of Maccabees*, Appendix A, pp. 247–250.

[2] Information concerning these groups in drawn primarily from the works of Josephus and Philo, both Jewish writers of the first century A.D.

through meticulous observance of moral and ceremonial laws. They supported the temple cult but were most uneasy about the usurpation of the high priesthood by one of non-priestly caste. More often they were identified with synagogues, the local autonomous gathering places of the masses, where prayer and study were conducted. In addition to the study of the scriptures, the Pharisees emphasized the teachings of the elders or oral tradition as a guide to religion. They professed belief in the resurrection of the body and in a future world where rewards and punishments were meted out according to man's behavior in this life. They believed in angels through whom revelations could come, and later were to develop a belief in a Messiah.[3] They tended to view alliances with foreigners with suspicion.

The Sadducees were pro-Greek, aristocratic priests, whose interests were centered in the temple and the cultic rites. Their name was probably derived from Zadok, the famous priest of the time of David and Solomon (II Sam. 8:17; 15:24; I Kings 1:34). Because the offices of high priest and governor were combined, the Sadducees tended to be deeply involved in high-level politics. Politically, they were committed to independence and to the concept of the theocratic state, as were most Jews. Although they were opposed to foreign domination, they did not object to the introduction of foreign elements into Jewish life. Like the Pharisees, they stressed the importance of observance of the Torah, but they rejected the authority of oral tradition. When confronted by situations not covered in the Torah, they enacted new laws. They rejected the Pharisaic doctrine of a resurrection and a future life and held to the older Jewish belief in Sheol. Nor did they accept the belief in angels.

The Essenes may have developed as early as the reign of Jonathan as a group of pious Jews within the Hasidim.[4] The derivation of their name is not at all clear, and it may mean "the pious ones" or "the holy ones."[5] For some unknown reason, they felt compelled to withdraw to the wilderness area on the shores of the Dead Sea, perhaps to mark their separation from the Pharisees.

The discovery and excavation of a Jewish religious communal center dating from this period at Qumran, and the recovery of numerous scrolls and thousands of fragments of manuscripts in caves nearby, have led many scholars to make some identification of the Essenes and the Qumran sect, despite the fact that nowhere in the Qumran literature is the sect identified as "Essene."[6] The scroll materials are from several different centuries and therefore may represent the evolving concepts of the wilderness community. The group appears to have been motivated in part by the expectation of the kingdom of God and in part by the belief that they had been, or were

[3] The messianic belief is expressed in the Pharisaic document "The Psalms of Solomon," to be found in the *Pseudepigrapha*.

[4] Cf. Matthew Black, *The Scrolls and Christian Origins* (New York: Charles Scribner's Sons, 1961), pp. 15 ff.

[5] *Ibid.*, pp. 13 f.

[6] For a detailed discussion of this problem, cf. Millar Burrows, *More Light on the Dead Sea Scrolls*, pp. 263 ff.

AN OVERVIEW OF THE RUINS OF QUMRAN. *The Qumran community was situated on a terrace above the ravine known as the Wadi Qumran overlooking the Dead Sea which can be seen in the background. The photograph was taken from one of the caves in which scrolls were found.*

being, misled and betrayed by temple authorities. They withdrew to the desert to prepare God's way in fulfillment of Isaiah 40, to live in accordance with their understanding of the Torah, and to fulfill the ethical ideals of the prophets. The proper or right way to live was expounded by a "Right Teacher" or "Teacher of Righteousness"—an unknown person. Righteousness was best achieved in a community of those committed to the right way, composed of persons who yielded up private possessions to the community and were formally initiated into the sect. The group was structured with officers and varied ranks. In the wilderness setting they awaited the end of time and the final battle between the Sons of Light and the Sons of Darkness, which could culminate in victory and appropriate rewards for the righteous.

John Hyrcanus had planned that, upon his death, his wife would take charge of civil affairs, and his son, Judas Aristobulus, would be high priest. When Hyrcanus died in 104, Judas imprisoned his mother and all other members of his family except his brother Antigonus. Judas Aristobulus had himself crowned king, taking the title Aristobulus I. In the single year (104) that he reigned, he seized the Galilee region for Judah and compelled the inhabitants, many of whom were of Syrian and Greek descent, to become Jews. His brother Antigonus was murdered, and his mother died of starvation in prison.

Jonathan, a brother of Aristobulus who had survived imprisonment, took control of Judah, Hellenizing his name to Alexander Janneus. During his relatively long reign (104–78), the Hasmonean kingdom reached its peak of territorial power, for Janneus expanded the borders. As a despotic Sadducee, Janneus waged open war against the

THE APERTURES OF CAVE FOUR AT QUMRAN. *This cave lies below the southern edge of the terrace on which the Qumran community lived and overlooks the Wadi Qumran which can be seen at the left. A large collection of manuscript fragments were found in this cave.*

Pharisees. They publicly objected to his mockery of certain rituals and to what the Pharisees considered to be degrading acts. In savage retaliation, Janneus released his mercenaries on the Pharisees and about 6,000 were slaughtered. The result was civil war with numerous battles, and Janneus was not always victor. The Pharisees appealed for aid to the king of Syria, Demetrius III, a descendant of the ancient enemy of the Jews, Antiochus IV. This was an error, for after the defeat of Janneus, many Jews sympathetic to the revolt balked at the thought of Syrian control and joined Janneus' forces. Janneus smothered the revolt and exacted a gruesome revenge in the crucifixion of 800 of his fellow countrymen and the murder of many of their families before them as they hung dying on the crosses.[7]

Janneus died in 78 and the throne was bequeathed to his widow, Salome, who had taken the Greek name Alexandra, and she became the second woman to rule the Jews (78–69). One son, Hyrcanus, was appointed high priest and another, Aristobulus, was left as a dis-

[7] It is possible that many of the events of this period are reflected in statements in the literature of the Qumran community; cf. John Allegro, *The Dead Sea Scrolls* (Baltimore: Penguin Books, Inc., 1956), pp. 96 ff.; Burrows, *More Light on the Dead Sea Scrolls*, pp. 214 f.

A Nabataean tomb carved into the living rock at Petra. *Nabataean structures
feature rather simple ornamentation using
straight lines and the stair-like pattern that
can be seen at the top of the facade. Later,
under Roman influence, highly decorative
patterns were introduced. The rock out of
which the tomb is cut is Nubian sandstone
with multicolored striations in pinks, reds
and blues. Within, the tombs are rather
spacious rooms in which rituals associated
with the cult of the dead were performed.*

gruntled, potential ruler. Alexandra was pro-Pharisee and released
political prisoners who immediately began a retaliatory persecution of
the Sadducees which soon got out of control. Alexandra favored a
positive Pharisaism with reform without revenge, improvement of the
administration and law courts and the introduction of a program of
elementary education. Leading scholars from Alexandria, Egypt, were
invited to Jerusalem to aid in the educational program. When the
aging queen fell ill and it appeared that the mild-mannered Hyrcanus
might be elevated to the throne, Aristobulus raised an army. He was
about to attack Jerusalem when Alexandra died. Hyrcanus was defeated at Jericho and retired as king and high priest. Upon the advice
of an Idumean official named Antipater, Hyrcanus took refuge with
Aretas III, King of the Nabataeans. At this same time Syria became a
Roman province.

Whatever success Aristobulus II (69–63), the pro-Sadducee king and
high priest, might have had in government was marred by civil war.
Hyrcanus, urged on by the Idumean Antipater and backed by King
Aretas, besieged Jerusalem. In 65, the Roman general Scaurus went to
Syria as a legate of Pompey, and both Hyrcanus and Aristobulus
appealed to him for aid. Scaurus, amply bribed by Aristobulus,

ordered Hyrcanus to lift the siege, and as the Nabataean troops withdrew, they were set upon from the rear and defeated by Aristobulus.

The victorious Aristobulus returned to Jerusalem and began a series of attacks on neighboring provinces. But the people were weary of him and his brother. When Pompey arrived in Syria in 64, several delegations of Jews appealed to him, representing Hyrcanus II, Aristobulus II, and a pro-Pharisee group seeking a theocratic government under the high priest. Pompey called for cessation of all hostilities, and when Aristobulus failed to obey, Pompey marched on Jerusalem. Aristobulus was taken prisoner and shipped to Rome. Hyrcanus was appointed high priest and ethnarch. Judah was reduced in size, losing all territories acquired since Simon's time, and was annexed to Rome as a part of the province of Syria, governed by Scaurus. Antipater was given charge of political relationships and served as a Roman puppet. The Jewish kingdom had ended. The Roman province of Judaea was born.

LITERATURE OF THE PERIOD

In addition to the dramatic historical document, I Maccabees, the literature of the late Hasmonean period consists of documents written in the name of former heroes or well-known figures, including Jeremiah and his scribe Baruch, Daniel, Esther, Solomon and a theologized version of some of the events included in I Maccabees. II Esdras, often called IV Esdras or Ezra, was written in the name of Ezra in the Christian era. The writings will be discussed in chronological sequence.

BARUCH

The work entitled Baruch is one of several writings attributed to Jeremiah's scribe.[8] The book can be divided into two major sections, one in prose, the other in poetry. Within this broad division, smaller independent units have been recognized. For analytical study, we divide the book as follows:

I. The Prose Section: Chapters 1:1–3:8.
  a. 1:1–14, the introduction, which sets the book in Babylon in 586. Baruch reads his text before Jeconiah (Jehoiachin) and seeks funds to purchase offerings for the altar in Jerusalem.
  b. 1:15–3:8, the confession of sin.
    1:15–2:10, the recognition that Judah's sin caused the Exile.
    2:11–35, a prayer for forgiveness.
    3:1–8, a plea for divine mercy.
II. The Poetic Section, Chapters 3:9–5:9.
  a. 3:9–4:4, a poem in praise of wisdom.
  b. 4:5–5:9, a poem of comfort for Jerusalem.

8 For others, see the *Pseudepigrapha*.

Read Baruch
1:1–14
The introductory section contradicts one bit of evidence found in Jeremiah and repeats one error from the book of Daniel. In 1:1, it is stated that Baruch was in Babylon after the destruction of the temple, but Jeremiah 43:6–7 indicates that Baruch accompanied Jeremiah to Egypt, making it impossible for the scribe to be with the Babylonian exiles in 586. Baruch 1:11 borrows incorrect information from Daniel 5:4–19 and reports that Belshazzar was the son of Nebuchadrezzar rather than of Nabonidus and this evidence enables us to date the collected work after 165, and to suggest that the editor was not Baruch but a Palestinian Jew. The editor interprets Jeremiah's recommendation to the exiles to seek the welfare of Babylon (Jer. 29:7) as a request to pray for Nebuchadrezzar (1:11).

Read Baruch
1:15–3:8
Like other confessions, the prayer reviews past history and recognizes that disobedience to the divine will results in punishment. Dependency on Daniel 9:4–9 can be seen in 1:15–20; 2:1 f., 7–14, 16–19, indicating that this section also comes from the post-Daniel period.

Read Baruch
3:9–4:4
The first poem praises wisdom and appears to be the product of a member of a wisdom school. Possibly the writer is familiar with Job 28 (cf. 3:29–34), Prov. 8 and the work of Ben Sira, Chapter 24 (cf. 3:35–37, 4:1). For this writer, the way of wisdom is the way of peace (3:13), and wisdom is to be understood as the Law (4:1). At one moment the author glories in the transcendent majesty of God, whose house is the whole world (3:24 ff.), and at the next expresses particularism in his gratitude for Israel's election and intimate knowledge of "what is pleasing to God" (4:4).

Read Baruch
4:5–5:9
The closing poem of lamentation defies precise dating but appears to have drawn inspiration from Deutero-Isaiah. Because 5:5–9 is a parallel to Chapter 11 of the Psalms of Solomon, a very late work which is preserved in the Pseudepigrapha, some scholars have dated this portion of Baruch in the Christian era, after the destruction of the temple in A.D. 70.[9] It is possible to argue just the opposite and to maintain that this parallel is irrelevant for dating because Chapter 11 of the Psalms of Solomon was based on Baruch. We have accepted the latter position. How early the poem in Baruch may be cannot be determined, except to say that it is post-Exilic. The poem looks to the glorification of Israel, the gathering of the scattered people and a period of blessing.

It would appear that in the Hasmonean period Baruch was edited by a Jew of Palestine who, through this composite document, set before his readers his convictions about the importance of repentance, the significance of wisdom and the Law and his hope for a peaceful future. Baruch has canonical status in the Roman Catholic and Eastern Orthodox Churches.

THE LETTER OF JEREMIAH

This one-chapter document is affixed to Baruch as Chapter 7 in the Roman Catholic Bible, where it is given canonical status, but appears

9 Brockington, *op. cit.* p. 88.

in the Apocrypha of the Protestants and Jews as a separate writing and is considered non-canonical. It purports to be a letter written by Jeremiah to the exiles in Babylon. Probably it is a post-Exilic document by an unknown writer.

The "letter" has two parts: verses 1–7 are an introduction, and verses 8–73 are a series of brief statements that terminate with the phrase "they are not gods, do not fear them" (vss. 16, 23, 29) or its equivalent (vss. 40, 44, 49, 52, 56, 69). Some effort is made to provide a Babylonian setting by references to a processional (vss. 4, 26) and cultic prostitution (vs. 43), but the procession seems to echo Isaiah 46:1–2, and the condemnation of idolatry echoes Isaiah 44:9–20. The "letter" appears to be a rather impassioned homily on the evils of idolatry.

Some indication of the time of writing may be found in the reference to seven generations of Exilic life, which would provide a date shortly after the time of Alexander the Great. We have followed R. H. Pfeiffer and placed the document in the Hasmonean period[10] and recognize it as part of a developing tendency to demonstrate the superiority of Judaism by attacking and denigrating other religions. The author delivers his mocking taunts, ignoring the basis upon which the ritual of the other faith might have rested (vs. 33), and insisting that the image was believed to be the actual god rather than a symbol. The effect of his scathing attack is to portray the beliefs and rites he dislikes as stupid and ridiculous.

Additions to Esther

The LXX version of Esther is much larger than the Hebrew edition, and the so-called additions of the Apocrypha represent the extra material. In Roman Catholic Bibles most of these additional verses have been gathered together as separate chapters (chs. 11–16) and appended to the shorter version of Esther. Actually, the additions were designed to fit into the text of Esther at specific places, as the notes in the Revised Standard Version of the Apocrypha indicate.

It is generally accepted that the shorter Hebrew version is earliest and that the additions were composed later to transform the secular book of Esther into a religious document by introducing passages affirming belief in and dependency on God. At times, the extra passages contradict or correct material in Esther. We will follow the Roman Catholic numbering of these extra chapters as they appear in the Revised Standard Version. As each section is studied, it will be wise to refer to the text of Esther to assist in grasping the context.

The first addition was placed at the opening of the story of Esther to introduce Mordecai. He is said to have been exiled with Jehoiachin (Jeconiah) in the first deportation. In the addition we are told that he discovered the plot against the king in the second year of Artaxerxes'

Read Chs. 11:2–12:6

---

[10] Pfeiffer, *History of New Testament Times*, pp. 413–417. For earlier dating, cf. Brockington, *op. cit.*, pp. 90–92.

reign (11:2), rather than in the seventh year (Esther 2:16–21). The remarkable dream is not explained until the end of the story.

Read Chs. 13:1–7

The next section is designed for insertion between 3:13 and 3:14 in the older text of Esther. By quoting what appears to be an official document, it brings to the story a touch of authenticity and historicity. The document changes the day for the proposed annihilation of the Jews to Adar 14 (13:6) rather than Adar 13 (3:13).

Read Chs. 13:8–15:11

Chapters 13:8–15:11 are to be read between Esther 5:2 and 5:3 and explain Mordecai's refusal to bow before Haman as the act of a pious Jew who, like Daniel, will bow only to God. Esther, too, is transformed into a pious woman who pours out her inmost feelings before God in an act of abject humility. We learn that her role in the royal harem is distasteful to her and that she has abstained from participation in pagan rites (14:15–18). She is made to appear more like Judith as the heroic aspects of her role are enhanced and her actions become almost sacrificial.

Read Ch. 16

The letter of Artaxerxes correcting his previous edict is to be read after Esther 8:12. The author of this addition transforms Haman into a Greek (16:10), whereas previously he was an Amalakite (Agagite), and states that like other Greeks he lacked "kindliness" and could not be trusted, for he was willing to betray his benefactors. Artaxerxes' high praise for the Jews honors Jewish law and religion. The 13th of Adar is set aside as a day of rejoicing, preceding what almost became doomsday.

Read Ch. 10:4–13

The epilogue follows Esther 10:3, explains the dream in the prologue, and presents the election idea in a different form. Here, perhaps some clue is given to the time when the additions were composed. Verses 10:8 ff. suggest that the "nations" that would have destroyed the Jews have failed, that the Jews have been saved, and that God has done great things for them. Such an attitude fits best into the period of Jewish independence—perhaps during the time of Simon (141–135).

Read Ch. 11

The concluding sentence is a translator's note giving the time when Esther was translated into Greek together with the additions. The "reign of Ptolemy and Cleopatra" is not a very precise clue, for several Ptolemys were married to Cleopatras: Ptolemy V (203–181), Ptolemy VI (181–145), Ptolemy VIII (116–108, 88–80), Ptolemy XII (80–58, 55–51) and Ptolemy XIV (51–44). The reign of Ptolemy VIII may be the time when the translation was made.

THE ADDITIONS TO DANIEL

During the second century several independent units were composed as additions to the story of Daniel. One of these, "The Story of Susanna," appears as an introduction to the Book of Daniel in some manuscripts, possibly placed there because Daniel appears to be very young in the story. In other manuscripts, it is added as Chapter 13. "The Prayer of Azariah" and the "Song of the Three Young Men" were designed for insertion at appropriate spots in Chapter 3 of Daniel, but in some manuscripts they follow the story of Susanna to form Chapter 14. There are no positive clues for dating in these stories, but they must have been composed between the time Daniel was written (165) and the period when it is believed that the book was made part of the LXX (about 100) .[11]

THE PRAYER OF AZARIAH AND THE SONG OF THE THREE YOUNG MEN

The two poems and their prose explanations were written for insertion between Daniel 3:23 and 3:24. The Prayer has nothing to do with the plight of the young men in the fiery furnace. It is a communal lamentation, perhaps composed during the early years of the Maccabean period before Judas had rededicated the temple (cf. vs. 15). The poem acknowledges God's justice in bringing the nation into the desperate situation, but calls to remembrance the covenant and traditions of the past and pledges fidelity to God. Verses 15 and 16 recall Micah's definition of true religion (Micah 6:6–8) .

Read the "Prayer" and the "Song"

In the Song of the Three Young Men, the plight of the heroes is ignored, except for Verse 66. The song is a hymn of praise modeled on Psalm 148, perhaps written originally for antiphonal chanting and adapted through Verse 66 to its present setting.

Apparently someone decided that the three young men in the furnace ought to do something other than walk around in the flames, and two poems, taken from other contexts, were added. Or perhaps someone believed that martyrs ought to pray, rejoice and witness to their faith. The Eastern Orthodox Church accepts these writings as canonical.

THE STORIES OF SUSANNA, AND BEL AND THE DRAGON

These three stories are among the earliest known "detective stories." Susanna employs the familiar motif of a woman falsely accused and rescued by a wise judge. In refusing to yield to the desires of the two lecherous elders and in maintaining her innocence despite threat of death, Susanna sets an example of ethical standards expected of a married woman. As the prosecutor, Daniel demonstrates the weakness of Deut. 17:6 and exhibits the need for intensive and careful cross-examination of witnesses to prevent collusion.

Read Susanna

The unmasking of the idol, Bel, and the destruction of the dragon, are tales designed to demonstrate the superiority of the Jewish religion by displaying the weaknesses in other faiths. Rather than announce that the priests of Bel practiced deceit as the writer of "The Letter of Jeremiah" did, this author prefers to use fiction to expose their nefarious practices. Scattering ashes to record footprints is a technique often found in fairy tales.

Read Bel and the Dragon

The story of the defeat of the dragon may contain reminiscences of

[11] Pfeiffer, *History of New Testament Times*, pp. 438–444.

the Babylonian creation myth and the defeat of Tiamat, the dragon symbol of chaos. Daniel's return to the den of lions is enlivened by the story of the miraculous delivery of food by the prophet Habakkuk. Only Bel and the Dragon are accepted as canonical, and only by the Eastern Orthodox Church.

THE PRAYER OF MANASSEH

Read II Chron. 33:11–19 and Manasseh's Prayer

The prayer of Manasseh is a non-canonical, penitential psalm extolling the majesty and glory and forgiving nature of God. It begins with praise of God's creative power (vss. 1–5) and forgiving mercy (vss. 6–8), continues with a general confession of sin (vss. 9–12) and an appeal for forgiveness (vss. 13–14), and concludes with a vow and a doxology (vs. 15). The psalm suggests that the author was a Jew familiar with the LXX. The earliest literary evidence of the psalm is in a Christian writing of the second or third century A.D., the "Didascalia," and in relatively late editions of the LXX (fifth to tenth centuries). Some scholars have attributed it to a Christian writer, but it betrays no peculiarly Christian emphases. It can be fitted nicely into the post-Exilic Hasmonean period when documents were being composed in the name of historical figures. Only the title links the prayer to Manasseh, probably on the basis of Manasseh's repentance as reported in II Chron. 33:11 ff.

I MACCABEES

We read I Maccabees previously as we developed the history of events of the Maccabean period; therefore, in analyzing the book it will only be necessary to consult specific passages for reference. I Maccabees relates the thrilling story of the revolt against the tyrannical efforts of Antiochus IV to Hellenize the Jews and records the ultimate establishment of an independent state. The account begins with Alexander the Great and ends with John Hyrcanus. The history is developed chronologically as the outline indicates:

> 1:1–9, a summary of Alexander's conquests and the acts of the Diodochoi.
> 1:10–64, the persecution of the Jews by Antiochus IV Epiphanes.
> 2:1–70, the story of Mattathias and the Jewish revolt.
> 3:1–9:22, the feats of Judas, the Maccabee.
> 9:23–12:53, Jonathan's leadership.
> 13:1–16:24, Simon's leadership.

The book is the work of an unknown Palestinian Jewish patriot who wrote during the latter part of John Hyrcanus' rule or just after his death (104).[12] Perhaps the author viewed his work as an extension of

---

12 Josephus did not utilize the last three chapters of I Maccabees, and it has been argued that the original work terminated with chap. 13 and that the final editing took place after the destruction of the temple in A.D. 70. Cf. Tedesche and Zeitlin, *op. cit.*, pp. 27–33.

the history of the Chronicler for like the Chronicler, he used genealogies (2:1; 14:29), gave the speeches of key persons, inserted poems and referred to official documents. He is well versed in Hebrew scriptures and knows the events of the period and the terrain of Palestine. Despite his efforts to be accurate, he is not free from error, for he stated that before Alexander died he divided his empire among the Diodochoi (1:6). The speeches composed for Judas (3:58–60; 4:8–11, 16–18, 30–33) and Mattathias (2:7–13) and others may have some basis in reminiscences, but they should be treated as artificial, written in the tradition of Hellenistic writers of the period. The poems include dirges, laments and hymns of praise and may rest on a tradition of real events, but they may equally well be the composition of the author of I Maccabees (cf. 1:24–28, 36–40; 2:7–13; 3:3–9). The reported diplomatic documents and official letters may have been drawn from such official archives as "The chronicles of the high priesthood" (16:24) or copied from such inscriptions as the bronze memorial tablets (14:18, 27) [13] and so represent official wording. They could equally well be semi-authentic reconstructions in the writer's own words. The simplicity of style and the general reliability of the record tend to convey an impression of historical accuracy. In the absence of other confirming or contradicting evidence, I Maccabees must be treated seriously.

The author was a religious Jew and the scriptural allusions as well as the speech attributed to Mattathias recalling the heroes of the past reveal familiarity with sacred traditions. He does not attribute victories to any intrusion or direct act by God (cf. 3:58–60; 13:3–6), but in the speeches of the Jewish leaders and through their responses portrays God acting through natural means. He avoids direct references to God, preferring to speak of the people blessing "Heaven" (4:55), or to say that Judas prayed to the "Savior of Israel" (4:30). Attempts to demonstrate Pharisaic or Sadducean leanings have been inconclusive, and one can only note that the writer, as a man of faith, viewed Israel as a holy congregation, a people separated from and in opposition to the outside world because of their religious heritage and particularistic relationship to the universal God.

II MACCABEES

II Maccabees is an abridged account of the Maccabean revolt based on a five-volume work by Jason of Cyrene (2:19–23).[14] The larger work has disappeared, and nothing beyond this one reference is known of Jason. The extent to which the editor of the abridged version imposed his own point of view on the work of Jason is a matter of debate,[15]

[13] Inscribed copper plaques found at Qumran indicate that such inscriptions were not uncommon. Cf. John Allegro, *The Treasure of the Copper Scroll* (London: Routledge and Kegan Paul, 1960).

[14] Cyrene was a Greek city on the Mediterranean coast of North Africa and the capital of Cyrenaica, an independent kingdom conquered by Alexander. At this time it was under Ptolemaic control.

[15] Cf. Pfeiffer, *History of New Testament Times,* pp. 510–522.

but there is no valid reason for denying that the bulk of the summarized work is Jason's. The two letters appended at the beginning of II Maccabees, which urge the Egyptian Jews to observe Hanukkah, are not by Jason, nor are the editorial introduction (2:19–32) and the admonition to the reader, which is written in the first person (6:12–17), nor, perhaps, the side comment in 4:17. The rest of the work, we believe, fairly represents Jason. Most scholars date Jason's original work after the middle of the second century and the abridgment shortly before the close of the Hasmonean period. Jason probably wrote in Alexandria, Egypt.

The purpose of the abridgment was to present a succinct outline of the struggle for independence (2:24–32), and perhaps also to reassure the reader that the afflictions suffered by the Jews were permitted by God for disciplinary reasons (6:12). Jason's purpose must be surmised, for it is not stated explicitly. The emphasis on the centrality of the temple has led some scholars to suggest that his aim was the exaltation of this holy place. Broadly speaking, Jason appears to have been interested in reporting the Maccabean struggle in terms of sacred history. To accomplish this, he does not hesitate to explain failures and victories as acts of God, rather than of men as the author of I Maccabees does. He introduces visions, angelic figures, theological concepts, festivals, and acts of worship as significant elements of his story. He extols the supremacy of God in universalistic terms and sermonizes on the way God responds to his people when they are faithful, and how they are punished when they sin.

The book may be subdivided a number of different ways, but if 3:40, 7:42, 10:9, 13:26 and 15:37 are statements marking conclusions of Jason's five volumes, then perhaps it is better to attempt to read II Maccabees recognizing the divisions that Jason made.

I. Correspondence with Egypt, Chapters 1:1–2:18.
    a. 1:1–9, the first letter.
    b. 1:10–2:18, the second letter.
II. The Abridger's Preface, 2:19–32.
III. The Five Books of Jason, Chapters 3–15.
    a. 3, the story of Heliodorus.
    b. 4–7, Jewish opposition to compulsory Hellenism.
    c. 8–10:9, the Maccabean revolt, the cleansing of the temple and the institution of the Feast of Dedication (Hanukkah).
    d. 10:10–13:26, battles with Antiochus V Eupator and Lysias.
    e. 14:1–15:37, the defeat of Nicanor and the institution of Nicanor's day.
IV. The Abridger's Appendage, Chapter 15:38–39.

Read II Macc. Chs. 1–2

The authenticity of the letters purporting to be from Palestinian Jews to Egyptian Jews has been the source of much discussion. Most scholars treat them as compositions of the epitomist,[16] but it is possible that they are compilations based on older documents. The second letter contains an interesting legend about the preservation of sacred fire, which may embody two separate traditions. One account states

[16] Pfeiffer, *History of New Testament Times*, pp. 506–508; S. Tedesche and S. Zeitlin, *The Second Book of Maccabees*, Jewish Apocryphal Series (New York: Harper and Brothers, 1954), pp. 31–40.

that the fire was hidden in a cistern by priests at the time of the Exile and discovered in Nehemiah's day. The other says that Jeremiah ordered the exiles to take the holy fire, and that the prophet concealed the tabernacle, the ark and the altar of incense in a cave. Whether there is an echo of an ancient fire festival preceding Hanukkah in these legends is not clear.

In the idealization of the high priesthood of Onias, Jason claimed that the temple was enriched by gifts from rulers of other nations and that it was this great wealth that Heliodorus sought. Perhaps he intended to demonstrate that the prophecy of Haggai had been fulfilled (Hag. 2:6 f.). The miraculous preservation of the treasure and the saving of Heliodorus' life came through the righteousness of those who cried out to God in the proper manner.

The order of events given by Jason differs slightly from the preferred chronology of I Maccabees:

Read II Macc.
Chs. 3–15

I Maccabees	II Maccabees
Judas defeats Lysias (4:26–35).	The death of Antiochus (9).
Judas dedicates the temple (4:36–61).	Judas dedicates the temple (19:1–8).
Judas battles hostile neighbors (5).	Judas defeats Lysias (11:1–15).
Antiochus IV dies (6:1–17).	Judas battles hostile neighbors (12).

Jason explained that the reason God failed to treat Antiochus' violation of the temple as he had Heliodorus' act was because the people had sinned (5:17). The treasure donated by the nations disappeared with Antiochus.

Divine forewarning of the struggle with Antiochus was given in the vision of the "golden-clad horsemen," which was improperly understood (5:1–4). The persecution of the Jews by the Hellenists echoes the horrors described in I Maccabees. Heroic Eleazar, who put faith above life, is cited as an example to every Jew. The speeches that Jason ascribes to Eleazar are homilies. The five young men who died gruesome deaths for their religious beliefs are counterparts of the heroes in Daniel, except that in the real life situation there was no miraculous deliverance.

Judas does not struggle alone in II Maccabees, and it is with God's help that the enemy is overcome (8:24). Grateful warriors remember their religious obligations (8:27–29). Antiochus' illness comes as a blow struck by God (9:5). Jason's account of Antiochus' repentance and acknowledgment of the supremacy of the Jewish deity, and the futile attempt to bargain with God, is mocking satire. The section ends in triumph with the restoration of worship in the temple and the institution of a day of remembrance (10:1–8). The defeat of Nicanor has an equally victorious conclusion and provides for the institution of Nicanor's Day, which was later incorporated in the festival of Purim (15:36).

In addition to giving a theological interpretation of the Maccabean revolt, Jason designed his work to edify and inspire. Schooled in the rhetoric of Alexandria, Jason did not hesitate to employ exaggeration, epithets, melodramatic situations and any other literary tool that would enhance his work. The details of the profanation of the altar are subdued and the acts that defiled the temple dramatically enlarged. He wrestles with theological themes—the silence of God when his people suffer fiendish tortures, God's failure to respond when acts of indecency were committed within the temple precincts—and discusses these matters in terms of discipline, martyrdom (7) and sin (12:40). The wicked would die an eternal death with no resurrection (7:14), but the righteous would enjoy resurrection of the body, the renewal of life to eternity (7:9–12). He believed in the efficacy of expiation rites and prayers for the dead (12:43–45) and in angels. It is not possible to label Jason a Pharisee for certain, but without doubt he accepted many of their beliefs.

I Maccabees and II Maccabees are accepted as canonical by the Roman Catholic and Eastern Orthodox Churches.

THE WISDOM OF SOLOMON

The Wisdom of Solomon, like Proverbs and Ecclesiastes, is composed in the name of the famous Hebrew monarch. The book was written in Greek, probably by a Jew of Alexandria who was trained in Greek rhetoric and philosophy, and whose knowledge of the LXX is apparent in his writing. The most suitable date for this work is between the beginning of the first century B.C. and the end of the Hasmonean period.

The book is an apologia of Jewish belief in God, aimed particularly at apostate Jews. It has three major parts:

1. Chapters 1–5, a poetic contrast of the wise and foolish.
2. Chapters 6–9, a mixture of prose and poetry addressed to kings and judges.
3. Chapters 10–19, for the most part a prose meditation on wisdom and salvation-history. This section is interrupted by a discourse on folly (chs. 13–15).

**Read
Chs. 1–5**

As a ruler Solomon addresses his peers and as a wise man instructs them, urging them to follow Yahweh to gain wisdom. Something of the style of older wisdom writing appears in the use of parallelism, but the short individual sayings have been replaced by long discourses or treatises. The writer, through Solomon, admonished those who use the arguments of Ecclesiastes concerning the meaninglessness of life to defend pleasure-seeking that includes persecution and baiting of the righteous (ch. 2). Belief in death as the end is countered by a defense of belief in the immortality of the soul (ch. 3). Like Ben Sira, the author questions the merit of large families and the sense of continuity that some expect to find in their heirs (ch. 4).

**Read
Chs. 6–9**

The repetition of the opening address to kings marks the start of a new section. The song of praise for wisdom (ch. 6) is followed by Solomon's explanation of his greatness as a gift of wisdom.

**Read
Chs. 10–19**

The meditation on Hebrew history as determined by wisdom and blessed by God, demonstrates that vicissitudes of the past proved to be blessings in disguise. Some of the implications border on the fantastic (cf. 19:1–7).

The writer appears to have had several reasons for writing his treatise. He is concerned with the question of theodicy, which in his day took the form, "Why, if orthodoxy is the right way, does God not reward his own? Why are the impious in better circumstances?" The author responds to this ancient query on two levels: individual and national. Justice for the individual comes in the afterlife where the scales are balanced. So far as the nation is concerned, he argues that God has always cared for his people, but that at times it is necessary to have the perspective of history to recognize and appreciate the fact.

He desires to confront the secular Jew who represented the attitudes given in Chapter 2 and who persecuted the pious Jew perhaps in reaction to the rebukes of the righteous. These unorthodox persons are warned of the day of judgment. It is possible that in addressing his words to kings, the writer hoped to influence non-Jewish readers and the contrast between the folly of idolatry and the superiority of Jewish monotheism might have been aimed at such persons.

Like other wisdom writers, this author speaks of wisdom as a manifestation of God (7:25 f.), existing before the creation of the world (9:9 f.). God is described as the creator, but wisdom is involved in the creation process (7:22; 9:1 f.). The impact of Platonic philosophical concepts is apparent in the writer's view of man. Man consists of a physical body and an indwelling spiritual soul (15:8). The body is a burden to the soul (9:15), and the soul is pre-existent (8:19–20). The soul is immortal (3:1–5) and after death enjoys rewards or suffers punishments. Man was robbed of the eternal life that was his at creation through the "devil's envy" (2:24). Mankind is divided into two groups: those who are of the devil's "party" and those who belong to God. For the first time, we encounter the devil as a personality, a power opposed to God but not identified here as Satan or any other specific angel.

The Wisdom of Solomon has canonical status in the Greek Orthodox and Roman Catholic Churches, but not among Jews and Protestants.

II ESDRAS (IV EZRA OR ESDRAS)

II Esdras, a composite apocalyptic document containing writings by Christians and Jews, was composed during the Christian era and therefore lies beyond the perimeters of Old Testament history. It is without canonical standing. Because it has been included in the Apocrypha it falls within the scope of this book and will, therefore, receive brief consideration, without any attempt being made to engage in the discussion of the historical factors that lie behind it.

The simplest outline of the book is as follows:

I. Introduction, Chapters 1–2, Christian additions.
II. The seven visions, Chapters 3–14.

a. 3:1–5:20, the first vision.
b. 5:21–6:34, the second vision.
c. 6:35–9:25, the third vision.
d. 9:26–10:59, the fourth vision.
e. 11:1–12:47, the fifth vision, the eagle.
f. 13:1–58, the sixth vision, the man from the sea.
g. 14:1–48, the seventh vision, the writing of the books.
III. Conclusion, Chapters 15–16, Christian additions.

**Read
Chs. 1–2**

The distinctive Christian character of the introductory chapters can be discerned in the echoes of New Testament teachings. For example, the statement "I gathered you as a hen gathers her brood under her wings" is reminiscent of Matt. 23:37. Other passages revealing dependency on Christian writings include 1:32 (cf. Matt. 23:34–35); 1:35 (cf. Rom. 10:14); 1:39 (cf. Matt. 8:11).[17] The people who are to receive the kingdom denied to Israel are, of course, the Christians, and the "mother" urged to embrace her children is probably "Mother Church" (2:10–32). The closing section of Chapter 2 reflects the imagery of the Revelation to John, and the "shepherd" (2:34), "Savior" (2:36) and the "Son of God" (2:47) are references to Jesus, the Messiah who is to return. No clear indication of date is discernible in these two chapters, but many scholars suggest that they were added to the visions after the middle of the second century A.D.

**Read
Chs. 3–14**

Like Job, Ezra raises the problem of theodicy, but unlike Job, he is unwilling to accept the answer given to Job. He presses for details and they come in familiar apocalyptic garb. The initial vision is a response to Ezra's perplexity over God's use of unrighteous Babylon (Rome) to harass Zion—the same problem that troubled Habakkuk. God's answer, delivered by Uriel,[18] is a challenge to Ezra much like that given to Job. Ezra, like Job, admits man's finitude, but learns that when the predestined number of the righteous has been reached, the time of judgment will come and the wicked and righteous will receive their just rewards. The time of the end, which, Ezra learned, was close at hand, is to be preceded by signs. Sin results from a "grain of evil" sown in Adam's heart (4:30), giving to man the impulse or desire for evil (3:21).[19]

In the second vision, Ezra reiterates his complaint concerning the treatment of God's people (5:21–40) and raises a new question about those who die before the end of the age has come (5:41). He learns that God planned all that occurs from before the foundation of the world and that all the righteous will be treated alike. The signs of the end of the age, like those of the first vision, are ugly and forbidding.

Israel's role in the world to come is the subject of the third vision.

---

[17] For additional references, see the notations in *The Oxford Annotated Apocrypha* (New York: Oxford University Press, 1965), pp. 23–26.

[18] Uriel, whose name means "fire of God," is the fourth of the chief angels, the others being Raphael, Michael and Gabriel, whom we have encountered before. Uriel is not only a messenger but, in the pseudepigraphaic book of Enoch, is both guide and supervisor of Tartarus, the lowest section of Hades.

[19] The Hebrew term *yetser* means "impulse" and can refer to an impulse for good or an impulse for evil. The theme is developed in the Qumran document popularly called "The Manual of Discipline."

Ezra learns that only Israelites will be saved and of these, only those who observe the Law. God's son, the Messiah, is introduced as one who will reign for four hundred years and then die with all living creatures as the world returns to primeval silence (7:28 ff.). After seven days, the resurrection of the dead will occur and judgment will take place. Ezra sought more information: how long does the soul rest after death before being judged (7:75)? He learns that the souls of the righteous return immediately to God, while the souls of the wicked wander in torment up to the time of judgment when they will be destroyed. The emphasis is upon the few who will achieve salvation either by their faith or by their good works (9:7–25).

The fourth vision depicts Zion as a mourning wife bewailing the fate of her children. Suddenly the scene changes, and Ezra is permitted to get a glimpse of the new Jerusalem that will come in the future.

In the fifth vision, Rome is depicted as an eagle, the world empire that disappears when the lion, the Messiah, comes. To make Rome the fourth kingdom of Daniel's vision, the apocalypticist is compelled to reinterpret Daniel (12:10 ff.). The Messiah is of the Davidic line (12:32). In the sixth vision, the Messiah is portrayed as a man coming out of the sea, and the tribes of Israel are gathered to him and the wicked destroyed. The contrasting views of the Messiah in the third, fifth and sixth visions illustrate the fluidity of messianic concepts in this period.

The final vision explains how the scriptures were rewritten by Ezra's men under the guidance of God, demonstrating their divine inspiration. Ezra is instructed to make twenty-four books public, which would be the twenty-four books of the Jewish canon,[20] and to reserve seventy books for the wise; these extra volumes would be the apocalyptic non-canonical writings. Perhaps, here, some clue is given to the time of writing, for the canon of the Jews was not established until A.D. 90, so that the visions would probably have been recorded after that time. Obviously, the writer is not one of those who accepted the dicta of Jamnia,[21] and he does not hesitate to inform his readers that the non-canonical books contain esoteric writings not for the common people but for the elite.

The Christian additions that conclude the book are often dated about the middle of the third century A.D., at the time when the Christian church was under persecution by Decius and the Roman empire was threatened by Goths, Persians and Palmyrenians. The attacks on the empire are interpreted as acts of divine retribution for harsh treatment of Christians.[22]

There is no way to identify the Jewish author[23] of the seven visions,

Read Chs.
15–16

20 *Supra*, Chapter 1.

21 See below, Chapter 31, the section on "The Jewish Canon."

22 E. J. Goodspeed, *The Story of the Apocrypha* (Chicago: The University of Chicago Press, 1939), p. 111.

23 The issue of single versus multiple authorship has been debated. F. C. Porter, *The Messages of Apocalyptical Writers* (New York: Charles Scribner's Sons, 1905), p. 336, and H. H. Rowley, *The Relevance of Apocalyptic* (New York: Harper and Brothers, 1947), pp. 103, 142, are among those supporting the unity of II Esdras. G. H. Box "IV Ezra," *The Apocrypha and Pseudepigrapha of the Old Testament*,

but he reveals a typically orthodox concept of God as creator and judge, harsh in the treatment of sinners, but merciful to his righteous ones. Sin is an act of rebellion against God that results in estrangement (6:5; 7:48) and leads to punishment. The concept of the Messiah which developed in the inter-testamental period is conveyed in two images. The man from the sea (13:25–52) is a pre-existent figure. His rule is not everlasting and little is said of him. The Messiah as the lion (7:28 ff.) is called God's son and his reign is for four hundred years, after which he dies. There is both harmony of thought and fluidity of image in the Messiah pictures. Death and eternal life are separated by an intermediate stage, which in itself provides intimations of the final state of each individual. The remnant concept appears once again in the number of those saved. Salvation is not universal, nor for all Jews, but only for that select handful who carefully fulfill the Law.

---

ed. R. H. Charles (Oxford: The Clarendon Press, 1913), pp. 542 ff.; W. O. E. Oesterley, *II Esdras (The Ezra Apocalypse)*, Westminster Commentaries (London: Methuen and Company, 1933), p. 148; and C. C. Torrey, *The Apocryphal Literature* (New Haven: Yale University Press, 1945), p. 116 are among those supporting multiple authorship.

Canon, Text and Translations

31

Development of the Canon

THE idea of a canon rests upon belief in revelation and inspiration: the revelation of divine will to and through inspired persons. In Jeremiah's day, those who opposed him referred to the three accepted channels of inspired utterance in ancient Israel when they declared, "The law shall not perish from the priest, nor the counsel from the wise, nor the word from the prophet" (Jer. 18:18). The will of Yahweh was made known to priests through the Urim and Thummin, or other means of divination, but the means of sanctification and atonement, particular concerns of the priesthood, had been disclosed to Moses on Mount Sinai/Horeb and had become means of sustaining the divine-human relationship. The words of the wise, revealed by divine Wisdom, were in harmony with the very principles that brought the cosmos into being. The prophets were spokesmen for Yahweh and their words were Yahweh's words. Some of the biblical materials are representative of these three classes of "inspired" persons. How their words came to be canonized can only be inferred from hints within the writings themselves, but it is clear that prior to the Exile these three kinds of literature were accorded some sort of special status.

In the development of the history of Israel we have been able to see how the Torah gradually took form and reached completion in the late Persian period. The beginning of the canonization of this portion of the Bible may go back to the ancient belief that the law of the land was a divine promulgation, an idea prevalent throughout the Near East.[1] The Bible bears ample evidence that the Hebrews believed that Yahweh himself wrote some of the laws (Exod. 24:12; 31:18; 32:16–16; 34:1), and that those written by Moses were dictated by Yahweh (Exod. 34:27). The formularies of the Shechem covenant were labeled "the book of the law of God" and were deposited in Yahweh's sanctuary (Josh. 24:26). The first clear move toward canonization can be seen in Deuteronomy. The Deuteronomists stated that their law was complete, with nothing to be added or removed (Deut. 4:2; 12:32); that the laws were revealed by Yahweh and were binding on all generations (Deut. 29:29); that they were designed for public proclamation (Deut. 27:4–8) but as holy writings were to be given special treatment (Deut. 31:24–26). The curses and blessings, the covenant setting, the attribu-

---

[1] Cf. Meek, *Hebrew Origins*, pp. 55 f.

tion of the laws to Moses and Yahweh, make Deuteronomy the equivalent of a divinely revealed national constitution, completely removed from the sphere of ordinary literature. The use of the book in cultic settings further enhanced its unique status. During the Exile, Ezekiel's teaching that disobedience to Yahweh's will had brought divine punishment underscored the importance of those laws that purported to reveal what Yahweh demanded.

Perhaps the most important step toward canonization is recorded in the Ezra tradition. During the New Year festival, Ezra read publicly from "the book of the law" and instructed the people in the law (Neh. 7:73b–8:18). What this "law" embraced cannot be determined from the account.[2] It is possible that the scroll included Deuteronomy and those parts of P compiled by Babylonian Jews during the Exile. It is unlikely that the bulk of the Pentateuch was read, although this document must have been nearing its final form. Ezra's law could not have been completely new to the listeners, and it is clear that the Chronicler is suggesting that the structure of the new community was to be determined by this law which was, therefore, automatically recognized as possessing divine authority.

About this same time, the Samaritan canon (see below), which includes the complete Torah, came into being, and in the third century the LXX translation was made. The Law had reached its final form and had attained canonical status, but the details of this process lie hidden in the obscure history of the Exilic and early post-Exilic periods.

The oracles of the prophets were preserved by disciples (Isa. 8:16; Jer. 36) and perhaps by the temple cult. Knowledge of what the prophets had said was not restricted to the cultus or to the inner circle of disciples. Micah's words were quoted by an elder in Jeremiah's time (Jer. 26:17 ff.), and it is possible that prophetic utterances enjoyed much wider circulation than we have been willing to admit. Hosea's portrayal of Israel as an unfaithful wife and Isaiah's parable of the vineyard became standard illustrations of apostasy during the Exile.

The fulfillment of some predictions, such as those forecasting the fall of Syria and Israel, gave eighth century prophecy special significance.[3] If a prophet had foreseen events that had occurred, there was good reason to heed warnings concerning that which was yet to happen.[4] When Judah collapsed in the sixth century, there could be little doubt that prophetic predictions had, once again, demonstrated their inspired basis, for only Yahweh could know and make manifest the future. One of the writers of Lamentations commented:

> Yahweh has done what he purposed,
>   has carried out his threat;
> as he ordained long ago,
>   he has demolished without pity.
>
> Lam. 2:17

[2] For a summary of different interpretations, cf. R. A. Bowman, *The Interpreter's Bible*, III, 733 f.

[3] Cf. Isa. 7–8; Amos 3:9 ff.; 4:1–3; 9:1; Hos. 8:11–13; 10:7–10; Micah 1:6–8; 3:1–4.

[4] Particularly warnings concerning the fall of Judah, cf. Amos 6:1 and possibly 2:4–5; Hos. 5:5, 10; 6:4; 8:14; Micah 1:10–16; 3:12; Isa. 5:5; 6:11–13.

During the Exile, the prophetic oracles were studied for signs of restoration. The hope of return appears to have grown out of the interpretation and expansion of the remnant concept. By the time of the post-Exilic era, prophetic writings were well on the way toward canonization.

In the post-Exilic period, perhaps because of the development of hope for an idealized eschaton, prophecy began to fall into disrepute (Zech. 13:2–3; Neh. 6:7, 14). If one had assurance of an idyllic future from sources that had been proven reliable (despite the fact that the restoration oracles were added to earlier prophecies during the Exile), all further prophecy became unnecessary. By the time of the Maccabees, it was a common assumption that there were no prophets (I Macc. 4:46; 9:27; 14:41), although there was hope that true prophets would appear.

The contents of the prophetic canon appear to have been established between the fourth and second centuries in two general groupings: the Former Prophets (Joshua, Judges, I–II Samuel, I–II Kings) and the Latter Prophets (Isaiah, Jeremiah, Ezekiel and The Twelve). The Former Prophets are part of what Martin Noth has recognized as a Deuteronomic history. Whether or not they were included as part of the prophetic canon because they have much to report about prophets and prophetesses or because they were ascribed to prophets cannot be known. Possibly because they had been part of a theological history that extended from Genesis through Kings, when the first five books of the collection were ascribed to Moses, the remaining volumes of the sacred history were given sacred status too.

The Hagiographa or Writings are an amorphous literary collection with a most obscure history. Perhaps the cultic use of the Psalms and the ascription of many hymns to David tended to set this collection apart from secular songs. Wisdom writings, attributed primarily to Solomon, stressed reverence for Yahweh (Prov. 1:7) and declared that wisdom was a gift of Yahweh (Prov. 2:6; Sirach 1:1; Wisdom 7:7). Other documents survived through popular appeal and common usage. The fluidity of the "hagiographic canon" raised problems when the Jews attempted to standardize authoritative writings. The earliest mention of the collection is found in the prologue to Ben Sira's work where reference is made to the "other books of our fathers," presumably the Hagiographa.

THE SAMARITAN CANON

The relationship between the peoples of Israel and Judah had always been marked with suspicion and distrust and, on occasion, open hostility. When Solomon's empire was divided after his death, tensions between the two nations were never resolved. The destruction of Samaria by the Assyrians and the deportation of thousands of Israelites had not eliminated Yahweh worship in the northern kingdom but had tended to center the cult in Judah. What form the worship of Yahweh took in the Assyrian-held province of Israel is not known. In the time of Ezra and Nehemiah, Jewish-Samaritan hostility reached a new peak, and the Samaritans became openly hostile to the reconstruction of Jerusalem and the temple, partially, no doubt, from fear of any form of neo-Judaean power that might affect Samaritan political or theological well-being. When the Samaritan temple was constructed (probably in the fourth century),[5] the Samaritans, like their Jewish neighbors, possessed a body of sacred scripture consisting of the Torah or Pentateuch, which differs at many points with the Jewish Hebrew text and in some instances supports LXX readings. The exclusion of prophetic and hagiographic writings suggests that the schism took place before these collections had attained authoritative standing, although it is possible that the many anti-Ephraim statements in the prophets may have made these works unacceptable.

THE "ALEXANDRIAN CANON"

In reality, there is no "Alexandrian canon," for the Jews of Alexandria never officially canonized the LXX. The term, a misnomer, is used to designate the combined Jewish canon (Tanak) and the Apocrypha.

When the LXX was formed, the Jews had placed limits only on the Torah and the prophets. The authority of the larger group of writings out of which the Kethubhim were to be selected, had not yet been determined, although some sort of selective process must have been at work, for the LXX did not include such other well-known Jewish documents as Enoch or Jubilees or other writings now relegated to the Pseudepigrapha. What principles determined the contents of the LXX beyond the Law and the Prophets is not known.

THE QUMRAN SCRIPTURES

Like their fellow Jews, the sectaries of Qumran made use of writings now included in the Jewish Bible, with the possible exception of Esther of which no fragment has, as yet, been found. They also possessed copies of Ben Sira's work and Tobit, as well as Jubilees (at least ten copies), Enoch and The Testament of the Twelve Patriarchs which are today placed in the Pseudepigrapha. In addition, they consulted writings that appear to have been uniquely their own, including a collection of thanksgiving hymns, a manual of the order of the community ("The Manual of Discipline"), an apocryphal scroll called "The Wars of the Sons of Darkness versus the Sons of Light," a Genesis Apocryphon, a copper "treasure" scroll, commentaries on the books of Nahum and Habakkuk and numerous other writings. Clearly, the library of Qumran was not limited to books later adopted by the Jews as authoritative. At the same time, there is no way to determine how the Qumran sect weighted the authority of individual writings. Jubilees, on the basis of manuscript counting, appears to have been a popular work, and is quoted in one of the sect's docu-

[5] Josephus, *Antiquities*, 11:8:4.

THE SCROLL OF THANKSGIVING HYMNS FROM QUMRAN. *Among the writings recovered from Qumran was a collection of hymns of thanksgiving, apparently composed by members of the sect. The hymns are not unlike the psalms of thanksgiving in the Bible. The scrolls were composed of parchment leather and were wrapped in linen. Decomposition was due to natural aging brought on by time and some moisture, and in some cases increased by rodents nibbling the edges of the manuscripts.*

ments, The Damascus Document, but one cannot assume that it was given more weight than the book of Isaiah which was also represented by several copies.

THE JEWISH CANON

The earliest reference to the Jewish canon is in Josephus' defense of the Jewish faith, *Contra Apion* 1:8, in which he states that the Jews have only twenty-two "divine" books. He explains that "of these, five belong to Moses," and that to encompass the period between Moses

Opening a scroll. *Some scrolls were opened with relative ease; others demanded meticulous care and a maximum of patience. Here Prof. H. Bieberkrant works on one of the more difficult scrolls.*

and Artaxerxes "the prophets, who were after Moses, wrote down what was done in their time in thirteen books," and "the remaining four books contain hymns to God." The thirteen "prophetic books" include Joshua, Judges, I–II Samuel (one book), I–II Kings (one book), I–II Chronicles (one book), Ezra-Nehemiah (one book), Isaiah, Jeremiah, Ezekiel, The Twelve (one book), Job, Daniel and Esther. Ruth was probably combined with Judges, and Lamentations with Jeremiah. The "hymns" incorporated Psalms, Proverbs, Ecclesiastes and the Song of Songs. Josephus' listing represents what came to be the Jewish canon, although scholars were wrestling with problems of the authority of certain writings at the very time he was writing.

After the destruction of Jerusalem in A.D. 70, a colony of Jewish scholars led by Johanan ben Zakkai gathered at Jabneh or Jamnia, a village located near the Mediterranean about thirty miles west of Jerusalem, and by A.D. 90 were in deep discussion about the canon. Ben Zakkai had escaped from Jerusalem during the siege—according to one tradition, in a coffin—and was permitted by Vespasian, who was then a general, to establish a school at Jamnia. Ben Zakkai was a Pharisee, a well-known product of the famous school of Hillel.[6]

Sacrifice had ceased with the destruction of the temple. It was clear that the future of Judaism would have to be anchored in the Scriptures. If the Scriptures were to be the norm for faith, it was imperative that the authoritative writings be separated from all others. Jews of the Dispersion had taken a somewhat freer attitude toward sacred writings than the Jews of Palestine. Moreover, the Christian sect, which was fast developing into a religion apart from Judaism, employed Jewish writings, including some of questionable authority, to demonstrate that Jesus of Nazareth was the Messiah. Because it was commonly believed that inspiration had ceased in Ezra's time, there was really little point in keeping the canon open, and there was danger that some Jews, not so well informed, might continue to use questionable material or begin to use Christian writings in matters of the faith. Finally, there was a growing desire to determine the official text and to keep that text free of scribal errors, and without an official canon this was almost impossible to accomplish.

There were no problems concerning the Law. Among the prophetic writings, only Ezekiel came under serious discussion. Certain conflicts with the Torah, which was considered to be the supreme and final source of revelation, had to be resolved (cf. Ezek. 46:6; Num. 28:11). It is said that Hananiah ben Hezekiah ben Garon, a follower of Shammai, labored day and night, burning 300 barrels of oil, to harmonize the discrepancies.[7] Esther was accepted after much debate because of its association with Purim, and because it was said to have been revealed to Moses.[8] The greatest controversies were concerned with Ecclesiastes and the Song of Songs. Ecclesiastes was judged by the followers of Shammai to be a product of Solomon's own wise speculation, but members of the Hillel school judged it a divinely inspired document. The final decision, that the book was a product of the Holy Spirit, was debated for centuries. The Song of Songs, after much discussion, was finally admitted to the canon as an allegory of God's love for Israel. Perhaps Rabbi Akiba, the famous scholar of the second century A.D., put the quietus to the argument with his emphatic declaration, "All the Scriptures are holy; but the Song of Songs is holiest of all."[9]

The principles guiding the rabbis in the selection of sacred books

[6] Hillel, a Babylonian Jew, had migrated to Palestine to study the Torah under famous expositors. He established a school and became known as an advocate of the oral law with decidedly Pharisaic leanings. He is usually dated between 60 B.C. and A.D. 20. His famous rival was Shammai, a native Judaean and a Pharisee, but one who favored a more stringent, legalistic bent. Like Hillel, Shammai headed a school in Jerusalem. From these scholars came a long line of teacher-scholars known as the Tannaim (from the Aramaic *tanna,* "to teach").

[7] H. G. May, "Ezekiel," *The Interpreter's Bible,* VI, 41.

[8] Moore, *Judaism,* I, 245.

[9] Moore, *Judaism,* III, n. 9, p. 65 f.

have not come down to us in any clear-cut delineation but appear to have included the following:

1. The writing had to be composed in Hebrew. The only exceptions, which were written in Aramaic, were Daniel 2–7, writings attributed to Ezra (Ezra 4:8–6:18; 7:12–26), who was recognized as the founding father of post-Exilic Judaism, and Jer. 10:11. Hebrew was the language of Sacred Scripture, Aramaic the language of common speech.

2. The writing had to be sanctioned by usage in the Jewish community. The use of Esther at Purim made it possible for it to be included in the canon. Judith, without such support, was not acceptable.

3. The writings had to contain one of the great religious themes of Judaism, such as election, or the covenant. By reclassifying the Song of Songs as an allegory, it was possible to see in this book an expression of covenantal love.

4. The writing had to be composed before the time of Ezra, for it was popularly believed that inspiration had ceased then. Jonah was accepted because it used the name of an early prophet and dealt with events before the destruction of Nineveh, which occurred in 612. Daniel, a pseudonymous writing, had its setting in the Exile and therefore was accepted as an Exilic document.

The canon produced by the Jamnia Council is usually dated in A.D. 90, but in reality represents the results of discussions taking place over many years. The canon was not closed easily. Debates over controversial books continued, and some writings, such as that by Ben Sira, continued to be pushed toward canonization. Ultimately the canonical norm was fixed in accordance with the decisions of Jamnia to include Torah, Nebhiim and Kethubhim. The three-fold division reflects the order of priority. Within the last two divisions, there was some fluctuation in arrangement of books. The poetic books—Psalms, Proverbs and Job—were grouped and placed first in the Kethubhim, perhaps because of the religious significance of the Psalter. Next, the five festal scrolls (Megilloth) used in Jewish festivals were brought together in the order in which they now appear in the Tanak: The Song of Songs, which was recited at Passover; Ruth, which was used in the Festival of Weeks; Lamentations, which was associated with the commemoration of the fall of Jerusalem; Ecclesiastes, which was associated with the feast of Tabernacles and Esther, which was read at Purim. Daniel, treated as a prophetic work, followed Esther, and finally came the historical works—Ezra, Nehemiah and Chronicles.

THE CHRISTIAN CANON

Missionaries of the early Christian movement used the LXX in their appeal to the Greek-speaking world and did not hesitate to draw upon documents later classified as uncanonical by Jewish savants. The canonization issue had not become a particularly serious matter when the New Testament literature was being produced, and there are numerous references to sources excluded from the Jewish Bible. For example, Jude 14–16 quotes Enoch 1:9, and Hebrews 11:35 f. refers to

II Macc. 6–7.[10] Even after the Jamnia decisions, Christians continued to use the LXX, for there was no theory about the cessation of inspiration among Hellenistic Jews or Christians.

Not all Christians approved of the use of Jewish scriptures. In Rome, Marcion, a Christian from Sinope, a city on the south shore of the Black Sea, rejected the Jewish Bible and pressed for the acceptance of what was to become part of the New Testament as the Christian canon. In A.D. 140, he was expelled from the Christian community in Rome and formed a church of his own. For 100 years his followers were to challenge the tenets of other Christian groups.[11] Apart from Marcion, no other Christians appear to have raised serious questions concerning the use of the LXX. For most Christians, the Jewish Bible was "Holy Scripture" and was to be understood and interpreted in the light of Christian convictions.[12] Some uneasiness about the authority of the Apocrypha was expressed by Jerome (ca. A.D. 340–420), whose translation of the Old Testament into Latin rested on the Hebrew text. Jerome was in general agreement with the Jewish position and separated the extra books found in the LXX, which he admitted could be edifying, from the Jewish canon. Jerome's views did not prevail, and in A.D. 393 at the Synod of Hippo, the LXX was canonized, largely because of the influence of Augustine, Bishop of Hippo (ca. 354–430). Later, in 397, the Synod of Carthage confirmed the action taken at Hippo, and once again, Augustine exerted significant influence.

Despite formal actions by the Synods, there were those who were uneasy about the canonization of books not found in the Hebrew canon, and up to the time of the Protestant-Catholic schism, there were scholars who made sharp distinctions between canonical and apocryphal writings.[13] With the development of the Protestant Church and the tendency of the reformers to base translations of scriptures on original tongues rather than upon the Latin version, statements were included in the Protestant Bibles indicating that the Apocrypha was not to be placed on the same level as the other documents. Luther's translation (1534) included the Apocrypha between the Old and New Testaments with this title:

> "Apocrypha, that is, books which are not held equal to the Sacred Scriptures, but nevertheless are useful and good to read."

A year later Coverdale's Bible was published with the Apocrypha placed between the two Testaments under this statement:

> "Apocrypha, the books and treatises which among the fathers of old are not to be reckoned of like authority with other books of the Bible, neither are they found in the canon of the Hebrew."

10 Other material excluded from the Jewish canon may be found in James 1:19 (cf. Ecclesiasticus 5:11) and Heb. 11:37 (cf. The Martyrdom of Isaiah). The sources of John 7:38; Luke 11:49; and James 4:5 are not known. Cf. B. Metzger, *Introduction to the Apocrypha*, pp. 151 ff.

11 For a brief discussion of Marcion, cf. W. A. Gifford, *The Story of the Faith* (New York: The Macmillan Company, 1946), pp. 162 ff.; A. C. McGiffert, *A History of Christian Thought* (New York: Charles Scribner's Sons, 1954), pp. 58 ff.

12 Cf. Robert M. Grant, *The Bible in the Church* (New York: The Macmillan Company, 1948), pp. 43 ff.

13 Cf. Metzger, *An Introduction to the Apocrypha*, pp. 178 ff.

There were doctrinal reasons back of the Protestant refusal to accept the Apocrypha, for it was here that the Roman Catholic Church found Scriptural authority for the doctrine of Purgatory and for prayers and Masses for the dead (II Macc. 12:43–45) and for the efficacy of good works (Tobit 12:9; Ecclesiasticus 8:33).

At the Council held in Trent (Tridentum), Italy (1545–1563), the Roman Catholic Church officially accepted the Jewish canon and the Apocrypha, except for I and II Esdras (III and IV Esdras in Catholic Bibles) and the Prayer of Manasseh,[14] as the official Old Testament (See Chart I). In response, various Protestant groups took formal action, either encouraging the reading of the Apocrypha for edification but not for doctrine, as in the Church of England,[15] or placing the Apocrypha completely outside of the Canon as in the Westminster Confession of Faith (1648) which stated:

> "The books commonly called Apocrypha, not being of divine inspiration are no part of the Canon of Scripture, and therefore are of no authority in the Church of God, nor to be otherwise approved, or made use of, than other human writings."

The Eastern Orthodox Church took separate action. From the earliest times, the Eastern Church, which used the LXX, was undecided about the Apocrypha:[16] some Greek Fathers quoted from these books; others preferred to follow solely the books accepted by the Jews. The matter of the Apocrypha was raised in the Trullan Council at Constantinople in 692, but no binding conclusions were reached. Again in 1672, at the Council held in Jerusalem, the issue of the canon was considered and I Esdras, Tobit, Judith, Wisdom, Ecclesiasticus, Baruch, the Prayer of Azariah and the Song of the Three Young Men and I, II and III Maccabees[17] were accorded canonical status. However, because the Jerusalem Council was a "Regional Council" and neither Ecumenical nor pan-Orthodox, its decrees were not obligatory unless accepted by all Orthodox Churches. Although there has been no official acceptance of the canon outlined at Jerusalem, all editions of the Bible published by the Orthodox Churches include the books selected in 1672.

In 1870, the Council of the Vatican reiterated the concepts set forth at Trent concerning the canon. Since this time, there have been no official statements issued concerning the canon either by Jews, Catholics or Protestants. It must be noted that in recent years there has been closer cooperation in biblical studies among the three faiths.

14 Manasseh and I and II Esdras were printed in an appendix.

15 Cf. "The Thirty-nine Articles," Article 6. These are often printed in Episcopal hymnals, and The Book of Common Prayer.

16 The Eastern Orthodox Churches reserve the term "Apocrypha" for books usually called "Pseudepigrapha" by Protestants and Jews, and use instead the word "Anaginoskomena" to signify books "suitable for reading in public or private."

17 III Maccabees is a second century B.C. work by a Hellenistic Jew telling of Ptolemy IV Philopater's attempt to enter the temple. Metzger, *An Introduction to the Apocrypha*, p. 194, lists IV Maccabees, which appears to be a first century A.D. work designed to encourage faith written by a Hellenistic Jew well versed in Platonic philosophy. The decree of the Council of Jerusalem mentions only "the three Maccabean books," and the Orthodox Church lists IV Maccabees as an "apocryphon."

32

Texts, Manuscripts and Translations

THE task of the textual critic, to recover, insofar as possible, what the original writer wrote, is formidable. No autographs have been found, and in some instances our oldest manuscripts are separated by many centuries from the original writing. We are dependent upon the work of copyists, and some of these made many errors. A glance at photographic reproductions of the Qumran documents demonstrates the fallibility of copyists in scribal schools,[1] for it is apparent that, from time to time, the scribe himself recognized and corrected his own errors.

The importance of protecting manuscripts from mutilation was slowly recognized by the Jews, and by the time this awareness had become a principle, numerous additions had been made to some documents, as we have seen in the literary analysis of the texts. Books were reproduced in quantity in scribal schools and, on occasion, by special request for some wealthy collector. Because there was no sense of literary ownership or copyright, there was no reason why additions or deletions might not be made. Only when books acquired sanctity and authority were efforts made to maintain the purity of the text. The first major step toward accurate preservation came with canonization, and even after that, both voluntary and accidental changes were made.

Before attempting to recover the text, the textual critic makes certain basic assumptions. First, he assumes that the original author would not deliberately write a text devoid of meaning. If the text before him is incoherent, it is because it does not accurately represent the original. Second, he works believing that no text is to be treated as though it were infallible in all of its parts. Even the best texts are based on earlier works that may contain errors, and the most careful copyist may make mistakes. Third, he does not assume that earlier manuscripts are automatically better than later ones. Late manuscripts may accurately reproduce good early copies, and an early copy may be the work of a careless scribe. When it is possible, the text critic may attempt to ascertain the ancestry of a document. Certain "families" of manuscripts tend to be more reliable than others. Fourth, he treats with cautious respect quotations from the Old Testament in the New

[1] Desks, benches and ink pots of the Qumran copyists were found, demonstrating the existence of a scriptorium.

Testament, early Church fathers and early rabbinic sources. Quotations may be from memory and may be generally correct, but not precise,[2] or may be a compilation of several sources.[3] Fifth, where the text appears to be meaningless, he may, with extreme caution, venture conjectural emendations. Such emendations presuppose exhaustive knowledge of the textual history and languages involved.[4]

A partial list of the most common errors found in manuscripts includes:

1. Dittography or the repetition of a letter, syllable, word, clause or sentence. Once such an error was made, it was faithfully reproduced. In the Hebrew text of Lev. 20:10, the first five Hebrew words "If a man commits adultery with the wife of . . ." are repeated. The translators of the King James Version of the Bible incorporated the dittography in the English text, but in the Revised Standard Version the repetition is eliminated by placing one statement in the footnotes.

2. Confusion in transmitting letters. Many Hebrew letters look enough alike that, unless care is taken in writing, confusion may result. Because the Hebrew letters "n" (נ) and "r" (ר) were confused, the name of the Babylonian king Nebuchadrezzar was transmitted as "Nebuchadnezzar." When the letter "m" (מ) was confused with a "b" (ב) the name Merodoch-Baladan in II Kings 20–12 appeared as "Berodoch-Baladan."[5]

3. Errors of hearing. When the reader dictated from a master scroll and the scribe misunderstood, something that sounded like the original words was often recorded. On this basis, Psalm 100:3 was written "and not we ourselves" rather than "and we are his." The change in preferred readings of this verse may be seen by comparing the passage in the King James Version and the Revised Standard Version.

4. Errors of seeing, such as homoioteleuton. When the scribe copied from a manuscript and his eyes skipped from a line ending in one word to another line ending in the same word, all intervening material was omitted. This is what happened in I Sam. 14:41, which reads:

> Therefore Saul said, O Yahweh, God of Israel
> *why hast thou not answered thy servant this*
> *day? If the guilt is in me or in Jonathan,*
> *my son, O Yahweh, God of Israel, give Urim;*
> *But if the guilt is in thy people Israel,*
> give Thummim.

The scribe moved from the word "Israel" in the first line to the word "Israel" in the next-to-last line and omitted the italicized portion. The full reading was preserved in the LXX.

---

[2] For example, cf. I Cor. 1:19 and Isa. 29:14; I Cor. 2:9 and Isa. 64:4; II Cor. 9:9 and Ps. 112:9. When the apostle Paul dictated letters, he quoted his authorities from memory.

[3] Cf. II Cor. 6:16–18 and Exod. 29:45; Lev. 26:12; Ezek. 37:27; Jer. 31:1; Isa. 52:1; and perhaps Hos. 1:10 or Isa. 43:6.

[4] When the biblical text is translated for use by the public, translators may, when confronted with a meaningless text, suggest what they think the original may have said. The translators of the Revised Standard Version were careful to note such conjectures in footnotes with the abbreviation "Cn," standing for "correction." For a statement regarding the text, see the "Preface" to the RSV.

[5] This error was preserved in the King James Version but was eliminated in the Revised Standard Version.

5. Deliberate changes. On occasion, a scribe might deliberately alter a reading to make it conform to his beliefs. We have noted the change in the name of one of Saul's sons from Ish-ba'al ("man of Ba'al") to Ish-bosheth ("man of shame") by someone who disapproved of Hebrew royalty bearing the name of a Canaanite deity.

These and other errors demand of the textual critic a high degree of perspicacity. Sometimes he can determine precisely what happened to cause a particular textual variation, but at other times he can only guess.

Until the discovery of the Qumran scrolls, the earliest Hebrew biblical manuscripts were from the ninth century A.D. Pious Jews destroyed worn-out copies to prevent them from falling into impious hands. There were, of course, earlier versions in other languages. With the discovery of the Scrolls, scholars were enabled to move back nearly 1,000 years in the history of the Hebrew text.[6] The fidelity of textual transmission was obvious, for despite numerous variations no major alteration of the text had taken place.[7] Some Qumran manuscripts are closer to the LXX or Samaritan than to the Hebrew text, demonstrating that manuscripts with varying texts were in circulation during the first centuries B.C. and A.D., and that no one text had attained unique priority among the scribes of Qumran.

As Hebrew and Aramaic continued to be living languages during the first 500 years of the Christian era, there was little cause for concern about proper reading of the text. When these languages began to die, a group of Jewish scholars known as Massoretes[8] came into being in Babylon and Palestine. Their work embraces a period roughly between A.D. 600 and 1000. They were, in a sense, successors to the scribes and deeply concerned with the purity and preservation of the text, but their efforts extended beyond care in copying because of the emergence of new problems. The Hebrew text had been written without any division between words.[9] Because Hebrew and Aramaic had become dead languages, the words were separated to give ease in reading. To keep the text constant, the Massoretes developed mechanical checks and counted the number of words and letters, noted the number of times the divine name was used or special words appeared, and determined the middle verses, words and letters of individual books. Any manuscript that failed on any of these counts was defective. Efforts were made to correct scribal errors, although some "corrections" appear to have been made on dogmatic grounds.[10] The Hebrew

[6] For a discussion of the textual significance of the Qumran scrolls, see M. Burrows, *The Dead Sea Scrolls,* pp. 301–325; and *More Light on the Dead Sea Scrolls,* pp. 135–177.

[7] For example, in the translation of Isaiah, the Revised Standard Version contains thirteen footnote references to alternate readings in the Qumran Isaiah scroll, all noted as "One ancient manuscript reads . . .," none of which is terribly significant.

[8] The word "Massorete" is derived from an Aramaic root *msr* meaning "to hand down" or "to transmit." The Massoretes were transmitters of tradition, or traditionalists.

[9] Divisions according to subject matter, called *parasha* (pl, *parashoth*), are known from the third century. The Torah was divided for Sabbath readings into *sedarim*.

[10] Cf. Eissfeldt, *op. cit.,* pp. 685 f. for a brief discussion.

text had been recorded without vowels.[11] The Massoretes invented a vowel system which was added to the text to preserve correct pronunciation. Where the Massoretes questioned the reading, special notations were added, and the Massoretes distinguished between *Kethib,* what is written, and *Qere,* what is to be read. Perhaps the best known alteration was the placing of the vowels of *'Adonai* under the tetragrammaton YHWH, indicating that although the name is written YHWH (*Kethib*) it is to be read *'Adonai* (*Qere*). Most other notations of this kind rest upon grammatical rather than dogmatic reasoning. Massoretic notes placed in the margins of manuscripts became so extensive that they had to be compiled separately.

Not all Massoretic traditions were in agreement. Babylonian scholars had developed a vowel system that differed from that of the Palestinian or Tiberias school. Because the Palestinian pattern prevailed, manuscripts with other notations fell into disrepute and began to disappear. Two of the most famous and most authoritative manuscripts by Palestinian Massoretes are from the tenth century: one by Moses ben David ben Naphtali is known as "ben Naphtali," and the other by Aaron ben Moses ben Asher is known as "ben Asher." The ben Asher text, the product of a family of Massoretes, is preferred and is the basic Hebrew text used by scholars and translators. The Massoretic text is designated by the letter M.[12]

EARLY TRANSLATIONS

The first translation of Jewish religious writings out of the Hebrew and Aramaic, the LXX, was the product of several different translators.[13] Unfortunately no early copies of the LXX remain, and those we do have were preserved by the Christian Church. Some manuscripts contain alteration by those who wished to make certain passages sustain Christian beliefs. By the middle of the fourth century, the LXX had become sadly corrupted.

During the second century A.D., Aquila, a Jewish proselyte from Pontus and a pupil of Rabbi Akiba, made a Greek translation of the Hebrew Scriptures. Although Greek was his native tongue, he chose to make a stilted word-for-word translation that imitated Hebrew language patterns and perpetrated outrages on the structure of the Greek language. Because of his anti-Christian attitude, Aquila translated certain passages differently from the LXX, rendering them unusable for Christian doctrine. For example, he translated *bethulah* in Isa.

---

[11] The Hebrew language consists of twenty-two consonants, of which three were sometimes used as vowels: *w,* which may stand for long *u* or *o; y,* which may represent long *i* or *e;* and *h,* a breathing symbol which may represent long *a.* The problems of interpreting, even in context, can be appreciated by considering the possible English readings of the letters rd: raid, ride, rode, red, read, reed, aired, rude, etc.

[12] For a discussion of the sources of the latest printed editions of the Hebrew text, see the introductions by Rud. Kittel, A. Alt, O. Eissfeldt, and P. Kahle in *Biblica Hebraica* (Stuttgart: Privileg. Württ. Bibelenstalt, 1951).

[13] Some of the later books of the LXX were, of course, originally composed in Greek, e.g. Wisdom and II Maccabees.

7:14 as "young woman" (*neanis*) rather than "virgin" (*parthenos*) and avoided the Greek term *christos* as a translation of the Hebrew word for "anointed." In 1897, a collection of manuscripts from the genizah of the old Cairo Synagogue was found to include a palimpsest,[14] containing portions of Aquila's work dated in the fifth century A.D.

Theodotion, a follower of Marcion according to Epiphanus (a fourth century writer), or an Ebionite [15] according to Jerome, revised the LXX, or some text closely approximating it, during the second century. Theodotion's version was closer to M than to the LXX.

Only fragments remain of the work of Symmachus who, near the end of the second century, made a Greek translation from the Hebrew text. According to Jerome, Symmachus was an Ebionite, but Epiphanus says he was a Samaritan who became a Jewish proselyte. Symmachus consulted various Greek versions in preparing his work.

As Christianity reached into new areas of the world, it became more and more important to provide converts with the Bible in their own language and dialect. The ancient Syrian Church produced a translation known as the Peshitta, a term that may be derived from a word meaning "common" or perhaps "simple." The Peshitta is relatively close to the Hebrew text but reflects the influence of Jewish targums.[16]

During the third century, Origen composed the Hexapla in an attempt to harmonize Greek and Hebrew versions. The text was written in six parallel columns. The first contained the Hebrew text; the second, the Hebrew text translated into Greek; the third, Aquila's version; the fourth Symmachus' translation; the fifth, the LXX and the sixth, Theodotion's version. The fifth column was, in reality, a new text, an adaption of the LXX, and only contributed to the textual confusion.

Perhaps the most important translation was the Latin Vulgate ("common"). In response to an appeal by Pope Damasus, Jerome, the great Christian scholar of the late fourth and early fifth centuries, undertook a revision of the Latin Bible. His work relied heavily upon the Hebrew text, but in some places Jerome drew upon the LXX to support Christian beliefs. For example, he retained the word "virgin" in Isa. 7:14. His translation met with strong opposition but ultimately found favor and became the official Bible of the Roman Catholic Church.

A Coptic version was prepared during the fourth century to meet the needs of Christian converts in upper Egypt. Ethiopian, Armenian, Gothic, Slavonic, Georgian and Arabic translation were made. The

---

[14] A palimpsest is a manuscript that has been imperfectly erased and used a second time.

[15] Ebionites were Jewish Christians who maintained Jewish customs and attitudes.

[16] The word "targum" means "translation." During the period of the Second Temple, Aramaic replaced Hebrew as the common language and in Synagogue services the reading of Hebrew Scriptures was followed by an Aramaic paraphrase or free translation. By the time of the Christian era, the targums were being recorded and thus acquired a fixed form. Two important targums are the Targum Onkelos (Pentateuch) and the Targum Jonathan (Prophets), both of which originated in Babylon. Cf. F. Kenyon, *Our Bible and the Ancient Manuscripts*, pp. 94 ff.

scroll form had been virtually abandoned by this time in favor of the codex or book form. Three of the most important Greek codices are Sinaiticus, Vaticanus and Alexandrinus, all representing texts which probably originated in Egypt.

When, during the early years of the fourth century A.D., the Emperor Constantine made Christianity an officially sanctioned religion, the Church entered one of its periods of great expansion. Helena, mother of Constantine, was devoted to commemorating religious sites. Her interest led her to determine the precise place on Mount Sinai where God had revealed himself to Moses in the burning bush, and there she erected a tower. Nearly two hundred years later, the Emperor Justinian built a church on the site, which was to become the Convent of St. Catherine. The convent became a popular place for pilgrimages, and those who came brought precious manuscripts to swell the rich library.

In the middle of the nineteenth century, a famous German textual scholar, Constantin Tischendorf, became convinced that ancient manuscripts were preserved in the libraries of Greek, Syrian, Coptic and Armenian monasteries. His search led him to St. Catherine's, and there he found a fourth century A.D. manuscript known as Codex Sinaiticus.[17] This codex is composed of pages fifteen by thirteen-and-a-half inches, with four narrow columns of writing per page, except for the poetic books, which have only two columns per page. There are no word divisions. The hands of three scribes can be discerned, largely on the basis of spelling variations. Of the estimated original 730 pages, 390 pages remain of which 242 belong to the Old Testament. Codex Sinaiticus was sent to Russia, where it remained until it was sold to the British Museum for $500,000 in December, 1933.

An earlier fourth century codex, known as Codex Vaticanus, was also of great interest to Tischendorf. The Vatican library was established by the scholar Pope Nicholas V in 1448. Just how the fourth century codex came into the possession of the library is not known, for it is first listed in a catalogue made in 1475. It had always been considered of extreme value and importance, but because of restrictive rules, was available solely to scholars officially connected with the Vatican. Napoleon had removed it to Paris, where it remained until 1815 before being returned to Rome, but no one appears to have taken advantage of its availability.

Tischendorf made two attempts to see the manuscript. The first in 1843 failed. The second, in 1866, succeeded, for by this time Tischendorf had won fame as the discoverer and publisher of Codex Sinaiticus. Contrary to his agreement with Vatican authorities, Tischendorf copied and published some pages of the codex. Soon restrictive policies were relaxed and an official photographic copy was released in 1890. Codex Vaticanus contains 759 leaves, and from the Old Testament only the first forty-six chapters of Genesis and Psalms 106 to 138 are missing. Vaticanus is, perhaps, the most valuable of all Greek manuscripts of the Bible.

---

[17] The dramatic story of the discovery is worth reading and is summarized in Kenyon, *Our Bible and the Ancient Manuscripts*, pp. 191 ff.

The history of Codex Alexandrinus is obscure. In 1624, it was offered by the Patriarch of Constantinople to King James I of England. James died before it arrived, and it was received by Charles I. It remained in the possession of the royal family until George II gave it to the British Museum. Alexandrinus is dated in the fifth century and is only slightly less significant than Vaticanus and Sinaiticus. About fifty pages appear to have been lost, but 630 pages of the Old Testament remain.

TRANSLATIONS INTO ENGLISH

The story of the English Bible is marred by tragedy, martyrdom, tyranny, bigotry and other aspects of human misunderstanding, stupidity and greed. The account can only be sketched here, but there are many excellent books that tell the story in detail.[18]

Christianity was brought to England in the second century, but the expansion of the faith did not occur until near the end of the sixth century. It can be assumed that Latin versions of the Bible were in the possession of monks and that the "message" of the Bible was conveyed to the non-reading laity through sermons and other modes of teaching. During the early years of the eighth century, the Venerable Bede, a monk of Jarrow, recorded the story of Caedmon, a gifted monk of the seventh century who made poetic paraphrases of biblical themes in Anglo-Saxon. The few fragments of his work that have been preserved make it impossible to call his efforts "translations," although they do represent an attempt to make the contents of the Bible known to the masses in their own language. Bede was also a translator of the Bible, but nothing remains of his work.

Toward the end of the seventh century, a certain Aldhelm, who became Bishop of Sherborne, translated the Psalms into Anglo-Saxon. An eleventh century manuscript in Paris is supposed to be based on his work. King Alfred (ninth century) is reported to have continued the work of Bede and Aldhelm and to have affixed to his own laws parts of the Mosaic code, including the Decalogue. He was supposed to have been engaged in the translation of the Psalms at the time of his death. Unfortunately, none of his writings has survived.

There is only limited information concerning English translations before the fourteenth century. The Abbot Aelfric summarized parts of the Bible in Anglo-Saxon in his sermons, and one of his manuscripts is in the British Museum. Following the Norman conquest (eleventh century), William of Shoreham and Richard Rolle made separate translations of the Psalter. By this time Anglo-Saxon, influenced by new words imported from the continent, was becoming the English language. Like their predecessors, William of Shoreham and Rolle

[18] Cf. Kenyon, *Our Bible and the Ancient Manuscripts;* M. L. Margolis, *The Story of Bible Translations* (Philadelphia: The Jewish Publication Society of America, 1948) ; J. Baikie, *The English Bible and Its Story* (London: Seeley, Service and Co. Ltd., 1928) ; I. M. Price, *The Ancestry of Our English Bible,* second revised edition (New York: Harper and Brothers, 1953) ; H. G. May, *Our English Bible in the Making* (Philadelphia: The Westminster Press, 1952) .

_____ CHART XVII _____

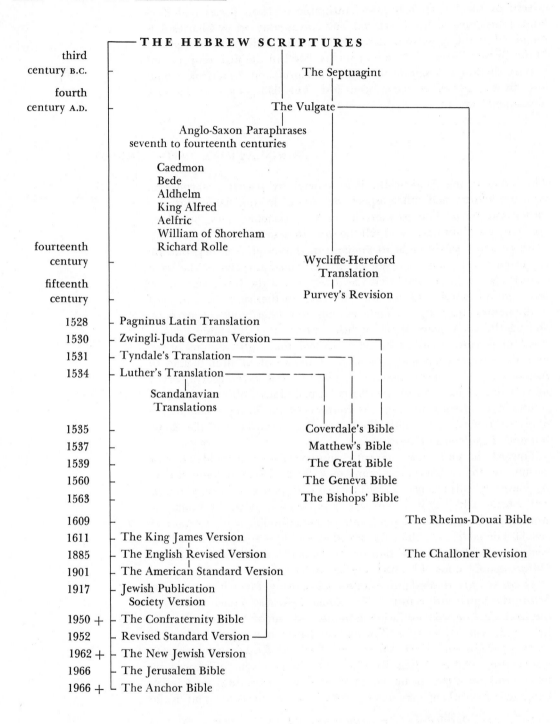

THE HEBREW SCRIPTURES

third
century B.C.

The Septuagint

fourth
century A.D.

The Vulgate

Anglo-Saxon Paraphrases
seventh to fourteenth centuries

Caedmon
Bede
Aldhelm
King Alfred
Aelfric
William of Shoreham
Richard Rolle

fourteenth
century

Wycliffe-Hereford
Translation

fifteenth
century

Purvey's Revision

1528 Pagninus Latin Translation

1530 Zwingli-Juda German Version

1531 Tyndale's Translation

1534 Luther's Translation

Scandanavian
Translations

1535 Coverdale's Bible

1537 Matthew's Bible

1539 The Great Bible

1560 The Geneva Bible

1563 The Bishops' Bible

1609 The Rheims-Douai Bible

1611 The King James Version

1885 The English Revised Version

1901 The American Standard Version   The Challoner Revision

1917 Jewish Publication
      Society Version

1950 + The Confraternity Bible

1952 Revised Standard Version

1962 + The New Jewish Version

1966 The Jerusalem Bible

1966 + The Anchor Bible

based their translations on the Vulgate. A most important contribution
to Bible study was made by Stephen Langton, Archbishop of Canter-
bury, who, about 1205, introduced chapter divisions into the Latin
Bible. It was not until 1330 that these divisions were first applied to
the Hebrew version.

Through John Wycliffe (also spelled Wickliffe, Wyclif, etc.) and his
Oxford associate Nicholas of Hereford (fourteenth century), great
strides were taken in Bible translation.[19] This was the age of Chaucer,
a time of literary and cultural growth. Hereford was responsible for
translating most of the Old Testament from the Latin, but his work
terminates abruptly at Baruch 3:19. During the early fifteenth century, John Purvey, a friend and disciple of Wycliffe, revised the Here-
ford-Wycliffe edition to produce a smoother, more readable work
which became extremely popular. Wycliffe's Bible was proscribed in
1408 by Archbishop Arundel, and in 1414 a law was passed stating
that those found reading the Bible in their own language "should
forfeit land, catel, lif, and goods." Despite legislation, the burning of
Bibles and killing of readers, the Bible continued to be copied and
read.

The second half of the fifteenth century introduced a period of
change in Europe that has been labeled the Renaissance. Men became
increasingly aware of "the world" through new explorations by travelers, scientists and thinkers. It was the century of Columbus, Co-
pernicus and Leonardo da Vinci. In 1453, when Constantinople fell to
the Turks, scholars from that great center of learning fled to Europe,
introducing classical knowledge of the ancient world. The Jews were
expelled from Spain in 1492 and five years later from Portugal, and
they moved northward in Europe, revitalizing interest in the Hebrew
Scriptures and Jewish scholarship. It was also the era of the Protestant
reformation. Most important for the literary world was the discovery
of the means of printing, using movable type. Now rapid and cheap
reproductions of written works, including the Bible, became possible.
The first printed Bible, a Latin version, appeared in 1456 and is
attributed to Henne Gensfleich or, as he is better known by his
assumed name, Johann Gutenberg (Gutenberg was his mother's
maiden name). About this same time, a certain Rabbi Nathan provided the Old Testament with verse divisions.[20] In 1475, the Jews of
Italy began to publish printed portions of the Hebrew text, and in
1488 there appeared the beautiful Soncino edition, the first printed
edition of the Hebrew Bible, to be followed in 1494 by the Brescia
edition, the version which Luther was to use.

In this turbulent era of developing concepts, William Tyndale grew
up (born 1484). After study at Oxford, Tyndale conceived the idea of
translating the Bible so that, as he put it to one clergyman, "ere many
years I will cause a boy that driveth the plough shall know more of the
Scripture than thou doest." His efforts received little encouragement
from the clergy or crown and only engendered growing hostility,

[19] For a discussion of authorship problems, cf. Kenyon, *Our Bible and the
Ancient Manuscripts*, pp. 278 ff.

[20] *Ibid.*, p. 299.

A PAGE FROM THE GUTENBURG BIBLE. *The words at the top of the first column are the last phrase of Baruch 1:15, and the large letter "P" in the first column marks the beginning of chapter two of Baruch.*

which caused him to flee to Hamburg and then to Cologne so that he might work in safety. His initial translations were of the New Testament, but by 1531 he had published a rendering of the Pentateuch and Jonah based on the Hebrew text. Shortly afterward he was entrapped by his enemies. After sixteen years of imprisonment, he was brought to trial, sentenced, strangled at the stake and burned. Tyndale's determination to place the Bible in the hands of the common man was to bear more fruit. His translations became the basis of subsequent English versions.

As Tyndale was publishing in England, translations were appearing in other languages. A new Latin version was made by Sanctes Pagninus in 1528. A German edition by Zwingli and Leo Juda was published in 1530. In 1534, Luther translated the Bible into German,[21] and his work became the basis for subsequent translations in Scandanavian countries. Chanteillon made a French translation in 1551.

It is not too surprising to find that when Miles Coverdale prepared his edition of the Bible (1535–6), he drew upon the translations of Tyndale, Luther and Zwingli-Juda. Coverdale's work was dedicated to King Henry VIII and was widely approved, for it appeared to meet the demands of both laity and clergy. For the first time, the books of the Apocrypha were printed separately.

More English versions followed, for it had become clear that there was a thriving market for Bibles. Matthew's Bible (1537) was little more than a compilation of the work of Tyndale and Coverdale, probably prepared by John Rogers, a disciple of Tyndale. In 1539, Coverdale brought out the Great Bible, a publication of splendid proportions and form, printed in France. This Bible was authorized by King Henry VIII. The Old Testament was a revision of the Matthew (Rogers-Tyndale-Coverdale) edition.

The English reformation encountered serious difficulties and Henry VIII took drastic action that can only be called anti-reform. In 1543, all Tyndale Bibles were proscribed, and by 1546, all Bibles except the Great Bible were outlawed. Bible burning became the order of the day. During the short reign of Edward VI, successor to Henry, Bible reading once again became legal.

When Mary Tudor, a Roman Catholic, became Queen of England in 1553, all use of the English Bible was forbidden. English Protestant scholars fled to Switzerland and began a revision of the Great Bible. Their finished product, the Geneva Bible (1560), was dedicated to Queen Elizabeth, who was now on the throne. This Bible became the popular version of the people, but the Great Bible, revised by a committee composed largely of bishops (1563–4), was the authoritative edition for ecclesiastical purposes. The revised Great Bible was known as "The Bishops' Bible."

The popularity of the English Bible among Protestants produced a demand by Roman Catholic laity for a version they too could read and understand. Roman Catholic refugees from England had opened an English College at Douai, France, and the official Catholic translation was begun there. Shortly afterward the seminary moved to Rheims. The New Testament was issued from Rheims in 1582. By the time the Old Testament appeared in 1609, the school had returned to Douai. The completed Bible is called the Rheims-Douai version, translated, according to the title page, from "the authentical Latin."

In 1603, James I became King of England. He inherited the benefits

[21] German language editions had been published before Luther's.

of the Elizabethan age: the developing attitude of tolerance, the strong spirit of intellectual excitement (prompted by such men as Shakespeare, Bacon, Jonson) and broad interest in religious matters. James was something of a Bible scholar, and is said to have tried his hand at translation. In an attempt to ease some of the tensions among Christians, he responded to a suggestion of Dr. John Reynolds of Oxford, a Puritan, that a new translation of the Bible be undertaken. Forty-seven scholars and learned clergymen were appointed to the translation committee (James' letter of authorization mentions fifty-four). Among the guide rules developed for translation were the following:[22]

1. The Bishops' Bible was to be followed and only altered where necessary.
2. Old ecclesiastical terms were to be retained.
3. No marginal notes were to be included except to give suitable alternate readings or to cite parallel passages.
4. Wherever Tyndale, Matthew, Coverdale, the Great Bible, or the Geneva Bible, were closer to the original text, these translations were to be followed.

The finished product, the famous King James Version of 1611, was not a perfect work, and in 1613 a revised edition appeared. As a result of sharp criticism, a third revision was made in 1629. Unfortunately, the Codex Alexandrinus had not arrived in England in time to be consulted, and eminent scholars were pressing for a new translation. The King James Version went through further revisions, one in 1638, another more extensive one in 1762 and in 1769 still another, in which spelling and punctuation were brought up to date. The Rheims-Douai version was revised in 1749 by Bishop Richard Challoner.

In the nineteenth century, a complete, scholarly, revision of the King James Version, utilizing codices recently available, was undertaken, and the finished product appeared in 1885 as the Revised Version. It immediately came under fire. It lacked the smoothness and beauty of the King James English, which by this time had become hallowed with age. In America, there were those who thought that too many English idioms and too many archaic words and phrases were included. An American Standard Version, a special revision of the English Revised Version, was published in 1901. The American edition had a better reception than its English counterpart, but remained second in importance to the King James Version.

In 1884, the first Jewish English language Bible was published in the United States. In 1917 another translation, called *The Holy Scriptures According to the Massoretic Text,* was published by the Jewish Publication Society.

In England the noted British scholar, Dr. James Moffatt, translated the Bible into what he termed "the English of our own day" and what he hoped would be "effective, intelligible English." The New Testament appeared in 1913, the Old Testament in 1924, and the combination of the two entitled *A New Translation of the Bible* in 1926.

---

[22] For a complete list of rules, cf. the item "English Bible" in *The Encyclopaedia Britannica,* ninth edition.

Shortly afterward, in 1939, *The Complete Bible: An American Translation,* the work of eminent Canadian and American scholars, was published. There were four translators of the Old Testament and a single translator of the Apocrypha, each of whom was free to follow individual style in all but basic essentials. The aim was to present "the Old Testament to the modern world in its own speech" making use of the latest and best knowledge of Hebrew linguistic studies. Despite the popularity of these modern language versions, the King James version continued to be the standard text used by Protestant churches and laity, and among Christian educators there was a growing conviction that the time was at hand for a revision of the King James Bible.

In 1937, the International Council of Religious Education, composed of representatives of forty major Protestant denominations in the United States and Canada, voted to begin a revision of the American Standard Version, which would "embody the best results of modern scholarship as to the meaning of the Scriptures, and express their meaning in English diction which is designed for use in public and private worship and preserves those qualities which have given to the King James Version a supreme place in English literature." The Revised Standard Version of the New Testament appeared in 1946. When the National Council of Churches was formed in 1950, the International Council of Religious Education was one of the merging agencies, and the Bible translation program came under National Council sponsorship. In 1952, the RSV Old Testament was published, and in 1957, the Apocrypha. Broadly speaking, the new version was enthusiastically welcomed, but criticisms by a vocal minority tended to be dogmatic and for the most part devoid of scholarship.[23]

Meanwhile, numerous other translations have been published. The Confraternity of Christian Doctrine Version, a product of Roman Catholic scholarship, has appeared. A new Jewish edition has been undertaken. Scholarly translations of individual books with notes and comments appear in the Anchor Bible series.

It is not anticipated that translations will cease. Agencies such as the American Bible Society have translated parts of the Bible into tongues ranging from Abor-Miri to Zulu, and they are still a long way from their objective of making the Bible available "to every man on earth in whatever language he may require." As the English language continues to change, new versions will become necessary, and perhaps, through the discovery of new manuscripts, troublesome passages will be explained and better readings emerge. No one version should ever be permitted to become authoritative for all time, but each translation must be measured on the basis of its faithful presentation of the best manuscripts.

[23] Cf. Gerald A. Larue, "Another Chapter in the History of Bible Translation," *The Journal of Bible and Religion,* XXXI (1963), 301–310.

CHART XVIII. CHART OF CENTRAL EVENTS IN THE ANCIENT NEAR EAST

	Aegean and Greece	Egypt	Asia Minor	Syria and Palestine	Assyria	Babylonia	Iran
2800		Egyptian writing	Early Bronze Walled cities			Cuneiform writing	2800
2600		Old Kingdom Pyramids				Early city states	2600
2400							2400
2200						Sargon of Agade	2200
2000		First Intermediate Period		Middle Bronze	Under Babylon	Amorite invasions	Under Babylon 2000
1900		Middle Kingdom				Lipit-Ishtar	1900
1800			Assyrian trade colonies founded		Commercial expansion	Rise of Babylon	Old Elamite Kingdom 1800

456

Date	Greece/Crete	Egypt	Hatti (Hittites)	Syria–Palestine	Assyria	Babylonia
1700	Minoan Linear A	Hyksos	Old Hittite Kingdom			Hammurabi Cassite Invasions
1600						
1500		New Kingdom				Hittites sack Babylon
1400	Minoan Linear B	Amarna Period: Akhenaten The Exodus	New Hittite Empire	Mitanni Kingdom	Nuzi	
1300		Rameses II	Hittite hieroglyphic writing	Ugarit 'Apiru		
1200		XX Dynasty	Sea Peoples	Hebrew conquest		
1100	Trojan War			Philistines Judges	Tiglath Pileser I	Nebuchadrezzar I
1000	Dorian invasion			Saul		

CHART XVIII (Continued)

Aegean and Greece	Egypt	Asia Minor	Syria and Palestine	Assyria	Babylonia	Iran
Greek alphabet 900			David Solomon Kingdom divides		Assyrian domination	900
800			Israel and Judah	Ashurnasir-pal II		800
Homer 700	Ethiopian domination		Fall of Samaria	Sargon II	Merodach-Baladan II	700
600	Assyrian invasion	King Gyges of Lydia	Hezekiah	Sennacherib Ashurbanipal Fall of Nineveh	Assyrian domination Chaldean Dynasty	Medes Rise of Achaemenids 600
Solon 500	Persian conquest	Cyrus defeats King Croesus of Lydia	Fall of Jerusalem Babylonian Captivity Return to Judah	Persian domination Cyrus rules	Nebuchad-rezzar II Nabonidus Persian capture of Babylon	Cyrus Darius I 500

						Xerxes I
						400
					Alexander	Alexander
				Alexander	Seleucids	**300**
				Seleucids		**200**
					Parthians capture Babylon	
						100

Persian Wars Age of Pericles		Rebuilding Judah Nehemiah, Ezra			
400					
Alexander	Alexander Ptolemies	Alexander Seleucids-Ptolemies		Alexander Seleucids	
300					
200	Seleucids forced out of Asia Minor	Maccabees			
Roman domination		Seleucids collapse Pompey takes Jerusalem Judea formed			
100	Roman province				

459

General Bibliography

THE BIBLE

Any accurate translation of the Bible may be used with this text, including *The King James Version, The English Revised Version, The American Standard Version.* Because of the advancement made during the past half century in language and word studies, and because of the new understanding of biblical language gained from the discovery of ancient manuscripts, a modern translation is recommended, such as *The Confraternity of Christian Doctrine Version, The New Jewish Version,* and *The Revised Standard Version.* Of particular value is *The Oxford Annotated Bible with the Apocrypha,* H. G. May and B. M. Metzger, eds. (New York: Oxford University Press, 1965), which includes useful notes, brief essays, chronological tables and maps.

ONE-VOLUME COMMENTARIES

Alleman, Herbert C., and Elmer E. Flack, eds., *Old Testament Commentary.* Philadelphia: The Muhlenberg Press, 1948.
Clarke, W. K. L., *Concise Bible Commentary.* New York: Macmillan, 1953.
Dummelow, J. R., ed., *A Commentary on the Holy Bible.* London: Macmillan and Co., Ltd., 1909.
Neil, William, *Harper's Bible Commentary.* New York: Harper and Row, 1963.
Orchard, B., E. F. Sutcliffe and R. Russell, eds., *A Catholic Commentary on Holy Scripture.* Edinburgh: Thomas Nelson and Sons, 1953.
Peake's Commentary on the Bible, rev. ed., M. Black and H. H. Rowley, eds. New York: Thomas Nelson and Sons, 1962.

MULTI-VOLUME COMMENTARIES

The Anchor Bible, W. F. Albright, D. N. Freedman, eds. Garden City, New York: Doubleday and Company, Inc., 1964 on. An interfaith and international series, semi-technical in structure.
Epworth Preacher's Commentaries, G. P. Lewis, N. H. Snaith, S. C. Thexton, *et. al.,* eds. London: The Epworth Press.

The International Critical Commentary. New York: Charles Scribner's Sons. This highly technical series has been in production for over half a century.

The Interpreter's Bible, G. A. Buttrick, *et al.,* eds., 12 vols. New York: Abingdon Press, 1952 on. Although important comments often appear in the homiletic expositions (bottom portions of the commentary), students should concentrate on the "Introductions" to the biblical books and the exegesis (upper portions of the commentary). The introductory articles in Vol. I are of immense value.

Soncino Books of the Bible, A. Cohen, ed. London: Soncino Press, 1945–1952, 14 vols.

Torch Bible Commentaries, J. Marsh and C. A. Richardson, eds. London: S.C.M. Press. This series is designed for the "general reader."

BIBLE DICTIONARIES

Corswant, W., *A Dictionary of Life in Bible Times,* A. Heathcote, trans. New York: Oxford University Press, 1960.

Dictionary of the Bible, James Hasting, ed., revised by F. C. Grant and H. H. Rowley. New York: Charles Scribner's Sons, 1963.

Encyclopedic Dictionary of the Bible, Louis F. Hartman, ed. and trans. New York: McGraw-Hill Book Co., 1963.

Horn, Siegfried H., *Seventh-Day Adventist Bible Dictionary.* Washington: Review and Herald Publishing Association, 1960.

The Interpreter's Dictionary of the Bible, 4 vols., G. Buttrick, *et al.,* eds. New York: Abingdon Press, 1962. This is the most recent comprehensive dictionary and is an indispensable tool.

Miller, Madeline S. and J. Lane Miller, *et. al., Harper's Bible Dictionary.* New York: Harper and Brothers, 1952.

The New Bible Dictionary. Grand Rapids, Michigan: Eerdmans, 1962.

ATLASES

Atlas of the Bible Lands. Maplewood, New Jersey: C. S. Hammond and Company, 1959.

Grollenberg, L. H., *Atlas of the Bible,* J. Reid and H. H. Rowley, trans. New York: Thomas Nelson and Sons, 1956.

Kraeling, Emil G., *Rand McNally Bible Atlas.* New York: Rand McNally & Company, 1956.

May, Herbert G., *Oxford Bible Atlas.* Oxford: Oxford University Press, 1964.

The Westminster Historical Atlas to the Bible, rev. ed., G. Ernest Wright and Floyd V. Filson, eds. Philadelphia: Westminster Press, 1956.

ANCIENT NEAR EASTERN TEXTS

The Ancient Near East: an Anthology of Texts and Pictures, J. B. Pritchard, ed. New Jersey: Princeton University Press, 1965. A paperback summary of the two following volumes.

The Ancient Near East in Pictures Relating to the Old Testament, J. B. Pritchard, ed. New Jersey: Princeton University Press, 1954.

Ancient Near Eastern Texts Relating to the Old Testament, 2nd ed., J. B.
  Pritchard, ed. New Jersey: Princeton University Press, 1955.
Documents from Old Testament Times, D. Winton Thomas, ed. New York:
  Thomas Nelson and Sons, 1958. (Also in a Harper Torchbook paper-
  back.)

JOURNALS

As research in biblical studies continues, new insights are developed
into Old Testament religion, theology, culture, history and literature,
and the results of scholarly investigations usually appear first in the
publications listed below. Those marked with a single asterisk (*)
tend to be technical and those with a double asterisk (**) highly
specialized and technical. Nevertheless, students with synagogue training in Hebrew can usually grasp the import of articles employing
occasional Hebrew terms, and those with high school or college
backgrounds in French or German can usually comprehend articles
written in these languages. All of the journals listed contain items in
English.

American Journal of Archaeology contains information on archaeological
  research in all parts of the world including the Near East, and in addition to excavation reports publishes special studies of artifacts, inscriptions, and facets of culture.
Archaeology (magazine) appears in a popular format with accurate, clearly
  written articles on facets of archaeology, including the Near East.
The Biblical Archaeologist publishes articles on archaeology directly related
  to biblical studies.
Bulletin of the American Schools of Oriental Research contains semi-technical
  articles on archaeological research in the Near East.
Bulletin of the Israel Exploration Society reports on archaeological research
  in Israel.
The Catholic Biblical Quarterly contains articles on various aspects of biblical
  study.
Hebrew Union College Annual nearly always carries articles pertaining to the
  Old Testament. Some articles are technical.
Interpretation: A Journal of Bible and Theology tends to publish articles
  that are hermeneutic rather than technical.
Israel Exploration Journal contains articles in Hebrew and English on
  archaeological research in Israel.
Jewish Quarterly Review usually contains articles on the Bible.
***Journal of the American Oriental Society* publishes material on the Near
  and Far East which is often highly specialized, but also publishes less
  technical items that are of great value.
Journal of Bible and Religion which is now published under the title *Journal
  of the American Academy of Religion* often publishes helpful articles on
  the Bible.
**Journal of Biblical Literature* tends toward technical articles but often
  contains valuable non-technical materials.
**Journal of Near Eastern Studies* includes articles on history, archaeology, art,
  religion and textual-linguistic studies which pertain to the Bible and the
  ancient Near East. Some items are highly specialized.

Journal of Religion often contains useful non-technical articles on the Bible.
Palestine Exploration Quarterly contains articles on Palestinian archaeology.
Revue Biblique usually publishes articles in French, but often contains essays in English.

*Vetus Testamentum often publishes highly technical articles, but also contains material that is broader and less specialized. Articles appear in French, German and English.

*Zeitschrift für die Alttestamentliche Wissenschaft publishes most articles in German, but also includes essays in French and English. Articles appearing in *ZAW* tend to be technical.

INTRODUCTORY TEXTS

An asterisk indicates a technical work.

Anderson, Bernhard W., *Understanding the Old Testament,* 2nd ed. New Jersey: Prentice-Hall, 1966.

Anderson, George Wishart, *A Critical Introduction to the Old Testament.* London: G. Duckworth, 1959.

*Bentzen, Aage, *Introduction to the Old Testament,* 2 vols. in 1. Copenhagen: G.E.C. Gad, 1952.

Bewer, Julius, *The Literature of the Old Testament,* rev. by Emil G. Kraeling, 3rd ed. New York: Columbia University Press, 1962.

Buck, Harry M., *People of the Lord.* New York: Macmillan, 1965.

Charlier, C., *The Christian Approach to the Bible,* H. J. Richards and B. Peters, trans. Westminster: Newman Press, 1958.

Cook, Stanley, *An Introduction to the Bible.* Baltimore: Penguin Books, 1945.

Davidson, Robert F., *The Old Testament.* London: Hodder and Stoughton, 1964.

*Driver, S. R., *Introduction to the Literature of the Old Testament,* rev. ed. New York: Charles Scribner's Sons, 1913.

*Eissfeldt. Otto, *The Old Testament: An Introduction,* Peter R. Ackroyd, trans. New York: Harper and Row, 1965.

Ellis, Peter F., *The Men and the Message of the Old Testament.* Collegeville, Minnesota: The Liturgical Press, 1962.

Flanders, H. K., R. W. Crapps and D. A. Smith, *People of the Covenant: An Introduction to the Old Testament.* New York: Ronald Press, 1963.

Gordon, Cyrus H., *Introduction to Old Testament Times.* New Jersey: Ventnor Publishers, Inc., 1953.

Gottwald, Norman, *A Light to the Nations.* New York: Harper and Row, 1959.

Harrelson, Walter, *Interpreting the Old Testament.* New York: Holt, Rinehart and Winston, 1964.

Kuhl, Curt, *The Old Testament: Its Origins and Composition,* C. T. M. Herriott, trans. Richmond: John Knox Press, 1961.

McKenzie, John L., *The Two-Edged Sword.* Milwaukee: Bruce Publishing Co., 1960.

Moriarty, Frederick L., *Introducing the Old Testament.* Milwaukee: Bruce Publishing Co., 1960.

Napier, B. Davie, *The Song of the Vineyard.* New York: Harper and Row, 1962.

Oesterley, W. O. E., and T. H. Robinson, *An Introduction to the Books of the Old Testament.* (A Meridian paperback, 1958.)

*Pfeiffer, Robert H., *Introduction to the Old Testament,* rev. ed. New York: Harper and Row, 1949. The abridged paperback version is titled: *The Books of the Old Testament.*

Sandmel, Samuel, *The Hebrew Scriptures: An Introduction to their Literature and Religious Ideas.* New York: Alfred A. Knopf, 1962.

Tos, Aldo J., *Approaches to the Bible: The Old Testament.* New Jersey: Prentice-Hall, 1963.

Tricot, A., and A. Roberts, eds., *Guide to the Bible,* I–II, E. P. Arbez and M. R. P. McGuire, trans. New York: Desclee, 1960.

Weiser, Artur, *The Old Testament: Its Formation and Development,* D. M. Barton, trans. New York: Association Press, 1961.

Young, Edward J., *An Introduction to the Old Testament,* rev. ed. London: Tyndale Press, 1960.

BIBLICAL RELIGION, CULTURE, THEOLOGY

Ahern, Barnabus, *New Horizons in Biblical Theology.* Notre Dame, Indiana: Fides Publishers, Inc., 1964.

Balthasar, H. Urs von, *Word and Revelation: Essays in Theology I.* New York: Herder and Herder, 1964.

Bentzen, Aage, *King and Messiah.* London: Lutterworth Press, 1955.

Burrows, Millar, *An Outline of Biblical Theology.* Philadelphia: Westminster Press, 1946.

Daube, David, *The Exodus Pattern in the Bible.* London: Faber and Faber, 1963.

Dentan, Robert Claude, *Preface to Old Testament Theology.* New York: Seabury Press, 1963.

DeVaux, Roland, *Ancient Israel: Its Life and Institutions,* J. McHugh, trans. New York: McGraw-Hill Book Co., 1961.

Eichrodt, Walther, *Theology of the Old Testament I,* J. A. Baker, trans. Philadelphia: Westminster Press, 1961.

Eerdmans, B. D., *The Religion of Israel.* Leiden: Universitaire pers Leiden, 1947.

Ferré, Nels F. S., "Notes By a Theologian on Biblical Hermeneutics," *Journal of Biblical Literature,* LXXVIII (1959), 105–114.

Finegan, Jack, *Handbook of Biblical Chronology: Principles of Time Reckoning in the Ancient World and Problems of Chronology in the Bible.* Princeton: Princeton University Press, 1964.

Gaster, T. H., *Passover; its History and Tradition.* New York: Henry Schuman, 1949.

Gelin, Albert, *The Religion of Israel,* Twentieth Century Encyclopedia of Catholicism, J. R. Foster, trans. New York: Hawthorn Books, 1959.

Gleason, Robert W., *Yahweh, The God of the Old Testament.* New Jersey: Prentice-Hall, 1964.

Glueck, N., *Ḥesed in the Bible,* A. Gottschalk, trans. Cincinnati: Hebrew Union College Press, 1967.

Heaton, Eric W., *Everyday Life in Old Testament Times.* New York: Charles Scribner's Sons, 1956.

Heinisch, P., *Theology of the Old Testament,* William Heidt, trans. Collegeville, Minnesota: The Liturgical Press, 1952.

Herbert, A., *Worship in Ancient Israel*. Richmond: John Knox Press, 1959.

Hopkins, Martin K., *God's Kingdom in the Old Testament*. Chicago: Henry Regnery Co., 1964.

Irwin, W. A., *The Old Testament: Keystone of Human Culture*. New York: Henry Schuman, 1952.

Jacob, Edmond, *Theology of the Old Testament*, A. W. Heathcote and P. J. Allcock, trans. New York: Harper and Brothers, 1958.

Jocz, Jacob, *A Theology of Election*. New York: Macmillan, 1958.

Kaufmann, Yehezkel, *The Religion of Israel*, Moshe Greenberg, trans. and abridger. Chicago: University of Chicago Press, 1960.

Key, Andrew F., "The Concept of Death in Early Israelite Religion," *Journal of Bible and Religion*, XXXII (1964), 239–247.

Knight, George A. F., *A Christian Theology of the Old Testament*. London: S.C.M. Press, 1959.

Köhler, Ludwig, *Old Testament Theology*, A. S. Todd, trans. Philadelphia: Westminster Press, 1958.

Kraus, H. J., *The People of God in the Old Testament*. New York: Association Press, 1958.

McAllister, Allan R., "Hebrew Language and Israelite Faith," *Interpretation*, XIV (1960), 421–432.

Mendenhall, G. E., *Law and Covenant in Israel & the Ancient Near East*. Pittsburgh: Biblical Colloquium, 1955.

Morgenstern, Julian, *The Fire upon the Altar*. Chicago: Quadrangle Books, 1963.

Muilenburg, James, "The Biblical View of Time," *Harvard Theological Review*, LIV (1961), 225–252.

———, *The Way of Israel*. New York: Harper and Row, 1961.

———, "The History of the Religion of Israel," *The Interpreter's Bible*, I, 292–348.

Oesterley, W. O. E., and T. H. Robinson, *Hebrew Religion, Its Origin and Development*. London: Society for the Publication of Christian Knowledge, 1937.

Oesterreicher, John M., *The Israel of God*. New Jersey: Prentice-Hall, 1963.

Pedersen, Johs, *Israel, Its Life and Culture*. Copenhagen: Povl Branner, 1946. Four volumes in two, I–II, III–IV.

Rad, Gerhard von, "The Origin of the Concept of the Day of Yahweh," *Journal of Semitic Studies*, IV (1959), 97–108.

———, *Old Testament Theology*, D. M. G. Stalker, trans. New York: Harper and Brothers, 1962 (Vol. I), 1966 (Vol. II).

Renckens, Henry, *The Religion of Israel*, N. B. Smith, trans. New York: Sheed and Ward, 1966.

Robinson, H. W., *The Religious Ideas of the Old Testament*. London: G. Duckworth (1959). First published in 1913.

———, ed. *Record and Revelation*. Oxford: The Clarendon Press, 1938.

———, *Inspiration and Revelation in the Old Testament*. Oxford: The Clarendon Press, 1946. (Now in an Oxford paperback.)

Rowley, H. H., *The Rediscovery of the Old Testament*. London: James Clarke & Co., Ltd., 1945.

———, *The Biblical Doctrine of Election*. London: Lutterworth Press, 1950.

Sales, R. H., "Human Sacrifice in Biblical Thought," *Journal of Bible and Religion*, XXV (1955), 112–217.

Segal, J. B., *The Hebrew Passover From the Earliest Times to A.D. 70*, London Oriental Series, 12. London: Oxford University Press, 1963.

Snaith, Norman, *Distinctive Ideas of the Old Testament*. London: Epworth Press, 1947. (Now in a Shocken paperback.)

Teeple, Howard M., "Notes on Theologians' Approach to the Bible," *Journal of Biblical Literature*, LXXIX (1960), 164–166.

Young, Edward Joseph, *The Study of Old Testament Theology Today*. Westwood, New Jersey: F. H. Revell Co., 1959.

Vriezen, Thomas C., *An Outline of Old Testament Theology*, S. Neuijen, trans. Oxford: Basil Blackwell, 1958.

Wright, G. Ernest, *God Who Acts,* Studies in Biblical Theology 8. London: S.C.M. Press, 1952.

———, ed., *The Bible and the Ancient Near East*. Garden City, New York: Doubleday & Co., 1961. (Anchor paperback edition, 1965.)

———, "The Faith of Israel," *The Interpreter's Bible,* I, 349–389.

Bibliography for Part One

THE NATURE AND AUTHORITY OF
THE OLD TESTAMENT

Abba, Raymond, *The Nature and Authority of the Bible.* Philadelphia: Muhlenberg Press, 1959.

Barth, Karl, *The Word of God and the Word of Man,* Douglas Horton, trans. New York: Harper and Brothers (1957), chs. 2–3. (Paperback.)

Beegle, Dewey M., *The Inspiration of Scripture.* Philadelphia: Westminster Press, 1963.

Bender, Harold Stauffer, *Biblical Revelation and Inspiration.* Scottdale, Pennsylvania: Mennonite Publishing House, 1959.

Blackman, E. C., *Biblical Interpretation.* Philadelphia: Westminster Press, 1959.

Bright, John, *The Authority of the Old Testament.* New York: Abingdon Press, 1967.

Burnby, John, *Is the Bible Inspired?* London: Gerald Duckworth & Co., 1949.

Daniel-Rops, Henri, *What is the Bible?,* J. R. Foster, trans. New York: Hawthorn Books, Inc., 1959.

Dodd, C. H., *The Authority of the Bible.* New York: Harper and Brothers, 1929. (Harper Torchbook edition, 1958.)

———, *The Bible Today.* New York: Macmillan, 1947.

Farmer, Herbert H., "The Bible: Its Significance and Authority," *The Interpreter's Bible,* I, 3–31.

Hebert, Arthur Gabriel, *The Authority of the Old Testament.* London: Faber and Faber, 1947.

McKenzie, John L., "The Social Character of Inspiration," *The Catholic Biblical Quarterly,* XXIV (1962), 115–124.

———, ed., *The Bible in Current Catholic Thought.* New York: Herder and Herder, 1962.

Moran, Gabriel, *Scripture and Tradition.* New York: Herder and Herder, 1963.

Mowinckel, S., *The Old Testament as the Word of God,* R. B. Bjornard, trans. New York: Abingdon Press, 1959.

Preus, Robert, *The Inspiration of Scripture, a Study of the Theology of the 17th Century Lutheran Dogmaticians.* Edinburgh: Oliver and Boyd, 1957.

Reid, J. K. S., *The Authority of Scripture.* New York: Harper and Row, 1958.

Richardson, A., *A Preface to Bible Study.* Philadelphia: Westminster Press, 1944.

Robinson, H. W., *Inspiration and Revelation in the Old Testament.* Oxford: Clarendon Press, 1956.

Snaith, Norman H., *The Inspiration and Authority of the Bible.* London: Epworth Press, 1956.

Tasker, R. V. G., *The Old Testament in the New Testament.* London: S.C.M. Press, 1954.

Warfield, B. B., *The Inspiration and Authority of the Bible.* Philadelphia: Presbyterian and Reformed Publishing Co., 1948.

Wilkinson, John T., *Principles of Biblical Interpretation.* London: Epworth Press, 1960.

Young, Edward J., *Thy Word Is Truth.* Grand Rapids: William B. Eerdmans, 1957.

BIBLICAL CRITICISM

Bright, John, "Modern Study of Old Testament Literature," *The Bible and The Ancient Near East,* G. E. Wright, ed. Garden City, New York: Doubleday & Co., 1961, pp. 1–26. (Anchor paperback edition, 1965.)

Coppens, J., *The Old Testament and the Critics,* E. A. Ryan and E. W. Tribbe, trans. Paterson, N.J.: Guild Press, 1942.

Grant, F. C., ed. and trans., *Form Criticism.* New York: Willett, Clark & Co., 1934.

Grant, Robert M., "The History of the Interpretation of the Bible: Ancient Period," *The Interpreter's Bible,* I, 106–114.

Grobel, K., "Form Criticism," *Interpreter's Dictionary of the Bible.*

Hahn, H. F., *Old Testament in Modern Research.* Philadelphia: Muhlenberg Press, 1954.

Kraeling, Emil G., *The Old Testament since the Reformation.* New York: Harper and Row, 1955.

McNeill, John T., "The History of the Interpretation of the Bible: Medieval and Reformation Period," *The Interpreter's Bible,* I, 115–126.

Rowley, H. H., ed., *The Old Testament and Modern Study.* Oxford: The Clarendon Press, 1951. (Now in an Oxford paperback, 1961.)

Steinmann, Jean, *Biblical Criticism,* Twentieth Century Encyclopedia of Catholicism, Vol. 63, Sect. VI, J. R. Foster, trans. New York: Hawthorn Books, Inc., 1959.

Terrien, Samuel, "The History of the Interpretation of the Bible: Modern Period," *The Interpreter's Bible,* I, 127–141.

Westermann, Claus, ed., *Essays on Old Testament Hermeneutics,* J. L. Mays, English ed. and trans. Richmond, Va.: John Knox Press, 1963.

HISTORY

Albright, W. F., *The Biblical Period from Abraham to Ezra.* Pittsburgh: Biblical Colloquium, 1950. (Now in a Harper paperback, 1963.)

———, "The Old Testament World," *The Interpreter's Bible,* I. New York: Abingdon Press, 1952, 233–271.

Bright, John, *Early Israel in Recent History Writing.* Studies in Biblical Theology, No. 19. London: S.C.M. Press, 1956.

———, *The History of Israel.* Philadelphia: Westminster Press, 1959.

Daniel-Rops, Henri, *Israel and the Ancient World* (originally *Sacred History*). Garden City, New York: Doubleday Image Books, 1964.

Dentan, Robert Claude, *The Idea of History in the Ancient Near East,* American Oriental Series. New Haven: Yale University Press, 1955.

Ehrlich, Ernst L., *A Concise History of Israel,* J. Barr, trans. New York: Harper and Row, 1965. (Paperback.)

Finegan, Jack, *Light From the Ancient Past,* 2nd ed. Princeton: Princeton University Press, 1959.

Guthrie, H. H., *God and History in the Old Testament.* London: S.P.C.K., 1961.

Heinisch, Paul, *History of the Old Testament,* W. Heidt, trans. Collegeville, Minnesota: The Liturgical Press, 1952.

McKenzie, R. A., *Faith and History in the Old Testament.* Minneapolis: University of Minnesota Press, 1963.

Mendenhall, George E., "Biblical History in Transition," *The Bible and The Ancient Near East,* G. E. Wright, ed. Garden City, New York: Doubleday & Co., 1961, pp. 27–58. (Anchor paperback edition, 1965.)

Mould, Elmer W. K., *Essentials of Bible History,* rev. by H. Neil Richardson and Robert F. Berkey. New York: Ronald Press, 1966.

Neher, A. and R., *Histoire Biblique du Peuple d'Israël,* I–II. Paris: Adrien-Maisonneuve, 1962.

North, Christopher R., *The Old Testament Interpretation of History.* London: Epworth Press, 1946.

Noth, Martin, *The History of Israel,* S. Godman, trans., rev. by P. R. Ackroyd, 2nd ed. London: Adam and Charles Black, 1960.

Orlinsky, Harry M., *Ancient Israel.* Ithaca, New York: Cornell University Press, 1964. (Paperback.)

Ricciotti, Giuseppe, *The History of Israel,* C. Della Penta and R. T. A. Murphy, trans., 2nd ed., 2 vols. Milwaukee: Bruce Publishing Co., 1958.

Robinson, H. Wheeler, *The History of Israel,* Studies in Theology, 42. London: Duckworth Press, 1957.

Robinson, Theodore H., "The History of Israel," *The Interpreter's Bible,* I, 272–291.

Soggins, J. Alberto, "Ancient Biblical Traditions and Modern Archaeological Discoveries," *Biblical Archaeologist,* XXIII (1960), 95–100.

Speiser, E. A., "The Biblical Idea of History in Its Common Near Eastern Setting," *Israel Exploration Journal,* VI (1957), 201–216.

Wellhausen, Julius, *Prolegomena to the History of Israel.* New York: Meridian Library, 1957.

Wright, G. Ernest, *The Old Testament Against Its Environment,* Studies in Biblical Theology, 2. London: S.C.M. Press, 1950.

———, "The Last Thousand Years Before Christ," *The National Geographical Magazine,* CXVIII (Dec., 1960), 812–853.

MYTH AND RELIGION IN THE ANCIENT NEAR EAST

Barr, James, "The Meaning of 'Mythology' in Relation to the Old Testament," *Vetus Testamentum,* IX (1959), 1–10.

Campbell, Joseph, *The Hero with a Thousand Faces.* (A Meridian Paperback, 1956.)

Childs, Brevard S., *Myth and Reality in the Old Testament,* Studies in Biblical Theology, 27. London: S.C.M. Press, 1960.

Davies, G. H., "An Approach to the Problem of Old Testament Mythology," *Palestine Exploration Quarterly.* London: Office of the Fund, 1956, 83–91.

Driver, G. R., *Canaanite Myths and Legends,* Old Testament Studies, III. Edinburgh: T. & T. Clark, 1956.

Eliade, Mircea, *Cosmos and History,* W. R. Trask, trans. New York: Harper and Brothers, 1959. (A Harper Torchbook.) First published by Pantheon Books, 1954.

———, *The Sacred and the Profane,* W. R. Trask, trans. New York: Harcourt, Brace and Co., 1959.

———, *Rites and Symbols of Initiation,* W. R. Trask, trans. New York: Harper and Row, 1965. (A Harper Torchbook.) First published as *Birth and Rebirth,* 1958.

Frankfort, H. and H. A., *et al., Before Philosophy.* Baltimore: Penguin Books, 1959.

Gaster, T. H., *Thespis; Ritual, Myth and Drama in the Ancient Near East.* New York: Henry Schuman, 1950. (Also available in Doubleday paperback.)

———, "The Religion of the Canaanites," *Forgotten Religions,* V. Ferm, ed. New York: The Philosophical Library, 1950, 113–143.

———, *The Oldest Stories in the World.* New York: Viking Press, 1952. (Republished as a Beacon paperback, 1958.)

Gordon, Cyrus H., *The Loves and Wars of Baal and Anat, and other Poems from Ugarit.* Princeton: Princeton University Press, 1943.

———, *Ugaritic Literature.* Roma: Pontificium Institutum Biblicum, 1949.

Gray, John, *The Legacy of Canaan.* Leiden: E. J. Brill, 1957.

———, *The Canaanites.* New York: Praeger, 1964.

———, *The KRT Text in the Literature of Ras Shamra,* Documenta et Monumenta Orientis Antiqui. Leiden: E. J. Brill, 1964.

Gunkel, H., *The Legends of Genesis.* Chicago: Open Court Publishing Co., 1901, and New York: Schocken Books, 1964.

Habel, Norman C., *Yahweh versus Baal; A Conflict of Religious Cultures.* New York: Bookman Associates, 1964.

Heidel, A., *The Gilgamesh Epic and Old Testament Parallels.* Chicago: University of Chicago Press, 1946. (Republished as a Phoenix paperback, 1963.)

Hooke, S. H., *The Labyrinth.* London: S.P.C.K., 1935.

———, *The Origins of Early Semitic Ritual,* The Schweich Lectures, 1935. London: Oxford University Press, 1938.

———, *Myth, Ritual, and Kingship.* Oxford: Clarendon Press, 1958.

———, *Middle Eastern Mythology.* Baltimore: Penguin Books, Inc., 1963.

Jack, J. W., *The Ras Shamra Tablets, Their Bearing on the Old Testament,* Old Testament Studies, No. 1. Edinburgh: T. & T. Clark, 1935.

James, E. O., *The Nature and Function of the Priesthood.* New York: Vanguard Press, 1955.

———, *The Ancient Gods.* London: Weidenfeld and Nicolson, 1960.

———, *Seasonal Feasts and Festivals.* New York: Barnes and Noble, Inc., 1961.

———, *Sacrifice and Sacrament.* New York: Barnes and Noble, Inc., 1962.

Jung, C. J., and C. Kerenyi, *Essays on a Science of Mythology,* R. F. C. Hull, trans. New York: Harper and Row, 1963.

Kapelrud, Arvid S., *Ba'al in the Ras Shamra Texts.* Copenhagen: G. E. C. Gadd, 1952.

———, *The Ras Shamra Discoveries and the Old Testament,* G. W. Anderson, trans. Norman: University of Oklahoma Press, 1963.

Kramer, S. N., ed., *Mythologies of the Ancient World.* Chicago: Quadrangle Press, 1961. (Also published as a Doubleday Anchor paperback.)

Loew, Cornelius, *Myth, Sacred History and Philosophy*. New York: Harcourt, Brace and World, Inc., 1967.

May, H. G., "Pattern and Myth in the Old Testament," *The Journal of Religion,* XXI (1941), 285–299.

McKenzie, John L., "Myth and the Old Testament," *The Catholic Biblical Quarterly,* XXI (1959), 265–282.

———, *Myths and Realities: Studies in Biblical Theology*. Milwaukee: Bruce Publishing Co., 1963.

Murray, Henry A., ed., *Myth and Mythmaking*. New York: George Braziller, 1960.

Obermann, Julian, *Ugaritic Mythology. A Study of Its Leading Motifs*. New Haven: Yale University Press, 1948.

Östborn, Gunnar, *Yahweh and Baal*. Lund: Lunds Universitets Arsskrift, 1956.

Raglan, Lord, *The Hero*. New York: Vintage Paperback, 1956.

Rank, Otto, *The Myth of the Birth of the Hero*. Vintage Paperback, 1959.

Toombs, Lawrence E., "The Formation of Myth Patterns in the Old Testament," *The Journal of Bible and Religion,* XXIX (1961), 108–112.

Van der Leeuw, G., *Religion in Essence and Manifestation,* J. E. Turner, trans., 2 vols. London: Allen and Unwin, 1938. (Reprinted as a Harper Torchbook, 1963.)

POETRY AND LITERARY TRADITION

Gevirtz, S., *Patterns in the Early Poetry of Israel*. Chicago: University of Chicago Press, 1963. (Paperback.)

Gray, G. B., *The Forms of Hebrew Poetry*. London: Hodder and Stoughton, 1915.

Hahn, Herbert F., "Form Criticism and the Old Testament," in *Old Testament in Modern Research*. Philadelphia: Fortress Press, 1966.

Irwin, William A., "The Literature of the Old Testament," *The Interpreter's Bible,* I, 175–184.

Nielsen, E., *Oral Tradition*. London: S.C.M. Press, 1954.

Robinson, Theodore H., *The Poetry of the Old Testament*. London: Gerald Duckworth & Co., 1947.

———, *The Poetry of the Old Testament*. London: Gerald Duckworth & Co., 1952.

THE NAME "YAHWEH"

Abba, R., "The Divine Name Yahweh," *Journal of Biblical Literature,* LXXX (1961), 320–328.

Albright, W. F., "The Names Shaddai and Abram," *Journal of Biblical Literature,* LIV (1935), 180 ff.

Bowman, R., "Yahweh, the Speaker," *Journal of Near Eastern Studies,* III (1944), 2–8.

Driver, G. R., "The Evidence for the Name 'Yahweh' Outside the Old Testament," *Old Testament Essays*. London: Charles Griffin & Co., Ltd., 1927.

Gray, John, "The God *Yw* in the Religion of Canaan," *Journal of Near Eastern Studies,* XII (1953), 278–283.

Reisel, M., *The Mysterious Name of Y.H.W.H.* Assen: Van Gorcum, 1957.

Carpenter, J. Estlin, and George Harford, *The Composition of the Hexateuch.* New York: Longmans, Green and Co., 1902.

Cassuto, Umberto, *The Documentary Hypothesis and the Composition of the Pentateuch: Eight Lectures.* Israel Abrahams, trans. Jerusalem: Magnes Press, Hebrew University, 1962.

Falk, Ze'ev W., *Hebrew Law in Biblical Times.* Jerusalem: Wahrmann Books, 1964.

North, Christopher R., "Pentateuchal Criticism," *The Old Testament and Modern Study,* H. H. Rowley, ed. Oxford: Clarendon Press, 1951.

Noth, Martin, *The Laws in the Pentateuch and Other Studies,* D. R. Ap-Thomas, trans. London: Oliver and Boyd, 1966.

Östborn, Gunnar, *Tōrā in the Old Testament.* Lund: Håkan Ohlssons Boktryckeri, 1945.

Rad, Gerhard von, *The Problem of the Hexateuch and Other Essays,* E. W. T. Dicken, trans. London: Oliver and Boyd, 1966.

Simpson, Cuthbert A., *The Early Traditions of Israel.* Oxford: Basil Blackwell, 1948.

———, "The Growth of the Hexateuch," *The Interpreter's Bible,* I, 185–200.

Winnett, F. V., *The Mosaic Tradition.* Toronto: University of Toronto Press, 1949.

THE CULT IN ISRAEL

Bentzen, A., *Introduction to the Old Testament.* Copenhagen: G. E. C. Gad, II (1958), 76 ff.

Buss, Martin J., "The Meaning of 'Cult' and the Interpretation of the Old Testament," *Journal of Bible and Religion,* XXXII (1964), 317–325.

Herbert, A. S., *Worship in Ancient Israel.* Richmond: John Knox Press, 1959.

Hooke, S. H., *The Siege Perilous.* London: S.C.M. Press, 1956.

Lohmeyer, E., *Lord of the Temple,* S. Todd, trans. London: Oliver and Boyd, 1961, 1–23.

Pedersen, Johs, "Canaanite and Israelite Cultus," *Acta Orientalia,* XVIII (1939), 1–14.

———, *Israel, Its Life and Culture,* III–IV. Copenhagen: Povl Branner, 1940, 725–745.

Rist, M., "The God of Abraham, Isaac and Jacob: A Liturgical and Magical Formula," *Journal of Biblical Literature,* LVII (1938), 289–303.

Wright, G. E., "Cult and History," *Interpretation,* XVI (1962), 3–20.

ARCHAEOLOGY

Albright, W. F., *The Archaeology of Palestine and the Bible.* New York: Fleming H. Revell Co., 1932.

———, *Archaeology and the Religion of Israel,* 2nd ed. Baltimore: Johns Hopkins Press, 1946.

———, *From the Stone Age to Christianity.* Baltimore: Johns Hopkins Press, 1942. (2nd ed. in paperback, an Anchor book, 1957.)

———, *The Archaeology of Palestine*. Baltimore: Penguin Books, Inc., 1960.

Anati, Emmanuel, *Palestine Before the Hebrews, A History From the Earliest Arrival of Man to the Conquest of Canaan*. New York: Alfred A. Knopf, 1963.

Barton, George A., *Archaeology and the Bible*, 6th ed. Philadelphia: American Sunday School Union, 1946.

Burrows, M., *What Mean These Stones?* New York: Meridian Books, 1957. (A paperback reprint of the 1941 edition.)

Clark, Grahame, *Archaeology and Society*. Cambridge: Harvard University Press, 1956.

Franken, Hendricus Jacobus, *A Primer of Old Testament Archaeology*. Leiden: E. J. Brill, 1963.

Gray, John, *Archaeology and the Old Testament World*. New York: Thomas Nelson and Sons, 1962. (Now in a Harper paperback.)

Kenyon, K., *Digging Up Jericho*. New York: Frederick A. Praeger, 1957.

———, *Archaeology in the Holy Land*. New York: Frederick A. Praeger, 1960. (Now in paperback.)

Pfeiffer, C. F., ed., *The Biblical World*. Grand Rapids: Baker Book House, 1966.

Pritchard, James B., *Archaeology and the Old Testament*. Princeton: Princeton University Press, 1958.

Williams, Walter G., *Archaeology in Biblical Research*. New York: Abingdon Press, 1965.

Wiseman, D. J., *Illustrations from Biblical Archaeology*. Grand Rapids: W. B. Eerdmans, 1958.

Wright, G. Ernest, "Archaeology and Old Testament Studies," *Journal of Biblical Literature*, LXXVII (1958), 39–51.

———, "The Archaeology of Palestine," *The Bible and the Ancient Near East*, G. E. Wright, ed. Garden City, New York: Doubleday & Co., 1961, pp. 85–138. (Anchor paperback edition, 1965.)

———, *Biblical Archaeology*, rev. ed. Philadelphia: Westminster Press, 1962.

———, *Shechem, The Biography of a Biblical City*. New York: McGraw-Hill Book Co., 1965.

Woolley, Sir Leonard, *Ur of the Chaldees*. Baltimore: Penguin Books, Inc., 1950.

Bibliography for Part Two

GEOGRAPHY

Baly, Denis, *The Geography of the Bible*. New York: Harper and Brothers, 1957.

———, *Palestine and the Bible*. London: Lutterworth Press, 1960. (Paperback.)

———, *Geographical Companion to the Bible*. London: Lutterworth Press, 1963.

Orni, Efram, and Elisha Efrat, *Geography of Israel*, 2nd ed. Jerusalem: Israel Program for Scientific Translations, 1966.

ANCIENT PEOPLES

Albright, William F., "The Old Testament World," *The Interpreter's Bible,* I, 233–271.

Astour, Michael C., "New Evidence on the Last Days of Ugarit," *American Journal of Archaeology,* 69 (1965), 253–258.

Baumgartel, E. J., *The Cultures of Prehistoric Egypt*. Oxford: Oxford University Press, 1955.

Ceram, C. W., *The Secret of the Hittites*. New York: Alfred A. Knopf, 1956.

Daniel, Glyn, *The Idea of Prehistory*. New York: World Publishing Co., 1963.

Engnell, I., *Studies in Divine Kingship in the Ancient Near East*. Uppsala: Appelbergs Boktryckeriaktiebolag, 1953.

Fairservis, Walter A., *The Ancient Kingdoms of the Nile*. New York: The New American Library, 1962. (A Mentor paperback.)

Frankfort, Henri, *Ancient Egyptian Religion*. New York: Harper and Brothers, 1948. (Harper Torchbook edition, 1961.)

———, *The Birth of Civilization in the Ancient Near East*. Garden City, New York: Doubleday Anchor Books, n.d.

Gurney, O. R., *The Hittites*. Baltimore: A Penguin Book, 1954. (Paperback.)

Guterbock, H., "The Hittite Conquest of Cyprus Reconsidered," *Journal of Near Eastern Studies,* XXVI (1967), 73–81.

Harden, Donald, *The Phoenicians,* Ancient People and Places. London: Thames and Hudson, 1963.

Hayes, William C., "Most Ancient Egypt," *Journal of Near Eastern Studies,* XXIII (1964), 74–114, 145–192, 217–274.

Kenyon, Kathleen, *Amorites and Canaanites,* The Schweich Lectures, 1963. London: Oxford University Press, 1966.

Kramer, S. N., *The Sumerians: Their History, Culture, and Character*. Chicago: University of Chicago Press, 1963.

Jacobsen, Thorkild, "Primitive Democracy in Ancient Mesopotamia," *Journal of Near Eastern Studies,* II (1943), 159–172.

Kassis, Hanna E., "Gath and the Structure of the 'Philistine' Society," *Journal of Biblical Literature,* LXXXIV (1965), 259–271.

Lloyd, Seton, *The Art of the Ancient Near East*. London: Thames and Hudson, 1961. (Praeger paperback edition, 1965.)

Montet, Pierre, *Eternal Egypt,* Doreen Weightman, trans. London: Weidenfeld and Nicolson, 1964.

Moscati, Sabatino, *Ancient Semitic Civilizations*. New York: G. P. Putnam's Sons, 1958.

———, *The Face of the Ancient Orient*. Chicago: Quadrangle Books, 1960. (Also available as an Anchor paperback.)

Murray, Margaret A., *The Splendor That Was Egypt*. New York: Hawthorn Books, Inc., 1963.

Piggot, Stuart, ed., *The Dawn of Civilization*. New York: McGraw-Hill Book Co., 1961.

Rahtjen, Bruce D., "Philistine and Hebrew Amphictyonies," *Journal of Near Eastern Studies,* XXIV (1965), 100–104.

Steindorff, G., and K. C. Seele, *When Egypt Ruled the East*. Chicago: University of Chicago Press, 1957.

Van Zyl, A. H., *The Moabites,* Pretoria Oriental Series, III. Leiden: E. J. Brill, 1960.

Wright, G. E., "Philistine Coffins and Mercenaries," *Biblical Archaeologist,* XXII (1959), 54–66.

———, "Fresh Evidence for the Philistine Story," *Biblical Archaeologist,* XXIX (1966), 70–86.

Yadin, Y., *The Art of Warfare in Biblical Lands*. London: Weidenfeld and Nicolson, 1963.

Bibliography for Part Three

THE EARLY HEBREWS

Astour, Michael C., "The Origin of the Terms 'Canaan,' 'Phoenician,' and 'Purple,'" *Journal of Near Eastern Studies*, XXIV (1965), 346–350.

Campbell, E. F., "The Amarna Letters and the Amarna Period," *The Biblical Archaeologist*, XXIII (1960), 15.

Danell, G. A., *Studies in the Name Israel in the Old Testament*. Upsala: Appelbergs Boktryckeriaktiebolag, 1946.

Glueck, N., "The Age of Abraham in the Negeb," *The Biblical Archaeologist*, XVIII (1955), 2–9.

————, *Rivers in the Desert*. New York: Farrar, Straus, and Cudahy, 1959.

Gordon, C. H., "The Patriarchal Age," *Journal of Bible and Religion*, XXI (1953), 238–243.

————, "The Patriarchal Narratives," *Journal of Near Eastern Studies*, XIII (1954), 56–59.

————, "Hebrew Origins in the Light of Recent Discoveries," *Biblical and Other Studies*, A. Altmann, ed. Cambridge: Harvard University Press, 1963.

Gray, Mary F., "The Habiru-Hebrew Problem, in the Light of Source Materials Available at Present," *Hebrew Union College Annual*, XXIX (1958), 135–202.

Greenberg, Moshe, *The Hab/piru*. New Haven: American Oriental Society, 1955.

Johnson, Aubrey, *The Vitality of the Individual in the Thought of Ancient Israel*. Cardiff: University of Wales Press, 1949.

————, *The One and the Many in the Israelite Conception of God*. Cardiff: University of Wales Press, 1961.

McCown, C. C., *The Ladder of Progress in Palestine*. New York: Harper and Brothers, 1943.

Meek, Theophile J., *Hebrew Origins*, rev. ed. New York: Harper and Brothers, 1950. (Now in a Harper paperback.)

Mendenhall, G. E., "The Hebrew Conquest of Palestine," *The Biblical Archaeologist*, XXV (1962), 66–87.

Newman, Murray, *The People of the Covenant*. Nashville: Abingdon Press, 1962.

Pedersen, Johs, *Israel: Its Life and Culture*. Copenhagen: Povl Branner, I–II, 1926, III–IV, 1940.

Robinson, H. Wheeler, "The Hebrew Conception of Corporate Personality," *Werden und Wesen des Alten Testaments*, B.Z.A.W., LXVI (1936), 49 ff.

Rowley, H. H., *From Moses to Qumran: Studies in the Old Testament.* London: Lutterworth Press, 1963.

Whitlock, Glenn E., "The Structure of Personality in Hebrew Psychology," *Interpretation,* XIV (1960) , 3–13.

Winnett, F. V., *The Mosaic Tradition.* Toronto: University of Toronto Press, 1949.

THE SETTLEMENT

Bright, John, "Joshua: Introduction and Exegesis," *The Interpreter's Bible,* II.

Burney, C. F., *The Book of Judges.* London: Rivingtons, 1930.

——, *Israel's Settlement in Canaan,* The Schweich Lectures. Oxford: Oxford University Press, 1919.

Cohen, A., *Joshua and Judges.* London: The Soncino Press, 1950.

Garstang, John, *The Foundations of Bible History: Joshua Judges.* London: Constable and Co., 1931.

Kaufmann, Yehezkel, *The Biblical Account of the Conquest of Palestine,* M. Dagut, trans. Jerusalem: Magnes Press, 1955.

MacLaurin, E. C. B., *The Hebrew Theocracy in the Tenth to the Sixth Centuries* B.C.: *An Analysis of the Books of Judges, Samuel, and Kings.* Sydney: Angus and Robertson, 1959.

McKenzie, John L., *The World of the Judges.* New Jersey: Prentice-Hall, 1966.

Moore, G. F., *A Critical and Exegetical Commentary on Judges,* The International Critical Commentary. New York: Charles Scribner's Sons, 1895.

Myers, Jacob M., "Judges: Introduction and Exegesis," *The Interpreter's Bible,* II.

Rowley, H. H., *From Joseph to Joshua,* The Schweich Lectures. London: The British Academy, 1950.

Rust, Eric C., *The Book of Judges, Ruth, I and II Samuel,* Layman's Bible Commentary, No. 6. Richmond: John Knox Press, 1961.

Simpson, C. A., *Composition of the Book of Judges.* Oxford: Basil Blackwell, 1957.

Tunyogi, Andrew C., "The Book of the Conquest," *Journal of Biblical Literature,* LXXXIV (1965) , 374–380.

Bibliography for Part Four

DAVID AND SOLOMON

Albright, Wm. F., *Samuel and the Beginnings of the Prophetic Movement,* The Goldenson Lecture for 1961. Cincinnati: Hebrew Union College Press, 1961.

Arnold, W. R., *Ephod and Ark,* Harvard Theological Studies III. Cambridge: Harvard University Press, 1917.

Bright, John, "I and II Samuel," *Interpretation,* V (1951), 450–461.

Caird, George B., "I–II Samuel: Introduction and Exegesis," *The Interpreter's Bible,* II.

Carlson, R. A., *David, The Chosen King: A Traditio-Historical Approach to the Second Book of Samuel.* Stockholm: Almquist and Wiksell, 1964.

Danell, G. A., "The Idea of God's People in the Bible," *The Root of the Vine.* Westminster: Dacre Press, 1953, 23–36.

Glueck, Nelson, "Ezion-Geber," *The Biblical Archaeologist,* XXVIII (1965), 70–87.

Hertzberg, Hans Wilhelm, *I & II Samuel,* The Old Testament Library. Philadelphia: Westminster Press, 1964.

Malamat, A., "The Kingdom of David and Solomon in its Contact with Egypt and Aram Naharaim," *Biblical Archaeologist,* XXI (1958), 96–112.

———, "Aspects of the Foreign Policies of David and Solomon," *Journal of Near Eastern Studies,* XXII (1963), 1–17.

Maly, Eugene H., *The World of David and Solomon.* New Jersey: Prentice-Hall, 1965.

May, H. G., "Some Aspects of Solar Worship at Jerusalem," *Zeitschrift für die Alttestamentliche Wissenschaft,* LV (1937), 269–280.

Morgenstern, J., "David and Jonathan," *Journal of Biblical Literature,* LXXVIII (1959), 322–324.

Neufeld, E., "The Emergence of a Royal-Urban Society in Ancient Israel," *Hebrew Union College Annual,* XXXI (1960), 31–53.

Parrot, André, *The Flood and Noah's Ark,* E. Hudson, trans. New York: Philosophical Library, 1955.

———, *The Temple of Jerusalem,* B. E. Hooke, trans. New York: Philosophical Library, 1955.

———, *The Tower of Babel,* E. Hudson, trans. New York. Philosophical Library, 1955.

Pfeiffer, Robert H., and William G. Pollard, *The Hebrew Iliad: The History of the Rise of Israel under Saul and David.* New York: Harper and Row, 1957.

Woolley, Sir Leonard, *Ur of the Chaldees*. Baltimore: Penguin Books, 1950.
——, *Excavations at Ur*. New York: Barnes & Noble, 1954.
Wright, G. E., "The Stevens Reconstruction of the Solomonic Temple," *The Biblical Archaeologist,* XVIII (1955), 41–44.
Yadin, Y., "New Light on Solomon's Megiddo," *The Biblical Archaeologist,* XXIII (1960), 62 ff.
Yeivin, S., "Social, Religious and Cultural Trends in Jerusalem under the Davidic Dynasty," *Vetus Testamentum,* III (1953), 149–166.

THE PENTATEUCH

Childs, B. S., "The Birth of Moses," *Journal of Biblical Literature,* LXXIV (1965), 109–122.
Cross, Frank M., Jr., "The Priestly Tabernacle," *The Biblical Archaeologist,* X (1947), 45–68. Reprinted in *The Biblical Archaeologist Reader.* Chicago: Quadrangle Books, 201–228.
——, and David N. Freedman, "The Song of Miriam," *Journal of Near Eastern Studies,* XIV (1955), 237–250.
Driver, S. R., *The Book of Genesis,* Westminster Commentaries. London: Methuen and Co., 1926.
——, *The Book of Exodus,* The Cambridge Bible for Schools and Colleges. Cambridge: Cambridge University Press, 1911, reprinted 1953.
Elliot-Binns, L., *The Book of Numbers,* Westminster Commentaries. London: Methuen and Co., 1926.
Finegan, Jack, *In the Beginning: A Journey Through Genesis.* New York: Harper and Brothers, 1962.
Fritsch, C. T., *The Book of Genesis,* Layman's Bible Commentary. Richmond, Va.: John Knox Press, 1959.
Gemser, B., and J. Hoftijzer, *et al., Studies on the Book of Genesis.* Leiden: E. J. Brill, 1958.
Gray, G. B., *A Critical and Exegetical Commentary on Numbers,* The International Critical Commentary. New York: Charles Scribner's Sons, 1903.
Griffiths, J. Gwyn, "The Egyptian Derivation of the Name Moses," *Journal of Near Eastern Studies,* XII (1953), 225–231.
Gunkel, Hermann, *The Legends of Genesis, The Biblical Saga and History.* Chicago: Open Court Publishing Co., 1907, reprinted as a paperback by Schocken Books (New York), 1964.
Haran, Menahem, "Shiloh and Jerusalem: The Origin of the Priestly Tradition in the Pentateuch," *Journal of Biblical Literature,* LXXXI (1962), 14–24.
Hay, Lewis S., "What Really Happened at the Sea of Reeds," *Journal of Biblical Literature,* LXXXIII (1964), 397–403.
Heidel, Alexander, *The Babylonian Genesis,* 2nd ed. Chicago: University of Chicago Press, 1951.
Hooke, S. H., *In the Beginning.* New York: Oxford University Press, 1947.
Marsh, John, "Numbers: Introduction and Exegesis," *The Interpreter's Bible,* II.
McCarthy, Dennis J., "Plagues and Sea of Reeds: Exodus 5–14," *Journal of Biblical Literature,* LXXXV (1966), 137–158.
McNeile, A. H., *The Book of Exodus,* Westminster Commentaries. London: Methuen and Co., 1917.
Micklem, Nathaniel, "Leviticus: Introduction and Exegesis," *The Interpreter's Bible,* II.

Morgenstern, Julian, *The Book of Genesis, A Jewish Interpretation.* New York: Shocken Books, 1965. First published in 1919 by The Union of American Hebrew Congregations.

Mowinckel, Sigmund, *The Two Sources of the Pre-Deuteronomic Primeval History in Genesis I–XI.* Oslo: Det Norske Videnskap-Akademi, 1937.

Neher, André, *Moses and the Vocation of the Jewish People,* Men of Wisdom Books, 7. New York: Harper and Brothers, 1957.

Niles, Daniel T., *Studies in Genesis.* Philadelphia: Westminster Press, 1958.

Noth, Martin, *Exodus,* The Old Testament Library, J. S. Bowden, trans. Philadelphia: Westminster Press, 1962.

———, *Leviticus,* The Old Testament Library, J. E. Anderson, trans. Philadelphia: Westminster Press, 1965.

Orlinsky, Harry M., *Genesis,* The New Jewish Version Translation. New York: Harper and Row, 1966. (A Harper Torchbook.)

Rabe, Virgil W., "The Identity of the Priestly Tabernacle," *Journal of Near Eastern Studies,* XXV (1966), 132–134.

Rad, G. von, *Moses,* World Christian Books. London: Lutterworth Press, 1960.

———, *Genesis,* The Old Testament Library, J. H. Marks, trans. Philadelphia: Westminster Press, 1961.

Renckens, M., *Israel's Concept of the Beginning Theology of Genesis I–III.* New York: Herder and Herder, 1964.

Rowley, H. H., *Israel's Sojourn in Egypt.* Manchester: Manchester University Press, 1938. Reprint from the *Bulletin of the John Rylands Library,* Vol. 22, No. 1, April, 1938.

Rylaarsdam, J. Coert, "Exodus: Introduction and Exegesis, "*The Interpreter's Bible,* I.

Simpson, Cuthbert A., "Genesis: Introduction and Exegesis," *The Interpreter's Bible,* I.

Speiser, E. A., *Genesis,* The Anchor Bible. New York: Doubleday and Co., 1964.

Vawter, Bruce, *A Path Through Genesis.* New York: Sheed and Ward, 1956.

Whitley, C. F., "The Pattern of Creation in Genesis, Chapter 1," *Journal of Near Eastern Studies,* XVII (1958), 32–40.

Wright, G. Ernest, "Deuteronomy: Introduction and Exegesis," *The Interpreter's Bible,* II.

Bibliography for Part Five

I–II KINGS

Cross, Frank M., Jr., and David N. Freedman, "Josiah's Revolt Against Assyria," *Journal of Near Eastern Studies,* XII (1953), 56–58.

Gray, John, *I and II Kings,* The Old Testament Library. Philadelphia: Westminster Press, 1963.

Montgomery, James A., and H. S. Gehman, *The Book of Kings,* International Critical Commentary. New York: Charles Scribner's Sons, 1951.

Rad, G. von, "The Deuteronomic Theology of History in I and II Kings," *The Problem of the Hexateuch and Other Essays,* E. W. T. Dicken, trans. London: Oliver and Boyd, 1966.

Rowley, H. H., "Elijah on Mount Carmel," *Bulletin of the John Rylands Library,* XLIII (1960), 190–219.

Snaith, Norman H., "I–II Kings: Introduction and Exegesis," *The Interpreter's Bible,* III.

PROPHECY

Anderson, B. W., and W. Harrelson, eds., *Israel's Prophetic Heritage.* New York: Harper and Row, 1962.

Bewer, J. A., *The Prophets,* Harper's Annotated Bible. New York: Harper and Brothers, 1949.

Buber, Martin, *The Prophetic Faith,* C. Witton-Davies, trans. New York: Macmillan, 1949.

Chaine, J., *God's Heralds,* B. McGrath, trans. New York: Joseph F. Wagner, Inc., 1954.

Clements, R. E., *Prophecy and Covenant,* Studies in Biblical Theology, 43. London: S.C.M. Press, 1965.

Davies, L. J. D. L., *The Origin and Development of Early Hebrew Prophecy in Special Relation to the Development of Yahwism in Israel.* Dissertation, University of Bonn, 1959.

Dheilly, Joseph, *The Prophets,* The Twentieth Century Encyclopedia of Catholicism, Rachel Attwater, trans. New York: Hawthorn Books, 1960.

Fohreh, Georg, "Remarks on Modern Interpretation of the Prophets," *Journal of Biblical Literature,* LXXX (1961), 309–319.

Fosbroke, Hughell E. W., "The Prophetic Literature," *The Interpreter's Bible,* I, 201–211.

Frost, Stanley B., *Patriarchs and Prophets*. Montreal: McGill University Press, 1963.

Gerstenberger, Erhard, "The Woe Oracles of the Prophets," *Journal of Biblical Literature,* LXXXI (1962), 249–263.

Gottwald, Norman K., *All the Kingdoms of the Earth: Israelite Prophecy and International Relations in the Ancient Near East*. New York: Harper and Row, 1964.

Guillaume, A., *Prophecy and Divination Among the Hebrews and Other Semites*. New York: Harper and Brothers, 1938.

Henshaw, Thomas, *The Latter Prophets*. London: Allen and Unwin, 1958.

Heschel, A. J., *The Prophets*. New York: Harper and Row, 1963.

Hoenig, Sidney Benjamin, *A Guide to the Prophets*. New York: Yeshiva University, 1957.

Huffmon, Herbert B., "The Covenant Lawsuit in the Prophets," *Journal of Biblical Literature,* LXXVIII (1959), 285–295.

Hyatt, J. P., *Prophetic Religion*. New York: Abingdon-Cokesbury Press, 1947.

Johnson, Aubrey R., *The Cultic Prophet in Ancient Israel*. Cardiff: University of Wales, 1961.

Kingsbury, Edwin C., "The Prophets and the Council of Yahweh," *Journal of Biblical Literature,* LXXXIII (1964), 279–286.

Kuhl, C., *The Prophets of Israel*. London: Oliver and Boyd, 1960.

Lindblom, J., *Prophecy in Ancient Israel*. Oxford: Basil Blackwell, 1962.

McKane, Wm., *Prophets and Wise Men,* Studies in Biblical Theology, 44. Napierville: Alex R. Allenson, 1965.

Milton, John P., *Prophecy Interpreted; Essays in Old Testament Interpretation*. Minneapolis: Augsburg Pub. House, 1960.

Mowinckel, Sigmund, *Prophecy and Tradition*. Oslo: I Kommisjon Hos Jacob Dybwad, 1946.

Napier, B. D., *Prophets in Perspective*. New York: Abingdon Press, 1963.

Rowley, H. H., *Men of God: Studies in Old Testament History and Prophecy*. London: Thomas Nelson and Sons, 1963.

———, ed., *Studies in Old Testament Prophecy*. Edinburgh: T. & T. Clark, 1950.

Scott, R. B. Y., *The Relevance of the Prophets*. New York: Macmillan, 1944.

Smith, G. A., *The Book of the Twelve Prophets,* The Expositors' Bible. New York: Hodder and Stoughton, 1902–1905.

Stuhlmueller, C., *The Prophets and the Word of God*. Notre Dame, Indiana: Fides Publishers, Inc., 1964.

Vawter, B., *The Conscience of Israel*. New York: Sheed and Ward, 1961.

Whitley, Charles Francis, *The Prophetic Achievement*. Leiden: E. J. Brill, 1963.

AMOS

Bentzen, A., "The Ritual Background of Amos 1:1–2:16," *Oudtestamentische Studiën,* VIII. Leiden: Brill, 1950, 85–99.

Cohen, Simon, "Amos *was* a Navi," *Hebrew Union College Annual,* XXXII (1961), 175–178.

———, "The Political Background of the Words of Amos," *Hebrew Union College Annual,* XXXVI (1965), 153–160.

Cripps, R. S., *A Critical and Exegetical Commentary on the Book of Amos*. London: S.P.C.K., 1929. (Reprinted by Macmillan, 1955.)

Driver, S. R., *The Books of Joel and Amos,* The Cambridge Bible for Schools and Colleges. Cambridge: Cambridge University Press, 1901, 1934.

Fosbroke, Hughell E. W., "Amos: Introduction and Exegesis," *The Interpreter's Bible,* VI.

Kapelrud, Arvid Schou, *Central Ideas in Amos.* Oslo: Oslo University Press, 1961.

McCullough, W. S., "Some Suggestions about Amos," *Journal of Biblical Literature,* LXXII (1953), 247–254.

Rowley, H. H., "Was Amos a Nabi?" *Festchrift Otto Eissfeldt,* J. Fueck, ed. Halle: Niemeyer, 1947, 191–198.

Snaith, Norman H., *Amos, Hosea, and Micah.* London: Epworth Press, 1956.

————, *The Book of Amos,* Study Notes on Bible Books. London: Epworth Press, 1946.

Watts, John D., *Vision and Prophecy in Amos.* Grand Rapids: W. B. Eerdmans, 1958.

————, "An Old Hymn Preserved in the Book of Amos," *Journal of Near Eastern Studies,* XV (1956), 33–39.

HOSEA

Brown, S. L., *The Book of Hosea,* Westminster Commentaries. London: Methuen & Co., Ltd., 1932.

Eichrodt, Walther, "The Holy One in Your Midst," Lloyd Gaston, trans. *Interpretation,* XV (1961), 259–273.

Ginsberg, H. L., "Hosea's Ephraim, More Fool Than Knave," *Journal of Biblical Literature,* LXXX (1961), 339–347.

Harper, W. R., *A Critical and Exegetical Commentary on Amos and Hosea,* The International Critical Commentaries. New York: Charles Scribner's Sons, 1905.

Knight, George A. F., *Hosea,* The Torch Bible Commentaries. London: S.C.M. Press, 1960.

Mauchline, John, "Hosea: Introduction and Exegesis," *The Interpreter's Bible,* VI.

May, H. G., "The Fertility Cult in Hosea," *The American Journal of Semitic Languages and Literatures,* XLVIII (1931), 73–98.

McKenzie, John L., "Divine Passion in Osee," *The Catholic Biblical Quarterly,* XVII (1955), 287–299.

————, "Knowledge of God in Hosea," *Journal of Biblical Literature,* LXXIV (1955), 22–27.

North, F. S., "Solution of Hosea's Marital Problems by Critical Analysis," *Journal of Near Eastern Studies,* XVI (1957), 128–130.

Ritschl, D., "God's Conversion," *Interpretation,* XV (1961), 286–303.

Rowley, H. H., "The Marriage of Hosea," *Bulletin of the John Rylands Library,* XXXIX (1956), 200–233.

Scott, Melville, *The Message of Hosea.* London: S.P.C.K., 1921.

Snaith, Norman H., *Mercy and Sacrifice: A Study of the Book of Hosea.* London: S.C.M. Press, 1950.

Tushingham, A. Douglas, "A Reconsideration of Hosea, Chapters 1–3," *Journal of Near Eastern Studies,* XII (1953), 150–159.

Ward, James M., *Hosea: A Theological Commentary.* New York: Harper and Row, 1966.

Wolff, Hans Walter, "Guilt and Salvation," Lloyd Gaston, trans. *Interpretation,* XV (1961), 274–285.

Blank, Sheldon M., "The Current Misinterpretations of Isaiah's She'ar Yashub," *Journal of Biblical Literature,* LXVII (1948), 211–215.

———, "Immanuel and Which Isaiah?" *Journal of Near Eastern Studies,* XIII (1954), 83–86.

———, *Prophetic Faith in Isaiah.* New York: Harper and Row, 1958.

Eaton, J. H., "Origins of the Book of Isiah," *Vetus Testamentum,* IX (1959), 138–157.

Fisher, Willis W., *Isaiah and the Nature Cults.* Chicago: University of Chicago Press, 1938.

Gottwald, Norman K., "Immanuel as the Prophet's Son," *Vetus Testamentum,* VIII (1958), 36–47.

Gray, George Buchanan, *A Critical and Exegetical Commentary on the Book of Isaiah I–XXXIX,* The International Critical Commentary. New York: Charles Scribner's Sons, 1912.

Jones, D. R., "The Tradition of the Oracles of Isaiah of Jerusalem," *Zeitschrift für die Alttestamentliche Wissenschaft,* LXVII (1955), 226–246.

Kennett, R. H., *The Composition of the Book of Isaiah in the Light of History and Archaeology,* The Schweich Lectures, 1909. London: Henry Frowde, 1910.

Kissane, Edward J., *The Book of Isaiah,* 2nd ed., 2 vols. Dublin: Browne and Nolan, 1960.

Leslie, Elmer A., *Isaiah.* New York: Abingdon Press, 1963.

Scott, R. B. Y., "Isaiah 1–39: Introduction and Exegesis, "*The Interpreter's Bible,* V.

Snaith, Norman H., *Notes on the Hebrew Text of Isaiah, Chapters XXVIII–XXXII,* Study Notes on Bible Books. London: Epworth Press, 1945.

MICAH

Haupt, Paul, *The Book of Micah.* Chicago: University of Chicago Press, 1910.

Marsh, John, *Amos and Micah.* London: S.C.M. Press, 1959.

Snaith, Norman H., *Amos, Hosea and Micah.* London: Epworth Press, 1956.

Wade, G. W., *Micah, Obadiah, Joel and Jonah,* The Westminster Commentaries. London: Methuen and Co., Ltd., 1925.

Wolfe, Roland E., "Micah: Introduction and Exegesis," *The Interpreter's Bible,* VI.

Bibliography for Part Six

ZEPHANIAH

Hyatt, J. Phillip, "The Date and Background of Zephaniah," *Journal of Near Eastern Studies*, VII (1948), 25–29.

Taylor, Charles L., Jr., "Zephaniah: Introduction and Exegesis," *The Interpreter's Bible*, VI.

Williams, Donald L., "The Date of Zephaniah," *Journal of Biblical Literature*, LXXXII (1963), 77–88.

DEUTERONOMY

Blair, Edward, "An Appeal to Remembrance," *Interpretation*, XV (1961), 39–47.

Cunliffe-Jones, H., *Deuteronomy*, Torch Bible Commentaries. London: S.C.M. Press, 1951.

Driver, S. R., *A Critical and Exegetical Commentary on Deuteronomy*, The International Critical Commentary. New York: Charles Scribner's Sons, 1895.

Erdman, C. R., *The Book of Deuteronomy*. Westwood, N.J.: Fleming H. Revell, 1953.

Kennett, R. H., *Deuteronomy and the Decalogue*. Cambridge: Cambridge University Press, 1920.

Kline, M. G., *Treaty of the Great King; the Covenant Structure of Deuteronomy, Studies and Commentary*. Leiden: E. J. Brill, 1963.

Mackintosh, C. H., *Notes on the Book of Deuteronomy*, Boston: J. A. Whipple, n.d.

Manley, M. A., *The Book of the Law; Studies in the Date of Deuteronomy*. London: Tyndale Press, 1957.

Moran, William L., "The Ancient Near Eastern Background of the Love of God in Deuteronomy," *The Catholic Biblical Quarterly*, XXV (1963), 77–87.

Myers, Jacob, "The Requisites for Response," *Interpretation*, XV (1961), 14–31.

Rad, G. von, *Studies in Deuteronomy*, Studies in Biblical Theology, 9. London: S.C.M. Press, 1953.

———, "Ancient Word and Living Word," *Interpretation*, XV (1961), 1–13.

———, *Deuteronomy: A Commentary*. Philadelphia: Westminster Press, 1966.

Rowley, H. H., "The Prophet Jeremiah and The Book of Deuteronomy," *Studies in Old Testament Prophecy.* Edinburgh: T. & T. Clark, 1950.

Weinfeld, M., "The Origin of the Humanism in Deuteronomy," *Journal of Biblical Literature,* LXXX (1961), 241–247.

Welch, A. C., *The Code of Deuteronomy.* London: J. Clarke & Co., 1924.

———, *Deuteronomy: The Framework of the Code.* London: Oxford University Press, 1932.

Wright, G. E., "The Lawsuit of God: A Form-Critical Study of Deuteronomy 32," *Israel's Prophetic Heritage.* New York: Harper and Brothers, 1962.

———, "Deuteronomy: Introduction and Exegesis," *The Interpreter's Bible,* II.

NAHUM

Haldar, A. O., *Studies in the Book of Nahum.* Uppsala: Lundequistska Bokhandeln, 1947.

Maier, Walter A., *The Book of Nahum.* St. Louis: Concordia Publishing House, 1959.

Taylor, Charles L., Jr., "Nahum: Introduction and Exegesis," *The Interpreter's Bible,* VI.

HABAKKUK

Albright, W. F., "The Psalm of Habakkuk," *Studies in Old Testament Prophecy,* H. H. Rowley, ed. Edinburgh: T. & T. Clark, 1950.

Brownlee, William Hugh, *The Text of Habakkuk in the Ancient Commentary from Qumran.* Philadelphia: Society of Biblical Literature and Exegesis, 1959.

———, "The Placarded Revelation of Habakkuk," *Journal of Biblical Literature,* LXXXII (1963), 319–325.

Good, Edwin Marshall, *The Text and Versions of Habakkuk 3; a Study in Textual History.* Ann Arbor, Michigan: University Microfilms, 1958.

Holt, John Marshall, "So He Who Runs May Read It," *Journal of Biblical Literature,* LXXXII (1964), 298–302.

Humbert, Paul, *Problèmes du livre d'Habacuc.* Neûchatel: Secrétariat de l'Université, 1944.

Irwin, W. A., "The Mythological Background of Habakkuk, Chapter 3," *Journal of Near Eastern Studies,* XV (1956), 47–50.

Sanders, James Alvin, "Habakkuk in Qumran, Paul, and the Old Testament," *Journal of Religion,* XXXIX (1959), 232–244.

Taylor, Charles L., Jr., "Habakkuk: Introduction and Exegesis," *The Interpreter's Bible,* VI.

JEREMIAH

Blank, Sheldon, *Jeremiah, Man and Prophet.* Cincinnati: Hebrew Union College Press, 1961.

Bright, John, "The Date of the Prose Sermons of Jeremiah," *Journal of Biblical Literature,* LXX (1951), 15–35.

———, *Jeremiah,* Anchor Bible. New York: Doubleday & Co., 1965.

Cunliffe-Jones, H., *Jeremiah,* The Torch Bible Commentaries. London: S.C.M. Press, 1960.

Gerstenberger, Erhard, "Jeremiah's Complaints: Observations on Jer. 15:1–21," *Journal of Biblical Literature,* LXXXII (1963), 393–408.

Harrelson, Walter J., *Jeremiah, Prophet to the Nations.* Philadelphia: Judson Press, 1959.

Holladay, William L., "Prototype and Copies: A New Approach to the Poetry-Prose Problem in the Book of Jeremiah," *Journal of Biblical Literature,* LXXIX (1960), 351–367.

———, "Style, Irony, and Authenticity in Jeremiah," *Journal of Biblical Literature,* LXXXI (1962), 44–54.

———, "The Background of Jeremiah's Self-Understanding: Moses, Samuel and Psalm 22," *Journal of Biblical Literature,* LXXXIII (1964), 153–164.

———, "Jeremiah and Moses: Further Observations," *Journal of Biblical Literature,* LXXXV (1966), 17–27.

———, "The Recovery of Poetic Passages of Jeremiah," *Journal of Biblical Literature,* LXXXV (1966), 401–435.

Hyatt, J. Philip, *Jeremiah, Prophet of Courage and Hope.* New York: Abingdon Press, 1958.

———, "Jeremiah: Introduction and Exegesis," *The Interpreter's Bible,* V.

Leslie, Elmer A., *Jeremiah: Chronologically Arranged, Translated, and Interpreted.* New York: Abingdon Press, 1954.

Milgrom, Jacob, "The Date of Jeremiah, Chapter 2," *Journal of Near Eastern Studies,* XIV (1955), 65–69.

Rowley, H. H., "The Early Prophecies of Jeremiah in their Setting," *Bulletin of the John Rylands Library,* XLV (1962), 198–234.

Skinner, John, *Prophecy and Religion.* New York: Cambridge University Press, 1922.

Welch, A. C., *Jeremiah, His Time and His Work.* Oxford: Basil Blackwell, 1929, 1951.

Bibliography for Part Seven

EZEKIEL

Broome, E. C., "Ezekiel's Abnormal Personality," *Journal of Biblical Literature,* LXV (1946), 277–296.

Cooke, G. A., *A Critical and Exegetical Commentary on the Book of Ezekiel,* The International Critical Commentary. New York: Charles Scribner's Sons, 1937.

Gaster, T. H., "Ezekiel and the Mysteries," *Journal of Biblical Literature,* LX (1941), 289 ff.

Greenberg, Moshe, "On Ezekiel's Dumbness," *Journal of Biblical Literature,* LXXVII (1958), 101–105.

Howie, Carl Gordon, *The Date and Composition of Ezekiel.* Philadelphia: Society of Biblical Literature, 1950.

Irwin, W. A., *The Problem of Ezekiel.* Chicago: University of Chicago Press, 1943.

May, Herbert G., "Ezekiel: Introduction and Exegesis," *The Interpreter's Bible,* VI.

Rowley, H. H., *The Book of Ezekiel in Modern Study.* Manchester: Manchester University Press and John Rylands Library, 1953.

Smith, James, *The Book of the Prophet Ezekiel.* New York: Macmillan, 1931.

Spiegel, S., "Noah, Daniel, and Job," *Louis Ginzberg Jubilee Volume.* New York: Academy for Jewish Research, 1945.

Torrey, C. C., *Pseudo-Ezekiel and the Original Prophecy.* New Haven: Yale University Press, 1930.

LAMENTATIONS

Gottwald, Norman K., *Studies in the Book of Lamentations,* Studies in Biblical Theology, 14. London: S.C.M. Press, 1954.

Meek, Theophile J., "Lamentations: Introduction and Exegesis," *The Interpreter's Bible,* VI.

JOB

Buttenweiser, M., *The Book of Job.* New York: Macmillan, 1922.

Carstensen, Roger N., *Job: Defense of Honor.* New York: Abingdon Press, 1963.

Crook, M., *The Cruel God.* Boston: Beacon Press, 1959.

Driver, S. R., and G. B. Gray, *A Critical and Exegetical Commentary on the Book of Job.* The International Critical Commentary, 2 vols. New York: Charles Scribner's Sons, 1921.

Eerdmans, B. D., *Studies in Job.* Leiden: Burgerdijk and Niermans, 1939.

Ellison, H. L., *From Tragedy to Triumph: The Message of the Book of Job.* Grand Rapids, Michigan: Wm. B. Eerdmans, 1958.

Fine, Hillel A., "The Tradition of a Patient Job," *Journal of Biblical Literature,* LXXIV (1955), 28–32.

Freehof, Solomon B., *Book of Job.* New York: Union of American Hebrew Congregations, 1958.

Genevieve, Sister M., "Job, a Drama: The Battle of the Soul." *Catholic Educational Review,* XXIX (1931), 345–348.

Gordis, R., "The Temptation of Job: Tradition versus Experience," *Judaism,* IV (1955), 63–76.

Hanson, Anthony and Miriam, *The Book of Job: A Commentary.* New York: Collier Books, 1962. (Paperback.)

Hone, Ralph E., *The Voice Out of the Whirlwind: The Book of Job.* San Francisco: Chandler Publishing Co., Inc., 1960.

Irwin, W. A., "Job's Redeemer," *Journal of Biblical Literature,* LXXXI (1962), 217–229.

Jastrow, M. *The Book of Job.* Philadelphia: J. B. Lippincott Co., 1920.

Jung, C. G., *Answer to Job,* R. F. C. Hull, trans. London: Routledge & Kegan Paul, 1954.

Kallen, H. M., *The Book of Job as a Greek Tragedy.* New York: Moffat, Yard & Co., 1918.

Kissane, Edward J., *The Book of Job.* New York: Sheed and Ward, 1946.

Kraeling, Emil G., *The Book of the Ways of God.* New York: Charles Scribner's Sons, 1939.

Kuyper, L. J., "The Repentance of Job," *Vetus Testamentum,* IX (1959), 91–94.

Laks, H. J., "The Enigma of Job: Maimonides and the Moderns," *Journal of Biblical Literature,* LXXXIII (1964), 345–364.

Larue, Gerald A., "The Book of Job on the Futility of Theological Discussion," *The Personalist.* Los Angeles: The University of Southern California, 45 (1964), 72–79.

MacKenzie, R. A. F., "The Purpose of the Yahweh Speeches in the Book of Job," *Biblica,* XL (1959), 435–445.

Nairne, A., *The Book of Job.* London: Cambridge University Press, 1960.

Nichols, H. H., "The Composition of the Elihu Speeches," *American Journal of Semitic Languages,* XXVII (1911).

Peake, A. S., *Job.* Edinburgh: T. C. & E. C. Jack, n.d.

Pope, Marvin H., *Job,* The Anchor Bible. Garden City, New York: Doubleday & Co., 1965.

Robinson, H. Wheeler, *The Cross in the Old Testament.* Philadelphia: Westminster Press, 1955. (Also in an S.C.M. paperback.)

Rowley, H. H., "The Book of Job and Its Meaning," *Bulletin of the John Rylands Library,* XLI (1958), 167–207.

Sarna, Nahum M., "Epic Substratum in the Prose of Job," *Journal of Biblical Literature,* LXXVI (1957), 13–25.

Shapiro, D. S., "The Problem of Evil and the Book of Job," *Judaism,* V (1956), 46–52.

Stevenson, William B., *The Poem of Job, a Literary Study with a New Translation.* London: Oxford University Press, 1947. The Schweich Lectures of the British Academy, 1943.

Stockhammer, M., "The Righteousness of Job," *Judaism,* VII (1958), 64–71.

Strahan, J., *The Book of Job Interpreted.* Edinburgh: T. & T. Clark, 1913.

Sutcliffe, Edmund F., *Providence and Suffering in the Old and New Testaments.* New York: Thomas Nelson and Sons, 1958.

Terrien, S., *Job: Poet of Existence.* Indianapolis: Bobbs-Merrill, 1957.

———, "Job: Introduction and Exegesis," *The Interpreter's Bible,* III.

Thompson, K. T., Jr., "Out of the Whirlwind. The Sense of Alienation in the Book of Job," *Interpretation,* XIV (1960), 51–63.

Tsevat, Matitiahu, "The Meaning of the Book of Job," *Hebrew Union College Annual,* XXXVII (1966), 73–106.

Williams, R. J., "Theodicy in the Ancient Near East," *Canadian Journal of Theology,* II (1956), 14–26.

Wood, I. F., "Folktales in the Old Testament Narratives," *Journal of Biblical Literature,* XXVIII (1909).

Zink, James A., "Impatient Job," *Journal of Biblical Literature,* LXXXIV (1965), 147–152.

DEUTERO-ISAIAH

Anderson, B. W., "Exodus Typology in Second Isaiah," *Israel's Prophetic Heritage,* B. W. Anderson and W. Harrelson, eds. New York: Harper and Brothers, 1962.

de Boer, P. A. H., *Second Isaiah's Message* (Oudtestamentische Studien XI). Leiden: Brill, 1956.

Cross, Frank M., Jr., "The Council of Yahweh in Second Isaiah," *Journal of Near Eastern Studies,* XII (1953), 274–277.

Knight, George A. F., *Deutero-Isaiah.* Nashville, Tennessee: Abingdon Press, 1965.

Lindblom, J., *The Servant Songs in Deutero-Isaiah.* Lund: Lunds Universitets Arsskrift, 1951.

Lindhagen, Curt, *The Servant Motif in the Old Testament.* Uppsala: Almquist & Wiksells, 1950.

Morgenstern, Julian, *The Message of Deutero-Isaiah.* Cincinnati: Hebrew Union College Press, 1961.

Muilenburg, James, "Isaiah 40–66: Introduction and Exegesis," *The Interpreter's Bible,* V.

North, Christopher Richard, *Isaiah 40–55; Introduction and Commentary.* London: S.C.M. Press, 1952.

———, *The Suffering Servant in Deutero-Isaiah, an Historical and Critical Study.* London: Oxford University Press, 1956.

———, *The Second Isaiah: Introduction, Translation and Commentary to Chs. XL-LV.* New York: Oxford University Press, 1964.

Pallis, S. A., *The Babylonian Akitu Festival.* Copenhagen: Andr. Fred. Host & Son, 1926.

Ringgren, H., *The Messiah in the Old Testament,* Studies in Biblical Theology, 18, Ch. 3. London: S.C.M. Press, 1956.

Roth, W. M. W., "The Anonymity of the Suffering Servant," *Journal of Biblical Literature,* LXXXIII (1964), 171–179.

Rowley, H. H., *The Servant of the Lord and Other Essays on the Old Testament.* London: Lutterworth Press, 1952.

Smart, James D., *History and Theology in Second Isaiah: a Commentary on Isaiah 35, 40–66.* Philadelphia: Westminster Press, 1965.

Smith, Morton, "II Isaiah and the Persians," *Journal of the American Oriental Society*, 83 (1963), 415–421.

Smith, Sidney, *Isaiah, Chapters XL–LV*, The Schweich lectures, 1940. London: Oxford University Press, 1944.

Stuhlmueller, C., "The Theology of Creation in Second Isaiah," *The Catholic Biblical Quarterly*, XXI (1959), 429–467.

Torrey, Charles Cutler, *The Second Isaiah; a New Interpretation*. New York: Charles Scribner's Sons, 1928.

Zimmerli, W., and J. Jeremias, *The Servant of God*, Studies in Biblical Theology, No. 20. Napierville, Illinois: Alec R. Allenson, 1959.

Bibliography for Part Eight

HAGGAI, ZECHARIAH, MALACHI, OBADIAH

Dentan, Robert C., "Malachi: Introduction and Exegesis," *The Interpreter's Bible,* VI.

Mitchell, H. G., J. M. P. Smith and Julius A. Bewer, *A Critical and Exegetical Commentary on Haggai, Zechariah, Malachi and Jonah,* The International Critical Commentary. New York: Charles Scribner's Sons, 1912.

North, F. S., "Critical Analysis of the Book of Haggai," *Zeitschrift für die Alttestamentliche Wissenschaft,* LXVIII (1956), 25–46.

Thomas, D. Winton, "Haggai: Introduction and Exegesis," *The Interpreter's Bible,* VI.

———, "Zechariah: Introduction and Exegesis," *The Interpreter's Bible,* VI.

Thompson, John A., "Obadiah: Introduction and Exegesis," *The Interpreter's Bible,* VI.

RUTH AND JONAH

Bertman, Stephen, "Symmetrical Design in the Book of Ruth," *Journal of Biblical Literature,* LXXXIV (1965), 165–168.

Childs, Brevard S., "Jonah: A Study in Old Testament Hermeneutics," *Scottish Journal of Theology,* XI (1958), 53–61.

Crook, M. B., "The Book of Ruth," *Journal of Bible and Religion,* XVI (1948), 155–160.

Gerleman, Gillis, *Ruth,* Biblischer Kommentar, Altes Testament, 18 (Neukirchen Kreis Moers). Neukirchener Verlag, 1960.

Myers, Jacob M., *The Linguistic & Literary Form of the Book of Ruth.* Leiden: Brill, 1955.

Smart, James D., "Jonah: Introduction and Exegesis," *The Interpreter's Bible,* VI.

Smith, Louise Pettybone, "Ruth: Introduction and Exegesis," *The Interpreter's Bible,* II.

Staples, W. E., "The Book of Ruth," *American Journal of Semitic Languages and Literatures,* 53 (1937), 145–157.

THE WORK OF THE CHRONICLER

Albright, W. F., "The Date and Personality of the Chronicler," *Journal of Biblical Literature,* XL (1921), 104–124.

Avi-Yonah, M., "The Walls of Nehemiah," *Israel Exploration Journal,* IV (1954), 239–248.

Batten, L. W., *A Critical and Exegetical Commentary on the Books of Ezra and Nehemiah,* The International Critical Commentary. New York: Charles Scribner's Sons, 1913.

Bickerman, Elias, *From Ezra to the Last of the Maccabees.* New York: A Schocken Paperback, 1962.

Bowman, R. A., "Ezra and Nehemiah: Introduction and Exegesis," *The Interpreter's Bible,* III.

Bright, J., "The Date of Ezra's Mission to Jerusalem," *Yehezkel Kaufmann Jubilee Volume.* Jerusalem: Magnes Press, 1960, 70–87.

Burrows, M., "Nehemiah 3:1–28 as a Source for the Topography of Ancient Israel," *Annual of The American Schools for Oriental Research,* XIV (1934), 115–140.

Curtis, E. L., and A. A. Madsen, *A Critical and Exegetical Commentary on the Books of Chronicles,* The International Critical Commentary. New York: Charles Scribner's Sons, 1910.

Elmslie, W. A. L., "I–II Chronicles: Introduction and Exegesis," *The Interpreter's Bible,* III.

Freedman, David Noel, "The Chronicler's Purpose," *Catholic Biblical Quarterly,* XXIII (1961), 436–442.

Kelly, Balmer H., *Ezra, Nehemiah, Esther, Job.* Richmond, Virginia: John Knox Press, 1962.

Myers, J. M., *I Chronicles,* The Anchor Bible. Garden City, New York: Doubleday and Co., 1965.

———, *II Chronicles,* The Anchor Bible. Garden City, New York: Doubleday and Co., 1965.

———, *Ezra-Nehemiah,* The Anchor Bible. Garden City, New York: Doubleday and Co., 1965.

North, R., "Theology of the Chronicler," *Journal of Biblical Literature,* LXXXII (1963), 369–381.

———, "The Cain Music," *Journal of Biblical Literature,* LXXXIII (1964), 373–389.

Rad, G. von, "The Levitical Sermon in I and II Chronicles," *The Problem of the Hexateuch and Other Essays,* E. W. T. Dicken, trans. London: Oliver and Boyd, 1966.

Richardson, H. N., "The Historical Reliability of Chronicles," *Journal of Bible and Religion,* XXVI (1958), 9–12.

Rudolph, W., "Problems of the Books of Chronicles," *Vetus Testamentum,* IV (1954), 401–409.

Slotki, I. W., *Chronicles,* Soncino Books of the Bible. London: The Soncino Press, 1952.

———, *Daniel, Ezra and Nehemiah,* Soncino Books of the Bible. London: The Soncino Press, 1951.

Snaith, N. H., "The Date of Ezra's Arrival in Jerusalem," *Zeitschrift für die Alttestamentliche Wissenschaft,* LXIII (1951), 53–66.

———, *The Jews from Cyrus to Herod.* New York: Abingdon Press, 1932.

Stinespring, W. F., "Eschatology in Chronicles," *Journal of Biblical Literature,* LXXX (1961), 209–219.

Torrey, C. C., *Ezra Studies.* Chicago: University of Chicago Press, 1910.

———, *The Chronicler's History of Israel: Chronicles-Ezra-Nehemiah Restored to Its Original Form.* New Haven: Yale University Press, 1954.

Welch, A. C., *The Work of the Chronicler,* Schweich Lectures, 1938. London: The British Academy, 1939.

Zeitlin, S., *The History of the Second Jewish Commonwealth: Prologemena.* Philadelphia: Jewish Publication Society, 1933.

THE PSALMS

Baggott, L. J., *The Seven Penitential Psalms.* London: A. R. Mowbray and Co., 1963.

Barth, Christopher, *Introduction to the Psalms.* New York: Charles Scribner's Sons, 1966.

Blackman, A. M., "The Psalms in the Light of Egyptian Research," *The Psalmists,* D. C. Simpson, ed. London: Oxford University Press, 1926, 177–197.

Boylan, Patrick, *The Psalms,* 2 vols. Dublin: M. H. Gill and Son, Ltd., 1948.

Briggs, C. A. and E. G., *A Critical and Exegetical Commentary on the Psalms,* The International Critical Commentary, 2 vols. New York: Charles Scribner's Sons, 1906–1907.

Buss, Martin J., "The Psalms of Asaph and Korah," *Journal of Biblical Literature,* LXXXII (1963), 382–392.

Buttenweiser, M., *The Psalms, Chronologically Treated with a New Translation.* Chicago: University of Chicago Press, 1938.

Cohen, A., *The Psalms, Hebrew Text, English Translation and Commentary,* The Soncino Books of the Bible. London: The Soncino Press, 1945.

Cooper, Charles M., *The Psalms in Life; a Study of the Psalter and Its Place in the Life of Christians Today.* Philadelphia: Muhlenberg Press, 1959.

Crim, Keith R., *The Royal Psalms.* Richmond, Virginia: John Knox Press, 1962.

Cross, Frank M., Jr., "Notes on a Canaanite Psalm in the Old Testament," *Bulletin of the American Schools of Oriental Research,* CXVII (1950), 19–20.

Cumming, C. G., *The Assyrian and Hebrew Hymns of Praise,* Columbia University Oriental Studies, Vol. XII. New York: Columbia University Press, 1934.

Dahood, Mitchell, *Psalms I (1–50),* The Anchor Bible. New York: Doubleday and Co., 1966.

Dalglish, E. R., *Psalm 51 in the Light of Ancient Near Eastern Patterns.* Leiden: E. J. Brill, 1962.

Drijvers, Pius, *The Psalms, Their Structure and Meaning.* New York: Herder and Herder, 1965.

Driver, G. R., "The Psalms in the Light of Babylonian Research," *The Psalmists,* D. C. Simpson, ed. London: Oxford University Press, 1926, 109–175.

Franken, H. J., *The Mystical Communion with Yahweh in the Book of Psalms.* Leiden: E. J. Brill, 1954.

Freehof, S. B., *The Book of Psalms, A Commentary.* Cincinnati: Union of Hebrew Congregations, 1938.

Gaster, T. H., "Psalm 45," *Journal of Biblical Literature,* LXXIV (1955), 239–251.

Gressmann, Hugo, "The Development of Hebrew Psalmody," *The Psalmists,* D. C. Simpson, ed. London: Oxford University Press, 1926.

Gross, M., *Blessing and Cursing in the Psalms.* Chicago: University of Chicago Press, 1937.

Gunkel, H., "The Poetry of the Old Testament: Its Literary History and Its

Application to the Dating of the Psalms," *Old Testament Essays*, D. C. Simpson, ed. London: Griffin, 1927.

————, "The Religion of the Psalms," *What Remains of the Old Testament and Other Essays*. London: Allen and Unwin, 1928.

Guthrie, H. H., *Israel's Sacred Songs*. New York: The Seabury Press, 1966.

James, F., *Thirty Psalmists*. New York: G. P. Putnam's Sons, 1938.

Johnson, A., "The Psalms," *The Old Testament and Modern Study*, H. H. Rowley, ed. London: Oxford University Press, 1951.

Kalt, E., ed., *Herder's Commentary on the Psalms*, B. Fritz, trans. Westminster, Maryland: The Newman Press, 1961.

Kilpatrick, A. F., *The Book of Psalms*. London: Cambridge University Press, 1902.

Kissane, E. J., *The Book of Psalms*, 2 vols. Westminster, Maryland: Newman Press, 1953.

Kraus, Hans-Joachim, *Die Königsherrschaft Jahwes im Alten Testament*. Tübingen: Mohr, 1951.

————, *Worship in Israel*, G. Buswell, trans. Richmond, Virginia: John Knox Press, 1966.

Lamb, John A., *The Psalms in Christian Worship*. London: Faith Press, 1962.

Leslie, Elmer A., *The Psalms, Translated and Interpreted in the Light of Hebrew Life and Worship*. New York: Abingdon-Cokesbury Press, 1949.

McCullough, W. S., "Psalms: Introduction and Exegesis," *The Interpreter's Bible*, IV.

Mowinckel, S., *The Psalms in Israel's Worship*, D. R. Ap-Thomas, trans., 2 vols. Oxford: Basil Blackwell, 1962.

Oesterley, W. O. E., *A Fresh Approach to the Psalms*. New York: Charles Scribner's Sons, 1937.

————, *The Psalms*, Vol I. London: S.P.C.K., 1939.

Paterson, John, *The Praises of Israel*. New York: Charles Scribner's Sons, 1950.

Patton, J. H., *Canaanite Parallels in the Book of Psalms*. Baltimore: The Johns Hopkins Press, 1944.

Ringgren, Helmer, *The Faith of the Psalmists*. Philadelphia: Fortress Press, 1963.

Simpson, D. C., ed., *The Psalmists*. London: Oxford University Press, 1926.

Smith, J. M. P., *The Religion of the Psalms*. Chicago: University of Chicago Press, 1922.

Snaith, Norman H., *Studies in the Psalter*. London: The Epworth Press, 1934.

————, *Hymns of the Temple*. London: S.C.M. Press, 1951.

Taylor, Charles Lincoln, Jr., "The Psalms," *Munera Studiosa*, Massey H. Shepherd, Jr., Sherman E. Johnson, eds. Cambridge, Mass.: The Episcopal Theological School, 1946, 3–21.

Terrien, Samuel, *The Psalms and Their Meaning for Today*. Indianapolis: Bobbs-Merrill, 1952.

Weiser, A., *The Psalms*, The Old Testament Library, H. Hartwell, trans. Philadelphia: Westminster Press, 1962.

Westermann, C., *The Praise of God in the Psalms*, Keith R. Crim, trans. Richmond, Virginia: John Knox Press, 1965.

Widengren, George, *The Accadian and Hebrew Psalms of Lamentation as Religious Documents*. Uppsala: Almqvist & Wiksells Boktryckeri-A.-B., 1937.

Worden, Thomas, *The Psalms Are Christian Prayer*. New York: Sheed and Ward, 1961.

Bibliography for Part Nine

ESTHER AND JOEL

Anderson, Bernhard W., "Esther: Introduction and Exegesis," *The Interpreter's Bible,* III.

Doniach, S., *Purim and the Feast of Esther.* Philadelphia: The Jewish Publication Society of America, 1933.

Gaster, T. H., *Purim and Hanukkah.* New York: Henry Schuman, 1950.

McKane, William, *Tracts for the Times.* Nashville: Abingdon Press, 1965.

Myers, J. M., "Some Considerations Bearing on the Date of Joel," *Zeitschrift für die Alttestamentliche Wissenschaft,* LXXIV (1962), 177–195.

Thompson, John A., "Joel's Locusts in the Light of Near Eastern Parallels," *Journal of Near Eastern Studies,* XIV (1955), 52–55.

————, "Joel: Introduction and Exegesis," *The Interpreter's Bible,* VI.

Treves, Marco, "The Date of Joel," *Vetus Testamentum,* VII (1957), 149–156.

DEUTERO-ZECHARIAH

Dentan, Robert C., "Zechariah 9–14: Introduction and Exegesis," *The Interpreter's Bible,* VI.

Otzen, Benedikt, *Studien über Deuterosacharja,* "Acta Theologica Danica," Vol. VI. Copenhagen: Prostant apud Munksgaard, 1964.

WISDOM LITERATURE

Baumgartner, W., "The Wisdom Literature," *The Old Testament and Modern Study,* H. H. Rowley, ed. Oxford: Clarendon Press, 1951.

Irwin, William A., "The Wisdom Literature," *The Interpreter's Bible,* I, 212–219.

Lambert, W. G., *Babylonian Wisdom Literature.* Oxford: Clarendon Press, 1960.

McCullough, W. S., ed., *The Seed of Wisdom: Essays in Honour of T. J. Meek.* Toronto: University of Toronto Press, 1964.

McKane, William, *Prophets and Wise Men,* Studies in Biblical Theology, 44. London: S.C.M. Press, 1965.

McKenzie, John L., "Reflections on Wisdom," *Journal of Biblical Literature,* LXXXVI (1967), 1–9.

Murphy, Roland O., *Seven Books of Wisdom*. Milwaukee: Bruce Publishing Co., 1960.

Noth, Martin, and Thomas D. Winton, eds., *Wisdom in Israel and the Ancient Near East,* Vetus Testamentum Supplement III. Leiden: E. J. Brill, 1955.

Rankin, O. S., *Israel's Wisdom Literature*. Edinburgh: T. & T. Clark, 1936.

Rylaarsdam, J. Coert, *Revelation in Jewish Wisdom Literature*. Chicago: University of Chicago Press, 1946.

Toombs, L. E., "The Old Testament and Wisdom Literature," *Journal of Bible and Religion,* XXIII (1955), 193–196.

PROVERBS

Crook, Margaret B., "The Marriageable Maiden of Proverbs 31:10–31," *Journal of Near Eastern Studies,* XIII (1954), 137–140.

Fritsch, Charles T., "Proverbs: Introduction and Exegesis," *The Interpreter's Bible,* IV.

Scott, R. B. Y., *Proverbs and Ecclesiastes,* The Anchor Bible. New York: Doubleday & Co., 1965.

Torrey, Charles C., "Proverbs, Chapter 30," *Journal of Biblical Literature,* LXXIII (1954), 93–96.

Whybray, R. N., *Wisdom in Proverbs: The Concept of Wisdom in Proverbs 1–9,* Studies in Biblical Theology 45. London: S.C.M. Press, 1965.

ECCLESIASTES

Dahood, M., "The Language of Qoheleth," *The Catholic Biblical Quarterly,* XIV (1952), 227–232.

Gordis, Robert, "Was Koheleth a Phoenician?" *Journal of Biblical Literature,* LXXIV (1955), 103–114.

——, *Koheleth, the Man and His World*. New York: Jewish Theological Seminary Press, 1951.

Murphy, Roland E., "The *Pensées* of Coheleth," *The Catholic Biblical Quarterly,* XVII (1955), 304–314.

Rankin, O. S., "Ecclesiastes: Introduction and Exegesis," *The Interpreter's Bible,* V.

Smith, L. L., "A Critical Evaluation of Ecclesiastes," *Journal of Bible and Religion,* XXI (1953), 100–105.

SONG OF SONGS

Gordis, R., "The Song of Songs," *Mordecai M. Kaplan Jubilee Volume on the Occasion of His Seventieth Birthday,* M. Davis, ed., Vol. I. New York: Jewish Theological Seminary of America, 1953.

——, *The Song of Songs: A Study, Modern Translation and Commentary,* Text and Studies of the Jewish Theological Seminary in America, Vol. XX. New York: The Jewish Theological Seminary of America, 1954.

Meek, T. J., "The Song of Songs and the Fertility Cult," *The Song of Songs, A Symposium,* W. H. Schoff, ed. Philadelphia: The Commercial Museum, 1924, 48–69.

———, "Song of Songs: Introduction and Exegesis," *The Interpreter's Bible,* V.

Pouget, William, and Jean Guitton, *The Canticle of Canticles,* The Catholic Scripture Library. New York: Declan X. McMullen Co., 1948.

Rowley, H. H., "The Interpretation of the Song of Songs," *The Servant of the Lord and Other Essays on the Old Testament,* 2nd ed. Oxford: Basil Blackwell, 1965, 195–245.

Schoff, W. H., ed. *The Song of Songs, A Symposium.* Philadelphia: The Commercial Museum, 1924.

Schonfield, Hugh J., *The Song of Songs.* New York: The New American Library, 1959. (A Mentor paperback.)

APOCALYPTIC LITERATURE

Block, J., *On the Apocalyptic in Judaism,* Jewish Quarterly Review Monograph Series, No. 11. Philadelphia: Dropsie College, 1953.

Burkitt, F. C., *Jewish and Christian Apocalypses,* The Schweich Lectures. London: Oxford University Press, 1914.

Frost, Stanley B., *Old Testament Apocalyptic.* London: Epworth Press, 1952.

Klausner, Joseph, *The Messianic Idea in Israel from Its Beginning to the Completion of the Mishnah.* New York: Macmillan, 1955.

Mowinckel, Sigmund, *He That Cometh,* G. W. Anderson, trans. New York: Abingdon Press, 1956.

Noth, Martin, "The Understanding of History in Old Testament Apocalyptic," *The Laws in the Pentateuch and Other Studies,* D. R. Ap-Thomas, trans. London: Oliver and Boyd, 1966.

Porter, F. C., *The Messages of Apocalyptical Writers.* New York: Charles Scribner's Sons, 1905.

Rowley, H. H., *The Relevance of Apocalyptic: A Study of Jewish and Christian Apocalypses from Daniel to the Revelation,* rev. ed. New York: Harper and Brothers, 1955.

Russel, D. S., *The Method and Meaning of Jewish Apocalyptic,* Old Testament Library. Philadelphia: Westminster Press, 1962.

Teeple, Howard M., *The Mosiac Eschatological Prophet,* Journal of Biblical Literature, Monograph Series X. Philadelphia: Society of Biblical Literature, 1957.

DANIEL

Charles, R. H., *A Critical and Exegetical Commentary on the Book of Daniel.* Oxford: Clarendon Press, 1922.

Cornfield, Gaalyahu, *Daniel to Paul: Jews in Conflict with Graeco-Roman Civilization.* Tel Aviv: Hamikra Baolam Publishing House, 1962.

Driver, S. R., *The Book of Daniel,* Cambridge Bible for Schools and Colleges. Cambridge: Cambridge University Press, 1922.

Emerton, J. A., "The Origin of the Son of Man Imagery," *Journal of Theological Studies,* IX (1959), 138–157.

Ginsberg, H. L., *Studies in Daniel.* New York: Jewish Theological Seminary of America, 1948.

Heaton, E. W., *The Book of Daniel,* Torch Bible Commentaries. London: S.C.M. Press, 1956.

Jefferey, Arthur, "Daniel: Introduction and Exegesis," *The Interpreter's Bible*, VI.

Montgomery, James A., *A Critical and Exegetical Commentary on the Book of Daniel*. The International Critical Commentary. New York: Charles Scribner's Sons, 1927.

Porteous, Norman Walker, *Daniel*, The Old Testament Library. Philadelphia: Westminster Press, 1965.

Rhodes, Arnold B., "The Kingdom of Men and the Kingdom of God," *Interpretation*, XV (1961), 411–430.

Rowley, H. H., "The Meaning of Daniel for Today," *Interpretation*, XV (1961), 387–397.

———, *Darius the Mede and the Four World Empires in the Book of Daniel*. Cardiff: University of Wales Press Board, 1935.

THE APOCRYPHA

Bickerman, E., *From Ezra to the Last of the Maccabees*. New York: Schocken Books, 1962.

Booth, H. K., *The Bridge Between the Testaments*. New York: Charles Scribner's Sons, 1929.

Box, G. H., *Judaism in the Greek Period*. Oxford: Oxford University Press, 1932.

Brockington, Leonard Herbert, *A Critical Introduction to the Apocrypha*. London: G. Duckworth, 1961.

Bruns, J. E., "Judith or Jael," *The Catholic Biblical Quarterly*, XVI (1954), 12–14.

———, "The Genealogy of Judith," *The Catholic Biblical Quarterly*, XVIII (1956), 19–22.

Charles, R. H., ed., *The Apocrypha and Pseudepigrapha of the Old Testament*, 2 vols. Oxford: Clarendon Press, 1913, 1963.

———, *Religious Development Between the Old and New Testaments*. New York: Henry Holt, 1914. London: Oxford University Press.

Dancy, J. C., *A Commentary on I Maccabees*. Oxford: B. Blackwell, 1954.

Davies, W. D., *Introduction to Pharisaism*. Philadelphia: Fortress Press, 1967.

Dentan, Robert C., *The Apocrypha, Bridge of the Testaments*. Greenwich, Connecticut: The Seabury Press, 1954.

Di Lella, A., "Conservative and Progressive Theology: Sirach and Wisdom," *The Catholic Biblical Quarterly*, XXVIII (1966), 139–154.

Dimier, Catherine, *The Old Testament Apocrypha*, Twentieth Century Encyclopedia of Catholicism. New York: Hawthorn Books, 1964.

Farmer, W. R., *Maccabees, Zealots, and Josephus*. New York: Columbia University Press, 1956.

Finkelstein, Louis, *The Pharisees, the Sociological Background of Their Faith*, Morris Loeb Series. Philadelphia: Jewish Publication Society of America, 1961.

Gaster, Moses, *The Samaritans: Their History, Doctrines, and Literature*. Oxford: Oxford University Press, 1923.

Geyer, J., *Wisdom of Solomon*. London: S.C.M. Press, 1963.

Glatzer, Nahum N., *Hillel the Elder*. New York: Schocken Books, 1966. (Paperback.)

Goodspeed, Edgar J., *The Story of the Apocrypha*. Chicago: University of Chicago Press, 1939.

Hadas, Moses, *The Third and Fourth Book of Maccabees,* Jewish Apocryphal Literature. New York: Harper and Brothers, 1953.

Herford, R. T., *The Pharisees.* New York: Macmillan, 1924.

———, *Talmud and Apocrypha.* London: Soncino Press, 1933.

Hughes, Maldwyn H., *The Ethics of Jewish Apocryphal Literature.* London: Robert Culley, 1909.

Johnson, Norman B., *Prayer in the Apocrypha and Pseudepigrapha: A Study of the Jewish Concept of God.* Philadelphia: Society of Biblical Literature and Exegesis, 1948.

Marcus, Ralph, *Law in the Apocrypha.* New York: Columbia University Press, 1927.

Metzger, Bruce M., *An Introduction to the Apocrypha.* New York: Oxford University Press, 1957.

Oesterley, W. O. E., *II Esdras, The Ezra Apocalypse,* Westminster Commentaries. London: Methuen and Company, 1933.

———, *An Introduction to the Books of the Apocrypha.* London: S.P.C.K., 1935.

Pfeiffer, Charles F., *Between the Testaments.* Grand Rapids: Baker Book House, 1959.

Pfeiffer, Robert H., *History of New Testament Times, With an Introduction to the Apocrypha.* New York: Harper and Brothers, 1949.

———, "The Literature and Religion of the Apocrypha," *The Interpreter's Bible,* I, 391–419.

Reese, J. M., "Plan and Structure in the Book of Wisdom," *The Catholic Biblical Quarterly,* XXVII (1965), 391–399.

Skehan, P. W., *The Literary Relationship Between the Book of Wisdom and the Protocanonical Wisdom Books of the Old Testament.* Washington, D.C.: The Catholic University of America, 1938.

Suggs, M. Jack, "Wisdom of Solomon 2:10–5: A Homily Based on the Fourth Servant Song," *Journal of Biblical Literature,* LXXVI (1957), 26–33.

Toombs, Lawrence, *The Threshold of Christianity.* Philadelphia: Westminster Press, 1960.

Torrey, C. C., *The Apocryphal Literature.* New Haven: Yale University Press, 1945.

Wright, A. G., "The Structure of Wisdom 11–19," *The Catholic Biblical Quarterly,* XXVII (1965), 28–34.

Zeitlin, S., and S. Tedesche, *The First Book of Maccabees,* Jewish Apocryphal Literature. New York: Harper and Brothers, 1950.

Zimmerman, Frank, *The Book of Tobit,* Jewish Apocryphal Literature. New York: Harper and Brothers, 1958.

Bibliography for Part Ten

TEXT AND CANON

Duncker, Peter G., "The Canon of the Old Testament at the Council of Trent," *The Catholic Biblical Quarterly*, XV (1953), 277–299.

Filson, Floyd V., *Which Books Belong in the Bible?* Philadelphia: Westminster Press, 1957.

Flack, Elmer, and B. Metzger *et al.*, *Text, Canon, and Principal Versions of the Bible*. Grand Rapids: Baker Book House, 1956.

Hebert, A. G., *The Authority of the Old Testament*. London: Faber and Faber, 1947.

Jeffery, Arthur, "The Canon of the Old Testament," *The Interpreter's Bible*, I, 32–45.

——, "The Text and Versions of the Old Testament," *The Interpreter's Bible*, I, 46–62.

Lewis, Jack P., "What Do We Mean by Jabneh?," *Journal of Bible and Religion*, XXXII (1964), 125–132.

Murphy, R. E., A. C. Sundberg, Jr. and S. Sandmel, "A Symposium on the Canon of Scripture," *The Catholic Biblical Quarterly*, XXVIII (1966), 189–207.

Noth, Martin, *The Old Testament World*, V. I. Gruhn, trans. Part IV: "The Text of the Old Testament." London: Adam and Charles Black, 1966.

Östborn, Gunnar, *Cult and Canon: A Study in the Canonization of the Old Testament*. Uppsala: A.-B Lundequistska Bokhandeln, 1950.

Roberts, Bleddyn J., *The Old Testament Texts and Versions: The Hebrew Texts in Transmission and the History of the Ancient Versions*. Cardiff: University of Wales Press, 1951.

Sundberg, Albert C., Jr., *The Old Testament of the Early Church*, Harvard Theological Studies XX. Cambridge: Harvard University Press, 1964.

Wurthwein, Ernst, *The Text of the Old Testament*. New York: Macmillan, 1959.

Zeitlin, Solomon, *An Historical Study of the Canonization of the Hebrew Scriptures*. Philadelphia: Jewish Publication Society of America, 1933.

ENGLISH TRANSLATIONS

An Introduction to The Revised Standard Version of the Old Testament by Members of the Revision Committee. New York: Thomas Nelson and Sons, 1952.

Baikie, J., *The English Bible and Its Story*. London: Seeley, Service and Co. Ltd., 1928.

Bruce, F. F., *The English Bible, A History of Translations*. Oxford: Oxford University Press, 1961.

Butterworth, C. C., *The Literary Lineage of the King James Bible*. Philadelphia: University of Pennsylvania Press, 1941.

Herklots, H. G. G., *How Our Bible Came to Us*. New York: Oxford University Press, 1954.

Kenyon, Sir Frederick, *The Story of the Bible*. London: J. Murray, 1936.

————, *The Bible and Modern Scholarship*. London: J. Murray, 1949.

————, *Our Bible and the Ancient Manuscripts*, A. W. Adams, rev. New York: Harper and Brothers, 1958.

Larue, Gerald A., "Another Chapter in the History of Bible Translation," *The Journal of Bible and Religion*, XXXI (1963), 301–310.

Margolis, M. L., *The Story of Bible Translations*. Philadelphia: The Jewish Publication Society of America, 1948.

May, H. G., *Our English Bible in the Making*. Philadelphia: Westminster Press, 1952.

Mozley, James F., *Coverdale and His Bibles*. London: Alex R. Allenson, 1953.

Price, I. M., *The Ancestry of Our English Bible*, 2nd ed. rev. by W. A. Irwin and A. P. Wikgren. New York: Harper and Brothers, 1949.

Robinson, H. W., ed., *The Bible in its Ancient and English Versions*. New York: Oxford University Press, 1954.

Rypins, Stanley, *The Book of Thirty Centuries*. New York: Macmillan, 1951.

Wikgren, Allen, "The English Bible," *The Interpreter's Bible*, I, 84–105.

THE DEAD SEA SCROLLS

Allegro, John, *The Dead Sea Scrolls*. Baltimore: Penguin Books, Inc. 1956.

Black, Matthew, *The Scrolls and Christian Origins*. New York: Charles Scribner's Sons, 1961.

Burrows, Millar, *The Dead Sea Scrolls*. New York: Viking Press, 1955.

————, *More Light on the Dead Sea Scrolls*. New York: Viking Press, 1958.

Cross, F. M., Jr., *The Ancient Library of Qumran and Modern Biblical Studies*, rev. ed. New York: Doubleday & Co., 1961.

Gaster, T. H., *Dead Sea Scriptures*. Garden City, New York: Anchor Books, 1964.

Milik, J. T., *Ten Years of Discovery in the Wilderness of Judaea*, Studies in Biblical Theology, 26, J. Strugnell, trans. London: S.C.M. Press, 1959.

Ringgren, Helmer, *The Faith of Qumran*. Philadelphia: Fortress Press, 1961.

Vermès, Géza, *Discovery in the Judean Desert*. New York: Desclee Company, 1956.

SUBJECT INDEX

AUTHOR INDEX